IN MEMORIAM

SO·THE·HEART·BE·RIGHT

Joanna Defrates

1945-2000

Late Roman painting

Wladimiro Dorigo

Late Roman painting

A study of pictorial records 30 BC – AD 500

Foreword by Sergio Bettini
Translated from the Italian by James Cleugh and
John Warrington

J. M. Dent & Sons Limited London

First published in Great Britain 1971
Pittura tardoromana Copyright by
© Giangiacomo Feltrinelli Editore Milano 1966
© Translation J.M. Dent & Sons Limited 1970
All Rights Reserved. No part of this publication may be
reproduced, stored in a retrieval system, or
transmitted, in any form or by any means, electronic,
mechanical, photocopying, recording or otherwise,
without the prior permission of
J.M. Dent & Sons Limited

Photoset by BAS Printers Limited Wallop Hampshire
and printed in Great Britain by Lowe & Brydone
(Printers) Limited London NW10
for J.M. Dent & Sons Limited
Aldine House Bedford Street London

ISBN 0 460 07718 X

Contents

PLATES

The word *painting* in the title of this work covers mosaics, inlays, coloured illustrations in manuscripts and designs on textiles as well as panels, all executed in the territory of the Roman Empire by both pagan and Christian artists between the first century BC and the sixth century AD. Sculpture is treated comparatively only, in its relation to painting, not analytically, for its own sake.

Textual references to the illustrations are indicated by marginal numbers, bold type (in separate series) being used for the coloured plates. Capital letters refer to maps and plans.

Author's preface

This book grew out of an enquiry, modest and enthusiastic as a degree thesis can be, into the crisis of Roman pictorial art between the end of the third and the beginning of the fourth century. That work had been encouraged and guided by the richly humane personality and magisterial example of Sergio Bettini. After completing my university studies and beginning those of specialisation I felt bound to make a second attempt which might enable me to deepen my criticism and carry out an adequate revision of my ideas, not only in order to verify conclusions but also to extend the actual framework of my research.

The cultural significance of the theme, expressing one of the fundamental aspects of the great political crisis of antiquity, and the profound 'topicality' of the subject-matter, led me, in cases where the scientific motive would not have sufficed, to patient amplification of my enquiry, in the first place by numerous expeditions to the places concerned, beyond the nodal point which my initial labours had enabled me to confront directly. I included a critical itinerary which had even then begun with the end of the first century. I also added a more systematic examination of the early manifestations of the era of late antiquity and above all a more comprehensive collection of monuments as late as the first half of the fifth century. The purpose here was to account historically for the diversification of medieval artistic idioms which was already about to commence when the two *partes* of the Empire divided to face their different destinies.

I need not say how very conscious I always was of the difficulty of the task. I was affected not only by the intrinsic complexity of the facts and the possibly premature character of any efforts I might make at synthesis in the existing state of research, above all in the field of related disciplines, but also by the limited time my numerous and varied duties allowed me to devote to the undertaking. The study of monuments, library research, the further elaboration of the text and its actual composition were therefore prolonged excessively, from an objective point of view, in comparison with the concentration I was able to achieve in the finished product.

The typescript was ready for printing in 1961, when Sergio Bettini dictated his generous preface. Equally generous opinions, even when critical of the methodological basis adopted, were given by those who read the work in an editorial capacity. I hasten to thank in this connection Giulio Carlo Argan, Ranuccio Bianchi Bandinelli and Carlo Ludovico Ragghianti. But some considerable time elapsed before the typescript reached Giangiacomo Feltrinelli, who courageously consented to face not only the uncertainties of its reception by scholars but also the heavy burden of publication.

During the last five years many possible amendments of the text have of course suggested themselves to me. But although the publisher allowed me every freedom to integrate them, especially in the Bibliography section, the work has remained practically unchanged, except for a few pages. Such is the reason for possible omissions, for which I ask the reader's indulgence, of researches and discoveries occurring after 1961.

I am indebted to the many persons who have aided me in this labour, above all to Professors Giuseppe Fiocco and Sergio Bettini, my teachers at the University of Padua, who first inspired me with affection for these studies.

I desire further to mention Professor Biagio Pace and to thank for their advice, help and courtesy Professors Giovanni Brusin, Aldo Ferrabino, Carlo Verdiani, Bruno Zevi, Maurizio Bonicatti and Giuseppe Mazzariol; also Dr Licisco Magagnato, Father Antonio Ferrua, Monsignor Theodor Kempf, Dr Gino Vinicio Gentili, Professor Libero D'Orsi, Dr Alessandro Bettagno, Dr Claudio Morgagni of Ravenna, Dr Gose of Trier, and Professor Eva Petrova of Prague. Thanks are also due to Dr Francesco Papafava and Signor Federico Arborio Mella for taking photographs, to Professor Guido Marzari for the drawings, to Signorina Luigina Franco and Signorina Emma Scalvini for typing services and to many anonymous assistants and custodians at archaeological excavation sites and museums of the former Roman world.

I dedicate this book in gratitude and filial piety to the beloved memory of my father Luigi Dorigo, who waited so long to see it.

Wladimiro Dorigo
Venice, 1 April 1966

Concetto Marchesi has drawn attention to a remarkable passage in one of Gustave Flaubert's letters to Mme Des Genettes: '*Les dieux n'étant plus et le Christ n'étant pas encore, il y a eu de Cicéron a Marc-Aurèle, un moment unique ou l'homme seul a été. Je ne trouve nulle part cette grandeur*'. The splendid isolation of man in the absence of gods, here referred to, may perhaps however be thought to have been already present in Lucretius, a disciple of Epicurus but himself a Roman.

While Epicurus had said: '*Time is the happening of happenings*', therefore a series or duration, and had ended by affirming the metaphysical reality of eternity, Lucretius used the extraordinary phrase: '*Tempus per se non est*', i.e. cannot be categorised, being always relative to some particular *hic et nunc*. Gods no longer exist and man is alone, because his time has ceased to be guaranteed solely by a system. For the Roman of the Empire it was not only the Greek notion of a world extending in space but confined by the impassable circumference of its environment that had collapsed. The *saeculum* too, the marvel of '*cyclic time*' accepted by Vergil and Horace, was fading away.

A similar mood of alienation or existential anguish is again evident, not long after the age of Lucretius, in Seneca. His tragedies, according to Ettore Paratore, reveal beneath their submerging floods of rhetoric 'a profound and tragic sense of human desolation, which felt a need to express itself in such exasperated and sonorous language because that style alone seemed adequate to convey the vast despair of a solitude so embittered'. Seneca did in fact 'doubt the existence of a future state . . . (and) in a famous chorus of *The Trojan Women* he affirmed the mortality of all things and the nonentity of hell'. He was 'the philosopher of inherent desolation'. It is my own belief that the time has come when criticism should advance beyond such positions as that of Dvořàk (*Kunstgeschichte als Geistesgeschichte*) in phenomenology, with a view to identifying the 'presence' of a particular *Weltanschauung* as well as a particular *Kunstwollen* deep down among the terminologies applied to the arts, that is to say, located in the actual history of the works concerned. For example, Seneca's metrical practice involves the breaking down, by a capricious series of stresses, of metres originally Greek or assimilated to such measures, so as to disrupt them and introduce far-reaching alterations of their arrangement. The iambic trimeter is combined with the minor sapphic, the adonic, the dactylic hexameter, the anapaestic dimeter and monometer, the glyconic and minor asclepiad. Quantitative organisation, in fact, is thus replaced by expressionist accentuation, which itself implies paratactical construction. Parallels can easily be found in the idiomatic structure of the figurative arts: for example, with reference to painting, in the now celebrated heads on the ceiling of the Stabia dining-room, built before the year 79. In this case too a similar process of disintegration of the Greek 'tactile' form can be seen to follow an analogous principle, by this time far from that of Hellenic representation. 'Organic' design and shading are no longer practised, but simply a 'roughing in' which emphasises the controlling function of light, caught at the instant of the event depicted, in the construction of the image. The illumination is not in fact 'permanent' but momentary. It does not suffuse the faces but strikes them laterally, while the shadows coagulate in a few rapid brush-strokes, consisting of two or three capricious but precise tones.

The 'naturalistic illusionism' (Wickhoff's phrase) of the Augustan age was by this time discredited. A little later, even the 'continuous style of historical narrative', that is to say the securing of objectivity in the record by means of a chronological (though no longer in the Greek manner spatial) sequence of incidents, as in the frieze of Trajan's column, gradually lost its vigour during the seventy years that elapsed before the column of Marcus Aurelius was erected. In the latter monument the serialisation of the facts in an 'objective' temporal order is nullified by their implication that *'tempus per se non est'*. Accordingly, the 'personal time' of the observer – or beneficiary, as he is called nowadays – comes more and more into play, being somehow foreseen in the actual figurative structure of an art which seems to conform in however elementary a fashion with an 'open' (or mobile) theory of poetics.

Naturally enough, expressionist motives may also emerge in this figurative manner and bring about associated crystallisations of the parameters of a paratactic composition. Flaubert goes on to remark that the men of that epoch were afflicted with an incurable melancholy *'plus profonde que celle des modernes, qui sousentendent tous plus ou moins l'immortalité au delà du trou noir. Mais, pour les anciens ce trou noir était l'infini même: leurs rêves se dessinent et passent sur un fond d'ébène immuable'*. This dreamlike character continued to be stressed more and more in the images produced by the arts of the Empire. Their works were shadowy, lacking substance and depth. The background of changeless ebony came more and more to symbolise a spatial 'nothingness' until in due course Christianity imposed its new vision, inverting the old. The black background that had blocked further progress in the field of human endeavour became light itself, typified by the incorruptible gold of the heavenly Jerusalem.

It is helpful to recognise that the phases of this development were and still are identifiable and can be followed up mainly through criticism of the poetry and prose literature, in other words the language, of the Empire. In fact, it may seem superfluous to call attention to the numerous contributions to this subject, those of Auerbach above all, both in his early *Mimesis* and in his later admirable essay on *Literary Language and Society in Late Antiquity and the Middle Ages*. His observations, for example, on the clear affirmation of expressionism, especially during the fourth century in the *History* of Ammianus Marcellinus, but with precedents reaching back to Sallust and even Tacitus, are illuminating. (Not only does the language employ dazzling words and ostentatiously distorted syntax to depict a perverted, ghastly and spectral reality, but the verbal structure and syntax themselves reinforce the effect . . .'. In his disposition of nouns, particularly that of the subject in the nominative case, as well as in the abundant prominence given to adjectives and participles in apposition and in his tendency to indicate by word-order the reciprocal limits of the accumulated appositions, Ammianus continually reveals his power of suggesting a monumental, surprising and usually most animated vision. . . . It is obvious that his style of representation has carried to extremes a mode of expression which began with Tacitus and Seneca, that is to say, one of highly pathetic character, in which the sensual and the dreadful run riot. His is a dark realism, the very acme of pathos, utterly alien from the taste of classical antiquity. . . . In this passage 'realism' must of course be understood in the sense given to the word by Auerbach.)

It would be easy to multiply such quotations. While they would provide further proofs of the fundamental structural analogy between the literary and spoken language of the Empire and its figurative diction and *Kunstindustrie*, it is to be feared that they would throw into greater relief the residual discrepancy which still persists between the literary and the art criticism dealing with this period. Not very many years ago the 'originality' of Roman art, even of Roman architecture, was denied. Since then the pioneer work of Wickhoff, Riegl, Schlosser and the whole of the great Viennese school, together with that of numerous archaeologists, especially Rodenwaldt and other Germans, in Rome itself, has not been in vain. Its effects can be perceived even in quarters where questionable intolerance has entrenched itself or where the critical myopia of traditional 'archaeological method' is to be found. Some impression has also been made on those who only appear to oppose the latter tradition in their undeniably fanciful attempts to construct a self-styled Marxist theory of criticism (or one which overstrains 'dialectics'). Confining our attention to Italian contributors, it is not without significance that an essay so admirable, not least for its sobriety of tone, as that of Doro Levi on *Roman Art* (1950) did not have the success that might have been expected in Italy, considering that all its cards were played with the utmost fairness even from the professorial standpoint. But the essay probably disturbed certain ingrained mental habits. Such prejudices are not only academic; nor are they exclusively Italian. For it may be observed that even in Paris, the recognised centre of all advanced thought and a hotbed of nonconformity, so 'enlightened' a critic as Malraux insisted on disparaging the 'uncouth Colossus of the Tiber'. It should be added, however, that reaction, from one source at least, was almost immediate in Paris, and all the more significant as coming from Georges Duthuit, a scholar who had in the past appeared to uphold the conventional archaeological view of this matter. But he was too intelligent and too subtle an interpreter of contemporary art, especially that of the Fauves and of Matisse, to remain 'blind' for long to the true structural characteristics of the art of the Roman Empire. Duthuit in fact, in the second volume of his *Musée Inimaginable*, has presented one of the most brilliant and acute essays, for all its look of a pamphlet, which it has been possible to read during the last few years. Yet I am afraid that not many people, in Italy at any rate, have read it.

Nowadays the danger appears to be, if anything, just the opposite. For since the dispute as to the originality of Roman art has lost much of its point, if only because the adoption of more modern standards of criticism have rendered it unreal, there has been a tendency to draw over-close parallels between the cultural situation of the Empire, especially in its later developments, and that of our own century. The attractions of this line of thought are unquestionably numerous, manifest and even showy. There is in the first place, from a general and macroscopic standpoint, the process of coagulation and solidification of society under the later Roman Empire, resulting in the hopeless solitude, the *Entäussern* or alienation of the individual, and initiating the 'expressionist revolt'. The imposition and control of a *Kulturindustrie* and its consequences, though in proportions different from our own, may be added. Such phenomena may well be considered open to denunciations very like those addressed by Adorno, for example, to modern society. It is undeniable that not even the Roman world, as judged in terms of the *Aufklärung* philosophy, could have saved itself, for all the 'exception' of its Christian environment, which might, according to an optimistic and widespread view, have cured its 'crisis' by reconstituting the nucleus of the mass, the individual 'personality'. But in fact this entity, as considered within the framework of the philosophy mentioned, is merely one which remains closely attached to the theories of a *philosophia prima* unalterably convinced that truth resides in 'what is left' after the abstraction of historical contingency and accident. 'Residual' truth, however, far from being the remedy for any crisis, is no more than the transposition into ideological or mythical terms of 'nest-egg' economics and accordingly reconsecrates a power founded upon property and authority. It is not by such means, as incidentally the later history of the Church seems to show, that the *proton pseudos* inherent in all metaphysical and ontological systems, even the existential, can be overcome. It is an expression which can only be translated as a 'codification of power'.

More urgent and clear invitations to draw analogies arise from critical analysis of the formal structures of Roman Imperial art, particularly that of the period between Marcus Aurelius and Constantine. In addition to the generic imposition of 'expressionism' a growing corrosion of the image can now be observed, parallel and consonant with the obliteration of the ancient 'objective space' which had been implicated from the earliest times. The scenic and atmospheric 'surroundings' are gradually eliminated. The field of operations is steadily reduced to the *fond d'ébène immuable*. The image comes to the surface and stays there. Counter-tendencies and neoclassical reversions can of course be noticed. But the guiding principle of stylistic development is the progressive decline of the old organic syntax, accompanied by the progressive establishment of the fundamental outlines of a new language, paratactical in structure.

It is also significant that pictorial 'decoration', for example, becomes more and more indifferent to the gratuitous feature of Greek 'contemplation' and more and more frankly 'functional' in its applications. It collaborates closely, even on the figurative plane, with architecture, entering into its forms and following its ramifications, underlining, for instance, the diagonals of vault intersections or the convergent ribbing of roofed calottes and larger domes. The architecture itself is closed 'outside', even the windows being no longer, in a figurative sense, openings, but areas of colour grafted into the interior surface of the walls. The architectural treatment accentuates the character of the building as a form based on a continuum which demands to be investigated and appreciated by walking round it. Hence, on a stylistic idiom of this kind, less and less anchored to an 'objective' space and, though geometrically measurable, more and more subject to the influence of time, there was gradually imposed the compositional 'principle' related more to temporal than to spatial considerations. Accordingly, rhythm governed even the plastic forms of classical origin, such as pillars, etc., and also pictorial elements, such as windows, etc., derived from the 'naturalistic' practice of the middle Roman period. Painting consistent with such structural ideas could only adhere to the same type of 'dimension'. Figures, for example, are arranged in rows, facing the spectator, since to show them in three-quarter profile or even simply in profile would suggest depth. At the same time, as already noted, the ancient perspective of environment disintegrated. It was often inverted, as when the axes of scenes in depth open out fanwise to become horizontal. Individual figurative subjects are also 'stylised', losing their original organic quality and plastic consistency and being recomposed in an order no longer 'spatial' but rhythmic, as for example in the case of balanced heraldic symbols or the 'infinite product' series, etc.

In agreement with this trend, the colours of Roman painting also became more and more unrealistic. The critical moment can be approximately set at the time of the Tetrarchy. The painting of the Piazza Armerina masters or those of the Theodorean pavement at Aquileia betrays not only a 'deformation' or disintegration of the plasticity of the figures, as in cubism (a feature characteristic of Western art during the third century), but also a new and arbitrary employment of colour, which is 'invented' and might almost be described as *fauve*. This circumstance is one of the easiest and most dangerous encouragements to the drawing of analogies. It is not difficult to perceive a difference between the colours of a Roman painting of the Augustan era and those of one executed under Diocletian, a difference which corresponds with that between Impressionist and Fauve treatment of colour. A green by Monet and a green by Braque differ semantically as well as formally, because the first includes natural space-light and the second excludes it. Monet's green, drenched in atmospheric light, records the variability of naturalistic 'weather' and the changing influences of place, season, day and hour. Braque's green has 'eliminated contact' with nature in that sense and with those dimensions. Every atmospheric variation and every contamination by the environment had been squeezed out of it. Consequently, it is a mere area, of an arbitrary, invented and 'permanent' stamp, fixed in a hard, gem-like pallor.

Such a treatment of colour, in my view, characterises idiomatically the basic current of western Roman art throughout the fourth century (until, say, the date of the Dioscuri pavement at Trier), while at Constantinople, in the wake of the masters of Constantine's court (for instance in the pavement of the Seasons at Antioch, etc.), there was in progress that recovery (in some sense neo-hellenistic) of the lost formal organisation, together with a semantically gnomic spirit, in which I believe the 'origins' of Byzantine art may be sought. It should be borne in mind, of course, that the bipartite division is highly schematic. Works in the 'fine style' will be found in the west; typical examples are the paintings on the ceiling of the Constantinian hall at Trier and the structural trend which culminates in the sarcophagus of Junius Bassus, etc. In the east, for instance at Antioch, works employing stained and 'arbitrary' colour will also appear. But exchanges, borrowings, overlappings and reciprocal contaminations will be endless and accompanied by the most minute traces of dosage and articulation. It may therefore seem a hopeless undertaking to attempt to distinguish between the two divisions, to unravel one by one the threads of so intricate a skein, to follow their secret routes, to verify their idiomatic action and where possible their poetic validity, and finally to connect them with the spiritual structures, also modulated to an infinite extent by local and temporal influences, of the expanded Roman Empire.

Wladimiro Dorigo has undertaken this enterprise with admirable courage in the following closely reasoned essay on Roman painting up to the fifth century, to the point, that is to say, of the establishment in the West as well as in the East of that particular type of Constantinopolitan neoclassicism which was to lead under Justinian to the preeminence throughout the Empire of a style properly designated as Byzantine. The author could not have hoped to attempt this task if he had not possessed, in addition to a thorough knowledge of the subject and its relevant sources, a powerful critical faculty.

His work is better known to Italian scholars in other fields. Few people are aware, perhaps, that his 'training' has been that of a critic and historian of art, especially, as it happens, of late Roman and early Christian art. He belongs to a school which will be readily recognisable and makes no secret of its derivation, methodologically, from the great example set by Alois Riegl. In other words, this school adopts a method of phenomenological research based on the verification of formal structure, the elements of which 'give form to', i.e. present directly, the structures (capable of various semantic connotations under various kinds of analysis) characteristic of a civilisation, of an epoch, of a period, of a territory, in short of an 'individuality', historically determined.

Perhaps one of the most notable aspects of this essay by Dorigo, and one which may be expected to cause considerable stir among archaeologists, is his far-reaching and novel attempt to define critically in each case the 'individualities' of the outstanding artists whom he discusses. It is not impossible that on this account particularly he will be accused of 'betraying' or at any rate tampering with the principle of a rigorous structural analysis in order to comply with those of the traditional Italian school of art-history based on the recognition of such 'individualities'.

It may be recalled that the point was in fact made against Riegl's method, both in his own time and later, of a failure in this respect. The charge was brought still more recently by my greatly beloved and lamented friend Carlo Antoni in a review published by *Il Mondo* of the Italian edition of the well-known volume by Wellek and Warren on *Literary Theory*. Wellek asked, in reply, what personalities he was rebuked for having sacrificed. He asserted that they were abstract entities, biographically and psychologically speaking, unnecessary for critical judgment of the works produced. For the *Iliad* and the *Odyssey* would still be what they are, whether they had been written by Homer or by some unknown individual or group. The personality which they reveal cannot be deduced *a posteriori*, except from the structure of the texts themselves. Consequently, the critic must invariably return to the concrete source, the work itself, from which he should never have departed. Antoni could find no convincing answer to this argument. Wellek ended his retort with a statement by no means new. Once one has set out in this direction there is no reason why one should not go further and approach in this way a single work, or even the smallest part of any such work, with which there is no comparison. Conversely, the category could well be enlarged so as to include entire periods or territories of artistic culture with their specific *Kunstwollen*. The doubt remains, itself open to criticism, whether certain critics are induced to concentrate upon 'individualities' by what is in the last analysis a Vasarian 'humanism', in short, a history of art made up of 'lives'.

I myself incidentally, if I may be excused for mentioning my own work, had used similar arguments to defend Riegl's Introduction to his *Kunstindustrie* from the same sort of charge of neglecting 'individualities'. I remarked that if they are discovered from sources outside their works, viz., in documents or records, the result will be of a biographical and psychological, if not merely registrational character, not logically assimilable to the concrete historical substance of the works. If on the other hand the individuality of the artist as such is deduced only from his works, the operation is valid but not privileged as having no concrete alternative. In fact, it too is a 'construction' built up by the combination of certain common traits judged to be characteristic of the category applicable to the personality concerned because they recur statistically with more regularity in a certain group of works. In this way an 'assembly', a 'grand total' is established by a method which as such differs only by the choice of 'index figures' from that of the assessment, on the basis of formal structural constants, of a given idiomatic dimension or a given period of *Kunstwollen*.

A critical exercise of this kind obviously proceeds through concentric circles of approximation. Unquestionably the circle of *Kunstwollen* in Riegl's *Kunstindustrie*, embracing the constants of an artistic idiom covering a whole epoch and an immense area, includes the smaller circle of works produced by a single generation or in one place. A still smaller circle, in turn, includes the works which it may be possible to assign to a single creator. But if research, in accordance with Riegl's method, relies on structure, no methodological contradiction is involved in passing from one circle to another. Extrapolation, if any, properly consists in the passage to a different semantic dimension, which is carried out in the course of the critical operation by interrupting it at the level of the 'individuality' taken as *a priori*.

The concrete quality of the operation also of course suffers when it begins from the circle of a *Kunstwollen* abstractly hypostatised and the formal structures of the works are deduced from it. On the other hand it will be found useful to proceed from the central nucleus of the works in their concrete structural cohesion and thence to 'aim at' the horizon of the *Kunstwollen*, going on to intercalate a polarity extending from the work to the *Kunstwollen* and back again. It is the latter which permits access to the 'form' of the art, in other words the concrete historicity of its existence in a framework of space and time.

Such is the method adopted by Dorigo. The reader will judge with what articulated subtlety he employs it, with inflections due to his familiarity with the problems of modern art, He shows much prudence in avoiding the above mentioned danger of forcing or even underlining analogies, however apparently conspicuous and alluring. His plan of research, however, leaves no doubt as to his sense of actuality. It can be discerned, first, in his recognition of relativity, which Riegl himself continued to regard as the indispensable footwear of history. In the background of this critical treatise, moreover, one is conscious of the presence of certain problems which exercise a silent influence but eventually renew our way of interpreting even the forms of ancient art. Such problems include, for instance, that of the radical reconsideration of idiom, of new systems of equivalence set up in modern painting especially and arising from the search for non-figurative constants, or again the question of the growing importance of the 'poetic elements of form in movement' which anticipates the integration of the 'beneficiary' and so on.

Certain reactions may be conjectured, even forecast. I myself might disagree with the author here and there. But everyone remembers that Spitzer, for example, ventured to describe Auerbach as a 'theologian of criticism'.

For the most part one is conscious at least of fresh air pouring into the stale atmosphere of Italian culture, particularly that of archaeology, on to which Dorigo has flung a window wide open.

Sergio Bettini
Padua. July 1961

Glossary of terms used

Aedicula	a niche or small shrine
Angusti Clavi	narrow bands of material
Apatheia	spiritual calm
Arcosolium	a vaulted niche
Asaroton	lit. 'unswept'; used of a mosaic floor showing a variety of scattered objects
Auctoritas	authority
Carceres	starting stalls for chariots in the Roman circus
Concinnitas	skilful arrangement
Didaskaleion	school
Domus Aurea	Golden House, Nero's palace covering the S. slope of the Oppian Hill
Domus ecclesiae	church-house
Ductus	linear style
Emblema (pl. Emblemata)	a mosaic picture executed as a central feature to which the rest of the floor was subordinated
Enthousiasmos	frenzy
Fasti	calendar; hence lists of eponymous magistrates
Felicitas Temporum	temporal happiness
Frigidarium	large swimming pool in Roman baths
Gnosis	knowledge
Graecia capta	captive Greece
Hortus conclusus	an enclosed garden
In-der-welt-sein	common sense; lit. 'to be in the world'
Institutiones alimentariae	child-welfare boards
Insula	a tenement block
Koine	common style
Kunstwollen	artistic intention
Laudator temporis acti	admirer of the past
Limes	frontier
Lithostroton	mosaic pavements; perhaps originally an irregularly paved, patternless floor
Logos spermatikos	the dynamic rational principle active in the Stoic world–whole and its parts
Medium	middle doctrine
Mega palation	Great Palace
Metanoia	change of outlook
Nec sunt nec fieri possunt nec fuerunt	neither are nor can be nor have been
Opus sectile	form of mosaic executed with thin slabs cut into patterns
Opus tessellatum	form of mosaic in which the slabs of opus sectile were replaced by small cubes (*tessellae*) of uniform size
Opus vermiculatum	form of mosaic in which the *tessellae* were irregularly shaped and adapted to the field
Ovilia dei	folds (i.e. churches) of God

Paideia	education
Pars occidentalis	western part of the Roman Empire
Pars orientalis	eastern part of the Roman Empire
Pictor imaginarius	designer of mosaics
Pistis	faith
Potestas	power
Rotuli	cylinders
Sermo nobilis	superior mode of expression
Spina	a barrier down the middle of the Roman circus
Taberna	tavern
Tablinum	principal apartments of a Roman house
Terminus ante quem	lower chronological limit
Terminus post quem	upper chronological limit
Tessellarii	cube mosaicists
Theophania	apparition
Traditio clavium	delivery of the keys
Traditio legis	delivery of the Law
Venationes	wild-beast hunts; hence fights of man against beast or beast against beast
Venatores	hunters
Vicennalia	festival of the twentieth anniversary of an emperor's accession
Vir bonus	good man
Viridarium	a room with walls painted to resemble a garden
Virtus	fortitude
Völkerwanderung	mass migration
Weltanschauung	outlook on the world
Xenia	friendly gifts
Xystus	an open colonnade
Zeitgeist	spirit of the age

Introductory

Aspects of the ideological crisis of Roman society in the Imperial age

Between the assumption of the imperial power by Septimius Severus (AD 193) and the end of the age of Theodosius (AD 395) the Mediterranean world experienced two eventful centuries heavy with consequences. An epoch which had opened while the secular radiance of the Aurelian day still lasted closed upon an entirely different panorama of the Roman world. The turbulent waves of the *Völkerwanderung* were about to take more permanent shape in the new barbarian kingdoms, and political control of the Empire was preparing to divide into two centres of power whose respective destinies would set their seal upon a whole millennium. Meanwhile the Christian Church, which during the reign of Commodus had been hardly distinguishable from other obscure religious sects, was already permeating the imperial body with her own *Weltanschauung*, and would eventually, after the Theodosian edict of Thessalonica (AD 380), become the State religion and expel the image of Victory from the Chamber of the Roman Senate, despite the opposition of the Symmachi, those last champions of the old Roman faith.

That age of tremendous crisis, in which a civil catastrophe of gigantic and unfamiliar proportions coincided with a vast religious movement of revolutionary significance, was also the age in which material events were accompanied by a spiritual upheaval, all proceeding from remarkably similar historical roots and bearing witness to an evolution of conscience which marked the stages of a quest for a new kind of internal serenity pursued by some fifty millions of persons, the probable population at that time of the area extending from Hadrian's Wall to the fortified posts maintained by the legions of Trajan in Mesopotamia.

The difficult problem constituted by the crisis of the Empire defies classification and even today remains unsolved despite the huge mass of historiography produced by its investigation. Its chronological, geographical, political and religious dimensions suffice to indicate the unavoidable complexity of the parallel (and from many points of view identical) question of the 'crisis' of late Roman art; a complexity that cannot be eliminated by any simplified picture of systematic decadence.

The 'crisis' is undeniable *a priori*: its rejection would be a most undesirable historical method, and would moreover remove, at least in one sense of the word, any justification for undertaking such a study of late Roman painting as is here presented. Nevertheless, in the interests of a more articulate and exhaustive critical recognition of the historical facts which alone can permit the use of such a term as 'crisis' in the artistic field, it may be useful to attempt in reasonably rapid outline a clear account (selective, but not for that reason unfounded or gratuitous) of those aspects of the ideological crisis of the imperial age which may best indicate, as signs or symptoms of historical tension, if not positively allied semantically, to what extent that crisis occurred simultaneously in the field of art and particularly in that of painting.

The result of a historical survey of nearly four centuries of Mediterranean painting, etc., such as is attempted in the following pages, will then be able to show the advantage of having examined the internal configurations of an age by studying a single monument no less than by relating it to the more extensive and lasting tensions of an entire artistic civilisation.

Philosophic speculation and religious practice are the two domains in which the transformation of the elements of the ancient *Weltanschauung* between the central imperial and the late Roman period seems most precisely delineated. Here above all, among all classes, from the most cultured to the most humble, one can trace a gradual disintegration of certain concepts of the classical world, a disintegration which involved first and foremost the idea of individual liberty – based on the substantially personal and rationalist view of life which Greek paideia had transmitted to Hellenistic culture – and with it the relations of man to external nature and the civil community, in fine his undisputed sovereignty of the world.

From the time of Augustus onwards, while men enjoyed the *felicitas temporum* that had been awaited for decades, and at the very moment when the cultural and civil edifice of classical antiquity was culminating in the reduction of the world to a unity under the empire of Rome, when immense possibilities of development in every field seemed open to a society which had only just laid down the sword and seized upon the promise that it would never have to be used again, there happened to be lacking what might have seemed the logical reward of so much effort: a humanistic-social situation in which would be recognised at one and the same time the self-confidence of Roman man victorious after centuries of conflict, his mission as the administrator of justice within a pacified society, and his right to civil and moral independence subject to the forms imposed by the needs of empire upon the juridical and legislative genius of the conqueror.

At the beginning of a millennium that witnessed the almost immediate structural subordination of philosophical to religious experience, and right down to the humanist revolution of the fifteenth century, both those forms of experience helped to show that the centre of ideological interest was shifting steadily from the collective employment of the religious factor in solving the problems of earthly happiness to the participation even of individuals in a promise of metaphysical salvation; from the needs of mere material satisfaction to longings for new spiritual certainties; from the problems of the individual's relations with his fellows and with the social community to that of the dialogue of man both with himself and with God. Moreover, that shift took place notwithstanding the continuation and development, perhaps not organic, of a dispute between the classes – fundamentally those of the senatorial and municipal nobility, the poverty-stricken masses of town and country, and the initially Roman but later barbarian military element.

This intense anxiety in the thought and feeling of Mediterranean society to give a more recognisable and reassuring centre to its meditation on the great problems was itself an advance on the attitude of antiquity, an effort to exchange a cold, scholastic contemplation, intellectual in character, for a more intimate, agitated and vital participation of the individual in the superior bliss of the celestial world. It did not, however, find a ready response in the schools of traditional classical theory which were exhausting themselves in the futile labour of interpretation, further elaboration and commentary. Their work, almost wholly philological, dealt with the great literature of antiquity, seldom if ever critically recasting its problems in the light of the mounting uneasiness of the contemporary spirit, and drawing from them no logical conclusions that might have led to some sort of intellectual expansion among the learned and executive classes of the Empire. Such was the case with the Peripatetics; such with the Platonic School, until it was supplanted by Neoplatonism; such with Scepticism, which revived in the new Pyrrhonic School with Aenesidemus and Sextus Empiricus; such with the Cynics, who could count on many disciples in Rome during the central imperial period. These last, however, did not so much express a philosophy as a rebellion against current conventions, thus bearing further witness to the spiritual torment of the age.

These pressing needs, already implicitly recognised in Eclectic thought, seem to have aroused some attention among the Roman Stoics of the first and second centuries AD, notably Seneca, Epictetus and Marcus Aurelius.

Even Stoic theory, however, had little new to say on its own account during the central imperial period; and the *apatheia* of the sage, coupled with the necessary pantheistic rationality of the cosmos, was certainly not sufficient to provide a dissatisfied conscience with fresh hopes. But the wide interpretative network of this outworn philosophy was penetrated by 'modern' sensibilities deeply aware of

4

the sickness of the times, well equipped for existential participation, for psychological introspection and for humane compassion.

Seneca was not a man capable of renovating any system, nor could he have initiated a rebellion of conscience. But a personalised moral characterisation of the ancient pan-logistic scheme is often present in his work, undoubtedly testifying to a rising tide of discontent. In Letter cxvii he rebukes Lucilius for asking him meaningless and deceptive questions which, besides depressing rather than stimulating his mind, embarrass him by forcing him to choose between the conformism of the Stoic fraternities and the serenity of his own conscience, which obliges him to speak frankly. In writing thus he is depicting simultaneously both the banal academic status of the practising philosopher and his own progressive retreat from the multiplication of problems in his day. 'What is the use of devoting to vain imaginings the greater part of this present time, so fast and narrow a stream of events, which carries us too along with it? Consider also that the mind grows accustomed to pursuing the objects of its amusement rather than those of its cure and rendering philosophy a delight rather than a remedy. Tell me: when I have thoroughly learned the difference between wisdom and being wise, shall I be wise? Why then do you hold me to the discussion of wisdom instead of the actions which wisdom performs? I wish you to make me stronger, more serene, equal to my fate or superior to it. . . .'[1]

Philosophy, Seneca warns his friend, should aim at providing medicine for the soul rather than intellectual pleasure, and it does not suit him because it spends too much time in the quest for formal charm. 'Fundamentally, we should try to say what we feel and to feel what we say. Our language should be in harmony with our lives. We shall not be dissatisfied with one who whenever seen and heard is always the same' (lxxv). Even the recurrent, almost obsessive, sermons on death and declarations of mortality assume in this philosopher a tone which will shortly become customary among the cultivated classes of the Empire. Length of life is not so important as the ability to live virtuously (ci). On the other hand, the soul is made to affirm that 'when the day comes for the dis-solution of this mixture of human and divine I shall leave the body here where I found it and return to the gods. I am not separated from them even today. But I am ill at ease with my earthly weight. My sojourn in this mortal life is a prelude to a better and more permanent existence' (cii).

Such recognition of the unsatisfactory nature of life includes not only the traditional precipitate of Stoic thought, but also the deep disgust with the inequalities of value which earthly organisation, even that of the highest administrative apparatus, appeared structurally incapable

1 Seneca, *Ad Lucilium Epistulae morales*, cxvii.

of levelling out. While the problem remained unsolved even by Seneca's comprehensive and heartfelt preaching, this soil seemed the best adapted, the most congenial, for propagation of the redemptive doctrines of the Orient, which were now, towards the end of the second century, beginning to take account of the message of Christianity. When Seneca derides the means chosen by his colleagues to counteract the fear of death – 'Am I perhaps to say, "What is evil does not confer glory, but death does confer glory, therefore death is not evil?" That would indeed be a convincing syllogism!' (lxxxii) – his criticism of the vanity of wisdom, unable to solve the human problem, is already radical. Yet the critical passages in Seneca which, from the time of Tertullian onward, have been interpreted in various ways as Christian 'openings', scarcely affirm a crisis in his own system. They are not solutions of the problem, nor even projects for its solution. For they not only lack any content qualitatively analogous to the Christian, but also any sign, at any rate as they stand, of a potential departure from Stoic logic.

Even the imperturbable morality of Epictetus and Marcus Aurelius, no matter how clearly one may recognise a psychological evolution in the latter especially, is far from affording any promise of redemption capable of establishing a vital and responsible relation between human existence and its fate. Epictetus and his master Musonius Rufus share indeed the ethical impulses of Seneca's philosophy, but they do not supplement the minor force of intellectual participation with doctrines justifying it at a deeper level. According to the pupil of Musonius, continual reflection upon death will banish ignoble thoughts and desires from the soul;[2] but the root of this moral system and of the hope of another world remains natural, even rational. It is in true knowledge, reason, that there resides the essence of the good, rendering man equal to the gods. While the practice of virtue remains more than ever the prerogative of wisdom, any escape from the natural order of things is still inconceivable, all the more so because that order continues to be upheld by an immanent, universal necessity.

Marcus Aurelius may perhaps be said not to represent imperial society's most powerful attempt to deal effectively, in an extrinsic and active sense, with the spiritual problem of the age; for the very form of the *Meditations* illustrates the contemporary solution of a retreat to intimism. But with him that society did bear explicit testimony to the ability of its most sensitive and frank exponents to understand the direction which religious sentiment would have to take in order to afford the conscience of mankind the support of a new legacy of values in place of those which no longer sufficed to meet the needs of the community.

The meditations of Marcus Aurelius found expression

2 Epictetus, *Encheiridion*, 21.

in a lofty code of living, which was as yet beyond the reach of contemporary morality, but with a logic now sufficiently transformed, as compared with the preceding classical type, to represent repeatedly as new the basic arguments for goodness, tolerance, solidarity, the duty of communion with the divine and even the readiness to face death. But although such accents were already fully integrated in the ramifications of the traditional philosophy, they are now inserted as a form of human piety in the context of an ideological cosmos still governed by the familiar iron Stoic law of rational necessity closely combined with the destiny of men and things. The universal order of Marcus Aurelius is not disturbed by his special emphasis on philanthropy and the practice of virtue, and the *apatheia* of the sage remains entirely within the Stoic concept of rational imperturbability. Consequently, the cosmos of the Christians, freely animated by the existential adventure of persons attracted by divine love and the acceptance of suffering by the Son of God, an act destined to transform semantically the *pathos* of classical thought even in its Stoic guise of acceptance, would appear revolutionary to the conscience of the early third century, even as compared with the ideas of Marcus Aurelius.

The Emperor tells himself he must not sit in judgment on others. One seems to hear the Gospel injunction. But his motivation is different. 'You are not even sure that they actually do wrong; for many actions are done to serve a given purpose.'[3] Again, if for Marcus Aurelius the necessity he affirms of repeating continually to oneself, 'I am a member of the system made up of reasonable beings', is one which ought to permit a true love of mankind, it may be observed that to consider oneself part of that system is not enough to draw such a conclusion. The argument allows man to benefit his fellow-men, but solely 'as a bare duty, not yet as though doing good to yourself' (vii, 13). Or lastly, one is warned by the Emperor to see that 'the governing and sovereign part of your soul is undiverted by the smooth or broken movement in the flesh, affections of the bodily parts . . . are diffused into the understanding, as needs must be in a united system, then you must not try to resist the sensation, which is natural, yet the governing part must not of itself add to the affection the judgment that it is either good or bad' (v, 26).

In so far as this philosophy succeeds in permeating or expressing the territory of the Empire its results necessarily appear in the first place fatal to the basic structures of conscience through which is intimated the conscious mastery of this world by the *civis romanus*. The preaching of Roman Stoicism has been viewed as endangering (theoretically or practically) the fundamental institutions of the Empire. That danger has come to be identified with the very person of Marcus Aurelius, and can therefore best

3 Marcus Aurelius, *Meditations*, xi. 18.

be estimated by considering the aridity of the consolation offered by his final resort to a vague and inadequate system of reason. His thoughts uproot an active morality, trusting in human experience and historically justified, in order to replace it by a scheme of natural rationality lacking sufficient personal impulse and issuing solely in a frigid interior composition. It might be called a somewhat pretentious 'lay' religion, confirming by its very existence the participation of the Roman ruling class in the cultural and religious strivings of the Mediterranean peoples, expressed at the philosophical and theological level mainly through Neopythagorean declarations clearly directed to a mixture of rational and supra-rational acts of pacification.

While stimulating the crisis of the conscience of antiquity, this school of refined wisdom, suited only to very restricted intellectual circles, stresses also in Seneca's pronouncements the humanist inadequacy peculiar to that classical *paideia* of which it now represented the final and most rigorous exposition.

Cultural life in antiquity had always been a luxury confined to the social *elite*, a *hortus conclusus* accessible only to the ruling class and the urban middle classes. But in Rome especially, ever since the epoch of *Graecia capta*, it had been little more than a fashion which made philosophers and mathematicians, rhetoricians and men of letters acceptable in good society, though the philosophers met with a good deal of contempt. When the Hellenistic arts, represented by thousands of masterpieces seized in captured cities throughout the Mediterranean area, entered the new capital of the world, rhetoric was studied as a model for speech, and great numbers of portrait busts were ordered from sculptors (without, however, improving the social standing of the artists); but not much attention, at any rate in the early period, was paid to philosophic discussion. As for experimental science, it certainly never became domiciled in Rome, while its cultivation steadily diminished throughout the Empire, with grave economic and social consequences, owing to the lack of technological development.

This structural weakness on the cultural side continued with the growth of intellectual and spiritual dissatisfaction in the second century, when classical culture began no longer to satisfy even the ruling class of the masters of the world, and appeared devoid of meaning, so that the refinements of Hellenistic civilisation formerly imported and enjoyed ceased to provide an ideal of life and a recipe for happiness, and an alternative was sought in the nascent philosophical and religious syncretism, since the latest form of traditional rhetoric, that of Aelius Aristeides for example, had nothing more to offer.

The State made some effort at planning a more enlightened educational policy: teachers were granted exemption from taxation at various times; Trajan and his successors established *institutiones alimentariae*; municipal schools were founded and became much more numerous in the late imperial period. But the 'liberal studies' which constituted their only instrument of instruction showed an astonishing indifference to the growing cultural and spiritual problems of the day, to such an extent that after the *Metamorphoseon Libri XI* of Apuleius literature proved incapable of any fresh vitality. Production in the traditional literary forms imitated the archivistic method of Suetonius in history, the formalistic and artificial degeneracy of Fronto's rhetoric, the arid grammatical rigorism of Aulus Gellius, and finally the impassioned but languid preciosity of the poetry of Claudian and Rutilius Namatianus.

The poor quality of education and scientific research lapsed into formalism and rhetoric during the imperial period, without educative value or any possibility of successful development, owing to the inability of intellectuals to apply their methods and ideas to the real problems of everyday life. Such is the explanation of the crisis of classical humanism. It arose from the impracticability of repairing a shattered culture, from the preference for pettifogging specialisation, from the dichotomy between one discipline and another, as well as between the backwardness of science and the urgency of religious aspiration, and between the barren revivalist efforts of a philosophy incapable of any new direction and the tumultuous ferment of public and private life.

For Quintilian, as for his successors who grew progressively more detached from reality, a thorough familiarity with the precepts of rhetoric still remained, in fact, the surest passport to complete success in the public and private duties of life, in politics, in legislation and in jurisprudence.[4] His attitude accounts for the fact that the intellectuals of the late Empire wrote such inferior history, despite their continued show of lively interest in public events. Seneca had already noted this shortcoming as he ruthlessly dismantled the questionable machinery which should have produced the *vir bonus* in series. 'A learned man studies language, and, if he wants to go further, history, and, if he wishes to extend his range as far as possible, poetry. But which of all these disciplines smooths the path of virtue? Can it be the scansion of syllables, a careful attention to phrasing, a knowledge of legendary tradition or the regulation and modulation of his lines of verse?' (lxxxviii). His inability to discriminate between the liberal arts of leisure and practical studies directed to the foundation of a new *paideia* does not prevent us from recognising that the polemics of the Stoic philosopher had hit the mark.

One of the most dramatic and significant aspects of the

4 Quintilian, *Institutiones oratoriae*, proem, 10.

crisis of civilisation in the Empire is thus explained by the growing dichotomy between two situations: firstly the impetuous and even anarchical movement of the religious component of the collective conscience, ranging from disputes on the gravest problems of cosmogony and theology to mystical and ritual experience; secondly, the uncritical and indolent stagnation of the profane component, ranging from ideological dialectics to varieties of custom, and from the practice of the arts to that of experimental science. The more this last activity proved itself incapable of replacing the traditional forms of culture, and revealed its poverty and inertia in the spheres of technological rationalism and experimental behaviour, the more the erudition of antiquity disclosed the formal and practical aridity of its pan-logistic deposit, so much so as to inject into the charismatic expectancy of every kind of soteriological religion all their hopes for the future, thus causing their further exaltation. It is not surprising, therefore, that the Church showed no fear, at least until the fourth century, of injury to her disciples from the organisation and ideas, even if didactic, of the classical culture to which the younger Christians were exposed.

In the East philosophical speculation made earlier and more remarkable advances than in Rome towards its future reduction to theology. At the cross-roads of Alexandria, open to all types of civilisation and intelligence no less than to the commercial traffic linking Roman Europe with the Far East (including India and China), the first imperial century was already witnessing the irresistible collapse of Hellenistic rationalism, which was submerged in the inexhaustible mysticism of its original oriental subsoil, but which had failed, above all, to meet an imperative challenge to provide the peoples of the *pars orientalis*, already once united by Alexander, with the stability of a global outlook, a canon adequate to the attainment of truth and to the internal solution of the greatest of problems. Such assurances were no longer demanded from 'reason'. The questions were asked of 'faith'. For some centuries, as thought declined into a systematisation of dogmatic messages from beyond the world, the syncretistic crucible absorbed magic, rites and mysteries, antique or influential cults and the most diverse doctrines from all quarters. The unsatisfied conscience of mankind welcomed this re-emergence of 'pre-history' into 'history' and offered citizenship and disciples to every belief. There was even a clear tendency to fuse them all into a single instrument of internal contentment.

On the religious plane, only Jews and Christians showed any signs of an independent attitude. The need, however, to confront a new world, the fate of which they controlled between them, induced both to take over from the preceding apparatus of classical thought such of its methodologies, varieties and elements as might prove useful for the establishment of a firmly based theology, as Philo may be said to have done, or else positively for the conceptual systematisation of the new Christian teaching. The exponent of Alexandrian Judaism, from which Gnosis later borrowed the demiurgic metaphysics of the Logos, was accordingly called the 'Hebrew Plato', while Apollonius of Tyana, the 'Pagan Christ', flourished in the non-Christian climate of Neopythagoreanism, which had nevertheless been affected by certain contributions from the Gospels. These extreme cases are precisely those which indicate the breadth of this reforming front, whose members were pledged in various ways to meet a spiritual and substantially unitary requirement of the epoch, through the most diverse forms of juxtaposition between ancient myths and new mysteries, between the old victories of 'reason' and the recent gifts of 'faith'.

Amid all this speculation, which constantly refers to the great spirits of the past – bards like Homer or philosophers like Plato – as discoverers of truth but above all as masters of life, the complexity of the discussion between soul and body, between the world and God, deepens. It had originated in the breakdown of the structures of the classical '*in-der-Welt-sein*' built up into rational unity. First Philo, after rejecting as illusory the logical and scientific disciplines which had come to nothing, had proclaimed salvation of the soul and contemplation of divine glory to be the result, not of any human victory, but of the gift of God's grace. Then the Neopythagoreans, who, together with the Neoplatonists, were later to introduce the greatest of the classical efforts to meet the moral needs of the conscience of late antiquity, reformed the terms of redemption by recognising substantial merit in the human soul, which by cutting itself off from the world, the body and evil, either by asceticism (Apollonius) or by its own nature (Numenius), renders itself worthy and able to comprehend divinity.

It was in this spiritual climate that the 'saviours' arose, with whom theological and philosophical doctrines underwent a process of further reduction to soteriology. 'In a disintegrating society,' writes Toynbee,[5] 'creative genius assumes the role of a Saviour.' He classifies such beings according to whether they operate with the sword, as the small Hebrew people on the whole expected, or by social reform, philosophic teaching or divine incarnation. But whatever form this social demiurge may take, it undoubtedly replies under various aspects to an identical interior request. Consequently it is necessary to recognise a common character between the Christian proposition and others put forward simultaneously, at any rate so far as concerned the requirements to which all were concurrently directed. As Seeck explains: 'It is a fact that the

5 Toynbee, Arnold (1939), vi, p. 376.

ideas which conform with the spirit of an epoch are passed rapidly from mouth to mouth and sometimes appear in different places at the same period without their exponents being necessarily dependent upon one another. Is Christianity really indebted for its Platonic or Stoic elements to the disciples of Plato or Zeno? Or is it simply the case that the same ideas were conjured up, even in Christian thought, by an identical *Zeitgeist*? That is not a question to which any definite answer can ever be given. The only incontrovertible fact is that the teachings of Christianity are not entirely novel or original, but to a great extent rooted in the spiritual life of the epoch.'[6]

A glance at the Christian camp, however, shows, besides the separate aspects of the relation between religion and philosophy, the innovating peculiarity of the extended range of Christianity as compared with its current rivals. In the first place it is to be remarked that Christianity is less entangled with any of the other contemporary forms of reply to ideological and spiritual anxieties, owing to the fact that it arose in the character of an essentially religious message and as such did not have to pay substantial tolls to the wisdom of antiquity, which might well have conditioned or retarded its vital impetus. As compared with the ancient doctrines which were beginning to be overturned and reduced to syncretist theosophies, the values of the Gospel seemed free to develop in the conscience of humanity beyond the limits of any cultural system, and if anything to go some distance in the opposite direction.

Philosophic preoccupation did in fact make its way into the structure of Christian thought when its preachers penetrated pagan cultural environments and realised that they would have to employ a universally comprehensible language. At that stage Christian circles were assuming attitudes of acceptance or rejection in dealing with the Greek ideas which still permeated the mental structure and the constituent laws of the world open to discovery and conquest by the new Church. Towards the middle of the second century the charismatic approach of the earliest period was yielding to a practical motive, the intention to graft the Christian community into the social network. Moreover, it often happened that a convert had adopted the faith after an intellectual struggle, and was turning his attention to the new problems arising to a considerable extent from the contact of the revolutionary declarations of the Gospel with the obstinately surviving pagan ways of life. Now therefore he felt the need to preserve a cultural legacy which he recognised would be of service in the formation of his new status, if only as an earthly catalyst of the existing dialectical encounter.

These second-century attitudes gradually led the infant Church to feel that she ought to recover and redeem what was now recognised as light evolved by human thought,

6 Seeck (1910–21), iii, pp. 203–4.

if only by way of preparation for the 'fullness of time' in which the 'good tidings' had been announced.

The euhemeristic attitude of the first Christian apologists, who adopted the theory of the gods having become such after an existence as wise and courageous men, in order to use it polemically against pagan beliefs, was therefore very soon succeeded by the positive consideration, in an allegorical sense, of classical mythology. Many of its tales were utilised in the same way as were those of the Old Testament, that is to say as 'images' prefiguring New Testament history. Some singular parallels between classical myth and the Gospel narrative were thus exploited, leading Justin Martyr to declare that the stories of the gods and heroes were nothing more than imitations of the Biblical prophecies.[7] He proceeded accordingly, on the basis of the doctrine of the *Logos spermatikos*, to assert in the name of his coreligionists: 'Whatever truth they spoke belongs to us Christians.' And Christianity, assuming responsibility for all history, went on to extract from it, reviving it in her own way, the sum total of civilisation.[8]

By so doing the Christian Church at once ensured that she would no longer remain an isolated part of the ideological and spiritual context of antiquity. Confronted with the conversion of philosophy to theology by means of the imposing elaboration of syncretism, the Church realised that she must not be excluded from the contest but must cover her own section of the road by moving against the growing religious anxieties of the class which was still, though no longer firmly, in the saddle of the Empire. The Christians needed a language, in other words the ability to proclaim the message of salvation on an intellectual level. The Church had therefore to enter into the mentality, the intellectual category, the lines of reasoning, the concepts and the idiom which were the principal characteristics peculiar to an educated man of high social standing.

The attitude initially assumed by the intellectual *élites* of the Christian community in making this effort was logically apologetic and polemical. The Church fortified her position and defended it with weapons similar to those of the classical reaction, which was resorting to philosophic and religious syncretism in order to satisfy the universally felt longings for spiritual novelty. By proceeding in this way she was really establishing her right to conquer classical thought, and her consciousness that she would do so, thus providing evidence of the unfamiliarity and unprecedented range of what she had to offer. Such an attitude is confirmed in other fields: it is amply attested by treatises on constitutional loyalty, as well as by appeals to common juridical guarantees made by such apologists as Minucius Felix and Tertullian.

A similar importance attaches to the fact that the

7 Justin Martyr, *Apology*, 54. And elsewhere (46): 'All who live according to the Logos are Christians, even if they are called impious, as was the case among the Greeks with Socrates and Heraclitus'.
8 Justin Martyr, *Second Apology*, 13. Gilson (1952), p. 18.

Church never feared, in her pastoral teaching and literature or in the decoration of liturgical and funerary manufactures, to make use of images adopted from ancient classical mythology, despite Bréhier's view that responsibility for the birth of 'Christian art' rests with the laity rather than with the clergy and the leaders of the Church. The fact should also be stressed that this step was taken not only as a necessary defensive measure at a period of persecution, but that it was also in vogue after the Edict of Constantine, as is proved simultaneously by very numerous texts of the apologists and Fathers and by innumerable paintings and reliefs.[9] Carcopino concludes: 'In their art as in their literature the Christians had adapted the old myths to their beliefs as an illustration, warranted by antiquity, of their youthful certainties.'[10]

A final proof is offered by the very vicissitudes of second-century apologetics. In this connection it appears significant that the rigorism of Tatian and Tertullian, who were bitterly hostile to Greek thought and to the intellectual and moral habits of the day, led the former to the heresy of Encratite Gnosticism and the latter to the austerity of the most extreme Montanism. Yet the social loyalty of neither is in doubt.[11] On the other hand, intemperance was by no means a rarity in the militant wing of the 'Conciliators'. Here apologetics took shape in the unexceptionable doctrine of Justin, who opened the door for the first time to a free exchange of views and consequent admission of Christians to cultural citizenship, which after him facilitated the leavening and conquest of society; it was nevertheless followed by the sometimes rash irenism of Clement of Alexandria, and by the excesses of Origen in the greatest effort of rationalisation yet made by Christianity.

This conciliatory wing of the Greek apologists sometimes appears, on the other hand, bent upon grafting the Christian ecclesiastical organism into the organisation and spirit of late Roman civilisation, as if it were endeavouring to transform the matrices of ancient humanism by adopting the educational structures and classical heritage of that civilisation. The Church's educational programme had never been exposed to any serious danger from the official schooling or from traditional literature; and thus, finding herself in one respect in more lively and perhaps dramatic contact with the Gnostic peril, she proved indirectly her eagerness to test a formula that might permit an intellectual apostolate among the upper classes of Alexandrian society, which at the beginning of the third century were ready to swallow all forms of cultural novelty and which might accordingly be saturated with orthodox doctrine. The *Didaskaleion*, above all as typified by Clement of Alexandria, the 'rival of the Gnostics',[12] in fact inclined to the notion of a practical convergence of classical and Christian

9 Bréhier (1928), p. 16. *See also* Courcelle (1944).
10 Carcopino (1956), p. 199.
11 Tertullian, *Apologeticum*, xxxi, 3.
12 Tixeront, J. (1905), i, p. 262.

factors so as to form a new sort of man. This new man would be capable of living up to the new values taught by Christ, who would be regarded preferably as the Logos; capable of so living in accordance with doctrinal ideals that were rational and consequently within the purview of 'gentile wisdom'. In the eyes of a society which, although baptised, was still half pagan, the true Christian, the 'Gnostic', seemed to be one who practised mildness in speech and action, and avoided rashness and violence, adorning his aristocratic courtesy with graceful rhythms and walking majestically, as though conscious of divinity and sanctity.[13] It was to such an audience that Clement addressed his mild, well balanced, never harshly-phrased lectures. In the *Protreptikos*, *Pros Hellenas* and *Paidagogos*, he outlined a Christian paideia that did not require excessive heroism. In the *Stromateis* he praised the result of an education simultaneously human and divine, truly 'Gnostic', never entrapped by melancholy, convinced that all is for the best. The Christian does not lose his temper, for nothing can move him to anger. He loves God continuously, tenderly and more than any person or thing. He does not expose himself to desires and appetites. He is induced, in a word, to resemble his Master in *apatheia*.[14] But, as already pointed out, this attitude was very much more Stoic than Christian, and led to such statements as 'Everything that is contrary to right reason is sinful.'[15] These, though in themselves apparently capable of withstanding orthodox criticism, were none the less highly ambiguous, particularly in the ideological climate of the age, where pronouncements from all quarters, including themes of salvation pitched in a rationalist key though based emblematically on myth, were still the order of the day.

It is hardly surprising that the Church took not a single step on the road opened up by Clement. The 'Gnostic Christian', fashioned in the Alexandrian lecture-rooms not only as a secular *élite* but also as a reliable source for recruits to the ecclesiastical hierarchy which by this time was well on the way to institutional status, could not really come to terms with the more jealous guardians of the unique character of Christian values. Consequently, quite apart from the rigid attitude of those who opposed Christian participation in the humble profession of teaching, a view due as much to the old classical prejudice as to dislike of the educational programmes, it may be affirmed that during the fusing process of the third and even the fourth century the Church had neither the wish nor the practical opportunity to found a Christian educational system, to produce a new theory of didactics in place of the pagan scheme or to create an independent cultural organisation. In taking over certain predominantly instrumental aspects of classical philosophy the Church acted basically in defence of the legitimacy of her mission and in

13 Clement of Alexandria, *Hupotuposeis*, 44.
14 Clement of Alexandria, *Stromateis*, vii, 10, 57.
15 Clement of Alexandria, *Paidagogos*, i, 13.

order to improve her prospects of reducing the danger of syncretism by fighting on ground upon which no one else had taken his stand. It was remembered, moreover, that Christian apology itself had been almost wholly the work of separate individuals, acting independently and privately. It had at times lost its equilibrium by according sometimes too much and sometimes too little respect to the comprehensive doctrinal line assumed by the Church. Such seems to have been the position in literature, art and secular affairs. Accordingly, instead of undertaking such arduous tasks, which would certainly have strengthened her missionary effort, the Church preferred to run the risk of sending Christian boys and young men to the private and official classical schools, trusting that family responsibility and the day-to-day relationships of community life would render posterity immune to the 'poison' it might imbibe from its studies. At a time when the Empire had already become Christian, Jerome could therefore still imagine Christ uttering the curt reproach: '*Mentiris, Ciceronianus es, non Christianus!*'[16] He felt himself obliged to blame the priests who neglected sacred literature to dwell upon profane works. If the boys read such books, the Father warns his readers, it is because they are forced to do so. But it is a heinous offence to read them for their own pleasure.[17]

It is true, on the other hand, that the deeper level of Alexandrian speculation, which seems almost to anticipate the extreme classical reaction of Plotinus, marks the stage of a more ardent and authentic philosophy among the Christians, corresponding to the indefatigable polemic of the Gnostics.

The mythological syncretism represented by the Gnostics had incidentally and by way of reaction served to recall Christian apologists to the true incentives of religion. These could be satisfied, in a supra-rational sense, by faith alone, though an incautious overdose of philosophy might have substituted the discounted certitudes of intellectual learning. *Pistis* captured by *Gnosis* might have in fact meant the complete reduction of Christianity to a secondary component of philosophical syncretism. It would have permitted, in effect, the absolute predominance of the old pagan lexicon over the new Christian semantics. On the other hand, the closed philosophical terminology would not have assumed the unrestricted religious sense capable of transforming internally the already weakened rationality of the classical conception in such a way as to reorganise its construction. The pagan wisdom would have remained intact. Paul would have proclaimed in vain the superiority of the preaching of 'Christ crucified, unto the Jews a stumbling-block and unto the Greeks foolishness.'[18]

The Christian victory over Gnosis did not annihilate it, for the Church salvaged and adopted as much of that

16 Jerome, *Epistulae*, 22, 30.
17 Jerome, *Epistulae*, 21. 13.
18 Paul, 1 Corinthians, i, 23.

doctrine as she considered acceptable. Her triumph actually preserved the final revolutionary burden of the Gospel message, which had been undermined by the disciples of Basilides with the affirmation of the redemptive power they assigned to mere erudition. Against Marcion, however, Christian optimism denied that the universe had come into existence saddled with an initial error on the part of its creator. The Christian concept of moral responsibility bound up with free will thus fostered the Christian vocation to transform mankind. It was precisely this responsible autonomy assigned to the individual in conforming with the 'folly' of the Cross for the salvation of his soul, that best met the demand for new metaphysical certitudes. An alien element was thus introduced to the classical '*in-der-Welt-sein*'. On the ruins of the ancient world the freedom to attain salvation would slowly create in the Christian mind the idea of 'personality'.

The inventive inferiority of the Gnostic doctrine, as compared with Christian apologetics in this particular field, became more apparent than ever, and was confirmed by the manifest inadequacy of the last attempt at syncretism in the Alexandrian age, the Neoplatonism of Plotinus, which collected and systematised the elements of previous philosophies, especially in their religious connotation, in order to test an extreme type of classical response to the demand for a new religious product, a demand that was being satisfied by Christian thought now penetrating in all directions. Appreciable competition with it could be found only in two complex and multiform cults prevalent at various levels in the religious life of the third century, the worship of the sun and of Hercules respectively.

Consideration of the solar, Herculean and Plotinian religious theories appears highly instructive if it treats them all together. In these three diverse experiments of the religious conscience during the late imperial period there may be in fact discerned the pattern of the attempt made by classical culture – and thus by the ruling class of the Empire then undergoing a rapid process of transformation – to convert a licentious cult of oriental mysticism to the dignity of popular theological doctrine; to transfer the myth of Hercules to the plane of religious asceticism, especially among the upper classes; and to recover the elements of traditional Platonist-Pythagorean thought in a philosophical synthesis adequate to the new age. The enterprise was directed, in short, to resisting Christian subversion by a fusion of old and new materials drawn from classical thought and myth, together with foreign importations susceptible of vast expansion, in a system of cults and ideas, moral principles and cosmic notions sufficiently wide and articulated to include all the various anti-Christian reactions.

Rome had never been unwilling to absorb the ritual and

doctrinal expressions of her vast and variegated network of Empire. The cults of Cybele, of Isis, of Serapis and of Dionysus were only the most considerable among those imported by the capital during the early centuries, and thence disseminated by the legions and by trade throughout the Empire. But they had all undergone a process of romanisation, in other words an elimination of their more licentious features and those foreign to the conventional morality of the metropolis; so much so that the first scandalous contact of the solar divinity of Emesa with Rome, which occurred during the reign of Elagabalus, was almost immediately annulled on the death of the young emperor. Thus, as Altheim[19] has shown, it was only later that the god was fully and permanently accepted in Rome, under the influence of Heliodorus's *Aithiopika*, a novel which, about the middle of the third century, presented Helios in a new form, assimilating him to the greatest of the gods in a context not prejudicially polemical in relation to the classical system of theogony, of which he was made practically the central essence. A further influence was that of Neoplatonic preaching, which performed on the philosophic plane a similar operation of divine reunion, while preserving the traditional polymorphism. It was upon such foundations that Aurelian was enabled to introduce to Rome the new god, whom Plotinus and Porphyry had already identified as the universal demiurge of their system superior to the traditional family of Olympian deities. This he did in the year 274, after conquering the Palmyrene realm of Zenobia where the cult of Helios had originated. The significance of his act resides less in its relation to the theogony of Olympus than in its character as a pledge of spiritual reunification throughout the Empire, from the restless religious territories of the East to the barbarous populations of the *limes* called upon to serve in the legions, who were easily induced to recognise and adore in the new cult the ancient solar divinities of their native soil. This work expressed a simultaneously religious and political effort on the part of the ruling class to provide a surer defence of the imperial power, the destiny of the State and the safety of its peoples.

This, however, was not achieved without Neoplatonic mediation, which alone gave the new solar cult theoretical justification, so as to permit not only the imperial political decision but also the attempt to impose it as a revised official religion. But that mediation proved both the philosophical inadequacy of the new system and the means by which it could be finally resolved into the more coherent and consoling Christian message. Compared with the open, historical and communicable form of the Synoptic and other New Testament writings, Plotinian theology was closed, dogmatic and impracticable, even though its effect was to saturate classical metaphysics with mysticism.

19 Altheim (1960), *passim.*

Hence a desire to ignore it altogether. Besides, there was fundamental agreement that in a wide historical perspective the system of Plotinus appeared to be a *medium* of compromise between moribund tradition and the Christian theory, without either preserving the secular values of the former or impeding the triumph of the latter.

Plotinus, when one comes to think of it, enjoyed exceptional opportunities. He taught in Rome for a quarter of a century, and was in high favour with the court, particularly with his friend the Emperor Gallienus. He was also endowed with extraordinary philosophical energy, exceeding that of any other personality during the first four centuries of the Christian era; and the growing discredit into which the classical tradition had fallen enabled him to make use, without the least sign of prejudice, of a vast mass of material which no one could any longer revive and animate. He faced a great gap which needed filling, namely the religious conscience of his day, which was now surrendering to any imported deity; and he had only one enemy to fight, Christianity, against which its persecutors were increasing their final assaults before leaving a free field, somewhat unexpectedly, for the first juridical recognition of the Church. If he succeeded, his victory might theoretically lend wings to the process of recomposing the tissue of classical ideology by means of a traditionalist philosophical and moral answer proportionate to the questions of the age, so as to lead the Empire to discover the moral sources of a 'renaissance' in a renovated syncretism, if not in its more intimate original idealisms.

The essential cause of Plotinus's failure is immediately evident, if we recall that the victory of the Christian apologists over the Gnostics had been mainly due to the inability of classical thought to emerge from the rationalistic straits of the relationship between God and man, where the individual of the age of Plotinus, was still struggling without finding compensation in the form of a liberating answer to his questions. The external power of the Empire had been subjected during fifty years of military anarchy to the most arduous and humiliating ordeals; a disorderly succession of internal social rebellions was in full swing; science had made no advances, wealth was disappearing, economic security was becoming a gamble with fate; the 'atheist sects', such as Christianity, were gaining ground and beginning to obtain tolerance and satisfaction of their demands from the emperors,[20] who were necessarily preoccupied with economic and military problems of the gravest nature. The vague prophecies of the apologists foretelling disaster to the age were beginning to seem well founded, and Cyprian's warnings[21] of catastrophe were apparently already justified. Contemporary syncretism was being revealed as tragically inadequate for the solution of problems and the allaying of fears; and the

20 The decree of Galerius guaranteeing freedom of worship to the Christians and restoring confiscated ecclesiastical property was issued in 311. For this period *see* in particular Alföldi (1939).
21 Cyprian, *Ad Demetrianum*, 3.

total darkness that veiled the future combined with the anguished uncertainty that tormented the present.

At a historical juncture pregnant with such interrogatives the emanational character of the doctrine of Plotinus did not go substantially farther than preceding theories. The utter lack of determinateness in the One, so unknowable and inexpressible as to render a positive theology out of the question, led even the Roman citizen to point to it as grounds for his metaphysical despair. The divine imperturbability in its multiple act of emanative procession, the almost unrelieved malignity of matter, the necessity of separation of the soul from the body (which of itself 'exists without subsisting',[22] like light in the atmosphere), together with the futile mechanism of the circle of descent and re-ascent to the One, were even psychologically less suited than any other conceivable concept to satisfy a religious conscience primarily concerned to seek in the Deity the assurance of a redemptive standard. Moreover, the utter indeterminateness of the One and the cold, purposeless repetition of its emanative cycle could not appease the longing for a superior fatherhood which mankind, despoiled of every certitude and deprived of any pledge from a higher sphere, cherished as its last hope.

The demand, ever more urgent, was for a 'personal' citizenship in the world, that made by the illegitimate son in search of his father: a 'theological declaration' that the father exists, that he has a certain name and lovingly awaits the return of his son, to whom have been given a name, a promise, a capital of affection invested on high, the certainty that upon himself in the last resort depends the use of love for finding his way home. Plotinus gave no answer to that demand, and it is not illogical that the classical *Weltanschauung* thereupon acknowledged its own demise and that its fabric, long since impaired, soon (one might almost say straightway) collapsed.[23]

Despite a strong formal coherence of thought, destined to have a great deal to teach later Christian philosophy, upon which now depended the preservation of classical values by way of Neoplatonism, the doctrine of Plotinus reveals a substantial measure of internal incoherence, thus proving historically the inability of the classical *Weltanschauung* to fulfil the expectation of the age without self-contradiction. The unknowable god of Plotinus, by reducing the solar deity to the rank of demiurge, assumed the form of an ineluctable will cognizant of but fatal to the latest palladium of the Empire.

But these final years of the third century, marked by the uncompromising restoration of the Tetrarchy, were also those of a further and last attempt to introduce a new religious cult, the Herculean.

At first sight it appeared no novelty. A devotion to

22 Plotinus, *Enneads*, iv, 3.22.
23 Among the best studies of the position of Plotinus in the context of the spiritual philosophy of his time are: Guitton (1933) and Puech (1938). The reader should also keep in mind the *Enneads* of Plotinus himself.

Hercules had been for some time widely current in the capital and in many other Mediterranean centres; its remote Phoenician origins, overlaid at a later period by the Hellenistic tradition, had been recovered in an official exaltation of the divine hero steadily augmented from Trajan to Hadrian and from Commodus to Septimius Severus. But the various traditional elements of the myth had already passed into a work of clearly Stoic significance, the *Hercules Oetaeus*, possibly attributable to Seneca. It may therefore be deduced that when the problems of the religious crisis of the Empire came to notice in the first century the tale began to be used as a model for ethics – moral purposes. From the second century, however, certain parallels and correspondences between the life and death of Hercules and those of Christ must have become so evident as to fan the flames of debate between Christian apologists and pagan authors, proving that certain replies of Justin, or of Origen in his *Contra Celsum*, were prompted by the need to demonstrate to a cultivated public, by this time incredulous of all myths, the substantial differences between the son of Alcmene and the Son of Mary.[24]

The elements of a Herculean theology eminently Stoic in character were therefore already in place and operative in the Empire between the first and second centuries, after the traditional figure of the hero had undergone a certain transformation. That figure had not only been idealised in relation to its primitive mundane characterisation and transferred to the plane of a redemptive model of philosophical type, but had also been invested with cosmic and redemptive features tending to identify it with a kind of universal demiurge ransoming the world by self-sacrifice from the bondage of evil. The archaic demigod was now a mortal who, because of the extraordinary holiness of his earthly strife, had been deified and raised to a key position in an Olympus that retained very little of its ancient fable, since the chief divinities tended towards a gradual identification among themselves and in a Logos differently qualified at different times, in which Hercules himself was often recognised.

At the end of the second century Herculean mythology and theology became an integral part of imperial ideology and the official religion of the monarchical State. The Emperor received his power on earth from God just as Hercules, as the son of God, received it in heaven. Thus were laid all the premises required for the hallowing identification of monarch and god, leading to the conjunction in a single idealogical compound of the religious and secular bases for the survival of the Roman Empire. This unifying theological process was naturally also a form of compromise in which the sacred history of Hercules took on the religious and anthropomorphic form of the deity to which he was assimilated, but without finally

24 Justin Martyr, *Apology*, 21; *Second Apology*, ii; Origen, *Contra Celsum*, 3.22, and 7.53.

absorbing the entire complex system of the classical Olympus, and without that system being able objectively to signify an enlargement of the area in which classical religion operated. The two processes simply varied, were integrated, and took charge, alternately, of the cultural spheres by this time incapable of proselytism on their own account. Such is undoubtedly, from the time of the Tetrarchy onwards, the most conspicuous and certainly the most ambitious of the Herculean personifications, that of the Sun.

The imperial cult of Hercules, and the identification of the two divine persons, Jupiter and Hercules, with the tetrarchs Diocletian and Maximian, favoured (and drew profit from) this vague conjunction, which tended to accord with Neoplatonic ideology in the final attempt to restore unity in religion, law, economics and politics to the Empire as a whole. But as early as the time of Constantine the frequent identification – a markedly Christianising process – of the newly sole and supreme monarch with the Sun appears to show that restoration of a religious form to the now parched spirit of mankind would require something more than a progressive and mystifying reduction of the polytheistic universe to the poetic polymorphism of a unique metaphysical reality. The emperor, in fact, had only to grant religious liberty and show sympathy with the Christian Church, and the solar sign tended to lose in him all Herculean significance, all its Neoplatonic implication, or at any rate to withdraw sufficiently to allow his assimilation to the Son of the Christian God and to the Logos. It even appears that henceforth the very fate of the classical doctrine – Hercules, Logos, Sun – was inextricably bound up with that of Christian doctrine.

Very many similarities between the two doctrines are to be found not only in religious literature, through increasing analogies of the revised Herculean story with the Gospel narrative, but also in their respective philosophical speculations, their written polemics and the political aims of the acts of the imperial government. The various beliefs were widespread among the masses. Yet during the fourth century, from the time of Constantine onward, all of them, in a more or less advanced state of metamorphosis, were engaged in a final struggle for supremacy, mainly on the political plane, where the emperors looked to them for the most convincing integration, the most charismatic enrichment of their *auctoritas* and *potestas*.

The classical restoration of these ideological elements under Julian, for example, is so often substantiated, and its teaching resembles so closely the doctrinal structure of patristic Christianity, that the acts and writings of the Emperor inevitably appear, a century after Plotinus, to have been guided by the same purpose, though with less philosophical vigour and a more evident preoccupation with practical politics. That purpose was to bring into the closest possible approximation the structure of ancient cosmogony and morality and those which the success of the Christian propositions showed to be more congenial to human expectations, in such a way as not to limit the recovery of the classical heritage to the domains of philosophy and religion but rather to make it an essential component of the institutional and political fortification of the Empire. In the last political attempt at classical revival, as Simon has emphasised, the importance of the figure of Hercules in Julian's theology was due largely to the affinity this image had acquired with that of Christ, to such an extent as to render the former apparently the true pagan replica of the latter.[25] The same significance is to be attributed, incidentally, to the identification of Hercules with the Sun, which also developed mainly from the Hercules-Logos identification, whether in Julian's propaganda or generally in all the Neoplatonic philosophy of the fourth century.

In short, the intellectualist and allegorising transfiguration of the classical Olympus in the Neoplatonic cosmic system, the identification within that system of Hercules with the Logos and gradually of the Logos with the Sun, and of Hercules also with the Sun, even when he is personified by Eastern theology as Helios and Mithras, reveals in the fanciful articulations of an adopted and variously interpreted myth the almost frantic attempt of a whole oecumenical culture – oecumenical because of its syncretistic fusions and its wide field of operations, if not because its original sources were identical – to conform with the *metanoia* of its members, in positive theology as in liturgical rites, in their conception of the world as in the institutional ideology of the Empire. The endeavour to absorb within a revived classical *Weltanschauung* interpretations, rites, moral usages and sacred legends devised in oriental countries – where from Persia to Israel the cosmos of religion and the philosophic heritage of Greece and Rome had met with relentless opposition – was bound in the end to prove itself an artificial and substantially impracticable measure. The crisis demanded, on the contrary, the preservation of the deposit of classical civilisation in the framework of religious and secular structures originally alien from it, though now organically compounded therewith. The redemption required was one of internal conversion. Of all the forms of the spirit of antiquity only specifically plastic art, ranging from architecture to painting, managed to survive.

25 Simon (1955), pp. 143–9.

Chapter One
Post-Hellenistic developments and liberation of the idiom of Roman pictorial art in the first and second centuries

While Vitruvius, *laudator temporis acti*, was disparaging in the seventh book of his *De Architectura* the direction recently taken by artistic taste which was rapidly spreading in the capital in the form of pictorial interior decoration, the last twenty-five years of the pre-Christian era were beginning in the golden age of the principate of Augustus. The city of Rome was proclaiming her consciousness of empire not only by adorning herself for the first time with stone and marble, but also by her unprecedented activity in the buying and selling of artistic products – chiefly copies of the famous masterpieces of classical Greek and Hellenistic statuary and painting. This activity had begun in the preceding century with the sudden passion of the Roman ruling class for the art of '*Graecia capta*' and the massive emigration to Rome of artists of the Hellenistic *oikoumene*, who had been attracted both by the opportunity to dispose of their academic works among the wealthy new masters of the world and especially by the demand of these latter for portraits. The trade was intermittent and each commission differed from the last, but there was practically no end to the market.

The first wave of fashion had very soon been followed in the capital and the neighbouring Italic cities by a progressive alteration of taste, due partly to Rome's growing interest in the East which had begun with the acquisition of Pergamum (133 BC) and culminated in 31 BC with the victory of Actium. A second factor was the increase of both material and cultural intercourse, which linked more and more new classes – contractors, business men and intellectuals, as well as political and military authorities – with a world till then little known. Consequently, the Roman social fabric became more and more deeply penetrated by agents capable of inducing it to abandon rapidly, almost abruptly, the former provincial character of its civilisation. This first transformation resulted in the establishment of what Mau[1] has called the 'second style' of interior pictorial decoration. Its early development is exemplified on the walls of the Casa dei Grifi on the Palatine, which dates from the republican period (the style of building recalls that of the age of Sulla). Those walls present in perspective a pictorial decoration almost wholly imitative of casings in precious marble slabs, which in specimens of the 'first style' were rendered by coloured plaster.

But the passage between the two decorative systems, the

1 Mau (1882). Of more recent studies *see* Beyen (1938; 1960).

second of which attempted to replace the first exclusively by pictorial means, could not remain at this initial stage. The very principle of illusionism upon which it was based led to a more imposing use of the system devised.

Thus, probably under the influence of examples borrowed from the more baroque practice of the Hellenistic East, the architectural scheme began in the first phase of the 'second style' to use columns, pilasters and cross-beams in order to create the illusion of more ample internal space, which ultimately made room for the wonderful large-scale murals in the dining-room of the Villa at Boscoreale (now in the National Museum at Naples), and those of the dining-room of the Villa dei Misteri at Pompeii. Its function as providing larger apertures belongs to a second phase, of which we have good examples, illustrating its progress, in a room of the same Villa dei Misteri and in another (now at the Metropolitan Museum in New York) from the Boscoreale Villa. In place of the wall, which has been reduced almost to vanishing point, optical illusion presents increasingly complex perspectives of external architecture, fantastic and even improbable. Sometimes the aim is naturalistic, a closer contact between the house and its environment, the latter either mythical or (as already attempted in the Odyssey Landscapes from the Casa dell' Esquilino, now in the Vatican) realistic; examples are the *Viridarium* of the Villa of Livia at Prima Porta (now in the Museo Nazionale, Rome) and the garden with pavilion from the room of the Boscoreale Villa. At other times, and more often, the aim of an exciting perspective of open spaces is achieved with amazing skill, as in the Boscoreale room and the House of Livia on the Palatine, where the primary coefficient is the understanding from without of architectural space which had originally been confined to Greek builders and town-planners.

It is essentially this type of painting that Vitruvius attacks when, in a polemic against the more fantastic and mannered developments of the 'second style', he condemns the travesty of reality and the 'utter falsehoods' told by those who paint things which *'nec sunt nec fieri possunt nec fuerunt'*.[2] The long road of formal experiment taken by this fashion remained always within the domain of imported Hellenism, and accordingly with no symptom of radical stylistic renovation. It ended with the metamorphosis of Hellenistic into Roman painting, tested and approved by history; but in the last quarter of the first century BC that end was by no means yet in sight.

The same taste was to produce a final phase, the most Egyptian and redundant of decorative art, which introduced the 'third style', the painting, that is to say, of interiors most obviously and almost exclusively ornate in character, more akin to rococo in its treatment of colour

2 Vitruvius, *De Architectura*, vii. 5.

and repertory of symbols and patterns. Finally, after this 'degeneration', when preoccupation with ornament appeared to react strongly against the 'second style's' nevertheless exuberant invasion of perspectival architectural space (much reduced in the 'third' style), there followed a new release of luminous, aerial space in the scene-painting of the 'fourth style'. Here the achievements of the 'second' were revised in heavier fashion as a consequence of the traces of Egyptian influence on taste left by the 'third'.

Examples of these last phases of Hellenistic mural painting at Rome and elsewhere in Italy can be seen in both painting and stucco work on the walls of the House of M. Spurius Mesor (VII, 3) at Pompeii, on those from the Casa della Farnesina at Rome, now in the Museo Nazionale, as well as on those of many other houses at Pompeii, including those of Frutteto (I, 9, 5), of the Gilded Cupids (VI, 16, 7), of M. Lucretius Fronto (V, 4, 10), of L. Ceius Secundus (I, 6, 15), all in the 'third style'; on the walls of Nero's *Domus Aurea*, of the Pompeian houses of the Vettii (VI, 15, 1), of Pinarius Cerialis (III, 4, 4) and of the Dioscuri (VI, 9, 6–7); and in the fragment from Herculaneum preserved in the Naples Museum. Such examples are revealed by an exact judgment which operates outside the limits of the usual historical framework and gives due consideration to the development of taste which anticipated the essential exhaustion of the ancient model, as appears from its own strongly marked inclination towards a decorative mode becoming steadily more abstract and an excess of chromatic mannerism more and more calligraphic. An examination of the monuments mentioned above, or of copies transmitted from past centuries in the case of those which have meanwhile disappeared, proves that although the taste in decoration grew progressively complex and diverse, and the approach to lacework and the miniature (exclusively cultivated by much painting in this style) more and more astonishing, yet no substantial, significant change of idiom can be detected.

Representational painting occurs repeatedly in the airy architectural panels of the 'second style'; in the 'third' it creates the illusion of variously sized pictures forming part of the flattened and closed ornamental display; at a later stage it places its subjects within the redundant scene-painting of the 'fourth'. But the idiom in these cases merely shows fluctuations between (*a*) Campano-Italic interpretations of the great Attic tradition of large-scale design; (*b*) coldly correct neo-Attic copies derived therefrom; and (*c*) Hellenistic variations drawn from the more naturalistic Alexandrian manner, tending in its way to that of Egypt or of the different styles current in such areas of Asia as Pergamum, Antioch and Rhodes. The pictorial language shared to the full in the *koine* which Hellenistic art had imposed on the whole Mediterranean basin, the scheme including a variety of general decorative patterns. Its grammar remained that of the Hellenised East. But the syntax, in its multiple embodiments, could to a large extent be regarded as due to the influences of metropolitan taste and culture (not forgetting those also of other towns in Italy) which had by this time created a market undoubtedly bigger and in the long run harder to exploit than that of the Mediterranean Orient, if only because the concentration at Rome of every kind of fashion, workshop and artistic corporation from many different backgrounds produced a greater diversity in the works on offer and so in the logical considerations, preferences, conditions and reciprocal effects operative on both sides.

Without for this reason assuming that Rome was the only such centre, it may nevertheless be supposed that during the century between 50 BC and AD 50 the city became to some degree an extremely active agent in the evolution of taste and thus of artistic experiment. It is therefore quite natural that transformation of the mural decorative system, as well as the parallel changes in floors and ceilings, should afford evidence of certain structural motives already closely connected with the possibly somewhat unco-ordinated and confused investigation of the ever-changing and problematical experience of space, an investigation characteristic of all art in the imperial age until its reconstruction by the Byzantines in one direction and its submergence by the artistic vernaculars of medieval Europe in the other.

In the 'second style', from the illusionist painting of large-scale interiors and of *viridaria* to that of aerial perspectives contrived by fantastic architecture and no less fanciful panoramic views of nature, the progressive widening of interior spaces by means of wall-painting tends to accompany the articulated expansion of architectural structure in the closed environment which constitutes one of the most original, decisive and prolific aspects of architecture for the next thousand years. Its most significant stages are well known, stretching from the Pantheon to the temple of Minerva Medica, from the varying courts of the imperial baths to the Tivoli buildings erected under Hadrian, from S. Costanza at Rome to S. Lorenzo at Milan, from the rotunda of St. George's at Salonika to St. Gereon at Cologne, and from SS. Sergius and Bacchus at Constantinople to S. Vitale at Ravenna. This burgeoning of architectural structure, this progressive enlargement of internal space, deriving always from the need for a vision beyond one's immediate surroundings, for a breath as it were of the beyond, for a winding and centralised pathway into the distance, accorded well with the tendency noted as beginning with the 'second style'. It is no accident that the human figure is represented where the wall breaks off, whether set in the new 'space' produced by the decoration, whether discernible in a simulated picture on the wall – a pretence itself illusive of pretence, since the Hellenistic picture supposedly hanging there represented a 'copy' of nature – or whether, finally, the figure appears against the greenery or landscapes shown beyond the invented architecture of the locality.

With the 'third style', as already mentioned, we witness a strongly marked phase of reaction against this tendency. But despite the preponderance of imaginary figures drawn as an integral part of the ornamental complex, there are instances of pictures inserted in the wall-surfaces, a feature destined, incidentally, to survive in many examples of the 'fourth style'. In these last, however, the development of spatial evolution again takes place in the setting of a composition where figures are closely associated with the open-air architectural background, such as had been achieved in the 'second style'. For example, the scene from the *Iphigenia in Tauris* in a room of the House of Pinarius Cerialis at Pompeii (III, 4, 4), and also the decorations of another Pompeian house, the Apolline (VI, 7, 23), already achieve a fully monumental result by the architectural employment of the backstage wall of a theatre as a setting for the characters in a mythological scene, a setting which provides them with an environment suited to their function and foreshadowing the enhancement of Roman painting and sculpture from the end of the first century onwards, when architecture and frame came to play a part subsidiary to the personages of the narrative. The same result is also attained through the use of stucco decoration, rising to a still higher degree of integration between figures and ornamental structure, in the wall-painting of a Dionysiac subject in the Casa della Caccia (VII, 4, 48) and again in the Stabian Baths at Pompeii. Another illustration may be found on a spacious wall of the *Domus Aurea* of FABULLUS. An eighteenth-century reproduction by Mirri and Carletti[3] shows once more how the characters and the brief episodes are inserted – almost like sculptures and reliefs, a manner inherited from the 'third style' – in the repetitious context of the *aedicula* forming part of a colossal, though light and extremely elegant, backstage wall, closely resembling those of the Roman theatres at Sabratha and Aspendus, or the Septizonium of Severus on the Palatine. The result is less cold and academic than the large-scale decoration, which, however, enables them to preserve a certain personality of their own.

It is not only on the walls that this occurs. Unfortunately very little is known about the decoration of Hellenistic ceilings and vaults, but the great Neronian monument enables us to obtain some idea of it. No more precise knowledge could be expected at the end of the seventh decade of the first century AD, when the structure of the

4

6

3 Mirri and Carletti (1776), pl. XXVII. Another similar wall of the *Domus Aurea* is well reproduced in colour in *Enciclopedia dell' Arte Antica classica e orientale*, vi, Rome, p. 944.

'fourth style' can be judged to be within sight of its maturity. The evidence proves that compositional development, analogous to that on the walls, had become manifest on the ceilings. Once again, for the Gilded Vault of the Neronian *Domus*, we are lucky to possess a reproduction, a sixteenth-century water-colour by Francisco d'Olanda.[4] From this it is easy to see how the complicated texture of columns, pilasters, podia, cross-pieces, friezes and pediments on the walls is reflected on the roofing in a similar arrangement of frames, ornamental fillets, plaster borders and the coloured surfaces which form the requisite medallions containing subsidiary circular and square panels of a figurative character. These, though resembling framed canvases, like the reliefs and statues on the wall, nevertheless retain their function as representing moments and episodes in an organic and complete narrative symphony composed from the teeming repertory of materials in Greek myth.

In this example the figures in the various stories depicted on the ceiling all appear in postures axially co-ordinated with the central circular picture and at right angles to the four sides of the ceiling with the feet nearest the walls and the heads nearest the centre. Such a compositional solution of the problem satisfies, both practically and above all conceptually, the same criterion of organisation as has governed the decorative and figurative arrangement of the mural structure. As on the walls so also on the ceilings – and, as will be seen later, on the floors – painting served to simulate breaches in the outer walls leading from the interior of an environment to the infinite perspectives of the surrounding universe, either actual or imagined. To these immense vistas towards all points of the horizon there thus correspond equally far-ranging views upward to the sky, even though the latter is reduced in the gilded vault to the central circular picture and the eight scenes along the diagonals to the corners of the hall. Myth, history, epic, incarnate virtues and religious symbolism are all represented in this comprehensive organisation which contributed to the pomp of palaces and, on a smaller scale with less magnificence, to the modest decoration of private houses and the damp darkness of the catacombs, bearing its gift of inspiration, peace or encouragement.

As already mentioned, the points made so far apply also to floors. Hellenistic civilisation brought to Rome more than sculptors and fresco painters. It introduced also a taste for the kind of work which had already produced admirable masterpieces at Alexandria and throughout the eastern provinces of the Empire. The few surviving examples include the great floor of the 'Battle between Alexander and Darius at Issus', found in the House of the Faun (VI, 12,2 – 5) at Pompeii (now in the Naples Museum),

7

4 Egger, H. (1906), p. 64, pl. III. *See also* F. Weege in *Jahrbuch des Deutschen Archäologischen Instituts*, XXVIII (1913), p. 127 ff.

and *emblemata* such as those of SOPHILUS (from Tell Timai, now in the Alexandria Museum) and DIOSCORIDES OF SAMOS (showing scenes from the New Comedy, found in 'Cicero's Villa' at Pompeii, and now in the Naples Museum, nos. 9985 and 9987). These Alexandrian *emblemata* whether concerned with epic or idyllic poetry, landscape, comedy, still life or portraiture, soon met with appreciation at Rome. They were often bordered not by ovulate fillets, dentils and the like, as was usual in connection with normal architectural cross-pieces, but by ornamental frames more or less rich in figurative elements, in relation to an axis usually perpendicular to the side on which these elements were placed. In most instances the frame was a highly elaborate piece of work, which was probably meant to arouse particular admiration, but which no longer represented, except in a wholly pretentious manner, an artificial, imaginary window and hence the rational framing of space from and within which it had hitherto been possible to compose the image, as though accidentally caught in a realistic or illusory scene of nature, characteristic of Alexandrian Hellenism as revived by Roman taste.

Very many examples could be cited. It will suffice to mention among the best known *emblemata* those of 'Eros Riding the Dionysiac Panther' from the House of the Faun (VI, 12, 5−2) at Pompeii, 'Plato Among the Philosophers' at the Naples Museum or the so-called *asaroton* of HERACLITUS in the Museo Profano of the Lateran; or again, not to confine ourselves to Italian soil, such subjects as the 'Judgment of Paris' in the dining-room of the House of the Atrium at Antioch and 'Narcissus and Echo' in the Banquet House at Antioch-Daphne.[5] The first two of the works mentioned date from the first century, the third and the fourth from the second century, and the last from the beginning of the third century. They are all framed by ornamental fillets representing festoons of fruit with masks, specimens of Nile fauna, *asaroton* with masks, and grotesque faces. Figurative work of this kind is always axially related to the line of the frame containing it, obviously inviting the spectator to move round the *emblema* itself in order to obtain a precise understanding of each side of the surrounding fillet.

There seems little doubt that this development of the pavimental frames, from its geometrico-linear or architectural decorative function to a character of more or less stylised figuration, henceforward independent of the *emblema*, indicates a transition in significance from the original idea of a window opening on to nature − or rather, as already mentioned, on to the artist's 'copy' of nature − to an integrating part of the picture, standing as such in apposition to the representation of the subject framed by a succession of didactic, qualifying or com-

5 Levi (1947), i, pp. 16 ff and 132 ff; ii, plates Ib, CXLVI b and XXIIIc, CXLII b.

plementary images, like the stage scenery of many centuries later which was introduced to mark temporal and spatial changes in the action of the play. Thus it is perhaps no accident that in the Lateran mosaic referred to above the inscription *HERAKLITOS ERGASATO* already appears on the frame, not in the *emblema*.

This wealth of figurative interest within the ornamental scheme, which incorporates the frames in the enlarged context of the *emblema*'s story, is already to be found, as we have seen, in the mosaic flooring of the Empire during the first century. But its consequences, incidentally as various in character as they are equal in significance, were delayed for some considerable time during a slow phase of maturation and metamorphosis, until late Roman art reached its culmination when the third century was already far advanced. During that interval, however, the compositional scheme did not remain unaltered. Experimentation with problems of space continued steadily, with increasing recognition of their growing conceptual divergence from the original Hellenistic ideas. During the neo-Attic period under Hadrian, the most conservative of the imperial age, the fashionable trends encouraged by the monarch seem to have favoured an extreme development of decorative arabesque in mosaic flooring. It involved a clear subordination of the *emblemata* to complicated geometrical arrangements, as if echoing the predominance of architectural taste in mural decoration. This evolution had already begun under Trajan with the tendency to multiply framings. Additional features were both free and stylised ornamentations of a floral character, varied to the highest degree by graceful zoological motives, such as the representation of birds, etc.[6] But the succeeding Antonine age is characterised by a marked revival of figurative interest, for which the exaggerated style of abstract decoration typical of the preceding period may have furnished the organising network through a distinct sub-division of the content of the emblematic narrative into a series of interconnected sections each illustrating some part of the fable.

It is undoubtedly to this phase, as will be seen later, that we can assign mosaic floorings such as the Genazzano fragment with its remaining 'Heads of Pan and a Young Satyr', now in the Museo Nazionale at Rome, and the so-called Dionysus at Cologne, where the integration of the figures and the warm baroque quality of the ornamental scheme is fully evident. If the first schematic shaping, however substantially illusive, of five different spatial areas (four by the frame and one by the image proper) can reasonably be connected with the shaping of the *emblemata* frames, it seems legitimate to recognise at any rate some link between this revival of figuration in the late second century and an immanent negation of physical three-dimensional space. That negation was certainly not

36

38, 39

6 Blake (1935), p. 206.

derivable in any positive sense from alteration in the decorative purposes of the frames; but it expressed through such alteration a changed attitude to the picture itself or a new view of nature and the reproduction of nature, as well as an evident freedom of expression enjoyed by the *pictor imaginarius* in confronting the sources of his inspiration. It is therefore clear that between the end of the first century and the beginning of the second the utilisation of space, especially within the picture, had progressed significantly beyond the classical space-time unity of ancient painting. It is likewise clear that a new theory of aesthetics had been introduced, whether consciously or not, by the initial tendency (due simply to contemporary taste) to achieve decorative variety not so much through the employment of exotic, 'Egyptianising' ornamental motives predominant in the 'third style' as through the illusionist breaching of closed walls characteristic of the 'second' and 'fourth' styles, in order to acquire with the aid of the whole repertory of Alexandrian figurative resources a new standard for disposition of the subject in the picture.

The truth is that in this age Roman art produced in the great sculptured *rotuli*, in a style of continuous historical narrative and correspondent with the artistic ideals of the central period of the Empire, its first great monumental creation. One might think that this first authentically Roman achievement necessarily outclassed those of the 'fourth style'. But examination shows that such a verdict cannot be delivered without hesitation. In the matter of spatial setting or general artistic conceptions the storied columns of Trajan and Marcus Aurelius provide an adequate parallel to the aesthetic theory which can be deduced from the development noted in mosaic flooring and in the decoration of walls and vaults. The time-scheme of the narrative, governed historically by the 'fasti' and 'annals' of the imperial undertakings, requires indeed continuous qualification and transformation of the spatial environment, as a changing scene of action. And yet, as has been authoritatively stated,[7] this space is continuous, flowing onward without interruption, just as does the action in front of and within it. But that continuous space, the uninterrupted line of scenery, is far from assuming the independent significance implicit, for example, in the Odyssey Landscapes of the Esquiline, where the precisely delineated presence of the human figures adds its own comment and qualification to the picture. Owing to the Hellenistic origin of their artistic purpose, the illusionist walls and vaults of the 'fourth style' are widely different from the columns; but the continuity of space in these latter has a value analogous to that imposed upon such walls and vaults by the distribution of numerous elements derived from architecture and having a pseudo-structural function, which cut up the surfaces in order to obtain from them, in

29, 49

7 Bettini (1948), p. 51.

this case merely for the purpose of telling a story, the temporal scheme and scansion of the various motions, forms and aspects of the event concerned. The latter, lacking also true historicity, cannot be scanned in the countless active and reactive phases and in the innumerable contrasting forces which make up the historical episode, but appears in its paradigmatic content (not usually taken at random from the form of the *emblemata*) and in the simultaneous presence of the contours (persons or things) which constitute its attributable connotation.

The illustrations mentioned below afford proof that the tendency so far noted began to develop in the late second-early third century. The very variety of content involved, by turns Hellenistic myth, Roman religious and secular subjects and Christian religion, enables the start of the new and thenceforward irreversible movement to be chronologically identified. It is exemplified by the Genazzano and Cologne floors referred to above, by the 'Dionysus and Ariadne' floor at Seleucia, by mosaic niches such as that of 'Silvanus' from Ostia (now in the Museo Profano Lateranense); by mural paintings such as those of the Via dei Dipinti at Ostia (I, IV) and of the Via dei Cerchi at Rome; by vault decorations such as those of the Mausoleum of Clodius Hermes, the Sepulchre of Caivano, the Mausoleum of the Aurelii on the Via Flaminia and that of the Pancratii on the Via Latina, followed by those of the 'Greek chapel' in the catacomb-cemetery of Priscilla or those of the Cemetery of Lucina.

36
38 39
56
45
46, 47
48
81
10
8
9

At this date the wall decoration of the 'fourth style' and the late Hellenistic framing of the *emblemata* are still the vital structures, invigorating and conditioning every effect in the most complex no less than in the simplest representation. These ornamental items, more or less redundant according to the taste of the painter or *musivarius*, the cultural level of the patron and even the material state of the environment and the technical potentialities of execution, have by this time eliminated every naturalistic trace of landscape as a permanent qualificatory datum of space. The ivory-white background of the surfaces, and the richness or faintness of the superimposed colouring, now serve almost exclusively to eliminate any attempt at illusory effect, so as to make the figures rise to the surface, whether singly or in small groups, within the frames or decorative fillets as though set in niches which form an integral part of the latter. It is at this point that there appear certain instances of the violation of the so-called 'law of the frame': space has vanished and its last manifestation is actually confined to the local significance supplied by the bodily image and the frame which encloses and often adheres to it. Moreover the time required to examine the isolated presence thus signified, at the moment that qualifies it with the attribution of its existence, becomes syllabic, limited, partitioned and, in short, quantified.

At this point, too, there arises the compositional freedom of the third- and fourth-century *lithostrota*, and eventually that of the decoration of vaults and domes, a freedom enabling this ultimately explicit negation of space to express itself through the complete conjunction of the figurative element with that of abstract geometrical ornamentation. Compositional procedures are then imposed, in which the elements of a representation formerly unified are distributed in a series of diverse and distinct medallions, areas, planes and spaces resulting in an ever-increasing complication of the geometrical divisions of the frames and plaited borders which determine them. Those procedures continued until on the one hand they lost their function in the artistic idioms of medieval Europe and on the other were promoted to become the decorative characteristics of the gold materials used by the Byzantine artists.

The unitary style of antique art had incorporated, and thereby figuratively translated, the theatrical function of actors on the stage and of their attendant chorus. From it the separate medallions, etc., mentioned above were now cut, so to speak, almost like pieces of organic tissue for study under the microscope. In late Roman art they presented both the ancient and the new material of the story, its requalified gnomic capacity and its episodic form (this last regularly subordinated to the emotional and spiritual participation of the spectator), in a pre-logical succession which repeats its organisational potentiality, and hence the possibility of its organic development in an objective process. This they did by means of a 'time' individual in its action – that of the spectator. He recalls them one by one and, through their linked evolution whose history he re-interprets, reconstructs them in their vital meaning, in their physical and metaphysical situation in the one cosmos and in the other.

On the road of idiomatic liberation, which runs almost without a break from the Hellenistic type of Roman painting to that of the central imperial period, there are certain monuments which, after the first century, may be regarded as important forerunners of innovation. They undoubtedly bear witness to active tensions in the final development of the arts deriving from Alexandria, and form an essential part of the connected works making up the entire *corpus* of what is known as Campanian painting.

This last phrase certainly covers a Hellenistic culture and taste in workmanship usually ascribed to Alexandria, although when it first reached Italy (second-first century BC) it was modified by native experience, technique and taste. This circumstance, of course, even in borderline cases, in no way affects the unquestionable dependence of

Campanian painting upon that of the great Hellenistic province, to which it continued to be bound by compositional schemes and iconographic allegiance, by spatial conception and idiomatic affinity. Nevertheless, if the initial statement has any meaning, it can be referred to the new modulations and resonances, due to a certain 'new style' of pictorial language, which are already to be found clearly distinguishable in some of the Campanian paintings of the first century. There is a theory that this kind of initial disturbance in the internal line of development of late Hellenistic painting in Italy was an element of formal dissolution, and thus a prelude to later 'decadence' resulting from a spiritual and civil upheaval in the ancient world so recently unified under the Empire. That theory, however, can safely be left to the few remaining authorities who deny the existence of a Roman art. The notion is one which, no matter how shrewdly argued, remains narrowly dependent on a cultural outlook that uses Winckelmann's procedure of erecting an abstract type of the beautiful on the basis of fifth-century Greek sculpture in order to draw more modern conclusions, deriving only Hellenistic art from that model. Today the theory appears no less untenable than the legend of the East as root and precipitate of every new structural and formal solution applied to either architecture or painting, a supposition which had met with considerable support during the first decades of the nineteenth century, thanks to the studies of Strzygowski.

Another debatable and even dangerous proposition[8] asserts that the stylistic upheaval in question occurred as the first direct consequence of the polemical insurgence of the native Italian masses against the oppressive alien weight of the refined figurative resources imposed on them by official Hellenistic art imported after the Roman conquests in the East. This suggestion is perplexing, if only because it does not explain how crude objects of popular handicraft and works of art produced by an educated and sophisticated middle class, each group intended for utterly different social strata[9] and for utterly different purposes, were suddenly brought together and fused into a single artistic product for a single, dynamic and changeable purpose. It seems more likely that such tension was, in the abstract, the result of a time of independent practice (including stages of bold exploitation) in the stylistic workmanship learned from Alexandrian Hellenism by Italian craftsmen accustomed for centuries to express themselves in forms which were only occasionally 'popular' and which came to be known collectively as non-Hellenic. Or, again, it may have resulted from the spiritual crisis that came to a head throughout the Mediterranean basin in face of new philosophical, religious and socio-economic problems, and therefore had nothing to

8 Bianchi Bandinelli (1952), now in *Archeologia e cultura*, Milan-Naples, 1961.

do with race. Or, finally, it may have been due to the presence in the conventional classical organism of a congenital impulse to development, so that its own internal evolution led it on the one hand, especially under the influence of Pergamene, Rhodian and Alexandrian Hellenism, to the baroque fantasy and coloristic preciosity which replaced the chromatic simplicity of the ancient rules of painting (which in Augustan Italy found new application in the academic coldness of the neo-Attic artists), and on the other hand, in the mid-imperial age, to seek a new stylistic standard which would offer a more problematical formal balance than had been available under the old, strictly limited convention. Consequently, however fruitful the search in this field may appear, however full and free the possibility of effective critical results, it was that incalculable burden itself – bearing in mind the stated proviso 'in the abstract' – which, quite apart from historical and cultural influences, enabled the will and inspiration of the artist at the creative stage to be retained in the qualifying determination of stylistic structures.

Almost a century after the bitter polemic of Vitruvius already quoted, Pliny, though starting from similar theoretical postulates concerning the necessity for works of art to resemble reality, developed certain remarkably different ideas about the painting of his time, which was already deeply affected by new tremors. It was he who, while acknowledging LUDIUS to have anticipated him, praised the new landscape-painting for its small genre pictures and its instantaneous renderings of ordinary or comic scenes of daily life.[10] Many examples of this kind of art, appreciated by the conservative Pliny, have been preserved. They include small-scale works and sketches painted in Campania before the dramatic year AD 79 and traceable to the alleged manner of LUDIUS. They often reveal attempts, visionary and stylistic, clearly indicative of the qualities and limits of the first experiments in departure from the Alexandrian tradition. But above all they, like the paintings of which Vitruvius disapproved, evidently belong to the great current of Roman Hellenism.

These documents, moreover, are not confined solely to the artistic experience of Campanian Hellenism, if it be true, for example, that the fragments of wall-paintings discovered in the so-called Grottoes of Catullus at Sirmio (galleries which recent excavations have dated with reasonable accuracy to the second half of the first century, probably during the Flavian era), or in the Roman villa of Valdonega at Verona (late second century), show, by their alternation between a style deriving from strict traditionalism and frank participation in a certain development of the taste exemplified in Campania, that even in northern Italy, a region of unquestionably different background, the phenomenology of this artistic stage, common at least

9 Bianchi Bandinelli (1956, pp. 77–78) advances a theory concerning the new idiom of late Roman sculpture which it seems difficult to accept. 'When the "decadence" of any particular artistic form is observed, it is invariably brought about by decadence of the craftsmanship developed under the domination of that artistic form, and the decadence of craftsmanship is primarily due to an economic cause. A certain technique becomes too expensive . . . and is replaced by a more economical because more rapid process, even though its products turn out to be second-rate and less durable. This new technique, popularised by the craftsman as "fashionable", is accompanied by a change of taste, which obtains new formal effects, a new style, from the new technique' (pp. 77–78). Considering that this assertion was made in connection with the 'Decennial Tables' of AD 305 in the Roman Forum, the author's theory appears to agree paradoxically with the judgment of Berenson on the figures of Victory in the Arch of Constantine (Berenson, B. (1952), pp. 35–38), thus causing the latter to share, in a sense, the view of decadence as founded on economic considerations. On the other hand such an argument would have no validity if checked against the changes of style and taste in coinage, which faithfully reflect the evolution or decadence of the 'finer' contemporary arts. What stylistic effect could any technical or economic consideration have on the preparation of the matrix of a new coin? Or does coinage, as a channel of taste, depend mechanically on stylistic changes already induced for economic reasons in other forms of art? And when its innovations of style precede those of the other arts, what then?

10 Pliny the Elder, *Historia Naturalis*, XXV, 37, 5.

throughout the Italic area, does not seem to be contradicted.

The novelties of Romano-Campanian painting, therefore, are to be found in a clearly circumscribed framework without appearing alien or inexplicable therein, as is proved by the more significant examples which may be identified by a rapid examination. They may perhaps be regarded as simple foreshadowings rather than as definite precursors, even though certain details of paintings at Herculaneum, Stabia and Pompeii show new characteristics already highly individualised. These are signs, or rather a single sign, of coming events already arising and seeking on the artistic plane a formal expression of at least more immediacy and conviction.

The frescoes painted on a slightly concave wall-surface formerly in the Basilica at Herculaneum and now in the Naples Museum[11] in fact exemplify the particular tension which inspired such works. They were probably accompanied in some aspects by other pictorial influences current in Italy during the first century AD and also elsewhere, as will be conspicuously evident in the first frescoes of Palmyrene gods at Dura Europos. The situation was affected by, but progressively less connected with, the structures of a style that was to prove unnecessary for the execution of the Hellenistic cartoons themselves.

For example, in the large-scale work we may call 'Theseus the Liberator' (No. 9049) Maiuri considers that the hero's figure derives from a sculpture used as a model by the artist.[12] The Liberator's face in fact, though rendered mobile by vibrant and luminous touches, gives the painting all the plastic force of a work in bronze. Maiuri, however, relates the whole work to the baroque Pergamene style, a highly chromatic type of sculpture which has a very special position in the Hellenistic domain; and for that very reason it appears that the vivacious but broad and firm brushstrokes depicting the ardent gaze and full-fleshed features of Theseus, and the splashes of shadow which set his hair in movement by a technique to be surpassed only by the Christian painting of the catacombs, do more than merely animate the plastic rendering. Those touches do not destroy the finish of the form. It would perhaps be too much to expect them to do so in the middle of the first century. But they already indicate new methods of work.

The painter of this very fine large-scale design, for whom Ragghianti has justly claimed creative independence,[13] nevertheless betrays a certain carelessness which does not escape notice, not so much in his technique, which is always studied and refined, as in the psychological differentiation of his personages, only sustained in a few cases by novel syntactic accents. There is a remarkable difference, for instance, between the countenance of Tellus in the picture 'Hercules and Telephus' from the same Herculanean

58, 59

11

12

11 According to Maiuri (1953, p. 66) it is a question of 'a possible recognition of this point by painting in cultivated circles at Naples, susceptible to the arts and literature of the first century of the Empire during the period from Claudius to that of the first Flavian emperors'.
12 Maiuri (1953), p. 68.
13 Ragghianti (1954), pp. 203–6. He assumes on archaeological grounds that the TELEPHUS MASTER was active between 35–50 and 68–79.

basilica (No. 9008), where the absorbed intensity of the gaze does not impair the classical figuration,[14] and the liveliness expressed in the little satyr close by, in whom the accent of vivid realism is substantiated by the originality of formal signs which, together with the detail of Telephus suckled by the doe, permit an evidently deliberate contravention of the 'law of separation of styles'. The same point may be made again with reference to the majestic head of the Liberator, whose overwhelming personality, expressed in the eyes imperiously reporting victory and extending thence to all the features, is reflected in those of the boys surrounding the hero and of the multitude that welcomes him. The accentuation in their faces differentiates them from the range of impersonal feelings closer to the tradition, as illustrated in the less well-known Pompeian representation of the same subject preserved likewise in the Naples Museum (No. 9043).

These hints of future practice in the large-scale paintings at Herculaneum, which must be dated on stylistic and archaeological grounds to the beginning of the second half of the first century, do not yet amount to a new aesthetic method. The work of the TELEPHUS MASTER suggests that a highly cultivated and skilled artist belonging to the Hellenistic *koine* could dominate contemplation of the myth in magisterial fashion and sometimes break into the ancient framework with bursts of intuition possibly autonomous but not yet exceeding the bounds of virtuosity. The strain put upon the Hellenistic structure is not in fact applied so much by the personal idiom of the master as by his extraordinary ability to load his model with so much psychological depth of feeling, expressed in the faces depicted, as occasionally to invest the subject with a poetry unusual at his time and place.

Similar novel but more purely impressionistic methods became even more apparent in certain small votive pictures preserved in the Naples Museum. They need not be regarded as more than sketches; but their reduced dimensions would not have sufficed to encourage innovation by the artist. The iconographic models in the small picture 'Sacrifice to Dionysus' from Herculaneum (No. 9127) and in the 'Centaur between Apollo and Aesculapius' from the House of Adonis (VI, 7, 18) at Pompeii (No. 8846) cannot be said to have been subverted. Here too the ideal classical structure of the human figure, dignified in posture and anatomically correct, retains its amplitude of composition. But colour is used to indicate all vital effects in determining the plasticity allowed to the figures. They are of solid bodily build, and yet hardly more than sketched, above all in their extremely vivid and alert cast of features. The personages are defined by broad, juicy brushstrokes and held together by shadow and bright counterpoints of light falling laterally upon the image, so as to confer

14 According to Rizzo (1929, p. 42) both subject and style are strongly reminiscent of Pergamene sculpture. *See also* Lubke *et al.* (1958), p. 392.

rhythm, direction and animation. These forms alternate with certain objects and details of the composition treated with equally fluent rendering of their essence, such as the garlands and wreath in the 'Sacrifice', the flowering branch in the Centaur's hand and his sinewy, quivering legs. For the rest, Campanian painting of the first century is conspicuous for the light which draws from its surfaces illusive effects of surprising mobility. This is particularly the case with inanimate objects and landscape, where such effects are already sought in a fashion alien from the rational objectivity of the Greek style, the Hellenistic vision of nature having substantially preserved this character even in fragmentary decorations and small-scale genre pictures. In the Campanian mode the sudden flash of light is designed to reveal, not the formal, objective totality of the phenomenon, but its appearance at the existential juncture.

The Naples Museum also possesses a highly individual and wonderfully composed painting of the nocturnal transport of the 'Trojan Horse', formerly at Pompeii (No. 9040). It constitutes a further anticipation of the innovations of late Roman painting, showing not only a notably full range of impressionistic grammar but also a first instance of undefined depth in space, which, going beyond the experience of contemporary landscape painting, combines the already frigid representation of the myth with a sympathetically intimate participation in the historical expression of an event.

The poetic revival of so hackneyed a classical theme is here complete. The portrayal of the army in the background, surmounted by the emblems of war, is reduced to the minimum required for its individuation. In the foreground a dazzling wave of light exposes the men who, unknown to themselves, are hauling the instrument of a sinister deception which is unknown to them. The horse emerges from shadow, while other figures surround the scene in agitated movement and the notabilities of the city look on from the foreground. The greatest tension is evident in every attitude. As though to sustain this feature, the compositional device of a column and a tree, still further distinguishing without dividing two diverse moments, is visible behind the foreground group; and beyond these two objects again the statue of Athena stands above the anguished form of Cassandra, convulsed in the useless outcry of her gloomy prophecy. In the background, scarcely perceptible in the darkness of night, loom the walls of the now doomed city, a strange avenging Fury hovering above them.

In this extraordinary perspective, a sort of bird's eye view, it is easy to detect a polemical aim, still unprepared to offer complete solutions. Indeed the figures, which, with the movement of their bodies and their enwrapment in the atmosphere of night, indicate the intense *pathos* of the situation, to a great extent merely record the plastic finish of contemporary Hellenistico-Roman portrayal of persons, but without thereby losing anything in comparison with many Campanian paintings. Not only the disturbed silhouettes of this admirable work, but also all the details of the landscape, have clearly been built up by colour alone. The air itself, providing a homogeneous connection between the forms by broad patches of colour subtly aligned, adds its effect to a formative qualification of the chromatic scheme which prevails throughout the composition. Hence arises the great poetic merit of this artist, whose ingenuity is evident in other directions of his restless research. For example, the attempts to unite the various planes of the picture by means of the three excited figures in motion between, respectively, the army and the horse, the horse and the men hauling it, and these men and the lower edge of the frame, betray the incapacity of even illusionist devices to nullify the separation of one plane from another.

Landscape panels, pastoral views and small-scale genre paintings include certain items of the first century that sometimes carry the chromatic luminism of the MASTER OF THE TROJAN HORSE to its highest point. In a Pompeian panel with 'Houses and Figures' in the foreground, at the 17 Naples Museum, the result, under a dazzling noonday sun, becomes unreal. Apart from the neutral tone of the background, representing a far distant sea, the houses are rendered by nothing more than an extremely bold play of warm white and chestnut counterpoints, in front of which strange figures, expressed by identical means of rhythmic chromatic composition, stand out against the light. That is all.

Elsewhere, even when similar levels are not attained, the impressionist painter builds luminous perspectives of harbours with a rich palette of blue, pink, ochre and chestnut; see particularly a specimen found in the first eighteenth- 14 century excavations at Stabia (Naples Museum No. 9514), where bold white accents and scribbles animate the foaming of the water, and another from Pompeii (Naples 15 Museum No. 9414). In the foreground of these pictures human figures roughly outlined, with limbs in movement and rendered by long, thin strokes of reddish-brown, reveal an agitated unity with the landscape, a region of incessant transformation in its continuously animated variety. Even the pastoral subjects, so dear to the idealising Hellenistic dealers in myth, are semantically altered: the timelessness of the legendary idyll is often replaced by a touching reanimation of the theme by the artist, who creates indefinite tones of light and atmosphere, in which the herdsman's condition shares intimately in the life of his mysterious environment, as seen in the goatherd of the 'Ram at Temple', also in the Naples Museum (No. 9418). 16

Here we have merely technical and grammatical innovations, within the ambit of a developed lyrical impressionism or luminist divisionism. More than the Herculanean murals, the votive panels and even the nocturnal Trojan epic from Pompeii, the idylls as revived by the Campanian artists seem to have been drawn out of the calligraphic abstraction of the myth and committed to the direct emotional participation of the beholder; they constitute environments formative of existence, not pedantic copies of being. They no longer enclose, like decorative backgrounds, a fact caught for ever in an eternal moment as a function of narrative explanation, but are themselves the event, beyond the operation of any kind of casual recall or representative symbol.[15]

In a theme still generically human, a pastoral, marine or genre setting recalls the spectator to the sense of life, to the true human situation of all men who labour, enjoy and suffer on earth. A new poetry, beyond academic realism, endows the traditional structures with a pathos not to be found in the Alexandrian aesthetics represented, for example, by earlier Hellenistic painting in Campania, which is the concrete form of a moral obligation with deeper roots. Thus it was, as Marchesi so brilliantly perceived, that Vergil in the peaceful climate of the Empire had transformed the Theocritean idyll into a poem breathing the very spirit of lyrical feeling experienced in the calm of the endless countryside, and Hesiod's chant into a drama of man's labour within the destiny of creation, thus managing to fashion from the epic of the ancient Roman historians a poem which, by its poetic resuscitation of the national past, might ensure in the citizen a consciousness of Rome's universal mission to impose and guarantee peace throughout the world.

But what would Vitruvius have said about those tendencies which are represented with so much artistic power in the paintings recently discovered at Stabia, in the luxurious surroundings of the two villas excavated in the hillside at Varano and securely dated between the earthquake of 63 and the eruption of 79, in accordance with the *terminus post quem* and *ante quem* of the archaeological discoveries around Vesuvius? The villa discovered at the higher site on the hill yielded, essentially, classical Hellenistic compositions for a dining-room: the 'Marriage of Dionysus and Ariadne', the 'Ganymede and Eagle of Zeus with Eros', a probable representation of 'Ambrosia and Dionysus' and the majestic figure of a 'Hero', perhaps Theseus. But the finds and the patient work of restoration carried out at the great building in the San Marco region led to the recovery of myriads of smaller decorative fragments, many of which had fallen from the architectural ornamentation of the walls and especially from the aerial perspectives of the ceilings. These, when rearranged,

15 Bettini (1952, p. ix) writes: 'Hence the Roman painter, for example, of the so-called Yellow Frieze of the House of Livia, was less interested in the classical expression of plasticity in volumes by a balanced relation between the full and the empty than in pursuing the effect of indefinite space. For this reason he created in the first place a "view" of fantastic aspect with hills, rivers, bridges and shrines, where human beings and animals moved busily about. They were represented as actual momentary components of the space in question, not given once and for all, but in course of formation in the very relation between the individual shapes, which are accordingly not defined and plastically hardened but depicted in motion with a few rapid and dexterous touches. They are more like shadows than solid figures of flesh.' Maiuri (1953, p. 180) adds: 'From the time of its first appearance in the great Yellow Frieze of the House of Livia, accompanied by highly classical architectural and figurative subjects, landscape is painted by rapid and summary technical means, in gradations of chiaroscuro throughout. The theme is boldly reduced to the essential notations of form, colour and movement. The ancients called this manner *modus compendiarius* (the short method). It recalls vividly certain illusive effects of modern impressionism . . . therein lay the technical revolution achieved by ancient painting. It illustrates both in landscapes and in scenes of common daily life the new spirit of Roman painting'. Ragghianti (1954, pp. 76 and 85) attributes some of these works to an AMANDUS MASTER and a VISIONARY MASTER.

made it possible to recognise the essential developments of Roman art in Campania during the fifteen years prior to the fatal date AD 79. Two artists of high culture and great innovating powers came to light as a result of these investigations.

Naturally enough, the work of recognition and assignment at first proved difficult. But it was possible at least to identify the contributions of different hands among the smaller fragments of portraits and the mythological compositions which could be most definitely ascribed, on structural grounds, to the tradition of Hellenistic narrative, even if they happened to be particularly rich in the expression of intense vitality. For example, the discoveries in the first of the two excavations originally convinced Elia[16] that an anonymous master 'disposed of a numerous staff responsible for all the decorative painting in this building, whence the finest of the Stabian pictures were obtained', and therefore named him the MASTER OF STABIA. But today more thorough understanding and more detailed criticism have become possible.

In particular, it now seems safe to recognise in the patiently rearranged fragments of the ceilings of the building with lofty arcades discovered in the region of San Marco the hand of an artist of extraordinary compositional inventiveness. Following the example set by FABULLUS in the Neronian *Domus Aurea*, he presents a new type of aerial ceiling-painting, in a style which had a certain influence on later Roman practice in this direction.[17]

This artist unquestionably conceived the great ceiling of the upper gallery at the villa in the San Marco region, which Elia has called the Loggia of the Planisphere.[18] The design is developed in broad spans of complex decorative structure, very similar in taste to the 'third style'. It includes architectural details supported by caryatids, ornamental fillets of varying composition, small lateral panels and a great central square. The figurative items are clearly indicative of a tendency to stylistic reform. It is also easy to see in the decorative lay-out a dominating cultural significance obviously related, even in the mural ornamentation, sometimes to the traditional pastoral subjects of late Hellenistic work and sometimes to the more distinctly 'Egyptianising' mode. The artist was therefore not a solitary figure. It may be conjectured that he was assisted not only by a number of manifestly separate mural decorators, but also by the skill of an assistant of neo-Attic taste to whom may be attributed such figures in the villa as those of Perseus, Cassandra and Melpomene, executed with marked classical finish.

In these ceilings of the Loggia of the Planisphere, as well as in those of the corridor leading to the great four-sided colonnade which contains the 'Medusa Roundel' and the 'Victory Shield', we can observe a distinct artistic personal-

16 Elia (1951), p. 49 ff.
17 Elia (1957), p. 14: 'Stabian painting . . . introduces a new formula with its rapid and evident representation of change, and by removing its sphere of operation from the wall to the ceiling concentrates all the interest of the work on that part of the building's architecture.
18 Elia (1957), pp. 20–1 and 26–9.

ity, the MASTER OF THE PLANISPHERE. The stylistic structure of his portraits appears to be re-echoed in some tiny fragments from the hand of an artist of striking individuality, who worked in the neighbouring Stabian villa called by Elia that of the 'Woman Selling Cupids'. He was a painter of great formal audacity, whom I shall call the INNOVATING MASTER OF STABIA. He is associated in the second villa with the painter of the more extensive finds of large-scale dining-room work already alluded to, the TRADITIONALIST MASTER OF STABIA.

The merit of the MASTER OF THE PLANISPHERE, as suggested above, is not confined to his singular ability to create aerial perspectives, in which the central *emblema* seems to burst its framework, sending out fresh spatial accents, sometimes of cosmic magnitude. He is also capable of a special skill, conferring a conscious expressive clarity on all his painting, in minute figurative delineation. The novelty of this artist's formal research is attested by the fragmentary 'Seasons' of the imaginary zodiacal composition of the planisphere, a subject also to be found in the black and white mosaic floor of a tomb in the Ostian Necropolis,[19] as well as by the 'Glorification of Minerva' in the following section of the gallery, by the 'Sun's Chariot' in another ceiling panel, by the dramatic 'Apollo and Daphne' on the back wall of the arcade, and by some smaller miscellaneous fragments. Starting probably from Hellenistic models of Pergamene type, perhaps indicative of his original professional training, he applied an often astonishing baroque invention to a sequence of open skies on the ceilings, with occasional broad and daring perspectives. These mythological scenes of celestial life, composed with a very bright palette of pink, green, yellow grey and blue, and conveying, one need not hesitate to say, a flavour of Tiepolo himself, are nevertheless no mere technical exercises in virtuosity. Close scrutiny of the minute delineation of the faces and the more delicate details of the figurative structure shows them to derive from a dramatic classicism, as in the faces presumed to be those of Summer and Autumn, in the portrait of Minerva, in the face of Daphne and in the fragment of the 'Veiled Woman'. In these cases the assurance of the traditional lay-out is combined with deep psychological content and full expressive vigour through the employment of an idiom rich, for all its dexterity, in tokens of boldness and freedom, in broad brushstrokes and in rapid touches of colour, which are particularly evident in the context of representation because of their references to identifiable and recurrent models in the Hellenistic painting of Campania. It is obvious, for instance, that the basic pattern of the faces of 'Summer', 'Autumn' and the 'Veiled Woman' derives from a single such predecessor. It is, moreover, this very consideration that emphasises the

18

19

19 i.e. Tomb No. 101. Cf. Calza, G. (1940), pp. 183–4, f. 92.

noted, but also that the facial structure of the first two recurs in the Stabian fragment, so that the same cartoon was undoubtedly used by several artists. Up to this point there is nothing unprecedented in the situation. The gap between the three faces can well be accounted for by reference to two skilled masters, provided we recognise, with Richardson, that the two Pompeian paintings may be ascribed to an ACHILLES MASTER, or else that three masters were concerned if it should turn out that, on the contrary, the MASTER OF THE HOUSE OF THE LUTENIST studied under the MASTER OF THE ACHILLES OF THE HOUSE OF THE DIOSCURI.

The classical stamp of the two Pompeian faces, from which (or from the common model of which) the Stabian face unquestionably derives, is confirmed in the first case by a plastic solidity illustrated in a dense and warm luminosity, in which the best type of Alexandrian formalism expresses the subject's dramatic absorption in a climax of moral sentiment, as if already in the grip of bellicose excitement. In the second case classicism appears in a now more emphatically chromatic transverse direction of the facial planes, immersed in a compact atmosphere which gives an effect of greater frankness, simplicity and clarity. Taken as an expression of myth in various terms, the iconographic model of this heroic countenance is evidence of the extreme freedom with which formal means were employed by the master or masters of Pompeii. This fact justifies the progressive distortion of the actual structures that convey the sentiment, and permits the INNOVATING MASTER OF STABIA to follow his own inspiration in adopting the figurative scheme as modified and revived by novel stylistic experiment. It is possible therefore to regard this manner as truly late-Roman by anticipation, in a sense which will become clear when we consider certain tendencies of catacombal painting, but united and infused with a classical imprint almost entirely forgotten by Christian hypogean painters. The character here suggested is recognisable in the great assurance of the brushstrokes, which are capable of introducing a new poetry into the framework itself of the ancient pattern, and which, in the Stabian head, not only countersign the lit and shaded areas of the Pompeian works, but also present the first organic signs of a more typically Roman taste.

The painter or painters of the House of the Dioscuri and the House of the Lutenist made a patient use of tone to define through the play of light and shade the perspective composition of the bodies, fully accepting their plastic nature, and employed to the maximum individual luminist touches by way of augmenting expressive effect. But the INNOVATING MASTER OF STABIA, with a palette more simplified and reduced to a few tints, achieved a richer articulation, in which the patches of background colour, conjoined without the intervention of shading and boldly countersigned by rapid and precise flashes of light apparently from within the piece of illuminated surface itself, take shape, with impressive neatness, in a few black synthetic strokes, which at the same time and with extreme virtuosity construct the architecture of the face, the syntax of the form and the expression of the feeling involved.[22]

The idiom we suppose to be that of LUDIUS seems to have been revived and organically surpassed by the INNOVATING MASTER OF STABIA to a far greater extent than through its handling by the TELEPHUS MASTER. In the Stabian works the forward-looking and genial maturity of an authentic new style leads to an unhesitating judgment of its superiority to the nevertheless admirable stylistic command of dramatic power in the TRADITIONALIST MASTER.[23]

The abundant evidence preserved for posterity by the Vesuvian catastrophe, which provides excellent opportunities for comparative study of works created at the same stage of culture and taste, in many instances within the very short period of seventeen years between the earthquake of 63 and the eruption of 79, might certainly lead to the false belief that Roman art of the Flavian age already included in embryo all the tendencies and developments of tendencies of the imperial art that followed. In reality, the Campanian records provide us on the one hand with an exceptionally rich collection testifying to the kinds of shading and working methods operative at that time; though in certain provincial cities they operated in cultural conditions fairly close to those of the capital, even where the Hellenistic background was richer and older and such cities differed conspicuously in their sociological level and type of refinement. On the other hand, those records furnish an incomparably poorer harvest of works created after the fatal year 79. There is therefore some risk that, with the capricious sectarianism of which archaeological history provides so many examples, such works may illuminate only certain aspects of the succeeding artistic phenomena.

It is accordingly obvious that no positive statement can be made that such and such a Stabian manner or such and such a Herculanean taste had no creative consequence or none which differed from any other. We have indeed good reason to suppose that the taste for impressionism again matured, in general, during the last twenty years of the century, and even until at least the death of Trajan. In support of this assertion we may adduce not only certain paintings among the admittedly very few that have survived from the thirty years between AD 80 and 110, but also the very many items of authenticated sculpture produced so extensively in the age of Trajan.

The special style of that period, undoubtedly the first

22 Maiuri (1951), who recognises the hand of a single artist in the first villa excavated at Stabia, and attributes to him 'a fresher, less constrained manner than those of the academic and neo-classical conventions to which the Pompeian painting of interiors remained more or less bound, and at the same time a more sonorous tonality of colour and a more richly expressive modulation of feature and gesture, as if the Campanian artist had responded more adequately, in the warmth of his natural temperament, to the Hellenistic tradition from which even he unquestionably derives.'

23 These paintings, fragmentary though they are, provide partial confirmation of what Franz Wickhoff (1895) wrote at the end of the nineteenth century: 'The older art tried to achieve its effect by the organic and essential reproduction of the person or object represented. Its degeneration was due to a stylistic mutation that altered the forms, or to an exaggeration of those it considered essential. The new art, however, selected from the whole reality only so much as seemed particularly suited to convey in illusory fashion the impression of its appearance at a given moment. It was not a question of two artistic manners, one of which might easily develop out of the other, nor even of different methods, but of substantially diverse conceptions of art.' And again: 'Stylists and naturalistic artists take care to render the form with an extreme degree of refinement and the spectator then perceives it as something alien from himself. The illusionist on the other hand constrains the observer to effect by his own efforts the final fusion of the impressions into forms, and by simultaneously inducing him to create them arouses in him an imperative certainty of the reality of what he is looking at, for the very reason that the artist had made him collaborate spiritually in the completion of the illusion.'

concrete example of genuinely Roman sculpture, first appears, already reasonably mature, in the reliefs of the Arch of Titus, which are attributable to the end of the ninth decade of the century. They afford remarkable proof of the substantially parallel development of painting and sculpture, for the friezes of the Arch of Titus indicate, ten years after the Vesuvian catastrophe, the logical continuation of the taste and methods attested with greater originality in the painting of the Vesuvian region. They are those of the INNOVATING MASTER OF STABIA, who is thus found to be not a dead branch in the development of Roman art but a representative of its most novel and lively tendency.

The reliefs of the 'Capture of Jerusalem' correspond exactly with the stylistic developments which can be considered proper to Roman painting of the same period. As in the latter, the ingenious experimentation in the Arch of Titus, in Trajan's Column, in the Trajanic Friezes of the Arch of Constantine, and in the panels of the Arch at Beneventum, is developed in the break-up of the background plane, which no longer retains any traces of the scenographical apparatus peculiar to Alexandrian Hellenism, but reveals itself as the animated and experienced environment of the persons who are present there as living beings and 'make' it. The study of the third dimension in painting, as for instance by the establishment of several planes in the Naples 'Trojan Horse', develops in the imperial processions of Titus into an illusionist mingling of reliefs of different thickness, represented by the mutual interplay of light and shade – and 'breath' as Wickhoff[24] puts it. The forms are accordingly placed in an animated perspective called by Eugenia Strong, in her masterly work on the subject, a 'defect' in the 'knowledge of perspective'[25] owing to the undeniable contradictions involved in the classical view of this problem. But it may be more indulgently judged as the provision of an indispensable antithesis between a mobile treatment of space and the rigid, unequivocal, neo-Attic classicism of Augustan art. In any case, the same contradictory perspectives are surely to be found in the Pompeian picture of the Trojan night scene.

The highly skilled impressionist illusionism of the reliefs in the 'Capture of Jerusalem', capable of suggesting space in perspective, acquires further precision and matures in the more complex compositional audacities and innovations in general stylistic structure characteristic of the Column of Trajan. There, as Bettini has noted, 'a typically Roman subject, the exploits of an army commanded by the Emperor, takes shape in a *continuous narrative*, illustrative of the Roman sense of "time", and represented by *illusionist style* illustrative of the Roman sense of "space".[26]

The very nature of this indefinite space created by light was bound in the end to turn it into colour. The effects

29

2

29

24 Wickhoff (1895), p. 107.
25 Strong (1923), p. 112. But the following observation (pp. 109–110), which the author equates with that of Wickhoff regarding these reliefs, should be recorded: 'The neutral background, which may be called tactile, a wall lacking any sense of uniform depth, against which the figures stand out, is now transformed into a 'living' mass from which the sculptor's chisel evokes movement, light and shade, as would the painter's brush working on the flat surface of canvas or board. In other words, sculpture, after groping for centuries, has discovered the third dimension. This was certainly not because, as has often been alleged, it was trying to imitate painting, but because it, like painting, had by then also reached a stage at which the natural requirements of its development insisted upon an immediate confrontation with the problem of space.'
26 Bettini (1948), p. 49. *See also* p. 51: 'The classical unity of time and place, concentrated in and limited to the single moment of representation, has now therefore been superseded by spatial *continuity*, which obviously proves that the *dimension of time* has overcome the classical principle of pure spatial extension.'

achieved by the various stages indicated in 'fourth-style' murals are reflected exactly in the Column of Trajan. In the former, architecture and figures, particularly in the above mentioned landscapes, very soon become, though in an indefinite depth of perspective, mere contrapuntal notes of colour which establish precise relations of light and shade. In the Column, the Roman soldiers and their adversaries are immersed in the life of the uninterrupted landscape and form in combination with that same feature a luminist *continuum*.

The now widespread and recently revised understanding of the great sculpture produced under Trajan, and later under Hadrian and the Antonines, renders unnecessary any specific consideration of those monuments, which in the present context could only be marginal and partial. We cannot, however, disregard the presence therein of certain stylistic novelties, upon which the scarcity of contemporary evidence will not allow an adequate judgment in the field of painting, but which later pictures show to have been absorbed and to have been long in use.

In the first place, the concept of space apparent in the monumental sculpture of the age of Trajan indicates a phase of development which lasted from that of impressionist illusionism to that of the formative elements of two-dimensional chromaticism at the end of the century. The introduction of perspective illusion, by siting on different planes figures rendered in violently contrasted light and shade, leads from the paintings of Campania and the reliefs of the Arch of Titus to substantial variation. The Trajanic Reliefs of the Balustrades from the Roman Forum, and that preserved in the Louvre, first exemplify an approximation of the background wall to the narrative planes (two at most), on which are represented the Emperor's sacrifices and grants of favour. Here the spatial conception of the sculptor of the Arch of Titus has been substantially simplified, though the lavish luminosity is undoubtedly similar.

In the Column reliefs, and those incorporated in the Arch of Constantine, the uninterrupted course of the background landscape, as the existential historical scene of action, intrudes very much more into the main links recording the deeds of men. The figures are no longer, as in the earliest examples of Campanian painting, subordinate to the depth, to the actual physical characteristics of the landscape. Here it is the elements of the landscape, reduced, simplified to symbols and sometimes stylised, that mingle with the persons linking the action, to such an extent as to become wholly identical with them. The traditional bird's-eye perspectives of connective spatial components such as harbours, ships, rivers, bridges, city walls and military encampments appear; but they never succeed in regaining naturalistic control over the human figures. It is they that supply the action, regulate the space and sustain the time factor in the story within the environment of the background, which is brought to the surface.

This new dynamic balance between figure and environment, between men and landscape, between history and nature, already noted in certain basic examples of 'fourth-style' painting, is in itself a constituent element of the Roman *Weltanschauung*, which lends coercive power and directive capacity to the human will in its struggle with all the mysterious opposition of the world, to the *virtus* of the Roman soldier as representing a people in arms against the military and political existence of an enemy.

The lucid and potent idiom, which Bianchi Bandinelli considered to be the work of a single sculptor,[27] is sometimes expressed in a formal vigour of great plastic force, and elsewhere tends to change the effect of the carved surfaces in accordance with the repetitive rhythm of a handling that varies with the variation of light. The sculptor nevertheless composes a panorama of disconcerting expressivity, in which illusionism is by now close to diminution under the pressure of its constituent elements as they melt into a synthesis most maturely illustrated in the Trajanic reliefs of the Arch of Constantine. Here the few ingredients of the environment of the action, such as archways, trees and leaves, are finally overwhelmed by the movement, the plastic amplitude and the figurative composition of the continuous decoration, so much so that the residue of spatial illusion is contributed only by the forms of the men and horses. The illusion of space, however, enters so completely into the siting of the figures as to be more than ever prefigurative of effects to be found only in the painting of the end of the century. The figures have enclosed the space, and they alone constitute it. Transformation of the secluded, emblematic fixation of the figures in classical sculpture is accordingly complete. It may safely be affirmed that from this moment the neo-Attic Augustan school had come to the end of its task, since a fully independent style of Roman art was now in existence.

Unfortunately no works of this period have survived at Rome of sufficient significance to document the status of the new idiom in the domain of painting, whether by the wet or dry method of fresco, on panel or as mosaic. But in the provinces, where refinement in this art is better attested, some few items of illustrative value remain.

Among the scanty pictorial relics of the last quarter of the first century a site of exceptional importance for the whole history of imperial art is that of the paintings and mosaics of the Villa of Dar Buc Amméra, near Zlitan in Tripolitania.

The fragmentary murals and the mosaic floors of this

27 Bianchi Bandinelli (1950), i, pp. 217–8.

villa were first brought to light in 1913. They still remain, after more than fifty years, insufficiently studied by scholars, except for the notable crop of publications dedicated to them by Aurigemma, their discoverer. In this monumental complex there are present, bound together in a whole made up of separate pictorial works, the most diverse techniques in use during the last decades of the century: the pavimental mosaic in its varieties of *tessellatum* and *vermiculatum*, the marble *crusta* (*opus sectile*), frescoes on walls and vaults. From amid a panorama of widely differing material there emerges a substantial uniformity of taste, at any rate in much of the floor decoration, which is repeated and reflected in style and patterning, though not by the same hand (as was noted from the start),[28] in floors, walls and ceilings, thus affording unquestionable proof of a co-ordinated if not unified conception of the decorative scheme of the villa.

Among what may be considered the more significant specimens of this impressive art, and such as to represent solid ground for the identification of independent impulses in the history of painting under the Empire, we may mention the fresco of 'Drunken Dionysus riding the Panther' and the fragments of 'Artemis-Selene', 'Victory', 'Dancing Girl' and 'Nereids', all fallen from the vault of the crypto-portico of the villa; the large mosaic fragment depicting animals and scenes of ordinary life surrounded by spirals of acanthus ornament from the floor of the room with the quadrant; the whole pavimental 'Mosaic of the Seasons' and the whole pavimental 'Mosaic of the Gladiators'.

Despite a degree of stereometrical typology in a few faces, which resembles that of very late human and imaginary masks occurring throughout the Empire, there seems no doubt that the fresco painters and *tessellarii* were at work during the last two or three decades of the first century. It has been suggested that the 'Mosaic of the Gladiators' represents the punishment of the Garamantes (AD 70), which would give it a fairly precise dating. But we need not rely upon this identification, or upon Aurigemma's weighty arguments as to classification; for the decorative scheme of the vault of the crypto-portico containing the Dionysus picture, which was preserved and afterwards reconstructed thanks to the fall of an entire section of the plaster of the vault itself, will suffice to prove a decorative system clearly of the 'third style'. Furthermore, the proposed dating seems to be confirmed by the Alexandrian and Nilotic ancestry of certain subjects which later became unfashionable and disappeared from the pattern books, by the minutely fine *vermiculatum* and the tiny dimensions of the cubes employed, and also by the vigorous, sketchy style of certain pictures (the 'Dionysus' for example) indubitably connected through their execu-

25, 28

26, 27

28

25

26

28 *See* especially Aurigemma (1960; 1962, p. 36 (reports by Vincenzo Rosati) and p. 53); *also* Aurigemma (1926), pp. 107–27, including the subject of the connections between mural and parimental decoration. As to mosaics, *see* Aurigemma (1962), pp. 15–7.

tive characterisation and techniques with some fragments from the two Stabian villas.

The frescoes of the Dar Buc Amméra villa seem to be of outstanding importance in the art of the Flavian age and of that immediately following it. The picture of 'Drunken Dionysus riding the Panther', which the artist tried so far as possible to design from below, the belly and claws of the animal being visible, suggests for instance – within the limits of the expressive capabilities of the Alexandrian school of painting, intent on a realistic vivacity combined with the most approved iconography – a boldness of form, a rapidity in formative accentuation, a skill in the use of light and an effect of psychological agitation which instantly recall Stabia. These characteristics prove that the Campanian finds were neither isolated nor casual phenomena in a far larger field of art under the Empire. The same conclusions could be drawn from the Pompeian 'Houses and Figures' already mentioned, from the small picture (though it is much less strained) of a 'Seaside Village' belonging to the same section of the crypto-portico vault, or from the human face as depicted either in the 'Medusa' or in the fragment displaying 'Nereids, Cupids and Sea Monsters'.

In sketching small, summary images within an area of a few centimetres, where the forms nevertheless indicate an underlying narrative and figurative discipline of most remarkable quality, this MASTER OF THE ZLITAN FIGURES commands as much virtuosity as when he has to design on a scale of almost mural proportions. The comments made above on the 'Dionysus' apply even more emphatically to the 'Artemis-Selene' fragment, with its animated bust, and to the fragments, of progressively smaller dimensions, of the 'Victory' and the 'Dancing Girl', the last two having evidently been taken from the same model.

The first fragment, 'Artemis-Selene', is over 80 centimetres high, the head alone measuring about thirty; the second is over 70, the head being about fifteen; and the third over 35, with the head approximately five. In all three works, naturally with more definite structural results as dimensions increased, yet always with the same technical ability and formal refinement, the master achieved effects of indubitable merit within the limits of a renovation of the traditional style he was still cultivating. The slender and ardent beauty of the female bodies (especially of the 'Victory'), the almost baroque mutability (from red to green and yellow tones) of the splendidly unrealistic draperies, and above all the peculiar, melancholy vivacity of mind expressed in the 'Artemis-Selene', with its admirable countenance of lengthened, roundish features, notable for the strong, straight line of the nose and the practically monochrome result of the varied tinting, all bear witness to outstanding achievements, and in the case of the 'Artemis-Selene', one of perfection itself, by imperial Roman painting at the start of its most independent creative course.

The masters employed in the mosaics of this villa, in particular the ACANTHUS MASTER and the ZLITAN MASTER OF THE SEASONS, were no less accomplished than the painters of the walls and vaults. The problem of the identity of the *imaginarius* or executant of the faces in 'Artemis-Selene' and of those of Autumn and Winter need not be considered here. But it is necessary to emphasise that the skills of these artists were unquestionably exceptional and in fact such – if the dating proposed for each should ever be archaeologically confirmed – as to introduce duce at a remarkably early period two of the most genuinely outstanding personalities in the history of late Roman mosaic. From a strictly stylistic point of view, which would appear decisive if only because the faces of the 'Seasons' are portable *emblemata* inserted in terracotta cases and therefore less likely to have been executed *in situ*, it seems nevertheless more prudent to conjecture a later date, far into the third century, for the four panels.[29] For their resemblance to the 'Artemis-Selene' in physiognomical structure may well be thought due to subsequent imitation, exceptional as that may have been, or more plausibly to a common iconographical derivation, as is clear in the case of many faces of late date found in different parts of the Empire. (*See* in this connection Chapter IX.)

The school and the taste to which the MASTER OF THE SEASONS and the ACANTHUS MASTER belonged were certainly Alexandrian. The fact is attested above all by their repertory, by certain special figurative ideas, and by the techniques and materials with which they worked. Yet these artists, disposing of an altogether peculiar set of creative resources, were passing through a stage of spontaneous transformation.

The ACANTHUS MASTER represents a school of high formal standing, a refined aesthetic taste and a vigorous chromatic originality, one of the most striking in the immensely wide field of mosaics surviving from late antiquity. A globally comprehensive aesthetic judgment should certainly be able to recognise in this case the early date of the evidence and its intimate cultural link with even the Egypt-influenced painting of the beginning of the century. The panels themselves, the still life, the successful excursion into zoology and the unreality of certain unexpected chromatic changes are all in that style. But in the grandiose, and unfortunately for the most part missing, design of the floor, which is entirely dominated by circular rhythm, with every curve finding analogies and correspondences in a continual repetition of arcs, scrolls and spirals, there also emerges a warm love of nature as

25

27

28

29 A late dating, to the third century and beyond, has recently been supported by Rumpf (1953, p. 176) and Parlaska (1959 b) p. 122.

1 Rome, Museo Nazionale. *Viridarium*, from the Villa of Livia at Prima Porta.

2 New York, Metropolitan Museum. Room from the Boscoreale Villa

3 Pompeii, House of the Vettii. Dining-Room

4 Pompeii, House of Pinarius Cerialis. Room

5 Naples, Museo Nazionale. Fragment of wall, from Herculaneum

6 Rome. Wall of the *Domus Aurea* (from L. Mirri and G. Carletti, *Le antiche camere esquiline*, t. xxxvii)

7 Rome. Gilded Vault of the *Domus Aurea* (from H. Egger, *Codex Escorialensis*, t. iii)

8 Rome, Mausoleum of the Pancratii. Vault

9 Rome, Cemetery of Callistus. Vault, Crypt of Lucina

10 Rome, Mausoleum of the Aurelii. Vault

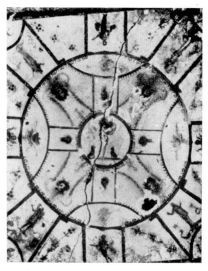

11 Naples, Museo Nazionale. 'Theseus the Liberator' (detail), from the Basilica of Herculaneum

12 Naples, Museo Nazionale. Hercules and Telephus, from the Basilica of Herculaneum

13 Naples, Museo Nazionale. Sacrifice to Dionysus, from Herculaneum

14 Naples, Museo Nazionale. Panorama with Harbour, from Stabia

15 Naples, Museo Nazionale. Landscape, from Pompeii

16 Naples, Museo Nazionale. Ram at Temple, from Pompeii

17 Naples, Museo Nazionale. Houses and Figures, from Pompeii

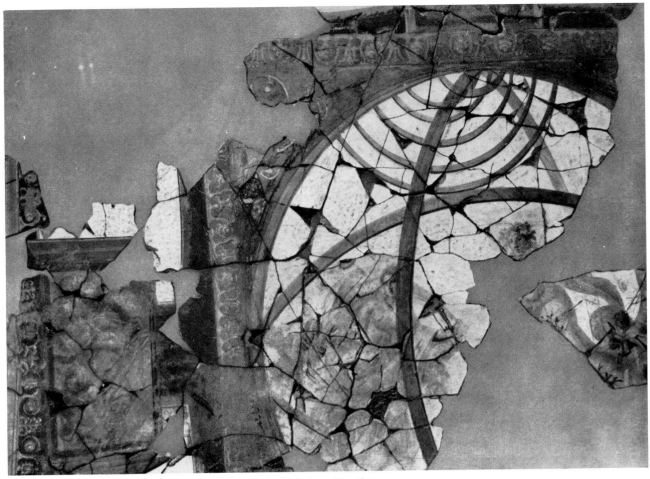

18 Stabia, Villa in the region of S. Marco. Loggia of the Planisphere (detail)

19 Stabia, Villa in the region of S. Marco. Fragment: Veiled Woman

20 Stabia, Villa of the Woman Selling Cupids
Fragment: 'Melancholy Youth'

21 Stabia, Villa in the region of S. Marco. Fragment of roundel: Medusa

22 Stabia, Villa of the Woman Selling Cupids. Fragment: Face of a Young Man

23 Naples, Museo Nazionale. 'Achilles at Scyros' (detail), from the House of the Dioscuri, Pompeii

24 Naples, Museo Nazionale. Orestes and Pylades before Iphigenia (detail), from the House of the Lutenist, Pompeii

1 Stabia, Villa of the Woman Selling Cupids. Fragment: Hero.

2 Naples, Museo Nazionale. Trojan Horse, from Pompeii.

3 Naples, Museo Nazionale. Centaur between Apollo and Aesculapius, from the House of Adonis, Pompeii.

4 Rome, House on the Caelian. Fresco: Mythological Seascape.

5 Ostia, Baths of the Seven Sages. Toilet of Venus.

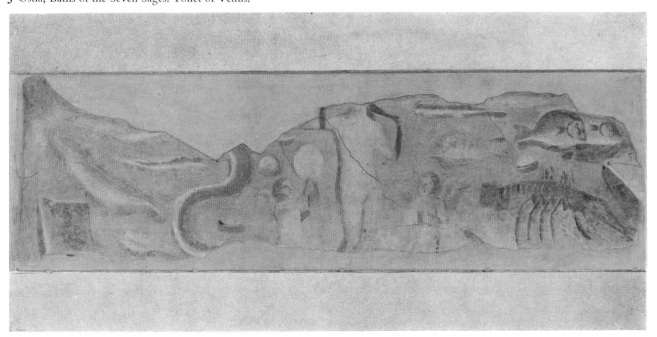

6 Rome, Cemetery of Priscilla. Praying Girl (detail), end lunette of cubicle 5.

25 Tripoli, Archaeological Museum. Mosaic of the Seasons, from the Villa of Dar Buc Amméra, near Zlitan

26 Tripoli, Archaeological Museum. Drunken Dionysus Riding the Panther, from the Villa of Dar Buc Amméra, near Zlitan

27 Tripoli, Archaeological Museum. Fragment: Artemis-Selene, from the Villa of Dar Buc Amméra, near Zlitan

28 Tripoli, Archaeological Museum. Mosaic: Animals and acanthus spirals, (detail) from the Villa of Dar Buc Amméra, near Zlitan

29 Rome. Column of Trajan (detail)

30 Antioch, House of the Calendar. Mosaic: Oceanus and Tethys (detail)

31 Paris. Louvre. Fragment of linen and wool tapestry, from Antinoë

32 Antioch, House of the Calendar. Mosaic: Oceanus and Tethys (detail of Oceanus)

33 St. Albans, Verulamium Museum. *Emblema*: Oceanus, from Verulamium

34 Palestrina, Archaeological Museum. Barberini Mosaic

35 Berlin, Staatliche Museen. Centaurs and Wild Beasts, from Hadrian's Villa, Tivoli

36 Rome, Museo Nazionale. Fragment: Pan and Satyr, from the Imperial Villa at Genazzano (detail)

37 Rome, Museo Nazionale. Fragment: Fishing Boat, from Via Portuense

38 Cologne, Roman Villa. Central *emblema* of the dining-room: Drunken Dionysus

39 Cologne, Roman Villa. Dining-room *emblema*: Satyr and Maenad

40 Nennig, Roman Villa. Mosaic: Circus Combats (details)

41 Trier, Landesmuseum. Anaximander with Sundial, from the   42 Nennig, Roman Villa. Mosaic: Circus Combats (detail)
Johannisstrasse

43 Rome, Antiquarium of the Capitoline Museums. Rape of Persephone, from Via Portuense

44 London, British Museum. Rape of Persephone, from the Tomb of the Nasos, Via Flaminia

45 Rome, Museo
Profano
Lateranense.
Mosaic Shrine of
Silvanus, from
the Mithraeum
near the Maritime
Baths at Ostia

46 Ostia, House in the Via dei Dipinti. Male figure (? philosopher) in the Red Room

47 Ostia, House in the Via dei Dipinti. Male figure (? poet) in the Red Room

48 Rome, House in the Via dei Cerchi. Figures of waiters on the dining room wall (detail)

49 Rome. Column of Marcus Aurelius (detail)

apprehended and studied in this part of the world. It is a feeling experienced as new, the object of perpetual investigation, and has forgotten the aesthetic frigidity apparent in some of the Hellenistic mural decorations found in Roman Campania. The flowers, the fruit, the luxuriant, never casually placed tufts of acanthus, the tiny animals busy with their modest affairs, the miniature separate scenes within the great plaited rim surrounding the heart of the wonderful story are observed with frank and trustful affection. The free account of this splendid image of creation, while subject to a rigorous aesthetic organisation of space, is all the farther from a naturalistic style and the epigrammatic realism of some late Hellenistic and imperial literature through its rejection of current artificial mannerisms in the articulation of its vision. The narrative is presented in its totality and exclusively in its own terms. The acanthus, that exuberant protagonist, becomes at the same time a kind of scansion, both temporal and spatial, the rhythmic palpitation, as it were, of the multiform and inexhaustible life of nature.

The four busts of the 'Seasons', on the other hand, may 25 be considered as absolutely model achievements of a now mature didacticism based on myth, ready in both form and inner meaning to occupy a space reorganised for the operation of mythical elements, at last, as henceforth independently active aesthetic entities. The four wonderful *emblemata* of the Dar Buc Amméra villa are in fact already at variance with the premises of the 'refrigeration' of late antiquity, and this is one of the grounds of their importance. Three of the four heads, viz. 'Winter', 'Autumn' and 'Summer', are done from the same cartoon. All four are shown almost full-face; their robust typology, with extraordinarily expressive vigour, sets the eyes, nose and mouth within the meshes of the low-toned chromatic surface, which have been widened until they almost form a single plane. The exceptionally sharp contrast of light and shadow suggests powerful frames or at any rate such as are alien from any traditional dimension of idealised beauty. The pupils of the eyes are accordingly rendered exceptionally conspicuous with their globular forms emerging from the dark hollows of the sockets and dominating each image by their strong opposition to the broad whites behind them. This is one of the distinctive features of late imperial portraiture and was passed on through the expressionism of the third and fourth centuries and successive formal modifications to the more active Byzantine tradition.

On the other hand, taste in colour tends to clotted streaks and chromatic patches in which the ancient imperceptible changes of tone disappear in order to achieve, even in works composed of very small tesserae (9–15 per sq. cm.), numerous and surprising mutations which rely

F

for the rendering of outline and depth on a vision comprehensive but already of itself maturing an autonomous value in single sections of the surface. This chromatic taste anticipates certain technical and aesthetic effects of the later *vermiculatum*, though at the same time it permitted traditional passages of virtuosity, rare erudition and vivid imagination of a more thoroughly naturalistic kind. In the face of 'Autumn', for instance, those parts of the *opus* concerned with the face, the arms and the wings may be compared with those relating to the coronal of flowers and fruit. Similar comparisons may be made in the case of the 'Spring' emblema, but they are less justifiable in the cases of 'Winter' and 'Summer'.

Very different considerations undoubtedly come into play with regard to the six naturalistic panels (two of domestic creatures, two of fish and two of pigmy hunters) flanking the 'Mosaic of the Seasons', and with regard to the eight, also displaying fish, placed at the centre of the 'Gladiators'. These too are cased *emblemata*, most probably purchased (their respective dimensions are often diverse, so that in order to assemble the floor it was necessary to employ optical tricks, involving the addition of strips of cubes to the edge), which express the level of fashionable production now industrialised and of a commercial standard.

The makers of these *emblemata* also loved Nature and her diminutive brood, but their works, as compared with the floor of the ACANTHUS MASTER, differ in outlook, sensibility and poetic quality. The panels, sometimes resembling *xenia*, sometimes inspired by the well-known Nilotic art, and sometimes introducing, without the slightest attempt to create an environment, the abstract white background characteristic of the painting of late antiquity, are often examples of mere virtuosity; but the images, lively and convincing though they are, lack the mysterious and highly original rhythm of the ACANTHUS MASTER's floor. The organisation of the subjects in the picture is here external to the images, symmetry being varied but imposed from without. Creatures of a different world, subject to rigorous compulsion, seem to have been enclosed alive under glass. A rather different aesthetic system is produced by a sort of immobility, which is not rigidity of form but actually the result of different rhythms conditioned by the interior time of the image, ruling out the unexpected and customary as a biological repertory of natural forms. That system will be combined at a later date with the congealed figurative residue of division by clusters of acanthus to issue in such pre-medieval masterpieces as the nevertheless classically influenced vaults of S. Costanza, the floors of the *xystus* and of the four-sided portico at Piazza Armerina, and finally the floor of Justinian's basilica at Sabratha. This aesthetic theory, which on the one hand tends to arrange the narrative in wholly self-explanatory stages, and on the other hand fixes its images by congealing them in a programmatic series of signs which must necessarily lead to expressionism, then sets up the temporal scansion identified in the subjects themselves of each scene, dissecting the latter into various 'times' organised, as it were, typologically, each subject with its own space.

Finally, the large narrative framework of the 'Mosaic of the Gladiators' suggests by its subject, technique, inspiration and artistic energy a practitioner from another region, probably Africa. Like the ACANTHUS MASTER, the MASTER OF THE GLADIATORS unquestionably worked directly *in situ*, a circumstance which is only probable in the case of the MASTER OF THE ZLITAN SEASONS and must almost certainly be excluded in the case of the abovementioned naturalistic *emblemata*. The 'Mosaic of the Gladiators' is shown to be foreign in culture and derivation by the arrangement of space, by the pagination of the figures adrift on a white background, by the utterly casual way in which they are linked (making them look like a series of disconnected sketches with two, three or four figures of men and beasts), by the much cruder feeling for colour, by the very originality of the themes in their neglect of Alexandrian sources, and by the coarse naturalism of certain scenes.

The general hypothesis accordingly suggested is that of a personal or professional co-ordination between such artists as the MASTER OF THE ZLITAN FIGURES, responsible for [26, 27] the frescoes of the crypto-portico vaults; the MASTER OF THE ZLITAN SEASONS, *imaginarius* of the four mosaic busts; [25] the ACANTHUS MASTER, who designed the naturalistic floor; [28] and the MASTER OF THE GLADIATORS, executant of the fillet of the floor so called. On this view the fourteen naturalistic *emblemata* inserted in the 'Mosaic of the Seasons' and in [25] that of the 'Gladiators' would be imported works. If the dating indicated is accepted, the Dar Buc Amméra villa as a whole would support the belief that as early as the end of the first century, on African territory very close to the great Alexandrian art market, competition had started between workshops and individual practitioners of varying education and origin. It would be mainly attested by a great deal of diversity in poetic and stylistic expression, constituting foundations by this time ready for free experiment in late Roman art.

At Antioch, the House of the Calendar is one of the most securely dated buildings excavated by the University of Princeton expedition. Its reconstruction has been proved to have been carried out during the period immediately following the earthquake of 115. Moreover, the edifice preserves, even though in largely mutilated form, one of the best surviving mosaics of Roman imperial art attributable to any part of the second century. While cutting short life of flourishing cities, the Vesuvian disaster of 79 preserved intact the *status* of art at the beginning of the last quarter of the first century; and the long gap extending from that date until far into the second century is largely covered by the Antiochene house together with the Dar Buc Amméra villa.

Between two fillets representing waves is a border, a plaited strip of exquisite workmanship. This border contains a panel showing 'Oceanus and Tethys' against a marine background teeming with fish, no fewer than thirty-nine species of which have been identified.[30] Adjoining the panel is the circular picture of a Calendar with personifications of the twelve Months and the four Seasons, unfortunately almost all missing.

The representation of fish, as well as that of sea divinities, which is very frequent, occurs fairly commonly in Hellenistic art also. But the great stylistic gulf which separates these illustrations from the Antiochene 'Oceanus and Tethys' may be sufficiently estimated by examining some of the best surviving examples, such as the first-century *emblema* preserved at the Naples Museum. The latter comes from a Pompeian dining-hall (VIII, 2, 16) and consists of very small cubes depicting a marine background with fish and crustaceans. Another is an *emblema* of the same subject, also at Naples, from the House of the Faun at Pompeii (VI, 12, 2–5); it dates from the phase of transition between the 'first' and the 'second' style at the beginning of the first century BC. In these mosaics the objective space, lacking any variation of light, as though it were a pre-ordained and absolutely unalterable cavity, receives the beings which populate it without in the slightest degree varying their nature or disturbing by alterations of colour or light their physical, rationalised volume. The rocks scattered here and there round the picture merely constitute components of realistic connotation, typical of the more traditional Hellenistic taste. They do not, in fact, perform any temporal function in setting the scene, the background of which, being rendered without modulation or shading, simply supplies a conventional plane of materialised support, a glazed section, so to speak, of the watery element which sustains the various species of fish.[31]

Very different is the spatial structure of the Antiochene seapiece, one and two centuries later, respectively, than the above. Here, unlike the purely descriptive images at Naples, the fish are animated with an intense, expressive vitality. Sudden flashes of light vary the colours of the polychrome surfaces by means of glazed cubes which produce multiple refraction and thereby afford a progressive revelation of altering form, subject at Naples to motionless, objective

30 Levi (1947), i, p. 39.

31 Naples National Museum, Room LXIX, No. 120777 (Blake (1930), p. 139), and Room LX, No. 9997 (Blake (1930), p. 138). Other fragments dealing with this subject may be seen in the Roman Municipal Antiquarium (*see* Jones, H. Stuart (1926), p. 280, pl. 109). Excavated near the church of S. Lorenzo in Panisperna, their free but controlled impressionism seems to indicate their execution towards the end of the first century AD. Others are the frescoes of the 'Fishing Cupids' executed about the year 125, taken from the Via Portuense and now at the Museo delle Terme (*Archäologischer Anzeiger*, LV (1940), pp. 482–7). Here fish of every kind, sometimes ridden by little fishermen, depicted with some degree of bold impressionism and free fantasy, among boats beautifully painted with scenes from history or fiction, positively leap from walls to vault, almost flying along the sea and composing a continuous, multi-dimensional picture of the watery world. These fish emerge from the background through shading, like those of the House of the Vettii (VI, 15, 1) at Pompeii. *See also* in this connection Jacopi (1943).

illumination. But above all, the darting shapes come out clearly against the background, on which shadows of variable outline are also distinguishable, in the same way as the dominating figures of the two deities. Thus the illusionist dimension of infinite depth, invented in atmospheric space by the execution of certain Pompeian works, is found at Antioch in the unfathomable liquid abyss of the sea. A similar process can be identified on the stylistic plane, though as yet resulting in less expressive liveliness, in some fragments of linen and wool tapestry excavated at Antinoë and now shared by the Louvre[32] and the Musée historique des Tissus at Lyons. In these fragments, which are probably of later date (second to third century), shading gives the fish the same impressionistic detachment from their green background, while their moving bodies are also wonderfully illuminated from below, so as to bring out their diverse structure synthetically. It is interesting to observe here the homogeneity of formal development, though one may be inclined to attribute slower growth to it in the neighbourhood of Alexandria, at any rate when the subject is, as here, typically Hellenistic.

The sea of the Antioch mosaic is composed entirely of greenish and blue cubes, which set the general tone of the scene. The scales of the fish glitter amid the infinite facets of clear blue light, and the bodies of the two divinities, one seated and the other half reclining in the water, stand out even more against a whole range of dark blues in the mantles that cover their lower limbs. Oceanus has a robust torso tending towards rather warm reddish tones. The perfect Hellenistic design of the half-nude form of Tethys comprises an expanse of surfaces varying from white to pink, which further brightens an already luminous general composition.

A close study of the countenance of Oceanus (that of Tethys is half lost) clearly reveals the stylistic significance of the whole work. The features are unquestionably classical, in direct derivation from the great Attic school of sculpture through Pergamene Hellenism, which was evidently still operative in the second-century Antiochene artist. They are powerfully incised in vigorous lines, violently expressive in their detachment, giving the laterally-lit figures an almost dramatic animation. It is the light, in fact, rather than any chromatic brilliance, which, by means of a technique approaching divisionism and within the scope of a mature impressionism full of inspiration and plastic potency, defines lineaments, planes and chromatic surfaces in such a way as to attain an effect of organic, majestic vitality.

In terms of pure style, comparison with the more significant works of the first century (e.g. 'Theseus the Liberator' from Herculaneum, and the faces designed by the MASTER OF THE PLANISPHERE and the INNOVATING

32 The Antinoë fragment of tapestry with fish, in the Louvre, is catalogued No. GU. 1242.

MASTER OF STABIA) and with the great Trajanic sculpture of   18, 22
the years immediately preceding, the Antioch mosaic
reveals an increase of the sharp intervention of colour and
light in the process of pictorial disintegration of Hellenistic
plasticity. This advance was contained, nevertheless, within
a channel of strict formal tradition, so that there emerged
a cohesive factor in the physical pattern which was
actually to prove capable of rejoining the attempted return
to classicism that reached its height in Rome after the
accession of Hadrian. But the conditioning of the Hellenistic cultural environment at Antioch, though in substantial agreement with the artistic development of the
capital, may have remained in force at this point owing to
its loyalty to an idea of form which, notwithstanding its
conscious combination with impressionist modes, had
remained undisturbed. Such was the great tradition of
Pergamum and Antioch. Wherever composition could be
allowed more freedom, as for instance in the case of the
darting fish, the impressionist originality of the artist
found means to give further proof of its existence.

An interesting comparison, more profitable than any
with traditionalist faces of Oceanus such as are common in
mosaics of northern Africa (e.g. at Sabratha), can be made
with the face of Oceanus depicted in the *emblema* at the   33
Verulamium Museum, St. Albans, discovered in a building
erected there in the second half of the second century, at
the extreme limit of the Roman world. The *emblema* is set
in a geometrically tessellated pavement, clearly typical of
the time of Hadrian, and was probably made by an artist
subject for some decades in that distant province to a taste
by then outmoded in the capital and certainly uninfluenced
by the rich figurative style that enlivens the Antiochene
floor. Nevertheless, the vigorous, though cramped and
simplified, plasticity of the face, the unmistakable significance of the presentation, the formal synthetic capacity
shown in the reinforced shading, are all characteristics to
some extent echoing those of the Antiochene Oceanus,   32
otherwise so remote in style, though the St. Albans
emblema remains in the orbit of a classicism filtered through
a local taste, the graphic evidence of which would emerge
in the third century and still more in the fourth.[33]

In Rome the age of Hadrian, so far as has been ascertained, affords little proof of the stylistic progress already
to some extent documented by the Antiochene mosaic.
The tendency to the full revaluation of neo-Attic works of
art appeared naturally for the most part in court circles and
in the items most affected by the aesthetic dictatorship of
the emperor. Here, therefore, little benefit would be
derived from a thorough analysis of such time-wearied
though not unskilful bits of work as the *emblemata* from
Hadrian's villa at Tivoli (now in the Vatican Museum,
Nos. 113A and 125A, and the Berlin Staatliche Museen),

33 *See* especially Toynbee, Jocelyn
M.C. (1962), No. 178, pl. 207, pp.
196–7; Wheeler, Robert E.M., and
T.V. (1936), p. 144, pl. 41 and 45a.

representing 'Pastoral Scenes' and fights between 'Centaurs and Wild Beasts'. A direct Hellenistic, undoubtedly Alexandrian, influence dominating the choice of subjects must be recognised. But at the same time, behind the rustic vivacity of these *emblemata*, executed in wonderfully fresh colour with very small cubes, one significant detail should be emphasised. The protagonists, whether separate animals, flocks or centaurs, stand out against the landscape, in itself remarkable and given a highly illusionist life of its own. This feature is certainly to be attributed to the stylistic development of painting and sculpture during the fifty years covering the end of the first century and the beginning of the second. This period, as already noted, saw a modification of the specifically Hellenistic notion of space. The change would therefore appear to have involved, actually in the most authentic and significant specimens of art under Hadrian, a clear adoption of some of the basic elements of the new Roman idiom.

It is not, perhaps, by chance that the return of lyricism as an independently expressive factor in landscape (sometimes occurring in a more precisely traditional manner, as in the Albanum Landscape from the villa of the Quintilli) and the greater compositional and semantic weight assumed by the figure in the representative pattern of these works undeniably approximate to the imposing Palestrina mosaic and the equally impressive 'Mythological Seascape' fresco in the pagano-Christian Caelian House under the basilica of SS. Giovanni e Paolo at Rome.

The former of these two productions, one of the most famous ancient Roman mosaics ever discovered, cannot here be subjected to a fresh analysis. Only certain general and stylistic considerations can be advanced with regard to its composition, with a view to determining, on valid artistic grounds, its historical position. The 'Barberini Mosaic' in fact, though always ascribed to a Hellenistic artist inspired partly by an Alexandrian original and partly by the well known stories of animal life written in Greek by Claudius Aelianus of Praeneste, is nevertheless clearly an adaptation, though probably a very free adaptation, from an original of the Ptolemaic era. The treatment of the extensive landscape, while organic in its general narrative structure, shows signs of a performance now chiefly concerned with the most meticulous rendering of historically recognisable localities, of animals, and of human beings seen in their day-to-day activities. The original panorama unfolds *en plein air*, no longer the main subject of a discounted field of art but a mere storied framework, the *hic* of a *nunc* which, in the several extracts from an only superficially unified narrative, becomes a single humanised and differentiated event. In this great Praenestine production Nilotic literature seems not so much *demodée* in the Rome of Hadrian – to which I should be inclined, notwithstanding recent opinions, to ascribe the mosaic – as revived, with much artistic freedom, to accord with a taste that is now historical and specifically Roman. It appears reasonable, therefore, to view the 'Barberini Mosaic' as dating from a period slightly later than the fragmentary Hadrianic pavements at Tivoli, with which individual scenes can legitimately be compared in respect of the prominence given in the passages of landscape to the human and animal forms or to the natural and architectural environment.

This view, at one time accepted by the majority of scholars, has recently been called in question once again, for example by Gullini, who has studied with particular care the reassembly of the 'Barberini Mosaic' in the Palestrina Museum. He was able, in so doing, to give closer attention to certain aspects of the executive technique of this great lithostroton than they had ever before received. He distinguished the components supposed to be original from the later refurbishings and distortions applied up to 1855, and made some useful comparisons with the fragments of the 'Fish Mosaic' from the Cave of the Lots at the Praenestine Sanctuary.[34] His conclusions, although they appear illuminating in many respects, do not seem to me to justify the antedating of the Nilotic pavement, as well as that of the Fish, to the age of Sulla. For while the 'Fish Mosaic' may well be dated upon various grounds to the first century BC, this is not necessarily the case with the 'Barberini Mosaic'. Gullini's proofs were technical, iconographical and stylistic. He recognised, though with another end in view, that the cubes of the former were smaller than those of the Nilotic mosaic[35] and that the mortar was coloured. He also pointed out that representations of the same model are not known after the beginning of the second century.[36]

His conclusion is essentially based on the identity of the materials used in the two pavements, on the identical way in which the cubes are arranged so as to avoid every geometrical principle in their placing, on the analogy of 'plastering with mortar and pounded earthenware in the interstices' and on the identity of a good part of the tessellating material used with that employed in the famous 'Battle of Alexander' mosaic and others in the House of the Faun at Pompeii. But he is obliged to record the results of Fuhrmann's petrographical examination, according to which the cubes of the frames of the mosaics in the House of the Faun and the cementing ingredients themselves in the fixing mortars came from the neighbourhood of Vesuvius.[37] But obviously these arguments from identity cannot preclude the possibility that in the one case, involving the lapse of two hundred years, workshops of mosaicists moved from Alexandria to Palestrina or Pompeii in order to execute important commissions of the kind

34 Gullini and Fasolo (1953), p. 312 ff. Of the more recent studies *see also* Schmidt (1929), especially p. 10; Helga von Heintze in *Gymnasium* II (1956), p. 102; Jacopi (1959), p. 23; Heinz Hahler's review of the study by Gullini and Fasolo, in *Gnomon*, XXX (1958), p. 366–83; Aurigemma (1957–9).
35 Gullini (1956), p. 6.
36 Cf. note 31 to this chapter, and Gullini (1956), pp. 20–4.
37 Gullini (1956), pp. 6 and 19.

here referred to. They would naturally bring with them supplies of many varieties of stone unobtainable in Italy but certainly much used for many centuries at Alexandria. In the other case immigrant Alexandrian artists or Italian artists educated in Alexandria may have executed both works, in the first century BC and the second AD respectively, using the same sort of materials. In the first case very few changes would have been made in the methods of laying the cubes, while in the second it may be supposed that notable alterations would have been introduced.

All things considered, it appears that while perceptible and steadily increasing differences in workmanship may have arisen in course of time between Alexandrian and Italian *tessellarii*, the latter having undoubtedly learnt their technique from the former and progressively adapted it to a new taste, it is more difficult to identify a similar process at Alexandria itself, the fountain-head, where a much greater technical, iconographical and stylistic fidelity to the more ancient Hellenistic forms of art is attested throughout the development of painting under the Empire.

In fact, unless a judgment based on the technical features observed by Gullini is regarded as decisive, it seems legitimate to assert that not only does a different spirit and cultural status permeate the Nilotic and Fish pavements, but also that the differences from a purely stylistic point of view are more than remarkable. It accordingly appears reasonable to give diverse datings to the two mosaics, thus rendering more logical the fact that Pliny (*Naturalis Historia* XXXVI, 189) mentions only one lithostroton, even on the theory that by this term he meant the 'Fish Mosaic' and not the other Palestrina *pavimenta*. I do not intend to refer here to the zones so carefully marked out by Gullini, though they ought to be considered, at least in part, as restorations carried out in late antiquity (3rd–4th century). I shall confine myself to those which are certainly original, stressing either the evidence of the single episodes with a landscape background; or the inconsistently perspective drawing of ships, environments and buildings; or the brisk sketching of the rapid silhouettes given historically motived relief in the narrative, though this fact does not impede their resemblance to the style of pastoral and harbour scenes in the late Hellenistic painting of Campania. Sometimes, as in the scene of the soldiers under the tent, they approach the treatment in the famous 'Trojan Horse' or else, as in the case of the warship, the formal concision, all shadows and atmospheric colour, of the ships represented in certain Pompeian frescoes at the House of the Vettii (VI, 15, 1) and those from the Temple of Isis (VIII, 8, 28) which are now in the Naples Museum (Nos. 8527–8529). Such considerations concerned with form, culture and taste might be developed at some length. They seem to indicate that a dating prior to the beginning of the second century AD, and hence · a classification in the purely Hellenistic-Alexandrian category, would not be the best way to reach a better understanding of the great Praenestine *lithostroton*.

As to the large mythological seascape preserved on the west wall of the House on the Caelian hill and measuring about 2 by 5 metres, it was probably meant to extend on both sides over other long walls, perhaps for a distance of some thirty metres covered with figures.[38] It is certainly unprofitable to dwell on the question of the identities of the deities represented.[39] On the contrary, the fundamental problem in the case of this mural, 'the greatest picture surviving from ancient Rome and preserved in all its wonderful freshness of colour',[40] is also that of its date, a matter still in dispute among scholars. There is a considerable difference of opinion, not only on stylistic but also on archaeological grounds. Wirth, for example, relies also on the character of the mural structure in attributing the work to the time of Hadrian or the first Antonine age,[41] while Colini considers it impossible to go lower than the third century, to which period he assigns the method of extending paintings over a lateral wall.[42] Gasdia, in his long monograph, leaves it open to date the picture to the second century or at latest to the beginning of the third.[43] Finally, Levi[44] restores the dating to that proposed by Wirth, basing his argument on certain detailed comparisons, particularly with some faces found in the House of the Calendar at Antioch.

Accordingly, whether the mural in the present case represents Aphrodite and Ares or some other myth, it is certain that the artist, the MASTER OF THE CAELIAN SEA, did not intend to confine himself solely to the subject of the fable, to which he had undoubtedly been led by the traditional cartoons, nor to the usual type of seascape. This conclusion is reinforced by a description given by Cassiano dal Pozzo of a similar scene in which the central group on a rock, surrounded by Cupids in boats, lacked the male figure of Ares or Bacchus. It decorated one of the lunettes of a vaulted hypogean structure excavated in 1639 in the adjoining garden of the Fathers of St. Gregory and immediately destroyed.[45] In that picture the aggregate of divinities was much less clearly defined, being absorbed more organically into the natural surroundings. The compositional fusion between the latter elements and the large figures set among them accordingly seems in itself singularly favourable to a dating within the second quarter of the second century, that is to say after the close of the age of Hadrian, when a formal interest of neo-Attic type in the human figure had been re-established, though without eliminating the compositional achievements of the preceding style of painting. The classical build of the personages, deities and Cupids in this mural seascape also

38 Wirth (1934), p. 80.
39 Gasdia (1937, p. 254) recognises in this picture Ceres, Proserpina and Bacchus; Colini (1944, p. 173) agrees. Wirth (1934, p. 80) prefers Proserpina or Tethys, Venus and Bacchus. Levi (1947, i. p. 527) refers to Aphrodite and Ares.
40 Lugli (1924), p. 152.
41 Wirth (1934), p. 82.
42 Colini (1944), pp. 172–3.
43 Gasdia (1937), p. 252.
44 Levi (1947), i. p. 527.
45 Colini (1944), pp. 208–9, f. 169 b. (from Bartoli and Caylus, 1783).

supports reference to such a period. The elongation of the figures, common towards the middle of the second century; the static frigidity of their attitudes; the clarity of line, concentrating upon the definition of physiognomy rather than the usual shading; the reappearance of impressionistic peculiarities and the further though still incomplete progress in the representation of the figures and other components of the scene on a single plane, all inevitably impose the conviction that, while stylistic excellence may not have been fully achieved, the signs of an important phase in imperial painting of the second century are certainly explicit. It was a phase that linked the traditionalist era of Hadrian with that of the Antonines and the unmistakable maturity of traits which would be eventually combined under the Severan emperors to form a uniform artistic whole.

Indeed, the possibility of dating this great Caelian composition any later than the second century, or at most the beginning of the third, is excluded by the traces of traditionalist resistance and the manifest classical stamp of anatomies and physiognomies. But this period probably also produced the extensive fresco which, as in the case of the Caelian House, decorated three sides of a hall in the Baths of the Seven Sages (III, X, 2) at Ostia with widely dispersed scenery representing the 'Toilet of Venus' attended by Cupids against a background of extremely beautiful marine animals. It is a picture of brilliant and lavish chromatic effect and skilful impressionist technique, of which unfortunately little remains. But enough is left to prove that, with the elimination of the problem of perspective, the painting of the Empire had already advanced into the late Roman epoch.

An adequate view of the stylistic modes of expression current in the Antonine age is obtainable with the aid of certain surviving mosaics and murals, such as those of Genazzano and the Via Portuense respectively, the large mosaic of Dionysus at Cologne and the lunettes of the Caivano Tomb. None of these works reveals an especially talented hand. Almost invariably they are by good artists whose skill appears in the sound proportions of their composition and their combination of realism and impressionism in an idiom proving the extent to which they had resumed, after the forced reaction under Hadrian, the free stylistic development of Roman painting.

The Genazzano fragment at the Museo Nazionale in Rome was found in a villa proved by its wall structure to belong at latest to the Antonine age and thought to have been owned by the emperors Marcus Aurelius and Lucius Verus.[46] A meticulous tessellation technique and the refined, still over-emphatic, taste shown in the distribution of ornament, achieved with a baroque subtlety of chromatic modulation, are accompanied by the insertion of tiny

36, 37
38, 39

36

46 Mancini (1910).

circular *emblemata* exhibiting against uniformly but richly coloured backgrounds heads of a Dionysiac type, of which a bearded and grinning Pan and a very youthful Satyr survive. Marion Elizabeth Blake has assigned the medallions of this fine pavement, qualitatively the best of all those here examined, to the 'category of false *emblemata*',[47] emphasising 'the realistic modelling of the features' as reflecting the taste of the epoch.[48] In fact, the Genazzano Mosaic is not isolated in this connection. It will be sufficient to mention, among the suggestive survivals of Ostian painting, the 'Niche of the Horseman' (Tomb No. 19 of the Necropolis), which revives the neo-Attic pattern of the Hadrianic roundels on the Arch of Constantine by introducing the personalised animation of the portrait of a youth. Another example might be the freshness of line and the satirical statement in the figures of the 'Antique Sages' lecturing on good digestion in the Ostian *taberna* included in the Baths of the Seven Sages (III, X, 2).

The realism of portraiture in the persons of this Dionysiac *thiasos* is expressed in the Genazzano Mosaic with a pungent and highly individualised expressiveness, certainly altogether different from the traditional style and not wholly lacking in the characteristic stresses of impressionism. But it is the general placing of the heads in the encircling, ribbon-like bands and frames that affords definite proof of the re-emergence of the taste for figures in a cultural sense which excludes neo-Atticism within the luxuriance of arabesque that had been developed to the maximum by the preceding era. This manner concealed the organic significance borrowed from neo-classical taste in order to stabilise the fusion which had occurred in idiomatic usage between elements of diverse origin, leading to a result of comprehensive novelty. The same considerations can be applied, in dealing with a work of much greater importance, to the large pavement at Cologne.

Excavations undertaken for military reasons in 1941 near the south door of the cathedral resulted in an archaeological surprise. There was brought to light a great mosaic floor, almost intact, whose splendours had once adorned the dining-room of an imposing peristyled villa, a type of structure which, as Fremersdorf, the excavator, noted, had never before been discovered among the relics of Roman civilisation in the Rhineland.[50] The 'Dionysus Mosaic', as the multicoloured pavement was named from its figurative subject, measures 10.5 metres by 7, and is composed of cubes with an average lateral dimension of one centimetre. They are slightly smaller in the *emblemata*, in which many of the tesserae are glazed. The panelling is organised in thirty-one figured sections. A great central *emblema*, bordered by a double-plaited fillet, represents an intoxicated Dionysus supported by a satyr. Six octagonal panels portray Eros, maenads and dancing satyrs. Eight square,

38, 39

38

39

47 Blake (1936), p. 179.
48 Blake (1936). p. 132.
49 The works were finished in 1949; in 1959 the mosaic underwent thorough restoration.
50 Fremersdorf (1949), p. 3. *See also* Parlaska (1950); Fremersdorf (1956).
51 Lübke *et al.* (1958), p. 437.

smaller panels exhibit pots and baskets of fruit, the Dionysiac panther and other simpler scenes with satyrs. Lastly, sixteen marginal panels of auxiliary decoration contain the minute forms of animals such as ducks, pigeons, rabbits, peacocks, parrots and guinea-fowl harnessed to farm-carts loaded with fruit and labourers' implements, etc. Fruit is also shown separately in these panels. Between the various decorative fillets framing the scenes, all executed on a white ground with the cubes arranged fanwise, small rhomboid components displaying stylised flowers are introduced. The whole design is contained within a double border of ropelike braid and plain Greek fret.

A warm tonal range of yellow, pink and red combines with the white of the backgrounds to dominate the colour scheme. In general, an elaborately baroque style can be detected throughout the extensive surface, while the artist's highly developed decorative taste reveals an entire cultural and formal dependence upon neo-classical models. The DIONYSUS MASTER appears on the whole to have been a provincial artist, though belonging to a province still relatively new to Roman civilisation and with no recollection of previous independent figurative traditions. (I refer to him as an individual, because the evident stylistic unity of the whole work leads me to suppose, in opposition to Fremersdorf and Berta Sarne,[51] the hand, or at least the direct supervision, of a single artist responsible for this mosaic.) His great sensitivity to established taste is shown by the superfluity of geometrical decoration in the constitution of the work as a whole and by his resort to warm tones of colour. But he seems still rather resistant to the new tendencies of imperial art then coming to maturity, especially in Rome. He keeps remarkably close to his models so far as traditional anatomy is concerned and the significance of forms in objective space. The rigorous perspective maintained in the scenes of birds harnessed to carts is symptomatic in this respect. Consequently, the formal simplicity with which certain anatomical structures are treated appears as surprising as a grammatical error.

These general observations at once corroborate the archaeological assumption of a dating between the middle and the end of the second century, and rather earlier than later in that period. One is inclined therefore to place the pavement somewhere in the Antonine age and to regard it not so much as a platform for the celebration of secret rites as setting a joyous and uninhibited mood for banquets held in a hall where it was certainly unnecessary to recall the more important episodes of the myth, as was subsequently the function of floors in Christian or late pagan times. The aim was simply to take pleasure in *genre* pictures dealing with the story of the god only casually, as a fable, not liturgically. The decorative arrangement thus

51 Lübke *et al.* (1958), p. 437.

supplies a geometrical and architectural framework of diminutive illustrations to be assessed in exactly the same way as the painting of the 'third style'.

Spatial unity is nevertheless implied and clearly evident among the various scenes owing to the subjects themselves of the individual figurations, which acquire integration as diverse aspects of an episode of Dionysiac *enthousiasmos*. The missing element at Cologne, as in the Genazzano fragment, is the definition of the background. It does not affect the coherence of the narrative. But as already noted, there is no trace of environment in the white, abstract setting of any individual scene. Accordingly, the intermediate, transitional stage undoubtedly represented by the Genazzano and Cologne mosaics has to be traced through the retention of figurative shapes derived from the Hellenistic repertory, though at Genazzano these already differ very considerably in idiom from the originals, in a pictorial space environmentally negative, consisting of surfaces of undifferentiated colour, almost as if the figures had been imposed on cuttings from the ancient work, which thereby regained control of their significance. 36

The bodies of the satyrs and maenads (as well as the details of the plumage of the birds), bearing the stamp of classicism in the anatomy of their limbs, in the colour scheme and in the accurate delicacy of the mosaic lines, are conspicuous for their graceful ease of movement, caught in felicitous dance postures which lift their transparent veils and garments in such a way that the artist's understanding of form finds opportunities to assert itself in the highly coherent indication of rosy areas of flesh by means of noticeably stressed chromatic shading. The idiom of the *tessellarius* is even more apparent when compared with the models relevant to some of his designs in the mosaic. The Drunken Dionysus of the central panel, for instance, is one of the best reproductions in this medium of a subject, here treated with every resource of technique, the model for which, extremely familiar in ancient art, was employed on innumerable occasions. It will suffice here to refer to the 'Farnese Bacchanal' relief at the Naples Museum, which affords decisive confirmation of the source not only of the present subject but also of the two music-making and dancing maenads in two of the octagonal panels at Cologne. The *emblema* of the so-called House of the Intoxicated Dionysus near Antioch, dated by Levi from the first years of Hadrian's reign, shortly after the earthquake of 115, is another case in point, as is also the scene of Dionysus between two satyrs at the Museo Nazionale in Rome.[52] As compared with the work at Antioch, due to a more refined hand and tradition, the figures at Cologne, executed about fifty years later,[53] show a greater admixture in their chromaticism of a warm, unified tonality interrupted only for the sake of contrast by the fluttering 38, 39

38

52 Levi (1947), i, p. 40; ii, Ps. VII b; Museo Nazionale Romano, No. 125594.
53 Parlaska (1959 b, p. 178) suggests the alternative date AD 220.

blue garments of the Dionysiac procession. The still vivid hues of the Hellenistic tradition at Antioch had been succeeded – as convincingly exemplified in the splendid bowl loaded with fruit – by a sumptuous and vibrant baroque style.

The Cologne pavement, though its subject is entirely different, is in many ways similar to the mosaic of 'Combats in the Circus' at the Nennig villa, well known for having been discovered in 1852.[54] This second mosaic covers a large area (15.65 by 10.30 metres), and contains nine *emblemata* within a complicated decorative system of intersecting rhombs and squares. Seven of the *emblemata* survive. They show Circus scenes of gladiatorial combats, games and the hunting of wild animals. The lavish ornamentation is singularly close to that of the Cologne mosaic, but the latter has more chromatic content and a more academic expressive structure. In certain iconographical respects and in similarity of subject the 'Mosaic of the Gladiators' at the villa of Dar Buc Amméra (Zlitan) is also comparable with the Nennig pavement, which is, however, superior in composition and care of execution. It has been ascribed by Parlaska to the years 230–240,[55] but may perhaps be reasonably pre-dated to the beginning of the third century. As another specimen of this imported taste, which probably lasted for a long time in the Rhineland, we may cite such a fragment as the roundel of 'Anaximander with Sundial', taken from the Johannisstrasse at Trier. On the strength of its design in a compositional and chromatic structure even more frankly Hellenistic, it may be dated to the end of the second century.[56]

Yet another example of the development of the understanding of space in Roman painting of the second half of the century is provided by the incomplete *emblema* representing the 'Rape of Persephone' from the Via Portuense, now in the Antiquarium of the Capitoline Museums.[57] The fragment preserves the chariot of Hades, driven by the god who is carrying off the girl, together with Hermes, who restrains the horses, and a nymph crouching in astonishment at the abduction. The figures appear against a white background furnished with a Greek inscription, their shadows mingling at the base of the design. They are depicted with great assurance in a small area, in a lavishly impressionistic style which makes spirited use of an almost summary technique of shadow and rapid lighting. Keen psychological insight marks the otherwise stereotyped emotions of the characters, who are caught in balanced movement at the height of the dramatic action. This feature recalls some of the most outstanding pictures of early Campanian impressionism which date from the preceding century but are still within the orbit of Alexandrian figurative tradition. Likewise, though less emphatic-

40, 42

41

54 Wagner (1908); Lafaye and Blanchet (1909) no. 1295.
55 Parlaska (1959 b), p. 38.
56 Parlaska (1959 b), p. 29.
57 Jones, H. Stuart (1926), pl. 106; Blake (1936), pls. 45–6 I.

ally, it reminds one of the probably contemporaneous little panel (now in the British Museum) from the Tomb of the Nasoni on the Via Flaminia,[58] which treats the same theme in a stylistically more traditional manner, though figuratively the design is quite similar.

On the other hand, the impressionism of the Via Portuense fragment is highly individual and also significant in other ways, as compared with the Via Flaminia scene and the livelier of the paintings from Hellenistic Campania. The violence of the action, conveying the lightning speed of the abduction, seems to concentrate the power of the work in the straining hoofs of the horses as they start to leap forward, their extremities being certainly elongated in a physically exaggerated fashion, according to a convention as old as that of Attic vase-painting. For the rest, a certain expressionist tendency is recognisable in the features of the two divinities, seen full-face in their stern psychological involvement with the exploit and looking in a direction contrary to that of the movement of their bodies. Even the blown robe of the nymph surprised by the sudden assault has an expressionist touch. Her whole figure, in its smooth outline, bright colouring and bodily attitude, contrasts with the agitated statement of the event represented. Everything in the picture, then, conspires to reveal in the artist a desire to qualify his work stylistically with a traditional reference in this particular passage, which Levi found 'a little affected'.[59]

Turning, on the other hand, to a production which preserves more fully the stamp of the Hellenistic treatment of scenery, and where the floating of the figures on an abstract ground, characteristic of all the painting of the Antonine age, is absent, we find for example the 'Seascapes' of the lunettes in the Caivano Tomb, now in the Naples Museum and probably belonging to the early Antonine age.[60] Here it will be necessary to note that 'the masterly use of light to obtain an illusion of space', which Levi emphasised,[61] nevertheless states, by means of its fierce luminosity from background and atmospheric space, together with the extreme vivacity of its silhouettes, the objective which Hellenistic scenery painting had itself reached within a century after reinforcement by the novel techniques of LUDIUS and transfiguration by the Italian painters from the 'fourth style' onward. Beyond the identification of dazzling light and indefinite space, and more probably implicit, potential, in it, there could only be the white, abstract ground of Roman painting in the third and fourth centuries.

The expressionist touches evident in the 'Rape of Persephone' were not unique in the second half of the century. The 'Mosaic Shrine of Silvanus', perhaps only a few years later, was found in the nineteenth century at the Mithraeum of Ostia, near the so-called maritime baths

43

45

58 Hinks (1933), no. 72a, p. 48, pl. XIX.
59 Levi (1947), i, p. 532.
60 Elia (1931), pls. I–VII. The author dates these works in the last quarter of the first century.
61 Levi (1946–8), pp. 257–8.

constructed by Antoninus Pius, and is now in the Lateran Museum. This mosaic was severely criticised by Cecchelli, almost in the same terms as Nogara[62] had used. The former, for instance, went so far as to speak of 'effects deadened by uniform, rectilinear shading'.[63] The barely indicated drapery, the few strips of brown *tesserae* used for the features of the face, and the poor perspective of the rural altar, elements nevertheless recognised as integral to the dissociative process accentuated in the late second century even in reproductions of the human figure, induced Cecchelli to pronounce a substantially negative verdict on this peculiar work.

In the context of the present study, however, the Ostian 'Silvanus' appears to be not only a monument of much importance, for the reasons recognised by Nogara himself, but also a work of some merit on the artistic level and surprising for the abundance of stylistic innovations to be found there. In the first place it is to be noted that, as well as retaining the traditional iconography (see for example the slightly later 'Silvanus', in fresco, at the Ostian Museum),[64] the figure preserves, in spite of its new stylistic elements, an almost classical solidity of structure, where the head carries accents worthy of the best tradition of portraiture. The importance, however, of the mosaic lies in a different direction: it is in fact the first organic example of the use, here already very fully exploited, of the curved line as a factor in expressionism.

The halo alone, which encircles the head of the divinity, contributes to an unmistakably religious effect, calling to mind the active essence itself of the work, bound to attract the gaze of the faithful. Furthermore, the figure, being placed in the recess of a shrine, forms part of a generally concave structure of the composition. The expressionist aim is therefore facilitated by the compositive motion indicated, tending to comprehend the entire visual field, so as almost to give the impression, later to be the consistent intention of every apsidal mosaic in a basilica, of spiritually imprisoning the spectator in the picture, or rather in the actual space occupied by the god.

The figure of Silvanus and the altar standing to his right, though idiomatically appropriate to this situation, are not however entirely coherent. The personage, taken from a cartoon undoubtedly meant for representation on a single plane, looks rather isolated from the spatial context and the counterpointing items of trees, altar and dog. The rustic structure, presented in subtle tones of dark blue over pearly azure and pearl-grey over sky-colour, is placed, as Cecchelli observed,[65] in a wrong perspective. But the error is due mainly to the fact that at this point too the cartoon, designed for representation on a level, was used for curved reproduction. Matters are made worse by the altar being situated at a section of the mosaic curve where

62 Nogara (1910), p. 32.
63 Cecchelli (1922), 1–2, p. 9. The author writes: 'Drawing and execution are very rough; the importance of the work derives less from its artistic skill than from the singularity of the representation and above all from the fact that it is the one great example among these mosaics that goes back to the classical age. They were accordingly . . . almost an anticipation of the Christian mosaics . . .'.
64 Room V, No. 186. *See also* Wirth (1934), pp. 139–41, and pl. 37, where the approximate date 210 is assigned.
65 Cecchelli (1922), p. 9.

the eye would most naturally demand a very differently rendered perspective. Yet this result, after all, points to the dissociation of perspective planes, potentially cubist, which would be widely current in the third century and definitely dominant in the fourth.

Finally, the sky of deepest blue, against which the white tunic of the god with its red *angusti clavi* stands out most effectively, represents a substantial innovation, being to a great extent an addition, with respect to the impressionist landscape in which the painted 'Silvanus' of the Ostian Museum is embedded. This sky looks forward to the character of much later works: for example to the tonally sophisticated background of the fresco portraits on the ceiling of the imperial hall at Trier, dating from the age of Constantine; to the plainer background of the 'Patriarchs' in S. Aquilino at Milan; or, lastly, to the mysterious and exalting background in the Mausoleum of Galla Placidia at Ravenna, an abstract, unearthly azure destined eventually to be replaced by the still more magical field of gold.

In the present case the artist did not introduce the rhythmic punctuations of colour, for instance the concentrically arranged stars or the cross, such as were to be found later in the Naples Baptistery, the Mausoleum of Galla Placidia at Ravenna, the Casanarello Memorial and the Albenga Baptistery. Nor did he think of heightening the body of Silvanus, so as to set his head against the sky. But the method of disposing the cubes of the small apse appears in the highest degree significant. An infinite, interconnected series of arcs leads from the largest on the outer margin of the cavity right down to the tiny central conglomeration of dark blue *tesserae*, testifying to the desire of the artist to obtain by this spasmodic repetition of curved lines, slightly more counterpointed under the halo of Silvanus (five concentric strips of cubes ranging from white to deep blue through a succession of graded tones), a magical rendering of space. He achieved an infinite sky of inaccessible depth, obsessively repetitive of the hallowing arc, and at the same time a sense of the circular, impenetrable dimension of the universe.

Yet, even in works by traditionalist artists of this highly critical *fin de siècle* some aspects of the new aesthetics are clearly recalled, showing that a taste which must by now have been acceptable to the majority had been acquired to a considerable extent. The painters of the large Red Room on the ground floor of the Casa di via dei Dipinti at Ostia (I, IV) and of the 'Waiters' in the dining-room fresco at the House in the Via dei Cerchi at Rome produced results, at different levels of culture and of adoption of the new poetic outlook on space, which may be legitimately placed in this category. The first of these artists, who probably worked about the year 180, composed a series of scenes,

159

45

46, 47

including female figures, poets and philosophers of traditionally Hellenistic appearance, the sages being made to look very austere. These scenes are enclosed in a now distorted and architecturally disconcerting proliferation of threadlike structures taken from the 'fourth style' and almost indistinguishable from pure and simple linear decoration, such as appeared some years later on the walls of the Peacock Inn at Ostia. This mannerism already tends to abstraction in the almost exclusive adoption of red and yellow tints.

Such are the results of the process of setting figures in deliberately abstracted space, exemplified throughout the second century by the best paintings of the Ostian Necropolis on the Isola Sacra. Among these is the 'Fates' in Tomb No. II, of which Calza[66] stressed the 'classicising character' still reminiscent of Hadrian's time by the simplicity and a certain degree of solemnity in the figures. Another example is the 'Fates' of Tomb No. 16, dating from the third quarter of the century; here the intervention of bright colour and naturalistic energy marks the end of the tendency to flatten the figure against the background. Calza, incidentally, had already called attention to this development in the previous case as suggesting a 'lack of air and background elements between figuration and wall'.[67] Accordingly, the question automatically arises whether the isolation of the figure which basically accounts for it is merely academic, derived from the 'analogous figurations of Alexandrian funerary columns'[68] and classical statues in general, or whether it may not by now be expressive of the tendency to achieve space through the figure preparatory to the denial of space itself, which had been pronounced in the sculpture of Trajan's time.

The figures in the Casa di Via dei Dipinti, though almost obliterated, can be reconstructed in the lighter contours and surfaces plainly visible against the red wine-colour of the background. They leave the impression, however, of a tendency to monochrome in their execution, barely illuminated by touches of white. They invade the ornamental design with unhesitating audacity, the heads often interrupting the double linear border, thus developing the aesthetic unity of figure and background, figure and frame, which had already been implicit in the figurative insertions of the 'fourth style'. Such was the consequence of a fixed conception of space, an inexhaustible source of artistic practice not only in Roman antiquity but, as Focillon[69] has shown, throughout medieval Europe.

This assumption of the rise of the figure to the surface and of the abolition of background, already investigated by Hellenistic art on account of its *horror vacui*, and of the final identification of the figure with the background, appears at a less advanced stage, possibly one of more compromise, in the dining-room of the Roman House in

66 Calza, G. (1940), p. 122.
67 Calza, G. (1940), p. 123.
68 Calza, G. (1940), p. 121.
69 Focillon (1931; 1933).

the Via dei Cerchi. Here a complex architecture, with a flavour of the stage of a theatre, constitutes the background, where the environmental interest is only occasional, supplied by the lifelike figures of a group of busy slaves placed in front of monumental archivolts and in free rhythmical motion. The incomplete identification of the two planes, which preserve a trace of diversity in their lines and colours, does not interfere with the result, by now clearly indicated and already complete at Ostia, of the process of solution through colour and movement of the problem of relations between the figure, always the more prominent, and its environment. Thus the 'realistic' preservation of two elements in a work actually later than the Ostian decoration and executed at the beginning of the age of Septimius Severus[70] does not seem to involve any sign of restoration of the previous spatial illusionism. This point, incidentally, is attested by the absence of any dissolution of continuity between the architectural background, which divides the areas of colour, and the figures in clear chromatic relief inserted in casual fashion at the intervals in the architecture.

Such landmarks of painting in the Antonine age testify to the incapacity of the traditionalist neo-classical currents so often represented in Roman art (the Julio-Claudian art of the 'third style'; Hadrianic neo-Atticism; post-Gallienan realism; the Constantinian 'fine style'; Valentinianist mannerism) to arrest the anti-classical development of *Kunstwollen* in the central imperial period of late antiquity. This movement was most fully exemplified in all Mediterranean art, in the Roman provinces and above all in the Orient, to such an extent as to make the arguments of Strzygowsky appear remarkably persuasive at some points. Another imposing Roman monument, however, the Column of Marcus Aurelius, erected at the end of the second century, affords an indisputable example of the first organic employment of expressionist idiom with its 'disembodiment of space', combined with a demarcation of time and an allegorical evasion of the subjects.[71]

The historical interest already present in the great figured scroll of seventy-five years before, the Column of Trajan, now tended openly, through the frequency of its exact and continuous notation of scenery, to a stereotype in which the environmental element is almost always recalled for the sake of its function as instrumentally necessary to the action. It follows that the management of the work comes to be completely dominated by a narrative in which the historicity of the event tends on the formal level to appear only through the personages who took part in it, without any indications of locality. Hence typical scenes are often repeatedly presented (fording of rivers, execution of prisoners, capture of women, speeches to the soldiers, armies on the march), which would be wearisome

48

49

29

49

70 Strong (1916). Cagiano de Azevedo (1947–9) has recently suggested a dating between 220 and 240.
71 Bettini (1948), p. 66.

and trivial had not the craftsmen done their best in each case to introduce novel elements or attitudes. Furthermore, this system, if, as I believe, it is not derived *ipso facto* from some reproduction of the well known Antonine Reliefs of the Palazzo dei Conservatori and of the Attic of the Arch of Constantine, or from similar works, succeeds in concentrating the story in a series of episodes more or less ably linked. They hold up construction even on the narrative plane at arbitrary moments, largely detached and mutually independent, in such a way that the continuous historical style of narrative is distorted in favour of an extra-temporal, symbolical, allusive transfiguration regulated by the recurrent presence of the emperor's figure, given substance at important junctures and reduced essentially to allegories in which the historical event becomes universalised in the eternal presence of the myth.

In this novel system of periodicity, largely paratactical, certain elements of vocabulary and syntax are declared which became characteristic of all late Roman art and thereafter of medieval. These are the frequent frontal presentation of the persons, especially of the more important figures, their hierarchical arrangement (shown even in their relative proportions), their crowding of the surface and the resort to conventional perspectives of cartographical type. On the other hand the expressionist idiom, having now reached a coherent and unquestionable standard of artistic respectability, deepens the play of light – which in the illusionism of the first century had been mainly concerned with creating spatial atmosphere and depth, skimming over wide areas in a straight line – and enables it to achieve extraordinary chromatic effects with chiaroscuro, penetrating the representations of living flesh, garments and human action in a corrosion generously promoted by drill and chisel. Powerfully emphatic results were obtained, violently revealing sentiments and passions. The twist of the heads, the contrary directions of bodies in motion, the repetitive patterns of massed groups, the compositional skill that uses a progression of similar gestures to carry physical and spiritual agitation to a climax, and the physiognomical distortions displaying such states of mind as ferocity or terror, are so many utterances of a largely original instrumental complex which completes the general stylistic effect of the memorable art of those sculptors who in the penultimate decade of the century created at Rome a monument that may be regarded as indicative of the fundamental destination of the art of the central imperial period and the point of departure for the whole of late Roman art.

Everything which was later recognised on sound aesthetic as well as historical grounds as accomplished by the age of the Severi is already implicitly or explicitly contained in the column erected by Commodus to the glory of his father.[72] This, one need hardly now say, does not mean that in that epoch of ardent innovation there were no examples (even important examples) of a taste loyal to 'the good old days'. When studying the more significant masters of the third and fourth centuries, in other words of late Roman painting properly so called, it may even be useful to insist upon certain 'personal' characteristics. In this connection, however, it will not be surprising to meet with the assumption, though late and infiltrated, of expressions and forms of the idiom dominant throughout almost the whole of the third century, within the co-ordinates of two-dimensional parataxis, atonal chromaticism and the most violent expressionism.

72 *See* especially: Strong (1926), pp. 263–78; Wegner (1931); Rodenwaldt (1935).

Chapter Two
The rural labours master of Cherchel and Severan painting in Africa

I have already called attention in the preceding pages to certain mosaics which, as the second century advances, indicate an unqualified preponderance of traditional taste, not only in the Mediterranean East, through a numerous group of *magistri* of Alexandrian extraction who had obviously retained a formal tendency of Hellenistic character in their works and trained many native artists on that basis. With the beginning of the Severan age, this taste for classicism in artistic execution, which had been favoured by Roman or romanised clients, gradually turned on the one hand to the employment of a limited repertory of subject-matter and on the other to certain new modes of expression elaborated in the course of the second century. These latter came almost to dominate ancient art, being used in the production of works that, as they became progressively connected with the advocacy of experimental methods and forms, very soon acquired a remarkable homogeneity in the artistic *koine* of the late Empire, a manner that grew universal in the third century.

Consequently, before entering upon a detailed examination of the few surviving third-century monuments which in Rome itself decisively prove the irreversible advent of a new style, it seems advisable to verify the degree of development in this sense achieved contemporaneously by Roman Hellenistic painting in Africa, just as it will be necessary to estimate how far Roman painting at the farthest eastern limits of the Empire was able to adapt itself to this movement, in the presence of such vividly contrasting layers of substrate and adstrate.

Indisputable proof, on a very high artistic level, of the acceptance of the Roman proto-expressionistic style late in the second century, an idiom which had arrived at systematic formal coherence in the Column of Marcus Aurelius, is provided in Africa by the great (partially obliterated) pavimental 'Mosaic of the Rural Labours', brought to light in a richly adorned house at Cherchel (Caesarea) in Algeria and now in the local museum.[1] Among the various conjectures as to the date at which this exceptional mosaic was laid – conjectures as diverse as those in the case of Zlitan – it appears most appropriate in the interests of a precise stylistic analysis to incline to an opinion placing it in the age of the Severi and indeed at a fairly late stage of that epoch, in the course of the first or second decade of the third century.[2] It is in fact difficult, in the environment of a plastic culture that was clearly

50

25 28

1 Gsell (1926), p. 40 ff; Bérard (1935).
2 Picard, G.C. (1959). Bérard (1935, pp. 128–9) considers possible a date 'not earlier than the Severan age', at the beginning of or halfway through the third century. The beginning of the fourth century is the dating proposed by Rumpf (1957), pp. 195–6.

traditional, to imagine such a work as the Cherchel pavement being produced not only before the great frieze of the Column of Marcus Aurelius at Rome but also prior to 49 the decoration of the four-pillared Arch of Septimius Severus at Leptis Magna erected during the years 203 and 52 204. For in these monuments the expressionist idiom had gained further depth by the maximum employment of shading through hollowing out and piercing the stone surfaces, so that a relief of an emphasis hitherto unprecedented had been attained.

The Cherchel mosaic apparently consisted of five 50 rectangular panels, one above the other, representing respectively ploughing, sowing, hoeing, weeding and vintage. (This last subject is now almost entirely missing.) The scenes are not separated by the usual decorative mouldings but by simple streaks of colour across the background, isolating one episode from the other in very irregular fashion, so that the various attitudes of the labourers and animals, in the aggregate, have to be presented obliquely. They move against a white background without any real depth of perspective, casting heavy shadows on a confined area with no pretensions to landscape and leaving part of the space to luxuriant fruit-trees, though almost always so as not to overlap them, a process which would have obviously involved the solution of the problem of an effective rendering of distant perspective. Consequently, the result as a whole already indicates a method of figurative severance which would be adopted, from the third century onwards, by all the art of late antiquity and of the earliest medieval period. The classical conception of space was thus dropped, and with it the two-dimensional solution of spatial representation.

On the other hand Levi has repeatedly drawn attention to the existence in the Cherchel pavement of a particular illusionist aim, which accordingly ends by acquiring an appearance of depth in the setting of the figures in their environment. This in fact becomes clear when the details of the figures and natural objects are closely examined. They certainly carry on the great formal tradition of Alexandrian Hellenism with a minute descriptive realism and an unwavering adherence to the taste for plastic illusion, which is pursued with every refinement of tonal articulation in colour, and also by stressing physical bulk through strong contrasts of light and shade, actually in expressionist style. Levi himself concludes that 'the elegance and liveliness of the execution may sometimes produce a suggestion that the landscape elements are in a more distant plane. But when there is an overlapping of a detail with the figures the illusion is broken'.[3] This observation may call to mind the historical explanation of the phenomenon. Though worked out in the concrete idiom of a great artist, it is nevertheless definitely to be ascribed

3 Levi (1947), i. p. 542.

to the cultural origins of the RURAL LABOURS MASTER OF CHERCHEL. Though trained in an Alexandrian school, he was nevertheless extremely sensitive to the new problems which had at last reached Africa, from the art of the capital (Rome), perhaps through the Leptis Magna monuments which the African Septimius Severus had ordered to be carried out in the style then current in Rome and in accordance with the division of scenes appearing on the Arch of Severus in the Forum.

The RURAL LABOURS MASTER OF CHERCHEL did not, in short, forget his training in Hellenistic mosaic painting; but in this composition he gave it more emphasis in many respects. By relating the strips of his scenes of agricultural labour through antithetical movements of the figures, he adopted in substance, as already mentioned,[4] an alternating scheme of direction identical with the compensatory systematisation invented by the great MASTER OF THE ANTONINE COLUMN in his brilliant application of a motive of Pergamene sculpture when, for instance, he set in opposition the diagonals of shields and weapons carried by the soldiers of the advancing Roman army.

It should also be observed that the alertly straining bodies, the intense concentration upon movement, the psychological and physical connection established between the directive lines of the figures of the labourers and animals, and even of the conventional boundaries of the different scenes and the shaping of the branches of the trees, all contribute to a synthesis of organic motion which is neither disorderly nor casual. It has an almost classical stamp and at the same time an unsurpassable expressive force that seems to raise it to a level of universal, omnicompetent transcendence of historicity, by the compositional context of the negation of space, developing the narrative on a single superficial plane. It was this manner which, as background gradually faded out, came to be more and more the dominating principle of the late Roman artistic *koine*.

The brilliance of this fusion of the morphological and syntactical elements of two diverse artistic idioms is the special distinction of the RURAL LABOURS MASTER. He added to it a number of personal inflections significantly in harmony with the future variation, both in ornament and figures, which imperial art was to apply to the white, abstract ground of mosaics in such monuments as the pavement of the 'Triumph of Dionysus' at El Djem, now at the Bardo Museum in Tunis, the pavement of the 'Muses' at El Djem, the great *asaroton*-like vault of the circular ambulacrum of the Roman Mausoleum of Constantina[5] or the pavement of the House of the Aviary at Carthage. A fair proportion of the 'skies' of the rural scenes at Cherchel is in fact diffused by the branches, heavy with leaves and fruit, and even by the seed one of the

53

24

4 Levi, *ibidem*.
5 For the first and third mosaics mentioned see *infra*, in this Chapter and in Chapter X. For the second, Gauckler (1910), No. 68. For the fourth, *see* Gauckler (1910), no. 640. This is the *impluvium* mosaic of a luxurious dwelling discovered in 1903 on the eastern slope of the Odeon hill. The mosaic, now in the Bardo Museum, is in four sections. The subject is the same as that of the 'asaroton' vaults of the Mausoleum of Constantina, but is perhaps treated here with more realism.

labourers is scattering. This feature certainly anticipates, in its formal result, the more clearly indicated artistic aim of the later works mentioned.

But decisive evidence of this master's level of achievement is further revealed through concrete study of the executive detail of his wonderful pavement: for instance, the massive, pulsating forms of the yoked oxen, deeply incised in the chromatic sense by organically conceived shadows which bring out their majestic vitality. Similar effects are produced by the vivid alternation of colours and the wind-blown clothing of the labourers, or again by the significance of their facial expressions. All these points in the artist's work allow a sufficiently precise estimate to be made of its originality, as in the highest degree influenced by expressionist realism and constituting a creative transition to the new idiom in a cultural orbit unquestionably inured to a taste already degraded and outworn.

A conspicuously representative specimen of that taste can be detected in the mosaics of the Nile Villa at Leptis Magna particularly in those of the bath hall. Four remarkable panels about 1.2 metres in height and varying in length from 2.8 to 3.8 metres represent an 'Allegory of the Fertility of the Nile', 'The Adornment of Pegasus', 'Cupids in a Harbour' and a 'Fishing Scene'. More than the *emblemata* of *venationes* in the upper part of the villa, these compositions, perhaps inspired by Hellenistic short poems or epigrams, are more indicative of an advanced stage of degeneracy in the Alexandrian style to which they must clearly be attributed, even though their *imaginarius* was probably a native who handled his cartoons with a compositional freedom sometimes less than happy. The signs of decadence appear in the narrative structure, in the frequent iconographical repetition of the same model for different persons, in the use of tesserae of varying dimensions to depict either figures or background respectively, in frequent free chromatic changes at certain points of the design and in the development of colour preferences in the strips of *vermiculatum*. The dating of these mosaics as a whole, ascribed to the second century by Guidi and Aurigemma,[6] must be at least as late as its closing decades. In comparison with the free inventive capacity of the RURAL LABOURS MASTER OF CHERCHEL, the work shows certain delayed results of a cultural convention by then not susceptible of renewal.

Further highly significant proofs of progressive development in the important contribution made by African artists to late Roman art are to be found in two remarkable mosaic pavements with a Dionysiac subject, which certainly date back to the first and second halves, respectively, of the third century. The 'Triumph of Dionysus' at Susa (Hadrumetum) was taken from the so-called Vergil's Villa

54, 55

6 Guidi (1933); Aurigemma (1960), p. 49.

and is now in the local museum. The 'Triumph of Dionysus' at El Djem (Thysdrus) has already been mentioned. The first work, on the strength of which Picard felt it possible to date the entire villa,[7] can also be referred, in its figuration, to the compositional structure of the relief depicting the 'Triumph of Septimius Severus' on the Leptis Magna Arch, owing to a series of precise repetitions of detail. It can therefore be assigned to a date *post quem*, i.e. after 203–204.

The composer of this pavement, which differs noticeably from others in the same house, had clearly learnt thoroughly and accepted without reservation the lesson of the imperial relief; to such an extent, in fact, as still further to develop the plastic organisation. In other words, he carried to its extreme limits the elimination of space attempted by the sculptor of the Severan Arch, freely adding to the scene figures which introduce into the composition a further note of dismemberment. Above all, he thrust between the depiction of the triumph and its background on three sides an ornamental design of spiral vine-shoots growing from two pots placed at its angles. Cupids stand like harvesters among the leaves, They are accompanied by birds and large baskets of grapes. A very important aspect of this phase of the transformation of the distribution of ornament into an integrating part of the *emblema*, to which I referred on an earlier page, is accordingly documented here in a work which bears witness to the rapid evolution of taste among artists working in Roman Africa at the beginning of the third century.[8]

The SUSA ARTIST, though his line is somewhat rigid, also gives proof of a broadly Hellenistic training. There is in his idiom a certain ambiguity between enthusiastic acceptance of the new forms of expression and eclectic retention on the one hand of a degree of plastic solidity in his figures, especially in those of the wild beasts (the four tigers; the panther; the lion ridden by Eros), and on the other of a refined formal elegance (flying robe of the maenad beating a tambourine; emphatic muscular development of the naked satyr carrying a drinking-vessel; undifferentiated lineaments of Dionysus, Victory and the maenad). These considerations lead to a conclusion different from that adopted in the case of the RURAL LABOURS MASTER OF CHERCHEL. For the greater audacity in composition (perhaps not original, but important as evidence) of the *imaginarius* of the 'Triumph of Dionysus' does not attain the spontaneous stylistic coherence of the former, but keeps to an often redundant formalism unable to resolve the cultural contradictions between two artistic modes.

A similar judgment applies to the analogous 'Triumph of Dionysus' found in a sumptuous house at El Djem and now in the Bardo Museum.[9] Here the Susa compositional

7 Picard, G.C. (1959); *see also* Gauckler (1910), no. 142.

8 A preceding phase, attributable substantially to the taste for multiplication and distribution of the *emblemata* within elaborate ornamental compositions, characteristic of the Antonine age, is documented in the Lambaesis mosaic (De Pachtère (1911) no. 191), by the rich polychromy of the minute cubes, in which six tufts of acanthus, elaborately entwined, compose seven compartments containing as many representations of Dionysus. At this stage the artist is still proceeding separately to the *emblemata* conception and that of the decorative frame, not yet freed from the premises of geometric articulation. The second half of the second century (Levi also (1947, i, p. 522, n. 25) recognises on stylistic grounds a date preceding the age of Hadrian) has been named as the period of another similar mosaic, found in *oecus* no. 33 of the Villa of the Laberii at Oudna (*Uthina*) (Gauckler (1910), no. 376) and now in the Bardo Museum. In this pavement a remarkable border of garlands of flowers and fruit, interspersed with grotesque masks, encloses a complex system of vine-branches rising from four pots at the angles of the frame. The vines act as both support and environment for twenty-eight harvesting Cupids, while at the centre, still surrounded by the foliage, a quadrangular area contains an *emblema* of Dionysus and Icarus. This large mosaic (5.6 metres by 4.35) shows a more advanced stage of compositional development than that of the Lambaesis floor. It is closer to that at Susa and still more to that at El Djem, since it testifies to a compositional conception in which the emblematic element, which still survives, is immersed in a sea of vineyard efflorescence, which has completely lost its original function of decorative geometrical partition but now constitutes, with similar ornamental justification, a two-dimensional environment of secondary narrative character.

9 Gauckler (1910) no. 67. Of the same type, but of later date, between the end of the third and the beginning of the fourth century, is the 'Triumph of Dionysus' at the Oran Museum, originally at Portus Magnus (Saint-Leu). (De Pachtère (1911), no. 455).

structure employed at Susa is used again with even more precise references to the Severan relief at Leptis but going beyond the Susa work in the homogeneity of its narrative elements with those originally decorative. The EL DJEM ARTIST, in fact, further dislocates the still substantially unified scene of his Tunisian colleague, keeping the triumphal car but reducing it to a chariot drawn by two tigers and bearing Silenus and the winged Victory as well as the young god, while Pan leads the two beasts at ground level and a maenad dances beside the vehicle. I have referred to this work as a single scene, but it would be more exact to call it two scenes or possibly even four, since the material area occupied by the densely interlacing pergola of four vine-stems growing from the same number of pots at the angles of the square composition is once more preponderant with its unified level of luxuriance in grape-clusters, leaves, birds and harvesting Cupids. The original figural section is relegated to the four sides of the pavement, where the tangles of foliage contain the scene just described, a similar presentation of Drunken Dionysus accompanied by Silenus on an ass and the lion, and two short 'wings' with panthers approaching the bowl of wine.

In this composition, finally, there is evident not only the disappearance of the *emblema* and its multiplication into a number of emblematic pictures scattered about the pavement, as already seen clearly – even though within strictly defined compartments – in the dining-room at Cologne, but also the renunciation of the exclusively rigid, heavy baroque articulation of the frames and ornamental borders, and its replacement by the more elastic and variable tangle of vines (for which it will be possible elsewhere to substitute clusters of acanthus flowers and so on), which divides and encloses the various incidents of the fable without for that reason interrupting, even conventionally, the substantial unity of the unified space. The latter is now deprived of both height and base, top and bottom, and reduced to the abstraction of a screen, that is to say of any indeterminate section of reality for the reception and absolutely free disposal (subject only to extrinsic considerations of symmetry and decorative organic quality) of the particular narrative portions of the ancient Hellenistic *emblema* which no longer follow the *consecutio temporum*.

El Djem, therefore, provides more evidence than do Cologne, Genazzano or Susa of the almost complete accomplishment of the great revolution of the relations between 'picture' and 'frame'. It had definitely begun in the central and late periods of the Empire with the study of the problem of space, leading to a rejection of the preconceived rationality of Hellenistic naturalism. The space of the 'Triumph of Dionysus' at El Djem, in view of its historical origin, may be considered a cosmos

52
51
53

38, 39

53
38, 39, 3◖

53

animated by presences no longer of a logical, natural, historical order, but set in a spatial *consecutio* governed actually by the autonomous, organising form. In course of time, at Trier for example, in the second half of the fourth century, the already representative space in question came to constitute a universe open to personal access and exploration from one constellation to another. Hence, beginning from the still decorative harmony pre-established by the disposition of the various moments, there ensued the reconstruction of a new logic, wholly spiritual. Arising from the liturgy, it found an outlet in the event and so became a 'sacred' history in which every believer engaged in psychic adventure could participate anew, in a fashion entirely personal and original. 189–194, **32**

No such genetic responsibilities in the process of late Roman plastic (and not only plastic) conceptions can of course be attributed to the humble ARTIST OF EL DJEM, for all his introduction of remarkable chromaticism even into his interlacing vines, which are in themselves monotonous, dominated conspicuously by various tones of green and amber yellows. He was following a 'tradition' of development, if such a paradox can be excused, which certainly did not necessarily involve results, but obviously proceeded under inspired guidance. He sympathised, in other words, with a sentiment of the time universally prevalent and stimulating to the search for personal solutions, even if they could not be precisely forecast in every formal detail. Moreover, as usual, such a study as the present is obliged to regard the El Djem 'Triumph of Dionysus' as in some degree typical, since it is there that the Mediterranean lands have left their evidence, and to ignore the countless other testimonies that may have preceded it; and so it is likewise compelled to exercise organic and comparative caution in its research. The recognition in the artist's technique of an accent primarily professional in stylistic development certainly does not imply that the *imaginarius* in question, by discounting formal habits of Alexandrian origin, initiated or, more precisely, took over and inherited, a new, systematic artistic conception of space. His work is here simply regarded as documentary evidence, the first modest but significant fragment of a great structure now lost.

Chapter Three
The problem of the Orient posed by Antioch, Dura Europos and Palmyra

1 In this connection *see* especially, among the ingenious and illuminating contributions: Galassi (1930 and 1953); Rostovtzev (1935 and 1938); Levi (1946–8 and 1947); Morey (1938).

2 'The mosaics of Antioch', writes Levi (1946–8, pp. 296–7), 'are the expression of a provincial art at the extreme limit of the classical world, rooted in the very soil of the East. Consequently, their study should have brought out in a special sense the phenomenon of an unexpected and gradual retreat from the current of western art, and that of an increasingly sensitive and manifest penetration by a current inspired through opposite tendencies. If this last current had then succeeded in imposing itself on the West, more uncompromising evidence of it would have appeared at Antioch, which would have then seemed to be in the van of the movement affecting the art of Rome. But on the contrary, not only has a constant adherence of the art of Antioch to the general direction of classical art been noted but also, there in particular, a closer dependence than in the West upon the great legacy of the formal and spiritual world of Hellenism and a more obstinate reluctance to withdraw from it. Again: 'The outcome of this analysis excludes the notion of any real and important artistic current arising in the East at a given moment, submerging the tradition of Western classical art and setting the production of local art of a different course. On the contrary, it turns out that such elements introduced by the East increasingly assumed classical garb.' *See also* Galassi, *op. cit.*, II, p. 357: 'The entire cycle of Antiochene art furnishes the clearest evidence of a faithful copy, rejecting the inspiration of its subjects for the figurative style of their rendering.'

3 Levi (1947), i, pp. 141–9 and 546.

During the first few decades of the present century historians of art were worried by the problem of the Orient, which cannot even now be said to have been solved. Such writers were concerned, on the strength of Strzygowsky's arguments in *Orient oder Rom*, to set the problem of Roman art and still more the whole problem of ancient art up to its Byzantine and, generally, medieval limits in terms of cultural and stylistic derivation from a particular, though indistinct and incomprehensible, phase of plastic art. To start considering the question only at this point, implies clear recognition on the one hand of the partial disposal of the question by scholars in the interval[1] and on the other a critical and unprejudiced assessment, within the scope of the present work, of whatever may appear – principally as a result of the excavations undertaken during the inter-war years in Syria and Mesopotamia, notably at Dura Europos, Palmyra and Antioch – a historical monument concretely legible in its stylistic structure and of any exemplary value.

It has already been noticed, in the case of the 'Oceanus and Tethys' mosaic from the House of the Calendar at Antioch, that at the beginning of the second century the realist-impressionist manner of an artist working from tradition was to be found in the Syrian metropolis. The excavations at Antioch seem to show that he was not in fact isolated from the taste attested by the majority of finds. The consideration of certain remarkable mosaic pavements of Seleucia, dating from the first years of the third century, positively proves, as will also the analysis of other similar Antiochene monuments from the first and second halves of the fourth century, that a clear formal fidelity to the current mode, though evidently accompanied by elements actually belonging to the stylistic transformation of the artistic *koine* of the late Empire, may be discerned throughout the development of Antiochene painting, somewhat later though it undoubtedly was than the evolution found in other romanised provinces. The conclusion therefore appears incontrovertible that in this accessible field of history Levi is right in his deductions.[2]

30, 32

He has ascribed to the age of Severus[3] the pavement of the dining-room in a suburban house near the Musa Dagh at Seleucia in Pieria, the port of Antioch. This mosaic, one of the few surviving from that epoch, is the work of an artist of some individuality; it presents an interesting example of the stage of stylistic transformation clearly reached in this medium at the beginning of the critical third century in one of the cities most open to economic and cultural exchanges in imperial times. The myth of Dionysus and Ariadne is there represented within an elaborate architectural framework. But it is certainly not so much the subject, very hackneyed in ancient art, which attracts attention as the particular connection between the personages and their environment. Yet this does not seem by any means unusual at that period in the Syrian city, where it is illustrated in other noteworthy specimens of the kind. One of these, in the dining-room of the so-called House of the Drinking Contest, featuring Dionysus and Heracles,[4] comprises a wide geometrical mosaic similar to that which encloses the *emblema* of 'Dionysus and Ariadne'. Yet owing to the greater depth and decorative complexity of the architectural partitioning, as well as to the spatial structure and stylistic details of the scene, it appears less developed and more faithful to the original Hellenistic model, an impression, however, which does not imply any certainty that it was composed even a short time before the other.

The architectural setting of the 'Dionysus and Ariadne' pavement appears to be a facile copy of a Pompeian lay-out in the 'second style'. It is composed of four Corinthian pilasters based on a podium and carrying, together with two more Corinthian columns which project in front of the two central pilasters, an architrave decorated with a border of convex mouldings and festoons and another of dentils in harmonious perspective; a description, incidentally, which can be applied to the whole structure represented. On top of the architrave stand two eagles, two goblets and two griffins on either side of a large drinking-vessel. The illustrative field is thus divided into three scenes of which the two lateral are narrower and have the effect of theatrical wings, with a setting different from that of the central scene which they integrate.

The sobriety of the architectural and decorative partitioning is evident, especially in comparison with the richer and more elaborate designs of this feature in the 'Drinking Contest' mentioned above. Yet the latter does not, in my opinion, suggest derivation from one of the oldest patterns of the 'second style',. which might be represented, for example, by the room with the most ancient decoration in the House of Livia on the Palatine. In fact the Seleucid mosaic much more resembles one of the *cubiculi* of the Villa dei Misteri at Pompeii, which is certainly of later date and more complex than the room in the House of Livia. Accordingly it seems that the 'Dionysus and Ariadne' tends rather to establish the terms of structural and formal simplification intended by the artist after contemplating his model. Actually, it remains clear that the architectural design, while abandoning floral

4 Levi (1947), i, pp. 156–9 and 547.

variety and complexity of contour, retains decorative elements not found in the phases of the 'second style' which are classified as most ancient.

This extraordinary instance of stylistic conservatism belongs to a time when the whole Empire was already undergoing a radical subversion of the ancient concept of spatial dimension, and the Roman frescoes of the Via dei Cerchi had probably been executed, though perhaps only recently. On examination of its idiomatic structure the first point that strikes an observer is the substantial separation between the two parts of the work, its architectural partitioning and the scene with figures. It is remarkable, in fact, that while the former is in itself sufficiently connected and coherent, carefully and accurately placed in a classical visual perspective, the latter, though its formal vigour is strictly controlled, seems to have a life of its own, quite apart from the field of perspective framed and initiated by the columns, pilasters and architraves. It is, moreover, dominated by the internal tendency to unify planes and render the subject superficially, which was one of the basic features that reached definite maturity in the Antonine age and was passed on irreversibly to all later imperial art. Hence it is obvious that the first concern of the artist, probably to show his command of the new manner, was actually to recover in a substantially cultural sense, outside and contrary to contemporary currents (though not perhaps altogether foreign to Seleucia), an environmental structure originally of illusionist value in the framing of the old Hellenistic repertories, but no longer of living significance in the first years of the third century. He must also in the first place have been troubled by his inevitable nearness to the prevailing historical stage of pictorial representation through *emblemata*. It is true that some particulars in the figure of the satyr in the lateral area on the right indicate a certain correspondence between the picture and the vertical elements, column and pilaster, of the architectural setting. This circumstance, if the placing of the column behind the pilaster is borne in mind, might justify the hypothesis of a residual organic linking of the two parts of the composition.

But this hypothesis is not acceptable if it is realised that the identification of figure and frame and the infringement of the law of the frame had meanwhile been fully developed in Roman painting by such means, as in the figures of the Casa di Via dei Dipinti at Ostia (I, IV), through the advanced procedure of surface figuration that replaced the previous illusionist space, which was completely enclosed by the decorative framework of pavements and ceilings with *emblemata* or by the architectural framing in wall-paintings from the 'second' to the 'fourth style'. For the rest, the very emphasis on the advance towards the spectator of the column as compared with the pilaster proves that there is no residue of realistic notation to be detected here but something very different: the attestation that the figures of Dionysus and Ariadne and those of the maenad and the satyr, in the environment of their frames, have come wholly to the surface, to such an extent that one of them, the satyr, invades with one foot, his tunic and his right hand, the boundary of his own area. This effect is not the result of an illusionist convention aimed at situating the figure between the architectural frame and the 'real space' of the observer, but simply the consequence of an asyntactic process of fusion of illusionist 'second-style' structure with an *emblema* of the third century. In the former case perspective space is congealed within the idiomatic structure of the first Roman borrowing from Alexandria. In the latter case the particulars of spatial connotation indispensable to the narrative are stated in purely chromatic terms[5] by way of capricious counterpoint to the figures, from which they do not detach themselves substantially. Thus the figure of the satyr is not detached from but actually overflows the ideal surface of contact between frame and *emblemata*.

This experiment by the NEOHELLENISTIC ARTIST OF SELEUCIA assumes exemplary significance for the purposes of the present study, and provides historical evidence of the views hitherto maintained. Working in a metropolis at the extreme limit of the Empire, in almost direct contact with oriental cultures but saturated for centuries in the Hellenistic figurative tradition, this artist attempted at the dawn of the third century to recover the ancient modes of cultural expression. Thus, against his own will, he achieved a result which, with the skeletal rigidity of the ancient frame and the matured late-Roman scenic idiom, bears witness to the substantial irreversibility of the existing process. At the same time his traditionalist aims showed that this oriental province was even then, at the most critical period of imperial art, still entrenched in ideas and tastes by no means altogether innovatory. It is true that this second conclusion could not be correctly drawn merely from the instances so far adduced. But as these are truly representative of a manner widely illustrated at Seleucia during this period, the deduction will appear more convincingly legitimate.

A patient and detailed examination of the 'Dionysus and Ariadne' mosaic proves, moreover, the existence of a now pronounced taste for plastic resolution in terms of purely chromatic, two-dimensional variation of light and shade. It was in full agreement with artistic ideas in every part of the Roman world, from the Severan reliefs at Leptis Magna to the frescoes of the Roman Mausoleum of the Aurelii. Consider the satyr's torso, legs and right arm, the maenad's face and dress, and above all the clothing of Ariadne. Such details, determined by tessellar arrangement

5 Note, by way of contrast, the occurrence in the service of perspective illusion (though in a formal aspect vaguely recalling modern structures in the 'De Stijl' movement) of similar simple architectural shapes rendered in flat colour in the mosaic *emblemata* signed by Dioscorides of Samos, formerly in the so-called Villa of Cicero at Pompeii and now in the Naples Museum (nos. 9985 and 9987 in Room LIX).

H

and streaks of colour, which are the equivalent of a flattened structural skeleton of baroque drapery and modelling, were very frequent at Seleucia at that time, appearing also in the 'Seasons' of the above-mentioned House of the Drinking Contest. They show the perfect adherence of the most minute elements of idiom to the general spatial effect of the picture. The artist's Hellenistic neo-illusionism is thus revealed to have taken a new thread, against his will, into its texture.

Antioch, however, owing to its deep Hellenistic substrate and although it remained exposed to developments of the late imperial *koine*, should be recognised as the most satisfactory viewpoint for those who seek rather to identify what Levi himself has called an exhausted wave of Roman art dying at the extreme limit of the Empire, than to detect such novel structural features, external to Roman civilisation, as might in some way reinforce the theories of the orientalists. Attention is therefore inevitably attracted to Palmyra and Dura Europos, not so much with a view to following in the footsteps of Strzygowski towards the Iranian highlands as in order to operate in territory which, though not unaffected by Hellenistic culture, was less dominated culturally by the coastal metropolis. Those towns were flourishing centres in the third century. The former is of interest through its special character as an independent kingdom, overthrown, with its 'empress' Zenobia, by Aurelian. Dura, an ancient caravanserai, assumed military importance because of its situation on the banks of the Euphrates, confronting the Iranian menace, and it remained thus important until its fall in 256.

Dura in particular is believed, on the strength of the rich and very important discoveries made there by Yale University scholars,[6] to contain decisive evidence of a cultural invasion by the 'Orient' of lands formerly dominated by Hellenistic civilisation so as eventually to condition the entire evolution of late antiquity. The essential sources referred to are the pictorial works of the Temple of the Palmyrene Gods, of the Mithraeum, of the Baptistery of the *Domus Christiana*, and of the Synagogue. As regards Palmyra, it will be expedient to consider the so-called Tomb of the Victories.

58, 59 60
70, 62–67

69

The first monument in chronological order is the collection of paintings found on the walls of the Temple of the Palmyrene Gods. These works were discovered in circumstances of some risk at Dura Europos in the years immediately following the First World War, before the systematic excavations which rescued the valuable finds in the other religious edifices. The various paintings are of very different dates. The first, on the south wall of the *naos*, shows 'Conon Sacrificing', together with some priests and the members of his family; it undoubtedly goes

58

6 Cumont (1926). *See also* the series of *The Excavations at Dura-Europos. Preliminary Report (I–X), New Haven, 1929–1952, and lastly the Final Reports.*

back to the foundation of the building and the immediately subsequent years, approximately during the last decades of the first century. The other paintings, on the south wall of the *pronaos*, display other 'Sacrificers' on two super-imposed levels. The north wall of the same building carries a scene of 'Sacrifice by a Roman officer' (Jul. *59* Terentius, tribune of Cohors XX Palmyrenorum) in the presence of three Palmyrene divinities, Baalshamin, Iarhibol and Aglibol and the two Fortunes of Palmyra and Dura. A small room standing apart from the temple presents another 'Sacrifical Rite with Five Palmyrene Gods'. Cumont dates these, respectively, to an age close to that of the first 'Conon' fresco, and the age of Severus, but so as to contain them all within the period of the Roman occupation of Palmyra, from AD 164 to the middle of the third century.

Inspection of photographs of these paintings (unfortunately very much damaged), and of the oldest in particular, leaves one with a sense of profound and insuperable astonishment. In the group of Conon with his relatives, priests and other sacrificers, an effect of poetic *58* originality is produced by the stylised and elongated figures with their marked idiomatic elegance; by their ample, clearly defined white-and-rose draperies; by the warm complexion of each portrait of an individual of Arab race; by the pink-and-mauve background of admirable though shallow architectural relief (against which the figures, the foot of one sometimes overlapping that of another, 'float' in rigorous frontal presentation and rhythmic attitudes); and by the limpidity of expressive portraiture in the various physiognomies. The undeniably high formal standard of this work almost makes one forget that many of its features, taken together, constitute a tendency which may be said to be common to all the primitive periods of artistic civilisations[8] as well as, on the other hand, an aim conspicuously anticipating idioms customary not only in Rome but also throughout the Empire barely a century later, and then not always in such well organised compositions. It therefore seems certain that the Roman world, including its immediate confines, has revealed no artistic evidence of approximately equal date comparable with the earliest paintings in the Dura temple. These must be considered very near in time to those which portray sacrificial figures on the south wall of the *pronaos*. Their names are known to us from an inscription, as is also the name of the artist himself, one ILASAMSOS. He signs himself in Greek, and may be considered to have worked in the first half of the second century.

The other frescoes of the *pronaos* and of another room *59* in the temple present fewer problems. It is easy, in fact, to recognise that they were most probably executed late in

7 Cumont (1926), p. 143 and elsewhere.
8 So Levi (1946–8), p. 286.

the Severan age. The fragment of a dedication to Alexander Severus in 230 might be connected with the Roman soldiers depicted in the representation of a sacrifice on the north wall of the *pronaos*. But in these the style can clearly be seen to be developing in the direction of forms dominated by the western figurative tradition in its late Hellenistic manifestation. Furthermore, qualitative judgment in this case must be very different from that applicable to the 'Conon' group, because of the manifestly inferior skill in execution together with a certain lack of original inspiration. Several factors thus combine to give a general impression of progressive decline (not progressive development) from the confident originality of the MASTER OF CONON. Those factors are: the conventionality of the style, considering the date of execution; the growing cultural acceptance of the modes of the imperial *koine* (in a particular sense which, as Bettini[9] has emphasised, is not methodologically new, like 'style of the legions', in the peripheral provinces of the Empire) in an environment where for some time previously a certain independence of the Hellenistic figurative tradition had prevailed; and finally the less than masterly level attained by the second lot of paintings at Dura. The Palmyrene school to which the MASTER OF CONON belonged has left no reliable evidence of significant fecundity in the context of contemporary imperial painting, apart from the work of ILASAMSOS who continued that artist's manner.

Another monument at Dura which involves problems of stylistic derivation from the cultural area outside the Empire is unquestionably the Mithraeum, excavated by the Yale University expedition. It is one of the few temples of this kind which, especially in the East, has retained its pictorial decoration substantially intact. The paintings here referred to do not belong to the period of the first foundation of the shrine but to its middle (AD 210–240) and late period (AD 240–256). These works must be ascribed, in part, to an artist named MAREOS, according to a congratulatory inscription. Cumont and Rostovtzev incline to the belief that he was a Semite, serving in the garrison of Dura after the rise of Mithraism.[10] He is supposed to have painted the 'Cosmogony' and the 'Life of Mithras', portrayed on the arch of the cultic niche, and also the series of 'Signs of the Zodiac'. These works, however, are not the most interesting on this site; they are merely decorations of a rather modest character by a craftsman who based his work substantially on the repertory usually resorted to on such occasions, sometimes through the medium of sculpture.

More importance attaches to the 'Two Magi' painted in the well-known attitude of the prophet Mani, with ebony staff and Babylonian book, on the interior wall of the

9 Bettini (1952), p. xxii.
10 Cumont and Rostovtzev (1939), p. 104. For the observations by Rostovtzev regarding the scene of 'Mithras Hunting', *see* p. 113 ff. Among the best scenes of 'Mithras Killing a Bull', however, those mentioned and praised for their artistic merit come from the Mithraeum of Santa Maria Capua Vetere and from discovered recently at Marino in Latium, both from late in the second century.

60

niche, and to the scene of 'Mithras Hunting' on a lateral wall. These works are, in fact, on a higher artistic level, clearly derived from Iranian sources, both in the racial typology of the figures and in the stylistic convention of trees, animals, etc. The 'Two Magi', seated on chairs the four legs of which are set paratactically on the same surface plane, wear the Phrygian mitre and draperies which, in their precise and developed markings, bear unmistakable signs of stylistic autonomy. The figures are presented frontally to perfection. The colours employed, yellow, red and ochre, show a tendency to monochromatic effect. The same comment applies to the scene of 'Mithras Hunting'. He is pursuing two bucks, two gazelles and a wild boar in a forest of highly stylised trees. The same colours and composition, as Rostovtzev has noted, prevail in Iranian art during its last Partho-Sassanid phase, known also from pictures produced in southern Russia such as those of the Tomb of Kerch (Panticapaeum) in the Crimea, dating from the first or second century.

These decorations certainly attest the frequency of exchanges among various artistic civilisations, in the farthest provinces of the Empire, with elements of the artistic style which, crossing the often ill-defined frontiers guarded by the legions, and thanks to the busy commercial traffic along the caravan routes of the 'Indies road', maintained itself and at the same time repeatedly derived essential ideas and formal discipline from the imperial *koine*. In this sense the pictures in the Mithraeum at Dura indicate an intellectual intercourse of remarkable extent, tending in the imperial area to a hybrid mixture issuing in the acquisition of norms rather than in any profound stylistic reinforcement capable of original production. This, incidentally, appears natural in the light of what is known of the sociological and cultural structure of the city in the third century. Consequently, once one has recognised the part that might be played by such interchanges of idiom in so extremely mutable and individual a climate of civilisation as that of Syria, it is impossible, with the best will in the world, to deduce from it a genetic function of an activating, clearly differentiated and well defined nature in the supposedly static and academic context of eastern Hellenistic art and hence also in that of Rome.

For the rest, analogous and perhaps more convincing phenomena can be found in Sassanid regions, for instance at Bishapur, the city founded by Shapur I on the Iranian tableland at the time of his victory over the Romans (260) when he captured the emperor Valerian. Here a large pavement in the royal palace is decorated with a *lithostroton*[11] which, apart from certain compositional details in local taste, appears to be the work of Roman artists, probably from Antioch. This mosaic proves not only the prestige of late Roman painting among the warlike

11 Ghirshman (1956); Ghirshman (1962), pp. 140–7 and pls. 180–6. For the Kerch Tomb, *see* Rostovtzev (1922), pls. XVIII–XXIX.

Iranians across the frontier, but also the attainment of a particularly free stage in paratactical expression and chromatic line (an example is the 'Lady with Flowers') 61 during the Roman painters' experiences in Syria and beyond.

These views may probably be extended to a third monument at Dura Europos, though it does not provide such unmistakable proof of foreign figurative borrowings from a Romanised area. The persons responsible were Christians.

The pictures in the *Domus Christiana* were taken to the United States and placed in the Yale Gallery of Fine Arts at New Haven. On the strength of philological arguments and archaeological evidence they may safely be assigned to the first decades of the third century, not later than 235. As in the case of other finds at Dura, some authorities have attempted to attach to these frescoes, particularly to the scenes of 'Adam and Eve', the 'Good Shepherd', the 'Miracle of the Lake' and the 'Healing of the Palsied Man', exceptional importance as forerunners in both iconographical and stylistic terms. But the view that such historical judgments are not well grounded appears to be supported by iconographical differences between the Dura 'Adam and Eve' and its known analogues in the West, between the Dura 'Good Shepherd' and the Roman versions,[12] by the priority of the Christ and St. Peter compared with the older illustrations previously known, and finally by special observations of a stylistic character on these and other scenes in the Christian building at Dura Europos.

It is clear in the first place that this is poor, very modest artisan's work, little more than scrawls with a few basic tones, in which no incipient capacity for genetic influence on later Roman art can be detected historically. Certainly the pictures testify, at least iconographically and by a few signs of style (the 'continuous', for example, in the 'Healing of the Palsied Man'), the probable existence of models concocted from the New Testament story as early as the very first years of the third century. But the impoverished reflection of such images cannot permit any safe conclusions to be drawn with regard to their compositional conception and style; for in a scene such as the 'Healing of the Palsied Man' a composition in the continuous narrative style may well be the result of a contraction of two pictures dealing with the 'before' and 'after' of the miracle. In any case these productions could hardly be called new in relation to the *rotuli* of the Roman columns.

Rather more stylistic interest attaches to the damaged 'Women at the Sepulchre', placed below the scene of the 70 'Miracle of the Lake'.[13] In the first place, the work is by a painter of considerable skill, the ARTIST OF THE DOMUS CHRISTIANA AT DURA. It is very much easier to recognise

12 *See* Baur (1933), pp. 67–78, where it is stated, apparently with no good reason, that 'Roman art is pre-eminently devoted to symmetry' (p. 69).
13 Rostovtzev (1934, p. 281), who recognises the hands of five fresco painters in the Baptistery, also considers the artist of the 'Women at the Sepulchre' superior.

in his manner the modulation of certain data now absorbed by the artistic mind of the first half of the third century. Within a framework of black, red and white strips the figures of Mary Magdalene and her two female companions approach the sepulchre, atop which are two large, highly stylised stars. Each holds a lighted torch and a jar of perfumes. The bright forms of the Marys, all frontally presented, move against a uniform red background which throws into special relief the long, cloudy veils framing their heads almost like halos.[14] The hair-styles have been identified as resembling the fashion introduced by Julia Mammaea, mother of Alexander Severus. As she died in 235, this detail constitutes one of the elements of the dating *ante quem* of the fragment,[15] and also links it to the depiction of the maternal figure in the contemporary chamber of the *Velatio* in the Roman Cemetery of Priscilla.

82, 83, **6**

In this same Roman catacomb a similar phenomenon will be observed in the sacred significance attaching to the veil of the 'Praying Figure'. At Dura as in Rome it appears as wide on top of the head as are the parts hanging on each side of the face, producing paratactically the effect noted by Aubert. At the same time it is difficult to reach any conclusion as to the stylistic influence of one work on the other. At most it is possible to invoke the hypothesis of a common model, though this is unlikely. Certainly the almost contemporary presence on a frontier of the Empire and at Rome of such a detail cannot fail to lead to a recognition, by a critic both prudent and dispassionate, of the spontaneous occurrence of similar developments during the late Severan age in very different regions of Roman civilisation. Hence it is bound to follow that an objective judgment of the Christian frescoes at Dura must find that they prove a stylistic evolution common to other zones of the artistic *koine* in the central imperial period. In the same way it will appear profitable to suppose that, as Grabar has suggested in the case of the sacrificial procession in the Temple of the Palmyrene Gods, this short Syrian procession of women may contain *in germ* the great repetitive series at S. Apollinare Nuovo three centuries later. But, to confine speculation to a briefer period, it need not seem incredible that the *Domus Christiana* scene may be conceptually akin to the gnostic sequences in the Mausoleum of the Aurelii and those of the solar cult in the Mithraeum under S. Prisca, which were very probably painted in the capital during these very decades.[16]

6

58

71–75, **10**

Analogous considerations, though in a more complex and systematic setting, seem applicable to the extensive Old Testament decoration of the Synagogue of Dura Europos, now in the Damascus Museum. The building

14 Aubert (1934) stresses the importance of the bright veil, which almost amounts to a halo.

15 Baur (1933, p. 75) notes: 'It is possible to date this painting with great accuracy owing to the peculiar hair-style of the two pious women whose heads survive. This was the style which Julia Mammaea brought into fashion. She wore her hair waved over the forehead and descending on each side of the cheeks, covering the ears. The deduction is that the picture cannot be later than 235 AD'. *See also* Rostovtzev (1934), p. 274.

16 Grabar (1953), p. 38. For the Mausoleum of the Aurelii see Chapter IV. For the Roman Mithraeum under Santa Prisca, which an inscription below the cult niche would help to date before 202, see *Archäologischer Anzeiger*, 1940, coll. 478–479.

was excavated by scholars of Yale University and the Académie des Inscriptions et Belles Lettres, under the direction of Rostovtzev, between 1932 and 1935. It stood on an *insula* near the city walls and, as attested by two inscriptions, had been constructed for the Jews of Dura in its final form between 244 and 245. Eleven years later, under the menace of the Persian advance, the walls of Dura were strengthened both inside and out by an *agger* which engulfed both the Synagogue and other important edifices in the city, leaving buried in the former over half the area of walls decorated with four rows of sacred narratives. The emergency was fortunate, since it allowed so many valuable artistic productions to survive until the present day.

The wealth of subject-matter in the Synagogue certainly presupposes, even more than does that of the *domus ecclesiae*, the existence of a voluminous illustrated Biblical history as early as the end of the second century or beginning of the third. This consideration disposes, among other matters, of the claim that the religious culture of the Hebrews absolutely forbade iconography, in strict accordance with a Biblical precept (Deuteronomy IV, 16.) Above all, the presence among the incidents depicted on the walls of subjects evidently reduced from more comprehensive representation, or put together from several models by unifying a number of functions in the chief figure of the narrative, and more frequently by the preservation of two or three images of this protagonist in developing the sequences of the action studied, has permitted the supposition that the same original unified models, identified by R. du Mesnil du Buisson[17] in the ritual of Jewish festivals (*haggadah*), may have undergone slow transformation in order to fit them into the varying sections of the mural decorations.

The images of the Synagogue, however, appear to have been individually strained through the sieve of the local cultural *milieu*, which ranges from the clothes they wear to their racial type, and also through the idiomatic prism of the personalities of the artists, certainly at least three, who worked there. Grabar, though he recognises in the paintings of the Christian Baptistery an example of the 'style practised within the Empire',[18] seems in the case of the Synagogue to go beyond the identification of a local revival of general tendencies in the artistic idiom of the central imperial period. He mentions 'a distinctly local style' manifest in a monumental painting which in the second and third centuries foreshadows the Byzantine aesthetics of the sixth and even some of the very methods that Byzantine art was to apply under Justinian.'[19] This conclusion is nevertheless modified by the prejudicial observation that foreign suggestions of this kind would not have been welcomed at Constantinople if they had

62–67

17 Du Mesnil du Buisson (1939), p. 143. *See also* Cohn (1904). Roth (1963, p. 40) favours this hypothesis.
18 Grabar (1953), p. 38.
19 Grabar (1953), p. 39.

not been imported from court circles and found a favourable soil there. The reference is indubitably to the personality dominant at Rome under Gallienus, that of Plotinus, who in the third century was erecting a theory of aesthetics congenial to the taste of the new art.

It is clear that the question, put in this way, involves the hypothesis of a cultural intake of artistic methods operating at a distance of centuries, those that elapsed between the decoration of the Dura Synagogue, contemporary with the activities of Plotinus, and the artists at work under Justinian. The suggestion is rather perplexing to scholars inclined to see a less artificial, more natural origin of Byzantine art in the crisis of late Roman art during the third and fourth centuries.

Certainly it may be conceded without hesitation that the Dura Synagogue already exemplifies a type of 'decoration which simply juxtaposes scenes brought together in coherent historical cycles with a view to demonstrating religious ideas through the presentation of persons and buildings displayed as existing outside concrete space and illustrating a moral hierarchy which defines the relations between their magnitude and their placing in the picture'.[20] But it is relevant to remember that there were contemporary and only slightly subsequent examples of such work in other parts of the Empire, especially at Rome (Mausoleum of the Aurelii, Mausoleum of the Julii, to say nothing of the Column of Marcus Aurelius), which render unacceptable the theory that this form of aesthetic prompting was confined to Iran and Syria.[21]

Although systematic study of the art of the two critical centuries, the third and the fourth, proves this theory of exclusive responsibility to have been inadequately based, the Hebrew narrative paintings at Dura are nevertheless of unquestionable value. The most important of the surviving sequences, such as the Tales of Moses (the 'Flight and the Passage of the Red Sea', the 'Burning Bush', the 'Miracle of Water in the Desert', 'Aaron', 'Moses Rescued from the River'), the prophets 'Abraham' and 'Ezra', some of the Ark Episodes, the Tales of Elijah (the 'Widow of Sarepta', the 'Priests of Baal', the 'Altar of Jehovah', the 'Resurrection of the Little Boy') and the Tales of Ezekiel provide a combination of details, rarely so numerous in other monuments of the imperial period, which furnishes a new insight into the artistic idiom of the Empire, especially that prevalent in the Hellenistic East.

The general style of the Synagogue artists obeys an aesthetic of line which almost eliminates the narrative function of colour, which is reduced here to exclusively emotional significance, *Farbenrhythmus*. Line and colour accordingly act together, in undoubtedly anti-classical fashion, devoid of any spatial influence or motivation and of all investigation, in rational terms, of perspective. Apart

74, 79
49

66

64, 67
63

65

20 Grabar, *ibidem*.
21 *See also* in this connection, regarding the 'Syrian' thesis upheld by De Francovich (1951), the remarks by Galassi (1953, p. 557): 'There cannot be any doubt, accordingly, that many of the elements developed in the phase of transition to the Middle Ages reached Christianity by way of Syria. But they were elements proper to the Roman imperial "Commonwealth", no different essentially from those which, in the same evolution, could have been transmitted from other directions; though this consideration does not imply that in some cases Syria itself might not have been the channel, also, for the afflux, not the influx, of Mesopotamian or Iranian modes or motives. But to suppose that this circumstance amounted to formative or generative intervention, in other words, authentic influence, would be to go beyond what historical sources and the true logic of events permit . . .'. So also Bettini (1948, pp. 115–6), who concludes that the problem of the Orient is one of a 'special aspect of provincialism' constituted by the 'minor figurative aspects', which 'undoubtedly preceded similar aspects of late Antiquity'. But that observation does not in fact mean that the aspects of this provincialism' determined in any way the vicissitudes of figurative culture in the late antique period.'

from the frequent iterative assonance of figures repetitive of the same person, almost reminiscent of contiguous cinematographic shots, it is noticeable that the components of these narratives – animals, material objects and environmental details, in short everything required for representation of the desired scene – combine against a background in itself abstract within the framework of a logic which is not representative in the traditional physical sense and is not directed to cover 'resemblance' to a reality postulated as objective and hypostatised in the categories of the knowable, but which is merely evocative, allusive – in a word, suggestive in the manner of a series of symbols which, when mutually engaged, obtain from the very results of their composition a force both didactic and hortatory.

Fundamentally, we are here concerned with abbreviations, each charged with a liturgical rather than a historical power, and ready to communicate with the observer provided they are taken together in their relational placing, expressive of the event as reconstructed, rephrased and revived by various elements. This imperative, too, is obeyed by the use of colour, which is diverted from realistic significance and submerged as an emotional, if not positively magico-liturgical, connective in the texture of the design. The figures therefore often resemble one another rhythmically, in the colouring of their garments (where yellow, green and rose alternate, varied by *clavi* and blue and brown edges) as well as in the evident formal iteration of the folds of their drapery. Behind the personages extend continuous areas of background, sometimes themselves alternating between red and green so that, in compositions like that of the Temple of Jerusalem[22] or the Temple of the Sun (Beth Shemesh),[23] they assume predominant significance, though the colour is not particularly violent, with a series of streaks of white, black, mauve-pink, grey, red, white again and ochre, which R. du Mesnil du Buisson has linked with Mesopotamian regulations dealing with the arrangement of walls in a temple devoted to celestial or solar cults.[24]

As a result of these liturgical conceptions, which are implicitly those of the religious authorities commissioning the work, and which find explicit form and stylistic dignity in the artists' own refusal to follow Hellenistic aesthetic structures, the cultural deposit and the cartoon used as a model cease to be determining factors. The Synagogue masters did make a wide use of traditional models, perhaps not without translating them of their own accord into structures appropriate to the culture of the Jews of Dura Europos. But they took extreme liberties in this process. It might be said that they used scissors. The models thus appeared in cuttings, sometimes repeated again and again in the most diverse historical contexts.

22 Kraeling (1956).
23 Du Mesnil du Buisson (1939), pp. 84–92
24 Du Mesnil du Buisson (1939), p. 88 ff.

Some of the figures of Ezekiel, for instance, closely
resemble some of Moses, of the priests of Baal, of persons
in the 'Anointing of David' and of many other characters.
Again, the 'Apotheosis of Moses' can be compared with
'Ahasuerus Enthroned', the latter with the Pharoah in the
Tales of Moses, and this in turn, an extremely significant
case, with one of the 'Two Magi' of the Mithraeum
already mentioned. These figures were set up with such
compositional lack of bias that the iconographical results
within the pictures as a whole can certainly be called novel.
Finally, of all things, the figure of the fallen soldier in the
lower register of the 'Battle between Jews and Philistines
at Ebenezer', a traditional subject of the classical repertory,
was used by the MASTER OF THE ARCH OF SEVERUS AT
LEPTIS MAGNA and later by the HUNT MASTER in his mosaic
of 'Circus Races' at Piazza Armerina. Though it is now
certain that such work was in process at the same time in
Rome, it must still be recognised that the Hebrew monument at Dura constitutes in its own right a lexicon of
proportions, and hence of stylistic implications, of
decisive historical importance.

Closer examination of a feature such as the concept of
space entertained by these MASTERS OF THE SYNAGOGUE
reveals a number of highly instructive facts. In the 'Departure of the Ark from the Country of the Philistines' we
notice, for instance, that the defeated idol of Dagon has
been overthrown and lies broken on the surface, together
with all the latter's furniture. The manner is that of the
celebrated Hellenistic *asarota*; but it is used here with more
abstract effect and in any case lacks all spatial relations with
the environment, being reduced to a two-dimensional
structure, such as will be found again, late in the age of
Constantine, in the vaults of S. Costanza at Rome. Again,
the car of the allies is seen laterally, as well as the yoked
oxen, while the wheels and the canopy surmounting the
Ark face the spectator. This irregular perspective, due
ideologically to respect for the sacred object, inconceivable
if not frontally and therefore centripetally presented, is
linked however to earlier examples already known in the
Roman world, for example the contemporary figure of
the 'Mother and Child' of the *Velatio* Chamber in the
Cemetery of Priscilla in Rome, where the sitter faces the
spectator in a chair turned sideways. Similar and more
pronounced distortions of perspective appear in the
'Triumph of Septimius Severus' on the Arch at Leptis
Magna (AD 203–204), where the horses, wheels and side
of the imperial chariot are shown laterally, while its
front, in order to support the frontal presentation of the
emperor and his suite, is in full perspective.[25] If we leave
out of account *a priori* disputes as to the possibility of one
monument deriving inspiration from another, the above-
mentioned examples lead inevitably to the conclusion that

25 Levi also (1946–8, p. 208) pointed out
the 'distortion of the forepart of the
imperial chariot', out of line with the
procession so as to allow the emperor to
be seen from the front, though at the
centre of a picture still partially narrative.

the Synagogue paintings bear witness, at the extreme limits of the Roman world, to a development of the late Roman artistic idiom which is entirely similar, if also perhaps more complex and rich in highly diverse figurative implication, to that hitherto attested in various regions of the Empire.

On the basis of concrete stylistic examination, necessarily confined to a few of the more outstanding specimens, two fundamental characteristics of the manner of the SYNAGOGUE MASTERS need now cause no surprise. In the first place they composed a wholly and severely linear style, able in its graphic richness to transform every plastic function of shading and colour almost into 'negative relief'. Secondly, they showed a decided tendency to endow with emotion faces that are not always those of the chief characters or of those drawn on a larger scale. The features express a deep though not lively spiritual tension, revealing psychological determination and a physiognomical structure from which it is easy to see that the expressionist style which was to prevail, though in various forms, towards the end of the century already stood on the threshold.

In this sense the aspect of the Biblical heroes is directly related to the spirit of the great apostolic figures of the Roman Mausoleum of the Aurelii, however profoundly different the pictorial idiom of the former may be. In fact, the Roman MEGALOGRAPHIC MASTER was a great traditional artist who proved capable of reviving the values of classical culture in a 'modern' synthesis, permeating them with new spirituality and even making them a ceiling, as it were, adequate to support the problems posed by the new Christian personality. The ARTIST OF MOSES AT THE PASSAGE OF THE RED SEA, though Hellenistically trained, nevertheless carried to the maximum of linear tension the old formal apparatus, while his colleagues, to whom should be attributed the solitary figures of the prophets 'Abraham' and 'Ezra', sacrifice of the 'Priests of Baal' and the 'Anointing of David', after peremptorily nullifying the plastic function of colour, became graphic artists who took advantage of the old models only in order to extract from them effects of surprising formal novelty. This is especially true of the artist of the 'Anointing'.

In these stylistic procedures the methods of the Dura masters certainly recall one of the permanent characters of Byzantine painting, its fusion of the individualised treatment of the faces and the chromatico-linear abstraction of the other surfaces, even though their chromaticism, very close in taste to that of the Temple of the Palmyrene Gods, is entirely alien from the brilliant purity of the Byzantines. In this connection I feel bound to agree fully with certain observations by Grabar.

Nevertheless, the main problem is the extraction of the cultural root of such a phenomenon, particularly in view

71–72, ʼ

67
62

of the ancient objection of Jewish tradition to plastic and iconic narrative, which would seem to imply an absence of psychological interest and of appreciation of portraiture. The Synagogue frescoes, however, are contemporary with Rabbi Johanan of Tiberias, who is said by Avi-Jonah to have been the first to permit the decoration of walls with images, contrary to Jewish law.[26] Personally I have no doubt that the SYNAGOGUE MASTERS started from an artistic base of decidedly late Hellenistic stamp, from which they drew materials for the reinforcement of the figurative tradition underlying all their work. They varied, enlarged and transfigured it formally in the very ways that can be studied in the *pars occidentalis* of the Empire, though perhaps, considering the environment in which they worked, with fewer traditional obstacles and attachments. In their linearist views of the construction of form they invoked the taste of Iran which is so convincingly documented – yet here too not exclusively in the imperial area – in so many reliefs of third-century Palmyrene sculpture. But it is difficult to see whence they derived the seeds of portraiture, the highly individualised psychological charge, typical of many of their personages, without at the same time producing portraits in the Roman manner. It is well known that the Orient, whether considered mythically or historically and whether Jewish, Hellenised Antiochene or Sassanid Iranian, could not supply any such roots.

It is probably necessary to turn westwards, to Hellenistic, Romanised Egypt, and approach that extraordinary artistic phenomenon of the Fayyum Mummy Portraits, a phenomenon still not fully studied in its detailed formal development. It is here, within the limits of traditional realism of the artistic Alexandrine province, that we find a very strong inclination to portraiture. That inclination was certainly not native to the Egyptian substrate buried by the cultural victory of Hellenism, and it gained strength during the Roman period.

68, 77, 78

More than six hundred Mummy Portraits have so far been discovered in an extensive district of the Nile valley which includes Fayyum, Saqqara, Akhimim, Assuan, Hawara and Antinoë. They do not seem to be earlier in date than the Roman conquest of Egypt. Although they may also have been inspired by the portraits previously imposed on mummies of the pharaohs, they are clearly derived in their formal design from the traditional Roman portrait, grafted with stimulating effect and historico-sociological vivacity on the Hellenistic. They were produced from the first to the fourth century in successive techniques, from encaustic to tempera on wood or canvas, and in styles ranging from the psychological realism familiar in certain Hellenistico-Campanian portraits to an almost hieratic abstraction with exclusive stress on the

26 Avi-Yonah (1960), p. 920.

eyes, in every respect similar to the expressionist painting of the epoch of the Tetrarchy and Constantine. These Egyptian portraits in themselves represent a typical byway of imperial art, however well defined culturally and even racially its environment.

This impressive artistic material has so far been catalogued only in part and has been the subject of some general, still inadequate study, notably by Drerup and more recently by Zaloscer.[27] It might nevertheless form the basis for a history of the painting of late antiquity, so convincing appear the elements of comparison hitherto emphasised by certain typical specimens. When contrasted with the few works from other Romanised zones available for identification of the various phases of the advance of formal development, they afford an adequate basis for the more detailed reconstruction of the presumptive sequence of events throughout the Mediterranean basin. There is a close correlation of formal changes which, within the imperial *koine* and despite the influences of native substrate and of the subsequent non-Roman cultural adstrate, occurred spontaneously along a road travelled by the whole art of late imperial antiquity. That correlation is to be inferred from exact stylistic relations, first between the Mummy Portraits and Pompeian portraits of the first century; second, between the Mummy Portraits and Mesopotamian representations of the human figure, as in the Synagogue of Dura Europos and the Palmyra Tomb, also funerary mosaics at Edessa, such as that of 'Queen Shalmot with her father Ma'nu and grandfather Mokinu' attributable to the early third century and very similar in technique to the Synagogue portraits;[28] and third, as we shall see later, between the Mummy Portraits and late fourth- or early fifth-century frescoes at Rome, Naples and Constantinople. Examples at Rome are the 'Praying Women' in the Traso Cemetery; at Naples, 'Christ with Apostles' in St. Januarius *extra moenia*; at Constantinople, the 'Portrait of an Old Man' in the imperial palace.

As already indicated, the formal development reached in these portraits begins with realistic statements of great expressive efficacy, profound psychological insight and perfect physiognomical individuation. Among the factors which prove them to have been executed while the subjects were still alive is the apparent age of the sitters compared with that at which they died. The artists made use of a technique that is sometimes quite touching in its results, picking out and emphasising even slight and vivid facial defects, as if by means of a snapshot; and their work is carried out in a more or less vibrant impressionistic style imposed on a solid Hellenistic foundation, with lively colours, accurately toned shadows and a line that is subtle and precise. The final effect is clearly typical in the definition of the features. Here the psychological classi-

68

67, 69

162, **23**

27 Derup (1933); Zaloscer (1961). *See also* Guimet (1912); Reinach, Adolf (1914), p. 32 ff; Reinach, Adolf (1915), p. 2 ff; Strelkow (1936); Coche de la Ferté (1952); Pavlov (1965). Lastly, Parlaska (1965), the most recent work on this subject, which I was unable to consult before this book was printed in Italian. In opposition to the theory of 'Romanisation' advanced by Drerup and supported in various ways by Levi (1947, i, p. 523 ff), Zaloscer, Coche de la Ferté, Pavlov and others, De Francovich (1963, pp. 6–7) has recently declared that it reappears specifically in the editions of Drerup's book issued by Lippold in *Deutsche Literatur*, LV (1934), coll. 1922–4, and by Weigand in *Byzantinische Zeitschrift*, XXXV (1935), pp. 138–9. De Francovich finds 'closer analogies in the world of Eastern Asia and particularly in certain Syro-Mesopotamian regions and centres intimately associated with Parthian art'. He refers by name to Dura Europos and Palmyra. Such similarities are certainly convincing. But so far at any rate as concerns the specific portraits in the Egyptian paintings, it is here considered that the influence operated in the opposite direction. General chronology, moreover, certainly does not appear to favour the influence of Dura and Palmyra portraits on Egyptian.

28 Leroy (1957); Segal (1959).

fication actually becomes epochal; the expression hardens from one portrait to the next in stereotyped though not insignificant forms; and the pictorial idiom fixes the abnormal intensity of the gaze within a setting of almost anodyne areas of colour, except for a few strokes of rapidly applied hatching upon which the whole effect of three-dimensional space is left to depend. The colour itself is expressed in raw or pallid tones which appear solely through their own agency within the autonomous quality of the surfaces.

In the Pushkin Museum at Moscow[29] is the 'Portrait of a Man in a Blue Cloak', an encaustic painting on wood, undoubtedly belonging to the first century. The features express a fervour that seems still republican; the colour is naturalistically applied and worked up with minute brushstrokes. Then take, for example, the third-century 'Portrait of a Bearded Old Man' in the Seminary of Egyptology, University of Munich.[30] It is already 'arrested' in its psychological individuation, and worked in tempera with successful iteration of significant line. Comparison of these two works provides evidence of a remarkable divergence of style. Consider next the 'Portrait of the so-called Aline' in the Berlin National Museums;[31] it was painted in tempera on wood at the end of the second century and represents in admirable impressionist style a matron of still striking personality. Again, we have the third-century 'Portrait of a Middle-aged Woman' in the Pushkin Museum at Moscow,[32] painted in encaustic tempera on wood, where the prominence of the great expressionist eyes in a structure passionately dedicated to line denotes only, after the lapse of less than a century, an indifferent, heavy melancholy in the individuation of the features. The contrast between these last two pictures helps further to qualify the symptomatic significance and historical importance of this kind of portraiture in the creative experiments of late Roman painting.

Nor is this all. In fact, some full-length representations of deceased persons, ascribed by Galassi to the second and third centuries, have been said by the same authority to herald the 'style in which the Apostles are presented in the Ravenna baptisteries'.[33] This consideration applies less to the iconography than to the general idiom. For the diverse conditioning imposed on the work by the traditional portrayal of the face, and by the new tendencies so widely asserted in the construction of the body, could only confirm in the Alexandrian zone, though with greater fidelity, the phenomenon illustrated by the Dura monument. A comparison, for example, between the 'Abraham' of the Dura Synagogue and the second-century 'Deceased with Scroll' in the Moscow Pushkin Museum[34] appears to argue persuasively for a formal evolution which in the Dura fresco is, in the garments of the patriarch alone,

29 Pushkin Museum, Moscow, no. 5771. See Pavlov (1965), p. 67, pl. I.
30 Seminary of Egyptology in the University of Munich (unnumbered). See Zaloscer (1961), p. 64, pl. 40.
31 National Museums, Berlin, no. 11411. See Zaloscer (1961), p. 69, pl. 26.
32 Pushkin Museum, Moscow, no. 5783. See Pavlov (1965), p. 70, pl. XII.
33 Galassi (1953), p. 580.
34 Pushkin Museum, Moscow, no. 5749. See Pavlov (1965), p. 74, pls. XXIV–XXV.

more strongly linear but certainly (though more standardised) consonant with the much older Egyptian portrait.

It is in any case evident that the Hellenistico-Roman tradition of the Mummy Portraits did not fail to produce results in the Jewish painting at Dura. It was that tradition in the first place which acted as a formative element from the first to the fourth century in the stylistic climate which lasted without a break until the advent of the Byzantine manner. At the same time it proved itself useful, much more than and much earlier than at Antioch, to a process of formal transliteration from the individual mark to the general poetic treatment of surfaces, a movement which so strongly attracted the Dura Europos artists.[35]

This *nisus formativus* between the daring experimentation of the Judaeo-Oriental school at Dura and the Hellenistico-Egyptian figurative tradition of the Mummy Portraits is not, incidentally, an isolated feature of the complex texture of stylistic relations in the late imperial painting of the Mediterranean East. I referred earlier, in dealing with the foundations of modern knowledge in this region, to the so-called Tomb of the Victories in Palmyra, and it will be convenient to end the present Chapter with a brief consideration of that subject.

The Palmyrene Tomb of Magharat el-Djelideh, in the necropolis south-east of the city, is an extensive T-shaped sepulchre at the end of which several niches, with painted pilasters between them, had been built into the walls. The artist presumably worked about the middle of the third century. Levi, arguing from the inscriptions and some unmistakable data deciphered in the tomb, specifies the time as between 241 and 259.[36] A series of winged spirits or 'Victories' is depicted. The figures stand on globes, supported in turn on beds of acanthus leaves, and hold aloft large circular medallions containing portraits of as many deceased persons buried near by. The barrel-shaped vault, decorated with painted hexagonal caissons, forms a great lunette in the background which carries a mythological scene, almost unrecognisable owing to the sorry state of dilapidation in which it was found. The decorative borders encircling the walls and below the vault are clearly derived from the Antiochene tradition, characterised by winding perspective, ovoli, beams in lateral perspective, and so on. They can be paralleled in very many mosaic pavements, not only in the Hellenised East but also throughout the imperial area.

There can be no doubt that these paintings share substantially in the evolutionary tissue of the whole artistic style of the late Empire towards the close of the third century. The portraits and the heavenly figures contribute to this conclusion by their frankly frontal presentation, the meticulous symmetry of their structure and their

69

35 Commenting on the essay by De Francovich mentioned above, Bonicatti (1959 and 1963) has recently emphasised the importance of the Hellenistic tradition of Alexandria in the fifth century, to which convention he had already ascribed 'new' tendencies characteristic of late antiquity, as definitive of the succeeding 'Syro-palaeo-Christian art of the sixth and seventh centuries, and at the same time of the culture of 'Partho-Iranian origin' in the genesis of Coptic art. He also recorded the presence at Dura Europos in the third century of 'a popular art of particular vivacity', referring to the Christian Baptistery, while the walls of the Synagogue were being adorned with 'hieratic paintings', which De Francovich assigns, with the Temple of the Palmyrene Gods, to the 'Partho-Iranian' culture. Bonicatti's convincing essay, which draws illuminating comparisons with manuscripts and mosaics from Egyptian Hellenist sources, as well as from Syrian and later Constantinopolitan, illustrates from the *Rabula Gospels* of 586 a 'continuity of taste, indirect or otherwise, between northern Africa and Mesopotamia, expressing social attitudes which divert the *koine* style itself from adhesion to a single historical stage'. His research does not go so far back as the third century, and therefore does not directly involve the problem of Dura Europos, except marginally. The argument in the preceding pages of the present work may perhaps complete Bonicatti's theory *ab imis*.

36 Levi (1947), i, p. 551. *See also* Kraeling (1961–2).

graphic emphasis of line. But it is necessary to add that this share of the MASTER OF THE PALMYRA TOMB in the stylistic development of the late Empire was not due to external influence by way of novel borrowings and alien intrusions. It clearly arose from the constitution of the *koine* itself, even introducing into the latter's designs entire elements native to the Palmyra region which had been in the past, for instance in the 'Conon' paintings at Dura, of a different order of importance. Consequently, Levi has on the one hand correctly stressed the close connection of the Tomb pictures 'with the main stream of classic art, considering them much less subject to local influences and to provincial impoverishment than the paintings of Dura',[37] and on the other hand has rightly concluded that with them 'the substance of Roman art fully permeated the pictorial idiom of Palmyra'.[38]

Rostovtzev and Baur, however, have been able to find an analogy with the *nikai* of this tomb in a winged spirit discovered on a painted panel of the north tower of the Palmyra gate at Dura Europos.[39] The two scholars, after closely examining this work and dating it as about contemporary with the Palmyrene frescoes, considered it possible 'to ascribe the differences between the two pictorial productions to their execution by two different schools, of which the Dura establishment was the more practical and oriental in taste and that of Palmyra the more Hellenistic'.[40] This judgment appears reasonable and adds further support to a description of the Palmyra Tomb as Hellenistic, though not excluding elements of the Iranian tradition.

In the Tomb, the above-mentioned traces of psychological individuation in many of the faces in the Dura Synagogue seem to have been later eliminated in a conventionalised but expressionist physiognomical annotation, not so much reflecting the artisan status of the craftsman as symptomatic of a taste which had by then outstripped that of the preceding Hellenistico-Roman art. There appears no doubt, in fact, of the cultural connection between the Mummy Portraits of Hellenistic Egypt and the portraits of deceased Palmyrenes such as Simeon, Abbas, Mali, Bata and the rest. On the other hand it must be admitted that the latter, while taking over the stylistic linear inflections characteristic of the contemporary Fayyum 'Portraits', seem also to have reverted to an unvarying typological convention that was later to be accepted by the Egyptian artists.

Galassi[41] quotes a description by Sotiriou of an encaustic icon at the Monastery of St. Catherine on Mount Sinai, showing 'St. Peter' against an architectural background of clearly late Roman origin and three small faces on a shield-shaped surface representing Christ, the Virgin and a saint. This work, attributable to the age of Theodosius or to the

37 Levi (1947), i. p. 552.
38 Levi (1946–8), p. 291.
39 Rostovtzev and Baur (1931), pp. 181–93.
40 Rostovtzev and Baur (1931), p. 190.
41 Sotiriou (1950); Galassi (1953), pp. 581–2.

first decades of the fifth century, apparently affords valuable evidence, in a cultural zone of great importance, of certain links in the passage from a traditional manner of lucid sobriety to the assumption of morphological developments obviously derivable from the evolution of a certain tendency in the Fayyum to linear expressionism, classicist in origin, which reappeared in the vigorous fragment by the CONSTANTINOPLE PALACE MASTER.

Three factors, therefore, combine to illustrate a single operation: (i) the recognition in the paintings of Dura Europos and Palmyra of a crisis of the same sort as that occurring in one imperial region after another during the third century; (ii) its connection in certain details not only with the well known linear emphasis of all Iranian and Middle Eastern art but also with the illuminating developments of portraiture in Romanised Egypt, and (iii) the reference to this by no means exclusive context of the study of the formal precursors of the Byzantine idiom. It necessarily involves a standard of vigilance in historical consciousness in which the individuation of concrete poetic 'personalities' will certainly prove no obstacle to the consideration of the macroscopic and epoch-making movement of the aesthetic thought of late antiquity.

Chapter Four
Elements of the new idiom of Roman funerary painting in the mid-third century

The monument of the Aurelii in the Viale Manzoni at Rome is so closely connected by origin with Roman pictures of only a short time before that it forms an essential link in the development of painting technique in the late Severan age, some decades before the brief intervention of so-called realism after the reign of Gallienus. The frescoes of this underground cemetery, excavated in 1921, have been and still are the object of arduous research and extensive debate by specialists, especially on archaeological and historical grounds, owing to the difficulty of determining the ideological and social character of the community which owned it. It is generally agreed that the mural decorations belong to the second quarter of the third century; De Wit suggested a date not later than 235, Wirth argued for circa 240. But the dispute has continued: Mingazzini, for example, considered the monument to be an orthodox Christian cemetery; Bendinelli regarded it as representing generically a form of Christianity imbued with traces of ideas tending to paganism; while the vast majority, though not unanimous on points of detail, have maintained its heretical character – Montanist according to Cecchelli, Gnostic in some shape according to Marucchi, Paribeni, Wilpert, Achelis, Bettini and Carcopino.[1]

10, 71–75

The question is one of considerable importance to the history of the philosophy and religion of imperial Rome. But it is not entirely negligible from a purely artistic standpoint, which has to take into account the extent of orthodoxy in the probably very strict orders of the patrons, who are generally understood, from the dedication of a mosaic pavement, to have been the Aurelii Onesimus, Papirius, Prima and Felicissimus, whether these persons were related by blood or merely by membership of a common sect.

I do not propose to enter here into a dispute which has nothing to do with strictly artistic appreciation. The problem, especially after the recent studies by Carcopino, appears to be clearly approaching a complex but sufficiently illuminating solution.[2] The paintings in this hypogeum were no doubt influenced by the religious-cultural environment of the Severan age with its ideological and moral outlook unquestionably dependent upon various half-Christian and half-pagan notions, probably and specifically Pythagorean, which must have had some effect upon the artists, themselves perhaps members of the

1 See chiefly Mingazzini (1942–3); Cecchelli (1927; 1944); Bendinelli (1922); Marucchi (1921; 1922); Paribeni (1921); Wilpert (1924); Achelis (1926); Bettini (1952), pp. xv and xxvii; Carcopino (1956). This last exhaustive study is the most authoritative and recent consideration as to the religious beliefs of those who owned the monument.
2 Carcopino (1956, pp. 99–131) refers to the Gnostic sect of the Naasenes.

community. Nevertheless, it must be emphasised at once that the highly individual semantic connotation of those paintings indicates in itself a certain spiritual content; their style conveys a *Weltanschauung* so typically expressive of the ideological and moral unrest of the period as to constitute in relation thereto a most original record of that singular interaction between religion and poetry. 'It shows signs,' wrote Bettini,[3] 'of the so-called art of Plotinus'. Carcopino observed:[4] 'I know of no painting, whether of Pompeii or of Fayyum, that has produced ancient portraits in which idealisation appears less affected, and effort less falsifying to life and reality, or which breathes with a more natural simplicity a nobler air of gentleness, a more confident, pure and unpretentious aspiration', so that 'the touching beauty of these frescoes' allows them to define 'perhaps the most expressive of the male figures hitherto bequeathed by Roman antiquity'.

Carcopino was able to justify his assertion with a well-grounded comparison and comment. He contrasts the murals of the Aurelian monument with the plaster figures of the much older Pythagorean basilica close by at the Porta Maggiore, calling attention to the frigid dexterity of the latter's chiselling as opposed to the expressive power of the former, so that 'the differences between the two works are not so much those of degree as of kind. The spirit of the religion of Christ has given point and renewed vitality to the whole production'.[5] The faith of the Naasenes, considered by this scholar to have commissioned the hypogean murals, was so strong as to bring out previously unnoticed intonations in the ancient pagan music, which they believed they were understanding for the first time.[6]

To state the matter with greater critico-historical precision, this opinion may be summarised by observing that the Aurelian Monument furnishes useful evidence for the theory upheld in the present work, namely that the stylistic and semantic revolution in Roman painting arose less from external pressure on the structures of artistic inspiration and of moral conduct in the central and late imperial epochs than from the fact that there were available the means of revival and self-transformation, a fact implicit in the formal framework itself of Roman art, in accordance with a special native interpretation of the classical norm of Hellenism. Consequently, in the atmosphere of the spiritual event whereby it sought, in the satisfaction derived from a new mystery, to rejuvenate the ancient, outworn mythopoeic faculty, the artistic conscience showed itself capable of reintegrating forms indubitably classical, as in the unforgettable so-called 'Apostolic Procession'. Meanwhile in other paintings there appeared, under further highly skilled hands, the recognition of a spatial vision already positively anti-classical, 71, 72, 7

3 Bettini (1952), p. xxvii.
4 Carcopino (1956), pp. 219 and 183.
5 Carcopino (1956), pp. 218–20
6 Carcopino, *ibidem*.

tending to the total transfer of the narrative to the plane of the supporting scenery. This point will be made clearer by a brief consideration of the chief paintings in the north chamber. They are perhaps the oldest and certainly the finest in the whole building.

While it is easy to agree with what Bendinelli was the first to notice immediately after the discovery, namely, that the Aurelian hypogeum was decorated by at least three or four painters, the most able of them was, without the slightest doubt, the MEGALOGRAPHIA MASTER of the north chamber.[7] In my opinion he was also responsible for the sketch of the 'Shepherd Teaching on the Mountain', perhaps the first bearded Christ of all Christian iconography. In the same chamber I should be inclined to recognise the work of at least one other fresco painter of high accomplishment. I shall call him the GNOSTIC MASTER, responsible for the 'Ovatio' and probably also for the 'Lesson in the Forum', the 'Sacred Conversation in the Garden', the 'Banquet' and the 'Three Young Male Nudes and Weaving Woman Talking to a Seated Man' (who may be Ulysses). A further division of these latter paintings between two different artists might be attempted, but would be rendered most difficult by the poor state of preservation of some of them. Two other painters also may have executed frescoes in the other two chambers of the hypogeum.

As regards the megalographic painting – to which the 'Shepherd Teaching' is related by clear resemblances in the placing of figure and head, as well as in the more detailed though far smaller stylistic elements – Bendinelli has rightly noted that 'the figures are all set down firmly, like statues, only the drapery revealing a consummate understanding of anatomy whether at rest or in motion.'[8] The faces, not one of which is shown entirely from the front, are rendered with as much mastery as the bodies. A few impressionist touches, in colours gauged and lit to a tone that unifies them all, contrive to present, though as part of a completed plastic shape, expressions of an extraordinary vivacity. They might well suggest 'historical' characteristics of persons who perhaps belonged to the community, if the most reliable philological evidence did not point to their being philosophers or else members of the Apostolic College. This astonishing assembly, comparable in its suggestion of a formal occasion with some of the greatest masterpieces of palaeo-Christian and Byzantine art, including the 'Patriarchs' of S.Aquilino at Milan and the prophets and martyrs of the elaborately composed mosaics at Ravenna, does however imply a kind of portraiture in the perfect individuation of the separate personages, whose common spirituality favours their communication of private inner experiences.

The physiognomies themselves, in some of which it is

74

73

Bendinelli (1922), p. 494.
Bendinelli (1922), p. 416.

easy to recognise features traditionally employed in Apostolic iconography, may tell us nothing of the well-springs of their exaltation. Yet it is possible to believe that the inspiring fervour of these faces arose from the interior peace, individual, historical and in each case different, which the members of the sect attained in their communal life of faith.

Within the limits mentioned, the great figures of the north chamber constitute the summit attained in this age by the relics of classicism in Roman painting. The solid anatomy beneath the cloaks, the solemn pacing of the personages and the highly individual countenances presented in expert impressionist style, but all combining to form a single calm, triumphant whole, cannot fail, especially if compared with the remaining decorations of the building, to recall the rationalist spirituality of the 'Christian heretics' who raised the hypogeum for the dead of their sect. Those Gnostics, however, in their capacity for the formal idealisation of life, must have been very close to the doctrines taught almost contemporaneously, during the first and second decades of the third century, by Clement[9] to the *Didaskaleion* at Alexandria. It may well be thought that in these figures is achieved the *optimum* of the human state at that period, as Christians saturated in classical culture felt they ought to exemplify it. Hence the taste and refined pictorial sentiment of the MEGALO-GRAPHIA MASTER, employing an undeniable skill, were impelled to resuscitate the content of the Hellenistic tradition, stamping it with the most passionate intensity of line, combined with the chromatic modulations, which the figures bring out so well against the bright background of the wall and linear decoration in green and red, with a rhythm now predominantly optical in its accentuation.

It seems appropriate, in connection with the figurative typology, the style and the poetic animation of the MEGALOGRAPHIA MASTER, to mention at this point a remarkable fragment from the Cassia Catacomb at Syracuse, now in the Archaeological Museum of that city. Nothing else is known about its origin. Here we have the life-size image of a man's face, obviously a genuine portrait, whose dimensions are similar to those of the great figures of the Aurelian hypogeum and at once brings them to mind. The left side has been seriously damaged. But the whole facial area except the left eye survives. The portrait shows an expressive power rarely attained in funerary painting. The large eyes are wide open and extremely alert, the right being under the arch of an eyebrow which is continued so as to trace clearly the line ridging the nose, with an effect of restrained but tense energy. The almost imperceptible smile of the closed lips is very finely de-lineated, with the curves of the full, short and neatly trimmed moustaches setting off the arched eyebrows. The

9 The Naasenes, whom Carcopino suggests as the most probable proprietors of the hypogeum, in fact cherished ideas of a majestic purity, in some ways similar to those of the doctrine of Clement of Alexandria. *See* for example Doresse (1958, pp. 47–50). He also deals explicitly (pp. 99–100) with the sepulchral monument of the Aurelii, giving a summary but detailed interpretation of its paintings, and noting the close correspondence of one of the scenes (that of the weaving woman, the traveller and the 'Three Young Male Nudes', characters he identifies with Penelope, Ulysses and the Suitors) with the references to the *Odyssey* which the *Philosophumena* of Pseudo-Hippolytus allege to be peculiar to Gnosis and in particular to the Naasenes.

71, 72,

76

perfect oval of the face, correctly drawn, is rendered still more noble and sensitive by a broad shadow on the cheekbone, creating there a hollow which further spiritualises the expression of the features as a whole. The brushstrokes are firm, especially in the vigorous darks and the unexpected flashes of light illuminating, for instance, the ocular cavity, which is usually left in shadow, and the lower lip. In the opinion of Agnello[10] the fragment should be ascribed to the very first years of the third century or even more probably to the last decade of the second, when the echoes of Antonine art could still make themselves felt. On this reckoning the work would precede by three or four decades the great Gnostic figures of the Aurelian Monument, in which quite a number of expressive and structural resemblances to it can be detected.

Yet the careful observer will also remember a certain general effect to be found in the Mummy Portraits, to which again the work is linked by expressive realism and the life-size dimensions of the features. Indeed, a Fayyum portrait in the Pushkin Museum at Moscow[11] and another portrait from the same source, datable to the second half of the second century and preserved at the Louvre,[12] are surprisingly similar to that at Syracuse and therefore require further formal examination.

The Moscow portrait belongs to the end of the second century or the beginning of the third. Here is 'a masterpiece that seems to forecast certain portraits by Amedeo Modigliani . . . even in the bronzed tints,' a masterpiece achieved by the combination of 'ancient, substantially Nilotic tradition, Greco-Roman influence, form largely abolished by flattening, and unified but by no means neutral colouring.'[13] The portrait reveals the overwhelming contemporary (or perhaps slightly later) victory of Roman chromaticism, which monuments such as that of the Aurelii and others in the age of Gallienus would subsequently try to counteract, without of course being able to ignore or misunderstand the preceding stylistic conquests. For it was precisely in the extraordinary crucible of methods of expression represented by these portraits of the first half of the third century that the old and the new achievements of Roman painting were fused, and that the traditional psychological and historical allusiveness of Italian funerary portraiture confronted the pregnant phenomenon of new spiritual contents on the road that was to lead to the millennial art of the icon. Between the Syracuse fragment and the Moscow portrait, that of Paris constitutes a very close link, testifying to the way in which different materials and techniques can provide an exemplary instance of a single formal itinerary. About a century later the praying 'Virgin with Child' of the Coemeterium Majus supplied a conspicuous confirmation of the effects immanent in megalographic paintings of the Severan age.

78

77

76, 78, 77

21

10 'If the oldest parts of the Cassia Catacomb could be dated back, as Orsi considers, to the first half of the third century, if not to the end of the second, the chronology of this fresco, in view also of the evidence of its stylistic peculiarities, would be easily determinable, since it would then be possible to make it coincide with that of the most ancient catacombal nucleus. The important fragment in question might consequently rank as one of the oldest, if not the very oldest, of those which have survived from early Christian funerary painting (Agnello (1952), p. 102).

11 Pushkin Museum, Moscow, no. 5789. Encaustic tempera on wood. See Pavlov (1965), p. 70, pl. XI.

12 Louvre, Paris, no. P.201. Encaustic tempera on linen. See Coche de la Ferté (1952) pp. 14–5 and 30, pl. 9.

13 Galassi (1953), p. 579.

There are, as already enumerated, present in the MEGALOGRAPHIA MASTER's work elements of colour and space which are clearly late-Roman, though combined with the still classical internal form of the figures; and it is mainly because of the presence of those elements that it is possible to ascribe to the same artist the first scene in the chamber, that which, as both Wilpert and Carcopino have suggested, probably introduced the practice of preaching salvation, *ianua coeli*, through mural illustration. It is the first Christian example of that progress towards communion with the godhead which, already apparent in the initiation scene of the 'Dionysiac Megalographia' in the Villa dei Misteri, and a little later in the Christian and Jewish buildings at Dura Europos, subsequently bore 70, 62–6 majestic progeny in the floor and wall decorations of the basilicas. The layout of this decoration on successive levels ('Apostolic Procession' at the bottom, 'sacred stories' above, and sometimes 'metaphysical scenery' at the borders of the vault) is perhaps fully anticipatory of the several decorative 71, 72, 75 levels in basilican naves, e.g. that of S. Apollinare Nuovo, 73 and even more of the same feature in the Synagogue at Dura Europos.

The two forms of *Kunstwollen* present together in the 'Shepherd Teaching' are identical with those of the 74 MEGALOGRAPHIA MASTER. The figure retains a classical attitude, owing to its handling as a portrait and the plasticity of its physical constitution which is accentuated by the seated posture. But in the spatial vision it is easy to perceive, with Levi,[14] the adoption of the 'laws of inverse perspective later to be typical of the Middle Ages', since 'the sheep are proportionately very much smaller than the human figure, which is supposed to be at a much greater distance from the spectator'. This difficult and highly original choice of a position, halfway between the old figurative tradition and the new structures of pictorial vision, is a sure guide to recognition of the MEGALO-GRAPHIA MASTER.

The other decorations of the building, especially those by the GNOSTIC MASTER in the same north chamber, appear, as has already been remarked, to fit more coherently into the context of contemporary Roman painting. The great figures hitherto mentioned may recall, *servatis servandis*, 71, 72, 75 the similar images of attendants in the House in the Via dei Cerchi. But in the '*Ovatio*' scene, in the same room, the chromatic rhythm and the centralised placing of the rider between the procession and the group of *seniores* awaiting him outside the gate of the city clearly confirm the date 73 assigned to the monument on other grounds. In the procession following the rider, for instance, the heads, all almost frontally presented, evidently obey the compulsive practice of the Severan age. The same may be said of the group of elders near the gate at the other end of the mural.

14 Levi (1946–8), p. 273.

In the centre the rider passes in front of a yellow building with a decorated pediment. Flowers are shown scattered below, at his feet. At the time of painting, the artist could think of no better way to idealise the celebration of a triumph. The elements referred to are all in fact those which, developed both in the religious and in the secular field, would occur later in pictures of the *majestas Domini* on the Christian sarcophagi and in the Constantinian Reliefs of the Arch of Constantine, for example that of the *Congiarium*.

As for the scenery, the GNOSTIC MASTER at last expresses, with meticulous attention to the details involved and through an anti-rationalist feeling for nature, a single distant note of the function of light in the creation of spatial depth, like that found in the landscapes of the Caivano Sepulchre at Syracuse. The colours certainly grow gradually lighter and more evanescent than the bird's-eye views of the city and those of the 'Lesson in the Forum' and the 'Garden', thus setting their levels at a greater distance from the spectator. But one cannot fail to notice that the view of the city in the '*Ovatio*' has preserved very little of the ancient bird's-eye view. It can truly be said, as Bendinelli has noted,[15] that an effort of will has to be made to remember that 'despite every appearance to the contrary the city indicated . . . is perhaps situated in a plain and not climbing the slopes of a mountainside'. What in fact we see here is the transfer to the foreground of the architectural background, as already noticed in the Column of Marcus Aurelius. Consequently, the negative judgment   49 of Marconi[16] regarding the 'incoherence' between the perspective view of the city and the undifferentiated plane of the procession seems unfounded. Everything in the present case reverts to one level.

Together with this elimination of the perspective depth of atmosphere peculiar to the painting of the first and second centuries, and the consequent tendency of the various background planes to come to the foreground and unite with it, the art of the GNOSTIC MASTER acquires exemplary significance through having produced, by means of the variegated colouring of the garments of his figures, a practically unlimited chromatic modulation of the separate but crowded individuals of the two groups.   73 This kind of *Farbenrhythmus* proves that long before the mid-third century great strides had been taken by that tendency to dissolve the individual bodily form in colour which was to remain for many centuries a notable constant of Byzantine painting. Moreover, that tendency is strikingly confirmed, no later than the year 257, by the octagon of the vault of Tomb X, that of Clodius Hermes,   81 under the *Memoria Apostolorum in Catacumbas*, site of the present Basilica of S. Sebastian. The date is settled by that of the deposition of the remains of the apostles in the

15 Bendinelli (1922), p. 502.
16 Marconi (1929), p. 110.

triclia built over the actual tomb of Clodius Hermes and two other similar tombs adjoining it. The octagon shows an impressive figure wearing a red tunic and cloak, with a staff in his left hand, and surrounded by a throng of persons on a much smaller scale, each being rendered by a single flowing stroke of colour. Does he represent a Christian Saviour or a pagan psychopomp?[17]

The question is not of fundamental importance here. What matters is the chromatic and spatial structure of this scene, in which Christ or Hermes is delineated with a force hitherto unusual in Roman painting, as the masterful dispenser of metaphysical salvation. The uniform alignment on a two-dimensional level enables the figure of the Saviour to be transposed above the heads of the crowd of attendant souls; and since the latter are supposed to be nearer the spectator, here again, as in the 'Shepherd' of the Mausoleum of the Aurelii, the natural dimensions as 74 governed by the laws of classical perspective are subverted. These considerations suggest that the dating of this scene and the medallions surrounding it should be postponed to the mid-century, in other words a few years before the burial in the mausoleum, and that the other nearby decorations are clearly the work of another hand in the preceding age.

Look next at the figure of Christ as Sun-god, on an octagonal shield in a mosaic vault of the Vatican Cemetery under St. Peter's. Similarly dated on the same archaeo- 79 logical grounds, it leaves no room for doubt that it is the work of an artist who, like his colleague of the Clodius Hermes Tomb X, was experimenting with a new style in 81 contemporary views of space.

In the so-called Chapel of the Fisherman (Mausoleum M of the Julii), in the Vatican Grottoes under St. Peter's, there was recently discovered a mosaic vault showing the 'Triumph of Christ as Sun-god'. This discovery adds in 79 many ways to our understanding of tendencies still disorganised but very far advanced in the stylistic revolution of mid-third-century Roman painting. The novelties, and the developments of earlier revivalist movements, to be found in the mosaic of this vault and traceable also, so far as can be conjectured, from the impressions left by the cubes fallen from the upper part of the side walls of the chamber, are such as apparently to justify the entertainment of serious doubts concerning the date of the decoration, the same kind of uncertainty as surrounded the paintings in the Villa de Colle at Varano near Stabia and those of the vault of the Roman Mausoleum of Clodius Hermes *in Catacumbas*. Meanwhile this latest discovery 81 also cannot, for architectural and structural reasons, be much later than the first half of the third century.

The fairly early dating of the mosaic is confirmed by the

17 *See* full analysis of the problem by Carcopino (1956), pp. 333–76.

relatively small size of the tesserae (average 8 sq. mm.), even though that size is dictated by the short distance of the vault from the visitor's eye and the cubes are set close together. Nevertheless, as stated in *Esplorazioni sotto la confessione di S.Pietro in Vaticano*, the tesserae 'make not the slightest attempt to imitate the quasi-pictorial technique' of the *emblema*.[18]

The Chapel of the Fisherman is a small pagan mausoleum converted almost at once into a Christian tomb. That much may be inferred from the *titulus*, now lost, which was seen, together with the mosaics, by Alfarano in the sixteenth century, when the monument was uncovered during work on the foundations of the basilica and immediately reburied. Under a slightly arched cross-vault, whose shape is due to the small dimensions of the niche (2 metres in length, 1.6 in width and 2 in height), we can admire about two-thirds of a design of four tangled, luxuriant growths of vine. The remaining third, apart from the hole made by the sixteenth-century discoverers, can be reconstructed from the clear impressions left on the red cement by fallen tesserae, and from a faint brown tint, perhaps a sinoper used by the *musivarius*. The vines rise from the four angles of the vault and surround a central octagonal shield adorned with a easily recognisable Sun, haloed and rayed, with two white horses in front of it. From the iconographical interpretation of the murals, which include traces of a 'Good Shepherd', the figure of a 'Fisherman with Fish' (which gave the Chapel its name) and the scene of 'Jonah fed to the Monster', an identification of the Sun with Christ was established with equal facility.

That in this hypothesis the imagery may almost be said to be suspended between classical myth and the new Christian vision is clear, incidentally, from a brief examination of the nearby Sepulchre U fresco, also beneath St. Peter's. Here, presumably a little earlier, an artist personified the stars of morning and evening, Lucifer and Vesper. The iconography of Christ as Sun-god in Mausoleum M undoubtedly drew on some such figure as the Lucifer, haloed and on horseback, characterised by his fluttering cloak. An even more significant comparison can be made with a roundel representing Helios, painted on the vault of the arcosolium in the Tricliniarca Crypt, near the Agape of the Cemetery of Peter and Marcellinus, and flanked by two scenes from the story of Jonah. In the roundel, which is certainly later than the Vatican mosaic, Helios is depicted as 'clad in a sleeved tunic, furnished with a greyish-blue halo and driving a two-horsed chariot'.[19]

Finally, Galassi has not failed to record[20] the close genetic connection of this composition with one of the mosaic sections of the annular vault of the Mausoleum of Constantina, where the wide, prodigal tangle of vines is

79

80

166

18 Apollony-Ghetti *et al.* (1951), p. 41. But it is well known that by this time the technique in question had been very rare for at least a century.

19 Apollony-Ghetti *et al.* (1951), p. 62, pl. E. Perler (1953) takes the figure of Christ as Sun-god for that of Christ in triumphant resurrection from Hades to the Father. For the roundel in the Cemetery of Peter and Marcellinus, *see* Wilpert (1903, p. 30, pl. 160 (2)) who dates the work in the first half of the fourth century.

20 Galassi (1953), p. 345.

also present, framing at its centre a space for the portrait and leaving further space at the borders for the figures of harvesting Cupids.

Granted a date in the middle of the third century, and consequently a tomb decorated by Christians some years before the remains of the apostles were transferred *ad catacumbas*, the most cursory examination suffices to show the work as far in advance of its time, and thus to identify among contemporary finds a signpost towards the maturity of certain essential elements of Roman expressionist style. In the first place, the chromatic rendering of the vine-spirals attracts attention. Where they cross, one of them is always tinged for a brief part of its course with a decidedly dark tone of green, more intense and glowing than the normal colour of the leaves, though some of them are given the same chromatic accent. There seems no doubt that by this expedient the painter meant to indicate the various degrees of distance in the arboreal web, or rather that the imagined diversity of the ideal planes supporting the interlacing vines has been deliberately reduced to mere chromatic accentuation, chiefly by the use of only two tones of green. Moreover, it is singularly convincing to find that even on the bed of cement revealed by the fall of certain sections of tesserae, the depth of the brown tint increases wherever crossing spirals and leaves of darker tones were represented, exactly as in the undamaged part of the mosaic. This observation, in my view, confirms the artistic function, clearly conceived and intended, of such chromatic emphasis, which expresses a precise stylistic solution of the problem by the *imaginarius*, whom I call the CHRIST AS SUN-GOD MASTER.

On the other hand, this solution was not unexpected in the figurative development of the central imperial period. For several decades there had been present in Roman art a tendency to represent objects on a single plane. In order to be convinced of that, one need only look at the well-known pilaster in the Lateran Museum, adorned with tendrils, grape-clusters and other viticultural subjects, to which both Wickhoff and Riegl have drawn attention, or at the earlier vineal decorations on the vault of the gallery of the Flavii in the Cemetery of Domitilla. The effect of that tendency was defined by Wickhoff as 'rather of line than of plasticity';[21] it was contrived by what Riegl called 'the regular rhythmic alternation of the bright determinant (marble) with the dark background (shadow, space)', which 'throws into relief the chromatic charm, catching the eye by colour, which is so characteristic of all this kind of art and its specific purpose'.[22] The points hitherto made in respect of chromatic idiom are all precisely paralleled by the way in which the images are composed and given plastic form.

On a yellow background, similar in its intensity and

21 Wickhoff (1895), p. 95. *See* Toynbee, Jocelyn M.C., and Ward-Perkins (1956), p. 73 ff.
22 Riegl, Alois (1901); *Industria . . .* (1953), p. 124; *Arte tardoromana* (1959), p. 114.

vivacity to that of Byzantine gold, the representation of Christ as Sun-god, with halo, rays and wind-blown cloak, stands out from the octagonal shield like some of the riders in mosaics of mythological or hunting scenes. A few golden tesserae are dispersed around the head and across the chest. The face is shown almost exactly frontal, but the gaze is directed upwards. This detail, together with that of the fluttering cloak, which the artist, by his use of shadow, obviously meant to represent as lifted from the ground by the wind, introduces into the already un-mistakable two-dimensional quality of the composition, including vine-tendrils and leaves, a certain degree of depth. The phenomenon is repeated, but with quite different emphasis, in the two white coursers. Their heads and bodies, though seen in correct profile, afford evidence of the now customary distortion of perspective, since they contrast with the frontal posture of the divine driver, which would normally have suggested a similar attitude of the horses, racing towards the spectator. Contrary to the opinion of Cecchelli,[23] it is probable that there were originally four, two having been destroyed by the hole drilled in the vault by the sixteenth-century excavators.

As we have seen, this convention was already present in the reliefs of the Arch of Severus at Leptis Magna. It had also made its appearance in the two small pictures of 'Charioteers of Two Factions in the Circus' on the east porch of the Ostian *insula* called in fact that of the Charioteers (III, X, 2). Here the drivers are frontally represented and the horses in profile, except one belonging to the Blue Faction, which is seen strictly from the front. The wheels of the chariots are set among the hind legs of the horses, while a forceful expressionism, in the features and huge staring eyes, pervades the countenance of the Green charioteer. The two Ostian scenes are elegantly conspicuous on the ample white background, within a slender frame of red and green. Later in date than others of even more striking elegance in the same building, which belong to the late Antonine age, they should probably be assigned, mainly on stylistic grounds that do not conflict with archaeological considerations, to the years 260–280, and therefore be included in the transitional phase between post-Gallienan realism and the expressionism of the Tetrarchy.

But quite a different innovation is discernible in the slightly older Vatican solar chariot. The plane of the fron-tally presented Christ as Sun-god and the plane (at right angles to the latter) of the horses' heads in profile, are supplemented by a third plane, at right angles to the first two, which enables three-quarters of the surviving cour-sers to be seen from below. The continuous black outline of the animals' heads, in fact, alternates in the upper portions of their two bodies with an outline formed by

52

79

low-toned tesserae, while certain anatomical curves appear still more clearly lit. In the lower portions of the horses' bodies, on the contrary, the black line is accentuated and prolonged in two series of cubes so as to cover about half the bellies of the animals and delineate the shadowed front and rear hoofs. They are thus rendered by a double or triple row of tesserae, white in the upper part nearer the divine driver and seeming to reflect the light from that direction, and black in the opposite area, which is dominated by shadow. The entire presentation, from below, of the bodies of the two surviving horses is the fundamentally novel stylistic achievement of the mosaic and one of a precociously cubist stamp. By means of a twofold distortion of perspective the CHRIST AS SUN-GOD MASTER has thus managed to present the solar car and the divine Charioteer simultaneously from below, in profile and from the front, on three mutually perpendicular dimensional planes, disjoined and rearranged on a uniform surface.

This mosaic composition, on the vault of the Mausoleum of the Julii beneath St. Peter's, is one of the oldest that survives. Its unmistakable originality, with all its novelty of spatial notation and idiomatic technique, is not indeed matched by any exceptional skill of execution. But I thought it necessary to dwell upon the work, since it affords an opportunity to examine the grammar and syntax of the new language of late Roman painting at a still undeveloped cultural stage, that is to say apart from their lyrical transfiguration by certain outstanding creative personalities of a poetic cast of mind.

This and other examples previously cited prove that Roman art in the middle of the third century was perfecting not only those elements of the new style which clearly show its sensibility to the existing revolution in the spheres of morality, culture and social structures, but also a readiness to sympathise with Christian religious thought.

It is extremely important at the close of this investigation to stress the increasing abandonment by third-century Christian apologists and philosophers of concepts, conventions and frameworks of Greek, Hellenistic and rationalistic type, such as the Church had adopted in the first century of her existence – how Origen, for instance, gave place to Cyprian, how at Rome, Greek gave place to Latin in ecclesiastical usage. Similar discrimination was likewise at work in the artistic field. It is evident in the sarcophagi of the third century and in the catacombal paintings, where it tended to be accompanied by a remarkable change from the stock subjects, symbols and figures of the classical, Hellenist tradition to the new cultural soil of Christianity. The active spirituality of the new religious community distrusted the formalist perfection of standard Hellenistic art and readily took over the new Roman

idiom, even helping it – witness the Mausoleum of the
Aurelii, heretical though that group was, and the Mausoleum of the Julii – to develop and to take all-important
steps in the elaboration of techniques in conformity with
the new *Weltanschauung* which, quite apart from the influence of the Church, was inspiring the whole Mediterranean *koine*. The character of late Roman *Kunstwollen*,
the artistic will directing the original, spontaneous evolution of Roman painting, was thus enabled to offer
henceforward a common field of aesthetic civilisation and
culture to the Christian Church, to classical resistance and
to the innumerable forms of cultural and religious
syncretism throughout the Empire.

10, 71–75

79

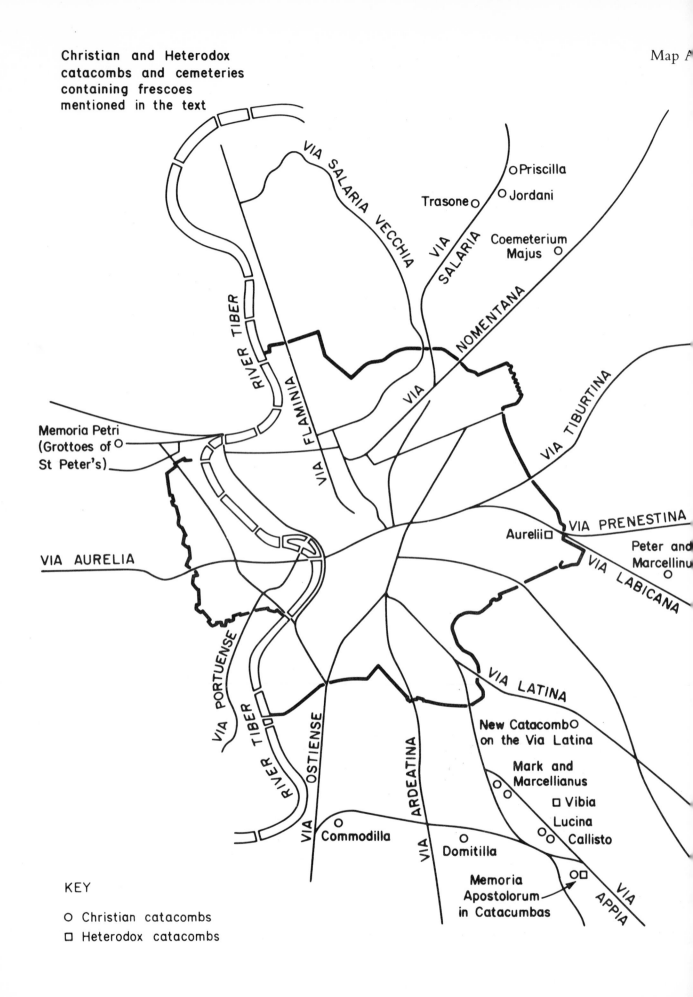

Christian and Heterodox
catacombs and cemeteries
containing frescoes
mentioned in the text

VIA SALARIA VECCHIA

VIA SALARIA

○ Priscilla

Trasone ○   ○ Jordani

Coemeterium
Majus ○

VIA NOMENTANA

RIVER TIBER

VIA FLAMINIA

VIA TIBURTINA

Memoria Petri
(Grottoes of ○
St Peter's)

VIA PRENESTINA

Aurelii □

Peter and
Marcellinus

VIA LABICANA

VIA AURELIA

VIA PORTUENSE

RIVER TIBER

VIA OSTIENSE

VIA ARDEATINA

VIA LATINA

New Catacomb ○
on the Via Latina

Mark and
Marcellianus
○○   □ Vibia

Lucina
○○ Callisto

Commodilla ○

Domitilla ○

Memoria
Apostolorum
in Catacumbas   ○□

VIA APPIA

KEY

○ Christian catacombs
□ Heterodox catacombs

Chapter Five
Christian catacombal painting at Rome in the second half of the third century

It is now recognised, ever since the appearance of three exhaustive studies by German scholars,[1] that the paintings in the Christian catacombs at Rome, and to a less extent at Naples and Syracuse, constitute an indispensable third-century link between the most significant works of Roman painting in the central imperial period and those in the Christian basilicas which were to prove definitely triumphant in the course of the fourth century. The slight importance formerly attached to catacombal painting has today been replaced, without opposition, by unqualified appreciation of the authentically Roman character, closely connected with contemporary secular painting, of Christian hypogean decoration.

This conclusion, which is naturally applicable only to the style, not to the content, of funerary painting in the third century, does not of itself solve the previously even more controversial problem of the iconographical derivation of basilican mosaic decoration at the beginning of the fourth century. Whence originated that collection of narratives which, for the most part in historical sequences, came almost unexpectedly to decorate the imposing Christian edifices built after Constantine and Theodosius? Could they be derived only from the large catacombal niches which late in the third century began to be more and more frequently adorned with iconographical designs and subjects drawn from the Old and New Testaments? Hypogean decoration had till then ignored such resources, preferring to dwell on funerary themes, although, as Wilpert had already noted, some Biblical references were made, but only symbolically, in relation to the deceased. Styger believed that 'catacombal painting probably repeated the pictorial symbols which for long formed part of the decoration of Christian houses',[2] whereas at a later date De Wit persistently maintained that in the third century even Christian houses, like all the rest, were adorned with illustrations of neutral themes, taken directly from the old Hellenistic cartoons dealing with classical myth.[3]

It may be true that much catacombal painting of the second and third centuries makes no explicit reference to the deposit of Faith, and that at least until late in the third century it presented 'Cupids, Psyches, divinities of rivers and springs, and other apparently pagan subjects'.[4] But it must certainly be recognised on the one hand that the decoration of the *Domus Christiana* at Dura Europos

Map A

70

1 Styger (1933); Wirth (1934); De Wit (1938).
2 Styger (1927), p. 90.
3 De Wit (1938), pp. 14–17.
4 De Wit (1938), pp. 16–17.

provides irrefutable proof of the presence of an early and specific use of New Testament narrative (just as is indicated at a later stage of evolution by the Old Testament pictures in the Synagogue), and on the other hand that the late development in the catacombs of a new pictorial repertory illustrating the Gospel story suggests that the latter did not originate in the cemeteries,[5] but had been worked out in the *domus ecclesiae* and thence transferred to catacombal decoration.[6]

It therefore seems now more prudent to admit that, from two quite distinct cultural and functional sources – that of the urban liturgical halls (the *tituli* of the later basilicas) and that of the underground cemeteries – there flowed alongside the simultaneous stylistic transformation in secular painting an extremely rich repertory of subjects, treated with even more variation, which was to constitute the material of art for a whole millennium. Bettini has thus been enabled to presume, with good reason, that in the *domus ecclesiae* 'there was elaborated that "continuous narrative cycle" which was destined to provide the basic material for the adornment of the great basilicas (e.g. the mosaics of S. Maria Maggiore), direct descendants of the *domus ecclesiae*'.[7] 'Christian painting had hitherto remained on the margin of the "official" stream, merely in contact, it might be said, with a "funerary" current, which was as yet ill-defined but which today can be studied through some most interesting details to be found chiefly in the Ostian necropoleis. . . . Now it returned to the idea of commemoration typical of Roman court art, adopting its canons, its characteristics and even its method of commemoration by means of narrative.'[8]

210

The finds in Christian cemeteries, at Rome and elsewhere, are naturally seldom of high quality. Most of them are frescoes rapidly executed on wet plaster, much less carefully prepared than was usual in secular painting. As a rule only two grounds were laid, the first being of pozzolana cement and lime, the second of lime and pounded marble, which, towards the beginning of the fourth century, were combined to form a single coat of lime and pozzolana and whitened with a solution of lime. The decorations were often executed over outlines drawn on the fresh stucco in lighting and other working conditions which left much to be desired. Perhaps for these and other practical reasons the artists employed were not generally the most skilled.

Such considerations, however, cannot weaken our assessment of the Christian hypogean *corpus*, not only because of its immense historical value, but also in large measure because of the frequent presence of paintings of singular artistic merit or at any rate faithfully reflecting the development of contemporary taste, as is confirmed by comparisons with contemporary mosaics, coins, etc.

5 Junyent (1932), p. 91.
6 Kirsch (1927).
7 Bettini (1943), p. 19.
8 Bettini (1952), p. xxvii.

De Wit has proposed a division of periods according to style: impressionism from the late Severan to the later Gallienan period; post-Gallienan realism and tetrarchic expressionism; Constantinian expressionism and the transitional period of the 'fine style'; Valentinianist classicism and Theodosian mannerism. These distinctions appear on the whole valid, though tendencies and manners were often displayed in many different ways. Within the framework of De Wit's scheme certain murals in the Christian cemeteries of Rome assume great significance, and to them we may safely confine ourselves in undertaking an investigation the purpose of which is to recognise in the hypogean field a further development of the new forms of idiom hitherto identified on the pavements and walls of secular buildings.

It is obviously not intended here to embark upon a comprehensive consideration of the subject by styles and by successive (and ultimately epochal) idioms. Such a proceeding could only be abstract, since, in attempting to achieve the necessary reconstruction of certain 'artistic modes', it would erect, at least methodologically, a theory of evolution which has nothing in common with an impartial view of the creative capacities of artistic freedom in history, or even with the actual modifications of social structure which accompany ideological transformations and the substitutions of secular values. It seems clear, however, that in settling the lines of our present investigation criticism must, *a fortiori*, sometimes be directed to surviving works of inferior quality. Two factors account for this. First, there is an almost complete lack of secular painting in these years. Second, catacombal painting in the third century has a certain peculiarity, being (as already explained) often the work of sincere and able artists but very seldom of masters with a style recognisable, so far as can at present be determined, in other important examples of secular Roman painting of the period. It will accordingly be understood why, at risk of lowering the standards of the gallery we imagine ourselves to be touring, these minor works have been chosen to represent possible productions of more merit which have not survived but which may have influenced the others to develop the particular idiom regarded as their own. But the extent to which such works may be considered exemplary must necessarily and manifestly be subject to more limited and cautious appraisal.

According to the results of Styger's[9] archaeological studies, which confirm Wirth's stylistic investigation, none of the Christian works in the catacombs can be safely dated before the beginning of the third century. The oldest sections of the Christian underground at Rome (the Crypt of Ampliatus in the Cemetery of Domitilla, the Crypt of Lucina in the Cemetery of Callisto, the Cubicle of Urania

9 *See*, in addition to his two works already mentioned, Styger (1935).

in the Cemetery of Praetextatus and the 'Greek Chapel' in the Cemetery of Priscilla) can all be dated between the end of the second century and the beginning of the third. They prove a persistence, especially symptomatic in the first of these examples, of mural decoration directly related to the manners of the 'fourth style' as interpreted in the second-century painting of interiors. During this later phase it was steadily giving way to a type of linear ornamentation in which the walls and even the vaults (particularly of the Crypt of Lucina, of the Cubicle of Urania and of the 'Greek Chapel') reproduce motives, later common in the catacombs, of which earlier secular specimens survive.[10] Moreover, the pictures in these older regions of the catacombs are derived almost exclusively from the usual secular stock. They show the first attempts at religious symbolism referring to the themes of death and the hereafter in their oldest expression through profane subjects.

As already noted, these profane iconographical origins of catacombal painting, universal at the end of the second century and beginning of the third, are to be found also in some famous hypogean monuments examined above, when the question of their religious orthodoxy was discussed: the Mausoleum of the Aurelii in the Viale Manzoni and that of the Julii in the Vatican Grottoes. Consequently, even though as early as the Cubicle of Urania scenes supposed to refer to incidents in the Gospels are accompanied by the figure of the 'Good Shepherd', it is not until the second half of the third century that we discover a wide range of Christian funerary painting progressively more and more free from symbolic constriction, which also includes an increasing flow of the 'historical' painting of the *domus ecclesiae* and the gradual assembly of that vast store of figures which was to be produced in the fourth century.

Cubicle 5, the chamber of the so-called *Velatio*, in the Cemetery of Priscilla, furnishes a remarkable example of mature impressionist painting, though the construction is firm and the decorative taste simple. Wilpert assigned to the second half of the third century[11] a decoration which De Wit, relying on the hair style of one of the figures attributed to the later Severan age,[12] while Carcopino inclines to a date *circa* 250.[13] The lunette of the rear wall of the chamber probably represents on one side the ceremonial preceding the 'Conferment of the Veil' upon a virgin by the bishop; at the opposite end Wilpert identified one of the earliest pictures of the Madonna and Child, which would thus be very little later than the date of the Cemetery of Priscilla. In the centre stands the tall figure of the consecrated virgin in the characteristic attitude of the 'Praying Girl'. In these three figures, especially in the first two, which are more summary and have less formal significance, paratactical re-arrangement of the perspective

10, 71–9
79

82, 83, 6

82

83

6

10 *See*, for example, the roof of the Stabian Villa at Colle al Varano, with its picture of 'Victory' on a central octagonal shield. In itself it merely represents, still more than do those of the Planisphere Gallery, a simply copy of the Roman 'Golden Roof' of Fabullus. The arrangement of the catacombal vaulting is in strict accord with that of Stabia.

11 Wilpert (1903), p. 517.

12 De Wit (1938), p. 29.

13 Carcopino (1956), p. 121. Volbach and Hirmer (1958, p. 44), with Grabar, date it on stylistic grounds to the end of the third century. Peirce and Tyler (1932, p. 52) refer it to the end of the fourth.

planes is very conspicuous. The face of the bishop, seated in profile on his throne, is presented almost wholly in the now customary frontal posture, though his eyes are fixed upon the girl preparing for the rite. She, however, has her back to the bishop and holds a *volumen* from which she reads the ritual formulae. Behind her a deacon takes part in the ceremony; but he is in the same spatial plane, thus throwing the figures out of perspective by setting them at an identical level, a practice that was to become more and more frequent in later painting. The frontality of the female figure is complete, except that, as in the great contemporary figures of the hypogeum of the Aurelii, the head is turned slightly to the right and the body slightly to the left. The impressionist rendering of the faces is quite remarkable, achieved by small but strongly marked touches of luscious colour. The bodies, however, show no sign whatever of that still classical solidity which we noticed in the Monument of the Aurelii; they are simply areas of colour, so flat that even the arm of the consecrating bishop, stretched forward for three quarters of its length, acquires no spatial depth.

At the other side of the chamber the figures of 'Mother and Child' show signs of cubist treatment not discernible in the representation of the bishop, seated in an almost identical posture, simply because his figure is partially obscured by that of the girl who is to receive the veil. The Virgin's chair is seen laterally, in perspective, but her attitude is almost entirely frontal; only the purple *clavi* of the tunic indicate the bending of the seated body. Behind her right shoulder the curving back of the chair suddenly reappears, this time in almost perfect perspective. Following the chariot in the 'Triumph of Septimius Severus' at Leptis Magna, the 'Departure of the Ark' at Dura Europos, and the Vatican mosaic of the 'Triumph of Christ as Sun-god', this picture of the Madonna and Child seems to provide yet another clear example of that reduction to a single two-dimensional plane of solid objects, formerly represented by the reciprocal intersection of normal planes, which was to be generally adopted in medieval painting. A similarly seated figure may be observed, for instance, in the 'Adoption of Moses' by Pharoah's daughter, the subject of one of the mosaics in the nave of S. Maria Maggiore. In the earlier work, three-quarters of the baby's rosy form, rendered like the mother's face by broad patches of colour retouched here and there, is seen from the back. But this distorted figure reveals more than does anything else in the composition the difficulties of the task undertaken by the painter and the provisional nature of his solution of them, an approach to the new cubist idiom still too clumsy and unconscious to be effective.

The same tendency is prominent also in the detail of the head of the 'Praying Girl', now wearing the veil, a figure which illustrates in the centre of the series the final stage of the rite. A dazzling streak of white light on the veil expresses with almost supernatural force the new divine illumination which has descended on the newly consecrated *sponsa Christi* and answers the light in her eyes, two conspicuous white crescents indicating her absorption in prayer. The perfectly rigid and even fall of the veil, and the equally plain though massive length of the purple garment uniform in its extent with the surface, are among the finest products of all Roman catacombal painting. The effect is heightened by the fact that the veil over the girl's head neither disappears nor is concentrated in a short line of perspective above the hair, but surrounds it with the full width of the material, projected on to the surface plane, so as almost to form a halo. In short, the skilled hand of the MASTER OF THE VELATIO here resorts to the stylistic expedient already referred to, which came to its full maturity at the end of the century in the formulation of the paratactical construction of cubism. The foreshortening of the veil placed on the hair appears in the two-dimensional projection of its surface, adding to the impression of a broad extension of the facial planes. This feature and the intensity of the large eyes in the rapture of ecstasy are such as almost to anticipate the cubist expressionism of certain portraits executed under the Tetrarchy.

We may now consider 'Moses Causing Water to Gush from the Rock' and 'Susanna and the Elders', which form part of the decoration of the so-called Chamber of the Water Miracle and of Susanna, in the Cemetery of Peter and Marcellinus. The first design appears on the pilaster of the arcosolium, the second in the lunette. Wilpert assigned these works to the second half of the fourth century.[14] But certain stylistic details, formerly insufficiently studied, besides the iconological point mentioned above, have induced De Wit to refer them to the twenty years between 270 and 290, thus quite logically including them in the period called by him that of post-Gallienan realism introducing the expressionism of the Tetrarchy.[15] The artist's preoccupation with anatomy, shown for instance in the strictly defined folds of the robes of Moses, who stands in the well-known slightly decussated attitude, seems an echo of the age's brief endeavour to return to traditional ways, an echo present to some extent in painting. These figures, nevertheless, recall only too clearly the relief which Riegl called negative. Consequently, although the flat chromatic surface of the robe in the *Velatio* of the Cemetery of Priscilla gives place about a generation later to an investigation of outward bodily configuration, even this concern tends, through its fierce insistence upon line (almost the only way in which form is expressed), to resolve itself into chromatic rhythm. This is true likewise of the figure of Susanna, exceptionally simple and nearly formless though it is.

86, 84

86

6

84

14 Wilpert (1903), p. 512.
15 De Wit (1938), pp. 33–4. Bovini (1957a, pp. 20–1) classifies those paintings 'in the last decades of the third century'.

This detail, together with the truly remarkable vivacity of the faces,[16] suggests that these pictures date from the end of the period conjectured by De Wit, or as near as possible to the expressionist assertions of art under the Tetrarchy. The colours are thinly and very loosely applied, thus increasing the rapidity of their flow. This method shows how far Roman mural painting had travelled since the time of the small portraits in the Stabian villas of Colle al Varano. It was not without reason that De Wit himself wrote in this connection of a 'rejection' of the impressionism exemplified in the decoration of the adjacent corridor.[17]

20, 22

In the crypt of the Five Saints, in the Cemetery of Callistus, the only portrait of a praying figure which remains almost intact (though damaged) for inspection is that of 'Dionysas', so called from the inscription *Dionysas in pace*. It may well be affirmed, with De Wit, that every specific trace of impressionism has disappeared from this countenance. Its facial planes are so separated from the physiognomical lines of eyes, nose or mouth as to amount to a formal dissociation which is wholly expressionist.[18] The lineaments appear self-contained and arid in their confident individuality, so much so that it is necessary to stress the lack of any unifying direction of interest. Yet the large eyes, deeply encircled by a heavy, continuous line which isolates them and superimposes them on the rest of the face, constitute one of the most suggestive examples of expressionist idiom in the entire *corpus* of late Roman painting. They are placed centrally in the face, which is framed in a heavy shock of hair. De Wit dates this figure and the others between 292 and 328.[19] These excessively wide chronological limits *post* and *ante quem* should not, however, lead to uncertainty. Classification of this work within the years of the first Tetrarchy is suggested by the stylistic structure of the figure, together with the surrounding paradisal-type decoration which is still rendered in markedly impressionist fashion, with varying tones of vivid colours intended to create spatial illusion.[20] Any later date, such as Levi[21] seems to favour, would appear unacceptable.

22

Such chronological placing would cause the 'Dionysas' of the Cemetery of Callistus to rank as the oldest surviving example of expressionist painting under the Tetrarchy. Of more importance, however, is the fact that for this period it is a work of accomplished poetic merit. The DIONYSAS MASTER, to whom may probably also be attributed the portrayal of the other four 'saints' in the crypt, appears accordingly to have been one of the few personalities of marked individuality among the decorators of Christian catacombs in the third century. The refined taste for paradisal ornament is attested by an undisguised and vigorous illusionistic arrangement, a relic of impressionism, which is conjoined as never before with the new com-

16 Above all in the 'Moses', where the penetrating and almost wild stare (De Wit (1938), pl. 24, I) may be profitably compared with that of another 'Moses' in Cubicle 6A of the same cemetery (De Wit (1938), pl. 18, I): a facial theatre in which a very few heavy, dark, horizontal and vertical strokes create not only a physiognomy but also strong spiritual feeling. It is particularly in the mouth and eyes that the resemblance between the two almost contemporaneous heads is so marked.
17 De Wit (1938), p. 34.
18 *Ibid.*, p. 42.
19 *Ibid.*, p. 43.
20 Bettini (1953), pp. xxxvi and li.
21 Levi (1947), i, p. 562, n. 13.

munication of form by expressionist figuration, the first authentic artistic idiom of late antiquity. It is manifested in a warmth of colour, through glowing, startling tones of yellow, red, violet and chestnut, that seems almost to anticipate the luminosity of the future, calling it from the funerary shades that were to give birth, with the *fauvisme* of the Tetrarchy and the expressionist classicism of the age of Constantine, to the splendours of the fourth century. We shall find this form of decoration, broken up into paradigmatic episodes of purely ornamental significance, in the pavements of Aquileia and in the Vaults of S. Costanza.

132–41, 25–27 166, 24–

On the first cross-gallery of the Agape region, in the Cemetery of Peter and Marcellinus, a lunette illustrates the factors at work in the revolution which introduced the art of the Tetrarchy, to which period it undoubtedly belongs. De Wit declares that it outdoes the treatment of reflected light in the impressionist period by its use of extended bright and dark strokes, extremely simple in form, to which, in defining the style, he is led to apply the epithets 'geometrical' or, directly, 'goniometrical'.[22]

In this picture of the Christian *agape*, framed in wide bands of red, the bright and empty background emphasises and repeats the tendency operative in the mosaic pavements, which as early as the second half of the second century were dissolving their most distant planes into ivory spatial abstractions, a prelude to the abandonment of every relic of perspective. In this case the very complexity of subject might well have allowed and suggested the affirmation of spatial perspective; instead, in obedience to the canons of the new vision, everything is brought to the surface. The curved, classical shape of the table and the location of the diners, do not suffice to create a perspective depth that was neither sought nor desired. The existence, however, of many earlier and well-known pictures of banquets proves that the cartoon was of strictly traditional origin, and therefore not such as to induce the painter to embark automatically on formal innovations, but rather such as to discourage anything of the sort.

But the most extraordinary aspect of the catacombal 'Agape' is furnished by the structure of the physiognomies of the diners. Their features are altogether unusual, shattered by a kind of wild geometry. There is no question here of great chromatic variety in the persons and objects depicted. For the ARTIST OF THE AGAPE, while retaining certain basic colours used by the DIONYSAS MASTER, was unable or did not wish to understand their revolutionary significance. Consequently, the picture tends to monochrome, the wide areas of colour being scarcely relieved by hard, dark lines applied with a nervous hand; tones of sepia, chestnut and black, for example, are superimposed on burnt ochre.

91, 92

22 De Wit (1938), pp. 34–5.

The long, liquid brushstrokes were neither inspired by nor, all things considered, in conformity with such accomplished artistry as may be seen in contemporary works of some importance (even though paralleled elsewhere) in various cemeteries. This fact introduces some perplexity into the problem of the origin and historical identification of what De Wit has called the 'geometrical style'. It may be asked, in fact, whether the 'Agape' of the Cemetery of Peter and Marcellinus, and the similar contemporary decorations of the Cemetery of the Jordani and the Cemetery of Domitilla,[23] amount to the literary expression of an idiom historically recognisable, which in other cases would also have produced works of unmistakable artistic individuality; or whether, on the contrary, such decorations are merely a less polished version of the very well attested and highly versatile pictorial cultivation of expressionism in the age of the Tetrarchs.

As De Wit has noted,[24] the first guest on the left, seen in profile, and the second, full-face, are stylistically very much akin to other portraits of the epoch, ranging from the porphyry 'Group of Tetrarchs at St. Mark's' at Venice to that of the Vatican, and to the heads of emperors on the coinage of Diocletian and the first years of Constantine. The rhythmically waved and geometrically treated hair reveals an intimate understanding of the value of line. The eyes, represented by white circles, convey the same abstract and superhuman effect as those of the porphyry portraits. It is therefore clear that this manner was adopted not only to render adequately the sacred character of an emperor, but also as the result of independent stylistic innovation, the desire above all to give artistic expression to ideas of form in full agreement with a new *Weltanschauung*. This point is confirmed by the rendering of a child on the ceiling of the arcosolium containing the picture of the *agape*: the same eyes, the same geometrical confusion of anatomical planes, the identical hair, the exactly similar technique of applying colour. The style reappears in another catacomb: the lunette of the arcosolium at the back of the eighth chapel in the Cemetery of the Jordani, showing Moses causing water to gush from the rock. If it is agreed with Wilpert[25] that these stylistic efforts of a revolutionary age in course of transformation belong as a whole to the first half of the fourth century,[25] at the climax of the great crisis, there can be no doubt of their vital importance, apart from their limited intrinsic value, for the assessment of a turning point between two epochs of the history of Roman painting.

Some other chapels of the Cemetery of the Jordani and two 'Praying Figures' on the tomb of the same name in the Cemetery of Domitilla illustrate similar methods. In both cases, according to De Wit,[26] the pictures in question are slightly later than those mentioned above, and may be

91, 92

100

90

23 *See infra.* Another funerary 'Agape', presumably of the same period, is preserved in the Syracuse Museum (No. 49824). It was taken from the local catacombs and is much more traditional in treatment, with its background floral decoration, etc., though not without echoes of the age of the Tetrarchy.
24 De Wit (1938), p. 36.
25 Wilpert (1924), p. 509. For the 'Moses' of the eighth chapel of the Jordani Cemetery, *see* De Wit (1938), p. 45.
26 De Wit (1938), p. 45.

27 The pictorial series which can be reckoned more representative includes, as well as the arch of the Jordani Cemetery, the *Collegium* of the Hermetes Cemetery, dated *ante* 337, two paintings in the Cemetery of Domitilla – one on an arch and one on the open arcosolium near the Ampliatus Crypt (*circa* 350) – and also one in the apse of the Region of the great apostles in the Cemetery of Domitilla, belonging to the last years of the century. In connection with the chain of development completed by this last composition in the Domitilla Cemetery, already fit for transfer to a basilica, the *Collegium* of the Jordani Cemetery has a very special compositional interest: on each side of the divine Master the apostles form two ranks, amounting to a double *theoria*, which the figures in pairs in a formal pattern very close to that favoured by the age of the Tetrarchy. On this point *see* also Chapter XI and Note 21 to that Chapter.

This picture of the apostolic college, certainly among the very earliest known, may suitably introduce a series of paintings culminating, by way of the series of great sarcophagi – from those of Junius Bassus (*c.* 359) and the Arcadii (*c.* 350), preserved in the Grottoes of St. Peter's, to that of the '*Traditio Legis*' of the Lateran and those of Concordius (*c.* 390) in the Arles Museum and Gorgonius (*c.* 380) in the cathedral at Ancona and to the Theodosian sarcophagus (*c.* 390) in S. Ambrogio at Milan, to mention none but the most noble and famous – in the great decorative mosaics of the basilicas, beginning with the apsidiole of S. Aquilino at Milan and the apse of S. Pudenziana at Rome, and the hypogean decorations, also in fresco, such as that of S. Maria in Stelle near Verona.

28 De Wit (1938), p. 43.

29 For these frescoes of the Jordani Cemetery, *see* in particular Josi (1928); p. 199, for the picture of 'Daniel among the Lions'.

dated between 305 and 315. The absence in some of them of features proper to expressionism in the age of Constantine is to be noted. The ascetic dignity in the countenances of the 'Christ with Apostles' on the inner side of the arch of the fourth chapel of the Cemetery of the Jordani is rendered, in comparison with the 'Agape' faces, in a more orderly and severe manner, technically quite similar but more powerfully expressive of individuality, more vivid and realistic. The style is inspired, in fact, by a taste not entirely absorbed by the strained inflections that lend such turbulence, on the other hand, to the usual interpretations of the current mode.[27] 'The wings of the nose are triangular . . . the lips oval, the corners of the mouth drawn down . . . the hair comes deep down over the forehead, the bony structure is strongly accentuated, the gaze is austere and the expression in both cases sullen and melancholy'.[28]

In this same fourth chapel,[29] on the interior lateral wall to the left, under a scene representing 'Jonah vomited by the Monster', the better preserved figure of a worshipper has been executed, presumably by the same artist, with spirit and remarkable skill. Here too, broad and decisive strokes of the brush have laid plain surfaces of colour, stressed the facial planes and hollowed mouth and eyes with expressive effect, to which the intact radiance of the wide crescents alone adds a penetrating spiritual power. But the artist himself was clearly capable of formal synthesis, not only in the face but also in the successful realisation of the figure. This gift enabled him to dispense with erratic line, though without losing anything of the personal expressive quality it had involved. in order to compose a finished structure. A similar consideration applies to the 'Praying Figures' of the Cemetery of Domitilla already mentioned, in which the formal reshaping is more evidently the result of a disciplined design functioning as a substrate.

On the right-hand wall of the same chapel the same artist was responsible for the scene of 'Daniel among the Lions', one of the boldest and most ardent pictures of this subject bequeathed by catacombal painting. The placing of the animals around the figure, the suggestion of the pit given by a simple circular sweep of the brush, and the shading, all combine to give an impression of synthetic perspective. Here too the powerful, unhesitating line conveys passionate emotion. Such figures, attributable to a JORDANI ARTIST in the closing years of the Tetrarchy, are truly representative of the spirit of their time. But by now men's eyes were beginning to re-open to a sense of wonder and to livelier modes of expression; lines were preparing to expand in an organic return of the form which had not forgotten the achievements of the preceding style. Without any break in continuity the expressionism of the age of Constantine and the so-called fine style had arrived.

Chapter Six
Late Tetrarchic painting and the Constantinian
'fine style' at Piazza Armerina villa

The wonderful assemblage of mosaic pavements in this late-Roman villa, brought to light near the 'village' of Piazza Armerina, constitutes for the purposes of the present study one of the most magnificent and epoch-making archaeological discoveries of modern times. It unquestionably sets at the central point of the crisis here investigated a pictorial *corpus* of exceptional importance, which has undoubtedly added greatly to our understanding of the stylistic transformation of Roman painting in the late imperial period. The sheer abundance of the mosaics revealed, covering in all an area of about 3500 square metres, and their obvious creation by a number of different masters, who probably worked in the villa over a period of some decades, are conclusive reasons for assigning to a region which has been called the Sicilian 'city of mosaics' a position of primary significance in the archaeology and art history of late Roman antiquity.

At first, immediately after the start of the new systematic excavations undertaken in the spring of 1950, the problems of identification, classification, and hence of dating, gave rise to remarkable differences of opinion. Above all, the question of ascription of the floors to one or other of the artistic tendencies expressed with such passion during the century of the great transition, the fourth, appeared peculiarly intractable. Essentially, the very originality and in so many aspects unfamiliar beauty of the polychrome surfaces suggested, amid the uncertainty due to the lack of decisive archaeological evidence, either that they were created during a period of transition between the expressionism of the Tetrarchy and the so-called Constantinian fine style, or that they were the handiwork of a group of craftsmen to be included in the period called by De Wit that of expressionist classicism of the age of Valentinian. The fact that these important works could be referred by various authorities to different stages in the development of late Roman painting, spread over at least three quarters of a century, is an accurate measure of the remarkable artistic standard and outstanding personalities of the masters simultaneously acknowledged to be capable of expressing in the sphere of art the tendencies of their own times, or of prefiguring the taste of the ensuing epoch with novel and prophetic power.

Pace maintained[1] that 'the Masters of Piazza Armerina . . . may be placed in the interval between the experiments which relied on the return to classical or academic ideals

---

1 Pace (1951), p. 470.

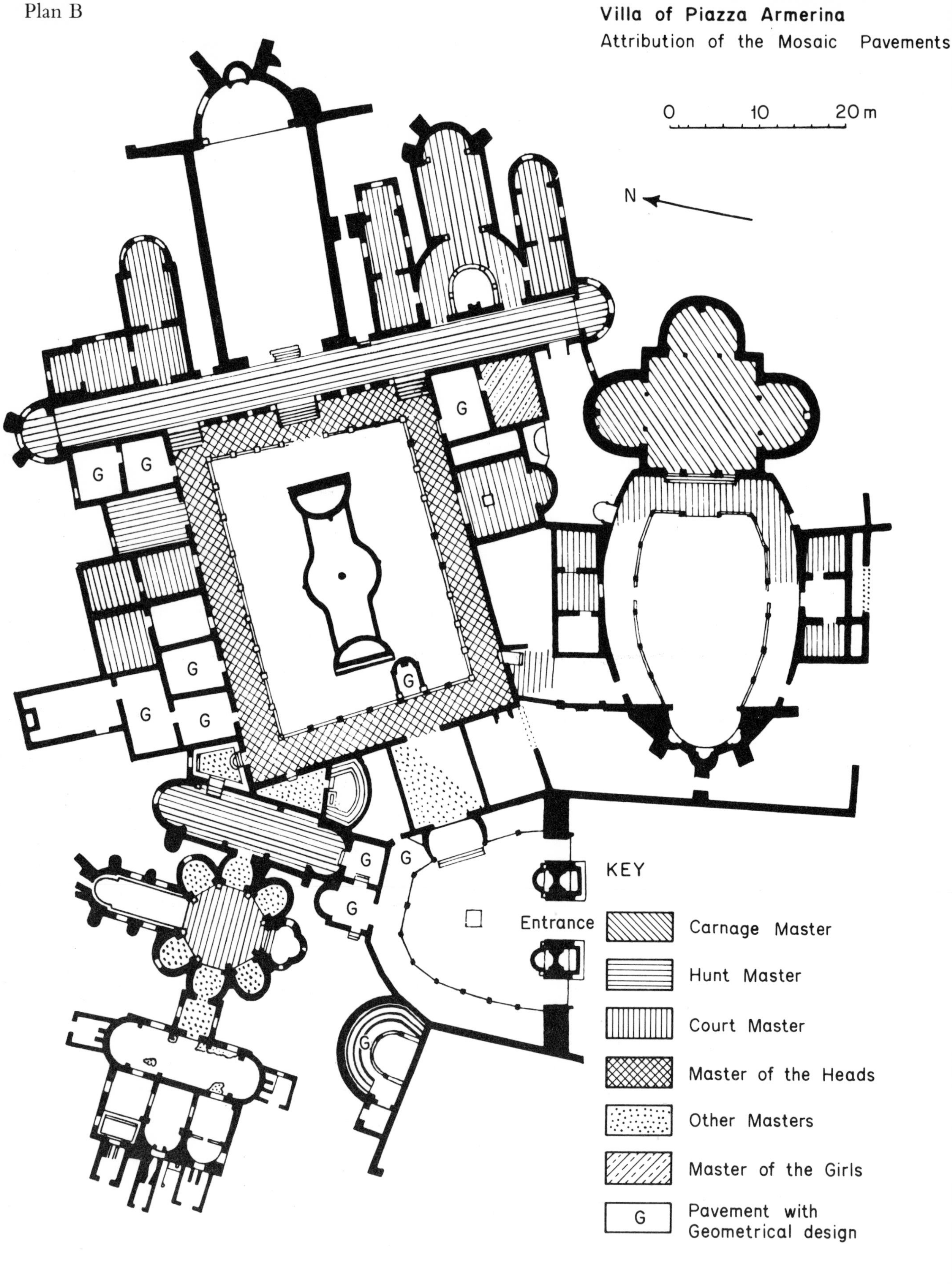

Villa of Piazza Armerina
Attribution of the Mosaic Pavements

0   10   20 m

N

KEY

Entrance

Carnage Master

Hunt Master

Court Master

Master of the Heads

Other Masters

Master of the Girls

G   Pavement with Geometrical design

of Hellenistic inspiration, or on impressionist research, and those later investigations which pioneered the adoption of purely linear decoration characteristic of Byzantine taste. This first cautious verdict was followed by that of Gentili.[2] He agreed in considering that the mosaics should be attributed to two movements, which, though operating within the same school, were quite distinct from one another, the second beginning some decades after the first; but he inclined to set the works as a whole in the first half of the fourth century – more precisely, in the Constantinian age.

Galassi, for his part, recognised the validity of the observations of L'Orange, favouring the hypothesis that the villa was occupied by the emperor Maximian Herculeus, and thus dating it between the end of the third century and the beginning of the fourth.[3] He remarked, however, that this archaeological assumption 'would appear to be somewhat at variance with certain stylistic features of the mosaics, in particular the considerable formal distortion in some of them and the carpet-like variegation of colour in others. Such features would be a striking anticipation of later developments if the mosaics were really to be ascribed to the age of the Tetrarchs'.[4] He concluded first by distinguishing 'two categories, one of mainly classical type and the other more in line with the new tendencies to dismantle the Hellenistic and Roman figurative structure'; secondly, by denying that 'the difference of outlook can be regarded as indicating more than a quite substantial difference in the period of their execution';[5] and thirdly, by assigning all the mosaics to a period between the middle of the fourth century and the beginning of the fifth.[6]

Pace later returned to the controversy, likewise favouring some time in the late fourth or early fifth century, while Gentili finally narrowed the limits of his original estimate, deciding for the age of the Tetrarchy.[7] This last dating has since been confirmed by archaeological evidence, in the shape of an 'antoninian' of Maximian Herculeus found in the mortar cementing the marble slab at the threshold of the south-east portico of the *frigidarium* of the villa. The coin 'was undoubtedly issued in the last years of the third century'.[8]

Lastly, two further specific contributions to the argument may be cited. Lugli,[9] on the strength of research into the history of the building of this imposing villa, proposed a complex dating system divided into five phases. Those more directly pertaining to the mosaic decoration comprise the years 300–380; 300–330 for the peristyle and the adjacent residential quarters; 350–370 for the *xystus* and the trilobate hall; and 370–380 for various repairs. Carandini,[10] on the basis of an exhaustive inventory of monuments studied in their antiquarian and stylistic

2 Gentili (1950; 1952 a; 1952 b; 1957, pp. 7–27; 1959).
3 L'Orange (1952). In opposition, Mazzarino (1953, pp. 417–21).
4 Galassi (1953), p. 626, n. 20.
5 Galassi (1953), pp. 367 and 373.
6 Pace (1955) pp. 105 and 111 ff. *See also*, for attribution of the villa to the Nicomachi family, Cagiano de Azevedo (1961).
7 Gentili (1952 b, p. 16; 1959, pp. 15–6). On page 33 of this last (1959) study Gentili dates 'the whole original series of figured compositions in the villa' to 'about AD 300, approximately in the final phase of the first Tetrarchy'. In this connection the superimposed fragment of the *Mutatio Vestis* in a lunette of the *frigidarium* and the pavement of the 'Girls at Exercise', both 'certainly of the age of Constantine', would constitute exceptions. This attribution, however, seems too limited chronologically, and in any case too early.
8 Gentili (1957), p. 25, n. 3.
9 Lugli (1963), especially p. 80.
10 Carandini (1964), pp. 66–7.

aspects, has suggested the period 320–370 for the whole complex of mosaic flooring, placing it within the cultural orbit of workmen operating between the bipolar co-ordinates of Africa and Italy.

Since the *post quem* dating provided by the coin of Maximian coincides with the lower limits of the chronology derived from the history of the construction of the villa, it seems obvious that it need be considered conclusive only in one sense. We must therefore seek in the architectural and decorative stages of the villa, in their antiquarian and above all stylistic elements, a safe course between the many chronological alternatives offered. In this way, now that the excavations are complete, it is possible to give a satisfactory answer to the question raised by Pace[11] in 1951. He asked himself whether the 'displacement of the axes and the lack of organisation in interconnection' to be found in the three constituent parts of the villa so far discovered, belonging respectively to the Trilobate Hall with its elliptic *xystus*, to the great peristyle with its adjacent 'Corridor of the Hunt', and finally to the short arcade and baths, should be attributed to the successive agglomeration of separate buildings or to an exceptional desire for variety, which would also be attested by the 'baroque' conformation itself at all curves of the first of the above-mentioned nuclei.

Lugli's answer seems very clear and enlightening; but even in the context of a comprehensive examination of all the mosaic decorations it appears to allow too long a period to the different stages of construction. Consequently, while accepting in substance the sequence given, I prefer to suppose a much briefer course of development, lasting no more than about fifty years, between 315 and 360–370; I have in mind particularly a much earlier date for the construction of the trilobate hall with *xystus*. On this view, even if the hypothesis of successive stages of building is accepted, their articulation still seems remarkable within a structurally unified design, even though resulting from a creative process through successive but almost continuous phases.

In any case, the polychrome expanses of the flooring at Piazza Armerina, where the vaults and walls, presumably richly decorated with legendary subjects, have disappeared, speak more distinctly. In surveying them we shall be able to make use of an historically determined itinerary, which sets each work as clearly as possible within the framework of the taste of the age of transition and renewal during which they were executed, and within that of the artistic culture of the masters employed on them.

To begin with, three artistic personalities are very clearly discernible in an attentive and detailed study of this immense pictorial *corpus* produced by masters who plied their craft from the foundation of the villa and for most of

Plan B

11 Pace (1951), pp.461–2.

the time it took to complete, a period which cannot have ended much before 335–340, even if Pace's cautious estimate[12] is subjected to the most drastic limitation. Subsequent works, after the first half of the fourth century, were entrusted to new craftsmen: it is certain that the first three masters were followed by others as time went on, and of these at least two may be stated with relative certainty to have carried out one work each in the villa. Accordingly, the present attempt at historical reconstruction of the genesis of the various artistic manners found at Piazza Armerina should leave few zones not ultimately attributable with some degree of certainty to artists of fairly well defined personality. The second phase, which is also the more difficult to identify chronologically, may have lasted for brief periods throughout much of the second half of the century.

We may call the first three artists the HUNT MASTER, the CARNAGE MASTER and the COURT MASTER, following the order which seems the most historically verifiable for the execution of the *lithostrata*; the others we may call the MASTER OF THE ANIMAL HEADS and the MASTER OF THE GIRLS. In the first group the HUNT MASTER would appear to have carried out the original instructions of the patron when the work began. He represents in fact, on unimpeachable stylistic grounds, the art typical of the Tetrarchy in all the disconcerting novelty of its expressionist content, its paratactic vision and its revolutionary feeling for colour, such as might have been seen by a craftsman probably educated in North Africa. The CARNAGE MASTER appears to have worked at Piazza Armerina somewhat later: a few years, but more than enough because the interval had witnessed many changes in the political and cultural life of the Empire. On the accession of Constantine the age of re-establishment had already begun, taking shape in art as the movement to recover form. The norms of the so-called fine style came into fashion. Meanwhile, the CARNAGE MASTER was neither an unthinking executant of orders nor a copyist: he was a very great artist and, as such, an innovator who in a highly personal fashion would attempt the recovery of Hellenism demanded by the formal revolution under the Tetrarchy. His version of Hellenism was derived at long range from Rhodes and Pergamum. But it was North African by extraction.

To these two artists of genius a third may be added. He was endowed with an exceptional degree of refinement, with extreme versatility and a subtlety of mind expressed in a manner lacking the CARNAGE MASTER's 'Michelangelo touch' but not far from it. He translated the style into a more elegant, more lightly fantastic and even humorous vein which often approaches with intelligent curiosity that of the HUNT MASTER, and also makes not infrequent use of

12 Pace (1955), p. 108, n. 1. Gentili (1959, p. 11) considers a period of three or four years sufficient for the execution of the 'Great Hunt' by six groups of four *tessellarii* each. But he calculates the daily productive capacity of one *tessellarius* as about one square metre 'of figured mosaic'. It is not clear how, with that unit of measurement, one arrives at an estimate of three-four years. The Hunt Corridor, including the lunettes, has an area of over 300 square metres, for which, accordingly, a year's work by a single mosaicist would have sufficed, or alternatively fifteen days' work by 24 employees. But the completion of one square metre of figured mosaic a day by each labourer seems an excessive standard, even if the laying of the white background cubes is included. A reproduction of the mosaics of the 'Circus Contests' and the 'Girls at Exercise' recently carried out by the Mosaic School at Ravenna may be of some assistance. The two tessellated areas, comprising in all some 120 square metres, needed about a year's work in copying and laying by between 8 and 10 specialists, not counting the time required for preparation of the cartoons. I am therefore inclined to think that the Hunt Corridor alone must have taken at least two years to complete. Even supposing that other *pictores imaginarii* and *tessellarii* from one or two workshops were employed on other pavements at the same time, a conservative estimate would appear to be a decade for all the works of the first three MASTERS OF PIAZZA ARMERINA. But wall and ceiling decorations must also be taken into account, together with probable frequent interruptions, whether seasonal or otherwise. Accordingly, a period of twenty-five years, between 315 and 340, seems to be the least that can be prudently conjectured.

13 Gentili (1959, pp. 33–34) identifies a designer 'substantially in full agreement with the Hellenistic tradition, which he continues to elaborate in his own way'. To this artist 'one may ascribe the compositions of the "Heracleia" and the pictures surrounding it in the same Trilobate Hall', as well as 'Africa', the south sector of the 'Great Hunt', the 'Ulysses and Polyphemus', the 'Arion', the marine mosaics and those of the plant spirals. He is the painter whom I have named the CARNAGE MASTER. But I would deprive him of the south sector of the 'Hunt' and all the other items enumerated. The latter I would attribute to the COURT MASTER, and the former, together with the rest of the same corridor, to the HUNT MASTER, apart from any particular cases in which another hand may have collaborated. To a second designer 'who, though maintaining in his figures the naturalistic form of Hellenism in its vivid pictorial quality, departing from the classical tradition in its addiction to composition in planes', Gentili assigns the mosaics of the 'Adventus', the 'Dance', the 'Boy Hunters' and the 'Musicians and Actors'. To a third artist, much resembling the second in his conjunction of more complex features, and 'undoubtedly talented but not exceptionally so', are attributed the 'Little Hunt', the north and later section of the 'Great Hunt', the *Mutationes Vestis*, the 'Family Portrait', the 'Circus Contests' and the 'Orpheus'. In comparison with my own classification, the second of these two artists is responsible for the work I assigned to the HUNT and COURT MASTERS, while other works by the latter are ascribed to the first.

Apart from the stylistic merits of single works, which Gentili seems to have omitted in favour of attributions based on more general principles of taste, of iconographical influences and of composition, it does not appear that his identifications adequately reveal the peculiarities of the three artists engaged, or, in particular, their reciprocal relations. This is a subject which I have tried always to keep in view in the following pages. Carandini sets out his detailed classifications without attempting to reconstruct the personalities of the artists concerned.

the same subjects, in such a way as to draw from them an extremely modern *corpus* of stock forms which might have been supposed exhausted. Such was the COURT MASTER. At this stage the greater part of the mosaic decoration of the villa might be said to be complete, though other hands of less individuality may have been concerned, and other zones may have been laid out by the first and third of the artists mentioned. After the lapse of some years or decades, two masters of very diverse mentality covered the great quadrangular pavement of the peristyle with stone tesserae and also an adjoining zone formerly decorated in geometrical style. The MASTER OF THE ANIMAL HEADS, who was certainly trained in North Africa, turned the classicising zoological garden of the elliptical peristyle into a 'modern' bestiary, with heads of wild and other animals composed in an idiom still African in its derivation, which can be described almost as medieval in its emphasis on pure chromatic juxtaposition within an outline nevertheless schematic and sometimes barely sketched. The second artist, the MASTER OF THE GIRLS, was an artist of undeniable culture, with a vivid sense of colour and influenced by those tendencies which, in addition to the new mannerist reaction of the age of Valentinian, were already prefiguring the character, the rhythm and the prolific invention of Byzantine mosaic. So much is clear from his pavement depicting daringly dressed girls playing and competing in the palaestra.

This attempt to assign the whole mosaic complex of the villa to recognisable artists may appear in the discussion which follows to be more detailed and meticulous than any made hitherto, excepting those of Gentili and Carandini, from which it differs, though often taking advantage of somewhat analogous stylistic research.[13] But it is certainly not the outcome of a wish to display mere virtuosity in this field; any such purpose would be deplorable in a matter of such difficulty. The endeavour is made on grounds which will now be presented in due order, manner by manner and work by work.

The HUNT MASTER is the artist who expresses most directly, though perhaps rather late in the day, the characteristic style of art under the Tetrarchy. He is therefore outside the scope of the complicated and formidable problems raised by the environment of a revived taste for tradition exemplified by the CARNAGE MASTER, and is also unaffected by the return of Hellenistic feeling, which, within the framework of a structure novel at the time, distinguishes the COURT MASTER.

The dramatic vitality, the desire to retrieve by new expressive methods the lost sense of classical balance and the attempt to introduce further plasticity into set formal patterns, all of which characterise in a creative sense the art of the 'Carnage', are facts and problems which do not

50 Cherchel, Museum. Mosaic: Rural Labours, from a house

51 Susa Museum. Mosaic: Triumph of Dionysus, from 'Virgil's Villa'

52 Leptis Magna. Attic relief on the Arch of Septimius Severus: Triumph of Septimius Severus

53 Tunis, Bardo Museum. Mosaic: Triumph of Dionysus (detail), from a house at El Djem

54 Tripoli, Archaeological Museum. Arraying of Pegasus, from the 'Nile Villa', Leptis Magna

55 Tripoli, Archaeological Museum. Cupids in a Harbour, from the 'Nile Villa', Leptis Magna

56 Antioch-Seleucia, House near the Musa Dagh. Dining-room mosaic: Dionysus and Ariadne (detail)

57 Antioch-Seleucia, House of the Drinking Contest. Dining-room mosaic: The Drinking Contest

58 Dura Europos, Temple of the Palmyrene Gods. Conon Sacrificing, south wall of the *naos*

59 Dura Europos, Temple of the Palmyrene Gods. Sacrifice by a Roman officier, north wall of the *pronaos*

60 Dura Europos, Mithraeum. Magus, on the right jamb of the niche

61 Bishapur, Royal Palace. Mosaic *emblema*: Lady with Flowers

62 Dura Europos, Synagogue. Anointing of David (copy by H. J. Gute, Yale University Art Gallery, New Haven)

63 Dura Europos, Synagogue. Departure of the Ark from the Country of the Philistines

64 Dura Europos, Synagogue. Moses rescued from the River (copy by H. J. Gute, Yale University Art Gallery, New Haven)

65 Dura Europos, Synagogue. Vision of Ezechiel (copy by H. J. Gute, Yale University Art Gallery, New Haven)

66 Dura Europos, Synagogue. Flight and the Passage of the Red Sea (copy by H. J. Gute, Yale University Art Gallery, New Haven)

67 Dura Europos, Synagogue. Abraham

68 Moscow, Pushkin Museum. Painted shroud showing deceased with scroll (detail)

69 Palmyra, Tomb at Magharat-el-Djehideh. Victory with *imago clipeata* of deceased

70 Dura Europos, *Domus christiana*. Women at the Sepulchre (detail)

71 Rome,
Mausoleum of the
Aurelii. Figure in the
'Apostolic
Procession', north
room

72 Rome,
Mausoleum of the
Aurelii. Figure in the
'Apostolic
Procession', north
room

73 Rome,
Mausoleum of the
Aurelii. Fresco:
Ovatio (detail)

74 Rome, Mausoleum of the Aurelii. Fresco: 'Shepherd teaching on the Mountain'

75 Rome, Mausoleum of the Aurelii. Figure in the 'Apostolic Procession' (detail)

76 Syracuse, Cassia Catacomb. Fragment: Man's face

77 Paris, Louvre. Male portrait (tempera and encaustic on linen), from Fayyum

78 Moscow, Pushkin Museum. Male portrait (tempera and encaustic on wood), from Fayyum

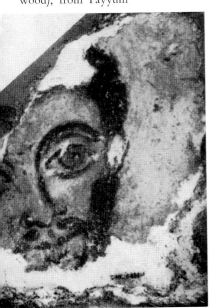

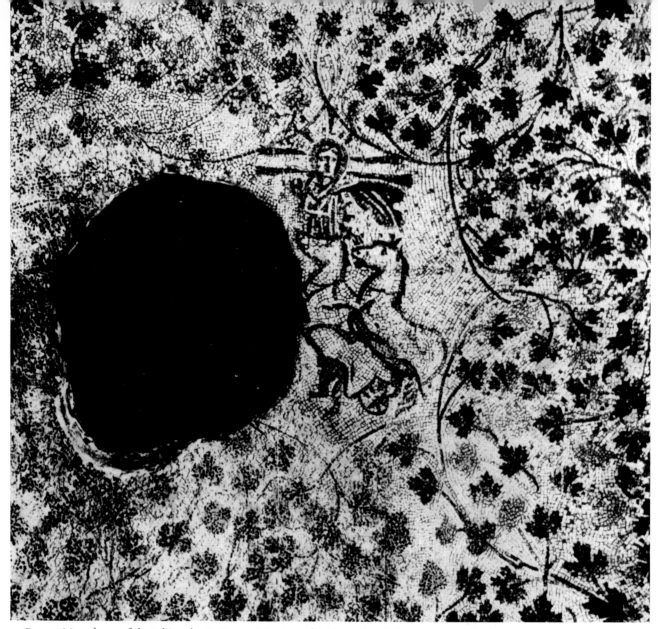

79 Rome, Mausoleum of the Julii under St. Peters. Mosaic vault: Triumph of Christ as Sun-God (detail)

80 Rome, Cemetery of Peter and Marcellinus. Vault of the *arco-solium* in the crypt of the Tricliniarch: Chariot of Elijah (detail)

81 Rome, Mausoleum of Clodius Hermes at S. Sebastiano. Vault with octagon of the Saviour (detail)

82 Rome, Cemetery of Priscilla. Conferment of the Veil (*Velatio*), end lunette of cubicle 5 (detail)

83 Rome, Cemetery of Priscilla. Mother and Child, end lunette of cubicle 5 (detail)

84 Rome, Cemetery of Peter and Marcellinus. Susanna and the Elders, Chamber of the Miracle of the Water and of Susanna

85 Rome, Cemetery of the Jordani. Christ with Apostles, vault of the arch of the fourth *sacellum*

86 Rome, Cemetery of Peter and Marcellinus. Moses Causing Water to Gush from the Rock, pilaster of the *arcosolium* in the Chamber of the Miracle of the Water and of Susanna

87 Rome, Cemetery of the Jordani. Worshipper, left pilaster of the fourth *sacellum*

88 Rome, Cemetery of the Jordani. Daniel among the Lions, right-hand pilaster of the fourth *sacellum*

91 Rome, Cemetery of Peter and Marcellinus. First guest on the left of the Agape, lunette of the first traverse of the Agape region

89 Rome, Cemetery of the Jordani. Jonah vomited by the Monster, left-hand pilaster of the fourth *sacellum* (detail)

90 Rome, Cemetery of the Jordani. Moses causing Water to Gush from the Rock, lunette of the arcosolium at end of eighth *sacellum* (detail)

92 Rome, Cemetery of Peter and Marcellinus. Second guest on the left of the Agape, lunette of the first traverse of the Agape region

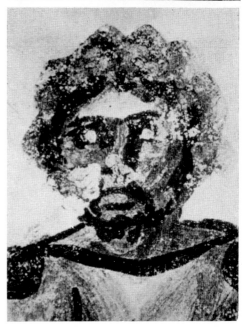

interest the HUNT MASTER or only very occasionally enter into his work. In some respects he is surpassed by the CARNAGE MASTER: for example, in the innovation of spatial modulation, through which individual personages or moments appear to be separated and brought together again in accordance with a general distributive convenience relative to the forms, which demands personal involvement of the spectator in the picture. This treatment of space, very differently systematised and applicable in cases where an interior event is supposed to take place, will be found some decades later (see below the Chapter on the cult-hall at Trier); but it is less evident in the compositions of the HUNT MASTER, who returns with a taste more typically Roman, though disguised, to the great tradition of the historical *continuum* in the Columns of Trajan and Marcus Aurelius.

29
49
Plan C

But the Corridor of the Great Hunt, though not without contradictory features, shows a general bird's-eye-view notion of space. The episodes, groups and moments are often seen at their starting and finishing points harmonised by the figuration itself. For instance, the episodes of the loading and unloading of captured animals at the stern and bows of the same ship ingeniously adapt the technique of the central imperial period, whereby an identical figure combines two different and successive movements of an action. Such incidents are also presented in a space defined less by trees, rocks and water than by the continuous line of hills, villas and greenery that stand out against the horizon. It cannot be denied that the memory of the storied imperial columns is more than compulsive. But it is chiefly and substantially limited by an inorganic and discontinuous narrative process, nearly always omitting any suggestion of 'before' and 'after'.

98, 103

7, 102

Essentially, the corridor has neither beginning nor end. It originated in the outward imitation of the structure of continuous narrative in the central imperial period, alien though this now was from its aim to relate history. Apart from the scene (itself highly generalised) of the presumed Tetrarch Maximian and soldiers of the Hercules Legion watching the capture of wild beasts, and a similar one of some officials, the paving contains not a single particular alluding to living persons or episodes recognisable on account of their originality as having really occurred, even on a hunting expedition and not in war. On the contrary, there is at least one detail of unquestionable symbolical significance, that of the winged griffin holding in its claws a cage containing a man.[14] Furthermore, almost throughout its course the mosaic presents in combination two or even three episodes of hunting or of desert life, arranged on what are implied to be different levels and given similar dimensions. There is no adequate perspective; in fact perspectives are sometimes the reverse of normal, as in the

101

99

14 I cannot share in this connection the views of Pace (1955, p. 66), who detected a 'hint of comedy' and consequently a realistic note, in this scene. It is not that touches of realism, even bold ones, are lacking in the corridor, as in the lamb used as a bait for the beasts of prey and the serving-man beaten by the soldier. But I consider that this illustration may rather be meant symbolically, by way of paradox, as if it were desired to call attention, in the midst of so much seizure of animals by human beings, to a potential fate recoiling upon man himself, confronted with a beast that had regained the upper hand. In this connection, *see* the article 'Grifo' in *Enciclopedia dell'Arte antica*, iii, Rome (1960), pp. 1062–3, where it is observed that in the imperial period the griffin symbolised Nemesis and a bibliography is appended.

scene represented at the south end of the corridor, where a small house is placed between a hunter and a tigress carrying off her cub. The procedure, therefore, of the great cylindrical records of history made during the central imperial period is distorted, incidentally following the methods illustrated by the reliefs on the Arch of Septimius Severus at Rome, by the comprehensive bird's-eye-view vision of the time, displaying very extensive panoramas, bounded by the line of landscape at the back and broken here and there by irregularities, all swarming with the encounters of men and beasts. The scenes are not accordingly descriptive of real environments, but the result of compositions wholly invented. 9

The casual nature of the narrative, in short, is undeniable. It is also clear that its structure, in content even more than in form, is derived almost exclusively from stock illustrations and the usual type of cartoon, without any concrete historical value whatever. Consequently, of all the efforts made (apart from the difficulty of that undertaken by L'Orange and Gentili, to identify Maximian in 101 the group with the old 'Tetrarch') to establish the great pavimental stretches of the corridor as a framework for any kind of coherent historical narrative, not one can be regarded as convincing. What is the subject, for instance, or the point, of the two terminal lunettes? 8

Pace describes as without 'sufficient foundation' the idea that they may signify the beginning and the end of the *venatio*, or the land of the hunt (Africa, Asia?), and the country for which the beasts are destined (Rome). He concludes with the more general identification of the goddess Earth (Ge). The two lunettes may really depict two regions or continents which supplied beasts for Roman entertainments. But it is not easy to ascertain which countries are meant, and in any case the answer to the question would be no great help to the present enquiry.

An alternative might be to recognise an organic narrative connection between the various scenes into which this wonderful mosaic is split up. It is worth noting, if only because scholars have not so far paid enough attention to this feature, that two fundamental divisions interrupt the continuity of the picture, episodic though it is. Almost exactly in line with the interior walls of the two long wings of the peristyle the sequence of events is interrupted by clearly marked breaks both in the background landscape and in the figures, so that the body of a boar, for example, is left incomplete, neatly cut off by the edge of that scene and conjoined with a tree-trunk in the next. This remarkable correspondence between the peristyle walls and the interruption of the mosaic narrative suggests that the corridor was originally conceived as the actual narthex of the basilica and consequently that its length was

Plans B, and C

limited by the nevertheless ample width of the four-sided portico to which it gave access. Clean breaks of this kind can be found in the picture near the north lunette, as above mentioned, and also near the south lunette with the figures of the 'Tetrarch group' and the start of a new landscape, the latter in front of a hunting scene in a marsh, to which 'Maximian' turns his back. 101

Hence ensues one feature of the narrative, but a feature that is not unique: between the north lunette and the first break we have various big-game-hunting scenes, in which soldiers only are engaged. In the central section of the corridor, between the first and the second break, there is a sequence representing successively the capture and transport of mostly harmless animals, their loading into a ship anchored in a sea full of differently coloured fish (composed of unusual glazed tesserae) which interrupts the background landscape; then, at the exact centre of the corridor, their unloading under the direction of some officials with Syrian staves and tetrarchal caps. Next in order, symmetrically placed, come the unloading of another ship, again in a sea which interrupts the landscape; the loading of the same ship (from the opposite end) with elephants and tigers; and the capture, partly in a marsh, of bison, hippopotami and rhinoceroses. Here occurs the second break. The third section opens with the group of the so-called Tetrarch, who, facing the south lunette at the end of the corridor, watches various scenes of the hunting and transport of wild beasts. The section closes with the picture of the griffin and the man imprisoned in a cage. Plan C 143, 98 99 7 101 8, 9, 102

A certain symmetry is therefore present in the figured strip and paralleled similarly in the background as follows: vegetation and landscape; first break; landscape with villas, sea, vegetal subjects, sea, landscape with villas; second break; landscape. Thus a further element is supplied which clarifies the purely external resemblance of the mosaic to the continuous historical narrative displayed on the great carved cylinders of earlier Roman work. Only one conclusion seems possible: the mosaic does not tell a story, which would demand a spatial and temporal dimension with a 'before' and 'after' imposing rhythm on the repeated appearances of the persons concerned, but constitutes a centripetal scene, tending to comprehensive presentation, where the central elements combine around the group of officials; while the two appendices of the corridor, marked off by the breaks, standing by themselves and differing in length, act like theatrical wings, closing the horizon at each end as in a panorama. Plan C 98 8

Moreover, if we turn from the general structure of the composition and its over-all concept of space to an examination of its planes, depth, colour, light and technique of tessellation, we are forced to conclude that this masterpiece in the corridor is the work of an artist participating, though with the originality characteristic of all outstanding masters, in the expressionist movement and chromatico-linear style peculiar to the art of the Tetrarchy and to that which followed it, without succumbing to the Constantinian court fashion of the 'fine style'.

The figures, in fact, are all given surface presentation, although, between one level and another, stylised elements of landscape, rocks, trees and bushes punctuate the abstract white background, and repeatedly create the altogether illusory effect of environmental depth. The now indestructible datum of two-dimensional or cubist parataxis is everywhere present. Notice, for example, the rendering of the carts: they are quite flat, lacking any indication of bulk (only two wheels), although the cages they carry are given full though very simple perspective. Again, six of the eight legs of the zebus drawing one of the two loaded carts are set on the same background plane. Look, too, at the capture of a bison: its hind legs touch the topmost foliage of a small tree (which from the spectator's viewpoint ought to cover the animal, and with far larger dimensions), while its tail sweeps the panorama till it is partially hidden behind some cypresses, which mark a much more distant area, beyond the beast's crupper as it struggles to escape. Look finally at the nearby capture of a tigress, where one of the *venatores* seems to be floating in the air in front of the left hind leg of the animal, though he is supposed to be standing on a plane farther back. The position is identical with that imagined during this same period by the artist of the *emblema* of the 'Good Shepherd' with his ewe, in the basilica at Aquileia. All these effects, and many others in the same mosaic, do not appear explicable, as Gentili maintains, by 'errors in interpreting the cartoons, with a consequent false rendering of perspective in the figures or groups of figures',[15] but are rather related, though still in fragmentary fashion, to an artistic outlook clearly illustrated in the practice of late antiquity.

Methodologically, the above examples apply to detail also: but such examples might be greatly multiplied. The characteristics in question, for instance, are natural consequences of the deliberate combination by the HUNT MASTER of a landscape which from the lowest level to the line of the horizon runs, apart from intervals of seascape, like a kind of bird's-eye view, and the human and bestial forms inhabiting the area thus defined but perfectly alien from it. The result, accordingly, resembles that of a photographic effect obtained by superimposing on a landscape individual figures all taken in close-up and of corresponding dimensions. The comparison helps us to understand how the decoration of the great corridor was inspired, substantially, by the new aesthetics of Plotinus, while the panorama as a whole remained secondary and of

102

7

7

137

15 Gentili (1959), p. 48.

ornamental significance, offering incoherent location to the personages or acting in a contrapuntal sense by occupying symbolically the empty spaces of an environment now distorted and not given any greater consistency by the very occasional use of stylised shadows of bodies in motion. Thus the examination of idiomatic syntax also helps to confirm that time is actually absent from the mosaic, with a consequent elimination of space. We have now to consider the grammar of the symbols, colour and light, and the poetry of colour and line.

This last, in the remarkable mosaic of the 'Hunt', is unique in summarising the whole taste of the beginning of the century. The exceptional vitality of the colour, in which form is achieved by means of a linear design the whole purpose of which is the bounding of chromatic areas, entitles us to recognise the author of this pavement as an artist of exceptional ability.

The palette of the HUNT MASTER, considered in its external relations, is first and foremost directly comparable with that of the masters of Aquileia, especially the one whom we shall identify (*see* Chapter VII) as the MASTER OF THE PORTRAITS. Two factors, however, gave the artist of Piazza Armerina an advantage over the latter. First, he undoubtedly possessed a more copious and refined taste. Second, he had at his disposal a more abundant supply of materials, because certain large workshops in Sicily, so near to Africa where their products were much in demand, must have had access to all kinds of stone. Consequently he displays a greater variety of colour, including some distinctly unusual tones which, by the very boldness of their juxtaposition, lend his work its first claim to originality. Reds from scarlet to deep crimson, sulphur yellows, violets and maroons of various shades, pinks, greys and greens of unprecedented subtlety, not to mention a revolutionary use of white, make up a repertory of hues which of itself constitutes a perfect example of the new art. *Fauve* colouring, familiar in modern times from the canvases of Matisse, Braque and Vlaminck, was not even here a caprice. The whole design, the entire composition of the HUNT MASTER, were functions of an avowed chromatic expressionism, without which his work would have sunk to the level of a pallid and pointless degradation of form. It seems, in short, that the artist was looking for something in pure colour, most evidently when, freed from the necessity to draw the outlines of the voluminous bodies of wild beasts and horses with reasonable fidelity to the model, he could give free rein to lyricism in treating elements of landscape with creative fantasy, and even more to the delineation, almost equal to that of a medieval tapestry, of the subtle and in themselves delicate variations which folds in clothing, *clavi*, *orbiculi*, protuberant metal ornaments, ribbons, shields and weapons can confer.

16 An interesting testimony to the diffusion of the didactic and idiomatic features of such representations of the Tetrarchs, which combine rather unexpectedly in the 'majesties' of the reliefs on the Arches of Constantine and Galerius at Salonika, is also provided by the watercolours executed by Wilkinson in 1859, after the subsequently lost pictures in the Temple of the Imperial Cult at Luxor, showing processions of soldiers and civil dignitaries of the Empire approaching the representation of the Tetrarchs. In this connection, *see* Monneret de Villard (1953). The dress of the Luxor figures, from the *campagi* to the tunics edged with all sorts of *clavi*, *orbiculi* and borders, clearly points to Egypt at the end of the third century. But the fashion was one which spread rapidly and lasted long throughout much of the Empire. It therefore reappears at Piazza Armerina, not only in the works of the HUNT MASTER but also in the lunettes of the *frigidarium*, in the *emblema* of the *tablinum*, and so on. Again, in a tomb at Gargaresh in Tripolitania (Pietro Romanelli, 'Tomba romana con affreschi del IV secolo d.C. nella regione di Gargaresh – Tripoli', in *Notiziario Archeologico del Ministero delle Colonie*, III (1922), p. 21 ss., ff. 8–9) the figures of the torchbearers are extraordinarily similar in expression and attitude, as well as in dress, to those of the slaves in the *frigidarium* lunettes at Piazza Armerina, while the shield-framed bust of Aelia Arisuth anticipates in important respects the resumption of proto-Byzantine mannerism in the age of Valentinian and Theodosius, not forgetting the special cultural influence of the Romano-Egyptian portraiture of Fayyum. Accordingly, it would seem necessary to set the date well into the fourth century. Similar considerations apply to the 'fine-style' figures, residually expressionistic, of the waiters from a Roman house on the Caelian now in the Naples Museum (Colini (1944), pp. 264–5, f. 222); and the scene of the parents on the arcosolium of the Tomb of Trebius Justus (Marucchi (1911), pls. 10–15; Cecchelli (1944), p. 135 ff.); etc. An individual specimen of the more striking continuation of this manner as seen in the *venatores* of the HUNT MASTER can be identified in the late octagonal and polychrome *emblemata* showing bearers of game and fruit; discovered during the laying of foundations for a new town hall at Constantinople and dating from the early fifth century. It is now in the local Archaeological Museum. The figures show signs of the neo-Hellenistic atmosphere still more evident in the mosaics of about the same date in

165

These last, incidentally, seldom if ever reveal a personality distinct from that of the rest; even as regards the slightly submissive and wholly typological fixity of the eyes, which conveys no suggestion of historical individuality, they are readily assimilated to one another within the wide context of fauna and flora that surrounds them. They are differentiated only by the functions of each and by the insignificant details of the conventional hunting scenes. They are diligent puppets made simply to provide support for an astonishing array of many-coloured garments which, often unrelated to the bodies they clothe, spread themselves gaily over the ivory background. Only 99 in the group of officials at the centre of the corridor, and in that of the so-called Tetrarch near the second break in 101 the sequence, does the artist show any sign of historical involvement, manifested among other phenomena by stylistic peculiarities that clearly suggest portraiture.

This exceptional flash of individual interest does not, however, contradict the general tenor of the work. It is centred on the expressive function of the unadulterated element of colour and line, sometimes, as in some of the hunters' clothing, accompanied by a clearly rhythmic and 7 iterative accentuation and always by the exploitation of 'negative relief' technique in the use of whites, reds and blacks on surfaces lacking volume and depth. The artist here repeats, in fact, that sentiment of conformity, not only in the civil but also in cultural and stylistic fields, which the Tetrarchy had adopted as an instrument of re-establishment throughout the Empire. The feeling was given typical expression in the famous and masterly 'Group of the Tetrarchs' at St. Mark's in Venice, carved in 100 porphyry, from which all trace of personality has disappeared, leaving only an awe-inspiring idea, the stereotyped symbol of an institutional conception of the State.[16]

It would, however, be unjust to forget that such formal preoccupations of the HUNT MASTER do not impede gestures and examples of great skill, occasional items revealing a versatility, an imagination and in short a poetic accomplishment and range which the subject of the hunt would undoubtedly tend to conceal and sacrifice. For instance, the extraordinarily supple articulation of line in the hunter carrying an ostrich aboard the transport is a true essay in 103 classicism achieved by novel means. The design of the two forms, certainly overlapping without any regard for volume, shows a facile elegance in the combination of the bird's many-coloured plumage with the shape, here evident, of the human figure. Notice also, close by, the exceptional formal vigour of the two soldiers bearing a captured wild boar, in which the iteration of the lineal element in their breeches and tunics is rhythmically counterpointed by the intersecting bonds that hold the animal motionless and even by the distant colonnade of the quadrangular arcade of the Imperial Palace, for which *see* Chapter XV. The colours are accordingly more fluid and brighter, and the drawing seems to concentrate progressively on a certain formal consistency. Lastly, an example of markedly Hellenistic influence on the Hunt Corridor may be seen in a provincial monument of contemporary or slightly earlier date, the mosaic remains of an apsed hall excavated at Gamzigrad in Dacia Ripensis (eastern Serbia) and containing *emblemata* depicting hunting scenes. The western *emblema* in particular, displaying three hunters and their quarry, has figures quite similar to those of the 'Great Hunt' in their frontal presentation and in the colouring of their dress and of the shield, though the facial expressions attempt the preservation or resumption of the traditional stamp. Mano-Zisi (1956, p. 79) observed that 'plasticity and modelling . . . are still preserved, but the painting is predominantly flat.'

17 The antelope captured near the bison in the 'Great Hunt' should be compared with the antelope to the left of the 'Good Shepherd' in the Aquileia Basilica (*see* Chapter VII), the stag of the pavement called the Worcester Hunt at Antioch, dated in the first quarter of the fifth century (Cf. Levi (1947), i, pp. 363–5; ii, pl. CLXXVII), and the goat of the Byzantine pavement at Qasr el-Lebia, datable from an inscription to the year 539. Cf. Goodchild (1957); Ward-Perkins (1958). It is quite clear that works belonging to four different schools of late antiquity, covering a period of about two centuries, shared a common stylistic development, of which the phenomena already noted of a lack of relation between the figure and its surrounding space are the integrating elements.

the villa in the background; likewise the refined elegance of composition in the various groups of soldiers and *venatores*, those for instance who have captured a rhinoceros and are trying to drag it out of the marsh, and those hauling an ensnared bison by the horns.

Incidentally, this last wonderful picture of a wild beast, and the one just above it showing the capture of an antelope, invite particular comment on the master's capacity for plastic synthesis. Though the forms of both creatures remain in a definitely two-dimensional environment, they are perceived with such evident longing for the restitution of volume, jointing and totality of structure in the organisms that a very highly individual attitude must be assumed in the mosaic work of every part of the corridor. The surfaces of these animals possess a wealth of solid geometry which is recognised with difficulty in the master's work, and only where one notices the existence of what we may call intermediate phases (e.g. those of the zebus drawing the cage on a cart, of certain horses and of the *venatores*, etc.) or different degrees of skill in the craftsmanship of the *tessellarii*.

Consequently, in seeking to trace the origins of the two prototypes, one cannot but infer that the artist was continually straining towards a progressively flatter representation, chromatically defined by weaker structural aims and wider concessions to colour. Most of the animal forms, in fact, show traces of inlaid framing, variously tinted, in which the significance of the organic bodily build is altogether missing. In this connection reference may again be made to the comparison suggested with the antelope of the Theodorean pavement (second section, south zone) at Aquileia, which proves stylistic resemblances between Theodore's artists and those of Piazza Armerina. The fleeing stag of the House of the Worcester Hunt from Antioch-Daphne and the late *emblema* of a goat in the Qasr el-Lebia basilica also afford useful comparisons, testifying to the formal stability of the same idiom until late in the sixth century.[17]

Such details, of which there are many in the Corridor of the Hunt, constitute, also, the most significant link with two other pavements in the villa, where the ideas of the HUNT MASTER can be traced. These are the *diaeta* of the 'Little Hunt' and the 'Circus Races' in the palaestra of the baths. The first is a wonderful version of the pseudo-continuous narrative of the Hunt Corridor in a co-ordinated scene of episodes of a *venatio*. It includes notes of historical realism in the conjunction of figures probably representing persons of rank belonging to the patron's family with others from the standard figurative stock of African cartoons already widely used in the 'Great Hunt'. In other words, the work shows greater fidelity to the customary sequence in mosaics of hunting

7

94

102, 9

94

95

96

97

104, 106

112

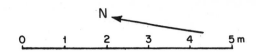

Villa of Piazza Armerina
Corridor of the Great Hunt

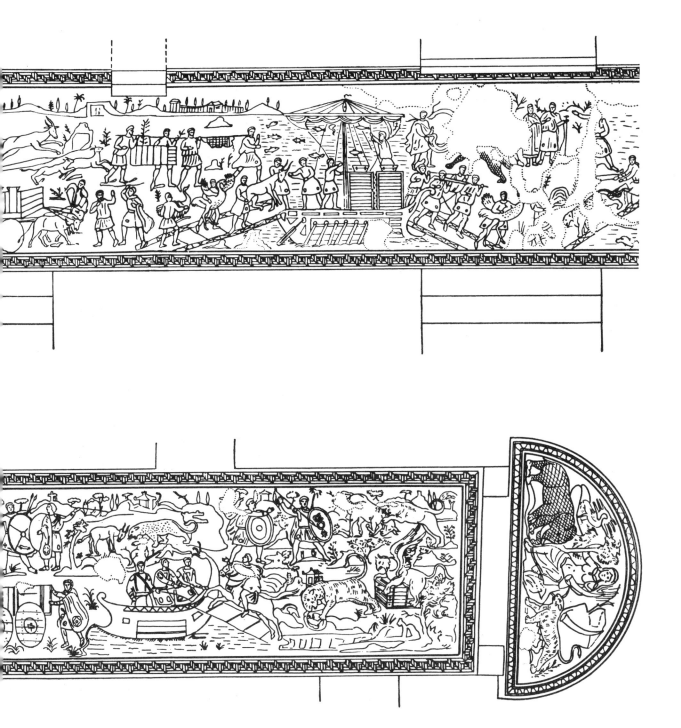

18 For certain of these mosaic pavements, *see* Chapter VIII. A special comparison has been instituted with the most ancient of the hunting scenes in mosaic, on three levels, which was excavated in 1955 at Cincari (Henchir Toungar). It is now in the Bardo Museum. The style is most meticulously realistic. *See* Salomonson (1965), p. 35, n. 18, pls. 14–16. On the other hand, this 'Little Hunt' has been regarded as the main source of certain larger or smaller mosaics, illustrating the spread in Italy of a taste, to great extent symbolical in its cult of *megalopsychia*, for African and Antiochene hunting scenes and their compositional variety. Finds in Roman Africa especially bear witness to this vogue. Attention is drawn in particular to the three large fragments found on the Esquiline, near the convent of Santa Bibiana, in 1903–4 now in the Capitoline Antiquarium (Blake (1940), pp. 116–7); to the mosaic of the Civic Museum at Chiusi (Levi (1935), pp. 89–90, f. 52); to the pictures of animals and Cupids in the Trilobate Hall of the Roman villa at Desenzano, of thoroughly late imperial stamp (*Bollettino del l'Associazione Internazionale di Studi mediterranei*, I, 1930; more recently, Ghislanzoni (1965), Beschi (1960), Degrassi (1960), and Zovatto (1963), pp. 27–31; and to the small fragments preserved in the Museo Opitergino (Zovatto, 1956; 1963, pp. 18–26). Nearly all these must be dated to the late or last years of the fourth century.

We are dealing with works by various hands, clearly derived from more skilfully executed models mainly based, with great compositional freedom, on traditional elements ('Killing of the Wild Boar', 'Netting of Antelopes and Trapping of a Bear', 'Hounds Pursuing Game', etc.), depending upon the space and the possibility of its organisation available to the craftsmen. The disappearance of shadows and the freedom of relations between the various figures that occur in these compositions are the most obvious features of a repetition relatively varied but by this time mechanically copied so far as significance of content is concerned, even when the models are much older. The 'Romanus' at Oderzo, for instance, may be compared with the scene of hare- and fox-hunting with greyhounds called *Ederatus* and *Mustela*, in the Bardo Museum, from the threshold of *oecus* No. 33 of the Laberii villa at Oudna (Gauckler (1910), no. 375).

The large fragments from the Esquiline in particular prove the permanence of success in the chromatic articulation and detailing of the figures, though accom-

produced during the central and late periods of the Roman Empire, especially in Africa, from El Djem to Oudna and Carthage,[18] where the distribution in superimposed levels perhaps indicates a further trace of the flattened and deformed vision of columns recording history in continuous narrative.

It is this pavement which reveals the traditional models to which the HUNT MASTER resorted for the great corridor. Here one cannot fail to recognise the lack of connection between the various groups, which the cartoons supplied in sets of not more than two or three and almost always on a uniform surface plane. But in the five levels allotted to alternate scenes, in no chronological order, of departure for the hunt, discovery and capture of game, struggles with and seizure of stags and wild boars, propitiatory sacrifice to Diana and feasting in the open air after the operation, it is clear that the artist intended some order in the composition, an original feature in the work of the HUNT MASTER. It actually forms the most conspicuous element in all Constantinian art, from the friezes of the Arch of Constantine onwards. The bringing together and centralisation of the key-moments of the business represented, the sacrifice and the banquet (like the unloading of beasts in the 'Great Hunt'), around which are set like a chaplet the events of the story, proclaim much more forcefully the intention to impose symmetrical order already observed in the 'Great Hunt'.

In this more readily identifiable compositional aim something more than an organic criterion of sequence is apparent. For it unquestionably takes for granted the Plotinian doctrine of perspective in an entirely temporal sense, and accordingly abandons the classical theory of events unified in a single representation, together with the continuous-narrative convention of the central imperial period, which had strictly followed the succession in time of historical occurrences. There is here already present the solution of the problem adopted in the Middle Ages in both west and east, whereby the climax of the event, whether a logical and chronological *consecutio* or a consecrated personage, was spatially centralised, the stages of the narrative framing the vision in a kind of radiant vista which required for its communication of the facts a spiritual fixity of contemplation summarising them *in unum*, starting either from their synthesis or from their *exitus*.

This 'Little Hunt' is also a brilliant lyrical exaltation of colour, with touches more lively and stylistically dramatic than those of its own greater model, possibly because the artist was able to concentrate more fully in handling so very much smaller a work. There are some examples of animals, such as the stags pursued till they finish in the net, in which he resumes his experiments with solid geometry panied by generally stiff and sometimes really clumsy drawing, even though there are occasional rapid and vividly expressive touches. Lübke *et al.* (1958, p. 419) date these works in the late third century, but they seem more likely to have originated in the second or third decade of the fourth. They can certainly not be referred to the sixth, as suggested by Rostovtzev, who relates the mosaics of Santa Bibiana to those of the palace of Theodoric at Ravenna. The second half of the fourth century appears preferable for the Desenzano scenes (Ghislanzoni (1965), p. 160) assigns them to the end of the third or beginning of the fourth; Roberti (introduction to Ghislanzoni, p. ix), to 330–40; Zovatto (1963, pp. 30–31), to the end of the third; Degrassi (1960, p. 72) to the end of the fourth; Beschi (1960, p. 547) to the first decades of the fourth). The evident preoccupation with realism in these scenes does not preclude, in the general conception of their decorative arrangement and in their stylistic characterisation, elements peculiar to the latest imperial epoch.

19 *See*, for example, the large mosaic of the same subject in the Archaeological Museum at Barcelona, attributable to the last years of the third century. Here the division into two planes appears simpler and attentive to traditional perspective. The dominant top section contains only the *spina* of the Circus, and the setting of the chariot race in the foreground of the lower plane completely dominates the whole composition. Or again, the more structurally complex relief of 'Chariot Racing in the Circus', now in the Foligno Museum, which nevertheless preserves, though it is closer to the mosaic mentioned in the text, a perspectival emphasis on dimension, once more in the race-track of the foreground. Another mosaic of circus racing with a perspective structure comparable with that at Piazza Armerina was found at Gerona and is now at Barcelona. (Cf. De Dios de la Rada (1880), p. 281 ff). It was presumably executed at the end of the third century by a certain Cecilianus (Reinach, S. (1922), p. 291, I). It may also be relevant to mention one from Auray, with a black background, preserved in the Lyons Museum (Lafaye and Blanchet (1909) I.1, no. 712), and the two African examples in the Bardo Museum at Tunis, originally at Dugga and Gafsa respectively (Gauckler (1910), nos. 540 and 321); the first named is of late workmanship, possibly in the middle of the fourth century, while the second is later still, in a local style by this time pre-Byzantine. The paratactical disorganisation of perspective arrangement brings about,

already noted in the cases of the antelope and bison of the 'Great Hunt'. But plenty of instances are also to be found where this method of treatment is replaced by more luminous variations, as in the bold 'brush-strokes' of white on the body of the dog following the fox to its hole. Workmanship of more meticulous virtuosity is certainly evident in the amazing variety of the trees, in the men's clothing, in the rural altar and in the details of the banquet (the *parapetasma*, the couches of the diners, the baskets of provisions), a common feature of iconography, and above all in the synthetic mounds of the landscape where the effusion of *fauve* colouring attains heights of genius, as in the fox's lair already mentioned. Consequently, here too the patrons' demand for portraiture is relegated to second place.

104

106

Notwithstanding concessions to the stricter requirements of narrative, similar remarks apply to the great hall, with apses facing its shorter sides, which has been identified as the Palaestra of the baths in the imposing aggregate of the villa. Here the Circus Scene of four-horse chariot racing includes human figures, the central *spina*, stands for the spectators, *carceres* and temples in a disconnected pattern of different perspectives, to some extent related to the compositional principle of the 'Great Hunt'.[19] Judging from the appearance of the *spina* of the Circus, the general view would seem to be bird's-eye; but the two levels, in which the chariots race, show at once the juxta-position on two parallel planes (both of the same size and both given foreground presentation) of the images that crowd the scene. On the other hand, the aisles and gates of the lateral stands on the two longer sides of the pavement are seen wholly integrated with the background in full perspective, as if viewed simultaneously by a spectator placed at the centre of the *spina*. Lastly, the same observation can be made in respect of the two curves at the short sides of the Circus. Integrated with the background and in full perspective, they represent in one direction the stand reserved for dignitaries – which has an extraordinary compositional and typological resemblance to the *Adlocutio* and *Congiarium* friezes of the Arch of Constantine – and in the other the *carceres* and three temples.

112

At least three different points of view, one external and distant, one external and overlooking the scene partly from one side, and one multiple, revolving and set at its centre, combine accordingly in a prismatic visual frequency in such a way as to appear actually to penetrate the objects represented. No earlier examples are known to exist in all Roman painting of such daring complexity and formal variety of perspective composition. Incidentally, the attitude in question is revealed also in the isolated groups and figures, representing chariots simultaneously from above and laterally (especially as in the detail of the

in a complex disposition similar to that at Piazza Armerina, a result arising from elements unquestionably more disjointed and erratic. The Dugga mosaic has a special bearing on the work here considered, owing less to fully frontal presentation of the charioteer Eros than to the precise correspondence of his dress and the *carceres* of the background with those at Piazza Armerina. The Eros charioteer, however, has a wreath of ivy suspended over his head.

A last, very late (fifth century) return to this type of illustration appears in the large mosaic of the Horkstow Villa, near Barton-upon-Humber, Lincolnshire, now in the British Museum (Hinks (1933), n. 36p, f. 124). *See also* Toynbee, Jocelyn M.C. (1962), n. 198, pl. 227, p. 202; (1958), p. 58 (b), n. I, pl. 22.

A superimposition of visual perspectives somewhat similar to that at Piazza Armerina, but very much later, is found in the well-known pavement of the so-called *Ecclesia Mater* of Tabarka (Gauckler (1910), no. 1021; *see also* Levi (1947), i. p. 617, f. 226), where all the possible projections and sections of the church are fused in a single pictorial plane.

20 Gentili (1957, p. 16) notes in this connection: 'The feeling for quality of space and perspective depth is still keen and warm in this marvellous group of chariots, one above the other. The composition is wedge-shaped, each vehicle being fully visible, since the legs of the horses and the wheels of the upper chariots barely touch the heads of the horses and charioteers below'. Yet, apart from the analysis of the composite perspective mentioned above, it is worth noting that at least one of the elements of this group seems clearly to have been inspired by previous monuments and given a different significance. *See* the detail of the fallen besieger in a fragment of the Arch of Septimius Severus at Leptis Magna in Berenson (1952), fig. 25 and already noticed in one of the scenes of the Synagogue at Dura Europos. The attitude is repeated in the figure of the defeated charioteer.

21 Pace (1951), p. 464.

naufragium[20]), or else simultaneously from below and from one side, with extraordinary effects of relief. In this connection the stylistic characteristics of the master closely resemble those of the other works here recognised as his.

Certainly the colour, compared with the *fauvisme* of the two Hunts, affords room for second thoughts, not so much with reference to the still very lively taste of the polychromy and to the daring juxtapositions, as in regard to its quality. It seems to have lost its crystalline character and also a certain tonal and expressive purity. Nevertheless, much of the work's poetic effect still relies on colour, so that although some of its reflected lights might seem to look back to the palette of the CARNAGE MASTER, the delicacy of the details of dress, the use of glazed cubes, the treatment of the horses' coats with streaks of colour, and many other particulars, prove that the dominant influence remains that of the Corridor of the Hunt. This judgment is confirmed, moreover, by an identical physical typology of the human figures, by similarity of movement in the animals and by the anonymity of expression in the faces.

The pavement of the great Trilobate Hall consists of four different commemorative mosaics, linked together by the minor scenes of the decorative border which separates the quadrangular central space of the hall from the three deep apses. As Pace has well observed,[21] its subject must be recognised as the 'Carnage of Hercules' rather than the story of his Labours. The historicity of the hero's several glorious enterprises is in fact here lost in the simultaneous presence of their total result – the 'Carnage'. The forms of the victims of his strength stand out as they draw their last breath against the ivory white background. The mosaic composition distributes their bodies in a fashion now devoid of the element of time. Most lie stretched in their death agony. The north apse displays the 'Glorification of Hercules', who stands naked, with the skin of a beast tied across his chest, and is crowned with laurel. The east, central apse contains the terrifying 'Giants Struck by Lightning', where the monstrous creatures are trying to tear from their bodies the deadly shafts in a paroxysm of dreadful but useless effort. The mosaic of the south apse presents one of the Hellenistic versions of the 'Dionysiac Myth of Lycurgus', that in which the Thracian king attempts to slay the maenad Ambrosia. In the minor borders, only partially preserved, synthetic illustrations of the myths of Daphne, Ciparisso, Hesione and Endymion complete the majestic decoration.

The perspectival conception of space is entirely absent also from this magnificent pavement, a fact particularly noticeable in the lunette of the 'Giants Struck by Lightning' and in the 'Carnage'. Here there is lacking even that

93, 11

10

108, 109

110

109

minimum of inclusive composition in the traditional taste which is just discernible in the other two lunettes. These however clearly show surface presentation of the figures and the abnormal proportions of the Hero's limbs. Above all, the decorative, nearly two-dimensional, abstract quality of the grape-gathering Cupids is obvious, forming a base for the scene of the 'Myth of Lycurgus'.[22]

It should be observed how, in the 'Carnage', men and beasts overlap, collide and compete with one another for space, carrying much further the aerial suspension, body on body, found in the Theodorean 'Good Shepherd' at Aquileia.[23] This mutual superimposition and invasion of free space was well understood by Pace,[24] who in this connection emphasised the CARNAGE MASTER's 'alienation from the principles of symmetry already rejected on theoretical grounds by the new aesthetics of Plotinus (vi, 7, 22). This attitude is responsible for the absence of composition, which is replaced by a distribution of masses dictated solely by the demands of space and adapted to the changing viewpoints of a spectator moving through the hall'.[25]

Similarly, a single rock on which the giant Enceladus crouches and a few shrubs scattered about the ivory background are the only scenic and environmental features (consequently 'denaturalised') of the toneless stage on which the fearful suffering of the Giants is played out. Their figures are all given surface presentation, without their position on three successive levels of the flattened space and the disordered agitation itself of their limbs creating the least hint of perspectival illusion. This result is accordingly achieved not so much by the use of the decorative partitioning border as by elimination of space. The frame acts like those of successive *emblemata*, providing an abstract and rhythmical reconstruction of environmental space – that for instance surrounding the Athletes in the pavement from the Baths of Caracalla (now at the Lateran), with which our Giants have been compared. The space eliminated, on the other hand, is that of the sequences themselves into which the aggregate of the elements of the ancient myth has been divided, abandoning the method of continuous historical narrative in an attempt to render each element independent of the other and to enable the spectator instantly to apprehend the various illustrative phases of the story.

At the Lateran, for example, the representation, though basically that of portraiture, has no 'historical' value but is a chronicle in itself didactic, lacking the time element. The temporal dimension, being absent, cannot be extracted in order to obtain spatial dissolution. It has, on the contrary, to separate the individual figures by the very act of denying them any mutual relations and any objective physical space. At Piazza Armerina the CARNAGE MASTER

22 It was not by chance that Pace (1955, p. 48) mentioned 'decorative intrusion' in this connection. I considered the possibility that the detail in question may have come from another workshop, possibly to be identified with that of the COURT MASTER, to be discussed later. But the remarkable differences subsisting between his Cupids and those of the 'Lycurgeia', in which the overflowing of the layers of polychrome tessellate still has the significance of chiaroscuro and is not simply chromatic, caused me to reject it. In any case, this is not the only incongruity to be found in the Trilobate Hall.
23 *See* Chapter VII.
24 Pace (1951), pp. 468, 469 and 471.
25 See the same idea differently expressed by Pace himself (1955, p. 52).

26 Pace (1951), p. 464.

27 Pace (1951), p. 463.

28 Galassi (1953), p. 372.

29 Pace (1951), p. 471.

30 The dramatic physical vigour of the Giants permits a reference to that of the far-famed 'Athletes' of the majestic mosaic fragments recovered from the pavement of the colonnades in the Baths of Caracalla and now almost all in the Lateran Museum (Nogara (1910), pp. 1–3). Of these twenty-eight lifesize figures, and of the twenty-six gigantic 'Portraits', much has been written concerning the date of their execution. It has been assigned by some, most recently by Levi (1949, p. 58), to the period of the building of the Baths, and therefore some time in the third century, and by others mostly to a later epoch, right up to the first decades of the fourth (Huelsen, Helbig, Nogara, Ippel, Blake, etc.). Although the cubes, except in the numerous cases of those repaired, are not of such a size as to ensure a late dating, the structure of the composition seems to point clearly to the last years of the third century at least, if not to the closing stage of the Tetrarchy. The repetitious and monotonous framing in double braids implies a taste by that time obsolete, with a subdivision of available areas too little differentiated. But the placing of the entire figure within the rectangle and the predominantly impersonal frontal rigidity of the colossal heads suggest the purely surface presentation of the single human form against a white, abstract background, lacking both depth and the time element, which is characteristic of the late Roman mosaic art prevalent from the start of the Tetrarchy. Those features also relate to the vogue for colossal statues which remained typical of that period. Various executants, of course, were responsible for these huge pavements. Their stylistic contributions were sometimes diverse. But they could always be unified in a tendency to linear representation, intent on contrasts of white and dark in bodies and clothing (see for example those of the Gymnasiarchs) and often resulting in pedantically stereometric shaping, with the whole muscular system of torso, arms and legs on view (photograph by Anderson, No. 24169), while at other times, especially in the case of Superintendents of the Games, careful attempts were made to restore classical attitudes and drapery (photograph by Anderson No. 24160). Again (photograph by Anderson No. 24167), the approach to the physical articulation of the Piazza Armerina Giants is closer in the attention paid to design, though it still remains very far from the stylistic result

tells a 'historical' story which includes the element of time even though the events themselves are legendary. Time is eliminated, by isolating the individual figures like monads, by abolishing any kind of relationship between themselves and between them and the environment, and by depicting each subject (excepting only the 'Myth of Lycurgus' with its more faithfully Hellenistic pattern) not only at the instant of the event peculiar to it but also in the simultaneous presence (already noted by Pace[26]) of the end of the vital *iter* of all – Hercules glorified, the Giants struck by lightning, the adversaries of Hercules slain. And that elimination of time is more than enough to eliminate space also, though at the same time connecting imaginatively all the features of the vast mosaic within the bounds of a decorative taste both versatile and refined.

The complete rejection in this monument of every classical convention is conspicuously proved, moreover, by the often violent distortion of the anatomy of individual figures, imposed, even though not finally resolved, in accordance with the principles of the most rigorously logical cubist parataxis. The muscular development, however powerful, required to express the superhuman strength of the sons of Earth and their agonised efforts would never of itself have required from the master's idiom such a contortion of compositional planes. The true impulse behind this extraordinary experiment must be sought in the *Kunstwollen* of this late Roman artist. It was no accident that he had inherited the style, aptly called tetrarchic, which is known best through the numerous colossal and (on coins) very small portraits of emperors upon which it has left its stamp, declaring the final and complete disappearance of every expressive effect reminiscent of classical plasticity. If Pace[27] and Galassi [28] are correct in asserting that the agitation of these twisted forms looks back to the Hellenistic Pergamene and Rhodian carvings (even on the iconographical plane there are exact parallels with the great frieze of the altar at Pergamum), it is certainly true that Pace himself[29] ventured to relate it, as a pictorial analogue, to 'that taste defined as stereometric in the sculpture which arose in the early fourth century, at the time of the Tetrarchs'. The masses of these bodies, he writes, 'project and are perceived in contoured volumes consisting of simple forms of geometrical type, modulated, so to speak, by their elements, each one of which seems to have a life of its own'.[30]

But it has also been remarked that those elements, without being thereby overwhelmed and betrayed, are accompanied in the five figures by attempts at further plasticity. It is no accident that even in modern analytical cubism the distortion of planes ends its structural research in the simultaneous vision of several parts of the same

110

10

109, 93,

109

attained by the CARNAGE MASTER. On the cultural plane, finally, analysis is helped by the feasibility of a comparison between these brutal 'Athletes' and the refined, graceful 'Girls at Exercise' of Piazza Armerina, undoubtedly of later date. The postures, the palms of victory, the crowns and the presence of supervisors of the contest all suggest a uniform epoch which could extend no further than from the early third century to the second half of the fourth. In any case, to sum up, the impersonality of the portraits itself is unquestionably enough to set them at a distance from the impressionism still prevalent in the Severan age and approximate them to the typical programmatic quality of portraits under the Tetrarchy and Constantine.

A period slightly anterior to that of the 'Athletes' from the Baths of Caracalla might be assigned to the heads of 'Athletes' from the Baths of Caracalla recovered from the extensive Aquileia Baths. These works are usually ascribed to a later date than that of the building (middle of the third century). The heads are more than lifesize, but still short of the dimensions of those at Rome, and reveal a continuing cult of personality in portraiture, with traces of psychological content. Stylistically they still retain residual classical form and some attempt at shading in their various chromatic touches. The cubes, on the other hand, are already much larger than those of the Roman Baths.

A final comparison may be made with heads of the athlete Nikostratos and another. Both were recovered in a damaged condition from the so-called Portico of Nicostratus in the House of the Porticoes at Antioch-Seleucia. (*See* Levi (1947), i, pp. 115–6). These finds, which are proved by archaeological evidence to belong to the Severan age, show the great fidelity to form that must have characterised the mosaic, which, as we have seen, was executed during the early decades of the third century in a Hellenistic region of strongly traditionalist outlook. The portraits of Nikostratos and his colleague exhibit a high degree of emphasis on character and an equal devotion to formal realism. An abyss separates them from the idiom of the Baths of Caracalla. Piazza Armerina, with better reason, is still more distant, having a more authentic expressive originality.

31 In the case of many of these figures, however, the model seems to have been well known to the artist and used in quite a long series of works, above all in the eastern frieze of the Altar at Pergamum. It is easy to identify other relations: for example, with sarcophagus

object, endeavouring, that is to say, to grasp the whole plastic corporeality by projecting it, disconnectedly, to the surface. In the pavements this aim, in harmony with that of glorifying the myth and with the almost homogeneous residue of classical form which can easily be detected in the work, combines to some degree the paratactical vision with the taste of the old Hellenistic style of chromatic gradation and tonal painting, drawing from these two sources a total effect unique and hitherto unknown in the whole history of ancient painting.

Paratactical vision, in fact, dislocates the supporting joints of the figures, preventing any kind of coherent rationality in the physical base. In the four Giants of the central lunette who face the spectator this result is particularly noticeable in the shoulders, where, as also in the Pergamene examples which the master certainly had in mind, the greatest effort is being made, and to a less extent at the groin, where the muscular system of the thighs begins. But the most original illustration is certainly provided by the last Giant on the right, seen from behind, who is trying to pluck out the shaft fixed in the middle of his back. Around the titanic torso, presented in a three-quarters profile that takes in the anatomical zone running from the left breast and the ribs below it to the spine, the arms and thighs are freely disposed. That zone is adjoined on exactly the same plane by the rest of the back and of the gluteous muscles converging in two very bold curves. The thighs are normally proportioned, entering the upper part of the body after a forced defensive twist. The left arm, flattened and with no indication of volume, rises to protect the head, while the right arm, straining to pluck out the bolt, is drawn in an excessively wide arc at the height of the shoulder, turning an organic bodily movement into a boneless alignment of the limbs with the surface. This figure reveals not the slightest resistance from the old anatomical conventions, so that the new idiom expresses without reserve, but also perhaps without cultural control, the artistic vision of the master.[31] With the breaking down of the bodily articulations the single, juxtaposed elements are brought to the surface. It is natural and significant that, in consequence, they should retain much less energy in motion than the figures of the other Giants. But the strength of this form, disjointed as it is, is revealed in unrestrained tension of colour and line, singularly neo-baroque in feeling. It proclaims with more obvious freedom the master's pictorial outlook, which was not fully investigated by Pace in his stylistic analysis.

The function assigned to colour is in fact decisive in defining the art of the CARNAGE MASTER; for colour is called upon both to express the moral significance and the figurative taste of tetrarchic expressionism, and to bring back into the orbit of the court culture of the most mature

108

414A in the Galleria delle Statue of the Vatican Museums and with the relief of the 'Battle of the Giants' by Aphrodisias, No. 1679/571–572, in the Archaeological Museum at Istanbul, both of the second century. Finally, an exact analogue can be seen in a detail of the architectural frieze represented in a mosaic fragment at Antioch (Levi (1947), i, pp. 140–1; ii, pl. XXVI, a, c).

32 Pace (1955), pp. 53–4.

33 In this connection Riegl's discerning remarks (*Industria* . . ., p. 223; *Arte*, p. 185) may be quoted: 'In these late Roman mosaics the most disagreeable impression made, for example in the treatment of the nude, is not the alternation of many different colours set one beside the other . . . but rather the failure to achieve chromatic unity, since each streak of colour is significant in itself. In other words, the object here as everywhere else in Roman art is isolation, not combination. A great deal of this painting remains polychrome, not pure chromaticism. It is an indelible feature of the tactile conception'. Riegl based this general view on certain mosaics of the fourth and fifth centuries, later than those of Piazza Armerina, such as 'Combats between Gladiators and Beasts' in the Galleria Borghese, vaults in the Mausoleum of Constantina and decorations in S. Maria Maggiore, etc. These were very far from the exceptional tonal unity of the CARNAGE MASTER and therefore display, as compared with the 'pure chromaticism' of the Byzantines, a complexity of colouring which appeared to Riegl fragmentary, and in a sense really was so.

34 Some examples of this technique have already been noted in the 'Athletes' from the Baths of Caracalla, now in the Lateran Museum.

35 Gentili (1950), p. 310.

Constantinian 'fine style' the remodelled remains of the formal Hellenistic tradition in their plastic significance[32].   11 Ample fields of warm, bright colour are punctuated by short, neat strokes of shading that only partially, and mostly in the faces, attains the divisionist character of this idiom,[33] the capacity to tone down being second nature in the master's *Kunstwollen*. The gradation is condensed at different depths of the colour used, almost as though contrived by a series of isometric lines, and reconnects the dissected zones and limbs in a new formal synthesis, often resorting to articulations frayed out into crenellations, so as to alternate cubes from different fields of colour and thus create a kind of marginal tessellar reticulation with the precise effect of illusionist shading.[34]

Gentili had already noted that these figures 'still retain a look of reality and acquire volume through the gradual merging of one colour into another. This expedient, through the fusion of shades and of other shadows, achieves sculptural effects, while the composition of the faces is governed by an impressionist tendency. Nevertheless, a principle of schematisation can already be foreseen. . . .'[35] Actually, in the 'Giants', as in the other apses, the faces show a highly developed function of line,   10 with streaks whose colours are in general less merged than those of the bodies. This feature, too, having originated in the first manifestations of expressionism, whether of court or catacomb, was to return in all subsequent painting, including Byzantine (where, however, the handling of colour underwent a profound transformation), and persists in the revivals of classicism. It will suffice in this connection to look at the perhaps somewhat earlier faces of the ceiling-fresco in the hall of the Palace of Helena at Trier: though they constitute one of the most evident   157, 159 examples of the courtly 'fine style', they retain in the rendering of the facial anatomy a more marked and self-sufficient stamp than appears in the other parts of the body.

Compared with the Gigantomachy, the 'Carnage' is inspired by a less agitated formal tension, but in no way falls below the masterly style of the 'Giants Struck by Lightning'. The colour, which here also fuses in a wonderful tonal unity despite its extensive divisionism and the wider variety of the tints displayed in the forms of warriors and animals, includes ranges of extraordinary beauty, though avoiding all crude emphasis. The beasts' hides are rendered in very numerous and carefully calculated tones of grey, red, ochre and maroon, occupying broad, variegated areas, interrupted and graduated by softly and subtly toned stripes which accentuate, reveal and hollow out the surfaces, exposing them to an ever-changing distribution of expert relief and shadow, and defining with the greatest skill the structures of physical framework.

The general syntax of the forms – as also, incidentally,

in the lunettes of the 'Glorification of Hercules' and the 'Myth of Lycurgus' – does not appear systematically controversial, considering the traditional Hellenistic structure. Yet it can be asserted that not even here, though there are fewer examples of out-and-out cubism, does the master repudiate his own cultural origins. It might even be said that the CARNAGE MASTER is at his most characteristic in the general traits of the 'Carnage', which lies halfway between the idiomatic audacity of the 'Giants', which perhaps never developed further, and the ultimate resurrection of the court style, in the traditional spirit, of the two lateral lunettes.

110

109

In the first place there exist, even in the 'Carnage', details of figures in which one cannot help noticing the desire for unaccustomed formal solutions, within the interpretation already described of paratactical cubism. In the north-east angle of the hall, for instance, the unhorsed Thracian knight shows much of the body (head and trunk) dislocated and twisted; they are treated with the same series of colours as the bodies of the Giants. Similarly, in the south-east angle, the stricken horseman exhibits a remarkable torsion of the back. In this last case the very strained and distorted chromatic handling, though no later retouching can be discerned, would lead one to suspect the unsupervised meddling of a less expert hand.

11

The figures of this extraordinary legend, represented simultaneously in their *exitus*, are the Mares of Diomedes and the Thracian Knights, the Nemean Lion and the Marathonian Bull, the Lernean Hydra and the Serpent of the Hesperides, three-bodied Geryon, the Erymanthian boar and the Arcadian hind. All were inherited from a refined civilisation and reveal to a large extent their derivation from old iconographical themes adapted from the classical repertory, though they receive a considerable increase of vigour from the concretion of colouring matter, from its density and from its thickness, all of which in themselves make for originality in the treatment of form. A less agitated but nonetheless animated and dramatic parataxis, composed within the limits of strict equilibrium, tells a story raised to philosophic dignity in the exaltation of the divine hero who teaches mankind how to break the bonds of matter. Thereby it expresses a revaluation of physical being, almost a recovery of compassion for the dignity of the flesh, translated into terms of line and colour, to which the expressive spirituality of the second half of the preceding century had been indifferent. It must again be stressed, however, that the colour in this case was not *fauve*, and therefore did not permit the brilliance which chromatic feeling often promoted in late antiquity and hence among the Byzantine *musivarii*; in other words, the brilliance of a metaphysical significance, of a direct reproduction of unearthly lustre or of the splendour of paradise.

93

The pigmentation, as stated in the case of the 'Giants', is earthy, warm and compact. It is generally fused in the interests of unity, in such a way as to express with dark intensity the revival of an ancient, highly sophisticated experience. Characteristic details are those of the right hind leg of the Nemean Lion, a testing ground for a range **11** of colours starting from various shades of greyish green and proceeding to ochre, pink and bright yellow; or again, the Marathonian Bull, where the powerful and **93** extremely subtle outline presents the neck in perspective and is lit up by various tones of grey and green of rare beauty. The same strong indications of bodily volume and figurative line reveal the culmination of the art of the CARNAGE MASTER, reached through the careful management of selected tints and the rejection of crude colours and staccato touches. The taste is baroque but perceptive and full of the new spatial vision, which in a climate of spiritual and political restoration avoids those manifestations of atonal chromatic sentiment which belong to the now distant period of the Tetrarchs.

The CARNAGE MASTER's reinterpretations of Hellenism are further substantiated, though perhaps with a less happy vigour of expression, in the lunettes of Hercules **10** and Lycurgus, where traditional taste is illustrated not **110** only in chromatic conjugation but also in figurative outlines classically inspired though in a spatial context permitting the flattest possible representation. This return to Alexandrian canons, unquestionably promoted by the renewal of imperial unity under Constantine, enabled the master to bring the multicoloured courses of the mosaic more clearly under the control of the plastic function of light. He did so by correlating the series maroon-violet-green-yellow-lilac-red-carmine and its reverse order, as in the legs of Hercules; or yellow-green-black, as in the spirals of vine leaves in the Lycurgus mosaic; or lastly carmine-pink-ivory white, as in the figures of the Cupids (where this series is directly related to the plastic function of light) so as to achieve a tonal gradation which defines by means of shadows the traces of volume perceptible in their bodies.

Such details might raise the question whether, if archaeological considerations are ignored, the decoration of the Trilobate Hall was one of the very first undertaken at the villa, thus enabling us to date it in the last years of the Tetrarchy, or whether it belongs on the contrary to a more advanced stage of the great enterprise, in which case it would be placed towards the end of the reign of Constantine.

This indeed is among the most difficult problems raised by the Sicilian villa, owing to the co-existence of elements and factors which, so far as they can be interpreted through the limited philological resources available, would appear to contradict one another. In the first place it is generally recognised that the situation of the hall and *xystus* within the plan of the whole villa, and the structure of their walls at the apses and ellipses, suggest a date somewhat later than that of the remainder. This opinion appears the more persuasive if, as Dyggve has suggested, the hall and the *xystus* are identified as a palatine *basilica Herculis*, open to the sky.[36] Secondly, the existence of a Constantinian 'fine style', which may be related in many of its aspects to the manner of the CARNAGE MASTER, and exemplified in monuments ranging from the 'Seasons Pavement' of the Constantinian villa at Antioch to the ceiling frescoes of the hall of the Palace of Helena at Trier, tends to confirm the belief that the CARNAGE MASTER was not an artist of such partly traditional taste as flourished under the Tetrarchy, but an innovator of later date working with ideas of his own in the courtly atmosphere of the age of Constantine. If so, a dating of the Trilobate Hall pavement in the third or fourth decade of the fourth century would lead to a critical conclusion entirely different from that which would identify the master as the first in time of the *imaginarii* employed at the villa.

As already stated, this hypothesis is opposed by certain considerations of varying acceptability. According to some authoritative interpretations the Herculean theme of the pavement, for instance, would be difficult to explain except on the assumption that it belongs to the age of Maximian. In particular, certain details of the critical judgment passed on the master would militate against the late dating suggested.

The CARNAGE MASTER's tradition, essentially Hellenistic though tending towards formal innovation, is expressed, as I have said, in an at least partial rejection of the most decisive revolutionary feature of tetrarchic taste, that of colour. The artist yielded, creatively to be sure, to the paratactical vision and expressionist idiom wherever he felt entitled to do so. Thus we find dissolution of space, elimination of shadows and discarding of plastic form in the scene of the agony of the Giants; dissolution of space and flattening of the bodies in the 'Glorification of Hercules', in the Lycurgus mosaic, in the central zone of the 'Carnage' and even in the borders connecting the latter with the apses. (*See*, for example, the border displaying the myths of Hesione and Endymion, where to the flatness of the female figure – undoubtedly copied from a statue – there corresponds some paratactical licence in the male body, and above all the spatially abstract placing of the dog, set against a bright background without depth, flattened and apparently condemned to fall into the void so as to preserve the perspectival illusion – the only instance of it in so much distorted two-dimensionality – revealed by the three-dimensional design of the mound,

19, 20,
147, 148, 152
157–9

108, 109

110
93, **11**

36 Dyggve (1957). *See* also, for the dating of the Trilobate Hall, Lugli (1963), *passim*, although the author does not share Dyggve's qualifying hypothesis.

which is already pre-Byzantine in its treatment of pattern, as will appear in the Hellenistic lunette in the Chapel of S. Aquilino at Milan.) But the artist excluded from the orbit of his otherwise impartial figurative culture that chromatic revolution which is represented in so many other pavements at Piazza Armerina. **29**

In more positive terms, the CARNAGE MASTER accedes to the demands made by chromatic expressionism on the methods of contemporary painters. which is actually deepens and raises to new heights of significance. He condenses and segments the tonal blending in an individuated series of aligned tints, which elsewhere disguises the aim of residual plasticity which he originated by granting independence to the separate colours composing it, in accordance with his own taste for chromatic juxtaposition. But actually he did not welcome the atonal freedom of such polychrome contiguity, a peculiarity, for example, of the almost contemporary (in fact slightly older) masters of the Theodorean Basilica at Aquileia.

Here we meet the argument against dating the master to the age of Constantine. It points to his chromatic (in the last analysis tonal) taste as indicating a contemporary unawareness of the new achievements of expressionist colouring, and to infer from that circumstance a cultural lacuna and a stage of traditional conformity unconscious of fresh developments. But it may safely be asserted, on more reliable evidence, that the lack in some respects of the very special feeling for colour preponderant among painters outside the court circles of this age and of that immediately preceding it was certainly not, in the case of the CARNAGE MASTER, the result of his having been active in any earlier period, but was due rather to deliberate originality of choice at a later date.

The master's genius is grounded, in fact, upon his attainment of a kind of 'chromatic plasticity', combining miraculously and, as it seems, with a success hitherto unprecedented and perhaps never more completely achieved, the triumphs of expressionism and of the paratactical cubism of the African school with an innate love of classical form in its nearest manifestation, that of the Hellenistic baroque which in the Mediterranean East had been for many decades the prevailing fashion, and was now often hard and lifeless. The continuance of this mode throughout the fourth century, as for instance in the great outburst at Antioch recently investigated with such brilliance by Levi, was no accident.

I mentioned earlier in this connection the phenomena of chromatic shading and tonal painting, and I must now justify the reference. The achievement of what I have called 'chromatic plasticity' was originally based not so much on the old Hellenistic technique as on the capacity to revive its taste compatibly with the new demands of vision and idiom matured under the Tetrarchy. The artist under consideration was capable of the shading directed to plastic illusion and also of tonal fusion. But he applied and relied upon the former gift less by a blending of tints passing imperceptibly one into another than by an organic succession of fields of colour. These fields were eventually composed in dissociated, but not for that reason subverted, proximity. They accordingly permitted assertion of the cubist structural vision within (a) a conception of space approaching the two-dimensional, (b) an idiomatic handling of light and shade which in its own way translated into pictorial terms the 'negative relief' of sculpture to which Riegl called attention, and (c) the kind of superficial and dissociated treatment of colour obtained by expressionism. The success of this experiment was total and striking.[37]

Now this 'chromatic plasticity', historically speaking, could imply either a continued belated adherence to ancient aesthetic theory, or an anticipation of new syntheses, provided only that developments of taste and pictorial technique proved to be reversible. Fulfilment of that condition, however, can be ruled out, since it is universally agreed that limited 'returns' to classicism, such as post-Gallienan realism, the Constantinian 'fine style', Valentinianist mannerism and Theodosian 'subtlety', cannot be considered as indicating reversibility of the tendency of the period. If the last-named movement in particular illustrates in its surviving monuments an almost complete preservation of the new chromatic taste already in vogue, so that the return to classicism involves nothing more than the attempt to recover logical composition, plasticity and the ancient formal freedom,[38] then the peculiarities of the CARNAGE MASTER's art may appear diverse but not contradictory. His traditionalism is indicated by his choice or exclusion of certain chromatic effects. But his form, his conception of space and the placing of his figures and areas of colour are clearly the result of a truly innovating creative audacity.

Certain Roman monuments (one of which may certainly be dated in a period very close to that of the CARNAGE MASTER) prove that a considerable range of stylistic influences can be traced back to the highly individual work of the great Piazza Armerina artist. Examples are the inlaid marble slabs of the Basilica of Junius Bassus, variously attributed to the years 317 and 331,[39] and the large mosaics of gladiatorial combats removed in 1934 from the peristyle at Torre Nuova to the Galleria Borghese.

The *opus sectile* was by no means a new departure for Constantinian Rome. Specimens of it survive, for example at Pompeii, dating from as early as the first century, and in

13, 113

114–6

37 I am not sure whether Galassi, in his cursory reference to the 'vigorous plasticity of some of the Piazza Armerina figures', meant, as it would appear, what I have called in connection with the CARNAGE MASTER 'chromatic plasticity'. It is, however, quite probable that the two definitions relate to the same unclassifiable aspects of the master's art. Pace, too, regarded his personality as exceptional but 'very difficult to classify'.

38 In this connection the Constantinople mosaics, for which see Chapter XV, may be regarded as exemplary. But supporting instances can also be found in the West. 'The Mosaic of the Nereids' in the Casa dei Dioscuri at Ostia may be compared with some of the illustrations by the masters successively employed at Piazza Armerina. In both these and the works of the CARNAGE MASTER, however, there is evident the new function of colour significance, containing and defining form, which would be handed on to Byzantium.

39 The various datings result from the doubts long felt about the date of the Basilica as between the time of the first Bassus, consul in 317, and the second, probably a relative of the first, who was consul in 331 and after conversion to Christianity was given a very famous tomb, the so-called Tomb of Junius Bassus, built in 359 and now beneath St. Peter's in the Vatican. In this connection *see* Krautheimer (1938), pp. 64–5, and Gerke (1936).

40 The very clear symmetry of the composition, extended even to the structure of the figures, is such as to make much of the illustration which it covers conform with an ideal curve towards the centre. This feature too exemplifies the now customary centripetal hierarchy, developed in the course of semi-deification of the personage honoured. The dark marble background throws into relief the figures of the consul and the four charioteers of the circus factions, which are brought to the surface in a fashion still more abstract than that of mosaics with a white background. The form of the horse of the first charioteer on the right slightly overlaps that of the consul, which, together with the two horses of his car, is clearly reminiscent of the winning charioteer Eros in the Bardo mosaic from Dugga (see Note 19 above). A further interesting comparison may be made with the mosaic fragment displaying the charioteer Quiriacus, preserved in the Louvre and probably of the late fourth century. A prototype, admirable for its symmetry and skilful perspective, even though it may be dated in the middle of the third century (Parlaska (1959 b), pp. 86–8, pls. 84–7), can be seen at Münster Sarmsheim in the mosaic of the solar car, seen from below and framed by the signs of the zodiac. Closely similar, too, is the very much later Monument of Porphyry recovered from the Hippodrome and now in the Archaeological Museum at Istanbul.

Hellenistic art earlier still. But most of such extant works are to be ascribed to the fourth century. Consequently the inlays from the basilica of the above named consul, now shared between the Palazzo del Drago and the Museo dei Conservatori, are only the items of most immediate figurative interest in a repertory that has left considerable traces or widespread memories in other Roman buildings, both Christian and pagan. The four remaining inlays are unquestionably due to various hands. A Hellenistic artist, deaf to the most urgent problems of the day, was certainly responsible for the Palazzo del Drago sample, with its lavish decorative use of Egyptian subjects and the myth of 'Hylas and the Nymphs' above; its composition is different from that of the Campagna mosaic now at the Hermitage in Leningrad. A craftsman probably of the Syrian school, and perhaps at a later date, produced the 'Consular Triumph'[40] where the typology of the faces and the garments worn recall the art of Dura Europos and Palmyra. Finally, the wonderful arabesque design and disciplined chromatic fantasy of the two slabs depicting 'Tigers and Calves' at the Museo dei Conservatori bear witness to the eminence of a skill employing many of the features of the CARNAGE MASTER's original idiom, though not always at the same level of accomplishment.

The two last-mentioned items represent in each case a tiger, one turned to the right and one to the left, seizing the crupper of a bovine creature. The technical methods of these marble *crustae* are such as to render it difficult to suppose that the stylistic outcome can be referred to traditional means. This circumstance, which cannot of course be regarded as decisive, nevertheless seems appreciable in the aesthetic character inherent in the material – strips of marble in slabs of varied chromatic texture dependent on the varying streak in the mineral aggregate. It suggests the unbroken surface of a uniform area of colour, its stratified variations being seldom capable of meeting the requirements of grading and shadow which in classical representation give a naturalistic appearance to the image. It is not by chance that the abovementioned inlay of 'Hylas and the Nymphs', with its clearly Hellenistic compositional structure and its visible aim at classical definition of form, presents the effect, although by a variety of accompanying factors, of a distressingly perverse absence of relief.

The two tiger panels, however, from the hand of an artist by no means subject to the dictates of tradition, though interested in a revival of plastic form, shows that a highly skilled draughtsman's restitution of three dimensions to the figure, even where the composition contradicts his achievement with two (notice the artificial postures of the two animals, with three of their four legs on the same side of the prey, in the plane between the latter and the

113

13

spectator), can achieve, however discontinuously, a most extraordinarily powerful effect of allusive plasticity, in a design executed with strips of serpentine marble rich in deeply expressive synthetic stylisations. In the two tigers this result is so conspicuous as to confer on the pictures an exemplary quality of style, even though the bovine creatures appear both drained of colour and in general poorly endowed with form. In fact, the depiction of the beasts' hides, so representative of their physical organisms, and that of their heads as fantastic masks, are enough to enable a verdict of unconditional admiration to be passed on these two items. It seems quite feasible, therefore, on the strength of such considerations, to relate to 'chromatico-linear plasticity' shown in the animals' images to the 'chromatic plasticity' revealed in the work of the CARNAGE MASTER, whose indications of form are based on the rendering of tonal gradations of colour laid on, nevertheless, in a marvellous series of mosaic courses producing a design simultaneously intelligible and aesthetically moving.

The precise chromatico-linear definition of anatomy by the ARTIST OF THE BEASTS in the Basilica of Junius Bassus is certainly not exactly paralleled in the large mosaic pavements of Torre Nuova, depicting 'Gladiatorial Combats' and 'Combats with Wild Beasts'. Unfortunately, when these compositions were transferred to the Casino Borghese they were so drastically restored, with very extensive refacing, that any confident assessment of their dates and original formal standard has been rendered almost impossible. But arguments based on the costumes and the inscriptions identifying the gladiators make it very difficult to date these works before the fourth century,[41] while at the same time the entirely different sizes of the tesserae remove their period from that of the large pavement of the 'Athletes' of the Baths of Caracalla.

114–6

111

Even apart from the pitiable state to which the work was reduced by later mosaic repairs, the dramatic vivacity of the compositions, the somewhat artificial attempts at naturalism and the attention paid to details of clothing and armour are not enough to raise the artistic level of these pavements to adequacy. They are poorly executed even if often fanciful or copied from models of considerable importance. These bloody and ferocious conflicts, however, recall in some ways the taste of the Piazza Armerina 'Carnage'. But they do so only on account of their cultural *milieu*, any stylistic comparison being of course unthinkable. Still, consider the harsh vigour of the forms of both men and beasts, in their death agony or already dead; the awkward attitudes of the fallen, their limbs apparently boneless and crushed, indicating, as Rocchetti has observed, 'the last moment of the games', and significantly resembling the last moment of the Labours of Hercules as represented

41 *See* Blake (1940), p. 113; Rocchetti (1961). Riegl (*Industria* . . ., p. 223) cites these mosaics in support of his theory that in late imperial mosaic work 'the greatest possible indifference was shown to "animation" (*Lebendigkeit*).'

in the 'Carnage';[42] and also a certain technique (obviously learnt, not original) in the laying of the tesserae in strata, streaks and indentations, which reveals an inclination to solid geometry in the nevertheless unquestionably flat rendering of the images. All these factors prove that the tendency illustrated with such genius by the CARNAGE MASTER found keen exponents at various levels in tetrarchic or Constantinian Rome.

Having thus defined the personality of the CARNAGE MASTER, we must next inquire what other works, if any, should be attributed to him. The question, though controversial, would appear to be easier to answer than those already discussed.

Pace believed the artist to have executed the 'Animal Heads' of the peristyle, the 'Orpheus' of the *diaeta* and, at a later date,[43] the 'Acanthus Spirals and Animals' of the *xystus* ellipse. It is my opinion, however, that only the decoration of the Trilobate Hall can be attributed to the CARNAGE MASTER with complete confidence. The peculiarity of his conception of space and of his chromatic tonality does not in fact seem to recur in any other pavement at the villa, which is dominated by different artistic views and notions of space, as well as by entirely diverse methods in the employment of colour.

128–30

Nevertheless, the master does not stand alone, nor is his work isolated in the total area of the great mosaic undertaking. The Cupids of the Lycurgeia, though not by him, are brothers of those engaged in grape-gathering and fishing in the *oeci* facing the *xystus*. (The chromatic structure of this last reveals no interest in grading and shadow; its merits are exclusively those of expressionism.) Moreover the Lycurgeia Cupids are linked with those of the *oeci* by a decorative accent similar to that of the vine-spirals or the surrounding marine fauna in the latter work. Accordingly, within the general baroque framework of all these ornamental fields, it seems perfectly justifiable to recognise a connection between two features: first, the sumptuous interlacing pattern, a superfluous but most elegant piece of work, which in the pavement of the elliptical *xystus* combines the vigorous theme and feeling of a complete early medieval bestiary with a luxuriant, many-coloured growth of acanthus; second, a whole series of mosaics which repeat in almost all parts of the villa a traditional decorative taste, frankly of the court and mythological. Consequently, if, as already anticipated, this very extensive ascription – which may of course refer to a whole workshop lacking the dominant personality of a single *imaginarius* rather than to a single craftsman – should appear acceptable, then few other *lithostrota*, but some of great importance, would be found, owing to an evident highly personal touch or to a no less evident supervising hand, unrelated to this third undertaking, which I shall call that of the COURT MASTER.

121

42 Rocchetti (1961), p. 82. The author also stresses (p. 104) 'the baroque manner of disorderly physical vigour' and (p. 105) the 'composition . . . predominantly plastic'. But he makes no comparison with the Piazza Armerina mosaic. These illustrations, however, are very far in their emotional effect from those of the overthrown Thracian horsemen in the Piazza Armerina 'Carnage', extremely daring as these are, though quite different in their formal coherence. The body of the fallen Astivus, for example, may be compared with that of the horseman in the north-east corner of the 'Carnage'. Similar considerations apply to the two *emblemata* of gladiators in the Archaeological Museum at Madrid (Reinach, S. (1922), p. 285, 3 and 4).
43 Pace (1955), p. 93. And in a previous passage (1951, p. 471).

The work of this craftsman is probably to be dated about the third or fourth decade of the century. Hence the problem of chronological relations between his production and that of the CARNAGE MASTER, to which Lugli's study of the building itself would tend to assign a later date. As the other masters who succeeded the COURT MASTER were active in the second half of the century, consideration of these artists at any rate should be postponed. Nevertheless, for the sake of a more orderly arrangement of this chapter it appears preferable to proceed with study of them without any break in continuity.

In comparison with the CARNAGE MASTER, the COURT MASTER, as already stated, had a very highly developed taste in decoration.

Whereas in the Trilobate Hall an artist of unprecedented genius created a world of epico-dramatic events isolated in the sudden tragedy of their doom, the works of the COURT MASTER present a gay, unbroken confusion of images. Animals and plants, creatures and elements, form a repetitive maze of immense vitality, substituting for the hackneyed personifications of myth an entranced contemplation of the myriad shapes of a single reality. While the figurative power of the CARNAGE MASTER can fairly be said to have something of Michaelangelo's spirit, the COURT MASTER transforms the simple pretext of mythological or conventional interest into an opportunity for the display of a multitude of decorative symbols and supports. These in themselves achieve the dignity of a pictorial result, illustrated, for instance, by the jocularity of the 'Fishing Cupids' and 'Grape-gathering Cupids' in the rooms leading to the *xystus* (*oeci*), the peristyle (hall) or the great corridor (entrance hall with porch and exedra), and by the chambers of the 'Boy Hunters' (cubicle), the 'Boy Charioteers' (vestibule) and the 'Musicians and Actors' (cubicle) adjoining the great corridor.

The same effect is produced by the *xystus* pavement of animals and plants, by the positively grandiose mythological compositions in the *frigidarium* of the baths, and by the 'Myth of Arion' and the 'Myth of Orpheus' in the *diaetae*. In these last-named works the narrative element disappears beneath the rich variety of forms, nor does even the highly expert composition invite a journey through the picture, as in the Trilobate Hall, but offers the spectator an expressive unity full of a thousand clever touches which can only attract curiosity or formal appreciation, not emotional participation in the successive stages of an event. Apart from such compositional and spatial aspects of the *Kunstwollen* of the two artists, their varied outlooks and degrees of accomplishment can be recognised in the actual syntax of their forms, their feeling for colour and the technique of their idioms.

It must be noted that the COURT MASTER shares with the

120, 121

118

117

122, 123

44 The mosaic pavement of the *diaeta* of the 'Myth of Orpheus', though much damaged, shares an iconography very common in the mosaics of late antiquity. About fifty of these subjects survive, found mainly in the West, from England to France, Italy, the Iberian peninsula and North Africa. Of the eastern remains those of particular importance were recovered at Sparta, where little more than an *emblema* was found, and at Cos (No. 1606 in the Archaeological Museum at Istanbul), both of quite late date. Of the African specimens, which constitute the most significant nucleus of the group, reference may be made to those from Henchir Thina (Gauckler (1910), no. 32 A), Oudna (Gauckler (1910), no. 381), both especially near in composition to that of Piazza Armerina, and Piazza Vittoria at Palermo, probably African, however, by derivation. It is now at the National Museum. (*See* Pace (1939), pp. 185–6). Of the Spanish finds that at the Saragossa Provincial Museum is one of the oldest, though the animals are clearly divided between two levels. In France that at Blainzy-les-Fismes may be mentioned. This mosaic was extensively restored in 1859. *See* Stern (1957), pp. 50–2; and especially Stern (1955). This last study contains a full acount of mosaic pavements dealing with the subject of Orpheus among the animals. The mosaic of the Piazza Armerina *diaeta*, related particularly to those of Tunis and Palermo, is also evidence of the influence of the African school on the COURT MASTER.

CARNAGE MASTER respect for the great Hellenistic iconographical tradition, but not for its special tendency or manner as expressed in Pergamene and Rhodian sculpture. Moreover, within this figurative convention, the first-named artist does not express the earthy dramatic vigour of the other, but turns in a different spirit to the setting of idyllic scenes and their reinterpretation in terms of leisure, cheerfulness, humour and ornament. Thus while the CARNAGE MASTER devised for Hercules, before his 'Glorification', the bloody series which accounts for the name here given him, the COURT MASTER, giving his own version of a Hellenistic model, chooses to record only one moment in the 'Myth of Polyphemus', the almost kindly and farcical scene in which Ulysses lures the giant to drunkenness.

It must also be added that the difference between the two artists is even greater in specifically stylistic matters. The CARNAGE MASTER's figures tend less to cubist dissociation of forms, reorganised and resolved in the neo-baroque variation of surfaces, than to organic flattening of the latter. His colours are not really directed to the integration of Hellenistic shading by toning down areas complete in themselves, but rather find their inspiration in the authentic expressionist feeling which, as already noted, is nowhere more ardent in the villa than in the work of the HUNT MASTER, of whose more rigid, less plastic linear quality they partake.

In this respect we may give qualified assent to the theory put forward, though in a different context, by Gentili.[45] According to him 'the confluence of the two tendencies' – here identified with the personalities of the CARNAGE and HUNT MASTERS – 'appears in the scenes of idyllic character, where the grape-gathering and fishing Cupids, still in the classical tradition of plump little winged and naked boys, are accompanied by sprites carrying off the grapes, who look like real people and wear stiff, straight little tunics. . .'

Through the enormous output that can be attributed on such grounds to the COURT MASTER, his assistants and workshop, the line of his development can be quite clearly traced. It remained suspended between and continuously under the influence of the two poles of the HUNT and CARNAGE MASTERS, while seeking a third direction, never found for certain, leading to a creative synthesis of the great but perhaps irrecoverable 'ancient' form of the last named artist and the 'modern', deeply suggestive pattern of the other.

The COURT MASTER's independent work perhaps began with the *oeci* of the 'Fishing Cupids' and the 'Grape-gathering Cupids' and the pavement of the *xystus*. Pace recognised[46] that the diminutive figures of the former work 'seem . . . formally closer to the sensibility of the "Carnage" '. Also, as noted above, he unhesitatingly

45 Gentili (1952a), p. 42. A comparison with the 'Grape-gathering Cupids' (167) of the porphyry sarcophagus of Constantia at the Pio-Clementino Museum of the Vatican is of use in thoroughly determining the stylistic difference between the Cupids of the CARNAGE and COURT MASTERS. *See* also in this connection the porphyry fragment with a similar subject, that of 'Grape-gathering Cupids' among enormous acanthus spirals (No. 806 in the Christian Room, XIX, of the Istanbul Archaeological Museum), probably taken from the sarcophagus of Constantine found at Constantinople.
46 Pace (1955), p. 90.

ascribed the *xystus* mosaic to the master of the Trilobate Hall. Indeed the elliptical pavement, which closes the perspective of the great Herculanean *triclinium* with a majestic nymphaeum, stands in a relation to the 'Carnage' similar to that in which the artist who carried the great corridor narrative to its conclusion in the paving of the peristyle would later stand to the HUNT MASTER. The subject is a courtly 'Zoophytomorphology' (a design combining animal and plant life) among acanthus spirals of the greatest elegance, many-coloured but in wonderfully fused tones, with touches of spirited naturalism in the tiny creatures peeping out everywhere, to produce a total result of such rich and fantastic baroque decoration as may be thought unequalled in the rest of the villa. The characters in this story with no beginning or end are animals of all kinds, each being 'narrated' in its peculiar vivacity and little affected by the taste of the trophies depicted in the *imagines clipeatae* of the peristyle. It is clear that these creatures are derived from the 'Carnage', just as the animal heads of the peristyle derive from the beasts upon which the series of the 'Great Hunt' is based.

128–30

Yet, as compared with the grandiose composition of the 'Carnage', where a classical vision revives to some extent in the Constantinian manner, that is to say through the solid geometry of the figures, the *xystus* pavement actually abolishes space in the inextricable tangle of its branches. One is reminded of the vaults of the Mausoleum of Constantina, at the same stage of aesthetic development, though earlier examples exist; but the fragmentary pavement of the ACANTHUS MASTER of Zlitan in Tripolitania, over two centuries older, presents, as already noted, a much more organic, elegant and logical pattern.

166, **24**

28

The pavings with Cupids and other boys, intent upon lending refinement to the pursuits of agriculture, hunting, fishing and theatrical and circus entertainments, follow in the wake of the Cupids in the 'Myth of Lycurgus' lunette: the expressionist V-marks which recur on the brows of the figures in all these pavements are only the most obvious indication of this provenance. But they appeal to the spectator by a passion for decoration and form so highly developed that neither the lack of relief noted by Gentili nor the vivacious and undoubtedly expressionistic polychromy, already noted, can obliterate the impression.

121, 118, 120, 117

110

In other works the COURT MASTER reveals a maturer, less complicated personality, expressed in decorations by turns majestic in their compositional skill or pleasing in their reinterpretations of mythology and tradition. In these productions his remoteness from the CARNAGE MASTER, though it never becomes absolute, seems greater the nearer he approaches a style that is 'modern' (even if chronologically earlier) and more closely in accord with the spirit of the time than is that of the HUNT MASTER.

From this moment onwards the development of the COURT MASTER can perhaps be followed almost step by step. The HUNT MASTER had laid down in the great corridor his imposing narrative of the chase. The COURT MASTER proceeded to decorate the chamber of the 'Fishing Cupids' [120] and the entrance hall with its porch and colonnade. He chose a similar subject, borrowing from the former master recognisable episodic and environmental suggestions and imparting realism and precision to his decorative aims. His Cupids are busy, as before, on a sea full of fish; but here a logical, positively perspectival order controls the picture. A symmetrical line of large seaside villas closes the horizon, which is defined by the green foliage of trees rising against it, while boats move to and fro upon the water. But the similarities of compositional structure to be noted in that part of the Hunt Corridor which depicts the loading and unloading of ships go no further. The figures [98] of the later master have a certain bodily volume, and the boats show some traces of depth in perspective. Such treatment was utterly unknown to the HUNT MASTER.

He went on to compose the complex 'Circus Races' in [112] the palaestra of the baths, one of the most realistic representations of the Circus Maximus which has survived from antiquity. Thereupon the COURT MASTER produced in the vestibule of the 'Small Circus' a remarkable minia- [117] ture of the same subject, showing boy charioteers racing on vehicles drawn by birds – not in itself a new idea – and synthesising with a few touches the environmental details so minutely described by the other artist. The division of the scene into two levels, again in defiance of the demands of perspective, repeats the chronological significance with a purely courtly and abstract intention, presenting the victory of the same *factio prasina* in a simplified rivalry from which the distinctive elements of the model are entirely absent. Moreover, the tendency to frontal presentation of all the chariots, which are seen from below notwithstanding the position of the wheels and the feathered coursers, shows a more marked concern with continuing the cubist experiments already noticed in the CARNAGE MASTER's work, in accordance with a plastic aim realised paratactically instead of by the smoother methods of the HUNT MASTER. As Gentili maintains in his exhaustive study,[47] glorification of the historical fact of a victory won by the imperial faction is thus transformed into a finicking and brilliant caricature which reduces the courtly celebration to the level of a frankly Hellenistic elegance symbolising, by the fruits with which the animals are adorned, the revolution of the seasons and the tireless march of time.

Again, no sooner had the HUNT MASTER finished work in the wonderful *diaeta* of the 'Small Hunt', than the [106] COURT MASTER composed his jesting comment in the cubicle of the 'Boy Hunters'. He likewise arranged his [118]

47 Gentili (1957), p. 24.

'story' on successive planes, with small scenes in exquisite taste of boys being pecked by a cock or bitten by a cat. Nor did he fail to enclose the whole production in a splendid floral border where once more the underlying narrative pretext yields without resistance to decorative magnificence, in the usual manner of many African mosaics and, as noted above, that of S. Costanza. The **24** artist's autonomous control is accordingly expressed by an abstract quality of composition completely devoid of environmental precision, arranged in narrative planes which are mere streaks of colour (very like the planes of the *Volta Quadrata* in the Crypt of S. Januarius in the Cemetery of Praetextatus), above and beyond which streaks move the little hunters, suspended among flowers, fruit and multicoloured branches, which punctuate a wholly artificial space. The same spirit and transition of the artist away from narrative and decorative aims seem also to have been responsible for certain pavements in the cubicles, vestibules and halls lying around the great peristyle. They alternate between the fancies of traditional idyllic illustration and devotion to a sophisticated mythological repertory.

The mosaic in the Cubicle of the 'Erotic Scene' is a **127** charming work despite the superfluity of its heavy and complicated decorative framing. Its *emblemata* contain theatrical masks and female heads of the Seasons, bordered by decorative festoons of laurel or by volutes, the former much more plastic and elegant than the later ones of the peristyle. These *emblemata* surround a centrepiece showing a young couple embracing, and thus form a symphony of faces in which the hair-styles, the structure of the features and the deep, melancholy gaze of the eyes are distinct reminders of the spirit of the age, but one combined and integrated most admirably with robes and forms of classical elegance. With this work there were most probably associated first the very badly damaged Hall of the Dance the few surviving fragments of which, especially the bust of the female dancer in the top left-hand corner, testify to the artist's inspiration by the feminine countenances of the Lycurgeia (in particular, that of Ambrosia), and secondly the Hall of the 'Seasons', the Cubicle of the 'Fruit' and a whole series of pavements purely ornamental in their geometrical and stylised floral passages, centred mainly on white, red and black; while the abovementioned compositional structure on successive planes, in the customary miniaturist style and with small figures rendered frontally in the expressionist idiom, reappears in the Cubicle of the 'Musicians and Actors', which constitutes the pendant to that of the 'Boy Hunters' beside the *diaeta* **118** of the 'Myth of Arion'. **122, 123**

With this last wonderful composition, preceded and prepared perhaps by the similar seascape in the hall of the *frigidarium* of the baths, the COURT MASTER achieved his finest work. It is also this pavement with which the artist proves his full artistic maturity and thus sufficiently justifies the attempt here made to reconstruct the COURT MASTER's personality and production. The subject constitutes in the first place a return to his highly individual 'Fishing Cupids', and, as a result of the more ample 120 figurative and compositional treatment required by the new personages, a close connection with the courtly and cubist-traditional orientation of the CARNAGE MASTER.

On the compositional plane, the decoration of the *frigidarium* already represents a free version of the scheme of the *oecus* of the 'Grape-gathering Cupids', centred on a 121 bust of Silenus, and of that of the entrance hall with its porch and exedra. But the new element is derived from 120 the majestic composition of the *diaeta*, where the separate groups of nereids, tritons, marine centaurs and sea-monsters are placed according to a partially free conception of space. Though it does not, like the 'Carnage', invite the spectator to enter with interest into the picture itself, it plays a definite part in the distributive balance, as does an organisation of various figurative groupings. Since these refer on every side to the central group with Arion, and reflect an arrangement preserving traces of the system of successive planes into which the neighbouring Cubicle pavements of the 'Musicians and Actors' and the 'Boy Hunters' are divided, they necessarily bring to mind the 118 *diaeta* of the 'Small Hunt' and therefore the HUNT MASTER. 104, 106

The structure of the figures, which are in general both graceful and robust, is also inherited from the unconstrained but flattened bodies in the 'Great Hunt', but not 102, 103 far from the plastic vigour of the stately divinities of the more Hellenistic lunettes in the Trilobate Hall. In fact, a **10**, 110 still noticeable and very vigilant consciousness of plastic form is expressed, so as to make it appear that in his female figures, of the *frigidarium* no less than of the *diaeta*, the master took advantage of appreciable elements of a tonality similar to that of the 'Carnage', though in a wholly different chromatic sense. This developed feeling for colour in the pavement of the *diaeta* facilitated, more than in all its predecessors, an authoritative expressionist statement, entirely free from tonal residues of Hellenistic type. The glowing bodies of the nereids, incorporating 122 warm flesh-tones of rose and amber, often fading into greys, greens and blues at the ankles and the feet under water, combine with the exquisite varieties of colouring in the marine fauna and the rigorous divisionism of chromatic line in the centaurs and tritons form a picture of such rich colouring and such refinement of tonal approximation as to be fairly judged among the greatest beauties of the whole villa. Here we are very far removed from the schematic Roman compositions of similar subjects in

48 Among the best black-and-white pavements are those of the Baths of Neptune at Ostia (II, 4), built in the Antonine age, and those excavated under the Roman church of S. Cesareo de Appia, laid at the end of the second century but extensively restored between the third and fourth. Among the African examples, because of the special importance of its classical composition and stylistic polish, reference may be made to the mosaic of a 'Nereid riding a Marine Centaur', from the second half of the third century, in the Timgad Museum (De Pachtère (1911), no. 139). The nude, bright figure of the aureoled divinity stands out to splendid effect, produced with much dexterous polychromy in very small tesserae, against the bodies of the centaur and triton beside her. The mosaic of the 'Triumph of Aphrodite' at the Djemila Museum is of the fourth century, despite the diminutive cubes of rich and varied colours. The central *emblema* (De Pachtère (1911), no. 293) is missing. Within a wide ornamental border the artist has tastefully distributed the figures of Oceanus with his trident, and Amphitrite in her sea-shell, accompanied by Cupid and supported by two marine centaurs. Similar groups of nereids and monsters are placed at each of the four corners, surrounded by waves and sea-creatures.

The neo-Attic mosaic from Lambaesis, illustrating a similar subject and signed by ASPASIOS (De Pachtère (1911), no. 190), is much older, dating from the middle of the second century. The 'Nereid and Sea-bull' tessellate at Aquileia, excavated in 1859 (Brusin (1950)), is probably of about the same date. Also of the second century, but later, the Susa mosaic (Gauckler (1910), no. 39) seems to be the oldest late Roman example of fishing Cupids.

Some interest, on account of their stylistic resemblance to some of the figures of the COURT MASTER, attaches to the mosaic representations of the nereid KLUMENE or THET(IS) and of a marine car recovered from a gymnasium in the baths at Aquileia and now in the local Museum. These mosaics, dating from late in the third century, are notable for distinctly plastic treatment of their rather stiff drawing, conveying on the whole a feeling of rigid and stylised heaviness. Attractive chromatic sequences of pearl-grey, violet, lilac, pink and serpentine green, together with a certain interest in flesh-tones delicately tinged with rose, are reminiscent of some aspects of chromatic sensibility in the line running from the CARNAGE to the COURT MASTER at Piazza Armerina. The execution of these works, partially

black and white during the second and third centuries, of which numerous examples survive. On the other hand, the best of the African mosaics, in spite of their earlier date,[48] appear quite comparable. Such artistic maturity significantly illustrates the capacity of the painting of this period to compete on vigorous and original terms with the most refined paintings and mosaics of Hellenistic civilisation.

The peculiar importance of the final achievements of the COURT MASTER, however, does not stop there. The plastic conception of form had not been altogether abandoned; it was still appreciable, despite the disappearance of tonality, through the maintenance of a residue of sfumato in selections of colours, though they were in themselves autonomous. But in the faces of Arion and the nereids we can detect a renewed interest in the traditional rendering of the head, similar to that adopted by the CARNAGE MASTER, especially in the figures of the Lycurgeia. Features are delicately modelled and the faces drawn out into a splendid oval resembling not only that of Ambrosia and the Roman 'Barberini Venus', but still more that of the *Dea Roma* on a fresco fragment recovered from a Roman building in the Via della Consolazione[49] and also those of the earlier female busts on the ceiling of the hall at Trier, striking anticipations of the Constantinian 'fine style'. As in those countenances, the firm and ample shading which provides the physiognomical relief in these marine forms fully retains every characteristic of expressionist portraiture. The features are strongly marked and distinct, the eyebrows widely arched and prolonged into the line of the nose, the eyes enormous and intent, with spacious white crescents beneath the pupils. Yet these elements seem to blend into an almost plastic rotundity of the head, expressed in colours which, because of their clear and unadulterated purity, appear subversive when compared with the heavy shading of the CARNAGE MASTER, and which are retained substantially at Trier, where, however, they are more closely associated in a rendering of graded shadows.

With the work of the COURT MASTER, now that the fullness of the new treatment of colour had been attained, the art of mosaic went on to attempt a new formal synthesis which, without misrepresenting the spirit of the time, would resurrect something of the great classical idiom which expressionism and cubism had for some decades been counteracting.

The rest of the Piazza Armerina mosaics, in addition to those so far discussed in the present study and those attributable to the MASTER OF THE ANIMAL HEADS and the MASTER OF THE GIRLS, are soon listed. They comprise the *emblema* of the *tablinum* in the vestibule of the baths, the lunettes of the *frigidarium* in the chamber of the *unctiones*

164

repaired in antiquity, may be referred to
about the middle of the century.
According to Giovanni Brusin they are
no earlier than the end of the second
century. (*Notizie degli Scavi*, 1923,
p. 230).
49 The 'Barberini Goddess' (Venus), a
fresco recently restored and reinstated
after being hidden by a wall in the
Palace of Fausta at the Lateran, may, as
suggested by Cagiano de Azevedo (1954),
belong to the period between 307, date of
the production of a similar statue in the
Temple of Venus and Rome, and 313,
when the Palace of Fausta was ceded to
the Church. The facial fragment of the
Dea Roma (Cagiano de Azevedo, 1954,
p. 131), now in the Capitoline Museum,
thought by some authorities to be
probably dated as late as the end of the
century, is in my opinion, particularly
when compared with the face of a
nereid in the *diaeta* of the 'Myth of Arion',
related to the pictorial phase of the 'fine
style' which even in Rome (*see*, for
example, the faces of the 'Great Praying
Women' in the Cemetery of Traso,
Chapter X) had a definite vogue for a
time in the catacombs themselves.

50 Some of these suggestions, in
accordance with a view of the artistic
personalities concerned which is at
variance with that here attempted, seem
also to be favoured by Gentili (1959,
pp. 33–4).
51 Pace (1955), p. 74.
52 Gentili (1952 b), p. 24; (1959), p. 18;
Lübke *et al.* (1958), p. 428. *See*
especially the study by L'Orange (1955).

and some fragments of the *tepidarium* pavement in some ways comparable with others already ascribed to the COURT MASTER, such as the Vestibule of the 'Myth of Polyphemus', the Hall of the 'Seasons', the Hall of the 'Dance', the Cubicle of the 'Erotic Scene' and the Cubicle of the 'Fruit'. These last could perhaps be taken together in any attempt to define them more accurately.[50]

127

The *emblema* of the *tablinum* has been much discussed. It has been taken, alternatively, to be the fragment of a scene representing a rite of the Mysteries or the imperial cult of the Augustales,[51] or of the ceremonial for the *Adventus* of the owner or the emperor.[52] It is certain that the *emblema* originally showed a double line of figures advancing in procession on two parallel levels and seen entirely from the front in the fashion so greatly admired at a later date in the two famous mosaics of San Vitale. The whole scene cannot of course be reconstructed from the narrow marginal fragment which has been preserved. But it seems obvious that the *emblema*, which must have measured about 3.5 metres across, cannot have included in this fragment the central personage concerned. There is therefore no point in trying, as some have done, to identify the figure holding a candlestick. It is more profitable to attempt to deduce the original composition from the dimensions and attitudes of the surviving figures. In view of the fact that the design is on two planes, somewhat abstractly divided by a course of grey tesserae, and lacks all concrete signs of spatial reference, it can hardly be dated among the older works at the villa, even though this type of figurative arrangement occurs within a period ranging from the Arches of Galerius and Constantine (friezes of the *Adlocutio* in the first, *Adlocutio* and *Congiarium* in the second), through exceptionally clear specimens such as the Sarcophagus of the Good Shepherd in the Split Museum, found at Manastirine (Salona), down to the base of the Obelisk of Theodosius at Constantinople. It is exactly to this type of organisation of figure-space that the *emblema* of the *tablinum* would be best assigned, upon the assumption that its central and most important part has disappeared, the part in which, probably on horseback between the two places, and perhaps with larger dimensions, must have stood the personage, frontally presented, towards whom the five surviving figures are looking. Their faces may usefully be compared with those of the HUNT and COURT MASTERS.

125

99, 103, 122, 123

There is less to be said about the collection of pavements in the baths. Apart from the octagon of the *frigidarium*, there seems no particular objection to seeing in them the hand of a single craftsman; for, leaving aside in this connection the archaeological question of identifying the different persons represented, their figures in any case could not add much lustre to the decorations of the villa.

93 Piazza Armerina, Trilobate Hall. Mosaic: Marathonian Bull, the 'Carnage of Hercules' (detail)

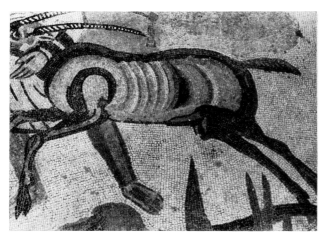

94 Piazza Armerina, Corridor of the Great Hunt (detail).
Captured Antelope

95 Aquileia, Basilica of Theodore. *Emblema*: Antelope

97 Qasr el-Lebia, Basilica. *Emblema*: She-goat

96 Antioch, House of the Worcester Hunt. Fleeing Stag (detail)

98 Piazza Armerina, Corridor of the Great Hunt (detail). Loading and unloading of beasts from a ship

99 Piazza Armerina, Corridor of the Great Hunt (detail). Officials with tetrarchic caps

100 Venice, St. Mark's. Porphyry Group of the Tetrarchs

101 Piazza Armerina, Corridor of the Great Hunt (detail). Group of the so-called Tetrarch

102 Piazza Armerina, Corridor of the Great Hunt (detail). Wheeled cage drawn by zebus

103 Piazza Armerina, Corridor of the Great Hunt (detail). Embarkation of Ostriches

7 Piazza Armerina, Corridor of the Great Hunt. Capture of Bison, Tigress and Antelope.

8 Piazza Armerina, Corridor of the Great Hunt. South lunette.

9 Piazza Armerina, Corridor of the Great Hunt. Episodes of *Venatio*.

104 Piazza Armerina, *diaeta* of the Small Hunt. Sacrifice to Diana

105 Tunis, Bardo Museum. Sacrifice before the Hunt, from a Roman house at Henchir Toungar

106 Piazza Armerina, *diaeta* of the Small Hunt. Combat with Boar

107 Rome, Antiquarium of the Capitoline Museums. Fragment: Boar-hunt, from the cloister of S. Bibiana

108 Piazza Armerina, central apse of Trilobate Hall. Stricken Giant, in the 'Giants Struck by Lightning'

109 Piazza Armerina, Central apse of Trilobate Hall. 'Giants Struck by Lightning,

110 Piazza Armerina, S. apse of Trilobate Hall. Dionysiac Myth of Lycurgus

10 Piazza Armerina, N. apse of Trilobate Hall. Glorification of Hercules (detail).

11 Piazza Armerina, central zone of Trilobate Hall. Thracian Rider Unhorsed (detail from the 'Carnage').

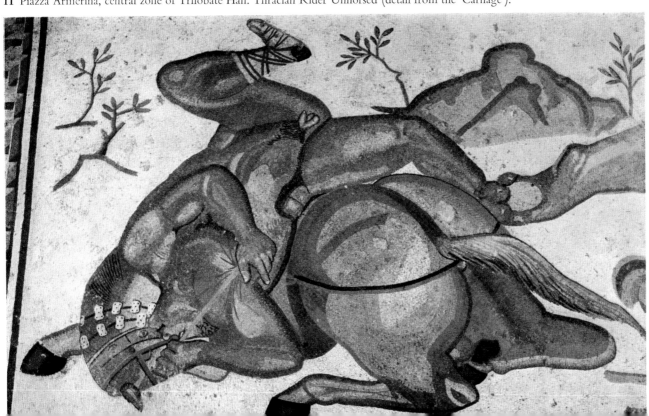

12 Piazza Armerina, vestibule of the baths. Family Portrait.

13 Rome, Museo dei Conservatori. Inlay: Tiger and Calf, from the Basilica of Junius Bassus.

111 Rome, Museo Profano Lateranense. Victorious Athletes and Gymnasiarch (detail), from the Baths of Caracalla

112 Piazza Armerina, Palaestra of the baths. Victorious Charioteer, in the Circus Races (detail)

113 Rome, formerly Palazzo Del Drago. Inlay: Consular Triumph, from the Basilica of Junius Bassus

114 Rome, Borghese Gallery. Gladiatorial Combats, from the peristyle at Torre Nuova

115 Rome, Borghese Gallery. Combat with Wild Beasts, from the peristyle at Torre Nuova

116 Rome, Borghese Gallery. Combat with Wild Beats, from the peristyle at Torre Nuova

117 Piazza Armerina, Vestibule of the Small Circus (detail). Boy Charioteers

118 Piazza Armerina, cubicle near the great corridor. Boy Hunters

119 Desenzano, Trilobate Hall of Roman Villa. Fishing Cupids

120 Piazza Armerina, porticoed atrium with exedra adjoining great corridor. Fishing Cupids (detail)

121 Piazza Armerina, *oecus* adjoining elliptic *xystus*. Grape-gathering Cupids

122 Piazza Armerina, *diaeta* of the Myth of Arion. Nereid and Marine Centaur (detail)

123 Piazza Armerina, *diaeta* of the Myth of Arion. Nereid

124 Rome, Capitoline Museums. Fragment: Face of *Dea Roma*, from Via della Consolazione

125 Piazza Armerina, *emblema* of *tablinum* (detail).
Adventus

126 Piazza Armerina. Mosaic in the room of the *unctiones* (detail)

127 Piazza Armerina. Cubicle of the Erotic Scene (detail)

128 Piazza Armerina, Great Peristyle. Lion's Head

129 Piazza Armerina, Great Peristyle. Bull's head

130 Piazza Armerina, Great Peristyle. Horse's head

131 Piazza Armerina. Hall of the Girls at Exercise

Nevertheless, these *lithostrota* were obviously commissioned to display ceremonial portraits. Their handling reveals a taste already conspicuously pre-Byzantine, both in the more prominent 'Family Portrait' of the vestibule and in **12** the *frigidarium* lunettes, where the setting blends easily with the graduated dimensions of the central figure and with those of the slaves assisting him on each side (*Mutationes Vestis*).

Notice the sense of rhythm conveyed by the bodies, their sumptuous and multicoloured attire, with its refined tones, and their hierarchical order, as well as the absence of any environmental element except the usual synthetic shadows at the feet, all of which features suggest that the mosaic should be dated among the later of the works hitherto examined, undoubtedly very near the middle of the fourth century. The figures, in fact, both in their attitudes and in their dress, look very like the 'Praying Women' of the Cemetery of Traso at Rome, to be studied later in the present work; they also bring to mind, even more strikingly, certain scenes of the arcosolium of the Roman Hypogeum of Trebius Justus on the Via Latina. There, with the clear intention to achieve symmetry and centripetal placing, the parents and slaves of the deceased youth are represented in clothing often similar to that worn by the Piazza Armerina personages. Their environment is still more freely and boldly paratactical in its two dimensions. In other words, it is less conditioned by residual stylistic aims of a traditional character[53] and is therefore well suited to join the company of later pictures in the new Roman catacomb of the Via Latina.

The pavement of the *unctiones* on the other hand, and the insignificant fragments of the *tepidarium*, turn back to the better known models of the past, those, for instance, in the baths fragments of the Aquileia Museum and the famous 'Athletes' of the Baths of Caracalla. But the later works, by comparison, show a clear organic disproportion in the bodies, a decidedly flabby shape in which the muscles and physical power are rendered by a series of chromatic passages varying from pink through violet to black, without the design giving any sign of integration or superficial organisation. This formal degeneration, a consequence not only of the continuous evolution of taste but also of technical deficiency in the *tessellarius*, can throw some interesting light upon the transition to the later pavement of the ten girls.

In fact, the Hall of the 'Girls at Exercise', or at the bath, **131, 14** is the last of the Piazza Armerina works to suggest any enthusiasm for the recovery of form within the limits of a taste which was by now well beyond that of the usual idiomatic structures of the late Empire and was accompanying or perhaps following the animal heads of the **128–30** great peristyle. They are certainly to be dated late in the century, probably in its sixth or seventh decade.

53 The decoration was assigned by Cecchelli (1944, pp. 135–46) to the second half of the third century. But it is much more probably to be referred (and not only owing to the presence of the *orbiculi* on the clothing, of the Chi-rho, etc.) to the age of Constantine, as already believed by Wilpert (1913) and maintained today by Becatti (1951a, p. 39), who also mentions the Carthaginian mosaic of '*Dominus Julius*' (for which *see* Chapter VIII), and by Rumpf (1953, p. 196).

The mosaic paving of the peristyle, indeed, sums up the villa's magnificent repertory of human and animal figures in an undoubtedly decorative way, by means of a repeated endeavour to create both expressive models of the various species and symbols of a great tradition – symbols now deprived of their ancient vitality.[54]

The African workshop which carried out this task numbered among its *musivarii* some craftsmen endowed with remarkable synthesising talents for design, certainly evident in many of the beasts' heads, almost all of which are drawn in perspective, where it is easy to see a complete dissolution of narrative intent in the full concentration on formal organisation of post-classical type. In others the undoubted mastery of form both cubist and expressionist, as understood under the Tetrarchy, is accompanied by a less satisfactory level of expressive power and a more broadly anti-classical outlook.

The MASTER OF THE ANIMAL HEADS, creator of this zoological gallery of frontally-presented forms, a true metaphysical interpretation of a *venatio* reduced to a series of trophies, sets out his images in a ponderous, solemn sequence, full of vigour and restrained preciosity, with no spatial content, in which last respect they differ even from the COURT MASTER's conception in the elliptical peristyle. The heads are arranged by tens in medallions which, owing to the almost invariable concentric disposition of the courses of *tesserae* in the background, seem to provide each animal with a halo. The beasts' expressions are sometimes wild and terrifying in the round, concentric fixity of the eyes and the characteristic contour of the jaws. They bring to mind the admirable and very differently finished *concinnitas* of form in the 'Tigers' marquetry of the Roman Basilica of Junius Bassus. The use of colour, precluding every attempt at tonal fusion even in comparison with the expressionist idiom of the *xystus*, is exemplified by changes and approximations often accompanied by daring 'negative reliefs' in white and black, typical of a taste by now definitely released from the Roman tradition, for all its complexity. If it were not for the familiar decorative partitions found everywhere in Roman mosaic, a spectator strolling at leisure through this quadrangular arcade might almost suppose that a different spiritual world, though heir to the techniques of previous art, had imposed itself, with no half-measures or compromises, on the cultural outlook represented by the villa, transitional though that outlook was. The Rome of the Tetrarchs was by this time very far from the atmosphere of these works.

The mosaic of the 'Girls at Exercise' is perhaps of later date, having been laid above another pavement decorated in geometrical style. On the other hand, it may possibly be taken to illustrate the other direction followed by the painting of late antiquity, leading to the resuscitation of form in Byzantine art.

128, 129

13

129, 130

131, 14

54 The return to tradition had a happy issue in the large mosaic of the 'Animal Heads' of the *tepidarium* of a House at Thuburbo Majus (Henchir Kasbat), comprising fifteen *imagines clipeatae* and five framed by hexagonal friezes, all composed of one marvellous laurel. In general the animals display only their heads, chests and forelegs. They are both domestic and wild, including bulls, horses, tigers, boars, stags, bears, ostriches and so on. The chromatic animation and dexterously expressive drawing of the 'Heads', the subtle, if solemn, refinement of the decorative composition, the attention paid to organic disposition of the various animals in the pavement, with their pendants and antitheses, as well as comparison with similar though less advanced African floorings, such as those mentioned by L. Poinssot and P. Quoniam (1953), all indicate the end of the third century and a phase of taste not yet acquired by tetrarchic aesthetics. It therefore appears entirely reasonable to date the Piazza Armerina *lithostroton* about two generations later than that of Thuburbo Majus, which can unquestionably be regarded as an important and significant predecessor.

In these ten female bodies, depicted in the most varied attitudes of open-air sport, the most conspicuous feature is the strengthening (I would not say reanimation) of the line, functioning less in the interests of form than in those of more accurate and organic application of colour. This last is organised in surfaces of diverse hue, mutually related in their promotion of muscular design and retraction of light, not in the tactile sense, but purely optically and chromatically. No relationship ensues between the external outline of the figure and the internal 'negative reliefs'. If, therefore, the articulated extension of the colour is ignored, it can be said that the images already contain *in germ* the medieval characteristic of chromatic filling of the design. Nevertheless, certain equally evident features prove that figurative study, after reaching a point so near to medieval ideas, had already chosen in this case to take a different line, anticipating through such extreme dissolution the Byzantine restoration. The latter, as we know, reinforced the classicising manner inaugurated by Constantine and imposed without difficulty in the courtly atmosphere of Constantinople, exempt from Western temptations, leading to consequences among which was the expressionist parataxis of the Tetrarchy and the Constantinian age. Such, properly observed, is the exceptional importance of the girl gymnasts of Piazza Armerina, who, in the rhythmic quality of this general composition, in the Hellenistic derivation of their attitudes and in the organic treatment of their faces, retain the fundamentals of that conservatism of the classical heritage which was to be the vocation of the Byzantine artists.

In this case, accordingly, the abovementioned characteristics suggest a further linear and chromatic simplification of the 'fine style', certainly some decades after the latter's appearance, within the ambit of a new palette in which prevailed colours plain and unmodified but not heightened in the *fauve* manner (bright blues, reds, yellows and greens), and through which the bodies reflect, if anything, the Aquileian style of the SEA MASTER with a series of such tints as ochre, pearl-grey, pink and violet. Thus, the design of the forms of the cupids appears, in certain difficult passages of the figures seen partially or entirely from one side, to re-echo that of the Cupids of the Theodorean Basilica. As regards the arrangement of the hair, the dancing or rhythmic attitudes, the shading of the legs, and the empty background, a still closer stylistic resemblance is to be found in the African mosaic of the 'Three Graces' at Cherchel (Caesarea), which copies the very well known model of the two Pompeian frescoes preserved at the Naples Museum[55] and is dated in the third quarter of the fourth century. In comparison with the 'Three Graces', however, the pavement of the villa, while retaining less of the stereotyped Hellenistic form,

141

55 De Pachtère (1911), no. 420. This mosaic from a Roman villa at Cherchel is now in the local museum. The two Pompeian paintings are numbered 9291 and 9236. *See* also the 'Medallion of the Graces', recently recovered from the Baths at Concordia Sagittaria and now in the National Museum at Portogruaro, where the female figures wear scanty pectoral bands, like those of the 'Girls at Exercise' of Piazza Armerina, but below the breasts (Zovatto (1963), pp. 50–2, f. 46) assigns this fragment to the third century, without further specification). The detail helps to confirm the belief that the Sicilian girls are not participating in an underwater spectacle. (*See* in this connection Traversari (1960), pp. 75–83). Pace (1955, p. 84) was the first to argue that the Piazza Armerina pavement represented an aquatic spectacle.

reveals an attempt at elementary syntheses in the chromatic structure of the bodies. This feature attests some progress towards the employment of autonomous formal indications complete in themselves, which was to constitute one of the imaginative splendours of Byzantine painting. (In this connection, notice the handling of the muscles of the arms, legs, abdomens, navels, and so on, of these figures.) A further very striking and illuminating comparison will be made in Chapter XIII with the 'Nereids' of the pavement in the House of the Dioscuri at **34–36, 19** Ostia, a mosaic perhaps executed a few years later.

The mosaics of the Theodorean Basilica at Aquileia are the first examples of pictorial art produced by Christians after its emergence into the light of day from the underground cemeteries and the halls of private houses such as the adjacent pre-Theodorean Oratory at Aquileia itself. It was immediately after the Edict of Milan that Bishop Theodore built the Basilica and paved it with the celebrated mosaics. Consequently, it seems reasonable and intelligible enough that the *pictores imaginarii* were not ready to conceive an original, extensive and organically composed cycle of *lithostrota* wherewith to express with new themes the Church's acquisition of doctrinal freedom, and that the decorators were obliged to have recourse on the one hand to the figure-painting in the catacombs and the *domus ecclesiae*, and on the other to that of secular art.

Iconographically, too, it does not seem that Christian catacombal painting, which was to a great extent crypto-symbolic, had as yet provided much for the new art of mosaic. It can safely be affirmed that at Aquileia only the 'Good Shepherd' and the 'Story of Jonah' in the Great Fishing show signs of any such derivation. Apart from these, the master mosaicists employed by Theodore sought their models in the still clandestine pre-Theodorean cult hall, in profane pictures, in Hellenistic cartoons resuscitated under the influence of a taste very close to that of certain African monuments, in the *emblemata*, and in the school of exuberant chromatic decoration. The same was to be done more than a decade later by the first master of the Mausoleum of Constantina.

Even the fresco-painters of walls and ceilings remained loyal to the traditional secular repertory. A scrap of fresco on part of the bottom of the south wall of Theodore's Basilica depicts Cupids, perhaps gathering grapes, against the background of a garden with paths and fountains. It is more than sufficient to give an idea of the richness of the wall decorations which the church of Theodore must have possessed in addition to its mosaic pavement.[1]

These observations strengthen the conclusion indicated above, which appears indisputable after careful consideration of the *corpus* of painting during the first half of the century: the mosaicists of the basilicas, who were given free rein by the Edict of Milan, were caught unprepared in face of new requirements. Little recourse was had to the figurative themes of Christian (particularly catacombal) painting, which were very few in comparison

Plan D; **15, 16,** 137–141

132, 133

137, **15**

24, 166

1 Cecchelli (1933), p. 158. Brusin and Zovatto (1957), pp. 116–9. Significant parallels can be drawn between the few fragments from the ceiling of the Basilica of Theodore and those from the ceiling of the imperial hall at Trier, dating from the years immediately prior to 326. *See* in this connection Cecchelli (1933), p. 172, pl. XXIII, 4; Brusin and Zovatto (1957), p. 118, f. 51.

Plan D

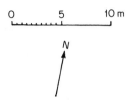
Complex of the Third-century
Oratory and the Theodorean
churches at Aquileia

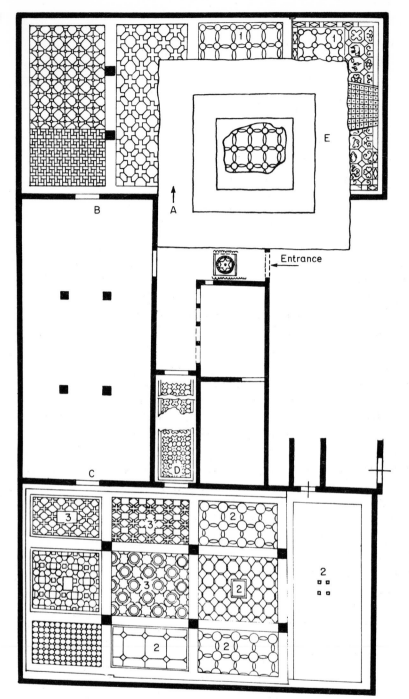

0   5   10 m

N

KEY

A   Entrance to third-century Oratory
B   Entrance to the Oratory. Church enlarged after 313
CD Entrances to the Basilica of Theodore (308 – 19)
E   Foundations of Poppo's Campanile (1019 – 42)

1   Pavements attributable to the Cyriacus Master
2   Pavements attributable to the Theodorean Sea Master
3   Pavements attributable to the Master of the Aquileian Portraits

with the flood of elements taken over from the traditional stock to be endowed with allegorical meaning and initiatory symbolism. This fact proves the unfamiliarity of the mosaic masters with certain types of commission, which in turn suggests that even in this field of activity the *Christifideles* continued for the most part to follow their old way of life, which a hundred years earlier, as Tertullian bears witness,[2] rendered them hardly distinguishable from their pagan fellow citizens, except by their profession of faith.

Apart, therefore, from a few isolated practitioners of catacombal decoration, it is highly probable that until well into the fourth century there existed no specifically Christian stream of development, school or repertory. This is particularly true in the field of mosaic, which required a more advanced technique as well as a more lively tradition of organised labour and artistic practice. It is accordingly natural that the Theodorean masters, like their predecessor in the hall adjoining the Basilica, should have used in their wonderful flooring not only an idiom but also a spirit and an iconography in no way different from those of official contemporary art. The fact that they did so constitutes further proof of the unity of Roman painting, and justifies reliance upon the Aquileian mosaics in evaluating the art of the period. In the pavimental complex of the Theodorean Basilica, that art is represented by the work of at least two masters with different artistic personalities, working at the same time, in the second decade of the fourth century. The two styles here distinguished were responsible for an almost infinite number of human figures and animals, constituting an exemplary record of high importance for the determination of the characteristic idioms of Roman painting as it emerged from twenty years of tetrarchic art, without the undeniable echoes of provincial practice being able to vitiate the understanding of its general tendencies.

Of these two painters the director of the workshop, whom I shall call the THEODOREAN SEA MASTER, indubitably conceived most of the work. In the climate of the radical artistic revival of those years, he seems to hanker after a taste, a culture, a vocabulary and an idiom not entirely remote from the ancient Hellenistic current. In addition to the large marine scene on the floor of the presbytery, I **15**, 141 attribute to him the central mosaic of the third area, containing the 'Offertory' and the 'Eucharistic Victory', as 139, 138 well as the two lateral pavements of this area, and the small section to the right of the second, containing a picture of flocks and the 'Good Shepherd'. The second 137, 140 craftsman of the Basilica was an *imaginarius* more in favour of the tetrarchic style and at the same time a highly individual artist, capable of a varied and penetrating expressionism, not much addicted to the fashionable

2 Tertullian, *Apologeticum*, XLII.

mannerisms of the day. He can be considered responsible for the 'Portraits of Donors and Seasons' in the mosaics to the left of the first and second areas, and for the central pavement of the latter. As a result of this smaller but remarkable contribution he may be called the PORTRAITS MASTER OF AQUILEIA

This first summary distinction becomes more evident as soon as the two Theodorean masters are compared with other Aquileian *tessellarii* active between the end of the third century and the first decades of the fourth, in other words during the fifty years that saw the solution of the problem of late imperial art. Very few of these artists seem to have any definite personality. They include the CYRIACUS MASTER of the *domus ecclesiae*, who in the last years of the century decorated the pavement of the small north cultic hall, which is to be distinguished from the *emblema* with the dedication *Cyriace vibas* and adjoins the Basilica of Theodore. The pavement in question was later partially destroyed (together with the large post-Theodorean church built at the end of the fourth century over and beyond the Hall of Cyriacus) when the patriarch Poppo decided to erect on the site a campanile for the restored Basilica of Theodore. Recently however, in 1962, it proved possible to recover the part of the mosaic covered by the construction of the campanile; it had been supposed lost, but was found *in situ* inside the tower. Another such artist is the MASTER OF THE CHRISTIAN ORATORY, which was recently excavated on the Della Cal estate near the Via Giulia Augusta. This mosaic is attributable to the second quarter of the fourth century.[3]

The CYRIACUS MASTER's work was undoubtedly the not too distant and very familiar model to which the THEO-DOREAN SEA MASTER addressed himself, though in the context of an idiom now quite remote. From him, and often in the form of an exact copy, the SEA MASTER took over the complicated, superfluous and somewhat geometrical-patterned ornamental framing which borders the figures in many areas of the Basilica. It is true that the exceptional chromatic taste of the CYRIACUS MASTER – his extreme virtuosity, for instance, in the production of greenish-blues and orange tints, and his sudden gleams of deliciously baroque quality – his refined talent for decoration and his subtle, arrogant feeling for classical form were not inherited by the SEA MASTER.

The tormented and decisive middle years of the century did not pass without results. The SEA MASTER continued to reveal his stylistic ancestry by remaining imprisoned in the lyrical, translucent flatness of his reading of tetrarchic art. But his striving for new solidity in the bodies of his animals, which conflicts with the prevalent two-dimensionalism of his figures and of the relations between them; his often manifest predilection for faint and almost

16

Plan D;
132
133

17

3 Brusin and Zovatto (1957, p. 214) consider it contemporary with Theodore's building 'if not a little earlier', drawing their conclusions from the one surviving portrait of the 'age of Constantine'.

tonalised colours, which contrast with his nonetheless present chromatic daring reminiscent of *fauve*; his ability to make idiomatic use of colour in order to forge a new link between elements whose separation had been brought about by the paratactical tendency – all three factors bear witness to a dialectic still unresolved. But they also prove the pre-tetrarchic roots of the master, an artist belonging to a province of such cultural and economic importance as Aquileia and brought up in the new climate of artistic taste, but nevertheless still highly sensitive to the more seductive and familiar suggestions of the past, and perhaps anxious for reconversion to the artistic gospel of restoration so recently announced.

Not unnaturally his production can be profitably compared with that of the CARNAGE MASTER, who represents at the Villa of Piazza Armerina a brilliant later synthesis of tetrarchic art with the Constantinian 'fine style', which for the time being had obtained the upper hand. The CARNAGE and SEA MASTERS differ greatly in their culture and significance; but for that very reason a comparison between them can show how two widely different artistic personalities, faced with very similar difficulties, solved a new stylistic problem.

In comparison with the pavement of the slightly later Christian Oratory, with its central representation of the 'Good Shepherd' recalling the vaults of the homonymous chamber in the Cemetery of Peter and Marcellinus at Rome, the inflections in the manner both of the SEA MASTER and of the PORTRAITS MASTER are likewise explained. When set beside the latter's method the probable 'Portrait of a Proprietress' or female donor by the ORATORY MASTER reveals an absolute pacification of expression, basically contrived perhaps by passage through examples of the court fashion in portraiture, which became dominant in the age of Constantine and may be likened to a recomposing filter. Traces of this mode can be detected in the preoccupation with shading in its plastic function, almost as if sfumato were desired. The 'Portrait' is also remarkable for the daring use of rather large tesserae under the influence of a somewhat insistent divisionist technique.[4]

This singular work, the only remaining portrait of four which decorated the Oratory pavement, is one of the finest and most original bequeathed by late Roman painting. The firm adhesive quality of the tessellate, with the aid of precise, brief touches to indicate lips, eyes, eyebrows and hair, and accumulations in themselves expressionistic of coldly animated chromatic material, demonstrates the formal pacification which, without injury to the new idiom, might have been occasioned by the temporary prevalence of the 'fine style', as if it had been demanded by patrons recently elevated to social and

17

4 *See*, for the description, Brusin and Zovatto (1957), pp. 221–3.

political power, not unmindful of former different conditions and above all of the preceding Christian funerary art. But even in the repertory more familiar to the SEA MASTER, such as animals and the 'Good Shepherd', the ORATORY MASTER illustrates the union of post-tetrarchic and late Constantinian manners in an idiom and vocabulary substantially uniform, in which the epoch-making *Kunstwollen* of the fourth century was now expressing the indisputable direction of contemporary art.[5]

Such being the historical framework in which the Theodorean masters operated, it is possible to approach the great mosaic carpet with a view to studying it in detail and tasting its worth. The faithful probably entered the Basilica, not by Poppo's gate, but by a side door in the outer wall of the left-hand nave, facing the second section of pavement.[6] They saw first a series of five 'Portraits of Donors', all placed opposite the entrance. Another four were arranged in the area to the right of it. The least that can be said of these portraits is that they show no sign whatever of formal serenity. Their violent expressionism is heightened by the tesselar field of the white background, disposed around each in radial bands directed with magical effect to the focus of the portrait, the eyes. These in their turn, together with the rest of the face, are rendered by an exclusive chromatic linearism, faithfully reproducing in the clearest and most emphatic manner the agitated expressionism of the bygone Tetrarchy. The planes are extended, abruptly cut off by the linear design and distorted in the highly individual fashion adopted by the PORTRAITS MASTER in the interests of psychology, with drastic enlargements of cheek, chin and jaw.

In the left-hand mosaic of the first pavement are four other female portraits in complicated decorative frames adorned with fish and birds. Leaving these on his right the visitor would move on till he reached the central nave beside the second pavement, where he could turn to the altar. But before he proceeded towards the ritual centre of the sacred edifice his attention would be drawn to a spacious and extremely graceful composition, dominated by the framed 'Portraits' of five other 'Donors' of the Basilica and by four 'Seasons'. The gaze of these last is more peaceful, vague though intense, under the natural wreaths that crown their foreheads. But the faces of the benefactors of the church, by turns expressing keen anxiety, stern inner resolution, wonder or pathos, show in the highest degree the ability of the new idiom to convey emotion. The novel methods, though still within the main stream of the individualised, historical tradition of portraiture characteristic of previous centuries, often exceeded it in poetic resources, if not in the mastery of idiom which the

5 Light can be thrown on the simultaneous development of taste in various parts of the Empire by comparing these birds at Aquileia and those decorating the border of the large pavement of the Constantinian Villa at Antioch, slightly earlier in date (Levi (1947), ii, pls. LX, d-g, and LXI, a-c). Singular formal refinement and complete programmatic frontality can be found in a pavement with an octagonal *emblema* representing a peacock, dating from the end of the third century and recently excavated at Aquileia.

6 Brusin and Zovatto (1957), pp. 69–70.

older art had been able to acquire. The 'wondering matron', for instance, retains the wide thickness of veil on top of the head, as first seen in the Cemetery of Priscilla and in the Baptistery of the *Domus Christiana* at Dura Europos; while the curve of the tesserae under the eye-sockets produces an enlargement of the planes of the cheek, and the hair parted in the middle of the forehead counterpoints the continuous line of nose and eyebrow.

The colours, comprising various tones of sulphur-yellow, white, rose-pink, grey, violet, ochre and maroon, tinge the restricted surfaces of the features with harmonies of great beauty, indifferent to naturalistic effect and organised in chromatic arrangements valid on their own account. The hair of the donor seen in half-profile is rendered in grey and yellow. On his face the black lines of an eyebrow, an ear and the mouth, while plainly indicating the facial planes, which are laid in the usual tones varying between faint and brilliant, lead to a complex result of great formal merit, which attains in its anti-classical structure an exemplary force of expression. The powerful artistic temperament of the PORTRAITS MASTER is here at its most impressive. His chromatic tonality stands out from the design in its own right as an independent, freely acting exponent of the new aesthetic of surface treatment. The very fact, moreover, that patrons of unquestioned social eminence, such as the donors of the basilica mosaic must have been, demanded portraits so clearly typical of the anti-traditional taste only very recently established, confirms its potential command of the artistic market which was now open to the idiom in question.

In the centre of the second contiguous zone, the mosaic to the right of the second area, the visitor comes suddenly upon the 'Good Shepherd', chronologically the first of known Roman mosaics on this subject. He is set in no recognisable environment within his frame of ovolos; only a single strip of three rows of chromatically neutral tesserae vaguely suggests the ground on which a ewe crosses his path. But the shepherd, though supposed to be behind (or rather above) the animal, covers its hind-quarters with his legs, as though he were hanging in the air. His motionless levitation further reinforces the already manifest flattening of the figures on the surface, a phenomenon reciprocal to the elimination of background.[7] The 'tetrarchic' expression, the deep and steady eyes, enclose this surrealist figure in the abstraction of the myth.

The 'Good Shepherd', the first notable production of the SEA MASTER to be met with in the worshipper's exploration of the Basilica mosaics, is flanked in the same pavement, and in the two left- and right-hand zones of the third area, by a magnificent representation of animals that live in flocks and herds, one of the finest of its kind bequeathed by ancient painting, which was so prolific of

16

137

95, 140

7 A significant anticipation in sculpture of this solution may be noted in the Roman sarcophagus of S. Maria Antiqua, to be dated at least a generation earlier (Gerke (1940), p. 259, pl. 59).

such work. The composition, neatly subdivided into areas and medallions copied directly from the north cultic Hall of Cyriacus, has of course a symbolic meaning. Here is depicted, in catacombal symbolism, the society of the faithful, guided by Christ and consisting of cattle and, by extension, all sorts of other animals (*ovilia Dei*). The idea will occur again later in the seascape which sets the scene for the story of Jonah in the upper level of the picture. It is given specific form in the human draught promised by Christ to His Apostles: men come in as *pisciculi Dei* to form part of the *ecclesia*, and the catching of them is represented by the presence in the lower level of twelve Cupids fishing from boats and rocks.

15

141

Sheep, goats, antelopes, stags, with the whole fauna related (even though in different mosaics) to the 'Good Shepherd', are admirable above all for the quite remarkable formal synthesis achieved by the artist. Following his inspiration as a whole, he seeks passionately in the para-tactical structure of the bodies, inherited from the taste of the Tetrarchy, a new plastic consistency relying primarily on colour. It has already been pointed out that in the work of the SEA MASTER this effort must be judged to have failed, since plastic illusion pursued by means of the boldest juxtapositions of colour does not succeed in re-creating on a flat surface the three-dimensional appearance at which every naturalistic painting must aim. Nor can it be attained by the suggestion of animated movement in the figures. Their rigid, static quality, despite the use of Hellenistic models, itself contributes to a result more suited to a medieval bestiary than to the stock forms of pastoral Hellenism.

95, 140

Nevertheless, in his study of various idiomatic details and in his choice of colours for these animals, where the shadows are in large part vainly allusive and synthetic because of their abstract projection on an empty white background, the master shows his interest in new formal solutions by attempting deceptive effects of a plastic character through an entirely asyntactic chromatic 'sfumato', contrived (as for example in the antelope on the left of the 'Good Shepherd' and in the goat at the extreme outer corner of the third area, right-hand zone) by alternate streaks of white and grey in very subtle tones, determining areas of corporeal masses only mechanically brought together, despite some resort to indented seaming, within a design of bodily contour which, in the form of a simple black line, reduces the figures to a meticulous pre-medieval calligraphy.

95

Elsewhere, as in the stag on the right of the 'Good Shepherd', the more markedly expressionist handling of colour ignores the more harmonious of the faint tones in favour of grey-green, yellow, brick-red, and again of pearl-grey, orange, lilac and violet, which tend to a more genuine effect. Particularly in the left-hand zone of the third area, however, chromatic assonance is less in evidence, the laying of strips of colour appears more original, and even the design seems more preoccupied with its own plastic importance. The single sheep browsing in the left-hand compartment of the first row from the bottom (the one farthest from the seascape) reveals to stylistic examination a more organic laying of the strips and consequently more appreciable syntax of volumes, so that the suggestion of bulk becomes less remote.[8]

The above description of cultural tendencies and stylistic practices makes it appear rather improbable that the same artist, the SEA MASTER, was responsible for the 'Great Fishing' scene and the central zone of the third area, culminating in the 'Eucharistic Victory'. The clumsy and at times positively surrealist colouring of this second subject and its frequently naive design, a feature almost always present in extensive maritime views, are reason enough for perplexity. But the chromatic taste already shown here and there in the representation of the divine flocks, the resemblance in figurative structure between the personages of the 'Offertory' and of the fishing scene (including Jonah) and the 'Good Shepherd', and the use of the same idiomatic filter in the handling of the bodies of the marine animals (monster and fish), as well as in the treatment of the flocks, are a convincing demonstration of an identity of poetic inspiration, though it may have been expressed in some cases by a craftsman different from and less skilled than the usual *tessellarius*.

15, 141
138

139, 141,
15, 137

The hand of such a craftsman might perhaps be often detected in the persons of the ritual 'Offertory'. His style, indeed, reflects almost exactly that of the SEA MASTER as it might have been understood and reproduced by local apprentices. It may be of interest in this connection to compare some of his figures with those of certain fragments in the Opitergino Museum, particularly with that of the young hunter attacking a boar, that of the beater Romanus setting dogs on a hare and that of the young cupbearer.[9] These fragments are all to be dated about the middle of the fourth century, and are therefore a generation later than the 'Offertory'. They show remarkable stylistic similarities to the seven surviving contributors represented at Aquileia.

139

More attention, therefore, should be paid to the 'Eucharistic Victory' at the centre of the third area. Here concern for naturalism, if present at all, is overwhelmed by the colour distributed with exquisite taste over the flowing robe, the face, the wings and the arms of the mystic figure. The wings are stressed surrealistically in green, grey and maroon. The arms are formed by a straightforward series of eight or nine courses of tesserae in various colours, with no indication of contour except the alternation of serial

138

8 All this has of course to be understood relatively. *See*, in this connection, Levi (1947), i, p. 584, where the animals of this pavement are mentioned as examples of 'purely schematic and superficial design'.
9 Zovatto (1956), ff. 5, 8, 9, 12; (1963), ff. 12, 14, 15.

order in the two parts of the right arm holding the laurel – an unquestionable sign of an attempt to create a three-dimensional effect through light and shade expressed in the colours. A rainbow of shrill, dissonant tones ranging from violet to lilac, pink, sulphur-yellow and red, transfigures the already tenuous corporeity of the image, so as to give it the insubstantiality of a dream, Just as in the bunches of grapes presented by one of the female offerers the black and violet border of the fruit encloses a circular corona of white tesserae, and these in turn a small pink centre, with quite remarkable effect, so here too the frequency of chromatic patchwork in the garments of many of the figures is metamorphosed into genuine notes of lively expressive content.

The spatial and chromatic concept, the formal taste and the repertorial preferences of the SEA MASTER, as hitherto described by way of anticipation, can be seen in their full development only in the great seascape of the last area of the Theodorean Basilica. The creatures in this symbolic picture are brought to the surface by the schematic shaping of the waves (two simple strips of tesserae one above the other, black and serpentine green respectively) with repeated formal distinction, in which is expressed the idiomatic structure already observed in the picture of the animals of the divine flock, but in which there are also and very frequently apparent the elements of a more completely linear aesthetic, related to a paratactical two-dimensionalism incapable of rendering the organic nature and volume of bodies.

This is true of the fishing Cupids, in which connection 141 the straining towards frontal presentation of the Cupids, seen in profile aboard the boats, is less illuminating than the flattened and almost dissected form of one who angles from the rock near the dedication to Theodore inscribed on the site of the ancient altar. It is true also of the figure of Jonah about to be devoured by the monster, a creature of 15 singular beauty on account both of its design and of the tessellar palette employed, comprising red, black, greyish brown, pearl-grey and pink. It is true again of the stretch of furrowed ground on which Jonah reposes after his release, and of those rocks from which the fishing Cupids throw their bait, rocks which are an authentic and chromatically expressionist foreshadowing of Byzantine crags, sometimes directly reflected in the sea-water with exact similitude of shape and perfect identity of colouring. It is true finally of certain syntactical details of the marine fauna, where in many of the fish the mouth is rendered frontally, not by a cut but by a perfectly round hole, or where the spherical mass of an octopus is composed in 15, 141 concentric strips of tesserae, which solve the problem of alluding to volume by means of a repetitive series of flat rings of colour.

The transposition, not without accents of lyrical grandeur, of all the infinite planes of perspective and three-dimensional reality to the surface of a single foreground plane occurs for the first time with the maximum of paratactical and two-dimensional coherence in this fantastic panorama by the SEA MASTER at Aquileia. The wealth of symbolism, the cultural curiosity, the conception of composition and the stylistic dexterity therein displayed all combine in an achievement which constitutes, in the present state of knowledge of the *corpus* of the art of late antiquity, a further effective point of departure and likewise a striking example of the maturity reached in the development of the new taste by painting which used the Roman idiom in the service of Christian inspiration, and which, through the mosaic *medium*, was about to culminate in the glory of apsidal bays and the world of the cupola.

Chapter Eight
Experiments and masters of North African mosaic in the fourth century

The prevailing view of the cultural and stylistic ancestry of the HUNT, CARNAGE, COURT and ANIMAL HEADS MASTERS of Piazza Armerina refers their manners in general, as noted above, to the *milieu* of North Africa (in particular of Tunisia) at the beginning of the fourth century. I have no wish even to sketch a complete itinerary of Roman art in Africa at this time; but the information supplied by some of the more important works excavated at Hippo Regius (Bône), Thysdrus (El Djem), Uthina (Oudna), Constantine and Carthage affords an opportunity to examine the lines of development and the most significant stylistic peculiarities of a phase of Romano-African mosaic painting in which the evidence of the Alexandrian tradition seems, in accordance with the movement already apparent in the Dionysiac mosaics at Hadrumetum (Susa) and El Djem, to be indicative of theories, stylistic practices and compositional results by now wholly involved (and sometimes, probably, as originally creative) in the tissue of the late Roman *koine*; indicative also of a future taste which may broadly be called Byzantine, although, until the beginning of the fifth century, Constantinople gave no sign, except in literary productions, of the revival of a neo-Alexandrianism perhaps not expressive of the real trend of contemporary culture.

The testimony of these and other African mosaicists of the fourth century is conspicuously endorsed by the development stamped with such magnificence at Piazza Armerina, where the mere presence of such an artist as the CARNAGE MASTER was enough to impart a very special accent to much of the evolving taste signified by the pavements of that extensive villa. Considering, therefore, not only the prevalence (itself perhaps not entirely accidental) of rural, hunting and marine subjects in the more notable remains of African mosaics, even during the fourth century, but also the extraordinary variety of such scenes in the Sicilian villa, it would appear reasonable to see in the mosaic pavements dealing with such themes the point at which grammatical and syntactical transformation of fourth-century Romano-African tessellates can be most usefully studied.

The pavement from the *impluvium* of the luxurious Villa of the Laberii at Oudna (Uthina) is now in the Bardo Museum, It appears to be earlier than the other pavements to be discussed here.[1] Nevertheless its chronological position may seem in this context very far removed from

145, 143
18, 144,

51
53

142

---

1 Gauckler (1910), no. 362.

the dating officially accepted, which was sanctioned from the outset by the recovery of coins issued during the long period between Trajan and Gallienus.[2] This large composition, with a border of double braiding, comprises on three sides, facing outwards, a series of scenes of 'Big Game Hunting and Agricultural Labour', while at the centre, facing the same way as the scenes on the longest side and almost touching the fourth side of the pavement, similar incidents of pastoral life are illustrated, surrounding a building used for farming purposes.

This arrangement of compositional elements is of itself enough to dispose of the argument for its origin in the second century, a period narrowed down by Gauckler to the last years of the first century or the very first of the second.[3] Nowhere in the entire Roman world has there been found a mosaic possessing such characteristics and assignable to any date prior to the early third century. Levi was therefore justified in opposing the long-maintained idea as to the chronological origin of this work, and in describing frankly as a 'wholly unreliable criterion' the judgment founded upon the date of the most ancient among the coins discovered in the Laberian villa.[4]

Indeed, from the stylistic point of view the mosaic shows, in addition to a manifest lack of continuity in the design, an often marked tendency to narrative weakness, expressed frequently in scribbled, slapdash forms, particularly in the lioness- and boar-hunting scenes, which looks back to the predelictions evinced (and often terminating in the linear style) during the last quarter of the third century, in the years preceding the full establishment of the Tetrarchy. There would certainly be no point here in denying that the pavement might easily be linked with the 'realistic style of Alexandrian painting',[5] because of its many lyrico-pastoral features – though there are present also indications of a more historical, documentary chronicle. But consider the defiance of the Hellenistic unitary concept of space; the purely contrapuntal significance of the pattern of landscape elements, including the very beautiful trees, all brought to the single surface plane; and finally the advanced stage of reintegration of the central scene (originally the *emblema*) on the white background confronting the lateral projections aligned on three sides. Those three factors together suggest that the designer of this mosaic, by now Alexandrian only in a generic sense and at long range, must have worked at the close of the third century, when he could have appreciated the virtual or operative attitudes of late antiquity, matured during that century even in Africa, where accurate reference could easily be made to work being done elsewhere in the Empire.

Owing to an evident similarity not only of content, but also of vocabulary, to the mosaics of Piazza Armerina, we

2 Gauckler (1896), p. 177 ff.
3 Gauckler (1910), no. 182.
4 Levi (1947), i, p. 522, n. 3.
5 Gauckler (1910), no. 362.

O

6 Gauckler (1910), no. 64.
7 Picard, G.C. (1959). In this connection
Pace (1955, p. 103) wrote: 'The
parallels are of greater significance . . .
and of still more is the mosaic of hunting
scenes from a house at El Gem, now in
the Bardo Museum at Tunis. The same
arrangement of the figures on levels with
indications of landscape recurs, as do the
same draughtsmanship of the horses and
other animals and the same human types.
But above all the same decorative sense
is found in the distribution of the figures,
in the representation of movement with a
"danced" rhythm, in the heaviness of the
drapery and in the ornamentation of the
clothing. Even the frame, with its
perspective plait-moulding, shows a
taste shared by the two mosaics. But the
Bardo pavement does not provide
reliable evidence of its date.'
8 A close comparative study of the two
pavements, exhaustive in every detail,
might ultimately have to postpone the
division between the hypotheses of two
artists from the same workshop and a
single *imaginarius*.
9 De Pachtère (1911), no. 45.

can profitably continue our inquiry by studying the *venationes* of El Djem and Hippo. The first of these was discovered during the excavations of 1905 in the same luxurious dwelling which yielded the third-century 'Triumph of Dionysus' already considered, and is today in the Bardo Museum at Tunis.[6] It illustrates some episodes of a 'Hare Hunt' organised on three levels, the narrative beginning at the top. Although Picard has found it possible to suppose this mosaic anterior to the 'Triumph of Dionysus' in the same house, its exact syntactic and idiomatic correspondence with the pavement of the 'Great Hunt', clearly distinguished by Pace,[7] suggests that it should be referred to at least the end of the century, too late probably for the laying of the Dionysiac mosaic. It may be observed, however, that the composition and certain figurative details recall the Piazza Armerina 'Small Hunt' even more precisely than the 'Great Hunt'.

53

143

104

The stylistic characterisation of this artist, though he may have shared an apprenticeship with the HUNT MASTER, becomes apparent in the freer search for a figurative articulation dominated by skilful draughtsmanship and by a concept of colour as the mere chromatic filling of a given outline, which undoubtedly gave rise to the same traits in the HUNT MASTER and which he progressively developed in the sense of endowing colour with some plastic significance.[8]

The Hippo artist, who decorated a wing of the *tablinum* of a villa with an elaborate 'Hunt Chronicle'[9] the events of which are set out in temporal succession, appears to have been formatively connected with the output of the school in which the Piazza Armerina HUNT MASTER and his El Djem colleague were trained. To the left of a broad, undulating landscape, part forest, two hunters on horseback, followed by two grooms, are pursuing ostriches and antelopes. In the centre, a serried rank of beaters, protected by shields and armed with lighted torches, are driving towards a cage containing domestic animals as bait a lion, a lioness and some panthers, one of which last has brought down a groom. Above and to the right is shown the capture of a wild ass by lasso; below, a picnic is being prepared among carts and tents.

145

This great pavement (6.70 × 3.75 m.) approximates to the 'Piazza Armerina style' through syntactic connections and the objective resemblance of the incidents, as well as by certain figurative details ranging from the shields of the beaters to the cage. Yet the mosaic from Hippo, as compared with some phases of the Sicilian 'Great Hunt', is notable for a more complex composition, sometimes laboriously assembled, certainly by virtue of the chronological sequences which the master retains. At Piazza Armerina, on the other hand, simultaneity of the terminal phases has now been achieved; a simultaneity which, at

Plan C;
102, 9, 1

the centre of the corridor, in the successive stages of loading and unloading the beasts, appears with a new symmetrical and as it were synchronous significance, where objective 'time' yields to the whole composition's demand for centripetal iteration.

This aim, to be sure, is indicated also at Hippo. Here, however, the central episode of the beat is not surrounded by simultaneous events, but more clearly by the 'before' and 'after' of the *venatio*, namely the departure for the hunt and the dinner off the spoils. Moreover, it must be pointed out that in the African villa the forms appear less refined and mature than in the Sicilian, and that the idiom, in its concrete definition of line and colour, certainly seems less confident and homogeneous and is unquestionably not on the same level.

The pavement of the HIPPO HUNT CHRONICLE MASTER can also be assigned to a date very close to that of the Sicilian hunts,[10] late in the period of the Tetrarchy. But it must at the same time be considered to belong to the entirely late-Roman phase, in Africa, of the preceding figurative culture of Alexandria.

A good example of African mosaic art in the age of the Tetrarchy is provided by the pavimental mosaic of the 'Triumph of Oceanus and Amphitrite', found in the environs of Constantine and now at the Louvre.[11] The composition is of medium dimensions and in frankly court style. It is organised strictly in accordance with the conventions of unemotional frontal presentation and meticulous symmetry, where everything combines to produce an effect of ceremonial majesty, from the Cupids riding dolphins in the foreground to others fishing from boats, and from the four sea-horses yoked to the divine car to the two Cupids hovering above the deities with a long purple cloth.

There are plenty of contemporary works, in reliefs for example, or in imperial medallions, and also works of earlier date, in which this type of syntactic organisation seems to have been solemnly invoked.[12] They prove that such productions were due less to the caprice of a patron than to a set standard of taste, whether directly imposed by the new policy of the Tetrarchy or itself a contributory cause of the artistic methods that paralleled those newly promoted in the political sphere by Diocletian and his colleagues and successors. But it is clear that in works of this kind, which drew their subjects from the abundant repertory of Alexandrian art and the later painting and sculpture of North Africa flourishing in the third century, men felt bound to undertake a thorough reorganisation of their models, on account not so much of any intentions of the artist at the time as of established secular ideals of a permanent character. This being so, it is hard to escape

18

10 So also Gentili (1952 b), p. 60.
11 De Pachtère (1911), no. 226.
12 *See* in this connection, for example, the gold medallion of Constantine and Licinius in the Cabinet des Médailles, Paris (Volbach (1952), p. 50, f. 21), and again: Picard, G. C. (1959), cc. 144 and 148; Levi (1947), i, p. 340, f. 138, n. 108; and the older *emblema* of the 'Triumph of Poseidon' in the fine mosaic at the Bardo (Gauckler (1910), no. 86) from Susa.

the impression of frigid and forced exaltation made on a modern observer by the 'Triumph of Oceanus and Amphitrite'.

A more precise stylistic judgment leads to the recognition of a certain severity, little inclined to effusive *fauve* chromaticism, relying entirely on tones of grey and blue, pink and red, and in the last analysis not much in favour of solving the problem of form by means of colour, such as had been seen at Piazza Armerina from the beginning. The hieratic frigidity of the composition, and the punctilious rigour with which figures in one half of the picture have their exact counterparts in the other (as in the case of the 'Consular Triumph' from the Basilica of Junius 113 Bassus), combine with an obvious poverty of chromatic invention in such a way as sometimes to allow the solecism of clashing juxtapositions, so that the result finally acquires a positive value, mainly by virtue of the role allotted to design and to certain techniques shared with the *musivarii* of a master of Piazza Armerina.

Actually, the restrictive need for symmetry causes the design to invent a coinage, so to speak, of repeated markings that lend to the whole a monotonous but not worthless rhythm. The tails of the sea-horses, for example, 18 and the repetitive pattern of their emergence from the waters, directly in front of the animals themselves; the sailing-boats with their fishing boys; the similar figures mounted on the dolphins; and even the marine fauna: all combine to present, in an often pleasing repetition of formal motives, a series of contrapuntal features which is the best element in the pavement. Moreover, this MARINE TRIUMPH MASTER of Constantine is a nimble exponent of a craft now recognised, for its expertise and brilliance, as unattainable in the CARNAGE MASTER of Piazza Armerina. It consists in varying the tones of the mosaic inlay within the same chromatic scale, or in altering colour in such a way as to recompose the tonality of the plastic texture of the organisms which tetrarchic parataxis tends to annul. The spirals of the sea-horses' tails, the bodies of some of the Cupids, the haloes of the two divinities, and the long purple cloth extended in their honour, all contribute to the result of movement and residual plasticity, through the well-known technique of hinged or indented tesserae.

It is undoubtedly in these points of style that the work of the MARINE TRIUMPH MASTER is subject to the most vigorous impulses of late Roman art and plays the most highly personal part in that particular phase of it which, with the ending of the Tetrarchy and the reunification of power under Constantine, tended to revive experiments directed to the recovery of form, on which the brightest light would be thrown by court art.

A stylistic step beyond the tetrarchic age's preoccupation with the developments of court art may be detected (outside the range of the latter's terminal mannerisms) in the conspicuously Roman texture, in some respects of markedly pre-Byzantine tendency, of yet another 'Hunt Chronicle', that of an *oecus* brought to light in a late fourth-century Carthaginian house and now in the Bardo Museum.[13] The narrative is set out in a series of five levels organised about a centripetal chronological base. The first and second levels from the top represent the departure for the hunt with muleteers, and encounters with a lion and a tigress. The third level, prolonged at the centre into the fourth, depicts sacrifice at a shrine of Artemis and Apollo. The fourth and fifth show scenes of stag-hunting, boar-hunting and the taking of a lion in a trap. The manner resembles that of the 'Small Hunt' at Piazza Armerina, but with a stricter division of time. In this sense the work shows more evident chronological depth than do others of the fourth century, and a possibly provincial predilection for the narrative structure brought to maturity in the preceding century. The repertory also, faithful to the usual cartoons, indicates a tendency to retain all kinds of objects and forms borrowed by Romano-African painting, though with variations in many works, from the highly fertile tradition of Alexandria.

But at the centre of the picture some points of unquestionable expressive originality prove once more that the most faithful adherence to tradition is frequently accompanied by a more progressive impulse towards novelty. On either side of the rustic shrine, consisting of two simple columns supporting a pediment beneath which stand the two haloed statues of the divinities, a group of three hunters in strictly frontal presentation stand with their backs to a row of cypresses which, by separating one hunter from another, lend additional emphasis to the rhythm of their static quality, which extends to a typological rigidity carried impersonally from face to face. These groups reveal the importance of the progress made since the appearance of analogous processions, already considered in these pages, both at Rome and at Dura Europos. This emblematical centre of the Carthaginian 'Hunt Chronicle' foreshadows the structure of the hieratic representations which, starting from the 'imperial majesties', and particularly from the Constantinian reliefs of the Arch of Constantine, recurred in a series of western Christian monuments from the small apses of S. Costanza to those of S. Aquilino, and from the triumphal arch of S. Maria Maggiore to the apse of S. Pudenziana, indissoluble links in a chain leading to S. Vitale.

Great significance also attaches to the mosaic design of the *temenos* and altar, which occupies the space of two levels of the narrative. Above, beneath the shrine and on the same level as the hunters, stand the two divinities; below, the altar, so roughly drawn as almost to suggest

144

15, 27

144

13 Gauckler (1910), no. 607.

the technique of a cartographer. A large bird, the sacrificial victim, appears to be falling stiffly from the altar but is in reality supposed to be resting upon it, and tends to connect two-dimensionally its upper surface with the side presented to view, so that the latter looks like the base of the object in question, seen from the zenith. Within the ambit of the capable representation, this strange design constitutes one of the clearest instances of subversion in all the painting of late antiquity. The rejection of classical three-dimensional harmony is no longer physical but internal, expressing an ideology. Yet this design may perhaps be classed as one of those asyntactic projections that would later swarm in the miniatures of manuscripts throughout the early Middle Ages. Again, only a little later, the aforementioned mosaic from Tabarka (ancient Thabraca) depicting the so-called *Ecclesia Mater*,[14] likewise preserved in the Bardo Museum, presents in a style even more complex, resembling the Piazza Armerina 'Circus Races' but with a clearer display of paratactical juxtapositions, the confluence of diverse planes within the anatomised configuration of the ecclesiastical building. Finally, there seems no reason not to suppose that a small sacrificial altar might really have been intended to appear at the centre of the reproduction of the *temenos*.

In reality, whenever taste or practical necessity drives the artists to faithful reproduction of existing monuments, the two-dimensional concept of space so often encountered in late Roman painting is destined to reveal itself with more astonishing clarity; and not only to reveal itself more clearly, but also to combine, within the figurative idiom by this time characteristic of the culture of late antiquity, the obsolete elements of an iconographical documentation which Christian realism in general, after passing its first expressionist phase, came to select, with new preoccupations in mind, from the inexhaustible heritage of ancient civilisation. The times had definitely gone by when the problems of human figurative environment could be solved exclusively in anthropomorphic terms. In tetrarchic expressionism, in the 'fine style' and in the mannerism of the closing century, they had been capable almost unaided of summarising the historicity of an event. A significant current of late Roman figurative culture, from S. Maria Maggiore to S. Apollinare, began to turn to the historicity of its monumental environment, which had certainly not been defined in classical terminology, for the achievement of its symbolical productions both in the religious and in the secular sphere.

A further step in pictoral representation, to be dated not earlier than the middle of the fourth century and probably very near the fifth, was taken in the large mosaic pavement discovered within the walls of another Carthaginian house, which contained other *lithostrota* attributable to

14 Gauckler (1910), no. 1021 (*see also* Chapter 6, note 19).

some time between the second and the fifth century. From an inscription on the mosaic here considered, the building immediately became known as the Villa of Dominus Julius.[15]

The composition, a panorama on three levels with a lavish outer frame of acanthus racemes and an inner edge of sea-waves, is no different structurally from many others of the North African school so far studied. The central level is dominated in the middle by the landowner's homestead, a building which by this time had assumed all the characteristics of a castle of late antiquity, with two lateral towers, a big entrance gate at ground level, and on the first floor a long, imposing gallery, certainly open to the local residents. Behind the façade and within the grounds of the villa, we catch a glimpse of four large domes, probably belonging to the baths, which complete the impression of a self-contained civil edifice on a great agricultural estate, able to support its owners, accommodate the labourers in smaller buildings and provide protection in case of disorders or hostile raids. This, then, is a type of architecture in many ways novel as compared with buildings such as that of Tivoli or even that of Piazza Armerina; it met a need for security and hence for experimental developments in fortification that would be widely adopted and elaborated all through the Middle Ages.[16]

Meanwhile, the novelty of compositional structure in the 'Dominus Julius' mosaic consists essentially in the mixing, one might even say the adoption, of the mythical and conjectural element into what was more clearly historical and commemorative. In fact, on all four sides, on the first and third levels, the DOMINUS JULIUS MASTER has presented the four 'Seasons', copied from ancient examples. It suffices, however, in this connection to study the work of the *imaginarius* of the Antioch Villa (see Chapter IX) in order to realise the difference between the two artists in both thought and feeling. The Carthaginian *imaginarius*, in fact, 'tells about' winter and summer, spring and autumn, with a meticulous realism from which the garlanded heads and the figures customary in all the traditional symbolism of the ancients are absent. Similarly, the same stereotyped allusions in certain scenes of a farmer's year are replaced by naturalistic presentations of modest peasant families intent on their seasonal labours and offering the fruits of the earth or the spoils of the chase to their master and mistress. These latter, like Dominus Julius, do not disdain the hunting of hares with the usual assistance of dogs and slaves; but they also take pleasure in being seen at their daily occupations and relaxations, the lady at her toilet and her husband seated for the reception of gifts and documents. We have already caught a glimpse of this varied society in the *Uthina* mosaic, but there the stock objects were more mechanically

146

147, 148, **19, 20**

146

142

15 Merlin (1921).
16 Mansuelli (1958), pp. 99 ff. and 104.

distributed. In the present wonderful pavement the figures seem, as it were, to have been photographed while engrossed in their pleasures and their business, in their surroundings and in the social and economic structure of the dying fourth century. Meanwhile more and more serious threats from the outside world were looming, and in every province of the Empire the social fabric was closing around its natural pivots, as if preparing to offer the maximum economic, cultural and civil resistance to the pressure of the Middle Ages enforced by migrations of the peoples of north-eastern Europe.

Even stylistically the 'Dominus Julius' pavement expresses the spirit of supervening forces, no longer necessarily or exclusively late-Roman, and appears sensitive to adstrate influences which, varying over the years, eventually prescribed cultural and formal changes throughout the area of the ancient *koine*. The work is certainly older, for example, than the mosaic of 'Hippolytus and Phaedra' at Sheikh Zueda in Egypt,[17] absurdly attributed to the first half of the second century, but which has also been placed very much later than the age of Constantine, to which Levi[18] refers as a *terminus post quem* in his argument for a date in the late fifth century under Theodosius II. And yet, if any stylistic affiliation with the 'Dominus Julius' mosaic is admissible, it must be sought in that mythological illustration, where the wide, inexpressive eyes that dominate wondering faces, generally devoid of any obvious meaning, clearly recall the Carthaginian pavement. In this latter the still animated impression given by the dancing movement of the figures is unquestionably tetrarchic, as is the taste for colour still conscious of its own formative function and the extremely keen attention to detail proper in a 'civil' subject (though one dealing with mythological personifications given a time dimension) as compared with the ossified Alexandrianism of residual content in the Sheikh Zueda mosaic. That movement and that taste for colour are to a great extent signs-manual of the great imperial art forged in the age of the Tetrarchy. In the same way interesting comparisons may be instituted with particular idiomatic details in the large mosaic of the *megalopsychia* of Antioch (Yakto Complex),[19] though here a formalist rigidity of neoclassical type is more evident. The neo-Alexandrianism of the *pictor imaginarius* seems very close to, even though it is later than, the formal refinement of the mosaics in the quadrangular porch of the *Mega Palation* at Constantinople.

146

39–41, 218, 221

17 Clédat (1915), Pace (1955, p. 103) accepts a date in the age of Theodosius I.
18 Levi (1947), i, p. 73, n. 32.
19 Levi (1947), ii, pls. LXXVI–LXXXIII.

Chapter Nine
Masters of the Constantinian 'fine style' at Antioch and Trier

Towards the end of the 1935 season an expedition from Princeton University excavated in the suburb of Daphne-Harbie at Antioch a villa of the Constantinian age, to be called hereafter the Constantinian Villa. The square pavement of the principal room was undoubtedly inspired by, being almost a reflection of, the decorative scheme of the four sections of a cross-vaulting. The mosaic is framed, like the surrounding rectangular area itself, by a winding margin, that displays various scenes of a predominantly pastoral character or busts of personified Virtues. Four diagonal strips, starting from the corners (where they meet a continuous lateral bounding strip adorned with conspicuous acanthus racemes and vegetable masks), divide the area into four trapezoids bordered like the lateral strip with ovolo mouldings and displaying hunting scenes. The four diagonals, on the other hand, contain the same number of winged female figures, supported by acanthus clusters and representing the four 'Seasons', as shown by their garments, by the agricultural products that they carry and by the type of vegetation that frames them against a black background. The central octagon formed by the meeting of the trapezoids and the strips illustrating the 'Seasons' was used as a pool, perhaps reflecting the decoration at the top of the vaulting, or else, if the summit ended in an aperture, as an *impluvium*.

The space provided by the adjacent rectangular field was subdivided into sections richly bordered with plaited mouldings and winding perspectives. It allowed room, more simply, for five circular medallions displaying the busts of members of the Bacchic *thiasos* and for three lozenge-shaped medallions facing the end of the hall. In an adjacent area, over thirteen metres long and only three wide, the oblong *emblema*, within a frame of acanthus sprays and Cupids against a black background, was devoted to the representation of full-length figures at exercise, of which only a few fragments survive.

The most remarkable and most important part of the whole pavement is unquestionably that depicting the plant-gathering figures of the 'Seasons'. The artist did not assign them the duty of symbolical caryatids metaphorically upholding the central tank of the *impluvium*; he gave them instead a morphological position which, together with the aforesaid explicit function, recurs in contemporary and later monuments, from the lost decoration of the cupola of the Mausoleum of Constantina in Rome to

147, 148

152

19, 20

156

147, 148,
19, 20

the vaults of the Archepiscopal Chapel, the Baptistery of the Orthodox and S. Vitale, all at Ravenna. More ancient examples are those of the winged spirits carrying funerary portraits in the painted Tomb of Magharat-el-Djelideh at Palmyra, already studied in the present work, and the still 69 older vault of the Roman Tomb of the Nasoni.

The substantial frames of the four 'Seasons' display, in the towering figures and the wonderful foliage from which they rise, examples of a pictorial style certainly not much practised by painters in the first half of the fourth century or, one may say more accurately, in its third decade. The undisguised classicism of the composition, though not altogether isolated, in fact illustrates an artistic procedure fashionable in the age of Constantinian restoration and directly promoted by its august leader. The mode was certainly not a natural outcome of the current of important stylistic development in imperial painting between the third and the fourth century. After the expressionist cubism of the Tetrarchy the trends most frequent at the beginning of the century showed signs of entering a more tranquil, but by no means in general reactionary, phase of paratactical expressionism, which lasted without a break for a full fifty years over a wide area.[1] It was the court culture, maturing in the shadow of the revived ideals of imperial unity cherished by the family of Constantine, which imposed on the best artists, whether or not summoned to work for the court, the recovery of a substantially classicist idiom which could not, of course, be unmindful of the traditions of taste and technique with which those artists themselves were naturally imbued.

At this juncture there suddenly appeared the great, though unclassifiable, work of the CARNAGE MASTER at Piazza Armerina, while other hands laid the mosaics in that house at Antioch (where the frescoes and other decorations that may be presumed to have covered the walls and ceilings have perished), and others again, whose productions will be discussed in due course, painted the ceiling of a hall in the imperial palace at Trier, at the other end of the Roman world.

Except for the figure of Winter, the Antiochene 'Seasons' wear transparent, light-coloured robes of white 147 or yellow. The surfaces are varied with delicate shadings of grey, rose and yellow in the interests of luminous effect, just as they give heavier relief to the wings. The cloths held up between the arms contain brightly coloured flowers, ears of corn and fruit, which like the different 147, 148, garlands and the luxuriant vegetation, characterise the four 148, 20 personified beings. The meticulous drawing, too, collaborates in a total result of narrative interest and plastic significance; so also, by way of lending the figures more decorative value (as Levi remarks),[2] does the return to the image of a richly dressed caryatid already proper to their

1 The mosaics of the Aquileian masters already examined, and those of the second generation at Piazza Armerina already deserted, are sufficient evidence of this development.
2 Levi (1947), i, p. 233.

primitive representations in Greek art, in obedience to a tendency natural at a later stage.

The highly elaborate design of acanthus shrubs, thick with greenish shoots and capriciously slashed with very strong light and very deep shadow, and the graduated and careful lay-out of the faces, caressed, as it were, by colour and tonality, and at the same time marked by a de-personalising line almost devoid of expression, do not of course suffice to establish a fully courtly effect, in the sense of a total recall of the structures of the most academic Hellenism.

Under deeper stylistic analysis the variations of light and shade in the figures and their botanical attributes, the plasticity of the female forms and their amply flowing robes and draperies, and finally the balance itself between crowded and empty space in the general arrangement of the compositions, actually convey an impression of deliberately flat ornamentation for its own sake, in which the harmony of the shapes and chromatic variants, the very contrast between the brightness of the figures and their dark background, as well as the mannerist subtlety of certain details in the flowers, tendrils and ears of corn, do not attain the total effect of a classical composition. As compared with the colourful impact of the supporting shrubs, the figures of the Seasons show no sign of even restrained movement or expressive animation. The entire decoration exhibits, on a plane which seems still unitary and without any real depth, a tireless exuberance of colour and line, in which Levi has stressed[3] 'a pleasant, rhythmic alternation of shaded and illuminated areas with created movement and life for the surface alone.' Did the 'fine style' of this MASTER OF THE ANTIOCH SEASONS develop, then, in an idiomatic culture of late antiquity vainly disguised in forms of classical tendency?

One might be tempted to reply at once in the affirmative to this question, but such an answer would elude the substance of the problem. Besides, the hunting scenes of 147, 148 the trapezoidal areas – which it seems may legitimately be attributed to the same artist, like the medallions of the rectangular section (Bacchic *thiasos*) – also show a similar coexistence of elements matured during the crisis of the Tetrarchy with those of an elaborately traditional taste in form. The scenes attest, to be sure, a highly accentuated tendency to organic re-composition of figurative structures. Gone are the clumsy liberties taken by cubist theory, with its geometrical and expressionist interests; and the chromatic surfaces can spread within the harmonious design of bodies with the calm assurance of an effort directed solely to the faithful reproduction of the solid volume of reality. The sense of movement, too – entirely absent from the 'Seasons', and certainly not because of their ostensibly static function – appears to animate with-

3 *Ibid.*, p. 561.

out stint these illustrations of the chase, where the hunters, their horses and the wild beasts, are poised in attitudes that for the most part suggest the sudden or sustained tension of their muscles.

But at the same time, and in particular, one cannot ignore the composition of these scenes, in which there is no trace whatever of traditional perspective. Individual figures appear to have been recomposed on the surface, and all transferred to the foreground, despite the abundance of landscape features; and yet there is not established between them, even when the action in which they are engaged demands it (e.g. hunter and quarry), any connection of accurately and 'realistically' determined depth, whether between one figure and another or between figure and background. In short, the individual figures clearly proclaim their derivation from organic classical models, originally disposed in a different spatial structure, and yet placed in natural mutual relations in accordance with the rules of the most precisely calculated Hellenistic perspective. In this case, however, men, horses and wild beasts, though they need a true relationship with the landscape (but one very different from that of a realistic creation, as will be seen later), are nevertheless all composed on a single plane, the same for their grouping, dimensions, shadows and background ratios. This circumstance inevitably entails, in their mutual spatial relations, subversions, deceptions and incongruities on which Levi has very properly and ably dwelt.[4]

One feels, therefore, as though present at a variety show, before the footlights of a stage with a painted backcloth which in each of the four scenes simulates an environment. It must be added, however, that this backcloth scrupulously and in most remarkable fashion presents the landscape features (trees, rocks, bushes, the rustic altar of Artemis, etc.) only so as to correspond with the spaces left empty by the persons moving about in front, so that it ultimately appears as though the two levels have become one, upon which the objects on the first take the greatest possible care to avoid contact with those on the second, and vice versa. A total effect of this kind can only identify the master's method with one of a symmetrical systematisation in the trapezoidal spaces, and in a two-dimensional compass, of forms taken from models of a much more active compositional complexity. There is no need to emphasise that such a proceeding takes place within the framework of a spatial concept wholly characteristic of late antiquity and, to be more precise, exactly paratactical. In any case it is extremely remote from Hellenistic spatial concepts.

The style was not, however, casual in origin. In analysing its structure, one need only study in isolation such features of the landscape as the rocks and certain sections

4 *Ibid.*, pp. 609–10.

traditional form; but they certainly indicate an identity of idiom within a common culture and sensibility.

At Antioch, then, the SEASONS MASTER confined his heads, so far as possible, within the same framework of courtly formal polish instinctive in all his work. It may be asked, therefore, whether a substantially negative judgment should be passed upon him.

Certainly not. While bearing in mind that the 'Vegetable Masks' of the frieze may just possibly have been executed by another hand, we may say that in those works at any rate which reveal more careful handling, e.g. in the busts of the Bacchic *thiasos*, the SEASONS MASTER's methods achieve results of more expressive vivacity and true beauty. In this connection the medallions of 'Dionysus' and 'Old 156 Silenus' should be examined. In the former the countenance of the god stands out, as already noticed in some of the Aquileian busts, against a background of white tesserae arranged in radial strips centred upon the eyes. It is stamped with majestic psychological dignity issuing from a firm tranquillity of form. The shading, contrived by means of tesserae which are fairly large (8 to 9 mm. wide), considering that the portrait is a little over life size, is imposed on the surfaces with the artist's familiar skill, though the expressive power and organic construction can only be called less negligible than those of the faces so far mentioned. It is true that in this case also Levi finds a 'contrast between the classic purity of lines and the lack of corporeal structure', which induces him to refer to the well-known 'Dionysas' in the Catacomb of Callistus.[10] 21 When the 'Dionysus' is compared with the 'Haloed 156 Female Head' on a fragment of linen and wool tapestry, of 155 unknown origin, preserved at the Detroit Institute of Arts, the latter will be found to be more rigorously conservative, formally speaking, in the structure of the image, while remaining within the limits of a resemblance not solely iconographical. The fabric, dateable between the fourth and fifth centuries, probably derives from the Alexandrian centre, and helps with the comparison suggested above to place the 'Dionysus' head, stylistically even if indirectly, 156 in the context of an interest in traditional values not uncommon at that period.

Levi's exact comparison, obviously valuable, must therefore lead to a conclusion of somewhat different emphasis. By placing 'Dionysas' among the more remote 22 origins of tetrarchic expressionism, and by drawing attention to its still partly impressionistic elements, I have already shown its relatively remarkable plastic significance. Its comparison with the 'Dionysus' of the Constantinian 156 Villa then becomes decisive, because the liveliness of expression and psychology, common to both and certainly more marked in 'Dionysas', manages in the 'Dionysus' and in the 'Satyrs' of the *thiasos* to overcome the conflict

10 Levi (1947), i, p. 562. *See also* above in Chapter 5. The tapestry fragment of a 'Haloed Feminine Head' is preserved in the Detroit Institute of Arts, No. 35103. De Francovich (1963, p. 136) proposes to date it between the second half of the third century and the beginning of the fourth. Werbel (1952, n.i.) in the 3rd and 4th centuries; Beckwith (1958, p. 18, f. 18) in the 6th–7th centuries; *L'Art Copte* 1964, p. 147, n. 151) in the 4th–5th centuries; Wessel (1963, p. 214, pl. 114) in the 6th–7th centuries.

between idiom and the claims of formalist theory, and thus to confer on these last Antiochene portraits a less shallow dignity. Such are the grounds of my judgment, rather than certain points noted by Levi: the 'oblique glance'; 'thick outline of the almond-shaped eyes', which certainly reveal and stress 'the spirituality peculiar to the Constantinian age,[11] if that phrase is taken in a very loose sense to indicate the period of about fifty years from the rise of tetrarchic expressionism to the decline of its Constantinian version in the 'fine style'.

The conclusion may be reached that the SEASONS MASTER undoubtedly lacks the admirable structural vigour and highly original treatment of surfaces characteristic of the CARNAGE MASTER of Piazza Armerina. On this view his art does not attain to the level of synthetic genius attributable to that of his Sicilian colleague. Nevertheless, it may be observed that the very elements constituting the glory of the latter remained unparalleled both at Piazza Armerina and throughout the later development of Roman painting, and that its brilliant synthesis of form, which has been called 'chromatic plasticity', does not appear to have been ever repeated from the time of its first manifestation.

Conversely, though not an artist of that high standing, the SEASONS MASTER appears to me, together with the COURT MASTER of Piazza Armerina, to have been an initiator, with many followers, of the 'fine style', in the full meaning of that phrase (even though it often shows signs of academicism and frigidity), and on the other hand unable to conceal, by incorporating them in a new synthesis, the aspects of idiomatic structure by this time dedicated to the art of the future. His experiment was that of a disciplined reconstitution, within the outward forms of neo-Hellenistic taste, of what still survived in thought and feeling of the legacy bequeathed by tetrarchic art to the new Constantinian age. He might have been able to improve upon that bequest by more straightforward handling, leading to a synthesis of greater distinction. But perhaps that would have made no difference to the influence he exercised on the painting of his century.

The above conclusions as to the somewhat Hellenistic viscosity in the development of mosaic painting at Antioch throughout the fourth century might well extend to the consideration of a further discovery in the Syrian metropolis, miraculously preserved amid the general destruction of the *lithostrota* of the D Baths at Antioch. This is the scene of 'Hermes with the Infant Dionysus', 149 which Levi dates to the beginning of the second half of the century:[12] he appeals both to extrinsic evidence and to certain details of dress, such as the fillet with central jewel over the forehead, which is characteristic of the imperial medallions of Constantine and Valens.

The fragment occupies the left-hand extremity of a

11 Levi (1947), i, p. 562.
12 Levi (1947), i, pp. 286–9.

14 Piazza Armerina. Mosaic: Girls at Exercise (detail).

15 Aquileia, Basilica of Theodore. Mosaic: Great Fishing and Story of Jonah (detail).

16 Aquileia, Basilica of Theodore. Portrait of a Donor.

17 Aquileia, Oratory near Via Giulia Augusta. Portrait of a Proprietress.

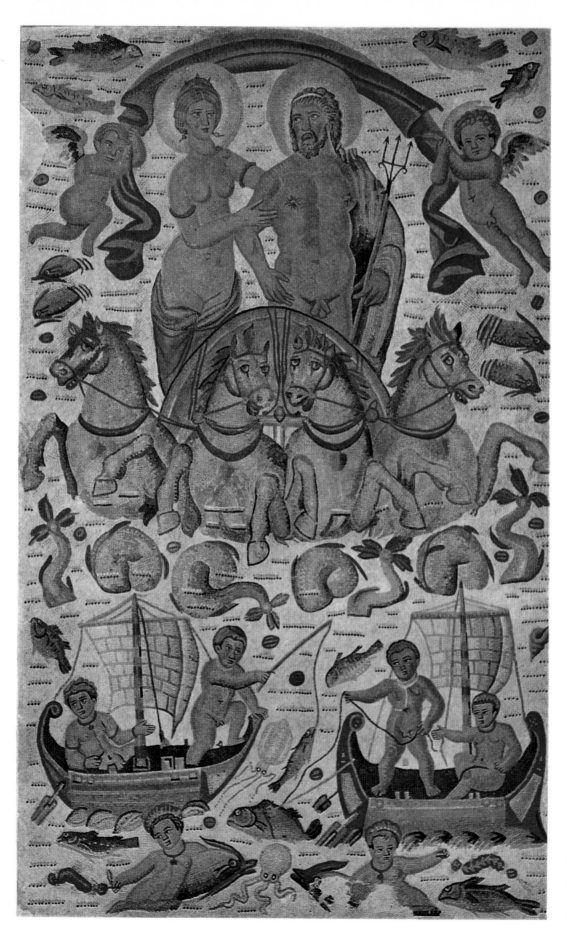

18 Paris, Louvre.
Triumph of
Oceanus and
Amphitrite, from
Constantine.

132 Aquileia, Hall of Cyriacus. Mosaic pavement: Goats and Birds (detail)

133 Aquileia, Hall of Cyriacus. *Emblema*: Ram with dedication *Cyriace vibas*

134 Aquileia, Oratory near Via Giulia Augusta. *Emblema*: Royal Duck (female)

135 Aquileia, Oratory near Via Giulia Augusta. *Emblema*: Royal Duck (male)

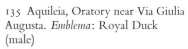

136 Aquileia. *Emblema*: Peacock, from a house

137 Aquileia, Basilica of Theodore. *Emblema*: Good Shepherd

138 Aquileia, Basilica of Theodore. *Emblema*: 'Eucharistic Victory'

139 Aquileia, Basilica of Theodore. *Emblema*: Offertory'

140 Aquileia, Basilica of Theodore. *Emblema*: 'Ovilia Dei' (detail)

141 Aquileia, Basilica of Theodore. Mosaic: Great Fishing (detail)

142 Tunis, Bardo Museum. Mosaic of the Great Hunt and Rural Labours, from the *impluvium* of the Laberii at Oudna

143 Tunis, Bardo Museum. Mosaic of the Hare Hunt, from a house at El Djem

144 Tunis, Bardo Museum. Mosaic of the Hunt Chronicle, from a house at Carthage

145 Bône, Museum. Mosaic of the Hunt Chronicle, from a villa at Hippo Regius

146 Tunis, Bardo Museum. Mosaic of Dominus Julius, from a villa at Carthage

147 Paris, Louvre. Scene of Meleager and Atalanta, from the Constantinian villa at Antioch (Daphne-Harbie)

148 Paris, Louvre. Bear, Lion and Tigress Hunt, from the Constantinian villa at Antioch (Daphne-Harbie)

149 Antioch, D. Baths. Mosaic fragment: Hermes with Infant Dionysus (detail)

150 Rome, Museo Nazionale *Emblema*: Spring, from the Villa of the Septimii at Baccano

151 Rome, Museo Nazionale. *Emblema*: Vegetable Mask, from the Villa Ruffinella at Tusculum

152 Paris, Louvre. Vegetable Mask on the cornice of acanthus spirals, from the Constantinian Villa at Antioch (Daphne-Harbie)

153 Antioch, F. Baths. Fragment: Head of Tethys among Fishes

154 Antioch, E. Baths. *Emblema*: Bust of Ge (detail)

155 Detroit, Institute of Arts. Fragment of linen and wool tapestry: Haloed Female Face

156 Paris, Louvre. *Emblema*: Head of Dionysus, from the Constantinian villa at Antioch (Daphne-Harbie)

157 Trier, Bischofliches Museum. Fragment: Head of Eros, from the ceiling of the hall of Helena's Palace

158 Trier, Bischofliches Museum. Framed picture of cupids from the ceiling of the hall of Helena's Palace

159 Trier, Bischofliches Museum. Framed portrait of woman (? Helena) with Jewellery and Halo, from the ceiling of the hall of Helena's Palace

160 Rome, Cemetery of Domitilla. Portrait of the boy Togatus (detail)

161 Rome, Palazzo dei Conservatori. Colossal marble head of Constantine

162 Rome, Cemetery of Traso. Left-hand Praying Woman, Sepulchre of the Great Praying Women

163 Rome, Hypogeum in Via Livenza. Artemis the Huntress, on wall of apse

164 Rome, Hypogeum of Trebius Justus. Trebius Justus with his Parents, lunette of the *arcosolium* (detail)

165 Gargaresh, Roman Tomb. *Imago clipeata*: Aelia Arisuth, on end wall

long, narrow *emblema* containing full-length figures and resembling the *emblema* of Room 4 of the Constantinian Villa. Hermes appears nude; a wide purple cloak, fastened at the shoulders by a large circular boss, forms a background to his moving body. The right leg is presented frontally; the left, in full profile and in the act of running, but set at an angle of 90 degrees to the rest of the body and consequently appearing almost out of joint. The god holds the baby Dionysus, also nude, and haloed, in a fold of the cloak, supporting the infant with his left arm and right hand, while grasping the caduceus with his left. Against the white surface of the background, between the god's feet, a naturalistic environment is suggested by a closely compact shadow shaped like the section of a convex lens.

The design of the model, apart from a few trifling variants, is extremely ancient; it occurs, for example, in a famous sculpture from Olympia, and can be traced, on the evidence of Attic vases and reliefs, as far back as the middle of the fifth century BC. In a centre such as Antioch, therefore, which is always associated with the perpetuation of Greek culture in unbroken continuity, it is not surprising to discover the affected compositional fidelity of this fragment, in which it is possible once again to recognise acceptance of the paratactical expressionism worked out at the beginning of the century. There appear to be no traditionalist intentions or modes in the work, nor is there any sign of its having been remodelled to suit the taste of the Constantinian 'fine style'. But it cannot be denied that the paratactical element has been filtered through a sieve of Hellenistic culture still very much alive.

It is easy to agree, in fact, with the accuracy of Levi's deductions from a suggestive comparison with the face of the right-hand 'Praying Woman' in the Roman Cemetery of Traso.[13] On the other hand, quite apart from the greatly superior quality of the Roman work, it is impossible to ignore the different levels of maturity evinced by the new idiom in Rome and at Antioch. In the Roman Cemetery the form appears hardly dependent at all on traditional cultural or syntactical conventions, and conveys an autonomous handling of surfaces, a notable feature of which is the advanced taste for rhythmic punctuations of the colour liberated in the necklaces and the adornments of the clothing, thus attaining truth and coherence of expressive fulfilment. So too in the Baths at Antioch the picture reveals traces of the Hellenistic psychological outlook, which remain as an active subsoil beneath the new idiomatic veneer.

The 'Hermes with Infant Dionysus' is later than the 'Praying Women' by at least two decades. But in this comparison, just as in those described earlier in these pages and many others which could be made, one must avoid schematic chronological classifications. They will always

23

149

13 Levi (1947, i, p. 569) notes with regard to the 'Hermes' face that 'the big pupils are eccentric and turned upward, showing a large section of the whites below. They are enclosed within thick frames with a lower semicircle and a more flattened arc above for the line of the eyebrows, which almost unite near the base of the nose, forming a single wide arch. The look has lost the expressive content of the Constantinian age and stiffened into an ambiguous fixity.' He goes on to compare it with the 'Praying Woman' of the Cemetery of Traso, which shows how 'the loss of any plastic depth in the rendering of heads has brought all the features into a single foreground surface, on which the temples and the eyebrows, the base of the nose and the eye-sockets, the cheeks and the lips, rest indifferently. The harmony of the relations of the single parts is destroyed. The features that produce expression dominate completely, while the smooth parts are out of focus. The oblique positions of the eyes, following the line of the eyebrow arches, is only an obvious derivation from the transposition of all parts into the surface, without any possibility of perspective relation. In the head of 'Hermes' – Levi concludes – 'slightly turned to the side, neglect of the plane surfaces of the face causes the cheeks almost to slip away. But the superficial flattening of the main features themselves produces the impression of an almost crushed nose'. It is easy, the author continues, to follow the evolution of a similar formation of the eyes in sculptures which can be dated with considerable confidence, such as, once more, the colossal head of Constantine in the Palazzo dei Conservatori at Rome.

be suggested by any monument, however late, that reveals marked elements of plastic disorganisation, clashing tones of colour, unification of the planes of representation and background, etc. The cloak of Hermes, for instance, falls with remarkable elegance behind the bright nudity of the figure, with which it composes an effective chromatic contrast, and is still classic in the variety of its folds, though it is rendered in a kind of 'negative relief' determined by the rhythmic use of cubes of different colours. Again, his body is in strenuous motion, though the legs, as already noted, are distorted. The fact that these phenomena retain some plastic value denotes in this case, as do other details in other cases, a later rather than an earlier dating, and explains it by the diversity of artistic and cultural intercourse and of the general *milieu* of civilisation, which, spontaneously affecting the various provinces of the Empire, also emphasises the active or passive character of their relations with the adjoining provinces, with the political capital, with the cultural capitals of the Hellenistic world and finally with neighbouring foreign kingdoms and their cultures.

Additional confirmation of this view will be found by turning from Antioch, one of the chief cultural capitals of the Empire and a city of very ancient traditions, to Trier, one of the new military capitals and very recently civilised.

Immediately after the Second World War deep excavations were begun on the site of the twelve-sided Memorial Building of which traces were found at a depth of 3.15 metres, lying beneath the pavement of Trier Cathedral. These led to the discovery, still lower down, of the remains of a magnificent rectangular Hall of the imperial edifice erected in the city in the time of Constantine and known traditionally as the Palace of Helena, his mother. The hall, containing beautiful frescoes, had been demolished a few years later, in 326, when work started on the first ecclesiastical building in Trier under the auspices of Bishop Agricius, to whom Helena had presented the site. The caisson-decorated ceiling had been destroyed with the Palace, but its ruins remained *in situ*. Consequently, the pieces of fresco collected from a total number of 50,000 allowed the reconstruction by patient labour of individual panels, which reveals the subjects of many, and makes 157–9 possible adequate study of six.

This persevering archaeological work, accomplished by Theodor Kempf, has resulted in one of the most exciting artistic revelations made in the present century, both because of the antiquity of the finds, which constitute (if we except the paintings in the catacombs) an exceedingly rare monument of late imperial ceiling-painting, and also because they are indubitable examples of court art in the Constantinian age, thus enabling us to make a fairly reliable estimate of the *Kunstwollen* of court fashion in the first decades of the fourth century.

Here follows a short summary of the excavator's first scientific report,[14] within the framework of a general hypothesis relating to the decoration of this ceiling which was divided into fifteen or twenty-one painted caissons. The special character of the subjects, the positioning of the figures in separate panels and the variety of their decoration (from the gilded frame of ovolo mouldings enclosing the representations of Cupids, and itself bordered by a red strip with a simple design of gilded plaiting, to the severely plain framing of the portraits) suggest that the ceiling must have been arranged in sections according to strict rules of court etiquette, requiring the alternation of the portraits with the panels of Cupids, the centralisation of the more important portraits, and the encircling of the latter with the rest of the decoration. In this way a chess-board pattern would be obtained of eight 'Groups of Cupids' and seven 'Portraits' if the arrangement comprised fifteen panels, or of eleven 'Groups of Cupids' and ten 'Portraits' if it comprised twenty-one. It was clear to Kempf, on the evidence of the precise data furnished by the fragments themselves, that the setting and mutual bearings of the panels he had reconstructed would fit exactly into such a design.

A first image, of which the upper part survives under the overlying foundations of the polygonal Hall, displays two heads of Cupids at play against a blue background. A second represents two other such beings, wearing double necklaces and playing with a reddish-violet cloak. The background is again blue, as it is in all the other pictures. A third has two dancing Cupids with short reddish-violet cloaks and double necklaces. They are flourishing cups in which incense is burning. In a fourth are head and shoulders, like the others more than lifesize, of a 'Young Woman in a purple tunic'; the tunic is sleeveless, she has a light-coloured greyish-blue nimbus, and on her head is a wreath of flowers. Her right arm is adorned with gold bracelets, and the hand holds a plectrum; the missing left hand perhaps held a lyre. Of a fifth image only a few fragments survive, but it is clear that the figure was not haloed. The sixth represents a pair of dancing Cupids with short cloaks and double collars. They are carrying a cornucopia. A seventh again shows the head and shoulders of a 'Young Woman wearing jewels and a halo', with a transparent veil over her head. The veil reflects yellow, reddish, chestnut-coloured and rosy tints. A purple tunic is worn under an ample, gold-embroidered *pallium* which hangs from the right shoulder. The jewellery consists of a necklace of large round pearls, another of sapphires, a large, drop-shaped pearl at the ear and on the diadem a circlet of pearls, a plaited wreath of laurel and a crown of

157, 158

14 Kempf (1950a, 1950b and 1951a). *See also* Alföldi (1955).

five rubies. The last picture reconstructed and described represents the head and shoulders of an older 'Woman with Jewellery and a Halo'. Her right hand raises a transparent veil of fine texture with heavy violet shadings. She is dressed in a tunic covered by a light-coloured dalmatic fastened on the right shoulder, while her hair, of a warm chestnut hue, is adorned with a string of costly, luminous pearls and a gold crown bearing three blue stones. A gold necklace of round sapphires encircles her throat. Of another panel Kempf could only assert that it represented a male personage.

The architectural development of the site provides a reliable *ante quem* dating of these frescoes: the year 326, when, after the celebration of the *vicennalia* and the imperial family tragedy famous for the murders of the Empress Fausta and her son Crispus, the Palace was demolished to make room for the construction of the polygonal Memorial Building which Helena on her return from Palestine had desired to be a copy of the Rotunda at Jerusalem, perhaps in order to deposit in the new building the sacred tunic she had brought with her from that edifice. The date *post quem* appears less accurately ascertainable from the content and style of the works discovered. But it could not be taken to the beginning of Constantine's reign; the usual evidence from coinage would point to a year subsequent to the period 308–313, and the conjecture of a date very close to 320 would not be far from the truth.

Clearly, no difficulties of interpretation are presented by the decorative panels of pairs of Cupids, since this type of subject had been known ever since the first period of Hellenistic painting and, as already noted, had left many traces throughout late Roman (including early Christian) art. The bearing of cornucopiae and censers was a characteristic function, among many others, of these figures. Such decorations, moreover, were especially logical in an imperial palace. It has proved more difficult, however, right from the start, to account iconographically for the heads in the Hall. It was natural enough for Kempf[15] to start by considering that no reasonably safe conclusion could be reached as to the general idea of the great ceiling and its political inspiration until the whole work of rearrangement and restoration had been completed. But today more informed criticism tends to recognise in this majestic composition an official representation of the imperial family. The latter view did not make its way without opposition. It is in fact of some interest to mention that the first inclination of the excavator, after reintegrating the large portraits, was to interpret them as 'symbolical figures, allegories of wealth, fertility and power',[16] very widespread in the fourth century. It was the repeated inclusion of imperial emblems and fashions

15 Kempf (1950a), p. 51.
16 Kempf (1959), p. 3.

in hairdressing which directed attention first to the theory that the portraits might be idealised representations of Helena and Fausta, and then to the notion that they could be actual likenesses of the great ladies of the house of Constantine.[17]

Unquestionably the most surprising feature in these frescoes is their undisturbed maintenance of an almost aggressively 'classical' style in the middle of the expressionist era under Constantine. Galassi refers in this connection[18] to 'Female heads, Cupids and floral items painted with a firm grasp of animation and rare formative capacity, noticeably without renunciation of the Apolline canons of ancient beauty', and proceeds to make a brief comparison of these frescoes with the remains of those, admittedly very much later, found among the ruins of the Imperial Palace at Constantinople.

These figures are in fact endowed with an undeniable plastic validity. Against a truly expressionist blue background, and in line with the fashion of the day, the painter has imposed surfaces rich in warm, resolutely toned colour, with summary, slight but effective shading, with certain traces of impressionism especially in the faces of the Cupids, where the chubby projecting planes create swift shadows and mobile, vivacious features.

The delicate texture of the limbs unfolds on a rosy ground with yellow overlay and touches of lilac, violet and maroon, with laboured chromatic effect, peculiarly refined in taste but undoubtedly mannerist in style. The wings are picked out in ranges of grey, blue, green and maroon. Reddish flecks model the masses of fair hair. The cloaks over which these beings are playfully quarrelling enliven the baroque versatility of the flow and structure of the drapery with a series of flashes and sudden shadows varying from lilac to violet. Not a single colour is left plain. Even the blue of the abstract, ceremonious background against which the images stand out carries overlays of black. The artist therefore shows a clear aversion from the preference, hitherto attested in the fourth century, for the pure tones, the shrill chromaticism which only a few years after the decoration of the imperial Hall at Trier is amply documented on the vaults of the Mausoleum of Constantina, though this latter building arose within the sphere of Constantinian court art. The TRIER CONSTANTINIAN MASTER,[19] however, is to be admired not only for the sense of colour which so clearly distinguishes him from the COURT MASTER OF CONSTANTINA, but also for a conception of plastic significance very close to that of such famous contemporary sculptured monuments as the porphyry Sarcophagus of Constantina in the Vatican Museums,[20] probably an Alexandrian work of the beginning of the century.

The anatomical clarity of plastic vision in the sculptor

24, 166

167

17 Kempf (1950a), p. 51.
18 Galassi (1953), p. 347. He adds that at Constantinople there can be found 'practically the same animation and perhaps a greater suavity in following, as though caressingly, the lineaments of the faces'.
19 I am at least inclined to share the opinion, which Kempf has confirmed to me verbally, that several different artists were employed on the Trier ceiling, of whom he would attach one to the presumed portrait of Helena and to the Cupid fragment No. 5, another to Nos. 1 and 6 of that series and the portrait presumed to be of Fausta, and a third to the other pieces found. On the other hand, it seems to me hazardous, in the present state of research, to attempt too strict a classification. While noting here, therefore, that various manners may be identified, I refer them for the time being to a single TRIER CONSTANTINIAN MASTER.
20 Delbrück (1932), p. 219, pl. 104; Volbach (1958), pp. 50–1, pl. 24.

of the Sarcophagus; his fondness for precise definition of decorative elements; the retention in his work, particularly, of much variety in degrees of relief, as if to attempt an ultimate immersion in the *plein air* of the idyllic subject and the extraction from it, though still in the frankly stiff manner of the *ductus*, of a Hellenistically elegant result: all these share with remarkable facility the sense of rhetorical accomplishment provided by the brushwork of the TRIER CONSTANTINIAN MASTER, with his rigorous notions of spatial division, framing, frieze and shadow. Consequently, though other stylistic comparisons with Italian monuments are possible, the most evident artistic ancestry of the painter appears to be, in point of fact, Alexandrian.

It is true, nevertheless, that some interruptions in the classicising linear fluency of this inspiration can be detected by close examination. A certain intensification of the function of line on a surface unprepared to receive it is recognisable in the face of the girl with the plectrum and in the features of some of the Cupids, in accordance with 157 a descriptive idiom traceable in many contemporary works, of which some examples have already been specified. There are even present a few instances of paratactical license, as in the position of the legs of the pair of Cupids 158 playing with the cloak. Furthermore, the conception of contour distribution is found to be very close to that prevalent at this period, above all in the panels of the Cupids, whose figures fit perfectly into the occasionally variant space of the caisson, so as to become unified with it, thus affording certain contrasts between the exuberant plasticity of the bodies and their enforced confinement within the limits of their frames. But, after all, these concessions are imposed by circumstance, not deliberate. They were by this time natural to the taste of the age and subsisted within an idiom which must be regarded as in the first place a cultural reaction, partly due to the restorative impulse applied in the political field, though also reinforced by the activities of the traditionalist Hellenistic workshops still maintained by Alexandria and even more by Antioch.

The word 'partly' has been used because one could not, in fact, reasonably argue that such painting as that at Trier was confined to the extraordinarily careful and 'purist' employment of a learned idiom re-established for motives unconcerned with artistic development. The Trier style dominated imperial society for about a generation, and was quite naturally resorted to for the decoration of an official ceiling at a time when Christianity itself, after the Edict of Milan, reached out to support the State and began to uphold on religious grounds the exercise of the restored civil authority of the Empire. The Trier ceiling certainly bears clear enough witness to an age of renewed, though brief and illusory, prosperity and greatness, and in particular to the partial awareness of this situation by the ruling class. The work was practically condemned by fate to suffer a judgment which, while acknowledging freely the high standard of its formal coherence and taste, was bound to detect the elements of redundancy and insincere rhetoric which nevertheless pervaded it. At the same time this work may, on careful scrutiny, logically be considered an erudite and ceremonious version of the phase of late Roman painting immediately but not exclusively succeeding that of the Tetrarchy, and as inheriting and transmitting to a further stage of development the characteristics which that phase of art had collected and absorbed into the rationalist rigour of its structure.

Chapter Ten
Constantinian expressionism from hypogean painting to the vaults of the Mausoleum of Constantina

The consequences of tetrarchic expressionism cannot, of course, be reduced to the frequent aulic frigidity of the classicist revival, found even in the surviving monuments of Constantinian palace art. In the Germanic capital and still more in the Syrian metropolis, where much evidence of its secular development remains, many works may undoubtedly reflect a controlled evolution of taste quite in harmony with the intentions of Constantine's principate. But at Rome the painting of the earliest decades of the century appears in several hypogean frescoes more preoccupied, though often within the limits of an actually analogous idiom, with a psychological animation, an emotive participation and, in short, an expressive quality more immediately influenced by and representative of a part of the contemporary conscience, religious or civil, to which the restoration had been less able to obtain access. During the very years when the masters of Piazza Armerina were engaged upon their vast undertaking, and edifices in the Constantinian taste were being admirably decorated throughout the Roman world, some momentous works, clearly distinguishable in the wide sea of catacombal paintings, were exhibiting in this area of post-tetrarchic art signs of profound poetic significance.

In the Cemetery of Domitilla the portrait of 'Togatus', 160 on the arcosolium of the same name, constitutes a first impassioned example of that phase of idiomatic transformation which, not unmindful of earlier successes, now emerged triumphantly as Constantinian expressionism. Indeed, once the fascinating animation of the eyes of its portraits had lost a little of their light, the physiognomical structure, already prone to extend in a neat, formal tranquillity, would reveal the stamp of the 'fine style'.

De Wit asserts that 'the attractive head of "Togatus" closely resembles the typical Constantinian portrait'. He specifies the characteristic features as 'large eyes under heavy brows, a highly convex and capacious skull, with hair low on the forehead, wide, protuberant eye-sockets and a cephalic structure spherical above and oval below'.[1] Apart from such considerations of facial morphology, this portrait can confidently be dated, for several reasons not solely stylistic, between 320 and 330. It can readily be compared, especially if the series of preceding portraits is borne in mind, with the type of the two 'Praying Women' in the Cemetery of Domitilla, with the 'Worshipper' in 87 the fourth chapel of the Cemetery of the Jordani, with the

1 De Wit (1938), p. 49.

style of imperial coinage in the second Constantinian period (there being, for example, a suggestive parallel with an effigy, though in profile, of Constantine's son Crispus on a coin dateable between 317 and 326), and above all, as De Wit himself mentions, with the medallions in glass and gold of Crispus and other sons of Constantine forming part of a cup in the Wallraf-Richartz Museum at Cologne and displaying the same stylistic traits.[2] Nevertheless, the work remains a *unicum* of magisterial virtuosity. In this astonishingly vivid portrait of a youth the TOGATUS MASTER has left us an important specimen of funerary art related to the best traditions of antique Roman portraiture and at the same time fully expressive of the spirit and the taste of the first decades of the fourth century.

To the same period must be assigned the lunette of the 'Virgin and Child' in the pose of a 'Praying Figure', with the monogram of Christ on either side, on an arcosolium of Room 5 in the *Coemeterium Majus*. The relief of certain physiognomical features (eyes and ears) is here very noticeable. The surviving ear of the child is almost detached from the head, and it is easy to see the resemblance of the structures of head and face to those of 'Togatus'. Although De Wit, a discerning authority on this work, has pointed out that 'the head of the Mother like that of the Child is designed with a powerful plastic sense',[3] it is necessary to admit that expressionist values remain unaltered in this revival of interest in form.

The work is, in fact, of a monumental character and has nothing to fear, as the same author remarks,[4] from a comparison with the most colossal of Constantinian heads. But a stamp very similar to that of the Constantinian 'fine style' has left great constructive lucidity on the very expressionism that moulds these faces. One might perhaps apply both to 'Togatus' and to this 'Virgin and Child' the term expressionist classicism in order to indicate how the relapse of a classical vocabulary into an anti-traditional idiom such as that of expressionism, far from leading necessarily to arbitrary compromise and gratuitous inflection, may sometimes create real masterpieces.

In this kind of painting, where every detail seems called upon to transform into an object of worship an image which fifty years earlier would merely have had the decorative value of funerary art, idiomatic affinities with the aulic 'Portraits' of the Trier ceiling are indeed numerous and far-reaching. They do not merely extend to such iconographical analogies as the very delicately textured veil of the 'Praying Woman' or her necklace of large mounted stones, which are found again in the so-called Fausta (and also in Helena) of the Constantinian fresco, though stress should be laid on the stylistic resemblance which can be detected even in these particulars, which are, however, more rapidly set down and more freely expressive in catacombal painting.

2 Delbrück (1933), pp. 122–35.
3 De Wit (1938), p. 48.
4 De Wit (1938), p. 49.

The most impressive points in this comparison are the identity of typological construction (already significant in such a century as the fourth, with its great variety of tastes in this field), and the frequent similarity of idiom. The technique of sfumato, though more hurriedly employed at Rome, might be called the same as that of Trier, were it not for the more fervent chromaticism of the catacomb artist. Of the same kind, limited to colour, are the distinctive marks of the hands, with their long, slender, restless and elegant fingers. As for the eyes, the broad white crescents characteristic of tetrarchic expressionism tend in both cases to play a larger part, perhaps less unexpected, which lends more stability to the intensely significant gaze. At Trier they are relatively smaller than at Rome, rendering their function in the 'Portraits' more objective and the liturgical effect of sacred inspiration less notable. Such stylistic divergences make possible a remarkably close estimate of the difference between the two works in matters of taste, function and type of execution. But for that very reason the discrepancies are worth attention in studying the undeniably common aesthetic conditions in which the Roman and Trier paintings flourished. There is no need, however, to emphasise the very much higher standard reached by this lunette in comparison with the aulic ceiling at Trier. The **21** cultural merits of the latter can do little to rival the lofty poetic effect of the rapid catacombal fresco by the MASTER OF THE COEMETERIUM MAJUS, yet another artist testifying to the importance of everyday art in an epoch known almost exclusively for the productions of the court.

Just as the marble Head of Constantine in the Palazzo dei 161 Conservatori remains the unsurpassed achievement of tetrarchic portraiture,[5] so the ultimate level attained by Constantinian expressionism in painting seems to be constituted by the faces of the two 'Great Praying Women' **23**, 162 of the sepulchre called after them in the Cemetery of Traso. They stand to right and left of the two niches, below a picture of the story of Jonah.

These female figures by the MASTER OF THE GREAT PRAYING WOMEN, which in their clothing and barely suggested forward movement, anticipate the fashion of the official processions at Byzantium, prove once again how deceptive it is to suppose that the classicising periods interrupted or diverted the creative course of late Roman painting. The two faces are in fact very like the aforesaid marble portrait of Constantine, not so much on the plane 161 of contemporary typology as in terms of stylistic morphology and poetic effect: the huge eyes and the conspicuous, intensely significant treatment of the eyelids; the low, straight brow; the short, straight nose; the dilated nostrils; and the indefinably expressive mouth, reinforcing the almost hallucinated gaze, symbolising absorption by a

5 For Bettini (1952, p. xxxi) this gigantic sculpture 'almost seems to be the final goal of a series of efforts in progressive expressionism'; it 'was certainly a portrait. But the extremely drastic simplification of the planes and the very size of the work turn it into something superhuman.'

mysterious anxiety. Consequently, a comparison with the older 'Virgin with Child' in the *Coemeterium Majus*, though it is clear that the features correspond precisely, must admit that the 'Great Praying Women' of the Cemetery of Traso go beyond the harmonious organisation of facial masses, which in the former work was determined by the plasticity already noted, and allow the complete control of the flat planes of the face by the eyes, eyebrows, nose and mouth, as the only carriers of expression, as though they had been removed from the presentation of the figure as a whole.[6]

21

23, 162

With the aid of convincing comparisons (e.g. with the bronze Portrait of Constantine in the Belgrade Museum) it is easy to recognise these faces as ardent and mature witnesses to the latest stage of expressionism in the Constantinian age, whereas the faces in the *Coemeterium Majus*, together with 'Togatus' in the Cemetery of Domitilla, certainly represent its initiation. Qualitatively speaking, the Praying Women almost justify this conclusion; but the MASTER OF THE GREAT PRAYING WOMEN was not working in an artistic *milieu* in process of expansion, as were his colleagues responsible for the productions quoted. His figures already forecast the exhaustion of effort in a school, and perhaps also the first self-critical review of a spiritual experience by now in contact with the disillusionment of the century.

21

160

It cannot be asserted that Roman hypogean painting of the first decades of the fourth century was uniform in the expressionist accentuation proper to the Christian works here mentioned. About forty years ago there was excavated on the Via Livenza in Rome a hypogeum whose purpose has never been satisfactorily explained. Wilpert, but not Cecchelli,[7] believed it to have been a Christian baptistery. At all events, on the apsidal wall were found two pictures of 'Artemis as Huntress with Nymph', and consideration of those two pictures will suffice to reveal a less problematical aspect of painting at that time; one more obvious, too, and settled in a kind of academic conformism.

163

The picture on the left shows the goddess in the act of drawing an arrow from her quiver. The image is static in spite of the mobile attitude. It stands between two stags fleeing in opposite directions against a background of suitably evanescent forest in lightly shaded tones of grey, green and rose. On the right, symmetrically depicted, a nymph in classical pose caresses a roebuck against a similar landscape. The composition is of itself such as to recall a taste which had been reinstated in the climate of the restoration. Consequently, I should be inclined to date it in the third decade of the century, in agreement with Levi[8] and contrary to the opinion of Ducati, who would postpone it by 70–80 years.[9]

6 De Wit (1938, p. 52) writes: 'The features are all out of proportion . . . it may be said of these heads that the filling of space, without which the linear style would already have made its appearance, is hardly present to the artist's mind.'
7 Wilpert (1923–4); Cecchelli (1944), pp. 201–8. *See also* Paribeni (1923).
8 Levi (1947), i. p. 565.
9 Ducati (1938), p. 366.

The paintings of the Via Livenza look back entirely to the manner of the 'fine style'. Technically, the figures are rendered by a meticulous definition of their plastic textures by means of an extremely refined sfumato, retouched however by highlighting on the faces and heavy shadows on the limbs. The composition, as in the hunting scenes of the Antiochene villa already noted, sets the structures of the landscape background in the spaces left available between those occupied by the persons and animals represented as in motion. The concept of space, appropriate to the compositional arrangement, does not disdain, in a painting of such academic flavour, to allow, for example, the stag pursued by the goddess to move in the same direction as herself, that is, obliquely towards the spectator, but from a point behind her, thus repeating, at least partially, the licence allowed by the Aquileian SEA MASTER in his 'Good Shepherd'.

147, 148

163

137

We have, then, a series of idiomatic structures in which conformity with the new taste lies as a cultural veneer and itself reveals an epoch of transition, in which a generation of artists adapts itself as best it can to the new aesthetic impulse. Once the clamours of the expressionist revolution had been suppressed by the disciplinary measures of the Tetrarchy, the stereometric standard and the cubist tendency became enfeebled in a sophisticated paring down of every previous characterisation of form. But this process, even on the level of such professional accomplishment as that of the ARTIST OF ARTEMIS AS HUNTRESS and after its cultural employment in the service of tradition, left in view the stamp of a manner which remains one of the most significant and original of all late antiquity.

These Roman pictures, beneath the pattern of cultural osmosis which animates them, are reminiscent in some ways of the *Leopard Hunt* depicted on two mural strips of the *frigidarium* in the so-called Small Baths at Leptis Magna. This decoration is the latest of those surviving in one form or another in that apartment, ranging from the wall mosaics, showing scenes from the myth of Dionysus and scenery on the river Nile, to the stucco work and the painted architectural views on the arches of the shorter sides. I mention it here, not because it repeats on African soil the tendencies already noted in the frescoes of the Via Livenza, but because at Leptis Magna they are clearly shown in a previous version, anterior to the aesthetic revolution of the Tetrarchy and unaffected by it in their provincial isolation.

The painter of the Leptis Magna hunt was no master. The figures of the *venatores* are repeated in stereotyped copies of both bodily and facial structure, industriously and plausibly reproduced, as if they were so many academic exercises. They do not show, substantially, the 'balanced composition of the entire scene' obtained, according to Pesce, 'by contrast and iteration of the same movements so as to form a series of points of reference',[10] but a more modest juxtaposition of figures, with the use of two or three model hunters given the names *Nuber*, *Inginus*, *Ibentius* and *Bictor*, to which correspond those of the beasts (*Rapidus*, *Fulgintius* and *Gabatius*). Yet the undoubtedly late form of some of these names, which occur first in the provinces and only subsequently in the capital, together with the kind of scanty clothing worn by the hunters, renders certain a dating of this work near the end of the third century;[11] though it must be granted that the artist was indebted to the workshops of Alexandria, which, as we have seen, were more than ever active at this period in northern Africa. Consequently the style, analogous in many respects to the Roman mythological scenes of country life found in the Via Livenza, is evidently to be referred to the fairly widespread Hellenistic practice of the day. In the Roman hypogeum, thanks to the artist's talent, it issued in renewed smoothness of form, though not unaffected by the aesthetic assumptions of tetrarchic parataxis. But at Leptis the outcome was complete fossilisation, in the sense of an absence of cultural and stylistic contrast. There the bright solidity of the figures, shaped like puppets and projected on to a background where the traces of environment are provided simply by chromatic variants and boomerang-shaped shadows, may perhaps suggest a taste unrelated even to the art of the whole third century, which the tetrarchic art violently assailed – and ultimately swept away.

After that digression we may now proceed to a final consideration of the achievements, unquestionably nearer in time to 340 than to 300, of Roman hypogean painting, which was now no longer characterised by a dominant interest in funerary decoration. For meanwhile the many-coloured mosaics of the first basilicas were already spreading their glittering surfaces to the light of day, and the same mode of expression was being continued in the *lithostrota* of the late Empire, proliferating throughout the provinces.

Hypogean painting has been briefly studied up to this point by reference to certain of its masterpieces and to some specimens of more limited merit but which nevertheless echo disturbing and innovating productions now lost. When it is judged organically, within the complicated but unitary context of late Roman imperial art between the mid-third and mid-fourth century, it returns completely vindicated from the exile of underestimation to which it had been banished by historical criticism based for over a century on standards of appreciation derived from Attic classicism, from popular handicrafts and from 'decadence'. It comes to participate, often with the fundamental efficacy of a high artistic level, in the art of the late

10 Pesce (1949). *See also* Ward-Perkins and Toynbee (1950).
11 Ward-Perkins and Toynbee (1950), p. 192. Pace (1955, p. 102) assigns it to the late fourth century. The dating by the two English scholars seems much more likely.

Roman *koine* and actually to represent some of the manners which have determined its development, as will incidentally be proved also by many discoveries dating from the second half of the century.

The substantial unity of this process will be conveyed by the perfect idiomatic agreement discovered between certain hypogean paintings and certain monuments, whether frescoes or sculptures, most fully representative of secular art, that of the court. These extremely diverse elements result in the predominance – not so much in terms of massive, unqualified victory as by way of fertilising permeation – of the innovating cultural impulse, its spiritual charge and its efforts to overcome the resistances undoubtedly interposed by the structural side of court and traditionalist convention linked to the more neo-Attic version of Hellenism. The consequence (better realised, perhaps, by concentrating on the age itself of classical revival in the 'fine style') was that a new concept of form, which in the natural course of further developments was to govern the future, proved itself irreversible. That future would be concerned not so much with the triumph of a Christian semantic revolution over the pagan vocabulary as with the assumption into a new, transfigured cultural climate of the secular burdens of a mighty past, together with the expectation of an ultimate, universal salvation. That is characteristic of every age of great ideological and social transition.

While Aquileia, with Bishop Theodore's seven hundred square metres of mosaic flooring, opened the basilicas to Roman *lithostrota*, the Mausoleum of Constantina or Costanza (S. Costanza) provides the earliest mosaic decoration of Christian vaults of which appreciable traces remain, if we except its most remarkable forerunner in the Mausoleum of the Julii below St. Peter's. Logically, even so complete and unexpected an instance of the decoration of vaults, apses and cupola (the last now unfortunately lost) inevitably raises the problem, as at Aquileia, of the derivation of, and of the cultural and technical preparation for, such an undertaking. In the case of S. Costanza, Bettini has spoken of the eminent suitability of mosaic as a means of expressing 'late Roman and Early Christian figurative ideas'.[12] He explains it firstly by the Church's adherence after the Edict of Milan to the 'commemorative purposes typical of Roman court art', for example the *majestas domini* repeated in the design of the imperial hieratic images such as those on the Arch of Constantine; and secondly by the basilican masters' use of the tradition and 'designs of the scenes presented in the most ancient paintings of the catacombs'.[13]

Cecchelli, insisting more upon the latter derivation, has noted in turn that 'the art of the catacombs was highly impressionistic. Constrained by the natural requirements

24–26, 1

12 Bettini (1942), p. 2.
13 Bettini (1952), p. xxvii.

of place, it practised from the earliest times division into zones of colour, preferring the more distinct tonalities. Hence the transfer to mosaic was rendered easy'.[14] But, still in Cecchelli's view, 'seeing that the development of technique runs parallel with that of the aesthetic ideal, it is to be observed that in the first century wall mosaic in large compositions with figures tends, like the *emblemata*, to approach so far as possible the condition of fresco . . . . Late in the second century the dissociative process became accentuated even for reproductions of the human figure ('Silvanus' in the Mithraeum at Ostia). By the fourth century straightforward divisionism was already fashionable; see, for example the figures on the annular vault of S. Costanza. This was the moment at which wall mosaic found its true nature and came to represent a separate form of art'.[15]

Cecchelli apparently considered that the impressionism of catacombal painting was partly due to the technique enforced by its environment, a theory to which Riegl would certainly have objected as being too close to that of Semper. But from the above quotation it would seem that the author supposed the style and artistic ideal of pagan mosaic in the first century and of Christian mosaic in the fourth to be derived from the same source. In this opinion he would be substantially in accord with the position of Bettini, who, when considering the explosion of new forms and the setting of new tasks, recognised the real genetic unity of the developments of Roman, especially funerary, art, from the pagan *lithostrota* and small shrines to the mosaics of Christian vaults. Moreover, with regard to technical evolution, he gave his own version of what Riegl had written concerning the character of mosaic, a 'speciality – progressively accentuated as the tesserae grew larger – of the last, distant-view phase of ancient art'.[16]

In dealing with a famous monument, the subject of so much previous study, attention must be paid above all to historical and critical considerations particularly relevant to the present work. Certain aspects and details will therefore be noted in so far as they throw light on the development of various elements of late Roman painting, naturally with separate reference to the decorative areas of the annular vault, and the two surviving lunettes of the decoration of the apsidioles.

In the first place it is essential to notice that the structure of the composition of the annular vault is rhythmic, not casual. It is divided into twelve areas decorated with six different subjects, which succeed one another in two semi-annular courses beginning from the zone of the vault overarching the entrance, proceeding in identical fashion and with uniform decorative patterns. Only the vault over the entrance and that facing it on the other side of the ring are different, the first bearing a geometrical

45

166

24, 166
25, 26

14 Cecchelli (1922), p. 11.
15 Cecchelli (1922), pp. 53–5.
16 Riegl (1901).

design of octagons and crosses, while the second is strewn with stars. Comparison is spontaneous, therefore, with the prototype of such itineraries in the Theodorean pavement at Aquileia, which ends its long series of figurative scenes with the 'Great Fishing' and the story of Jonah. So also 141, **15** with the annular vault of the Mausoleum, which soared to a cupola adorned with the same motif of the Cupids.[17]

In the planning of this concentric, rhythmic itinerary, always uniform and yet always new, there is conspicuous one feature now common but notable for the many different situations in which it occurs: the total disappearance of space. Only so can one describe the semantic abstraction of the white tesserae of the background, whether such background is strictly divided into the compartments of geometrical decoration, or is indecipherably varied by rambling vines in the scenes of grape- **166** gathering Cupids, or, finally, is covered with the picturesque disorder of animals and 'still life' in the vaults which incorrectly but with deliberately suggestive **24** intent can be called *asaroton*-like. This example of negation of space, the oldest surviving among many glorious vaults and domes, recalls similar cases in the Villa at Piazza Armerina: the 'Animal Heads' of the peristyle, the **128–130** *lithostrota* of the *xystus* with its spirals, and the paratactical confusion of the 'Carnage'. It is also to be found even earlier, as we have seen, in the so-called House of the Aviary at Carthage and other African pavements already considered. An exact parallel, in particular, can be established between the areas of the annular vault devoted to the labours of the 'Grape-gathering Cupids' and the fragment **166** of mosaic decoration from the Antonine Baths at Carthage, probably of the same period, representing little boys adorning a pavilion against a background of vegetation that invades the whole scene from all directions.

Noticeable likewise in the several areas of the vault, even in those we have described as *asaroton*-like, is the **24** strict attention paid to higher and lower levels in the placing of the figures on both sides of the central axis which divides the two gravitational fields at the top of the annular barrel. In the geometrically partitioned vaults, for example, there are two series of medallions (with small figures of Cupid and Psyche) in each section, and one series, also following opposed axes, at the centre. Riegl[18] accounted for this feature of the composition by the greater ease of vision thus afforded to the spectator. But apart from certain particulars in this vault which contradict such an arrangement (two Cupids of the central series in the areas with medallions, and some birds in the *asaroton*-like areas), the problem would be solved more logically by recognising that the lay-out of the vaults is similar to that of the decorative scheme of mosaic pavements, a fact recorded earlier in illustrations of the *Domus*

17 These two monuments, however, with an interval of less than twenty years between them, do not constitute the only evidence of the borrowing of a decorative section of pavement for a cupola. The central Rotunda of the so-called Baths of the Seven Sages at Ostia, preserving the mural of the 'Toilet of Venus' already mentioned, has a mosaic pavement in black and white showing scenes of 'Young Hunters Pursuing Wild Animals', framed in a most elegant border of interlacing acanthus sprays, while remains of polychrome tesserae, very delicately tinted, from the vault and lower course of one of the arcades which run rhythmically round the central space of the tunnel, are also adorned with stylised floral motives and scrolls. The date of these works, which cannot be long after the beginning of the third century, testifies to the origins of the relations between Roman and Christian decorative undertakings established over a hundred years later. In any case comparison with the Vatican vault of the Mausoleum of the Julii retains its point. The meaning of the rhythmic course of the annular vault was well understood by Adriano Prandi (1942–3), where (pp. 294–5) he drew attention to the notion of a 'crescendo' and a 'destination of every sentiment and every conscious formative planning' peculiar to this vault and its decorations.
18 Riegl, *Industria . . .*, p. 226; *Arte . . .*, p. 187.

Aurea and hypogean vaults of the second and third centuries.

7, 8, 9, 10

It is obvious, then, that there would be no advantage in any naturalistic placing of the figures arranged in echelons of medallions and other spatial delimitations, either with regard to their mutual relations or with regard to the spectator, whose point of view is imagined here also to be within the picture. Consequently, in representations which, like those of the Mausoleum of Constantina, are even more complex and crowded than some symbolical third-century vaults in the catacombs, figure and framework together may compose a single whole, but in accordance with the rhythm and the formal relations of the picture itself within the abstract structure of decorative geometry which coordinates and summarises the entire work. This is true, on the other hand, not only of one formal area, but also of the larger field comprising all sections of a monumental organism. Just as at Aquileia, the visitor cannot take in as a whole the entire figurative surface of the ambulacral system and of the cupola of the Mausoleum, as if it were objectively apprehensible from without; he must undertake a journey through it in order to penetrate the meaning of a succession based on the vaults of the ambulacrum, on the two semi-cylinders of the Mausoleum, a succession that culminates in the soaring efflorescence of the cupola. The logic of this itinerary, in other words its doctrinal and ascetic significance, completely coincides, however, with its unifying rhythm and is substantially absorbed in it. The didactic value of the story is summed up in the variety of its formal structure.

Plan D

Idiomatic considerations, briefly surveyed in isolation from iconographical and cultural estimates of some constants of the period, allow a critical estimate of the two artistic personalities responsible for the Mausoleum of Constantina. A fundamental distinction at once appears. A probably Constantinian palace master decorated with expert skill and refined classicising taste the vaults of the ambulacral system and most likely also the cupola, while a Christian *imaginarius* adorned the lunettes a generation later. Ignoring once again the dubious case of the Vatican Mausoleum of the Julii, we have at S. Costanza the earliest surviving mosaic wall decoration with Christian subjects. The above distinction, therefore, does not stop short at iconography; it declares itself, with results that I consider of fundamental importance to the artistic movement of the late fourth century, in the diverse elements of those works which represent the creative capacity of the two masters.

24, 166, **25**, 26 79

In the first of these, whom I may call the COURT MASTER OF CONSTANTINA, the characteristic note of court art, expressing itself both in its themes and in the formative resuscitation of the 'fine style', is closely associated with a special feeling for colour revealed in a peculiar mannerism. I refer to a pure chromaticism which prevails in almost all the areas of the ambulacral system, translating the strictly outlined but sufficiently rotund and plastic solidity of the grape-gathering Cupids into an extraordinary variety of gilded greenish blues, and the luxuriant interlacing pattern of vines into various shades of green. This often frigid, surrealist treatment of tone, which sometimes borders upon unearthly yellowish luminosity and elsewhere allows brilliant alternations of violet, is combined with the other tone characteristic of the master: a reddish veining, expressing itself here also in multiple shades, which joins the 'brushstrokes' of green in application to the clothing of the figures, to the faces of the two portraits, to the areas of geometrical decoration and even to the miniature forms of Eros and Psyche, as well as to the plumage of the birds in the sections where they occur.

166

Greater chromatic freedom, sustained by a wealth of hues and by liberal use of gold tesserae which do not, however, conceal the original two-colour scheme of the preceding areas, appears in the two final aerial vaults, where the composition is altogether anarchical. I have called it *asaroton*-like simply in order to stress its formal analogy to the Hellenistic representation of objects scattered over the unswept floor of a dining-hall; but, as already suggested, it is equivalent to the articulation of abstract space in medallions and geometrically adorned sections. In those last two vaults, then, the return to tradition imposed by the taste of the Constantinian court is illustrated by an endless collection of green plants, flowers, birds and inanimate objects (cornucopiae, pots, drinking-vessels, flasks) all fantastically polychrome, yet fused with a warmer tonal feeling of baroque quality. Consequently, in the absence of the lost cupola mosaic, the conviction grows that its disappearance deprived posterity for ever of the chance to become better acquainted with a most remarkable representative of that classical revival which is substantially delineated in manneristic or baroque forms by various monuments of the 'fine style' from Trier to Antioch.[19]

24

19 In certain respects the Santa Costanza annular vault and its lost cupola recall the complex, even if certainly less organic, remains of mosaic decoration in the Mausoleum of Centcelles (Tarragona). They present, within three concentric ornamental borders, compositions of classical type, containing images of probably Christian iconographical significance. The decoration has been insufficiently studied and appreciated even allowing for its little more than fragmentary state. It has been dated by Camprubi Alemany (1942, nn. 1–4; 1952) in the early fifth century, while Helmut Schlunk (1954) prefers the middle of the fourth. In any case the monument is of great interest, as it might well provide a better example than any hitherto known of the active conjunction of traditional classical themes and Christian subjects from both the Old and New Testaments not much later than their combination as shown in the Mausoleum of Constantina.

The tessellar palette of the COURT MASTER OF CONSTANTINA, as also his personal *Kunstwollen*, was divided between loyalty to a crude legacy of form and the laboriously creative elaboration of a new taste. Obvious components of the first of these impulses are (i) the now well-established two-dimensional treatment of figures and scenery, particularly examples of the gathering and transportation of grapes, and those of interlacing vines; (ii) preservation of the traditional two-colour scheme of decoration in red and green, particularly evident where it is employed mechanically, as in geometrical ornament; and (iii) the rigidity of many figures. The peculiar warmth

166

of the second component is illustrated by the highly personal accents of colour, their squinting lights, their surprising sudden gleams, and the extremely subtle effect of the two *asaroton*-like areas, where the courtly tone of jewelled iridescence indicates the refinement of taste animating the exuberantly vivacious baroque of the Constantinian 'fine style'.

24

The two lunettes with Christian subjects probably came a generation later. Their more recent origin is proved less by the indubitable novelty of their iconographical components than by the very conspicuous rejection of the courtly taste so evident in the adornment of the ambulacral system. The iconographical element is nevertheless of particular interest in this case. The two lunettes provide, in fact, the first mosaic example of a *Traditio clavium* and of a *Traditio legis* (or more precisely, perhaps in consequence of a late restoration, of the 'gift of peace'), which run in an almost endless series through basilican apses during the whole millennium of the Middle Ages. Very close parallels, for example, can often be established between these two lunettes and such later monuments as the modest *Traditio Legis* of the Catacomb '*ad decimum*' on the Via Latina near Grottaferrata,[20] the apsidiole of the Chapel of S. Aquilino in S. Lorenzo at Milan, the *Traditio Legis* in the Baptistery of the Cathedral of St. Januarius at Naples, the apse of SS. Cosmas e Damiano in Rome, the Sarcophagus depicting the same subject in the National Museum at Ravenna, and the apse of S. Vitale in that city.

25, 26

28

As always, it is advisable to concentrate upon the style of this PROTOCHRISTOLOGICAL MASTER OF CONSTANTINA. In the left-hand lunette, that of the *Traditio Legis*, Christ stands between Sts. Peter and Paul as He delivers to the former a scroll bearing the words *Dominus pacem dat* and the Chi-rho. Four sheep are represented at his feet, and an elaborate palm appears on each side of the group. Against the bright background of pearly sky there stand out fantastically the Divine Master's Halo, in concentric bands of grey, light blue and azure; next, the unearthly streaks of red cloud, another characteristic feature that was to dominate the Christian apses with apocalyptic gleams until the advent of the golden Byzantine backgrounds and even sometimes boldly to combine with them, as at S. Vitale; then the greens, greys and reds of the sketchy landscape; and finally the delicate chromatic variations of the robes. The figures and the recessions of the surfaces are distinctly and incisively outlined, while the colour accentuation absorbs all plastic relief, to the eventual elimination of every sign of solidity. On the other hand all elements extraneous to the figures are expressed in free chromaticism without restriction of the design. The colour rambles on in brief touches and authentic 'brushwork', sometimes in

25

20 Wilpert (1917), ii, pl. 132.

compact tones, sometimes giving the impression of underlying metaphysical essences. Consequently, in this lunette there is already an anticipation – perhaps a post-humous result of the most essential decoration of the catacombal vaults – not only of the iconographic theme, as already stated, but also of the taste for abstraction which would establish itself for centuries in the great basilican apses, forming with a few sacred figures the stylised symbolism of an unearthly landscape, where ancient vestiges of late Alexandrian pastorals lose themselves in delicate surfaces of celestial meadows spangled with flowers, branches, stars and crosses, in polychrome and golden symphonies.

The right-hand lunette, that of the *Traditio Clavium*, is even more highly significant in this respect. The landscape draws its life from the same sources, rendered even more conspicuous, if possible, by the bolder expressionist *fauvisme* of the red and blue clouds; by the beauty of the robes of Christ, alternating marvellously between red and greenish-blue, thanks to the systematic use of tessellar strips of these two hues; and finally by the graduated scale of greys and blues in Christ's halo. Here too no trace of naturalistic scenery remains; apart from late restorations, the palms reveal a maximum of stylised symbolist elegance, while the globe, despite the flattening of its spherical form, contrives to suggest the ephemeral quality of the cosmos upon which Christ is seated.

The PROTOCHRISTOLOGICAL MASTER OF CONSTANTINA was probably working about the seventh decade of the fourth century, and the important feature of his style is the indubitably preponderant expressionism. Religious solem-nity assumes attitudes of hallucination and utters terrible warnings, not only through the dramatic presentation of the faces and the hieratic fixity of their gaze, a feature certainly derived from the imperial 'majesties', but also through new shades of colour. Now that the traditional chromatic density had been abandoned, certain mannerist and baroque experiments had given the artist a taste for unprecedented, translucent lyricism and the skill to display it. The brilliant mutations and surrealist accents of the master expressed his discovery of a 'sense datum' of the new metaphysics, comprised in a spectroscopy of ethereal skies, the innermost essences of heaven.

It was not perhaps by chance that the Christian artist employed on the Mausoleum of Constantina expressed his feelings in so novel a creative language, while the traditional forms of the restored 'fine style' were favouring the evolution of the classicist reaction under Julian.

26

Chapter Eleven
Expressionism and mannerism in funerary and ceremonial painting of the second half of the fourth century

An exceptionally interesting assemblage of mural decorations is presented by the Roman Catacomb on the Via Latina. These paintings, recently published by Ferrua[1] shortly after their first excavation, have been ascribed from the outset to the fourth century on the strength of convincing epigraphical evidence discovered *in situ*, but especially upon the following grounds: their elaborate arrangement in trilobate, hexagonal and circular chambers, with multiple arcosolia and frequent niches; the wealth of ornament covering every available surface in the cemetery; the great number of architectural divisions (no fewer than twenty-two columns have been found, serving as fictitious supports of the vaults of almost all the rooms); and finally by the predilection for symmetry and the type of articulation of the enclosed spaces.

This extraordinary cemetery has been justly described as a 'great picture-gallery of the fourth century'. Its limited extent comprises fifteen rooms and some scores of paintings, with subjects drawn both from the Old and from the New Testament, as well as from classical myth. In general, they are framed in so ample a luxuriance of ornament as not to leave unoccupied the least space on walls and vaults. The content, rendered with extreme freedom of composition and application, displays a mixture of elements of the most various iconographical ancestry, to such an extent that it might well be supposed that an assemblage of this kind, undoubtedly completed within about a couple of generations, would be absolutely inconceivable, considering the predominantly Christian character of its themes, at a time when the Church had not acquired full liberty of action.[2]

Bearing these considerations in mind one may start by accepting the cautious opinion put forward by Ferrua as soon as this fortunate discovery was made public, to the effect that from the middle of the fourth century a Christian could probably look forward with a quiet conscience to the coexistence in his burial place of Christian paintings with decorations including, for example, even subjects taken from the myth of Hercules.[3]

Careful study of the monument nearly always confirms the view expressed by Stern,[4] that some rooms in the Catacomb may have served for the inhumation of Christians, and others for that of pagans belonging to the same family, since 'Christian and mythological subjects are never found together in one chamber'. It would seem

168–177

Plan E

1 Ferrua (1956a; 1956b; 1960); Josi (1956).
2 In fact, for the purposes of dating in general, the obvious stage of iconographical elaboration in monuments has to be taken into consideration. It was an entirely new departure, incidentally, in some catacombal painting. Actually, in many pictures compositional articulation and sometimes idiomatic specification of certain details are to be found, which would be inexplicable if they had not been taken from sarcophagi and miniatures or more often from fresco or mosaic decoration in ecclesiastical buildings. On these grounds even the oldest paintings in the catacomb might plausibly be ascribed to the advanced fourth century, arguably two or three decades later than the period fixed by Ferrua in the last of his works quoted above as between 320 and 340.
3 Ferrua (1956a), p. 129.
4 Stern (1958), p. 213, n. 304.

Catacomb on the
Via Latina (Rome)

Plan E

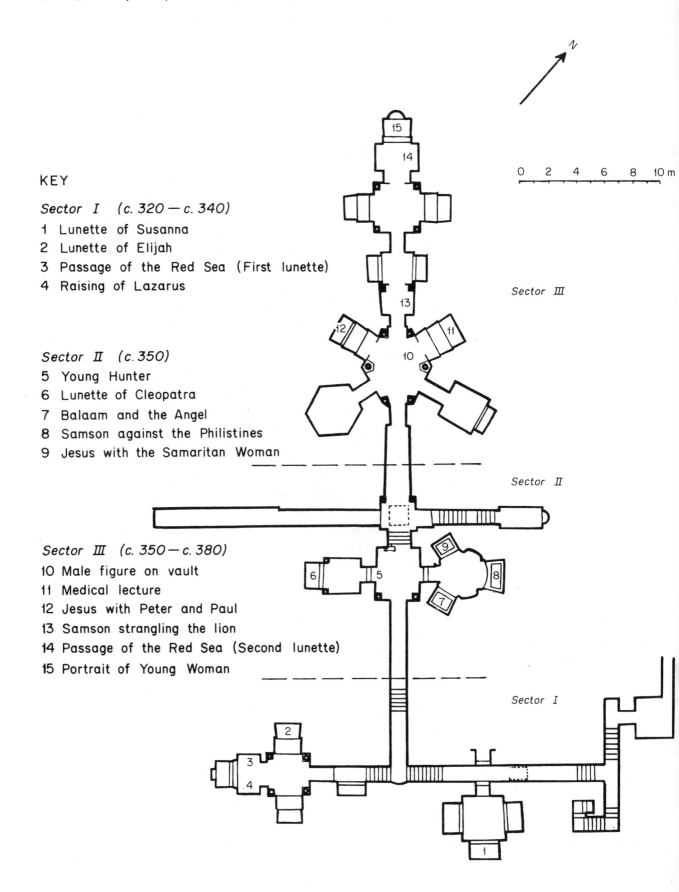

KEY

Sector I (c. 320 — c. 340)

1 Lunette of Susanna
2 Lunette of Elijah
3 Passage of the Red Sea (First lunette)
4 Raising of Lazarus

Sector II (c. 350)

5 Young Hunter
6 Lunette of Cleopatra
7 Balaam and the Angel
8 Samson against the Philistines
9 Jesus with the Samaritan Woman

Sector III (c. 350 — c. 380)

10 Male figure on vault
11 Medical lecture
12 Jesus with Peter and Paul
13 Samson strangling the lion
14 Passage of the Red Sea (Second lunette)
15 Portrait of Young Woman

0 2 4 6 8 10 m

Sector III

Sector II

Sector I

that this interpretation, accepted by Ferrua himself, can be reasonably admitted against the usual explanations based upon ideas of syncretism or of heretical influences which are seldom if ever supported by historical evidence. The Catacomb on the Via Latina would thus exemplify the workings of 'private equity',[5] under which it would receive the remains of the members of three or four groups of families during an age of transition when mutual religious tolerance reflected the presence in the same families of individuals converted to Christianity and others who adhered to classical traditions of belief. This fact would account for the close connection or rather intermingling in the catacomb of paintings and decorations of Christian, pagan and generically secular type. Such intermingling, however, implies no syncretism of any sort, because the fables depicted seem to be strictly orthodox and not reciprocally adulterated. All that they prove is a prevailing climate of tolerance in the sphere of ideology, or at least of symbolism, within a society in course of rapid transformation.

It would be as pointless and impossible in this work to undertake a complete philological and stylistic analysis of the pictorial content of the new catacomb as it would have been to do likewise with the enormous cemeterial complex of Rome. It will suffice here to deal with certain carefully selected paintings which may be usefully allowed a place in the panorama of monuments outlined in these pages. For this purpose I shall note some of the traits most in agreement with the taste predominant in palace art, both liturgical and secular, in the period between the last years of the reign of Constantine (fourth decade) and at least the first of Theodosius (ninth decade of the fourth century). Of these the first examples appear to be those clearly discernible in the 'Susanna Lunette' on the rear arcosolium of the first cubicle of sector I of the catacomb. They may be ascribed, though within the limits of two different techniques, to late Constantinian expressionism, but to a less agitated form of it than appears in the 'Great Praying Women' of the Cemetery of Traso. In obedience to a taste then rapidly imposing a progressively more linear and anti-plastic use of colour, the face of Susanna, the best preserved part of the lunette, retains in its not entirely frontal presentation a rigidly astonished expression conveyed by shades of rose and violet fused into one another with short brushstrokes, in a way that seems unquestionably derived from the creative treatment of surfaces by the TRIER CONSTANTINIAN MASTER. The 'Elijah Lunette' with its Hellenistic background and the prophet's chariot rising in correct perspective, is set at the far end of the right-hand arcosolium in the second cubicle of sector I. The general composition of the work reveals a different hand, not unrelated to the traditionalist reaction of the period but

23, 162

168

5 Ferrua (1960), pp. 89–90.

sufficiently mature to proceed to the further idiomatic achievements set on foot by imperial art as early as the Tetrarchy. The usual golden tones seem to be in retreat before a new invasion of pure colour. At the same time the faces clearly show work undertaken at two different periods, from the chromatically neutral first layer of the background surfaces to the rendering of the physiognomies by the confident use of a distinct and hard outline (probably on a dry ground), which carries the whole weight of expression and structure.

It appears certain, moreover, that the ARTIST OF THE ASSUMPTION OF ELIJAH worked in a cultural climate well acquainted with even the boldest experiments in composition. For in the very next cubicle (the third in sector I of the catacomb), opening out of the central space as does that of Elijah, a painter of glowing talent decorated the two large lateral niches with a 'Miracle of Lazarus' (on the left) and a 'Passage of the Red Sea' (on the right), both 170 exemplary specimens of the narrative style. This CATA-COMBAL ARTIST OF THE RED SEA, probably using very large and detailed models, divided his crowd of figures in the first work between the wall space and the interior face of the left-hand pilaster supporting the vault; in the second he employed the interior faces of both pilasters, thus creating a scene on planes interrupted and at right angles to one another, the two lateral ones serving as wings to the central stage of the wall. Accordingly, the representation of the Egyptian army in flight from the rising waves continues on the face of the left-hand pilaster, while that on the right shows the rear ranks of Israel delivered. In this case there is no such substantial contraction of form as is displayed, for example, by the picture in the nave of Santa Maria Maggiore, and is already suggested in the 210 Synagogue at Dura Europos. The catacombal painting 66 expands and continues, one might say, round the field of vision, being already organised in protomedieval fashion. The result on the whole much resembles the effect of some modern cinematic sequences on a very wide screen.

All the features of this procedure attest the spectator's full perspectival, and hence emotional and spiritual, participation in the scene, as is contrived, for instance (though on a single curved plane), in the apsidal bays of the basilicas. The fresco was not, moreover, without consequences in the catacomb, and is therefore not to be judged as an isolated and, in short, casual event.

Confirmation is supplied by the right-hand niche of the last cubicle of the catacomb, where some decades later another 'Passage of the Red Sea', facing another 'Miracle 171-3 of Lazarus', repeated the same 'winged' composition, though with an illuminating and fundamental difference. Here the ranks of the Egyptian army and of the Israelites 172 do not extend to the two sides of the lunette, which are occupied only by two figures representing the two hosts. The two peoples, divided by the waves of the sea, have also been reduced in numbers, and the iconography as a whole reveals a progression, reaching an extreme in the two lateral figures, towards a more synthetically expressive type of narration, more symbolically figurative. Such was the development which culminated a hundred and fifty years later in the apses of Ravenna, where the apostles would be transformed into diminutive sheep despite the fact that persecution was a thing of the past and there was consequently no longer need for symbolism.

A predominance of expressionist methods within a style bearing traces of a traditionalist culture may be detected in certain works of the middle sector of the catacomb. Their dates cannot be far distant from those of the rooms of the oldest sector, belonging perhaps to about the middle of the century. Here we have less of the superfluous decoration and baroque taste of the first cubicles, together with a more strictly controlled partition of the ornament, both in the two central spaces that lead along the axis of the cemetery and within the two lateral cubicles adjoining the first of those spaces. The general manner referred to is not without parallels among the other surviving monuments of the period. Examples are the frescoes in the Tomb of Silistra, which will be examined   181–4
later. These, with their partitioning (which includes large separate figures of the deceased and family groups) and their lunettes depicting peacocks *affrontés*,[6] repeat exactly certain aspects of the left-hand crypt in the middle sector of the catacomb, a crypt named also 'of Cleopatra' from the decoration of the lunette of the arcosolium.

Within the four chambers of this zone the prevailing hands are those of painters interested on the one hand in the last phase of the fine style, though not always sharing its tendency to decorative redundancy, and on the other more strongly attracted to the final message of expressionism. We may consider as representative of these tendencies the lunettes of the first central chamber, particularly that showing the small figure of a 'Naked Boy Hunter',   176
with an ample cloak hanging from his shoulders. The quality of the thickly laid colour, boldly fused in warm tones, together with the peculiarity of the large eyes and the almost archaic smile, proclaim this as one of the last of the vivid and yet still profoundly active figures before the breaking of that dramatic wave which events were about to bring upon the classical world. The picture somehow recalls the expressive character of the mosaic fragment of the 'Hermes and Dionysus' from Antioch,   149
already discussed.

Different technical methods characterise the author of the rear 'Cleopatra' lunette, in the left hand chamber, and   169
the painter of the lunette of 'Balaam and the Ass', in the   174

6 The peacock as a subject symbolising heavenly immortality in the starry luxuriance of its caudal plumage appears in both Christian and classical paintings, from the latter of which it was actually derived.

first arcosolium on the right of the right-hand chamber. The first is a master of colour still lavish of his abundant decorative gifts. He misses none of the opportunities afforded by colour for the display of vivid beauty. Thus the amber nudity of the woman reclining languidly in a garden of beautiful flowers and tall, threadlike verdure, rendered with quick touches of yellow and green, recalls, though with less joyous freshness, the well known scene of 'Cupid and Psyche among Flowers' in the oldest section of the Cemetery of Domitilla. The second is an artist more closely linked to the school of later tetrarchic expressionism, of roughened flatness and sober draughtsmanship, with hints of airy elegance in the trees and shrubs depicted in the lunette, and a touch very like that of certain details of landscape at Piazza Armerina, especially in the 'Little Hunt'.

The painters of the 'Lunette of the Samaritan Woman' and 'Samson with the Ass's Jawbone' in the same chamber on the right, were more interested in the substantially premannerist shallowness of volume frequent in the second half of the century. Similar in outlook were the artists of the central chambers of sector III, beyond the great quadrilobate hexagonal complex. Among the paintings in these central chambers, special importance attaches to 'Samson's Struggle with the Lion', where the undoubted resort to cartoons dealing with Hercules and the chase[7] does not prevent an effect of massed, flattened severity, such as was produced on a more elaborate scale in the Antioch hunting scenes of the fifth and sixth centuries[8] and had also been evident, though strictly controlled by an artist of much greater skill, in the mighty beasts of the CARNAGE MASTER at Piazza Armerina.

The small portrait at the top of the vault of the central arcosolium in the last cubicle of the catacomb definitely belongs to the first phase of Theodosian mannerism. This picture of a 'Haloed Girl' surrounded by flying Cupids, birds and festoons, retains, together with the typology which expressionism had by now bequeathed to the whole of the fourth century, a solid but agreeably rounded formation of the features, a look of meditative tranquillity in the eyes, and a general grace of structure, all of which relate the style of the artist in some measure to that of the heads of the Ivory Casket and Gold Glass by BOUNNERIOS in the Municipal Museum at Brescia and also to that of the so-called Sarcophagus of Nabor and Felix at S. Ambrogio, Milan.

The most imposing assemblage of paintings in the entire catacomb is found in the hexagonal chamber, where the six great sections of the vault are upheld by as many columns, which also mark the entrances to the spaces opening out on every side. It is indeed probable that sector III, which begins with this hexagonal chamber, was

177

7 It is probable that illustrations of the Samson story were based on models in the Hercules cycle, where there are, for example, many very similar scenes of the slaying of the Nemean lion, as well as from general subjects dealing with the chase and gladiatorial combats with beasts. Such is one of the many instances of direct iconographical intercourse between classical and Christian religious painting after the edict of Constantine.
8 *See*, for example, the scene of the 'Hunting Amazon' from the Yakto Complex, the hunting scenes in the Megalopsychia mosaic and the animals depicted in the 'Martyrion' at Seleucia, noted respectively in Levi (1947), ii, pls. LXIV, b; LXX, a, c; LXXXIX, a, b

the last to be decorated; but it does not seem possible at present, in the absence of satisfactory epigraphical evidence, to say for certain in what order the decorations in this room (very few of them Christian) were carried out relatively to others in the same sector. The paintings on the lunettes of the two arcosolia ('Christ between Peter and Paul' and the 'Medical Lecture'), both by the same hand, are of less importance than the remains of the vault portraits, showing busts of young and elderly men. These are executed in a peculiar style which owes little to expressionism and is certainly not inclined to mannerism. They reveal an attempt at portraiture which Ferrua has explained as represneting the great teachers of medicine. If true, this interpretation would undoubtedly carry weight in the cultural vindication of the physiognomical analysis evident in these busts. But the psychological naturalism and the detailed realism of the chromatic line leave some uncertainty as to whether these works, which we shall attribute to the MASTER OF THE CATACOMBAL PORTRAITS, should be dated to the sixth and seventh decades of the century or to a period nearer its end. I should prefer the latter date on grounds of idiom alone, with reference to the similar 'Patriarchs' and Apostles at S. Aquilino in Milan.

Some approximation to the spirit of these portraits, though it does not attain to any notable dignity of form, is to be found in the bearded and haloed 'Image of Christ', flanked by the letters alpha and omega, which appears among a set of caissons of the vault of a cubicle containing the portrait of one 'Leo officialis annonae', quite recently excavated in the Via Giovannipoli at Rome and now known to have belonged to the Cemetery of Commodilla, from which it had become detached by subsidence in the course of centuries.[9] The chamber, like the Catacomb on the Via Latina, is extraordinarily rich in frescoes covering every available wall-space, and this representation of the Saviour provides another example of non-mannerist painting at the end of the fourth century, to which period the entire zone is to be referred. Particularly in the scenes of 'Peter's Denial' on the right-hand arcosolium, 'Christ between SS. Felix and Adauctus' on the lunette of the central arcosolium, and 'Miracle of the Water' in the left-hand niche of the cubicle, the painter adopts a manner rooted in expressionism, which we shall find in the lunettes of S. Aquilino at Milan, in the pavement of the Dioscuri at Trier, and at length in the MASTERS OF SANTA MARIA MAGGIORE. This line of development, as will be shown later, often sought to recover the traditional treatment of the image, but it never surrendered in degenerate fashion to the manneristic taste of its day.

9 Ferrua (1958).

A singular development of Roman catacombal painting towards the end of the fourth century is exemplified by certain works that show a peculiarly solemn maturity of the mannerism of the age of Valentinian I. It is expressed by a very conspicuous elongation of the figures, to which the architectural handling of the robes lends an almost statuesque dignity; by a marked reorganisation of composition, not unmindful, however, of the preceding post-constantinian expressionist accentuations; and by an extremely free but symmetrical, autocompensatory setting of figures and objects against the white backgrounds of lunettes and vaulting. Particular reference may be made first to the Lunette of the cubicle of Veneranda (Cemetery of Domitilla), who ascends to the heavenly garden accompanied by the martyr Petronella (Petronilla) who is venerated in the adjacent Basilica of SS. Nereus and Achilleus; secondly, to the vault displaying 'Christ between Peter and Paul and the Agnus Dei with Four Martyrs' in the Cemetery of Peter and Marcellinus, where the composition by levels modifies the meticulous symmetry of the images; and thirdly, to the *Confessio* paintings under the Basilica of SS. Giovanni e Paolo.

180

179

The 'Lunette of Veneranda', variously assigned to the first two decades of the second half of the century, seems indeed to belong to the age of Theodosius. It may actually be a little later than the *Agnus Dei* vault, which some would be inclined to ascribe to the beginning of the fifth century.[10] These two paintings appear undoubtedly to have been the result of the same fashion in composition, but they actually differ quite noticeably. The *theophania* of 'Christ between Peter and Paul and the Agnus Dei with Four Martyrs' expresses a predominantly linear technique within the limits of the new taste, a technique that seems to involve the compositional *collage* remaining an end in itself, while the full rigour of ritual is imposed. On the other hand the scene of Veneranda's admission to paradise reveals more preoccupation with plasticity, more tranquillity in the management of the attitudes of the figures and a more concentrated and personalised solemnity in the depiction of the event.

180

179

180

This style is in many respects close to that of the elongated forms of the 'Praying Figure' and of the 'Martyrs' in the *Confessio* of the House of Pammachius under the Basilica of SS. Giovanni e Paolo on the Caelian, dateable to the penultimate decade of the century. In these pictures, fundamental for the study of the transformation of a *domus ecclesiae* (of the *titulus* Byzantis et Pammachii) into a basilica, the simple elegance of the scene-setting, the placing of the figures and the apt chromatic connections suggest a further blending of stylistic characterisation useful for the understanding of the *iter* of painting in the capital up to the end of the century. These works in fact

10 *See* for the *Veneranda* lunette Marucchi (1933), p. 161, f. 38, and Wilpert (1903), pp. 428–9, pl. 213; for the '*Agnus Dei*' vault also Marucchi (1933), p. 322, f. 114, and Wilpert (1903), p. 455, pls. 252–3; for the *Confessio* under the Basilica of SS. Giovanni e Paolo: Wilpert (1917), ii, pp. 637–8; iv, pl. 131. De Wit (1938, p. 58, pl. 51, 1–4) recognises the similarity of hair styles in one of the figures and in that of 'Petronella' in the '*Veneranda*' lunette.

prove Christian painting to have participated in the cultural and idiomatic evolution of official art and its tendencies, well known in sculpture, during the age of Theodosius.

The hypogean wall paintings found by Frova in 1943 at Silistra, the ancient *Durostorum*, in modern Bulgaria, seem on the other hand to constitute, though precise dating is difficult, a typical example of the painting now dependent on Constantinople. They were executed in the late fourth century, probably between the sixth and eighth decades, at a time when the 'fine style', Constantinian expressionism and the reaction under Julian were giving place to the so-called Valentinianate mannerism and that of the age of Theodosius, while the classical revival was being superseded by a more formalist and frigid echo of classicism.[11]

181–4

Close to the neighbourhood of the barracks, in the city from which Valens started against the Goths in 367, there was brought to light a Roman tomb in the form of a small barrel-vaulted hall, two metres and thirty centimetres high. On the stonework of the walls there survives a very lively decoration in fresco, which according to Frova[12] was retouched on the dry plaster. An overall pattern of framing in broad red bands and green lines divides the bright surfaces into compartments, with an effect of true funerary taste and tradition; as Wirth has shown,[13] it reproduces the type of red and green ornament which was already going out of fashion in Rome as the third century closed. Ten large figures up to 90 centimetres high occupy the compartments, three on each of the two lateral walls, four on the end wall, which is surmounted by a lunette, repeated over the entrance in the opposite wall, with the widespread subject of peacocks *affrontés*.

181–3

The little vault is summarily decorated with circles and octagons containing representations of various animals, in imitation of illustratious models ranging from the annular vault of the Mausoleum of Constantina to the later barrel-vaults of two large niches at Hagios Georgios, Salonika.

184

Following the conventions more often noted after the second century, the two deceased, husband and wife, whose figures occupy the central square of the rear wall, 'overstep the green frame with their feet; the man does likewise with his cloaked left side',[14] so that the line of the frame, previously drawn, reappears faintly under the cloak. Also, the flames of the chandeliers on either side of the entrance cut the upper side of the frame. The same thing happens in the painted caissons of the vault, where, for example, the spear of an ambushed hunter, aimed at a charging boar in the next compartment, crosses the dividing line of the frame. We have already noted in-

182

184

11 Frova (1943). The same author (1954) favours a dating in the early fourth century. Verdiani (1946, p. 35) prefers 'the last decades of the fourth century'. Bianchi Bandinelli (1955, pp. 98–100) argues for the mid-century, before the events of 376–8. More recently Dimitrov (1960), referring to the Theodosian *missorium* at Madrid and the Arles sarcophagus of 'Christ and the Apostles' (Gerke, 1935, p. 137, ff. 4, 5, 8), supports an attribution to the age of Theodosius, but within the last twenty years of the century, which seems to me too late. Finally, *see* Frova (1961), pp. 588–90.

12 Frova (1943), p. 11.

13 Wirth (1934), p. 224.

14 Frova (1943), p. 12.

stances of the surface unity of figures and background, where the decorative framing or border does not interrupt the substantial unity of the scene in space and time, though it is arranged in successive, coordinated moments. But attention must also be drawn to another clear though common characteristic of late antiquity, resulting in a vision of space now lacking volume and depth (e.g. the husband's right foot is placed upon the left foot of his wife), or from 182 paratactical structure: 'Thus in the picture of the thurible 181 and in that of the candelabra the third leg of the stand is aligned with the two in the foreground'.[15] (Incidentally, that 'thurible' looks to me more like a *cista*.)

Another important clue to the dating of the pictures is the architectural motif in decoration. An example of this is provided by the golden-backed architectural settings in the mosaics of the dome of the Rotunda of Hagios Georgios, Salonika, probably belonging to the age of 215, 216 Theodosius, or by the use of similar partitioning in many Antiochene mosaics of the third and fourth centuries. At Silistra sections of rafters are shown in perspective, the areas of red and green on a black background running rhythmically to their meeting-place on the shorter walls. Frova himself considers that this trabeate ornamentation may be the last memory of the Hellenistic tradition, which had been so fond of perspectival illusionism and fictitious architecture. But in the Silistra paintings one can detect no final provincial echo of Hellenism, congealed in forms of stiffly motionless pre-Byzantine mannerism. This conclusion is confirmed on the one hand by the idiom of the human figures, upon which is focussed the strictly artistic interest of this monument, and on the other hand by the vivacity and polychromy of the animals on the vault and the decorative organisation itself of their framing, the creatures being rendered by few but firm brushstrokes of much expressive merit. The duck, some of the birds in flight and other figurative work on the ceiling retain the taste of late Roman impressionism as it developed up to the mid-third century.

Again, the figures, particularly the two deceased persons, the maid carrying the *cista* and the manservant bringing a 181 belt, show some evidence of indebtedness to Roman 183 portraiture: they prove once more, though there are also signs of the incipient mannerism of the day, that recourse was had to Roman practice of earlier centuries. The eight waiters of the Roman House on the Via dei Cerchi, 48 framed in accomplished architectural perspective, recall, for example, even more forcefully than the figures of the Mausoleum of the Aurelii the no longer rhythmical but 71, 72, 7. deliberate stride of the figures at Silistra, naturally with quite different results due to the very marked divergence of style. The result in this case is a plasticity which echoes the Constantinian 'fine style', though its physiognomical

15 Frova (1943), p. 27. For the identification of the *cista* I rely on the convincing arguments in Verdiani (1946), pp. 28, 32.

syntax retains the expressive but crystallised and impoverished fixity of the countenances of the preceding age, which had developed under the influence of expressionism and not without traces of a peculiarly ingenuous accent, typical of the SILISTRA TOMB MASTER. Within the limits of this inheritance he reveals an original taste in form, which is displayed in a sure if concise mastery of line, in a care for the organic finish of surfaces, and in a capacity for the synthetic rendering of figures which causes his paintings to approach the smoothness of a polished bas-relief or ivory diptych. It is certain that, while his culture is that of a Roman province, his ideal comes closer to the manner being developed in Constantinople towards the end of the fourth century.

Even in northern Italy a similar direction of taste is authoritatively attested in the second half of the century, for example by the Brescia Casket and by the Sarcophagus of Nabor and Felix at S. Ambrogio. The mosaics here examined all represent on their own account and with variations of their own an artistic mode emanating from Milan.

The recent discoveries of large fragments of the mosaic decoration of a second apsidiole of the circular niched Chapel of S. Aquilino attached to San Lorenzo at Milan, and of decorative borders in the forceps atrium connecting the chapel with the basilica, have again raised the problem of the date of the mosaic in the apsidiole representing 'Christ with the Apostles', a work already known. Exhaustive study, however, in the light of philological and stylistic considerations, tends to support the views of Bettini, Galassi and Cecchelli, who were inclined to date both works about the year 400,[16] contrary to the opinion of Volbach, who judged them to be contemporary with the Mausoleum of Galla Placidia, erected in the middle of the fifth century.[17] On the other hand, Galassi's hypothesis of repairs which included partial refacing about fifty years after the original execution appears admissible.

As to the interpretation of the two lunettes, Cecchelli's observations are of interest. After expressing his belief that the Chapel of S. Aquilino may have been founded as a baptistery,[18] he goes on to present a largely convincing view of the iconography of the two apses based upon certain comparisons. The most striking of these is with the sarcophagus under the pulpit of S. Ambrogio dating from the end of the fourth century, which contains both the scene of Christ with the Apostles, in duplicate, and an Assumption of Elijah closely resembling that in the pastoral lunette with the 'solar chariot'.[19] Cecchelli also relies upon the clear translation into systematic theological terms of the iconographic details of the two San Aquilino lunettes.

28, 29

30

27

29

16 Bettini (1952), p. 52; Galassi (1953), p. 510; Cecchelli (Calderini et al., 1951, p. 209).
17 Volbach (1952), p. 71. F. Van der Meer (1960, p. 79, f. 190) also accepts a date slightly later than the end of the fourth century.
18 Cecchelli, in Calderini et al. (1951), pp. 226–7.
19 See Volbach (1952), p. 54, pls. 46–7; Bovini (1949), p. 232, pls. 249–50.

In the first lunette Christ, surrounded by the Apostolic College, is seated in a commanding position on an elevated rock, his right hand raised in an oratorical gesture, while some of the apostles turn their hands towards the Redeemer and seem to invite attention to his words. The picture might illustrate, rather than a normal *traditio legis*, evangelical teaching delivered by the Divine Master; for He holds an open *volumen* – as incidentally do some of the apostles, though theirs are closed – and a *scrinium* full of *rotuli* stands in the grassy foreground. The second lunette is enlivened by a pastoral landscape ('drenched in Hellenistic memories', as Galassi[20] justly observes), in which we see gushing springs of water; details of classical derivation, such as the solar chariot; and details of Christian origin, such as the usual attitude of Jonah in repose assumed by the right-hand shepherd, though this attitude is of more remote origin (e.g. Endymion asleep). This lunette might accordingly suggest a more complicated exegesis: the partly lost figure of the wayfarer at the centre of the apse, looking towards the solar chariot, might represent the prophet Elisha watching Elijah ascend to heaven, for in one of his homilies St. John Chrysostom draws a close parallel between the myth of the solar chariot and the biblical story; while the reclining shepherd, gazing at the spring of water and holding a *rotulus*, might symbolise the Christian contemplating the baptismal immersion which has purified him and clasping the book of the new faith he had learned and adopted.

While such points of interpretation to some extent clarify the iconographical connections between the figurative symbolism of the triumphant religion and the still powerful and readily accepted elements of classical myth, the pictorial vocabulary of these mosaics, rather than those of the atrium, proclaims especially in the 'Assumption of Elijah' a revival of classicising taste, discernible in the gradual dilution of colour and shadow, and in the attention to drapery, which, particularly in the first apse, assumes a basic function. Meanwhile there is evident an underlying reference to portraiture in the figures of the Apostles and in that of Christ, who is, however, shown beardless and with an Apolline look; they are not studied and composed as though they constituted a practically anonymous series of disciples surrounding the Master, but as if they were a collection of historically identified individuals, on which account Cecchelli has compared them with the 'Portraits of Donors' in the Aquileian Basilica.

But we are speaking of a tendency which could not, of course, resuscitate the past and which affords a new example of third- and fourth-century 'returns' to tradition; an example which certifies the dialectical and not passively retrograde value of those returns. In the bay showing the

20 Galassi (1953), p. 510.

19 Paris, Louvre. Spring (detail of the Seasons), from the Constantinian villa at Antioch (Daphne-Harbie).

20 Paris, Louvre. Autumn (detail of the Seasons), from the Constantinian villa at Antioch (Daphne-Harbie).

21 Rome, Coemeterium Majus. Virgin and Child (detail), lunette of arcosolium in Room 5.

22 Rome, Cemetery of Callistus. Dionysas (detail), Crypt of the Five Saints.

23 Rome, Cemetery of Traso. Right-hand Praying Woman (detail), Sepulchre of the Great Praying Women.

24 Rome, Mausoleum of Constantina (S. Costanza). Asaroton - like section of annular vault.

166 Rome, Mausoleum of Constantina (S. Costanza). Grape-gathering Cupids, in the annular vault

167 Vatican City, Museo Pio-Clementino. Porphyry sarcophagus of Constantina with cupids treading the winepress

168 Rome, Catacomb on the Via Latina. Lunette of Elijah (right-hand *arcosolium* of the second cubicle in Sector I)

169 Rome, Catacomb on the Via Latina. Lunette of Cleopatra (arcosolium of the left-hand chamber in Sector II)

170 Rome, Catacomb on the Via Latina. Passage of the Read Sea (right-hand niche of the second cubicle in Section I)

171, 172, 173 Rome, Catacomb on the Via Latina. Passage of the Red Sea (wall and pilasters of the right hand niche of the last cubicle in Sector III)

174 Rome, Catacomb on the Via Latina. Lunette of Balaam and the Ass (first right-hand *arcosolium* of the right chamber in Sector II

175 Rome, Catacomb on the Via Latina. Male Bust (vault of the hexagonal chamber in Sector III)

176 Rome, Catacomb on the Via Latina. Naked Boy Hunter (central chamber of Sector II)

177 Rome, Catacomb on the Via Latina. Head of Haloed Girl (vault of the *arcosolium* of the last cubicle in Sector III)

178 Rome, Cemetery of Commodilla. Cubicle of Leo: Image of Christ on the vault

179 Rome, Cemetery of Peter and Marcellinus. Vault: Christ between Peter and Paul, and the *Agnus Dei* with four Martyrs

180 Rome, Cemetery of Domitilla. Lunette in the cubicle of Veneranda (detail)

25 Rome, Mausoleum of Constantina (S. Costanza). *Traditio Legis*, in left-hand apse.

26 Rome, Mausoleum of Constantina (S. Costanza). *Tradition Clavium*, right-hand apse.

27 Milan, Chapel of S. Aquilino. Christ with the Apostles, right-hand apse.

28 and 29 Milan, Chapel of S. Aquilino. Fragments of the left-hand apse.

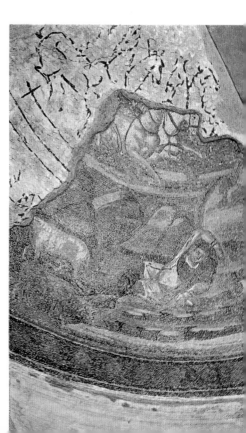

30 Milan, Chapel of S. Aquilino. Fragment: Figure of Saint, forceps *atrium*.

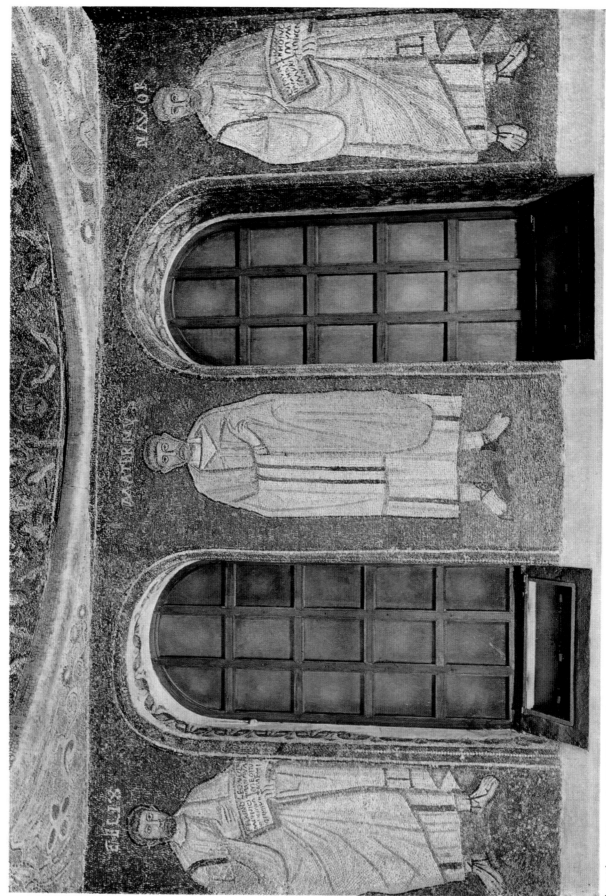

31 Milan, S. Vittore in Ciel d'Oro. Felix, Maternus and Navor, on a wall of the *sacellum*.

181 Silistra, Roman Tomb. Maidservant with *cista*, left-hand wall   182 Silistra, Roman Tomb. The Two Deceased, end wall

184 Silistra, Roman Tomb. Caissons of the Vault (detail)

183 Silistra, Roman Tomb. Servant with Girdle, right-hand wall

185 Trier, Landesmuseum. Mosaic of the Muses by Monnus (detail)

187 Trier, Landesmuseum. Mosaic of the Muses (detail), from the Neustrasse

186 Trier, Landesmuseum. Mosaic of the Muses, from the Neustrasse

188 Trier, Landesmuseum. Mosaic of the Muses (detail), from the Neustrasse

apostolic college where use is made both of the courtly concept of royal personages in the late Empire and of the vast repertory of philosophical gatherings, transmitted by way of the sarcophagi and the hallowed interpretations of them in the catacombs. Here, what remains of traditional taste is represented principally, as already mentioned, by the mannerist treatment of drapery, varied by extensive shading and sudden white highlights and 'brushstrokes' at prominent though not always organically justified points of the body, and by the generically austere appearance and thorough formal rendering of the individual personages. But these features did not succeed in distorting the merits of a picture in which, notwithstanding such experimental refinements, the white field of the clothing, shot with the most delicate tints of pearl-grey and watery green, is revealed as a formal superstructure hardly concealing a very different organisation of the bodies and of space. Galassi, Bettini and Volbach have correctly drawn attention to certain apostolic assemblies depicted in the Roman catacombs, notably those in the arcosolium adjacent to the Crypt of Ampliatus and in the apsidal bay of the Region of the Great Apostles in the Cemetery of Domitilla, dated respectively in the middle and later years of the fourth century.[21] The total absence of bodily structure and personal characterisation in these figures might help to isolate the professional skill of the SAN AQUILINO MASTER from his new interpretative effort to express a renovated historicism, and to show the impossibility of a full recovery of classical physical patterns even by a trained cultural vision clearly implying restoration of neo-Hellenistic taste.

It is thus possible to speak of an expressionist morphological vocabulary, which, while remaining for the most part alienated from the mannerist developments of the age of Theodosius, preserved within the limits of a process of new aesthetic acclimatisation appreciable elements of the parataxis of the end of the third century. Examples are: (a) the reclining shepherd, whose arms are so placed as to give the shoulders and upper back, drawn in continuity with the chest, an abnormal width, so that he appears to be leaning against the mountains of the background, with a result, formally speaking, that amounts to a union of figure and landscape; (b) the lack of balance between the heads of the apostles, all alike in the foreground, and their bodies aligned on a single ideal plane, which is turned by their dark contour lines into two separate levels, while their feet are again on the same plane and sometimes collide. On the faces of these persons expressionism is evident in the frequent lack of proportion between adjoining features, almost as though portrayal had relied on a distorting mirror. It is no less evident in the piercing protrusion of the eyes, spherical and often staring wildly,

21 The arcosolium was dated in the first half of the century by Wilpert (1924, p. 226, pl. 148, 2). De Wit (1938, p. 55, pl. 47) and Volbach (1952, pp. 44, pls. 7b and 10a), more recently, agree in preferring the mid-century. The apsidal lunette, assigned by Wilpert (1903, p. 127, pl. 193) and Ducati (1952, pp. 728–9) to the middle of the fourth century, was dated by Bettini (1952, pl. 38) to about 390, by Galassi (1930, p. 44) to the fourth century and by Bovini (1957a, p. 27) to the end of the century. For these two mosaics *see also* above, Chapter V, Note 27.
The recent rediscovery (1960) of an arcosolium decorated in mosaic in a new section of the entrance to the Cemetery of Domitilla adds a further monument to those hitherto mentioned. The work, quite exceptional for a catacomb, includes a lunette representing 'Christ as Teacher', with the right hand raised in an oratorical gesture and seated on a throne, with the Apostles Peter and Paul sitting at a lower level on each side. The foreground displays the *capsa* with its *rotuli*. The figure of the Master stands out against the background, beardless, and provided with a great gleaming halo of bright green, as though enveloped by a medieval mandorla. Above the lunette the inscription '*Qui filius diceris et pater inveniris*' leads the eye to the vault of the arcosolium, where three scenes are illustrated. They comprise the 'Resurrection of Lazarus', the 'Three Youths in the Furnace' and a third so damaged as to be indecipherable. The quality of the mosaic is remarkable. On other, archaeological, grounds Ferrua (1960a) has suggested the 'time of Pope Damasus, perhaps a little earlier, but not later', that is to say, between 366 and 384, as against a later date given by Cecchelli (1944, p. 196), who had indicated as a minimum the end of the fourth century or beginning of the fifth. The mosaic appears to constitute in certain of its idiomatic aspects an excellent introduction to the developments attested by S. Aquilino at Milan as part of the clear evolution of post-Constantine expressionism demonstrated in Rome by, for example, the lunettes of the Mausoleum of Constantina.

R

which with the other and usually darker outlines dominate oppressively the surface of the planes. In this connection Cecchelli[22] makes felicitous reference to the face of Hermes in the D Baths at Antioch, from which many and, I think, useful signs point back along a road to more distant origins, as far as the 'Great Praying Women' of the Cemetery of Traso and the tetrarchic portraits in porphyry.

149

23, 162

It is particularly to be noted with regard to the landscape environment and the marginal decoration of the two mosaic pictures in the apsidioles, especially that depicting Elijah, that the Hellenistic culture taken for granted in these surroundings is in fact substantially adulterated by a spiritual rather than idiomatic revival so as to transform the naturalism aimed at in the elements of the landscape, symbolical though they are, into a daring statement of a novel cosmology similar in many respects to the later concepts of Byzantium.

28, 29

This observation is confirmed to some extent by the stylistic renovation of the stock environment: schematisation of background mountains; distribution of foreground rocks; conventional treatment of running water; gilding of skies, and the use of gold-coloured tesserae in other details requiring a precious and brilliant appearance; transfiguration of flowers into abstract and stellar shapes; chromatic enrichment of the framing borders in ranges of pure atonality. But a greater weight of evidence is provided by the very considerable change of manner which, within the same narrative usages of the past, are revealed by the mosaics of S. Aquilino, which, as Volbach has pointed out, are spiritually close to those of the Mausoleum of Galla Placidia. The initially epic and then gnomico-psychological representation of historical events, which had replaced the Hellenistic mythico-idyllic form of storytelling, was carried a stage further by the S. AQUILINO MASTER. With him the historical statement is transformed into an event present and shared, exemplary and redemptive. The emotional charge carried by the picture came to be valued by the believer as sacred history full of meaning and vitality.

On the other hand, the Apostles of the south-west apsidiole of S. Aquilino show what experiments might accompany the efforts at formative recomposition, at first uncertain, then progressively more apparent, which are to be seen in the remains of the 'Patriarchs' of the adjacent forceps atrium, and in the more skilfully designed six 'Figures of Saints' (Protasius, Ambrosius, Gervasius, Felix, Maternus, Navor, besides the head of Victor) on the later walls and ceiling of the nearby Milanese chapel of S. Vittore in Ciel d'Oro, which were undoubtedly executed quite late in the fifth century.[23] The two 'Patriarchs' of S. Aquilino (de tribu Symeon and de tribu(Zabu)lon), whose faces stand out with magical effect against a splendid blue

27

30

31

22 Cecchelli (Calderini et al., 1951), p. 216.
23 Galassi (1930), p. 47; Bettini (1952), p. 52; Volbach (1952), p. 70.

background, varied with areas of grey and lettering in gold, show in their fragmentary figures and facial features, in their intensity of expression and in the chromatic richness of the tessellate, signs of the aftermath of mannerism, which help to declare them perhaps ten years later than the mosaics of the two apsidioles, if the latter are any earlier than the beginning of the fifth century.[24] The small emblematic picture, called 'Tamar' by Cecchelli, next to a third similar biblical figure,[25] shows a clear and bold advance in the divisionist technique of pure and 'blotted' chromaticism. It heralds the imminence of the full outburst of colour soon to occur in the twenty-seven pictures in the nave of S. Maria Maggiore at Rome and in the Mausoleum of Galla Placidia at Ravenna.

30

210

24 Galassi (1953, p. 346) notes that they 'do not yet show the monumental quality of the images created in the fifth and sixth centuries, but in compensation fading tonalities and slighter shadows where . . . the workmanship already noted in the Apostles of the Mausoleum of Galla Placidia is heralded'. Useful comparisons may be made between these figures of 'Patriarchs' and saints in the two Milanese monuments and certain similar mosaic fragments from other parts of the Roman world. If, for example, the figures are recalled of the 'Martyrs' in the Baptistery of the Cathedral at Naples or some sepulchral mosaics in the Tarragona Necropolis, the contemporary consolidation can be observed, if only in the expressiveness of certain details, of a formal syntax that unquestionably extended over a wide western area of the Empire. For instance, the frontally rigid drawing of the figure in the mosaic of the Tomb of 'Optimus' in the Early Christian Museum of Tarragona still in fact retains an organic quality in realistic structure which is vividly expressed, especially, in the face of the deceased. In the figures of the Neapolitan Baptistery, on the other hand, an evident memory of undoubtedly classical composition and colour appears in the attitudes depicting motion, the attention to anatomy and drapery and the attempts at colour shading. But both works belong to an executive context that fully shared the prevailing taste of the day. Hence it is reasonable to approximate them to the manner of S. Aquilino and S. Vittore in Ciel d'Oro, though this style is again characteristic of a very limited cultural area during the second half of the fourth century and the first half of the fifth. It was dominated by Milan, the leadership of that city being followed by that of Ravenna.

25 Cecchelli (Calderini et al., 1951), p. 239.

Chapter Twelve
Late manifestations of Roman painting on the Germanic 'limes'

In Gaul and along the Germanic *limes* the intensive work of Roman colonisation between the first and the fourth century resulted naturally in a widespread proliferation of monuments. The military outposts and the great centres on their supporting lines formed the woof of a system of communications and of residential settlement focussed mainly on the *castrum*, which was quickly organised as a *colonia*. A typical example was *Colonia Agrippinensis*, with its fortified camp beyond the river and its four-square city on the hither side. Such places would always afford opportunity for the gradual erection of such monuments and public buildings as were usual throughout the Empire (walls, gates, baths, basilicas), and also, in the case of Trier, a tetrarchic capital at the end of the third century, of imperial palaces. Nor was there any lack, among these extensive secular undertakings, of the traditional Roman architecture of privately owned country and town houses. Characteristic instances were the great Nennig Villa with its mosaic of 'Circus Combats', and the House of the 'Dionysus Mosaic' at Cologne.

40, 42

38, 39

Among such monuments, those just mentioned, together with many other pavements, mosaic fragments and wall frescoes the discovery of which was largely brought about by the Second World War, are very far from revealing the presence of an original contribution to art or of advanced stylistic progress in Roman Germania. The place of the 'Dionysus Mosaic' of Cologne in the development of second-century middle-class patronage has already been noted. The magnificent ceiling of the imperial palace at Trier is also of great importance, because it provides evidence of a contemporary palace-art the style of which recurs, with little variation, at Antioch, at the opposite extremity of the Roman world. It is reasonable, therefore, to suppose that it was not in itself an expression of a special culture at that particular time and place, even in a city which had become one of the most influential centres of the Empire.

157–9

Similar considerations apply to other works of high significance, discussed earlier, such as the Nennig Villa mosaic and the *emblema* of 'Anaximander' at Trier, or the so-called 'Mosaic of the Philosophers' (Socrates, Cleobulus, Diogenes, Sophocles, Chilon and two others now lost). This last measures 7.06 × 6.8 metres; it was excavated in 1844 at Cologne, near the church of St. Cecilia, and is dateable to about the middle of the third century.[1]

40, 42, 4

1 Lafaye and Blanchet (1909), no. 1640. *See* Parlaska (1959b, p. 82), who dates it in the second half of the fourth century.

The better known and more admired 'Mosaic of the Muses' at Trier itself, signed by MONNUS and measuring 5 metres across, is now in the Landesmuseum.[2] Rich partitioning with borders of a simple plaited design contain a whole world of mythology: the Muses with poets and sages in nine octagons; eight famous writers, the Months and masks in another set of quadrangular areas; the signs of the Zodiac and the Seasons in compartments nearer the periphery. The mosaic is assigned by general agreement to the 'second half of the third century'[3] (I would go so far as to place it shortly before the beginning of the Tetrarchy); it presents no stylistic features of any particular importance.

MONNUS was an undeniably ambitious *imaginarius*, capable also of keeping in touch with the fashions of the day. At the same time he desired that his great work should revive all the grandiose complexity of ancient myth, upon which he skilfully grafted the historical witness of great intellectual figures such as Homer, Menander, Ennius, Cicero and others. (Their presence was perhaps now more inspiring, in a land already familiar with the images of the great sages of antiquity, as indicated by works ranging from the 'Philosophers' of Cologne to the 'Anaximander' of Trier, and other fragments in the same city depicting orators.) Yet the whole of this splendid construction, this polymorphic search for a cultural value and a *sermo nobilis* adequate to such an undertaking, is cold, void of true feeling; it might be described as a refraction of the organic revival which was expressed at Rome in the realism of the post-Gallienic age and later reached the Germanic province enfeebled, deprived of critical emphasis, over-zealous and proclaimed in terms no longer viable.

The open country of the western *limes* had only recently been civilised by the advent of the legions. The inhabitants had no figurative tradition worth mentioning; they were prone, moreover, to sudden and violent military clashes, such as those which devastated Trier in 260 and 275. It was there, accordingly, more than elsewhere, that local cultural conditions, whether Celtic or Germanic, might develop in the long run into a force likely to corrupt any classical pattern upon which the structural crisis of the art of late antiquity might eventually come to rest. Meanwhile, even in this region the traditionalist phenomenology of the style imported from the capital prevailed decisively in its less effective forms.

Nevertheless, certain works do redeem the banality of formal repetition, on a high or low level, present in the surviving examples already mentioned, and in others such as the pavement of 'Theseus in the Labyrinth' from Salzburg, now in the Kunsthistorisches Museum at Vienna,[4] or the fragment of a 'Sacrificial Scene' on a piece of wall fresco from the Palastplatz, now in the Rheinisches

2 Lafaye and Blanchet (1909), no. 1231
3 Most recently, Parlaska (1959b), p. 43
4 Lübke *et al.* (1958), pp. 432–3, ff. 414–5.

Landesmuseum at Trier.[5] I have in mind also some other mosaics in the last-named museum, particularly the great pavimental 'Mosaic of the Dioscuri' from the Kornmarkt at Trier, which was brought to light by excavations following the Second World War.

A new pavimental 'Mosaic of the Muses' was found in the Neustrasse at Trier in 1942, and is now in the Rheinisches Landesmuseum. The enormous task of reconstructing the nine heads, which are frontally presented in as many square compartments all within borders of multi-coloured Greek fret, has unfortunately not allowed time for a critical assessment. The mosaic may have been laid at some time between the end of the third century and the beginning of the fourth, while its taste tends to place it among the forerunners of the 'fine style'. A comparison, at some remove, with the portraits on the ceiling of the Constantinian Palace reveals interesting similarities of external detail, even if so much as is clearly discernible of the original arrangement of the tesserae indicates quite a noticeable hiatus as regards the more significant aspects of the traditional courtly manner characterising those later frescoes.

A brief mention may also be made of the large *emblemata*, 'Octagons of the Muses', excavated in the Johannisstrasse at Trier.[7] These unquestionably valuable fragments are attributable to the second half of the fourth century. Consequently, though still within the limits of a figurative culture of traditional type, they demonstrate the active presence, even on the Germanic frontier, of a quality of colour in itself constructive of plastic relief in a very special interpretation of chromatic mannerism undoubtedly inclined to the predominance of frankly expressionist idiom. Such co-ordinates of category alone imply that a more precise location in time of the Johannisstrasse fragments, though it should probably be recognised somewhere in the age of Valentinian, is not from an idiomatic standpoint susceptible of more exact definition.

These works are informed not only by a marked sense of formal balance, but first and foremost by a classically inspired skill of figurative composition within the octagonal fields, which are defined by the usual decorative efflorescence now tending to abstraction. In them, too, there is at work a descriptive treatment of environment which had seemed in the third century to have been lost for ever behind the abstract neutrality of white backgrounds; but there is also apparent an almost excessive graphic refinement in the ornamental partitioning that frames the *emblemata*, a taste which may easily be found again in the figures, functioning as 'negative relief' and distinguished by a wealth of exuberant polychromy. In the classical attitude of those figures, though it is sometimes rigid because of the idiomatic means employed, there is much

32, 183-

186, 188

159

195, 196

5 *Trierer Zeitschrift* . . ., XVIII (1949), pp. 317–9.
6 The dating proposed by Parlaska (1959b, p. 33) is quite different, earlier than AD 220. Comparison with the similar mosaic of El Djem, now in the Bardo Museum, Tunis (Gauckler, 1910, no. 68) is useful.
7 Lafaye and Blanchet (1909), no. 1224. Parlaska (1959b, p. 61) attributes it to the late fourth century. *See also* Krüger (1933), c. 703.

in evidence a range of colour almost wholly free from tonal definition, often bright and garish, but given homogeneity by a repeated *vermiculatum* revealing the bodily structure as deliberately and rationally, never casually contrived.

The chromatic mutability of the garments, the pleasing and elegant impressionism of the faces, the uncompromising and undisguised outlining of the figures in black and the bold variations of hue in the chairs on which the Muses are seated, all combine to compel recognition of the lively executive talents of the TRIER MUSES MASTER, an artist of the traditional school yet capable of achievements unquestionably equal to those being carried out in these same decades both at Rome (apsidioles of S. Costanza and the mosaic of the House of the Dioscuri at Ostia) as well as at Milan (apsidioles of S. Aquilino).

25, 26
34, 36, 197
27, 29

More careful study should be devoted to the so-called 'Mosaic of the Dioscuri' of Trier, which was excavated in 1951 at the centre of the ancient city, among the ruins of an ancient building near the Kornmarkt. The pàvement is that of a hall measuring about seven by four metres.

33, 189–94

As shown by Eiden,[8] this mosaic, which is now in the Rheinisches Landesmuseum at Trier, belongs to the building's third period, other floors having been preserved beneath it. The constructional technique of the surrounding walls, as well as the iconography, have caused the work to be ascribed to the second half of the fourth century.

Iconographical interpretation of the mosaic has clearly established that the hall was the meeting place of a religious sect. The members celebrated a mystery-cult the nature of which remains obscure, but which certainly flourished within the limits of a late classical revival and included rites influenced both by Christianity and by certain oriental religions brought together in the syncretism of previous centuries during the central imperial age.

The picture is framed in a system of straightforward red and yellow plait, which criss-crosses so as to enclose six circular and seven almond-shaped medallions. These in turn frame two more spacious compartments, approximately octagonal, where the two principal scenes of the narrative are represented. It is therefore easy to identify at once a twofold subject in the two central shields which are integrated by full-length or half-length human figures in the separate medallions. But iconological examination of the whole work shows that the first scene represents only the mythical foundation of the second, which in turn records the liturgico-cultural celebration of the first. Consequently, these two scenes appear to be so closely connected as probably to have been regarded by the members of the sect as one episode, though divided into

194

8 Eiden (1950). *See also* Parlaska (1951); Egger (1953); Gregoire (1953); Moreau (1960); Parlaska (1959b), p. 56.

two successive moments: that of the mythical event occurring 'in history', and now universally and eternally present, ever since its translation to the supernatural sphere; and that of the liturgical event, the ceremony and rites of which provide the worshipper with the means of his initiation into its mysteries.

The mythological scene represents, so far as it can be **32** understood, the birth of the Dioscuri from Leda's egg. It has therefore been believed that the pagan legend lay at the root of the syncretistico-pagan beliefs of the sect. For some lines by Ausonius (Epigram LIV), written shortly before 370, suggest that it was still current in Gaul at the end of the fourth century:

> *Istos, tergemino nasci quod cernis ab ovo,*
> *patribus ambiguis et matribus adsere natos.*
> *Hos genuit Nemesis, sed Leda puerpera fovit*
> *Tyndareus pater his et Juppiter: hic putat, hic scit.*

So do the same poet's words from the *Griphus ternarii, numeri*: 'Triplexque Helenae cum fratribus ovum . . .'.[9] The sect in question enjoyed the state of religious freedom existing in the Empire both *de jure* and *de facto*, even though it was slanted in favour of the Christians. The egg, shown in section on an altar, contains the three children, while behind the altar, on a fluted column with capital, is the divine bird with outstretched wings. To the right Leda, nude and bejewelled, moves away from the altar as she dons a sumptuous robe; on the other side Agamemnon, with cloak and sceptre, seems to be ordering her, with a gesture of his right hand, to remain. The letters of the inscriptions, *Cas-tor*, *Po-lus*, *Ael-ena* and *Io-bis*, are distributed on each side of the column, while the names *Lyda* and *Agamemnon* are written above their respective figures. The meaning of the myth is clear. But the *pictor imaginarius* has varied it, as Louis[10] observed, by omitting the figure of the cuckolded husband, which would have introduced a jarring note of comedy into the scene. According to Louis this point serves to prove that the artist did not intend to give a 'historical' version of the birth of the Dioscuri but to illustrate a ritual 'miracle', not in the spirit of a delineator of myth, but in that of a liturgist.

The second scene is not so easy to explain. The priest **189** *Qodvoldeus* (an obvious popular corruption of *Quodvult-deus*), with a *simpulum* in his right hand, officiates in a short tunic, handing to his assistant (*Feloxsomedix*, whatever that may mean), dressed likewise, a trussed bird on a dish. The tunics worn by both these figures are provided with shoulder-pieces, or perhaps these are intended to represent a hood; for Louis considers that in a rite concerned with the divine bird it is quite logical that the celebrants should be disguised, just as the Christian were called by Tertullian *pisciculi* and *ovilia* of Christ, Himself pictured as a fish (*ichthys*) and a Good Shepherd. To the right of *Qodvoldeus*

9 Eiden (1950), p. 52.
10 Louis (1953).

a small kneeling figure, without the addition of shoulder-pieces, raises a bowl containing a white egg; his head is bent back, and he shades his eyes with his left hand. Above this personage an inscription reads *Andeg-asipone*. In the two upper corners are depicted a large tureen and a shovel. According to Eiden this second scene may well be related, because the egg and the bird are common to both. But he denies that the second scene can be concerned with sacrifice, for, notwithstanding the presence of the *simpulum*, there is no altar. It may, however, be maintained, with Louis, that as the two scenes illustrate events closely associated in the myth, as already explained, one altar could well serve for both pictures and correspond with the real, moveable altar in the hall, on which were placed the furniture and ingredients of the rite, certainly including an egg. I have already advanced a similar hypothesis in connection with the mosaic of the Carthaginian 'Hunt Chronicle' in the Bardo Museum.

The two scenes are separated, or rather conjoined, by 194 one of the ovoid areas, in which *Florus*, standing before a brazier, performs an act of doubtful significance, perhaps an offering of incense. Owing to the requirements of space he is at right angles with respect to the orientation of the mythological scene. In the other ovoids *Eleni* and 32 *Criscentia* dance to the rhythm of hand-instruments; *Andegasus* carries an object which may be another musical instrument; *Theodulus* and *Calemer* hold vessels used for some purpose in the rite; and *Secundus*, with a lamp, seems 189 by his gesture to invite worshippers to enter the hall. The six round medallions display in duplicate three male servants in dalmatics, seen full-face and half-length, and carrying above their heads various courses of food and delicacies. Their names are *Eusebius*, *Paregorius* and *Felix* 191, 193, 192, 190 (spelt *Felex* in his medallion).

So great a variety of explanatory inscriptions, typical of late Roman civilisation, has been the object of careful study. Eiden considered that only the names of the personages were thus indicated. Louis has refused to consider the two words *Feloxomedix* and *Andegasipone* as names unknown to Greek literature and epigraphy (in which case the correct names might be ★*Philoxomedes* and ★*Anthegasipone*), and has attempted ingenious subdivisions such as *Andegasi, pone*, which seems more convincing, and *Felox some dix*, a corrupt form of *Felix sume dis*, which is rather less acceptable. Since, however, it is not of primary importance in the present work to establish the meaning of this mosaic, the question may be dismissed by recognising the mystery rite of a syncretist sect which, like so many others, survived the triumph of Christianity by at least half a century. The sect probably reached the climax of its prosperity under the paganising reign of Julian, or at the time of Symmachus, and may have included in its beliefs some ritual practices related to those of the Christians.

To anyone who studies the composition of this work the figures in the central shields disclose a complete absence of connection between the planes, a legacy from the tetrarchic period. The altar is seen in perspective, and the three-dimensional effect is actually heightened by the most peculiar use of a rose-coloured area, applied in such a way as to give prominence to the frontal mouldings of the structure on two sides (one of them the upper horizontal), while for the other two sides the same function is performed by courses of black tesserae. The light therefore appears to come from below, where, beyond the border of the simple plaited pattern that frames the octagonal area, *Florus* stands at his brazier. This explanation may perhaps seem over-ingeniously logical. But no other has been advanced. It also raises some questions regarding the subdivision of the space by plaited-pattern borders or other framing. As a rule, the figures in the ovoids obey the 'law of the frame' whenever their axis is the same as that of the medallions, though there are some exceptions such as the relation already mentioned of the figure of *Florus* to the *Lyda* scene, the effects of light and shade on the front of the altar and the figure itself of *Lyda*, which ignores the marginal line, traversing its contour with one foot, the left arm and the robe, as in the case of the deceased couple in the Silistra Tomb.

Behind the altar, which is drawn in perspective, the column with the bird of Jove appears two-dimensional, without the least sign of consciousness of space. The figure of Agamemnon also, despite the streaks in his cloak, remains purely superficial, differing conspicuously from that of Leda, though both are by the same hand and the idiom of the *tessellarius* is, of course, identical. The face of Leda and her whole figure seem to have been taken almost directly from a sculptured model, so that the plasticity of form is retained, notwithstanding the entirely chromatic and linear mode of expression developed, as in the case of the MUSES MASTER, in layers of pure colour countersigned by firmly outlined strips of black tesserae. The classical drapery of this figure, in particular, should be noted. It had been out of fashion for many decades in Roman painting. More skilfully presented even than the robes designed by the MUSES MASTER, it would be enough of itself to indicate the talents of the DIOSCURI MASTER, who was capable of effects worthy of the best emblematic works of the first century, though he employed radically diverse modes of expression. In the figure of Agamemnon, however, the authoritative three-dimensional outline is wholly lacking, with the result that the face appears almost devoid of internal bony structure. Both figures are, moreover, wholly suspended in space and maintain no connection

32

189

182

32

whatever with the ideal centre of the scene, constituted by the altar and the egg, the importance of which the DIOSCURI MASTER may have intended to stress by obeying, naturally not altogether correctly, the ancient rules of perspective applied in Hellenistic modelling.

In the *Qodvoldeus* scene no such syntactical and psycho- 189 logical centre is present. Consequently, for the disposition of his figures, which are all carefully related to one another on a single plane of vision, the *imaginarius* found no better plan than to set their feet on the last row of white tesserae skirting the black margin of the octagonal area. The figures accordingly follow with perfect fidelity its various concavities, so that the master was obliged to use its two free ends for the placing of the other ritual objects, as if they were in flight and weightless. Yet even these articles, so strangely positioned to an eye directed in accordance with the naturalistic regulation of a classical perspective, will be seen as rationally distributed in the general order of the picture if considered as part of a 'radial' or extrovert perspective, when the true plane of vision would be found time after time in the marginal framing defining the octagonal field. In this 'liturgical' scene the figures are flat and the colours much less various and obtrusive than in the depiction of the mystic scene. The whole composition is organised in three basic tones of colour, a red combined with burnt brick-ochre, some ranges of greyish blue and a few shades of blackish-maroon. The faces belong to the period following that of the Constantinian 'fine style'; but now, along the course of development started by the 'Praying Women' of the **23**, 162 Cemetery of Traso, they lack all traces of such references to plasticity as coloured surfaces marked by strong, dark lines, large but inexpressive eyes, noses and mouths of considerable dimensions but also devoid of any residue whatever of psychological meaning.

In addition to the images of the two female dancers **32** (*Eleni* is more elegantly drawn), which were certainly derived from Hellenistic cartoons, a glance at the figures in the medallions discovers the more clumsy, flattened bodies of their companions, which seem to have no volume: no solidity can be discerned behind the unfilled expanse of *Florus*' robe or the simple diagonal across that 189 of *Secundus*, by which an attempt is made to suggest movement of the figure; or, again, behind the clothing of *Theodulus*, *Andegasus* and *Calemer*, where the tunic of the second and the dalmatic produce exactly the same effect of an empty hanging sack as does the dress of *Florus*. In the 189, **32** circular medallions, also, the same two-dimensional 189-93 flattening is apparent in the dalmatics of the food-bearing attendants, while the positively non-existent treatment of articulation in the arms gives the impression, not of flexible human bodies, but of rigid puppets.

But a study of these liturgical figures will not lead to an entirely negative judgment of them. For they are characterised by an expressive immediacy, a taste for abstraction in the attention to chromatic detail and tessellar constructive craftsmanship, and an intelligent pursuit of special formative effects, which enable us to suggest that the DIOSCURI MASTER possessed talents capable of raising him to a level of culture and inspiration anything but negligible, rather than of degrading him to the status of a mere artisan, as Pace[11] maintains. This view is supported by certain facial characteristics. For example, on the face of *Felix*, shown in half profile, a surprising play of shadows keeps the whole left side dark, and ingeniously allows us to divine the physiognomical features thus concealed. The result is an expression so striking, though summary, as to recall certain sketches by some of the less conventional masters of Pompeian painting. Noticeable also in this connection are the chromatic variants and capricious effects of light and shade in the clothing of *Felix* himself and of *Paregorius*, *Andegasus*, *Secundus* or *Theodulus*. They constitute a gallery of experiments in form, admittedly quite gratuitous and yet effective in their manifestation of a now complete and not unfruitful break with a venerable tradition. Surely one cannot help seeing in these figures the distant ancestors, for example, of certain famous tapestries of the early Middle Ages. Surely one cannot fail to observe the vast stylistic gap between these figures and the perhaps contemporary servants of the Silistra Tomb.

190

192, **32**,
189

It has already been stated that all the figures and all the objects represented in this mosaic floor compose a single figurative whole of which they constitute separate moments and separate aspects, conceived as interconnected and consequent upon one another, in a strict unity of space and time. A now mature example of this processional rhythm, which required the faithful to follow and take part in it stage by stage, had been provided, as noted earlier, by the Theodorean pavement at Aquileia. In other words, the method of partitioning and reorganising the spaces had managed after three centuries to accompany the believer in his liturgico-functional progress, the stages of the narrative being so arranged as to form a kind of bass counterpoint to the celebration of and participation in the sacrifice. In the cultic hall at Trier, it is possible, more precisely perhaps than in other monuments hitherto examined, not only to estimate the syntactical value of plait-partitioning[12] – which in this work, as in any other, apparently plays the part of an eminently decorative architectural segmentation, resulting from the reduction of figure and background to a single identical surface plane – but also to form an articulate judgment as to its semantic value, which seems to be that of distinguishing and correctly emphasising the separate figures and scenes,

Plan D

189

11 Pace (1955), p. 102. The manner of the DIOSCURI MASTER is recalled, in particular, though in this case with evident capacity for greater syntactical articulation and not without some aspects of pleasing virtuosity in forms of flattened plasticity, by the fragments of the 'Three Seasons' (clothing of the Cupids) from the triclinium of the Chedworth Villa in Gloucestershire, England, and by the scenes of 'Cupids as Gladiators' from the triclinium of the Bignor Villa in Sussex, England. *See*, for all these, Toynbee, Jocelyn M.C. (1962), nn. 187 and 191, pp. 199–200, figs. 214–7 and 225–6. These mosaics prove that the character of the forms in the Trier mosaic cannot be attributed to a modest level of artistic quality.

12 Entirely similar decorative borders are found at Aquileia in the pavement of the Theodorean basilica, at Antioch in the House of Aion (Levi (1947), ii, pl. CXXXVI, a, b, c), and in a mosaic from the Esquiline (n. 124703) in the Museo Nazionale, Rome. *See also* the damaged lithostrate of the very late fourth century showing 'Calendar Scenes', from a suburban building in the courtyard of Regions I, IV at Ostia.

13 On the basis of the different axes on which the figures are arranged within the limits of the 'law of the frame' the semantic feature might be more exactly defined as follows. The space in which the mysteries rites are performed is that decorated with the scene of Leda, the axis of which is that of the entire building. Florus stands, in the attitude required by the form of the picture, facing the altar with the egg, for which he seems to be burning incense. In view of the two-dimensional parataxis which dominates

the entire representation the figure itself could not, owing to its horizontal disposition, impair the closing rhythm of the movement. Furthermore, it is placed on the same axis as the 'Qodvoldeus' scene, at right angles to that of Leda. The reason for this arrangement is the same as that for the position of Florus, in the first place. But the possibility should be borne in mind that he may be facing the entrance to the hall, though the disappearance of the walls does not allow this conjecture to be verified. I believe that the entrance would in fact be in a side wall, as in the Aquileia basilica. If that is correct the figure of Florus would logically be seen facing the entrance. Below the above-mentioned scene Secundus, as required by the form of the medallion, is also horizontally placed, but reproduces the relation between the scenes of 'Leda' and 'Florus', being on this view the doorkeeper, inviting visitors to enter. Beside him Paregorius and Eusebius, in the circular medallions, remain on the axis of the 'Qodvoldeus' scene, and Theobulus also, in the ovoid above Paregorius, is orientated in the same way as Florus. At the other three corners of the hall, in the three circular areas, Eusebius, Paregorius and Felex have a diagonal axis, with their heads turned to the centre of the apartment, this being a rhythmically coherent attitude. The position of Felix is equally coherent, with his head nearest to Florus. Above the 'Leda' scene Criscentia dances on the same axis as that of Florus, while at the sides of that scene Andegasus and Eleni are axially in agreement with Leda and Agamemnon. The above arrangement does not include Calemer, who should be on the left of Qodvoldeus but whose figure is reversed with respect to that of Secundus, who faces the priest. But the disorder might also be only apparent here. In the four ovoid divisions of the two long sides the personages might all be meant as related to the 'Leda' scene, if Secundus did not have to interrupt the order of the forms with his duties as doorkeeper and his connections with the 'Qodvoldeus' scene. It would be for the same reason, as already noted, that the first Paregorius mentioned does not appear on the diagonal axis but on that of Qodvoldeus and placed so as to face the entrance.

If the reconstruction attempted in the above exposition is not regarded as too involved, the functional inspiration of the axes of the figures should be evident within the rhythmical and decorative modulations of the plait-work partitioning.

14 Brusin and Zovatto (1957), pp. 104–5, n. 99.

rendering intelligible their function in the *unicum* which is certainly implied by the pavimental picture.[13]

On entering, the visitor was introduced by *Secundus* and received by the half-length figures of *Paregorius* and *Eusebius*. He was at once confronted by the scene of the priest preparing the sacrifice, with the figures of *Theodulus* and *Florus* on each side. The axis of the figures of the second *Eusebius* and of *Calemer* invited him to turn right through an angle of ninety degrees, so as to come face to face with the central depiction of the myth, towards and with which all the other figures of the round and ovoid medallions were orientated. Something of the kind, though not divided up into compartments, is found, it will be remembered, in the Trilobate Hall at Piazza Armerina, where the visitor is led by the very act of bestriding individual figures to follow them step by step from one part of the picture to the next, but above all in the Basilica of Aquileia, where the same sort of itinerary can be reconstructed, and the same purpose of the axial functional arrangement of the separate scenes and figures in their frames.[14]

This dissolution of the classical unity of time and place is another revelation of the great stride forward taken by Roman painting. The architectural features of the 'fourth style', having been closely integrated with the plane of the figures, with which they had already been fully united at the end of the second century, subverted both the spatial unity of the representation and the temporal unity of what was represented. The first unity was replaced at Aquileia and Trier by segmentation of the representative spaces through the divisions created by the decoration, though these were not so decisive as to destroy the desired connection between the individual sections of the narrative. A substitute for the unity of time was found in a succession of periods, mutually isolated, however, and universalised, beyond their historical character, in the eternity of the myth. They came to life again in their chronological series whenever the spectator undertook a 'logical' itinerary through the picture, in accordance with the liturgy, and unified them by pursuing the successive instants of their 'history' through the spatial segmentation and the sung or rhythmically recited litany provided by the rite.

The separation of the unities of space and time led, therefore, to the fusion of individual spaces and individual times. It was the observer's duty to participate in what he saw in such a way as to reassemble, as soon as he became aware of the space-time relationship, the elements of the 'sacred' story, which was quite different for each believer because relived within his own personal history.

Plan D

Chapter Thirteen
The last Hellenistic experiments, from Egypt to Britain, and the two polarities of late Roman aesthetics

In the second volume of his *Roma o Bisanzio*, while considering *lithostrota* recently brought to light in the Roman world, Galassi gives a brief account of the large 'Mosaic of the Nereids' found in the House of the Dioscuri at Ostia. In this work the figure of Venus, supported by tritons, appears in a marine environment. The goddess is surrounded on every side by a troop of nereids mounted, in accordance with tradition, on sea-monsters.[1] The mosaic 'presents features which would appear at first sight to anticipate manners current at a later date, in the course of the fifth and sixth centuries'. But he adds: 'Were it not that the mediocre artistic level of the work precludes the bestowal upon it of such a responsibility'.

34–36, 197

Galassi's estimate of the intrinsic merit of the pavement may seem too hasty. But it cannot be denied, as indeed he recognised, that the idiomatic features of the work, reduced by Galassi to the category of 'stylistically negative', may have served in some degree as models for new usages in the pictorial vocabulary of late antiquity.

The Ostian seascape, inscribed in the margin with the exhortation '*plura faciatis, meliora dedicetis*', appears to be a late fourth-century mosaic floor which, though concerned with the narrative content of a waning myth, no longer exemplifies the traditionalist revival (with its social and political aims) of the Constantinian 'fine style' or of *fin-de-siècle* mannerism, but rather embodies an idiomatic experiment. This latter, apart from the question of its originality, constitutes proof of a genuine link between two movements. They were, firstly, the current of late Roman art, not exempt from reaction and neo-Hellenistic inflections, which were now being welcomed by the more courtly type of painting in that part of the eastern empire already dominated by Constantinople; and secondly, that of the prevailing manifestation of expressionist lyricism, wholly coincident with solutions of chromatic problems, whatever their tonality, and entirely identified with the more consistent aspects of the spirit of late antiquity and the pre-medieval age of imperial art during the interval before its encounter in the west with the Sarmatico-Iranian cultural tradition imposed by tribal migration.

The floor of Room I of the House of the Dioscuri,[2] a fourth-century building adjoining a large Hadrianic apartment-block with garden, has a compositional structure closely akin to that of numerous African mosaics of the same kind, and also to that of the COURT MASTER's *frigidarium* at Piazza Armerina.

1 Galassi (1953), pp. 375–6.
2 This work was made known by Becatti (1961), pp. 114–23, pls. CXLIX–CLIII and CCXIV–CCXVI. *See also* Becatti (1951a), p. 36, figs. 42–5.

At the centre is the naked goddess, seated on the sea-shell borne by two tritons, in a position similar to that of the analogous mosaic at Timgad, at least a century older. At the sides of the great room are eight nereids, clinging to various monsters, horses, panthers and sea-bulls, in a sea full of frisking dolphins. The waves are given a stiff, comb-like shape with streaks of dark tesserae forming right angles, especially at the corners of the room, where the suggested rippling of the waters necessarily assumes a right angle. This particular attempt to unify the various groups which compose the retinue, enveloped as they are in the narrative continuity of the environmental structure, expresses a meaning of the composition in which, over and above the original setting within a unitary and largely artificial perspective, there is imposed – besides the successive radial perspective which supposes the spectator to be at the centre of the picture – an aesthetic perception which obliges the spectator to undertake a journey through the various sectors of the mosaic in order to understand its spatial unification through his own personal 'time' as he walks, reliving the moments of the narrative.

This cultural implication has already been referred to in these pages. As early as the third century certain African mosaics, such as the 'Triumph of Dionysus' at El Djem, had exhibited, before those of Aquileia and Trier, model versions of such abstract and readily available means of spatial unification. From the standpoint of form the Ostian pavement did not far outstrip that achievement, considering that its complicated lattice of sea-waves performs the same particular function as the tangle of vines in the African floor, though it does so on a smaller scale. But the 'Mosaic of the Dioscuri' at Trier, discussed above, went further by including a liturgical element in that aesthetic disposition.

As to idiom, Galassi's judgment may be admitted to have some foundation in so far as it concerns the dry, almost laboured rigidity of line and the frequent relapse into poor quality of the chromatic aridity of the figures. On the other hand it remains undeniable that the design often shows an admirable capacity for organic and formal synthesis, together with a divisionist stylisation of expressionist type which at times almost amounts to a refined cryptography, and that the chromatic handling, which can hardly be ascribed to genuinely accidental consequences of inadequate feeling for colour, presents delicate conjunctions of a sober and sensitive polychromy, which a careful critic must decline to consider as due to chance.

That the OSTIAN SEA MASTER cannot be denied a skilful management of *ductus* will be clear to anyone who observes the remarkable subtlety of design, reduced to a few decisive strokes, in the physique of a nereid crouching on

35, 36, 197

53

32, 189-94

her seahorse and holding a casket in her left hand; or in the back view of her immediate neighbour, turning her back as she rides a bull; or, again, in the frontal figure of a nereid reclining on the back of another bovine sea-creature; **36** or, lastly, in the nearby naked and erect form of a fourth figure with a corner of her cloak negligently resting on her left shoulder and falling behind her. It may be asserted in **35** fact, without hesitation, that the brief range of mosaic materials here employed and the economy of tints in a manifest predominance of white, both in the figures and in the background, already foreshadow the silent, frigid and awkward poetry of the later western art that preceded the Carolingian age.

On the other hand, the style of graphic synthesis in the trunks of these nereids, so tall and slender, much resembles that of the marquetry tigresses in the Basilica of Junius Bassus, of the mosaic of the 'Three Graces' at Cherchel and **13** of the 'Girls at Exercise' in the Villa of Piazza Armerina. **14,** 131 In these cases, by means of a set of formally autonomous signs, the physical frame is investigated no longer in its bony skeleton, from which the classical organic quality was built up, but in the different formal prominence of the flesh surfaces, which defines a henceforth emptied corporeity of the human substance. Such treatment, it is superfluous to add, also constituted a prelude to Byzantium, more influential than in the case of Piazza Armerina. It renders historically tangible, in a monument presumably to be ascribed to the first decades of the second half of the century, the contemporary ability to distribute a firmly Roman vocabulary between the two great polarities of the aesthetics of late antiquity. On the one side stood the expressive, vitalist ruggedness of form, animated by a permanent interest in the existential condition of its time, which later became typical of the popular styles of European art in the early Middle Ages'3 and on the other a contemplative absorption in the transfigured metaphysical poetry of earthly matter caught up into the absolute, intrinsic purity of heavenly colour, which was to characterise the congealed forms of Byzantine court art.

Colour, in this context, is adequate to its task. By helping the paratactical decomposition of the planes in this diaphonous narrative, it animates the bare limbs of the female figures with tessellar strips of pinkish-white, yellow and lilac, ending in shades of greyish-blue at the extremities, **35** tints the bodies of the monsters with the addition of blues, greens, reds and greys, and blends into the hair of Venus **34** and her companions vermicular shreds (which would be called Matissian effects in a modern work) of yellow and red, or else yellow, red, black and lilac tesserae, producing linear harmonies of unmistakable charm, which often present styles of hairdressing already typical of the late Constantinian age. The pigmentation, however, never

3 *See* in this connection, as interesting examples of the tendency in question, the remains already mentioned of a large Ostian mosaic laid at the end of the fourth century, displaying heads and small allegorical representations of the Months. It was found outside the town and is now in the courtyard of Reg. I, IS.IV at Ostia (Becatti (1961) pp. 235–41 and 360–1, pls. CCII and CCXVII). *See also* the 'Seasons Mosaic', dateable to the late fifth century and now in the Museo Nazionale (n. 59585) in Rome. Here the drastic distortion of the physiognomical features of the heads with varying areas and strips of colour, expressed in great subtlety of tone, seems capable of relation to the procedure and taste shown in the work of the OSTIAN SEA MASTER. Concerning this remarkable 'Seasons Mosaic' Paribeni (1932, p. 88) and Blake (1940, p. 101) have observed that 'the great round eyes with their encircling shadows recall figures in mosaic at Ravenna.' In this case attention has been particularly drawn to the type of draughtsmanship, conspicuously defining, even more than in the 'Nereids Mosaic', the elements of the image with black or purple tesserae, and then entrusting their chromatic significance to a capricious colouration involving at this stage very little narrative significance, while preference is given to the expression of emotion in a free, anti-naturalistic, inventive lyricism.

completely covers the forms determined by the synthetic design.

If we ignore dimension (which in the white tesserae of the figures is less than that of the background cubes) and the fidelity of the white *vermiculatum*, within the figures themselves, to the form of the bodily image obtained by the coloured tessellar strips, the resulting illusion amounts almost to an X-ray photograph of the physical reality, printed on that abstract section of space which is void of all dimension and suggests the marine background of the work: a transparency which renders the residual physical quality of the image equal to the vagueness of the locality. Once again, this aesthetic option anticipates Byzantium, even though her artists would use a much more lively and vibrant chromatic feeling to reanimate the physical form, flattened though it was and brought to the same plane as the background; for the sophisticated chromatic purity of this Ostian pavement does not in fact clash with the refined beauty of their tones.

Finally, the idiomatic significance of this mosaic may be confirmed by comparing some of the nereids here depicted with analogous groups on Sarcophagus No. 1 in Room II of the Capitoline Museum, a monument certainly dateable to the fourth century and perhaps very near in time to the Ostian pavement. One of those groups was probably taken from the same model as served for the Ostian nereid reclining on the bull. The resemblance with which we are here concerned is obviously not so much that of the subject (which might be found in dozens of works throughout imperial territory) as that of idiom. On the Capitoline sarcophagus a capable stonemason, whose taste may unquestionably be referred to Constantinian classicism, with its obvious addiction to organic curvature of form, set out on two levels a series of marine deities, children and nereids playing amorously with tritons. On the upper level in particular, in lower relief, the artist carved a frieze of marine creatures, including a nereid, placed against a neutral background and flattened, though not to a disfiguring extent, so that the formal effect is very close to that at Ostia. In the relief shadows are simplified till they become equivalent to the precise lines of the mosaic structure. Consequently, the whole design appears to develop on a single two-dimensional plane. At a later stage the stonecutters of the sixth century would perforate the background and transform such projects into a complete lacework.

The idiomatic significance of the Ostian *lithostroton* was reflected in both the directions by this time discernible in imperial art at the end of the fourth century and beginning of the fifth. This fact becomes apparent when we consider the first, still broadly Hellenistic, phase in the manufacture

36

S

4 Cleveland Museum of Art, Cleveland, Ohio, U.S.A., n. 53. 18. *See* D. G. Shepperd (1954), where the date is tentatively ascribed to a period between the third and fifth centuries. De Francovich (1963, p. 136) proposes dating it in the second half of the third century or the beginning of the fourth, but within the compass of a chronology decidedly too early.

5 Paris, Louvre, *Antiquités chrétiennes*, n. GU 1230. The two fragments display respectively a scene of 'Apollo and Daphne' and one of 'Bellerophon and the Chimera'. Other fragments are preserved in the Textile Museum at Lyons. Peirce and Tyler (1934, nn. 92–3, pls. CLVI–CLVII) date the 'shawl' to about the year 500. *L'Art copte*, pp. 147–50, also assigns it to the end of the fifth century. De Francovich (1963, p. 141) considers it not earlier than the fourth century or beginning of the fifth. As mentioned by Galassi (1953, p. 366, fig. 224), the 'shawl' with its motives of Cupids and fish, recalls the *emblema* of the mosaic pavement of the Church of SS. Lot and Procopius in the city of Nebo, in Jordan, dating from the first half of the sixth century, and above all, with a figure of Apollo, some very important fragments formerly preserved in the Staatliche Museen at Berlin and lost during the recent war (*Frühchristlich Sammlung*, nn. 9240, 9241, 9243, 9244). They represent, respectively, a haloed female figure with a diadem and goblet, a female dancer with castanets, a female dancer, nude, with crossed legs, and a hermaphrodite, also with crossed legs. The figures, each about a metre in height, felicitous and delicate in design, the clothing rendered in wide layers of colour in strong 'negative relief' are set among stylised plants and clusters of laurel. They had been part of the decorations of a wall tapestry of the fourth century, a period, that is, culturally declining into that of the 'shawl of Sabina', but still notable for an alert interest in form. The work is disciplined and of the highest standard. *See* in this connection Wulff and Volbach (1926), pp. 7–8, pls. 4, 5, 44, where the fragments are assigned to the third or fourth century; Schlunk (1939), p. 74, pls. 80–1 (fourth century); De Francovich (1963), p. 136 (second half third century-early fourth). This Berlin tapestry probably included the Louvre fragment showing the head of a female dancer (*Antiquités chrétiennes*, No. X 4849); *see* *L'Art copte*, pp. 151–3, pl. 157. An interesting comparison may be made with the silver Meleager plate in a private collection in Munich (H. Kähler, in *Die Kunst*, L (1952), p. 321 ff; cf. Bianchi Bandinelli, 'Continuità ellenistica nella

of fabrics, sweat-cloths, tapestry and garment embroidery which is commonly known as the art of 'Coptic stuffs'. Some fragments of such work have already been mentioned, for instance the Fish in the Louvre and the Lyons Museum and the 'Haloed Face' at Detroit, of various dates in the second or third and fourth or fifth centuries. We may now consider some later specimens, belonging to the last, strictly traditional phase, prior to the iconographical and idiomatic adoption of the formal characteristics of Coptic culture: for example, the rectangular textile, a sort of *emblema* worked in wool on linen, depicting a 'Haloed Nereid on Blue Ground' within a stylised frame of vine-leaves and bunches of grapes, and apparently presenting a goblet. This masterpiece, probably of Alexandrian derivation, and dateable to the late fifth century, is now in the Cleveland Museum of Art.[4] Within the limits of an undeniable and strongly traditional taste it shows, about a century after the Ostian mosaic, singularly analogous tendencies (despite a different typology of form), especially in the treatment of the nude female figure, which is built up in synthetic pinkish shading, so as to give external definition to the curves of the breasts, abdomen and thighs against their pallid, flat background. Even the hair, though still essentially naturalistic, acquires distinction from the reddish lines on black that produce a result very like that achieved at Ostia. The whole simplification of form and the taste for simple, unobtrusive colours indicate in short, though at advanced date, a direction of this late Hellenistic textile art not so very different from that of the Ostian mosaic. A similar conclusion can be drawn from such other fragments, likewise almost contemporary, as the so-called Sabina Shawl from the tomb of a lady of that name at Antinoë (Musée du Louvre, end of the fifth century);[5] an ornamental square representing 'Nereids and a Haloed Female Portrait', also from Antinoë (Louvre, sixth century);[6] another showing a 'Female Portrait and Scenes of Cupids with Fish', with a related border displaying Cupids and fish, now in the Industrial Museum at Basel (sixth century);[7] another with a 'Haloed Nereid Riding a Dolphin', from Akhmim (Victoria and Albert Museum, London, sixth to seventh century);[8] and lastly, exhibiting the perfect union of idiom now fully Coptic with a Christian subject, the circular fabric with 'Scenes from the Story of Joseph', preserved at the Hermitage in Leningrad (seventh century).[9] This series of finds will clearly prove that in the neighbourhood of Alexandria, and certainly among local schools more or less influenced by the metropolis, a final phase of Coptic style corresponded substantially with similar phases in the West foreshadowed by the Ostian mosaic.

But between the fourth and the fifth century such production still remained very active, and numerous dis-

pittura di età medio- e tardo-romana' in
Archeologia . . ., p. 439, n. 108, pl. 86 a)
and with the fresco of Apollo in the
Barracco Museum at Rome.
6 Paris, Louvre, (*Antiquités chrétiennes*)
n. X 4153. Peirce and Tyler (1934, p. 120,
pl. CLXII) place it in the sixth century,
and do so again in *L'Art copte*, p. 161,
pl. 168. De Francovich (1963, p. 147,
fig. 82) assigns it to the fifth century.
7 Kesser (1960), p. 337, fig. 5.
8 Kesser (1960), p. 347, fig. 35.
9 Wessel (1960), pp. 242–4, pl. 131.

coveries could be cited as evidence of the similarity to the style of the Ostian mosaic. Another relevant example is that of the two 'Twin Portraits of Dionysus and Ariadne', in the Kunsthistorisches Museum at Vienna, attributable to the fifth century[10] in which the stiffly mannered ornamental border of acanthus frames two haloed busts, equally stylised and congealed in a frigid typology. Notice particularly the robe and necklaces of 'Ariadne', and the reiterated curls of the hair of 'Dionysus'. The work is, perhaps, of other than Alexandrian provenance; but it is not on that account unmindful of traditional structures, despite the massive adoption of non-Hellenistic traits. By far the most significant of these products continues to be the fragment of wall tapestry from Antinoë, now in the Metropolitan Museum at New York, comprising 'Twelve Hellenistic Medallions' dateable to the end of the fourth century or the beginning of the fifth.[11] I do not propose to intervene here in the dispute which has arisen among scholars as to the Christian or pagan implications of this set of images. Some, for example, might be either fauns or devils, others either philosophers or bishops. In the present connection it is above all important to point out the profound similarity between some features of these busts and of those of the 'Dionysus' and 'Ariadne' fragments at Vienna, for instance the high level of the design, with its conspicuously expressive synthetic quality in the delineation of the personages, who, though they certainly do not attain naturalistic individuality, are nevertheless successfully characterised typologically and in form. These last enigmatic *imagines clipeatae* truly illustrate the last stage of an artistic civilisation that ended not far from the metropolis which had for centuries provided the training ground and the leading market for its wonderful growth.

Another interesting comparison can be made with the Ostian tarsia in *opus sectile*, which, together with many other geometrical and decorative inlays, has lately been reconstructed by Becatti. It almost certainly represents a 'Head of Christ', haloed and bearded, dateable to the second half of the fourth century. While awaiting publication of this important discovery, one cannot fail to be struck by the fact that its composition (in which slabs of purple, brown and yellow are juxtaposed with an admirably coherent effect) is in complete accord with the aesthetic theory governing the pavement of the House of the Dioscuri. Its form is closer to the polished chromatic beauty characteristic of Byzantium, but does not for that reason lack the two-dimensional buoyancy of surface peculiar to the Ostian *lithostroton*.

There is a long series of earlier African mosaics in this kind of Hellenistic tradition: for example, the ASPASIOS mosaic at Lambaesis,[12] the 'Nereid Riding a Marine Centaur' at Timgad,[13] the 'Triumph of Amphitrite with

202, 203

202

207

202, 203

207

199

10 De Francovich (1963), p. 138 (early
fourth century); Wessel (1960), pp.
223–4, pls. 112–3 (inclined to fifth
century).
11 Metropolitan Museum of Art, New
York, gift of Edward S. Harkness, 1931.
12 De Pachtère (1911), no. 190.
13 De Pachtère (1911), no. 139.

Oceanus and Nereids' in the Djemila Museum,[14] the 'Oceanus and Nereids' at Ain-Témouchent[15] and the 'Triumph of Amphitrite' in the Tebessa Baths.[16] In relation to them the Ostian pavement shows an expressive originality which, though it may not bear the stamp of a master, nonetheless affords evidence of a particularly subtle and sensitive aspect of the victory of the principle of surface autonomy over the cultural relics of ancient taste. The work therefore now seems to have more spiritual affinity, for example, to certain British mosaic floors of comparable date.

34–36, 197

In the late fourth century Britannia, romanised but now abandoned by the legions, produced two exceptional mosaic pavements which were excavated after the Second World War. These bear witness to the same tendency as is revealed in the mosaic of the House of the Dioscuri at Ostia, and thus confirm, with a most remarkable approximation of idiomatic effect, the substantial unity of the transmutation of late Roman painting into that of the early Middle Ages. The great mosaic from the *frigidarium* at the Villa of Low Ham in Somerset, once the luxurious residence of a local magnate, dates from about the middle of the fourth century and is now preserved in the Castle Museum at Taunton. The no less remarkable apse-shaped *lithostroton* in the *triclinium* of the Villa of Lullingstone in Kent, of about the same date, remains for the present *in situ*.

204

205, 206

The pavement at Low Ham was inspired by the story of Dido and Aeneas (Books I and IV of the *Aeneid*), with a simplification of setting that is at once apparent on comparing its five scenes – (i) arrival of the Trojan ships and handing to Achates of the gift for Dido; (ii) Venus and Cupid, the latter dressed as Ascanius, rouse the love of Aeneas for Dido; (iii) Aeneas, Dido and Ascanius hunting; (iv) embrace of Aeneas and Dido; (v) Venus among the cupids symbolising life and death – with the illustrations in two famous Vergilian manuscripts, *Vaticanus Latinus 3225* and *Vaticanus Latinus 3867* (*Romanus*), dateable respectively to the first decades of the fifth century and to the fifth or sixth. The five scenes at Low Ham, whose composition represents a stage in the evolution of the tale as illustrated in late antiquity, alternate narrative stages of a rhythmic and continuous type (the arrival of the three ships, the three hunting figures) with moments of motionless and symmetrised confrontation (arousal of love, copula, central *emblema* with Venus and Cupids). The succession of events, which guides the spectator systematically around the great mosaic square, takes advantage even of the tumbling figure of Achates: situated diagonally at the angle between the scene of the ships and that of the arousal of love, he receives the wreath for the queen while literally falling backwards, in such a way, however, as to appear to be leaning forward to face the royal and divine

208, 209

204

14 Ibid., no. 293.
15 Ibid., no. 318.
16 Ibid., n. 2. *See* note 48 to Chapter VI.

persons grouped in the following scene. The two episodes are consequently brought together almost without any break in continuity. This procedure, well known in imperial art for more than two centuries, seems here to be peculiarly significant for the aspects described; but it does not afford the sole example of idiomatic evolution in the pavement of this villa.

The main points of resemblance between the Low Ham and Ostia mosaics are (i) the tendency of both to eliminate colour from the figures, all signs of form being set within their outlines, and (ii) the complete and absolute buoyancy of those figures on the white surface of the background, against which, though separated by their plait-work frames, they are arranged around the central picture of Venus, as in the House of the Dioscuri. The colours too, excepting a few special highlights, are blended in an overall chromatic effect including, through the use of local materials, sharp and clean tints for the contours and the capricious variety of the multi-coloured garments, and components in a lower key for the necessary filling up of certain zones in the pictorial narrative. Jocelyn Toynbee has rightly compared a certain formal conventionality of the figures (for example of the horses, of Dido and of Venus) with types often found in Tunisian and Algerian mosaics, and with the mosaic fragment of the 'Three Graces' excavated at Sabratha.[17] But it should be clearly understood that these approximations are due merely to the probable employment of the same cartoons or of models produced in the same workshops. This circumstance does not imply any idiomatic relationships, which are not in themselves discernible; on the contrary, innumerable elements are found which indicate important contributions from 'barbarian', or rather indigenous, sources in the execution.

The Vergilian mosaic at Low Ham seems therefore, on the grounds of technique, materials and style, to have been a local undertaking, but one clearly working on the tradition of ancient culture which at that period was glorified as never before in Britain. As such it confirms with all the more authority and significance the importance of the Ostian *lithostroton*.

The same considerations apply also to the almost contemporary pavement of the *triclinium* at Lullingstone. The central design, between wide zones of geometrical *tessellatum*, represents the myth of Bellerophon Slaying the Chimera, surrounded by four marine monsters, all within a quadrilateral field garlanded with 'Roundels of the Four Seasons'. The large apse displays the 'Rape of Europa', surmounted by an inscription alluding, as Toynbee has pointed out,[18] to the first Book of the Aenid: '*Invida si ta (uri) vidisset Iuno natatus / iustius Aeolias isset adusque domos*'. The Lullingstone *lithostroton* employs a stock of

206

205

17 Toynbee, Jocelyn M.C. (1962), p. 205, pl. 259. (The African fragment has not been published.) *See also* her note in *Journal of Roman Studies*, XXXVI (1946), p. 142 ff.

18 Toynbee, Jocelyn M.C. (1962), p. 200. *See also* Meates (1955).

tesserae in even plainer colours than those of the Low Ham pavement, to which it is related by a similar tendency to eliminate all chromatic solidity from its nudes. Coloured cubes are used mainly for garments and objects, but the figures are defined in even more radical and stylised fashion with a single strip of tesserae. In the floor of the House of the Dioscuri at Ostia articulation of the images was entrusted to a residual chromatic framework expressed by two or three rows of variously coloured cubes to imitate the rosy quality of flesh; and a no less evident relationship with Low Ham and with Ostia is recognisable in the second-century head of Oceanus from Verulamium, almost suggesting a permanent underlying tendency towards the adoption of a clearly graphic style which must, however, be recognised as typical of all non-classical artistic expression.   33

The Lullingstone artist, moreover, possessed remarkable skill and undoubted confidence in the handling of his material. Far and away the most astonishing feature in these *lithostrota* is the capacity to synthesise, with a single tessellar strip, complex forms from a learned tradition and to reveal their essence without afterthoughts or hesitation. In the group of Bellerophon, as in that of Europa, and also   206 20 in the very simple and successful presentation of the heads of the Seasons, it is as though the venerable imagery of antiquity had been subjected to the process of 'drop-out', as used today for the treatment of photographic prints. The ghost of the great Hellenistic tonal painting casts an impoverished shadow on the unadulterated purity of the white mosaic page. But the phantom still shows in these cases a potential style and poetry.

Analogous considerations might be applied to other British mosaics of the fourth century; for example to the apsidal lunette of 'Venus with Tritons' in the British   198 Museum,[19] easily recognisable as part of a rich tradition shared likewise, almost to the letter, by the central scene at Ostia and by such North African mosaics as the 'Triumph of Amphitrite' at Djemila;[20] to the fragment of the 'Frame with Fish' at the Lufton Villa in Somerset;[21] and to the *emblema* recently uncovered in the church of St. Mary, at Hinton, Dorset. This last is iconographically of Hellenistic descent, but markedly original in its draughtsmanship, presenting the head and shoulders of a 'Young Christ' who wears the *chrismon* instead of a halo.

In all these discoveries it is easy to recognise a very real correspondence with the polarity of mediaeval vernacular style, a correspondence conditioned solely by the cultural deposit of traditional models. Here must end the history of one artistic civilisation, and that of another begin.

19 Hinks (1933), no. 52 a, fig. 150. The tessellar strips of the hair-styles, the folds of the garments etc. noticeably echo the Ostian *lithostrate*, within the limits imposed by incorrect and untrained linear technique, typical of advanced *barbaritas* (barbarian practice in art).
20 *See* note 48 to Chapter VI.
21 Toynbee, Jocelyn M.C. (1962), p. 201, pl. 230.

Chapter Fourteen
The first illuminated MSS and the Romano–Italian
cultural area at the beginning of the fifth century

The end of the fourth century and the beginning of the fifth did not merely carry on the movement represented in the *pars occidentalis* by such monuments as the 'Mosaic of the Nereids' at Ostia, the Vergilian pavement at Low Ham and the pseudo-Hellenistic mosaics at Lullingstone, and in the *pars orientalis* by Egypto-Alexandrian textiles and tapestries which realised the last potentiality of the Hellenistic tradition. I have already shown how important in the art and culture of this time is the parallelism of some of the manners detected in decorations of the Catacomb on the Via Latina, in the mosaics of S. Aquilino and in those of S. Vittore in Ciel d'Oro. In the Roman lunettes depicting the 'Passage of the Red Sea' or the tales of Samson and of Elijah, as well as in the 'Assumption of Elijah' at S. Aquilino, there is exhibited, with greater iconographic distinctness than in the past and with a well-defined purpose of illustrating biblical history, a taste perhaps related to the confluence of a variety of idiomatic experiments, but which had not freed itself from the deposit of traditional classical culture. Meanwhile the attempts to restore realism to portraiture – naturally in the sense and within the limits that the times rendered possible – as seen in the Roman Catacomb and in the great figures of 'Patriarchs' and 'Saints' in the two Milanese chapels, proved the tumultuous interpenetration in the decisive closing years of the fourth century of the ancient fondness for historico-psychological significance in the image and the now fully developed and wide-spread tendency to abstract typology which, as already noted, matured so quickly in the vast gallery of Mummy Portraits during the third and fourth centuries.

This last enthusiasm for the materials and modes of the past among Christian painters at the end of the fourth century need cause no surprise, especially when it is compared with a very strong tendency to anticipate pre-medieval colour and line revealed in certain monuments of the final pictorial expression of the classical repertory, from Ostia to Britain and the Nile. In the examination of the latest surviving records which has been attempted in the preceding chapters it is true that no idiomatic anti-thesis was detected as a product of the two great ideological traditions that were now contending for the ancient world. Time and again, indeed, attention was drawn to the *koine* which offered a common idiom to the two contrasted tendencies. Now if ever study of idiomatic

34, 36, 197
204–6

170–3
168
28, 29

175, 30, 31

qualification in the sociological field might be usefully employed, not so much with a view to drawing a clearer distinction between the art of the *honestiores* and that of the *humiliores* as for the purpose of verifying in the extant records the terms of a fertile and integrating dialogue between a *sermo nobilis* and a *sermo humilis*, and the emergence of a popular and provincial idiom as the Hellenistic and traditional idiom became more and more insignificant. Yet even this task, when tainted with ideology and schematisation, met a stern challenge from numerous monuments which, with a variety of emphases, demonstrate that all the painting of the fourth century had a common platform.

A profitable undertaking in this connection is certainly offered by the study, as difficult and problematical as any, of the first illuminated manuscripts, produced during the fourth and fifth centuries both on the classical and on the Christian side. Antiquity had been familiar for centuries with the custom of illustrating *rotuli* – the decoration, for the wealthy and educated clients, of literary and scientific works with frontispiece portraits of their authors and with scenes descriptive of important passages in the text. During the first centuries of the Christian era the production of illuminated papyrus *rotuli* was gradually replaced by that of parchment *codices*, also illustrated. The principal advantage of the *codex* was that it allowed a saving of fifty per cent on materials, since it enabled both *recto* and *verso* of the page to be written upon. The illustrations were also better preserved, as the *codex* did not have to be rolled up. This type of product was in fact used by Christians from the outset. Affording an exactly determined amount of space, it also raised the problem of page-design as between text and illustration, as in the Canons of Gospel concordances based on rules laid down by Eusebius of Caesarea. That problem was occasionally solved by a combination of picture and script: by means not only of the tables of Eusebius, which framed in stately columns the parallel stories of the four evangelists, but also of the *technopaignion*, an equivalent of modern visual poetry (*carmina figurata*), which was employed by Publilius Optatianus Porphyrius, a poet of Constantine's court, who filled the outline of an image with verses referring to it.[1]

This sumptuous and often irrelevant page-decoration was of extraordinary value to ancient figurative culture. Owing to the ease with which the codices could be handled and transported, they did more than the collections of cartoons supplied by the workshops of the *musivarii* of the Dark Ages to transmit at least a part of the figurative repertory of antiquity to subsequent ages, when they became enormously popular for liturgical and ecclesiastical as well for cultural and court purposes, not

1 Nordenfalk (1936). A different but singular instance of illustration is provided by Carolingian copies of the *Chronographer for 354* by Furius Dionysius Filocalus, calligrapher and painter, who is known to have been active in Rome throughout almost the whole age of Damasus. The *Chronographer* comprises an astronomical calendar containing traditional symbols and personifications, representations of consuls and cities etc., lavishly illustrated and admirably handwritten. It unquestionably influenced the art of illumination. *See* in this connection Stern (1953); *also* Strzygowski (1888).

only in the eastern empire and (in the case of particular graphic images) among Islamic populations, but also in the West, as in Irish, Merovingian, Carolingian and Ottonian art, etc.

Apart from a few negligible fragments, the illuminated manuscripts that can be confidently assigned to the fourth or fifth centuries amount to only two. These are the fragment of Biblical texts known as *Itala of Quedlinburg* (Codex Theol. Lat. 485 of the Prussian State library in Berlin),[2] and the fragment of the works of Vergil called *Vergilius Vaticanus* (Vaticanus Latinus 3225 in the Vatican Apostolic Library).[3] A third fragment, possibly dating from the end of the century, is the so-called *Vergilius Romanus* (Vaticanus Latinus 3867, also in the Vatican Apostolic Library).[4] The first consists of four leaves; the second has fifty of the 245 miniatures which it is supposed to have originally contained. The third preserves nineteen. Three more manuscripts are probably to be ascribed to the early sixth century. They are the Ambrosian *Iliad* (Cod. F 205 inf. in the Ambrosian Library at Milan),[5] the so-called *Cotton Bible* (Otho B 4 at the British Museum in London)[6] and the *Vienna Dioscorid* (Cod. Med. gr. I in the Austrian National Library)[7] which is dateable, from the dedication to Juliana Anicia, to about 512.

The study of these documents, and of the first two which are of particular interest here, has been for decades among the most detailed and difficult, owing to the scarcity of accurate points of reference which might enable the locations and dates of the original *scriptoria* to be conjectured. Nevertheless, especially during the last few years, a wider consideration of these products has reached some extremely important conclusions which are now generally accepted in principle. For it no longer confines them to the level of so-called minor arts, and it carries comparison and research farther afield into the whole artistic field contemporary with their appearance.

The biblical fragments of *Itala of Quedlinburg* and the Vergilian fragments of the *Vaticanus* are now thought to derive from the same artistic culture, and by some authorities actually from the same *scriptorium*. The diversity of dates ascribed to the first manuscript ranges over about half a century, between 350 and 400. But in fact certain of the latest investigators, Nordenfalk[8] for instance, consider the two manuscripts to be so much alike as to induce the belief that they came from an identical establishment, 'though the *Vergilius* seems a little later', and they assign the *Itala* to the end of the century. Others, such as Böckler,[9] judge them to be contemporary and from the same centre. Schlunk too[10] has decided in favour of the second half of the fourth century in the case of the *Itala*. Byvanck[11] votes for the decade 350–360; Bianchi Bandinelli[12] for 360–370; Böckler for the age of

208

209

2 Degering and Böckler (1932).
3 Ehrle (1945); De Wit (1959).
4 Ehrle (1902).
5 Bianchi Bandinelli (1951; 1953a; 1953b; 1955).
6 Weitzmann (1955).
7 Premerstein *et al.* (1906).
8 Nordenfalk (1936), p. 31, n. 1; *also* Grabar and Nordenfalk (1957), p. 93.
9 Degering and Böckler (1932), pp. 166 and 169.
10 Schlunk (1939), pp. 81–2, fig. 93.
11 Byvanck (1938), p. 251.
12 Bianchi Bandinelli (1954).

Damasus;[13] De Wit[14] for the end of the century. On the whole it may safely be stated that this manuscript probably came from a Roman *scriptorium* at some date subsequent to the mid-century and was perhaps one of the very first of Christian illustrated books. On the other hand, the iconographical elements, still very similar to those of the *Vergilius Vaticanus*, indicate the employment of models usual in the representation of military feats and the events of classical myth, while the dropping of frequent zones of colour from the manuscript shows that the illuminator was given instructions suggesting that composition could still be remarkably free, almost improvised. Hence it is probable that a complete figurative repertory for Biblical decoration was lacking at the time of execution. It is impossible therefore not to subscribe to the following conclusions by Nordenfalk: 'No fundamental distinction existed in miniature painting at this period between the pagan and Christian styles of presenting form. Church and State were served by the same establishments.'[15] This had certainly been the case during the preceding centuries in the workshops of fresco painters and mosaicists.

But the *Vergilius Vaticanus*, which is fairly generally agreed to have shared the cultural environment of the *Itala*, is usually dated in the first years of the fifth century. Though Lowe[16] believed the *capitalis rustica* script of the codex to be of the fourth century, more recent and authoritative studies of the illustration have led De Wit,[17] Byvanck[18] and Bianchi Bandinelli[19] to recognise an approximate dating between 415 and 425 as satisfactory, while Nordenfalk[20] favours the early years of the century. At the same time, even those scholars who prefer an earlier period acknowledge the existence of a basic link between the manuscript in question and the mosaic cycle of S. Maria Maggiore. Hence there emerges a further important feature of this fundamental document.

Like the *Itala*, the *Vergilius Vaticanus* is the product of a western *scriptorium*, probably Roman, employing models which had been in use for some considerable time (as Bianchi Bandinelli[21] suggests) by Italian Hellenistic painters, very likely in book illustrations of the second and third centuries. The clumsiness sometimes evident in certain figures, the jarring juxtapositions of certain colours, the habit of calling attention to certain components such as personal clothing, fruit on trees, etc., by means of golden highlights, the manifest frequent indifference to coherent perspective and many other entirely late Roman features of these illustrations are never such as to rid them of the traditional deposit. They accordingly differentiate this manuscript noticeably from the *Ambrosian Iliad*, which Bianchi Bandinelli, as the result of exhaustive and detailed study, assigns to a *scriptorium* at Constantinople and to a date not earlier than the end of the fifth century, preferably at the beginning of the sixth.[22]

13 Degering and Böckler (1932), p. 192.
14 De Wit (1959), p. 156.
15 Grabar and Nordenfalk (1957), pp. 92–3.
16 Lowe (1934), p. 5.
17 De Wit (1935–6; 1959, p. 153).
18 Byvanck (1938), p. 247.
19 Bianchi Bandinelli (1954), p. 328.
20 Grabar and Nordenfalk (1957), p. 93. *See also* Bonicatti, *Traccia . . ., passim.*
21 Bianchi Bandinelli (1954), pp. 335–42.
22 Bianchi Bandinelli (1955; 1954, p. 329).

In these images, as noted above, late Roman painting was not yet dead. The memory of a coherent and complex composition in the scenes, the continuous search for a significant and allusive environment in the episodes, the precise and elegant arrangement on the page of illustration and script, and the sobriety of the explanations adjoining the figures of the miniatures, all combine in the reconstruction of a lost epoch, certainly by way of response to the demands of traditionalist devotees not only of a proper text but also of 'proper pictures' in the old style. Such products presented satisfactory answers to the cultural scruples of a class in search of the lost values to which they could cling in an age when the ancient certainties had been replaced for ever by new standards, texts and forms of civilisation. It may be agreed that different artists or different sources of repertory and inspiration can be detected in various groups of illuminations, as in the case of the Ambrosian *Iliad*. Yet it must be admitted that even in a product intended for a special and certainly most expensive market, in late antiquity, and claiming to serve, by its very existence, content and taste, traditional circles now in conflict with the general state of affairs, the aesthetic sense of the work as a whole was well suited to the inescapable sentiment of the time. The extraordinary result was that through a tendency to compositional crasis (*see* fol. XIII *recto* where Aeneas and Achates watch the building of Carthage – *Aeneid*, I. 419); through the bold use of colour, which already foreshadows the symphonies of blue, red, green, gold and white in the nave of S. Maria Maggiore; and through many iconographical particulars shared by that great and somewhat late mosaic series, this product of a conservative culture appears ready to inspire one of the most exceptional monuments of the painting of late antiquity in a Roman setting, a monument which really brought that culture to an end and started a new development.

S. Maria Maggiore did not in fact arise unprepared. The Roman artistic atmosphere at the end of the fourth century was extraordinarily stimulating, owing particularly to the commissions for mosaics placed by the ecclesiastical hierarchy. As noted earlier, the new Catacomb on the Via Latina proves that the Biblical repertory was growing rapidly and was now within the reach of private individuals, though they had to be wealthy. In the new Cubicle of Leo, in the Cemetery of Commodilla, a bearded image of the Redeemer had been placed among the caissons of the vault; together with that of the Agnus Dei vault of the Cemetery of Peter and Marcellinus, though they differed idiomatically, it showed that the iconography of the *Pantocrator* was ready for transference to the basilican apses. The small mosaic lunette in the

168, 170–4

178

179

Cemetery of Domitilla, with its inscription *Qui Filius diceris et Pater inveniris*, bears witness to the confidence with which the delineation of Christ in a celestial ovoid had been accomplished before the end of the century. Consequently, although it is not possible to deny the probable contributions of classical iconography (for example of the Ambrosian *Iliad*, deriving perhaps from Constantinople), it is certainly unnecessary to suppose that *pictores imaginarii* were summoned from New Rome or from the East to decorate the great Roman churches of the early fifth century: S. Pudenziana, S. Sabina, S. Maria Maggiore.

But more than one manner is perceptible in the large mosaics of these buildings. Notwithstanding extensive repairs in the eighth, seventeenth and nineteenth centuries, during which the surface was reduced, two figures of apostles were removed and many other figures completely remodelled, the apse of S. Pudenziana[23] reveals the hand of an artist addicted to classical composition, symmetry and a wide range of formal resources. Though the principles of his technique were undoubtedly of late origin (for example in the sky with coloured clouds, an organic development of ideas present in the apsidioles of the Mausoleum of Constantina), the MASTER OF S. PUDENZIANA depicted in the lower section of the apse something like a gathering of philosophers. Christ alone, related to the picture on the vault in the Cemetery of Commodilla mentioned above, seems already to have been composed in the form of the *Pantocrator* which the basilican apses in both West and East were to accept for centuries.

401–417

178

The scanty remains of the decoration of S. Sabina, with its two figures of the *Ecclesia ex gentibus* and the *Ecclesia ex circumcisione*, also belong to a tendency of Theodosian classicism, prolonged for some decades during the reign of Honorius, They may be dated preferably to the age of Pope Sixtus III rather than to that of his predecessor, Celestine I (422–432), in which the building was certainly erected, as attested by the great mosaic epigraph on the interior facade of the basilica, between the two *Ecclesiae* which have been preserved.[24]

The mosaics in the nave (formerly considered to date from the second half of the fourth century) and those of the arch of the Basilica of S. Maria Maggiore are generally believed by modern critics to belong to the period of Sixtus, despite recent proposals by Künzle[25] for an earlier date and the identification of the edifice itself with the Basilica Liberii or Sicinini. The discovery not long ago of the mosaic lunette in the Cemetery of Domitilla, and the many studies made of the apsidal mosaic of Hosios David at Salonika, of the two lunettes and figures in the forceps atrium of S. Aquilino, Milan, and of the Baptistery of Naples Cathedral (together with, from another stand-

210

27, 30

23 Wilpert (1917), p. 1066 ff., pls. 42–6. Matthiae (1937–9); Cecchelli (1933), p. 210; Volbach and Hirmer (1958), p. 70, pl. 130.

24 Bovini (1963a), pp. 67–74.

25 Künzle (1960–1; 1961–2); Bovini 1963b); Volbach and Hirmer (1958), pp. 69–70, pls. 128–9; Grabar and Nordenfalk (1957), pp. 34–9; Bonicatti (1963), pp. 79–103; Cecchelli (1956).

point, the Piazza Armerina complex) may perhaps help to revive the idea of an earlier general chronology for the monuments of this epoch. But in my opinion the stylistic character of S. Maria Maggiore as a whole militates against antedating it by three quarters of a century, as was urged thirty years ago by Diehl.[26]

Six of the mosaic pictures in the nave, representing Old Testament stories, were destroyed when two large arches were constructed in the sixteenth and seventeenth centuries to communicate with the Sistine and Pauline chapels, and another nine are lost. The twenty-seven that survive depict the adventures of Abraham, Jacob, Moses and Joshua, the Biblical 'figures' of Christ, whose infancy and the glorification of Mary are depicted in the great triumphal arch.

A somewhat immature phase in the presentation of a complex narrative is shown by arrangement of the various tales. Sometimes it reveals anomalies in the order of the scenes. Sometimes, for no apparent reason except possibly that of an improvised reduction of a figurative cycle too extensive to be contained within the limits of the forty-four spaces available for decoration in the nave, it alternates single with double scenes, and with others in which many separate incidents are shown in one picture (e.g. 'Abraham's Vision under the Oak of Mamre'). Sometimes, finally, it reduces to very hazardous compositional structures models of different sizes; for example the scene on two levels of the 'Capture of Jericho and the Ark Borne in Procession', where two aspects of the same event are displayed as if they were successive; or again the 'Passage of the Red Sea', a scene originally horizontal become vertical, without perspective, shows indeed a somewhat immature phase in presentation of a complex narrative. But the production of such effects in the mid-fourth century must appear almost incredible when we consider the imaginative design; the boldness in the use of pieces of models of different origin, as when a simple change of clothing in a figure denotes the assumption of a different part in the action; the exceptional taste in colour; the indiscriminate use of gold for the backgrounds, whether unmixed in abstract passages or combined with other bright colours in the reproduction of chaotically lyrical scenery; and the relations between both the figures themselves and between figures and environment.

210

In the triumphal arch the formula of make-up varies, using superimposed layers for a narrative which would normally be continuous though it appears even more emblematical and concentrated upon typical moments than was the case in the nave. The style, too, is less lively, more symbolical and tending to abstraction, culminating conspicuously in the gold background. These features indicate the hand of a differently trained artist and one more disciplined in composition, though the latest work of restoration carried out by Biagetti has revealed beneath the Annunciation scene traces of sinopers on the plaster which do not correspond with the form subsequently assumed by the work.

S. Maria Maggiore as a whole, briefly alluded to in the present study as being the first figurative result of a civilisation already beyond the scope of late Roman painting, displays certain essential aspects of manners which were to be in evidence a few years later at Ravenna, and also indicates some definite links with the mosaic idiom of S. Aquilino at Milan. The chromatic freedom of all the *musivarii* employed on these cycles; the expressionistic skill shown in the faces, the figures and the landscapes picked out with a succession of red, blue and green hills against fantastic skies animated by strips of gilded, grey and maroon tesserae; and the endless variety of garments worn by the personages, together with numerous idiomatic details; all show the existence of organic relations between these characteristics and those of S. Aquilino, in such a way as to exclude the possibility of this monument being necessarily the result of artistic intervention from Constantinople. That influence, however, might have been at least partially operative in the much damaged mosaic decoration of the aforesaid Baptistery of Naples Cathedral, which dates from some time between the end of the fourth century and the second half of the fifth. In this second case there would be a close connection with certain fragmentary frescoes of saints in the local Catacomb of St. Januarius.[27]

The stylistic manner found at Milan, in monuments such as S. Aquilino and S. Vittore in Ciel d'Oro extends to the hypogeum of S. Maria in Stelle, at Val Pantena near Verona, though the latter has a peculiar idiomatic character of its own. It was originally a funerary structure, known for centuries to historians,[28] and has probably been in almost continuous use until the present day. But it has only recently been brought to the attention of scholars.[29]

The architectural structure of this subterranean area is determined exactly by the course of a spring, conveyed in a narrow conduit, which reaches the entrance after having passed through a barrel-vaulted atrium at opposite sides of which are two cells with deep apses, and continues farther. It is attributed to a funerary building of the first half of the third century, ordered, as we learn from an inscription on an architrave, by Publius Pomponius Cornelianus for himself and his family. From another inscription, now in the Maffei Museum at Verona, he is known to have been *consularis* and *curator rerum publicarum*. There is a possible portrait of him in the statue of a man wearing a toga now standing in a niche near the entrance to the hypogeum.

27, 30, 31

27 Byvanck (1931); Cecchelli (1933), p. 214. Cecchelli, however, considers that execution should be dated 'in the second half of the fourth century, but a few years before its close', he recognises that 'in this case expressionist mannerism has crept in, while at Milan a plain style, truly classical, still prevailed; even at Naples a more refined palette had transformed compositions into a real riot of colour . . . but here all is fastidiously theological, taking place in an atmosphere of absorption, with even the most highly decorative passages obviously translated into symbol. The very shepherds are less naturalistic than those shortly afterwards to be seen in the S. Aquilino lunette. The Gospel figure is even more otherworldly in personality than the Martyrs.' *See also* Chapter XI, n. 24.
28 It is discussed by Moscardo, Maffei, Carli, Venturi, Da Persico and others, in that order, with reference to research on local history.
29 *See* Forlati Tamaro (1962), pp. 245–50. The author, citing also the oral opinions of Gerke, Palol, Salmi and Volbach, considers that the transformation of the hypogeum into a Christian chapel 'would not have been later than the fifth century'.

Here we have, in substance, two sepulchral chambers built by a provincial magistrate fond of a locality which had been dedicated in ancient times to the Nymphs because of the fertility conferred by the stream. As was usual (see for example the small hypogeum discovered in 1964 on the Via Ardeatina near Rome), the chambers were transformed, about a century and a half later, into a Christian chapel, as appears from the majority of the frescoes which deal with Old and New Testament subjects. It had not yet, however, become the small church called at a later date '*ad fontem divae Mariae stellarum*', from the fresco – unquestionably much later than the decoration of the right-hand cell where it appears – depicting the 'Virgin between Two Angels' and surmounted throughout the whole extent of the arch by a blue sky dotted with stars.

The decoration of the atrium includes on one of the side walls and in the lunette of the rear wall (*Traditio legis*) the remains of subjects attributable after careful examination to about the middle of the fourth century. The niche hollowed out in the right-hand cell is adorned on its inner sides with two figures of quite late execution. Finally, the traces of decoration on the left-hand cell reveal a hand in the act of blessing and an inscription certainly dateable to the eleventh century. This evidence is sufficiently indicative of the long life of the hypogeum, in which various hands have repeatedly, in the course of centuries, adapted its wall-paintings to illustrate changing functions and different religious themes.

The right-hand cell of S. Maria in Stelle is the most interesting in the present connection. In spite of the extreme humidity of the place it retains a decoration which until a few years ago had remained completely incomprehensible, as Orti Manara declared in 1848.[30] It has now been made reasonably intelligible by restoration work, and turns out to be of exceptional importance in the study of late antiquity and of the early Christian art of northern Italy. For it bridges a very large gap, helping in some degree to establish a convincing link between such highly significant monuments as S. Aquilino and S. Vittore in Ciel d'Oro, Milan, and the Mausoleum of Galla Placidia and the episcopal Chapel of St. Andrew at Ravenna.

The wall through which access is obtained to the cell bears a large lunette representing the Apostolic College **33** with Christ in the centre holding the Law, while two *cistae* containing other *rotuli* stand one on either side of the group. Below the lunette, at the same height all round the apse, runs a wide maze-pattern border, in perspective and brightly coloured (wine-red, golden-yellow and pale green), which separates the starred lateral arch and the vault from the series of scenes shown below them. (The vault is decorated with further sequences of variously coloured mouldings, such as were used in the construction

30 Orti Manara (1848).

of domes; and the mouldings in turn are set in concentric circles round a central aperture intended to admit light from above and to air the room.) The lower scenes consist of five almost megalographic pictures in which it is possible to identify, from right to left, the ox and the ass of the Nativity with the infant Jesus, the Massacre of the Innocents, the Three Young Men in the Furnace, the Magi before King Herod (or perhaps the same youths refusing Nebuchadnezzar's command to adore the statue) and the Triumphal Entry of Christ into Jerusalem.

213, 212

214

211

Perusal of the lunette of the Apostolic College and of the five scenes of the apsidal wall leads to the opinion that two different artists of diverse talent were engaged. The painter of the scenes from the life of Jesus and of the Old Testament episode of the three Babylonian youths was a local man with a lively gift for narrative in a popular style, but well trained.[31] He placed his large figures with rhythmic simplicity within the rectangle of the wall; they are functionally unequal in size, and express in a sometimes forced and persistently repeated linearism the full force of the story to be illustrated, as for example in the scenes of the Magi and the Youths. We may find it hard now to grasp the combinative significance of the subjects chosen (the 'concordantia veteris et novi testamenti' adopted by St. Paulinus of Nola and applied in his basilicas at Cimitile), which could easily be accounted for by the particular psychological requirements of the private patron. But we cannot fail to recognise the importance of the inter-mingling of Old and New Testament themes largely concerned with childhood and youth (the Nativity, the Slaughter of the Innocents preceded by the visit of the Magi to Herod, and the lads in the furnace) and with royalty (two scenes with Herod or Nebuchadnezzar and the Entry into Jerusalem). The evidently instructive intent of the painter unquestionably unites different cultural traditions. The Manger scene, taken from pseudo-Matthew and hardly intelligible in the present illustration, is not elsewhere exemplified in the first Christian centuries. Other sources appear to account for the story of the young Babylonians in the furnace, which is very common in catacombal art and on sarcophagi, and the scene of the Magi (if it is such; otherwise, if it is supposed to represent the young men confronting Nebuchadnezzar, we should note that this subject does not appear in the catacombs until the fifth century). The scenes of the Slaughter and of the Entry into Jerusalem appear more frequently after the fourth century. Incidentally, iconographical associations between the tales of the Magi and those of the Young Men are not rare at this period. Instances are the sarcophagus of *Adelphia* in the National Museum at Syracuse (*circa* 340), the casket of S. Nazaro at Milan (*circa* 400) and the Theodosian sarcophagus of S. Ambrogio at Milan,

31 Orti Manara, (1848, p. 54, notes 6 and 10 on pp. 87–8) suggests a date between the fifth and sixth centuries 'finding the movements of the figures, the clothing and other details similar to those of about this period also found in our region'; for example those 'of the chiesicciuola "chiselled out of the rock on the mountain called Scaglione or Costiglione near the Church of Saints Nazaro and Celsus".'

189 Trier, Landesmuseum. Mosaic of the Dioscuri: Scene of Qodvoldeus, from the Kornmarkt

190 Trier, Landesmuseum. Mosaic of the Dioscuri: Head of Felix, from the Kornmarkt

191 Trier, Landesmuseum. Mosaic of the Dioscuri: Head of Eusebius, from the Kornmarkt

192 Trier, Landesmuseum. Mosaic of the Dioscuri: Head of Paregorius, from the Kornmarkt

193 Trier, Landesmuseum. Mosaic of the Dioscuri: Head of Eusebius, from the Kornmarkt

194 Trier, Landesmuseum. Mosaic of the Dioscuri, from the Kornmarkt

195 Trier, Landesmuseum. Octagon: Muse, from the Johannis-strasse

196 Trier, Landesmuseum. Octagon: Muse, from the Johannis-strasse

197 Ostia, House of the
Dioscuri. Mosaic of Room I
(detail): Nereid on Marine
Panther

198 London,
British Museum.
Apsidal lunette:
Venus with
Tritons

199 Ostia, Museum. Marble inlay: Head of Christ

200 Ostia, Courtyard of Reg. I ins. IV. *Emblema* of the mosaic with heads of the Months

202 Vienna, Kunsthistorisches Museum. Dionysus

201 Cleveland, Museum of Art. Square of wool and linen with haloed Nereid on blue ground

203 Vienna, Kunsthistorisches Museum. Ariadne

32 Trier, Landesmuseum. Mosaic of the Dioscuri: Birth of the Dioscuri, from the Kornmarkt.

33 Verona, Hypogeum of S. Maria in Stelle. Lunette of the Apostolic College.

34 Ostia, House of the Dioscuri. Mosaic of Room I (detail): Venus on Sea-shell.

35 Ostia, House of the Dioscuri. Mosaic of Room I (detail): Nereid.

36 Ostia, House of the Dioscuri. Mosaic of Room I (detail): Nereid and Marine Monsters.

204 Taunton, Castle Museum. Mosaic of the Stories of Dido and Aeneas, from the *frigidarium* of the baths of the Roman villa at Low Ham, Somerset

205 Lullingstone (Kent), Roman Villa (dining-room apse). Mosaic: Rape of Europa

206 Lullingstone (Kent), Roman Villa. Bellerophon slaying the Chimaera (central zone of the dining-room) and roundels of the Seasons

207 New York, Metropolitan Museum. Fragment of tapestry with twelve Hellenistic medallions, from Antinoe

208 Vatican City, Apostolic Library. Folio 33 v. of the *Vergilius Vaticanus* (*Vaticanus Latinus* 3225) (detail)

209 Vatican City, Apostolic Library. Folio 18 of the *Vergilius Vaticanus* (*Vaticanus Latinus* 3225) (detail)

210 Rome, Basilica of S. Maria Maggiore. Mosaic in right-hand nave: Passage of the Red Sea

211 Verona, Hypogeum of
S. Maria in Stelle. Entry of
Christ into Jerusalem

212 Verona, Hypogeum of
S. Maria in Stelle. The Three
Young Men in the Furnace

213 Verona, Hypogeum of S. Maria in Stelle. Massacre of the Innocents

214 Verona, Hypogeum of S. Maria in Stelle. The Magi with Herod, or perhaps the Three Young Men refusing to adore the Statue

215 Salonika, Rotunda of Hagios Georgios. Figure of Saint, on the drum (detail)

37 Rome, Museo Nazionale. Mosaic of the Seasons: *Emblema* of Autumn.

38 Rome, Museo Nazionale. Mosaic of the Seasons: *Emblema* of Spring.

39 Constantinople, Peristyle of the Imperial Palace. Fragment of frieze: Vegetable Mask.

40 Constantinople, Peristyle of the Imperial Palace. Two Hunters Confronting Tigress.

41 Constantinople, Peristyle of the Imperial Palace. Guide Leading Boys on a Camel.

216 Salonika, Rotunda of Hagios Georgios. One of eight pictures on the drum with figures of Saints

217 Salonika, Rotunda of Hagios Georgios. Vault of a niche with animals and fruit (detail)

220 Constantinople, Peristyle of the Imperial Palace. Rural Labours

221 Constantinople, Peristyle of the Imperial Palace. Boy and Old Man Milking Goats (detail)

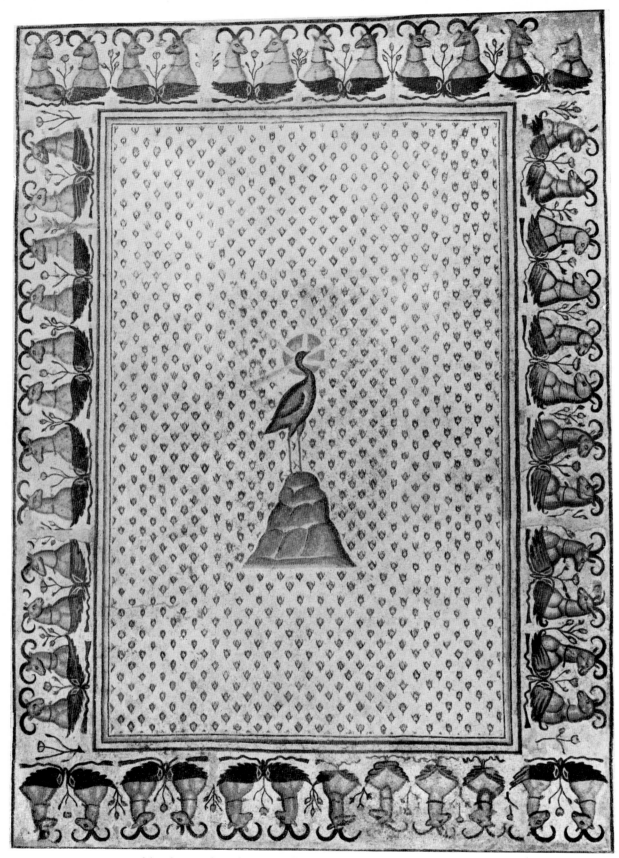

222 Paris, Louvre. Mosaic of the Phoenix, from the House of the Phoenix at Antioch

while on the mosaic Arch at S. Maria Maggiore and in the ivory *evangeliarium* of Milan Cathedral the Adoration of the Magi is accompanied by the Slaughter of the Innocents ordered by Herod. At S. Maria Maggiore there are three scenes: the Magi before Herod, the Adoration of the Magi and Herod ordering the slaughter.

This first artist of S. Maria in Stelle may safely be considered to have worked at the end of the fourth century and in the very early fifth. He shows a provincial style, unassuming and linear, but with much reference to the art of the Theodosian age and its successor; a style in some respects (e.g. the utilisation of line to function as a substitute for corporeality) akin to the manner of the lunette of 'Christ among the Apostles' at S. Aquilino.

The large lunette of the 'Apostolic College' at S. Maria in Stelle is undoubtedly the work of another hand, quite probably of a later date and certainly more individual and creative. An inevitable comparison with the mosaic of the Milanese apsidiole just mentioned at once reveals the lunette's alienation from a style clearly marked in the case of the apsidiole by subjective realism and traces of illusionist technique, here altogether absent. Unfortunately the face of Christ, which was presumably better defined originally, is barely decipherable. Those of the apostles, on the other hand, suggest the primitive emphasis on characterisation found in some of the portraits at the episcopal Chapel of St. Andrew at Ravenna, where the influence of the court still seems to have had little effect, and also recall the ingenious simplicity of the countenance of Adauctus in the fresco of 'Turtura' (chapel of Sts. Felix and Adauctus in the Roman Cemetery of Commodilla, dating from the year 528). The relation is cultural, stylistic and chronological, and implies for the large lunette of S. Maria in Stelle a date approximately at the end of the fifth century or beginning of the sixth. The APOSTOLIC COLLEGE MASTER was working in an atmosphere of uninhibited pursuit of the early Christian figurative tradition, independent of the palace taste later to be imported from Ravenna, and even anticipatory of a more accentuated popular expressiveness, such as that eventually to reach its most typical culmination in certain specimens of Carolingian art that survive in Alpine districts, at Malles for instance. A few decorative details, however, and perhaps the disciplined composition itself of the figures, in which the perfect chromatic simplicity does not disguise some effort at stylisation and rhythm (drapery, hands, etc.), suggests an artist not unaware of the more refined art which the *pars orientalis* of the Empire, once more exerting pressure on Italy, could still produce.

27
33

T

Chapter Fifteen
The NeoPlatonic and NeoAlexandrian masters of Salonika and Constantinople, and the origins of Byzantine art

It cannot be said that criticism of the *lithostroton* of the Great Palace of Constantinople, excavated between 1935 and 1938, and, more recently, between 1951 and 1954, has reached fundamental unanimity, either as regards the dating or as regards the more strictly idiomatic evaluation of the many works brought to light. Brett, who first systematically elucidated the results of the excavation so far as mosaics were concerned,[1] unhesitatingly assigned the large pavement to the age of Theodosius II, 'perhaps to its first half', in consequence of the finding *in situ* of scraps of mouldings bearing Christian symbols, which would give the years 400–410 as *terminus post quem*, and also of a capital typical of the very early fifth century.

Levi, however, about the same time, declared his belief that the *terminus post quem* announced by Brett should refer 'only to the construction of the portico and not exactly to the laying of the mosaics, which might be a little later, not far from the date' of the Apamea mosaics in Syria. 'Despite the high artistic quality of the work', he emphasised 'its close approximation to the style of the latest Antioch mosaics'.[2] By 1947, accordingly, the furthest limits had been set to a period covering the various dates suggested for the execution of the monuments. Other studies and authorities subsequently extended the time to well over a century. But it cannot be stated even today that the problem has been solved. In fact, while Mango[3] placed the pavement in the age of Marcianus (451–457), Galassi,[4] with Schede and Schneider, judged the date proposed by Brett 'anything but securely . . . based', and thought it should be 'put back to the fourth century, perhaps to its second half'. Grabar[5] and Bianchi Bandinelli[6] indicated that they shared Brett's view of the chronology. Lazarev[7] attributed the work to the middle of the sixth century. Talbot Rice,[8] in his second report on the excavations, has recently intensified the dispute by stating his inclination to a dating between the middle and the end of the fifth century, without excluding the first half of the sixth.

As already noted in the case of the mosaics at Piazza Armerina, so also the ones at Constantinople, more than a hundred years later, have set the most eminent scholars at variance on the question of their dating. The uncertainty arose in both cases not only from the usual diversity of critical standards, but also partly from the disagreement which seems inevitable between conclusions

1 Brett (1947), p. 91.
2 Levi (1947), i, p. 581, n. 101.
3 Mango (1951), p. 182 ff.
4 Galassi (1953), p. 352.
5 Grabar (1953), p. 76.
6 Bianchi Bandinelli (1957), p. 5.
7 Victor Lazarev, in *Vizantiniski Vremenik*, VII (1953), p. 373.
8 Talbot Rice (1958), p. 148 and p. 160. *See also* Talbot Rice (1958, pp. 43–4; 1955, p. 165 ff.).

founded on archaeological considerations and those derived from idiomatic analysis, partly and above all from the relative scarcity of corresponding monuments at the same 'depth', with which the pavements of both Piazza Armerina and Constantinople can properly be compared. Again, particularly as regards the Constantinople mosaics, the few known specimens are insufficient in themselves to constitute a satisfactory history of the rise of Byzantine art, since the developments of painting in the fifth century are still too little understood, particularly those in New Rome, which had rapidly become a dominant centre of artistic production. In these circumstances dating based on historical and critical considerations, to the exclusion of mythology, or, if the term is preferred, of convenience, is no easy matter.

Indeed, with more reason than in the case of any other surviving monument, the problem of the mosaics of the Great Palace at Constantinople is today, even though partially, the problem of the origins of Byzantine art. The very fact that it occupies a few pages at the end of a study which has tried to follow the contradictory but not un-related developments of artistic idiom in the Mediterranean area, especially between the age of the Severi and that of Theodosius, indicates in my view that the Great Palace, together with the mosaics of Hagios Georgios at Salonika, represent one of the two culminating points of late Roman painting, that of the introduction of Byzantine court influence, as closely as the present state of surviving works and their study will allow. Incidentally, the mosaics of Hagios Georgios have been attributed to the second half of the fifth century; but Dyggve, Volbach, Torp and Lazarev,[9] with whom I am inclined to agree, put them back to the end of the fourth.

The other monument of fundamental importance in the elucidation of this problem is the rotunda at Salonika. Built by Galerius close to his Arch, it was turned into a palatine chapel by Theodosius, and later called Hagios Georgios. It is most probably at that period, the end of the fourth century when the task of architectural adapta-tion was carried out, that it was decorated with the won-derful mosaic of the cupola, showing an enormous 'Christ Triumphant Crowned by Four Angels', much of which is now lost, and with eight majestic pictures standing below the main scene. Each of these, measuring ten metres wide and nine high, contains two figures of saints with inscrip-tions recording the *dies festus* of the martyr against a background of complex and most elegant *scaenae frontes* which recall the architecture of the Pompeian 'fourth style' as well as that of the rock tombs of the Necropolis, which are hewn out of the mountain-side at Petra of the Nabataeans (3rd–4th centuries) and explain the composite origin of the style of the eighth-century mosaics in the

216, 215

9 Dyggve (1957); Volbach and Hirmer (1958), pp. 25 and 68–9; Torp (1955); Lazarev (1959); Torp (1963); Matthiae (1962).

Mosque of the Omayyads at Damascus, unquestionably the work of Byzantine *musivarii*.

These wonderful mosaic compositions, in glazed tesserae of extraordinarily refined hues on a gold background, show clearly their Hellenistico-Alexandrian derivation in the very conception of the areas presented to religious contemplation, an aesthetic concentration of Neoplatonic type immobilised in a chromatic experiment which seeks to abstract from the materials every trace of physical quality in order to attain to paradisal colour. Certain elements of the later Byzantine court taste are already anticipated by the meticulous decorative motifs of arabesque and allegorical birds, perched on cornice and pediment, which adorn the splendid architectural features in grey, blue and amaranth against a sparkling gold background. Again, the work accomplished on the design of the praying figures (Porphyrios, Onesiphoros, Damianos, Cosmas, Philippos, etc.) shows that the essential quality of the courtly and paradisal images had already been acquired which was to be found in S. Vitale and S. Apollinare Nuovo at Ravenna, together with a distant echo of the manner of the 'Patriarchs' and 'Saints' of S. Aquilino and S. Vittore in Ciel d'Oro at Milan.

30

31

215

The technique of 'negative relief' has here at last provided a chromatically variant flatness with much graphic content in the garments, a flatness repeated in studies of drapery with endlessly inventive, frigid virtuosity, which finds individuation only in the faces of the several persons, completely characteristic of late antiquity in the structure of their planes and the methods of conveying physiognomical detail, but almost depersonalised by the effort to impart metaphysical significance. The hair, the eyes and all the particulars of these countenances testify fully that they adhere to the taste of their own time, recalling the most revolutionary features of expressionist portraiture as well as that of the tetrarchic and post-Constantinian periods of the fourth century. Yet they are immersed in the mode of the so-called Theodosian renaissance through their thorough formative recovery of the traditional Hellenistic type, exemplified by contemporary portraits in the 'subtle style'. Nor is it to be supposed that this manner, which I shall call that of the PROTOBYZANTINE MASTER OF SALONIKA, is the only one exemplified at this period within the boundaries of the Empire. The 'Bust of a Haloed Divinity', for instance, framed in a decorative border of discs and rhombs, excavated at Carthage near the Piazza S. Monica and now in the local museum of antiquities, is dateable to the end of the fourth century. The mosaic idiom closely resembles that of Salonika, while the pagan subject proves that the style was valid for varying ideologies and had an immense vogue.[10]

10 Heland (1964), n. 3; Salomonson (1965), n. 38, p. 39, figs. 29–30.

The rotunda of Hagios Georgios preserves also, in the vaults of its large Theodosian niches, mosaic decoration of entirely different significance. It is distributed in octagons with gold backgrounds divided into numerous geometrically shaped compartments in which animals and fruits in bright chromatic relief are depicted with lively delicacy of expression. The Hellenistic relationship, here untouched by Neoplatonic influence, is imbued with realistic humour and love of nature, even of a nature already again in the grip of the typological rigidity of late antiquity, and thrown into relief by the gleaming gold behind. Another vein of Byzantine art, chiefly concerned with silks, other textiles and auxiliary decorations, was to arise from this current of taste.

At Constantinople, by way of contrast, the artists who worked on the wonderful pavement of the great peristyle have left a work as simple as any in conception, from which it is easy to conjecture – notwithstanding the loss of much of the decorated surfaces – the imposing, though not oppressive and even in many ways exhilarating, grandeur of the original effect. This decoration is not without precedents, themselves of considerable importance: from the Corridor of the 'Great Hunt' of the Villa at Piazza Armerina (still retaining environmental features, illusionist though they were, and a panoramic expanse of continuous background) to the 'Gladiatorial Combats' and those with beasts from Torre Nuova in the Casino Borghese. The peristyle pavement's recovery of form, assumed the no longer unfashionable elimination of space which had been so very strongly asserted in those *lithostrota*; but it took place in the undoubtedly stimulating atmosphere of a recovery of colour, shading and design, and adopted the new fashion of using such valuable materials as enamel,[11] with the result that it constitutes a *unicum* of problematic character. The problem can be stated in the following terms. What is the documentary value, with respect to its epoch and the still embryonic – but now more definable – Constantinopolitan-Byzantine cultural area, of a mosaic of such colossal dimensions, in which a great number of masters, certainly the best in the capital, showed a convergence of idiomatic inflections truly surprising within a convention of taste so traditional as even to approach the Attic, yet still mindful of, indeed subject to, spatial and temporal conceptions derived from the most significant developments of all late Roman art? It is obvious that wherever we can recognise exemplary quality in the Constantinople pavement – pictorial skill, indeed, at the highest level of a tendency at one time existent and certifiable as the product in oriental territory of the continuous development of Roman painting – we may say that a fundamental link has been found indicative

39–41, 218–21

Plan C

114

115, 116

11 Talbot Rice, (1959, p. 43) is at pains to stress the co-existence in this mosaic of naturalistic and classical elements with features already medieval, such as figures superimposed on a flat background, etc.

of the idiomatic course of development running between Rome and Byzantium, such as to dispose once and for all of the abstract antithesis contrasting the two artistic centres.

Within a decorative border of complex composition, dominated by extensive ornament in the form of most elaborate sprays of acanthus, interspersed with bunches of grapes and large flowers, and framing birds and vegetable masks, an expanse of some hundreds of metres in length and about seven wide is bounded by the four sides of the great porch. It presents one of the most majestic figurative collections ever bequeathed, at least partially intact, by the whole of classical antiquity. From the few hundreds of square metres of mosaic fragments recovered in the course of excavation, one basic element above all can be identified with absolute certainty: that relating to the three levels of idyllic or pastoral illustration (with some trace of mythological statement) and also of hunting scenes (with the symbolical meaning of other large depictions of *megalopsychia*, such as the Hunt Corridor at Piazza Armerina and the mosaic of Room B in the Yakto Complex at Antioch), which is typical of this impressive work.

It is impressive above all, in a general sense, by its sheer scale. The extreme variety of subjects and of stock themes to be found in the mosaic does not allow, at least in that part of the pavement which has survived, any sort of organic or stylistic distinction among its contents. There is no break in the continuous presentation of peasants engaged in the innumerable humble tasks of every day; of races in the circus; of Cupids playing with animals or with the infant Dionysus and Pan; of the hunting of wild beasts, and of furious fights between the creatures themselves, displayed with every sign of dramatic force and splendour. A whole universe of human and half-divine beings, of animals and plants, of rocks and of buildings, constitutes both the subject and the place where action and life are represented in this ceremonious rendering of the great stage of the world.

In fact it has no other environment but itself throughout all the dozens of its closely packed scenes, many of which differ entirely from those adjacent to them. The paradoxical effect, therefore, is that of a choir of individuals, of prose full of genuine lyricism. The figurative elements producing it, whether men, animals, plants or mere patches of earth, have a life of their own, not dependent on any other condition. They are not selected in illusionist fashion from the inexhaustible panorama of creation, nor subject to a fanciful intervention which might impose on them significant relations or allusions to anything else or shed any interpretive light upon them. They were evoked in each case by a different need for the expression of an unfettered and novel appearance on the scene, in which they themselves alone had the opportunity to manifest

eir presence on the ivory mantle of the background,
hereon the tesserae, arranged like fish-scales, composed
infinite procession of repetitive arabesques in the void.
These presences bear a certain resemblance to phantoms,
anks to the revolutionary perspectives of late Roman
t, which comes between them and their authentic
ellentistic models, freeing them from the close ties that
und them to the environmental scenery, in which the
eat art of Alexandria had flourished for centuries. The
iguage which those rules had imposed continued
evant, though objectively it was no longer a classical
om but a structure which had undergone profound
eration in the climate of late Roman times that had
esided at its conception. By its recovery, due to cultural
rientation, of some of the stylistic features of Hellenistic
ilisation, it had attained in effect a new synthesis of
des of expression, in taste related to Hellenism, but in
rphological structure entirely changed. The resultant
ms cannot be regarded as less than astonishing in their
raint and elegance, which have been correctly, at least
ome respects, described as neo-Attic.[12]

s this effect leaves out the homogeneous background
he ancient models by the severely abstract method of
neating individual forms against empty space, it con-
utes the result of the new spatial conception and may
ear at first sight the outcome of a deliberately polemical
nique. But this is not in fact the case.

he matter may be clarified by a careful analysis of line,
our and perspective in the separate figures, showing
remote Alexandrian civilisation had now become
how organic, finally, the connection between the
cture of the images and their situation in space. This
the only way, it might as well be mentioned at this
t, in which at a later date the repetitive arabesques of
t-like forms could be set against a background, a
hod splendidly exemplified in pavements at Antioch,
before it came to be adopted in Coptic and Byzantine
les.[13]

t us start from the north-east angle of the four-sided
ico, with the wonderful picture of 'Two Hunters
fronting a Tigress':[14] the over-all effect is one of
ic solemnity, though it depicts a tense movement of
k. The body of the animal is represented in very warm
s, harmonised and fused in a gradual lowering of
ituation; the muzzle in particular expresses, by its
ity of form, a highly realistic ferocity. In a comparison
the heads of beasts of Piazza Armerina, to take one
ng parallel, one cannot fail to notice how far the
dimensional flatness and atonality of the latter had
rgone a process of linear reorganisation, thus in-
ably restoring the natural physical volume. The
considerations apply, indeed, to the two hunters:

40

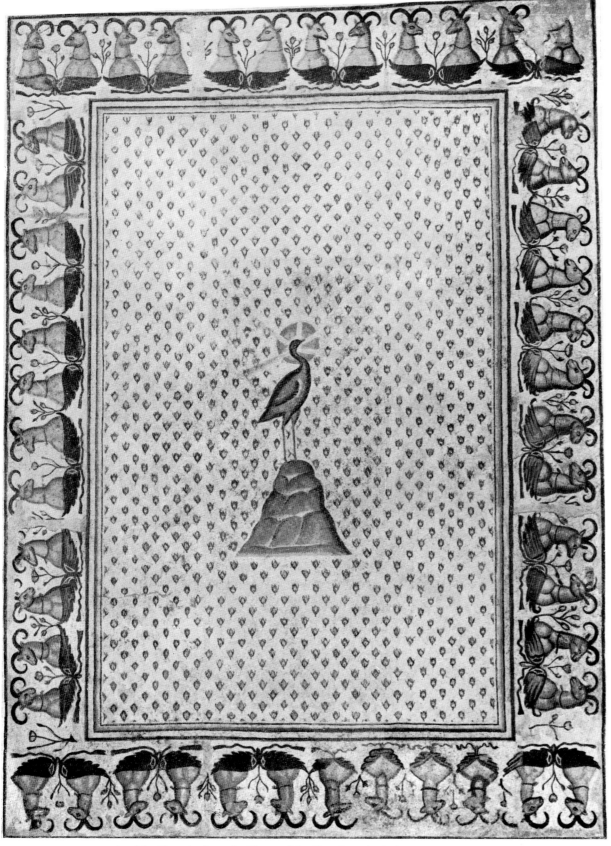

222 Paris, Louvre. Mosaic of the Phoenix, from the House of the Phoenix at Antioch

and in particular by the textiles of the Byzantine age. Many specimens of Coptic, Syrian and Constantinopolitan textiles surviving from antiquity in fact show their fidelity to the originals. It is easier in these copies to appreciate the adequacy with which the actual function of repetition to infinity of the figurative motives employed was carried out.

14 Brett (1947), pl. 37.

the varied torsions of their bodies and the diversity of superimposed planes in no way recall the paratactical, monotonous character of tetrarchic figures.

Similarly, in the extreme north-east corner, we have the group of 'Griffin and Prey',[15] in which the body of the monster is yellow and maroon, the head modelled in dark strokes, the beak grey and green; also the damaged 'Mounted Hunter',[16] where the brilliant colours of the clothing are skilfully associated. The Alexandrianism of these figures, which are clearly quite late, should not deceive the critic. He should be put on his guard, in particular, by certain idiomatic details in the capacity of the artists to achieve complex unitary and harmonious effects through the more extended, distributed and daring use of the chromatic *vermiculatum* line. It becomes, by union with the lines preceding and following it, something other than itself, as if the *tessellarius* had succeeded in distilling from an ancient compost of colour its simple, basic essentials and had materialised them in his stone cubes, trusting to their subsequent masterly arrangement for his customary result.

Look, for example, at the tree-trunk in the background.[17] It receives light and volume from an arrangement of strips of yellow, emerald green and light brown tesserae alternating along a considerable part of the trunk in the following order: first a row of monochrome tesserae, then one of two colours alternating, then another in monochrome and another in two colours as before, then two more in monochrome, the second being brown and constituting the shaded front of the trunk. At its base a different, still bolder structure is substituted, in the shape of a true chessboard pattern of yellow and brown tesserae. It is obvious that linked idiomatic formations of this kind were the outcome of the chromatic disunion and two-dimensional flattening typical of the crisis at the end of the third century. The resultant Hellenistic form cannot therefore deceive an observer who examines the pictorial line idiomatically.

A similar explanation will serve in the case of the 'Incomplete Fisherman', holding a fish he has just caught and with one foot in the transparent water of a stream. The figure appears in the upper part of the north-east corridor,[18] on the same level as the winged and horned griffin with a lizard in its talons. The organic laying on of colour, though in separate and alternate lines, along the dry part of the man's leg is found to result from the combined use of two bright chromatic tones to express the colour of flesh. But at the point where the foot enters the veiling element of water a system of alternating lines comes into play. This time they are horizontal, in white and blue, crossing the others in such a way as to produce a chequered pattern in four colours and achieving a surprisingly accurate im-

15 *Ibid.*, pl. 38.
16 *Ibid.*, pl. 39a.
17 *Ibid.*, pl. 37.
18 *Ibid.*, pl. 33.

Palace. Rural Labours

Palace. Boy and Old Man Milking Goats (detail)

pression of mobile, changeful realism. It might almost be said that the Constantinople master had anticipated the criterion of formative value employed in the modern process of selecting colours for printing; nay, more, that over the above the coldly mechanical four-colour process, he reserved to himself not only the wide range of technical resources apparent in these mosaics but also the fundamental right to extract from so stimulating a repertory the idiomatic micro-structure most adequate to the general poetic significance he intended as an artist to assign to each individual image.

A different hand may perhaps be perceived in the 'Group of Children' (one playing with a puppy and another stretching out its hands to a hare pursued by a pack of hounds), which covers some metres of ground in the eastern side of the portico, in the lower section of the decoration.[19] Here the design seems stiffer and more laborious, a more slavish imitation of the original cartoon. Nor is a complete exposition of form achieved by the colour: its tones appear indefinite, owing to the unstable effect of the tesserae, despite their linear structure, with different accents in multiple shades of red, pink and yellow. The same artist was apparently responsible for other similar groups:[20] the 'Rural Labours'; the 'Boy Driving Two Geese'; the 'Woman Suckling an Infant'; 'Pan Carrying the Child Dionysus on his Back',[21] which is notable for its expressive liveliness and careful attention to shadow; the 'Boy Feeding a Donkey', where the animal faces the spectator with curiously mocking effect;[22] and the 'Boy and Old Man Milking Goats' (in the central series), remarkable for its three-dimensional freedom, expressed with a tendency to compact definition of masses and a method involving concentric strips of tesserae, which sometimes alternate, as in the goats, and are sometimes more indefinite, as in the clothing of the boy and the old man, but always chromatically progressive.

An exception to the tessellar technique of colour hitherto described is constituted by the group of the 'Eagle Entwined by a Serpent' in mortal combat,[23] where the imaginative layers of yellow which range from sulphur to tawny achieve a singularly beautiful tonal rendering and juxtaposition of hues, not by the use of successive linear structures, but sometimes through a rich variety of tints of one colour in single tesserae, which in itself is capable of a gradation in which the tiny stone cube, equivalent to a minute and academically formless brushstroke, drops the idiomatic significance of the line operative as both form and colour, and retains only that of a dependent and auxiliary chromatic component. Stylistically this procedure undoubtedly represented a return to tradition, an old-fashioned gesture of self-conscious skill. No one would have supposed it an aid to poetic quality.

220

221

19 *Ibid.*, pl. 34.
20 *Ibid.*, pl. 32.
21 *Ibid.*, pl. 31.
22 *Ibid.*, pl 30.
23 *Ibid.*, pl. 36.

After the series of 'Large Horses Grazing' (in the upper level of the mosaic),[24] a convincing example of monumental though still academic vigour, another remarkable sequence claims our attention in the lower level. It shows a 'Circus Contest'[25] of the rival factions: four youths are competing in a race with two chariots driven parallel round a course barely indicated by the two markers at the ends, as well as by two great arches looming beyond them, typifying the architecture of the place. Between the right-hand marker and architectural wing stands one of the best representations of plant life[26] in the entire mosaic, which nevertheless offers a brilliant collection of neo-Hellenistic lyricism of this kind, resembling that of the *viridarium* in the dining-hall of the Villa of Livia at Prima Porta, and having in addition a scientific and botanical interest that anticipates the later production at Byzantium of illuminated manuscripts dealing with medicinal herbs. A most beautifully rendered 'Palm tree', with pendent fruit-bushes, perhaps rustic prizes for the winner, is shown in full flower, with rhythmically placed branches in yellow and ivory, pale green and grey emerging from the dark green background of foliage. Meticulous attention to refinement of idiom in detail is also evident in the alternate short lines of green and grey tesserae at the base of the trunk, in the careful use of pink and red in the faces of the competitors, and in the stripes of blue on the tunics of two of them, while the other two show that they belong to the green faction by exhibiting separate streaks of iridescent yellow, emerald-green and blue,[27] which lend even more lustre to the varied elegance of their garments.

The technique of chequered tessellate reappears on the trunk of another very fine tree in the zone of the last *in situ* fragment of pavement in the north-east side of the portico,[28] between the very lifelike images of a 'Goat at Pasture', its head turned towards the foliage, and a wrestling 'Hunter and Tigress'. Higher up, brightly coloured fruits are dotted against green and black leaves, which, in the complexity of their sinuous and mannered design, reveal the virtuosity of the artist.

Among the detached fragments, most of which were found during the 1951–1954 excavations of the south-west side of the portico, several pieces call for attention: the fine 'Guide leading a Camel Ridden by Children',[29] **41** where the man's face is alert with lively intelligence expressed with characteristically bold chromatic tonality; the background view of the 'Walls of a City' showing archways and elaborate fountains; the rather comic picture of a 'Mule Unseating its Rider'; and the ferocious 'Fight between Lion and Elephant'.[30] In this last the elephant has 218 wound its trunk round the lion's neck, causing a violent tension now almost stiffened in death. The feline's head is naturalistically delineated with harsh yellows, browns,

24 *Ibid.*, pl. 30.
25 *Ibid.*, pls. 29–30.
26 *Ibid.*, pl. 29.
27 *Ibid.*, pl. 69.
28 *Ibid.*, pl. 28.
29 Talbot Rice (1958), pl. 45.
30 Brett (1947), pl. 41.

reds, greys and greens. Its paws beat the air uselessly, while the coloured portions of the body, with their yellows and browns, faithfully reproduce its swelling muscularity, here not accentuated by line. Set against all that is the calm power expressed by the mighty form of the victorious beast, structurally rendered to perfection by broad areas of grey, green and yellow in every possible variety of tone.

Separate mention should certainly be made of the rocks, now thoroughly 'Byzantine', which form a vigorous set of punctuation marks between the images freely displayed in this mosaic. In most cases we can say of these rocks what we noted concerning those at Piazza Armerina. Wide layers of pure colour, here of more definite but also more opaque tint than at the Sicilian villa, with a definite predominance of greys, reds and greens, provide independent chromatic points of reference in the aesthetic arrangement of the pavement, as do also the human figures, the animals and the plants, all equally rich in expressiveness. It is not possible to determine what differentiates them from the fantastic rocks on the walls of the presbytery of S. Vitale, unless it be the fact that those at Ravenna do suggest an environment, no matter how fabulous and fanciful it may be, whereas there is no indication of any such thing in the white background at Constantinople. For it was actually there, at a stage of court art unquestionably anterior to that of Ravenna, that late-Roman abstract space, attested for centuries in the West, remained dominant, passing through the cosmic phase of blue before the eastern capital transmuted it to the gold of Areopagite theology.

Considering the undeniably close similarity of style among all the *tessellarii*, it may seem irrelevant in the present context to ask how many individual artists, each with his own method of expressing his ideas, may have worked on this pavement. Brett himself, who concludes his meticulous account by claiming to recognise in the pavement of the imperial portico the hands of at least nine masters (five on the north-east side, two on the north-west and two on the south-west), not counting the *tessellarii* who laid the decorative border, admits that 'the whole work was under the direction of a single person', though it is not clear how much control the supervisor might have been able to exercise over his subordinate executants.[31] In my own opinion there is no doubt whatever, in the first place, that at least three artists, each with a definite personality within the limits of the general manner of this single enterprise, took part in it. I should identify one in the north-east side of the portico, recognisable particularly through his idiomatic technique in the scenes of pastoral idyll and the chase; another in the fragments taken from the south-west side, especially in the scene of the 'Fight between Lion and Elephant', where a more vigorously formal taste is apparent, characterised by the originality of the three-dimensional chromaticism no less than by the skill in design; and a third in at least two of the 'Vegetable Masks of the Frieze' surrounding the whole floor. The tessellar work is here contrived to a very minute scale, Brett having counted no less than 437 tesserae per square decimetre, the maximum in the whole pavement.[32] These two masks are the most successful of the border in achievement of form with a baroque flavour, where an amazing variety of chromatic tones is triumphantly harmonised. Yet it seems necessary to recognise the unifying inspiration of talent on a high level, that of a PROTOBYZANTINE MASTER OF CONSTANTINOPLE, whose confident creative imprint is perceptible throughout the pavement.

A single master may therefore be postulated. Actually, he would be the leader of a school which, in common with that of the perhaps slightly older PROTOBYZANTINE MASTER OF SALONIKA, might be recognised in the present state of research as having 'fathered' certain fundamental stylistic structures of Byzantine painting.

A definition of such 'fatherhood' has already been suggested in the preceding pages, when studying the styles of various monuments of imperial painting. It is such a structural analysis, attempted here in mere outline because of the objective limits set by the plan of this present work, that submits to critical appraisal, as a matter of concrete history, the manner exemplified by the PROTOBYZANTINE MASTERS OF SALONIKA AND CONSTANTINOPLE, and thereby makes it possible to elucidate the basic features of the origins of Constantinopolitan art and to place them without breach of continuity within the vital process of imperial art as a whole. Consequently, a work such as the great mosaic pavement of Constantinople could not be anterior to the crisis of the third and fourth centuries, for the simple reason that that crisis came to a head in the spheres of taste, aesthetic principle and the transformation of spatial vision before doing so in that of stylistic structures.

All the late Roman artists mentioned in the preceding chapters show that the evolution of late Roman painting came to include the ancient stylistic structures of Hellenism after the general crisis of taste, culture and form of Hellenistic figurative civilisation within the climate of the transformation of imperial society. The *imaginarii* and *tessellarii* of the Great Palace and of *Hagios Georgios* attempted instead a rhetorical or metaphysical reconstruction of that general artistic spiritually expressive form, while clinging to the idiomatic conquests to which the crisis had led, although those conquests were certainly organised in such a way as to bring them to the forefront of cultural consciousness and were asserted on a very high

39

32 *Ibid.*, pl. 65.

level by artists of great gifts. Hence it becomes clear that the images presented by the mosaics of the majestic four-sided portico at Constantinople and of the Rotunda at Thessalonika are, as a phase of transition from the last innovations of late Roman painting of the fourth century, the most convincing archetypes, at least of all hitherto discovered, of Byzantine art.

Conclusion
Plotinus and Augustine, the late Roman masters of medieval art

Traditional historiography used to recognise in the domain of painting three great operative centres in the imperial age: Alexandria, Rome and Constantinople, in that order. It was inclined to locate within the civilisation of their workshops and of their economic and cultural environments – but especially those of Alexandria and Constantinople, in two distinct periods and admitting such later and contributory centres as Antioch and Ravenna – every creative skill brought to light by fresco and encaustic painting, by mosaics, by tablets and by such 'minor' forms of figurative art as glass, marble inlays, textiles and so on. The geography of style that supplied these ascriptions with content was equally well known and simple. It included the Hellenistic tradition centred upon the Nile; Romano-Campanian Hellenism, and its crude imitations in early Christian art, in the capital; Byzantine painting on the Bosphorus, with its later manifestations, partly under political inspiration, at Ravenna, in Africa and throughout the East; a sometimes ill-defined oriental tradition in the Syrian metropolis, which might even have influenced Constantinople and the early Christian painting of Rome in various ways; and lastly works of Alexandrian derivation almost everywhere in imperial territory.

It is necessary to realise that the discoveries and studies of the last thirty years have completely upset this pattern. The Villa of Piazza Armerina, the *corpus* of the Antiochene and Constantinopolitan pavements, the excavations at Dura Europos and Palmyra, the recovery of the majestic golden vaults at Salonika and of the Milanese mosaics, the evidence of the Trier Palace art, together with a number of fundamental studies, would themselves persuade most scholars[1] to accept (i) the different dimensions now allotted by history to the mythical category of the Syrian East; (ii) the critical recognition of the first Christian funerary painting as falling within the scope of contemporary painting in the capital; (iii) the more precise if still inadequate determination of the origins of Constantinople and of the original 'Romanism' of Ravenna; (iv) the settlement of the characteristics – fundamental for later developments – of a Constantinian court art at the extreme limits of the Empire; (v) the identification of constant and organic links between the expressionism of official and civil art in the third and fourth centuries and the expressionism of Christian funerary painting; and finally (vi) awareness of the existence of a *koine* of late antiquity

1 *See* especially in this connection Levi (1946–8; 1947); Wirth (1934); De Wit (1938); Galassi (1930; 1953); Bettini (1948; 1952); Grabar (1953); and lastly the three collections of Roman mosaics described by Marion Elizabeth Blake already mentioned. *See also* L'Orange (1933); L'Orange and von Gerken (1939); Strong (1923; 1926); Rumpf (1957).

throughout the Mediterranean area in the fourth century, leading to important modifications of the view that the great centres of production operated almost in mutual isolation, and to a tendency to see the situation as one of wide stylistic communication between the most civilised regions of the Empire, from North Africa to Italy, from the Rhine frontier to Constantinople and from Britain to the zones dominated by Antioch and Alexandria.

In the sphere of painting, with the rout of obstinate legends and preconceived notions, the progressive liberation of Roman production from Hellenistic scholasticism, its diffusion in provinces (from the Rhine-Danube frontier to Britain) never touched by Greek influence, the similar development (though more conditioned by the Eastern metropolis) of the provinces of Asia, and the crucial experiments of the great schools of mosaic in North Africa and their influence, are all movements that can now often be followed in detail almost from decade to decade, as the present study has tried to show particularly for the third and fourth centuries. Consequently, the practical dependence of Rome on the traditional oriental centres for its categories, models, materials and methods of production, still evident in the first imperial century, was already being counteracted in the second and had apparently almost vanished in the third. For instance, in a recent study of the celebrated Palestrina mosaic its attribution to the Christian era was denied on account of the proved employment of tesserae resembling those used in older productions of the Alexandrian workshops.[2] Accordingly, it now appears difficult, if not impossible, to believe that schools derived from that source were active in Rome under Hadrian or Marcus Aurelius.

The view, which no one dreamed of contesting until a few years ago, that Roman art, and painting in particular, was no more than a crude popular or provincial version of Hellenistic civilisation[3] hardly seems tenable in the light of the testimony advanced in the preceding pages. Moreover, scholars dealing with the imperial age have been busily refuting the older theory for some considerable time. The new argument treats the problem of Roman art as that of an organic succession to Hellenism, on the part of that artistic idiom which seems to have ripened progressively in all provincial production throughout the Mediterranean area. It was more free from the constricting doctrines of form which even in this territory might reasonably be called a 'second sophistic'. It was more keenly aware of the evolution of taste and the upheavals in every realm of the spirit. It was more capable of unifying, through the production of structures substantially homogeneous, areas of ancient, very high but no longer originative culture and other regions hitherto untouched by a securely based civilisation.

2 Gullini (1956), pp. 6 and 19.
3 In this vein the most recent Italian studies take the lead, though with noticeable differences of direction and level among the following authors. Rizzo (1929); Ferri (1931; 1933 a; 1933b); Pirro Marconi (1929); Bianchi Bandinelli (1952; 1953; 1956).

Such a succession does not involve sudden ruptures and worldwide subversions. It occurred, as its monuments prove, in the working out of new forms in certain sectors of artistic production, maturing only when – far from breaking the structural connection out of which they had grown – their ferments, actualised in standards of narration, methods of manufacture, ideas of representation and repertories of idiomatic solutions, were sympathetically received in other zones of production, discovering a market in centres formerly dominated by different traditions and imitated by artists and workshops already in a position to serve much larger areas of demand.

Historically, this sequel to the great Hellenistic tradition did not begin fully with the illusionist and impressionist specimens of the 'fourth style' of painting, of which striking examples have been found at Herculaneum, Stabia, Pompeii and Rome, however exceptional their renovating power of expression may appear. Nevertheless, in their romanticism or sophistication, psychological insight or homely character, they bore witness to the attempt to provide an idiom for the conveyance of new sensibilities. After entering upon the course illustrated by the great sculptural series executed under Trajan and Marcus Aurelius, these novel sentiments came to be expressed in 29, 49 that 'release from a rhythm and system of preconstituted proportions' and 'from the specific figurative characters inseparable from the predominance of plastico-linear movement congenial to that rhythm and system of proportions' in which Galassi has correctly observed 'the deep-seated conflict waged for more than half a millennium between the classical spirit of Greek origin and the native temper of the Romans'.[4] It appears reasonable, however, to take such ethnic categories as merely a general polarisation of elements very much more complex, and to allow for them in formulating any further sociological judgment of the methodologies of the first (Wickhoff–Riegl) and of the second (von Schlosser) generation of the School of Vienna.

The release described by Galassi cannot therefore be described as the stylistic caprice of a school of innovating artists, no matter how sincere and original their inspiration. It is rather the logical manifestation of a state of mind radically different from the Roman in-der-Welt-sein which, having attained a mature cultural level and effective control of its modes of expression, struggles repeatedly to break from the closed rationality of an inherited vision of Hellenic art through outlets similar to the different ratio vitae that inspires it. Those new idiomatic attempts and revolutionary movements, those strivings to break free and experiment with new idioms, as well as the calling in question of the form and content of ancient morality by thinkers from Seneca to Marcus Aurelius, unhinged the

4 Galassi (1953), p. 565.

classical *Kunstwollen*. And thus there matured during the critical third century the expressionist efflorescence, in which the forces disturbing and transforming imperial society made bold use of old materials in new systems of organisation till they were able to commission and obtain, with increasing zeal, the execution of works which, in both function and cultural activity even more than in the forms they produced, represented a moral requirement hitherto unknown in the ancient world.

It is hardly worth while to insist upon the point that the 'romanism' of this process is certainly not identical with racial characteristics, but with worldwide sociological perceptions. Within the limits of the Italian world, so largely assimilated to the civilisation of *Magna Graecia*, the part played by Rome developed from the start in an atmosphere that was generally speaking of anti-Hellenic outlook (perhaps because the Romans never intended to act aesthetically at all), which, owing to military expansion in the Mediterranean area and the advent of the Empire, was succeeded at first by an uncritical acceptance of Hellenistic production in its most obtrusive and ostentatious forms on the part of the ruling classes in the capital. From the time of Trajan, however, the Italian spiritual and cultural subsoil tended to reinforce and direct the wave of imported art, and to express itself first through peremptory demands which attacked and distorted the already weakened internal coherence of that production, and next by embarking upon independent treatment of form, only iconologically connected with late Hellenism, which was more and more requested and supported by the governing class, by now in a phase of rapid transformation. On the other hand, the 'romanism' in this domain also had long since reached frontiers of the Empire and struck root there with the settlement of political and military authorities, colonists, business men and soldiers. Consequently, it was inevitable that this second flood should be accompanied by a similar demand for 'new art' in all the provinces, though it is as well to recognise that that demand was supported (and often originated) locally. The movement, significantly enough, was more frequently resisted outside Italy than within the peninsula; but during the second half of the third century it strengthened the forms previously acquired and developed, adding many native elements which had been obstructed by Hellenistic civilisation in the peripheral areas of the Empire, and which often corresponded to certain Italian tendencies prior to the similar invasion consequent upon the Roman military campaigns of the second and first centuries BC.

The fourth century witnessed a proliferation of ideas unleashed throughout the Empire by a manifestation of expressionist art, which proved to be a means of communication far more 'popular' than any in the past.

U

During that period, and at least in that proliferation of ideas, it will therefore be possible to recognise in late Roman painting a degree of 'romanism'; for that painting expressed simultaneously the signs of a growing non-Hellenistic sociologico-cultural uniformity and collectivity, permitted by the new secular order, and also the signs of communal transmission, equally collective in character and increasingly typological and supernatural in reference, of the message of religious salvation. This extraordinary moment in history, as dialectical as any in its confrontation of political instrumentation and public consumption, can in fact be described as that of a single artistic language current for some decades all over the Empire. But it already contained the seeds of selective processes that were to last for several centuries, favoured by the divergent *iter* of the two *partes* of the imperial territory.

The main features of this process in the second century, after the preliminaries noted in the Stabian villas and the evidence of places such as Zlitan and Antioch, have been pointed out in two splendid monuments of imperial sculpture, the Columns of Trajan and Marcus Aurelius, as well as in that mosaic pavement from Palestrina, which, because it was too hastily excavated and consequently suffered centuries of deterioration and restoration, remains even today very difficult to interpret and hence of dubious representative value. In other words, the painting of this period is little understood and can only be assessed indirectly. The gap, in particular, between the great picture gallery provided by the region around Vesuvius and the frescoes and mosaics of the Dar Buc Amméra Villa on the one hand, and the surviving monuments of the age of Hadrian on the other, cannot therefore be bridged at Rome except by indirect conjecture, while the examples referred to at Antioch (House of the Calendar) and in North Africa (Lambaesis), though often marked by tendencies analogous to those found in Campania, testify only to slower development. Yet in the second half of the century, despite the intervening Hadrianic phase, it is already possible to collect sufficient evidence of the first results of the movement forecast earlier. First and foremost a new sensitivity to space, which is now created less by environment (Palestrina) than by the figures occupying it (House on the Caelian; Tivoli mosaics), in dynamic rather than calculable co-ordination of their relations, sets forth in original terms the situation and historical actions of man in nature or his contact with divinity.

In the new approach to figuration the cosmos is no longer an order given *a priori*, to be experienced in purely naturalistic fashion as if it were a stage-play without ulterior reference. It is a changeable scene, subject to transformation, in a perpetual state of becoming, not in

I, 18–20
25–8, 30,
29, 49
34

I–3, 11–2
25–8

30, 32

34
4, 35

itself measurable, influenced by its living creatures, tested by the tireless experiments of mankind and given meaning by the mysterious presence of the gods. That life, that experimentation, that presence are the creative element of space, its descriptibility, more particularly when, owing to the metamorphosis of decorative partitioning – in a way still illusionist, imitative and modelled on the scientific study of perspective – it becomes possible as it were to put space between brackets by means of temporal segmentation of the narrative which is reduced to the actions or gestures of the figures evoked, against a background originally based on nothing but the untranslatable ambiguity of the atmosphere (Stabian paintings), of water (Antiochene pavement) or of light (sepulchre of Caivano), till the solution is reached of an abstract, neutral, white ground. Consequently, ornamental divisions ended by expressing successive periods through an ever more complex elaboration of their disunion, full of implications of symbol and number, rhetorical figures of speech and allusions to rank (Genazzano fragment; Dionysiac pavements at Cologne, Lambaesis and Oudna).

14
30

36
38, 39

During the second century various currents of taste can be discerned in this metamorphosis of space, which implies not only the temporal qualification of the scenes depicted, but also, at a deeper level, the transformation of relations between the work and the spectator; in other words, a new artistic ideology linked with the sociological and psychological changes undergone by the population of the Empire. Instances have survived, often incompletely developed, of impressionist virtuosity and neo-Attic elegance of form, of naturalistic sketchiness and extremely vivid psychological realism, of baroque colouring and dramatic linearism, of miraculously effective expressionism and rhythmic figurative constructivism. If I am not mistaken, this efflorescence of idioms, in which the lines intersect without apparent direct causal determination by schools and centres of output, well represents the cosmopolitan movement of the mid-imperial age, its unpredictable cultural interests, its susceptibility to influences, demands and suggestions from every geographical and moral quarter, and the vigorous interchange of tastes and information which lay at the root of the rising growth of syncretism not only in religion but also in secular affairs and custom.

When we reach the twin peaks of imperial painting, under Commodus and Septimius Severus, and can study it more systematically on the threshold of the third century, the process of liberation from rationalist space, and of its subordination to the periods covered by the figurative event through geometrical and rhythmical transposition of its structures, turns out to have widened its area of inspiration throughout the Empire. It is no longer only

Italian monuments and those belonging to Africa Proconsularis, Numidia and Mauretania (among examples farthest from Alexandria), but also more numerous items in the artistic production of the provinces, and even of the ultra-traditionalist region of Antioch, that are found to have resulted from the same impulses. The masterly mosaic of rural life at Cherchel no less than the more modest records of Dionysiac enthusiasm at Susa, El Djem and Saint-Leu, as well as the splendid and still Dionysiac assemblages of architectural structures and polyptych *emblemata* at Cologne and at Seleucia in Syria, all bear witness, though in different idiomatic forms, to various phases of development of the same temporal problem of space as exemplified in Rome by the house in Via dei Dipinti, by the tombs of the Ostian Necropolis, by the frescoes and mosaics of the shrine of 'Silvanus' and by the 'Waiters' of the House in the Via dei Cerchi.

50

50, 53

38, 39
56, 57

46, 47

45

48

From the age of the Severi, however, to that of the Tetrarchy, the art of painting, like all expressions of spiritual and cultural life, not only showed the normal acceptance of the stage of elaboration prepared in the preceding epoch for the general treatment of surfaces in art, but also consolidated, in accordance with historical affirmations more evident in the field of philosophy and theology and preserved mainly in ritual and funerary literature, the stylistic experiments that had passed through the filter of taste to survive in a permanent condition of evolution and confrontation.

That turbulent and dramatic age preserved for us a proportionally greater number of records from public than from private sources; for if we expect the discoveries of successful archaeological expeditions to North Africa and Antioch, it provides insufficient evidence of wall painting and mosaic paving in dwelling houses elsewhere in the Empire. However, what we do know in this field suffices to justify the conclusion that there prevailed throughout the century a liking for the traditional stories of classical myth, with a preference for marine and Dionysiac themes. There was also a steady diffusion of agonistic, hunting and farming scenes, while more and more attention was paid to the cult of persons eminent in the thought and literature of both Greece and Rome. All those facts illustrate the gradual replacement of mythological by figurative symbolism (allegories and personifications of the virtues, narrative transfigurations such as *megalopsychia*, and so on). That range of subjects and that conception tended to take shape in virtuosity which was nevertheless closely in line with the general stylistic development. Its products were highly effective, richly expressive, solemn in the complexity of their framing, far-sighted and imaginative in their ideas, analogous to the trend of contemporary rhetoric.

When used in public works of a sacred character, painting reveals a severe and rigorous demonstration of expressionist grammar and vocabulary, with a manifest concern for didactic statement and functionalism of content. It cannot be too often repeated that the third century was a dramatic age in every sense of the word, an age in which metaphysical anxieties and the question of salvation were inextricably bound up with the problems of military defence, preservation of the constitution, the economic context and social levelling. It is not surprising that in the places intended for any form of religion – temples, synagogues and *mithraea*, *domus ecclesiae*, mausoleums and underground cemeteries, whether Gnostic, Christian or belonging to some other sect – a substantial community of emphasis indicated the similarity, if not of the doctrines of redemption, though such was often the case, at any rate of the inward attitudes of the congregation, their ways of asking and giving religious consolation and hope beyond the grave, which at that time lay at the base of the great theological dispute and of the rivalry between mystery cults.

In these circumstances chronological research, argument about priorities, discussion of native and imported influences or the directing functions of the various centres of production, seem to be reduced *a priori* to valuable auxiliary analysis and indispensable philological verification, which cannot however be relied on to offer responsible interpretation and ascriptions admitting no appeal. The bipolar distinction between Rome and the East, however prevalent in the realm of philosophic and religious concerns during the third century, appears to allow in the artistic domain, and especially in that of painting, a detailed study in which the same signs (often with illuminating, though not essential, coincidence in time) most often connote independent developments analogous in style, and exactly similar, though autonomous, solutions of the problems of form. The relations and comparisons established between the Roman hypogea and the sacred buildings at Dura and Palmyra, and between composition and portraiture in the capital, and Egypto-Alexandrian funerary production, have been scarcely mentioned in the foregoing pages. (Note that the mention of composition and portraiture in Rome refers to the years of Severan art, which were also important from the technological standpoint.) But those relations and comparisons do show that it is possible to identify the 'problem of the East' with the 'problem of Roman art' in the sense of recognising in the two spheres restrictedly diversified forms of idiomatic growth outside the classical order. At Dura Europos especially this process had been going on for a long time. Some examples of it are even outstanding, such as that of the Temple of the Palmyrene gods, where, 58, 59 in the paintings of the MASTER OF CONON and ILASAMSOS alone, it is impossible to deny this cultural implication and also, in the case of the former artist, a high level of expressiveness. The existence of such spontaneous analogies and natural reciprocity of influences proves the rise of a manner certainly unfamiliar in the area of Hellenistic civilisation but also rooted in a local *humus* that extended not only beyond the rivers of Mesopotamia, but more particularly in the *habitat* of form that reached the banks of the Nile and produced, by way of the Egypto-Alexandrian cultivation of portraiture, the extraordinary funerary tablets of deceased persons found at Antinoë and Fayyum. It is not suggested that these considerations completely solve the problem; but they do underline the significance of a by no means uncultivated provincial mentality, perhaps isolated from the artistic flood promoted by Alexandria and Antioch, but alert and active right up to the revelation of the third century and beyond, in the great Syrian and Coptic chapters of Christian art. Consequently, all that need be done is to reconstruct its history with due patience, in the expectation of surprising discoveries, at a time when the Roman panorama had already unrolled with conspicuous effect in such important hypogean records as the Mausoleum of the Aurelii, the Caves under St. Peter's, the Mausoleum of Clodius Hermes and various catacombs.

68, 77, 78

71–75
79
81, 82, 83,
6, 84, 92

In Rome the process in question matured through the practice of a Hellenistic discipline of form which came to concentrate more and more upon expressive quality, sharpened by recurrent linear tension, rendered surrealist by a heated and zealous use of colour and distorted by idiomatic experiments of cubist and geometrical tendencies, as demonstrated by works found in both public and private cemeteries, whether Christian or not. It was at this juncture that the tetrarchic restoration was already laying the political foundations of the new state. The almost complete absence of adequate records of secular public painting in the second half of the third century might appear a serious drawback to research. But scattered evidence throughout the Empire, such as the mosaic fragments from the Baths at Aquileia, the Leptis Magna frescoes, the Gerona and Barcelona circus mosaics, the colossal figures of 'Athletes' from the Roman Baths of Caracalla, the pavement of the central hall of the Baths of the Seven Sages at Ostia, certain works of uncertain provenance found in Gaul and the almost obliterated frescoes at the Temple of the Imperial cult at Luxor, indicates a more restrained development, closer to the official convention of taste and lacking the private figurative implications which were not required for the formal, playful elegance of artistic work in public buildings. Nevertheless, an examination confined to the idiomatic

III

field can only acquiesce in the dates of execution suggested by archaeological considerations and find that all the specimens mentioned take certain new directions, abandoning the forms now grown obsolete and assuming the more contemporary figurative consciousness.

At the beginning of the Tetrarchy, owing to secular events which one can only regret are not better documented, late Roman painting discarded all dialectic unrelated to artistic theory and all institutional conflicts engendered by the meeting of extremely diverse historical, philosophic, religious and social phenomena, such as had fermented in the crucible of the third century. More or less active resistance to the elaboration and diffusion of the new taste could be discerned, as well as more or less timely postponements and tendencies mainly either courtly or popular. But substantially the age of the Tetrarchs derived from the extraordinary vicissitudes of the dying century, as displayed in the radical crisis of ancient society, a single artistic mode of expression. The age of Constantine and Theodosius witnessed the development, not without hesitation and opposition, of a fully hallowed monarchy supported by the now temporal ambition of the Christian community; and it received from that of the Tetrarchy what might have been called a 'renascence', were it possible to speak of a 'decline' with reference to the preceding age. In excluding such terms, it must be recognised, in the domain of art and elsewhere, that the fourth century reached a high level of formal civilisation in which the political structure effectively shared as an element underlying the diffusion of a uniform idiom, not such as to stifle local achievements in the ancient tradition, but still capable of asserting to the very frontiers of the Empire the unity of a pictorial art of novel conceptions and elevating significance.

This specific activity of the fourth century in the artistic field was not paralleled in those of language and literature. The whole of the *pars occidentalis* having been released from the obligation to know Greek, two linguistic and cultural areas came into existence, where persons speaking both languages were by this time confined to a very few of the upper ranks of society and were less and less often to be found as time went on. But in architecture, for instance, the unity of constructive experiment led from the Pantheon to the Rotunda of Salonika, S. Costanza and St. Gereon at Cologne, continuing thence to S. Lorenzo at Milan, S. Vitale at Ravenna and to S. Sophia and SS. Sergius and Bacchus in Constantinople.[5] In sculpture the line of development from Trajan's Column to that of Marcus Aurelius and the Arch of Severus at Leptis continued to the Arch of Galerius at Salonika, the Constantinian friezes of the Arch of Constantine and the base of ·the Theodosian Obelisk at

29, 49

52

5 *See* in particular Bettini (1946). It was only the post-war works of reconstruction that permitted full identification of the Cologne building, called in antiquity *ad sanctos aureos*, as a rotunda with twelve apsidioles and an atrium, dating from the second half of the fourth century. *See* von Gerkan (1951).

Constantinople, from the Constantinian porphyry sarcophagi to the Sarcophagus of Junius Bassus, from the   167
Milanese Sarcophagus at S. Ambrogio to the ivory Casket
at Brescia.

In painting, a series of majestic monuments and modest
fragments, found in that great area of civilisation where
by this time a single artistic idiom prevailed apart from
certain details arising from the submerged native culture,
covered the movements, personalities and tendencies of a
whole epoch without leaving problematical gaps of any
appreciable size to be investigated by historians. It was the
first time this had been the case throughout antiquity,
except during the height of the classical age at Athens.
Generally speaking, the dates of these works have been
ascertained with a fair degree of certainty, either on
archaeological evidence or on that of critical analysis.
Accordingly it has proved possible to reconstruct their
chronology for almost the whole century, as a rule within
decades and sometimes even shorter periods. Similarly, a
remarkably close understanding of the idioms of the
various zones of production has been acquired. It is
therefore reasonable to attach to the resultant panorama
of art a character which, without being comprehensive, is
at any rate largely adequate for assessment and, unless
other monuments and other relations have in future to be
taken into consideration, exhaustive in regard to the extent
and quality of this development of late Roman painting.

Its structure can now be outlined as follows. It began
with the assertion of two expressions of renewal, distinct
in their specific definition of the figurative values arti-
culating their common source of expressionist significance.
Examples are (i) the manner authoritatively implied by
'Dionysas' in the Cemetery of Callistus, and (ii) the much   **22**
less individualised style well known from the 'Agape' in   91, 92
the Cemetery of Peter and Marcellinus, the chapels in the
Cemetery of the Jordani, and the 'Praying Women' in the   85, 87–90
Cemetery of Domitilla. Development continued at the
end of the third century and during the first decade of the
fourth with monumental accomplishment in 'tetrarchic'
art, both painting and sculpture. This stage evolved into
the dialectical re-establishment of a spiritual demand for
clear expressionist individuation, with a constantly changing vocabulary that oscillates between creative revelation
of the value of line and planes functioning cubistically and
the original employment of new chromatic meanings
drawn from the surface of the tonal veil, as in the Hunt
Corridor at Piazza Armerina and the Theodorean pave-   **7, 9**, 98, 99,
ments at Aquileia.   101–3; **15**,
This 'tetrarchic' painting survived in a few cases for   **16**, 137–41
some decades subsequent to the end of the system of
government after which it is called. It affirmed at the same
time both the aesthetico-political doctrine of lordship and

the drama of the Christian state of mind during the final decades of its persecution. Some of the resultant work was in a sense reactionary; but there was no break in continuity, since it was all full of the new spirit and technique. The accession of Constantine, and the atmosphere of religious and secular hopes which it initiated, permitted and in fact imposed an art devoted to restoration, the 'fine style', sometimes rich in majestically expressive sentiment and flourishing for more than thirty years, not only in the rarefied and politically preoccupied climate of the court, but also, significantly enough, in that of popular funerary and religious painting. *See* the pavement of the 'Seasons' in the Constantinian Villa at Antioch and that of the 'Carnage' in the Villa at Piazza Armerina; the ceiling of the Palace of Helena at Trier; Roman wall paintings, including the 'Togatus' in the Cemetery of Domitilla, the 'Virgin and Child' in the *Coemeterium Majus*, the 'Praying Women' in the Cemetery of Domitilla, the 'Artemis as Huntress' in the hypogeum on the Via Livenza; and the mosaics of the annular vault of the Mausoleum of Constantina. This evidence attests the full fusion less of two stylistic levels than of all painting, whatever its application and derivation, with the aesthetic theory in force from the beginning of the Tetrarchy and with the new imperial society that emerged, in profoundly changed economic and institutional circumstances, from the crisis of the third century.

From the Constantinian 'fine style' of painting, which abounded in revived Hellenistic inflections that permeated its courtly statements, and also in expressionist characterisation of its religious and secular works, there emerged towards the middle of the century a new phase. This was partly a tired repetition of forms recognised as in decay from the age of Julian's final classical outburst down to that of the so-called Valentinianist mannerism, and partly the miraculous rise of great liturgical painting, which often dared to include frankly 'popular' elements and some accents foreshadowing those characteristic of art during the barbarian invasions, together with the flowering of a new two-dimensional and strongly linear constructivism. Hence, beginning with some diversion of the courtly style in New Rome on the Bosphorus, and in the Italian context with an already essentially rhythmical quality, there arose long before the end of the century a few scattered examples of the mode later to be named Byzantine. Such are the lunettes of the Mausoleum of Constantina, the Tomb at Silistra, the new Catacomb on the Via Latina at Rome, the 'Mosaic of the Dioscuri' at Trier, the 'Animal Heads' and 'Girls at Exercise' at Piazza Armerina, the Carthaginian pavements of the 'Hunt Chronicle' and of 'Dominus Julius', the Ostian mosaics of nereids and 'Seasons', pre-Coptic Alexandrian textiles.

19, 20, 147, 148, 156
10, 11, 93, 108–10
157–9
160
21
23, 162
163
24, 166

25, 26 181–4
168–177
32, 189–94
128–30
14, 131
144–6
34–36, 197
37, 38
155, 201–3, 207

The peculiar course taken during the fourth century by fresco painting and mosaic expresses by its very nature an implication of unity in structural development. It can be regarded as the basis of a broader study of epochal transformation, of which the historian is always conscious, especially when, as in this case, the succession of cultures remains the most organically connective and expository phenomenon of the transition between two ages.

The present account of late Roman painting, ending in the first decades of the fifth century, is certainly not intended to suggest a new break between the *Spätantike* and the Middle Ages. The expression *Spätantike*, coined fairly recently to indicate a historiographical division of time, has also been used to bridge the too obvious gap, formerly allowed to exist, between antiquity and medieval times. To attempt the definition of another transitional phase between Late Antiquity and the Middle Ages would be an artificial and inconclusive undertaking, at any rate in the present state of research. It would be impossible, on the other hand, to prove any clear break to have occurred between those eras, even in any particular domain of art. Accordingly, to end a study in the age of Arcadius and Honorius, with the advent of the institutional-political as well as cultural division of the Empire, though bearing in mind the character of the artistic production that immediately followed, would not be to contradict the aim with which these pages have been written, that of delimiting the 'facts' and of seeking in them, with cautious criticism but also with thoroughness, what they can tell us.

As the fifth century advanced, though there were naturally exceptions – the latest of which have been called by Brandi 'resistances', 'revivals', 'returns' and 'fugitive but obstinate re-animations'[6] – the painting of late antiquity had already changed its character. After the chapels of S. Aquilino and S. Vittore at Milan, the authentic archetypal forms of the twofold Christian Middle Ages (though often closely linked with fourth-century painting) were represented, for example, by the Chapel of S. Maria in Stelle at Verona; by the classical and Christian manuscripts at Rome and Berlin; by the *naos* of S. Maria Maggiore, not to mention the Arch of Sixtus III; by the apses of S. Pudenziana, of S. Agnes and of SS. Cosmas and Damian; by the vaults of Galla Placidia at Ravenna, or, in a different category, by the interior of the dome of Hagios Georgios at Salonika; by the great crypto-porticus of the imperial palace at Constantinople; by the pavements of the Yakto Complex and of the Hunt at the Worcester House in Antioch; by the Hunters Pavement at Apamea; by the *martyrion* at Seleucia; by the textiles of Antinoë; and by the 'Mosaic of the Phoenix' at Antioch. Those works can undoubtedly be described as the last relics of ancient figurative culture. Yet, in the West as in the East,

27–31

33, 211–4
208, 209
210

215, 216
39–41,
218–21

96
201, 207
222

6 Brandi (1956), p. 210.

they were not waves that died upon a distant shore, but actually constituted the models for an artistic regeneration which, though destined to suppression for some time in certain territories under barbarian rule, ultimately recovered and retained its strength for a whole millennium throughout the Christian world.

The present study has kept in mind the cultural and social substructure of the age, tracing on strictly idiomatic grounds the inspiration or the aesthetic justification of the most significant records of late Roman painting. Within the general pattern outlined above, its results may very profitably be compared with certain aspects of contemporary development in the written and spoken language and of literary phraseology, which often closely paralleled that of the artistic sphere by moulding the Ciceronian idiom of the Golden Age to the physiognomy of the last imperial period, which in some respects foreshadowed neo-Latin vernaculars.

In fact, even in the sphere of language the profound changes which had occurred during the course of three centuries can be accounted for historically, not only by the tendencies which were already controlling the development of Latin in the central imperial period, but also by the introduction of new structural conventions to deal with contents originally unfamiliar in the culture and psychology expressive of the Roman spirit.

The ancient Roman dialect, little spoken in Italy even during the first century BC, was obliged, almost without warning, to undertake worldwide tasks connected with the political unification of the Mediterranean area. Complete supersession of the innumerable local dialects can only be discussed in terms of a slow process of cultural assimilation of the nations conquered in a military sense and not, as in the *pars orientalis*, already subject to the predominance of Greek. But it is certain that the availability of Latin for this purpose had been utilised, as soon as conquest began, by the policy of colonial settlement, by the need for defence, and by the consequent widening of the structure of commerce and social relations. Such factors in the imposition of a common language were also necessarily the means of bringing to the capital, by successive stages of expansion at the periphery, separate elements of all kinds, which affected vocabulary, morphology and pronunciation. Consequently, by the later years of the central imperial period, evolutionary elements of the now universal language were established, together with the impulses towards stable development natural in any active enterprise, an adequately unifying principle in all the provinces. But in the second half of the third century, above all under the reforming Tetrarchy, Rome and the rest of the peninsula remained in practice at the margins of the great currents of communication, as Trier,

Milan, Sirmium and Nicomedia took over the functions of capital cities. Instead of the original administrative and territorial plan with a single centre covering the whole Empire with a radiating system of roads converging on Rome, a new polycentric arrangement of political, military, economic, cultural and religious communications was established, founded on a network of arteries tangential to the Rhine-Danube *limes* and linking the provinces of the far north with those in the east. The civil organisation gradually conformed with this overriding necessity, vain though it was, of defensive strategy. Inevitably, therefore, a new phase began, leading from the Latin of the central and late imperial periods to the various neo-Latin tongues of Romània[7] by way of a pre-vernacular stage having different characteristics in the various provinces of the *pars occidentalis*, which had reached varying levels of development in accordance with influences that were native, imported or imposed from without. In the *pars orientalis*, on the other hand, owing to more successful military action, the continuity of the Roman (Byzantine) State and the ability of the capital to function centripetally, Greek took for some centuries a different road of evolution.

In the first, substantially uniform and more organic phase of this transformation, written Latin, by codifying the phrases most freely exchanged in oral communication, began by using such forms, constructions, words and pronounciations as seemed most effective, lively and emphatic. In morphology a tendency to periphrastic qualification appeared:[8] compound prepositional forms (e.g. *de ab ante*), verbal periphrases (e.g. *habeo dictum* or *erat amatus*), prepositional additions indicative of cases (e.g. *in de ad*), adverbs for comparatives (e.g. *magis*), alteration of pronouns, etc. Phonetically, quantity was replaced by a generalisation of the stress accent, expressive of the tendency to abandon even in literary usage the forms governed by such rhythm, always less noticeable in the spoken language than its values in musical tempo. As regards vocabulary, inevitable functional innovation resulted from the many cultures put into mutual communication through the single linguistic instrument officially operative within the State. But it was above all in phonetics and morphology that acquisitions and transformations were found to be decisive in the structural development of the language.

Their permanent significance was in fact that of a progressive disjunction of rational links, of a relaxation of the admirable but settled and intractable architecture of Latin grammar, syntax and pronounciation, which were no longer adequate for the semantic expression needed. The meaning of the traditional form began to seem no longer satisfactory when confronted with more intense expressive

7 Devoto (1953), p. 13 ff.
8 Devoto (1944), p. 265 ff.

demands with which it was intended to emphasise, articulate, colour and dramatise the structure. It was therefore considered advantageous to disconnect and juxtapose grammatical, syntactical and phonetic elements to be used for clarifying the components (in a spatial or temporal sense) of the thought, action or sound presented. The new linguistic form thus differed from the old through the practice of disjunction or structural articulation in such a way as to secure also a semantic modulation leading to more direct participation by both speaker and listener in a conceptual world caught in the act of its generative process, in its no longer secret internal union.

Such is the general view of all the structural changes undergone by Latin in the central and late imperial periods. They include (i) the signification and augmentation of the required period of time (e.g. by using the auxiliary verb *habere*) by cutting into two moments the action formerly expressed within the narrow limits of a single word; (ii) the looser connection with other parts of the sentence which is achieved by attaching a preposition to cases, which thus lose their endings, abandon all traces of their self-contained classical individuality and are obliged to commit themselves to a less compact verbal structure; (iii) the expressive accentuation obtainable by the addition to an adjective of an element (e.g. *magis* or *plus*) which heightens its meaning; (iv) the setting out on one level of the phrases of a sentence, which are freed so far as possible from hypotactical subordination to cause and time and unconstrained by the co-ordination of parataxis, so as to allow negation of the 'plasticity' of speech by attempting to give it 'chromatic' elaboration developed in only two dimensions; and finally (v) the tendency to alliteration, assonance and rhyme, which indicate in verse the progressive loss of the sense of syllabic quantity and the consequent replacement of the musical by the dynamic or exhaling accent, just as the vocalisation of vernacular Latin was indicated in the single word. This phenomenon amounted to the replacement of musical proportion in the words of a speech with the rhythmic accentuation apparently of the same nature as late-Roman artistic vision.

This happened not only in prose but also in verse composition. When the fourth-century African poet Commodianus, one of the last Roman men of letters, composed his hexameters in a rhythm founded upon accentuation of the words, and certainly not through ignorance of syllabic quantity, he expressed the final outcome of a movement that had actually lasted for centuries, showing what was by then the taste and almost certainly the kind of metrical ear possessed by the contemporary public. That accentual rhythm, moreover, is thus proved to have been already studied and defined by the grammarians. In the middle of the fourth century Marius Victorinus cast a vivid light upon its character in relation to classical metre.[9] But a century later Sergius acknowledged the difficulty of recognising syllabic quantity, since it was no longer automatically discerned, but had to be empirically determined.[10]

This general situation of self-conscious strain was especially reflected in the use made of language by the Christians from the second century onwards. Obviously, one cannot speak of the Church as making any conscious effort to transform the language, but only of the young Christian communities as responding more and more frequently, psychologically and with the means at their disposal, to an existing tendency due to the spiritual conditions and social structures of imperial society coalescing everywhere under the same inspiration. Later the Church herself preserved the instrument of ecclesiastical Latin for her own use, notwithstanding the continuous changes in cultural, social and ethnic circumstances in the kingdoms born from the dissolution of the Empire, an event which of itself rendered inevitable the death of its language. But until that time, from the second to the fifth century, a single tongue gradually came to serve the political society and, somewhat later, the religious community. That language was the Latin in process of transformation into vernacular, the only possible form of Latin.

The recognition of Latin as a liturgical language, which demanded a large measure of technical adaptation and semantic inflection, was delayed at Rome until the third century, Greek having been predominant until then. But contact between the Church and the language must by then have been customary for some time. Tertullian, for instance, normally used a Latin largely novel in its vocabulary, grammar and frequently paratactical structure of the sentence-construction.[11] Again, the *Vetus Latina* version of the Bible, attributable to the second century by virtue of its quotations from ancient authors, was already offering stable and organic solutions of the problem of expressing in Latin Christian technicalities mainly derived from Hebrew and Greek. Above all, the studies of Schrijnen and his school[12] have enabled us to distinguish various traditions in the formation of an initial stock of verbal technicalities for the new religion, such as Latin terms corresponding semantically with the original Hebrew, Latin versions of Greek expressions with the correct technical meaning, and imported Greek or Hebrew words taken over directly. Later, as Auerbach[13] has pointed out, semantic mutations of existent Latin vulgarisms, which 'passed into another sphere and acquired a new dignity', especially forms developed from Latin roots and attached to a context of new doctrinal meanings,

9 'Rhythmus quid estè Verborum modulata compositio non metrica ratione, sed numerosa scansione ad judicium aurium examinata, ut puta veluti sunt cantica poetarum vulgarium'. Keil (1856–79), vol. vi, p. 206.
10 'Syllaba natura longas difficule est scire. Sed hanc ambiguitatem sola probant auctoritatis exempla, cum versus poetae scandere coeperis', Keil (1856–79), vol. iv, p. 522.
11 Hoppe (1903), *passim.*
12 Schrijnen (1932); Mohrmann (1948; 1955; 1956); Blaise (1955).
13 Auerbach (1960), p. 60.

permitted, after the first stage of contact (useful especially for accurate translation of texts), the production of a Christian Latin language for the masses of the people and another suitable for propaganda among the educated classes. In both cases the new words which use rendered familiar to the faithful by emotional participation, and eventually their employment in apologetics, which took advantage more and more of the artifices tolerated in rhetoric, helped towards the codification of a vocabulary, a morphology and a style which, despite their adoption of barbarisms and vulgarisms, of syntactical innovations and of highly individual touches in the rhetorical and exalted transfiguration of the humility of the Christian content, ended by identifying itself in form with the written and spoken Latin of the fourth and fifth centuries. A perfect example of this language, adapted to the needs of a new, more energetic kind of oratory, was provided by Augustine.[14]

Early-Christian Latin was sometimes adopted as the form of a particular culture, which gradually entered into the texture of Roman life like others existent in the Empire but was destined, unlike those others, to constitute through the revolutionary significance of its teaching the predominant ideological form of the late Empire. Wherever that happened it is easy to see that the Christian use of language, neither exclusive nor sectarian, but more and more accessible to all ranks of imperial society, high and low, came in the long run to be one of the most active factors in the preservation of a tongue and of a literary taste which were nevertheless in process of transformation.

The fact that Latin underwent modification in all its elements, owing to the diverse structural influences which conditioned and stimulated it during the first three centuries of the imperial epoch, is clearly a positive phenomenon, which proves its vitality. Just as it would be impossible to maintain the decadence of artistic style in the same period as being the result of its progressive retreat from the Hellenistic canons transplanted to the workshops of the capital in the last years of the Republic, so the progressive abandonment of Ciceronian vocabulary and style by Tacitus, Apuleius and Ammianus Marcellinus reflects their uninterrupted contact with the cultural and social evolution of the composite Mediterranean world. It is accordingly hard to understand the slow but uncontrollable decline of Latin literature in production, diffusion, stylistic convention, recognised classifications and capacity to express and educate the society of the Empire.

The problem is that of the contents of an expressive structure and of the uses made of its idiomatic instrument. It arises from the question why good painting should not

14 Balmus (1930); Auerbach (1960), especially pp. 34–43 and 50–60.

be accompanied by good poetry or good prose. To such an enquiry no answer can be given within the limits of idiomatic study; but it may be convenient to indicate some attempts at solution of the difficulty, for the sake of their general interest.

The literary classifications, precepts and distinctions, and the rhetorical conventions, derived from ancient civilisation and Alexandrian Hellenism were certainly not so congenial to imperial society as they might have been at a time when the cultural outlook introduced by the Hellenistic invasion of Rome during the last century of the Republic had only just begun to dissolve. As the function of a superimposed culture which the arts, letters and philosophies of the highly civilised classical Orient had assumed in confronting Italy and the western provinces steadily weakened, the existential tendencies of Roman Stoicism, Pythagoreanism and Epicureanism, the 'temporalised' manifestations of the artistic *experiri* of Rome in painting, sculpture and architecture, and the realistic examples of the new novel as represented by Petronius and Apuleius, proved the instinctive cultural inclination of the central imperial period to employ in new works the doctrines of illustrious schools of thought, of artistically advanced civilisations and of approved literary types. Nor were those new works directed so much to the production of novelties in form as to responding with more energy and immediacy to the spirit of the times; for it was not only in the capital that sentiment had wearied of the discounted cultural practices which had induced literature, art and even philosophy to favour an otiose rhetoric.

This effort to emerge from the objectivist rationalism of Hellenistic culture, which had remained supreme for the first two centuries of the Empire, was naturally insufficient to save the structures of that civilisation, particularly its literature, despite the assumption of so many new modes of expression. In the face of unprecedented requirements in the fields of morality, eschatology and religion, cosmology and philosophy, the combination of Stoicism and intimist existentialism in Marcus Aurelius could no longer make headway. Nor could the evolution of artistic taste, to say nothing of the neo-Atticism under Hadrian, continue to be satisfied with the nevertheless powerful dramatisation, in a style of uninterrupted narrative history, of the spiral reliefs of Trajan's Column. Moreover, the educated public was losing its former intense interest in the 'second sophistic' applied, in the absence by this time of a true exercise of political and cultural liberty, to commonplace happenings or to academic, parasitical and mythological eulogy by the practice of a virtuosity in the treatment of form that had reached very high levels of artifice and pretentious refinement in the central imperial age. Actually, once form had submitted to utilisation by a stylistic instrument that was flexible because in real contact with life, new subjects, in other words new spiritual functions, inevitably imposed themselves. The development of conscience had to be accompanied by transformations of philosophy, literature, arts and sciences, to say nothing of customs and laws, if all were not to dry up and perish.

If that contingency was possible in the sphere of the 'mechanical arts', it was owing substantially to the indifferent attitude shown by the new social and religious bodies, including the Christian Church, which maintained the civilised life of the Empire from within and allowed the ancient symbols now in course of decay, as well as the exhausted classical tradition, to continue to furnish the outward structure of the new subjects and truths. If the Church, for example, like many mystery sects and priestly organisations among the numerous eastern religions, entered wholly, without reserve, into the architectural space (e.g. basilica, rotunda, apse, etc.) created by Roman life, utilised its reliefs and its paintings, and accepted its figurative representations, this state of affairs was due less to the employment, at least at first, of the same artists' workshops than to the practical attitude, partly casual and partly institutional, of all the new religious forms of antiquity: the exclusive attitude of the sect for initiates or the clandestine attitude of the 'subversive religion', and the didactic attitude which, while denouncing the inadequacy or falsity of the official cult and the classical Olympus, took over their forms, instutitions, personifications and rites, disguising their ancient significance in the service of the new teaching so as to enable the familiar mythical events to act as 'figures' or *exempla* of the truth which had at last been revealed. In the sociological sphere it was this fortunate circumstance that ensured in the artistic field the survival of the old and the new, and enabled the latter's vitality to penetrate instead of overthrowing the desiccated structure of the old, preserving and perpetuating its form, though with a complete reversal of meaning.

Different destinies awaited philosophy, literature, science, and juridical, economic and administrative organisations. These last, ever since the time of Marcus Aurelius, had been subordinated to the stern necessity of military defence, which eventually uprooted the very spirit of the Empire, crushing its ancient institutions under formally despotic rule and literally persecuting its citizens with the most incredible taxation and compulsory public labour, so that many inhabitants of the frontier zones fled to the barbarians in search of freedom. Meanwhile scientific research fell into disuse. Antiquity had hardly ever realised the significance of science for civil progress and the liberation of mankind; it had always feared the revolutionary implications of an experimental methodology as capable, if it spread, of fomenting social unrest. Classical philosophy, even in its last, Neoplatonic effort to compete with the new religions, had failed to make any real contact with the demands of widespread mystical yearnings, though admitting them to the categories of ancient rationalism. The literature of the central and late imperial periods was faced with the dilemma of either remaining firmly attached to the old culture and the usual rhetorical subjects or else passing to the other side of the ideological barricade to join the subverters of classical civilisation, whether named Tertullian or Heliodorus, who were proclaiming in more or less approved literary styles the challenge of civil revolution.

Thus it happened that several literatures were written in the Latin language, with a clarity perhaps unique in literary history. Substantially, they represented several types of civilisation. They all displayed, at least in certain periods, the same masterly skill, were equipped with the same technical abilities and were equally well armed for battle. That which differentiated them, and which was to ensure the end of one and the triumph of another, was not the cultural markets they controlled; not the degree of their adherence to social structures; not the occasional support accorded them by public authorities and powerful individuals, in whose hands antiquity had always left – in the form of private patronage or of clientship – the maintenance of men of letters and accordingly the future of literature, just as it had always limited mainly to the ruling class the enjoyment of artistic products, thus rendering the artists culturally helpless. No, the difference between those literatures lay solely in the capacity of their contents to promote moral decision and hence to separate the products of one from those of another in the field of choice between civilisations.

The exclusive departments of traditional rhetoric were steadily emptied of vital content. Even when invigorated by realism they followed the Alexandrian pattern, which was scarcely more animated or concerned with character. They dealt with fact according to a set of rules, making an event the occasion of an exercise in language and manner suited to celebration, drama, comedy or narrative, never representing it as requiring in itself the listener's participation, either in an aesthetic sense or ideologically and morally. The literature of the central imperial period, thus organised, showed progressively more skill in its forms of presentation, sometimes bold, astonishing and even fascinating in its tireless quest for novelty. But, as Auerbach[15] has clearly shown, the final stage of ancient literature, of whatever kind, is really that of a moralism which reduces every historical and social problem to terms essentially vacuous, static and ultimately meta-historical,

15 Auerbach (1956), pp. 36–44.

and that of the prevailing rhetorical convention, which moves a world of conformist and stiffly projected representations within the hackneyed repertory of an exhausted theatrical standard imposed from without.

During the central imperial period so high a degree of formal sophistication could certainly not be attained by Christian literature, which was nevertheless destined to succeed it in the end by the infusion of its impulsive talent for *raptus*. Auerbach[16] rightly declares that 'the first breach of classical theory' in the direction of the medieval conception of art was made by the story of Christ 'with its uninhibited mingling of everyday life and most sublime tragedy'. This revolution in literature did not arise as such, but simply as a form of the 'sacred book' transmitted as evidence of a story of Messianic subversion the events of which took place in a Roman province, in the social *milieu* of fishermen and peasants. From the viewpoint of the classical canons, it was revolutionary because it overthrew their individualist and rationalistic morality, which was imposed by the indefeasible laws of a society conceived almost as an object of natural science. It did so by conferring social responsibility on the individual, and also by means of a new ethic of human conduct extraordinarily congenial to the inarticulate aspirations of the masses, beneficiaries as they were to some extent of the cultural unification of the Empire, and responsive to the demands which the educated classes had been led to make upon themselves in face of the inadequacy of current convictions and practice. Moreover, so inextricable a mixture of stories, responsibilities and destinies, as well as the tragico-eschatological significance attached to the crucifixion of a Galilean agitator, which, according to the rules of classical literature, should have ranked, at most, as a comic event, upset the rigid casuistry of literary varieties and styles, later to recast them in a more detailed and comprehensive use of all the brilliant devices of rhetoric in the service of a theory regarding the universe as having been re-erected on new foundations. Therefore, while the gospel, in early-Christian Latin, and the first examples of apologetic literature may have seemed a very poor job to the trained ears of the cultivated public in the central imperial age, the language of the Fathers, especially that of Jerome, Augustine and other Christian writers of the fourth and fifth centuries, would fit perfectly into the rich formal context of imperial rhetoric, drawing from it – and finally elaborating upon it – every subtlety of expression, every variety of style, every figure of speech, to serve the disquieting novelty of the Christian message. Just as in the figurative arts, the Christian movement was to show that it had rescued the vast apparatus of form characteristic of an entire civilisation. But while in the artistic field this process – always preceded by figurative re-interpretation

16 Auerbach (1956), p. 587.

and hence by distortion – occurred without a break in continuity, in literature the discriminating factors of content and ideology at first impeded its redemptive application. It is therefore legitimate to distinguish, within the unity of Roman imperial art, at least two contemporary currents of writing, one of which was fated to be absorbed by the other.

The comprehension and philosophic systematisation not so much of the new taste as of the more or less conscious implications which in theory supported the stylistic development and moral change of late imperial art were not of course easy. Sudden worldwide replacement of an official aesthetic practically unchanged for centuries by a newly constructed doctrine, however authoritative and welcome, was not in fact possible. The network of the Platonic philosophy of art, which still underlay all the theoretical assertions of Antiquity, could be broken only by the shock of contact between artistic production obedient to the traditional rules and the new experiments in representation, which latter were in themselves almost always uninterested in the results of ancient aesthetic theory, striving rather to create not so much the prototypes of a new form of civilisation as the atmospheres, signs, symbols and statements in and by which a new conception of life could be evolved and disseminated.

Consequently, with the exception of a few incidental previous attempts, it is to Plotinus that students of either moral field look for the first synthesis and the first fully integrated conclusion, warranted by a general restatement of the philosophic problem, which can aspire not only to a logical representation of the contemporary spiritual demands but also to the dignity of a complete meta-physical system based on the highest possible authority. The aesthetic of Plotinus differed widely from that of the classical tradition hitherto based in one way or another on Plato and Aristotle, and was opposed in particular to Plato's stern rejection of art as 'third-rate labour'. It is also significant that the one substantial point of rupture with tradition, which the philosophy of Plotinus attempts to renew and defend, occurs in the *Enneads* in the philosophy of art, which is made an essential ladder of spiritual elevation and of attainment to the contemplation of God, culminating in the *ekstasis* (V, 5, 8), since the Good is the 'source and beginning of the beautiful' (I, 6, 9) and this is in reality Being, so that things are beautiful in so far as they participate in some way in the Beautiful through their form (V, 8, 9). The artist therefore, does not copy nature, but, intuiting the Beautiful, which he contemplates in the most exclusive and purest fashion, he almost necessarily projects it in his material (IV, 8, 8), creating a phenomenology of beauty which has no function other than that of relating to itself the soul of him who admires the work of art, so that perceiving 'something congenial, or at least the trace of such affinity, he rejoices in it; struck with dismay, the soul returns to itself and ascends to recollection of itself and of that which belongs to it' (I, 6, 2).

This practical identification of *theoria* and *poiesis* is first and foremost decisive for the liberation of artistic creation and aesthetic judgment from the canons, laid down in the course of imitating nature, which had controlled them throughout antiquity. Measure, proportion, symmetry and colour cease to act as rigid, indispensable co-ordinates for the production of beauty, since the latter, being wholly spiritual, cannot accept material attributes in themselves restrictive. Accordingly, aesthetic intuition, in creation as in judgment, is restored to a liberty which transcends nature and the sense datum. It is even called upon continuously to surmount the physical evidence of the phenomenon, whether natural or a product of artistic work, in order to attain the inexpressible. The abandonment of the canons entails, needless to say, that of the rigorous casuistry of styles, of realism in the representation of images, and of the scientific and rational notionalism tied to figurative production. Hence, though Plotinus may not draw from his treatises lessons for everyday life, which are in a sense outside his interests (a circumstance responsible in general for the abstract character of his metaphysics and the slightness of the moral effect of his teaching), it may nevertheless be maintained that his doctrine of the Beautiful founded a system completely new in the world of art, one that put an end to classicism and set its stamp on late Antiquity and the entire Middle Ages.

Works of art and natural beauties are only mnemonic traces of that transcendent Beauty, materialised signs in the sensible world summoning the beholder to the contemplation of the Ineffable, in order that the soul may attain to it and herself become a 'vision' (I, 6, 9), and hence a spectacle of beauty offered to herself (V, 8, 11). Naturally, therefore, in the works of Plotinus transcendent Beauty is not accounted for on stylistic grounds. Art as envisaged by Plotinus cannot of course be identified with the classical rationalism of the great Attic tradition, nor with the naturalistic classicism of Hellenistic civilisation. The work of art to which the philosopher alludes is perhaps rather, allowing for obvious differences, an 'open work' in the sense which might today define experiments which, whether or not they introduce new techniques or unexpected uses, require the spectator to complete the line, action, rhythm or tonal frequency, by way of an existential and original intervention which attempts on each occasion not the recognition of a representative datum, which does not exist as such, but the profitable opportunity afforded for his sharing in a project of aesthetic communication.

Since the expressionist and existentialist roots are the common denominator – apart from their significance in history – of the two concepts, it will not be necessary to dwell upon the remarkable uniformity of Plotinian *theoria* and the *poiesis* of late antiquity. What must be emphasised is the fact that since idiomatic applications, in other words a formal definition of the imitations of ineffable Beauty in the sphere of phenomena, are only implicit (and very rare at that) in Plotinus, articulations of the idiom considered less hostile to the assumption of form, and hence to the latter's reference to the contemplation of beauty, are also very scarce and difficult to interpret. It is indeed permissible to ask whether the philosopher, in his evaluation of the artistic and the natural concrete as an act of contemplation that goes beyond the form in order to reach beauty and is productive in itself (III, 8, 3; III, 8, 4), ever intended to concern himself with such modes of the 'image of truth' (III, 8, 4). It would not be difficult to reply in the negative to such a question.

Historically speaking, and in so far as the 'cubism' or 'expressionism' of late antiquity can be compared to the modern experiments which have helped to render them intelligible, it may be concluded that Plotinus was not the ideologue nor the direct critic of those works of the third and fourth centuries which have been studied in these pages. That, however, does not mean that one must fully agree with Grabar when he refers to the 'aesthetic insignificance of most of the works known to belong to the *milieu* of the third century',[17] or when, recalling that the Symmachi and Nicomachi commissioned neo-Atticist works at the instigation of Neoplatonist advisers, he concludes that the thought of Plotinus was eventually adopted by the Christians alone.[18] It is not the continued presence of classical reactions or survivals in the late Empire that can prove the permanence of an aesthetic of classical type in the last secular productions of ancient society. It is actually the planned traditionalist reaction of Symmachus that shows, *e contrario*, that the art of his time, even when commissioned and inspired by non-Christians, had a perfect right to be considered the idiom of late Antiquity.

There is no need here to raise the futile question as to whether Plotinus anticipated or adopted the mood of his age. But it may well be admitted that the 'founder of the mystic theory of aesthetics in Antiquity'[19] illustrated on a very high philosophical level the developments of taste and the meaning of idiomatic trends in the art of late Antiquity, so as to constitute its ideological justification throughout the Middle Ages.

On the other hand, the thought of Plotinus also includes

17 Grabar (1945), p. 16.
18 Grabar (1945), pp. 30–1.
19 Croce (1950), p. 177.

implications from which it is possible to derive a critical aesthetic standard specifically applicable to works of art. This matter has recently been investigated by Ferri, Grabar, Bettini, Michelis, Stefanini and others[20] with conclusions not altogether unanimous. These scholars were seeking a precise theoretical definition of the extent to which the artistic production of Late Antiquity and the Middle Ages differed from the classic tradition, the scientific perspective of the Renaissance and so on. Grabar in particular was able to interpret a certain passage in Plotinus (II, 8, 1) as representing two tendencies alien from the 'sound classical tradition' and found to be common in the art of late Antiquity. One was the refusal to place figures and objects at different distances from the spectator and the setting of them 'in the foreground, which thus becomes the only plane of the picture'. The other was the meticulous attention paid to such points of detail as costume, hair-style and other accessory matters, together with the replacement of chromatic shading 'by localised, flat and uniform tones, the same for all the objects represented'. This circumstance, 'according to Plotinus, would enable the spectator to recognise more clearly the *true* dimensions and the *true* colour, in other words the true characteristics of the object illustrated'.[21]

Other idiomatic consequences of the aesthetic theory of Plotinus, in Grabar's view, may be studied in the so-called inverse perspective, arising from the fact that 'the artist somehow identifies himself with the object depicted' and accordingly shows all the surroundings of that object – which is usually the chief figure in the scene – 'as a kind of panorama, such as he would himself perceive about him if he were identical with the object'.[22] Stefanini saw the position differently, asserting that 'the text of Plotinus throws no light on the subject, but argues, if at all, in favour of what might be called normal perspective'.[23] Again, 'when Plotinus tries to give some account of the illusion of perspective, he proves that he is acquainted with the normal type alone'.[24] In fact, when the question is considered on a purely physical level, there can be no doubt that the philosopher recognised that 'distant things appear smaller' (II, 8, 1) and that he also briefly investigated certain scientific explanations of the phenomenon. Yet it is actually from this recognition that he sets out to explain the need for a different kind of representation, consisting of a vision of detail, of unshaded colour and of aligned objects; in short, of reality divorced from the laws of nature, lacking the weight, volume and opacity of matter, which constitutes the negation of form. From such a picture he would derive the intellectual understanding which is the way to ecstasy, to the contemplation of the *Nous*. It is for this very reason that the 'mechanical quality', the material element attributed to artistic creation

20 Ferri (1936); Grabar (1945); Stefanini (1956). *See also* Bovini (1941); Gerke (1947); L'Orange and Nordhagen (1943); L'Orange (1947).
21 Grabar (1945), pp. 19–20.
22 Grabar (1945), p. 21.
23 Stefanini (1956), p. 100.
24 Stefanini (1956), p. 101.

in classical theory, is redeemed in Plotinus by a new dignity conferred upon the craftsman, who need no longer reproduce the object perceived in gross matter but may freely set forth in his material his vision, which is participation in metaphysical beauty, the form of beauty, thus performing an act which 'continues divine creation'.[25]

It was precisely because he understood that the phenomenon of sight does not consist in a mere imprinting of an appearance on the mind, in the moulding of the latter by the object seen as is wax by a seal, but that visual apprehension takes place 'where the visible object stands' (IV, 6, 1), that Plotinus emphasised that the true distances between objects[26] and their true dimensions could not be ascertained and estimated in any such manner.

Hence the Plotinian description of an aesthetic theory which finds its psychological basis in a recognition of depth. Why was the philosopher so interested in a more accurate knowledge of dimensions, distances and colours? Certainly not because he overestimated material understanding of them; such an idea would be inconceivable in the context of, his thought. In reality, if artistic creation (the aim of art) and the appreciation thereof afford the philosopher grounds for a metaphysical reference, for the contemplation of divine beauty, it seems not unreasonable to suppose that the object which is rendered a *medium* for such a function should be completely divorced from the deceptive laws of matter, the misleading veils of nature. Thus, through the mediation of art, everything would be seen in the truth of its life, which is also its beauty. 'Why is it,' Plotinus asks, 'that the most lively images are always the most beautiful, even if others are better proportioned?' (VI, 7, 22). Again, whatever allegorical and symbolical suggestions it may make to the contemplative soul, the object represented by art does not change through the laws of perspective the relationship between the figures, in which relationship the art of late Antiquity, from Constantine onwards, established the hierarchy of dignities even to the summit of cosmic creation. Furthermore, this kind of metaphysical geometry of things and creatures may give rise to an absolute rhythm of invention and design. What sort of rhythm would we have had in the processional figures at S. Apollinare Nuovo, if they had not been brought to the surface in gratuitous paratactical alignment, without perspectival overlapping, in defiance of physical laws, and making impossible demands, structurally, on the eye, in a manner that is certainly consonant with Plotinian thought?

In discussing the aesthetics of Plotinus it may be ambiguous to speak of 'inverse perspective'. But it is certainly permissible to speak of a complex of psychological, moral, allegorical and metaphysical perspectives, among which may be distinguished one that is no longer a 'represen-

25 Bettini (1948), p. 79.
26 '. . . hills where there are many houses, a number of trees and much else. Each of all these objects, if seen apart from the rest, will enable the whole to be measured, beginning from the separate objects seen.' (*Note by W.D.* That is to say, aligning the objects on a single plane and taking a single parameter for calculating the distance between each and hence the total space.) 'But if the form is not actually apprehended by taking one object after another the eye, in measuring the underlying extension, will not be able to ascertain, in relation to each single form, the whole in its true entity'.

tation' but a spiritual happening, an approach to *ekstasis*.

In the aesthetics of late Antiquity beauty as conceived by Plotinus possesses a singularly expressive power not so much because it is a decisive innovation with respect to the formulae of classical philosophy as because it laid the foundations of a doctrine of Art and of the Beautiful such as to be taken over unreservedly by medieval philosophers. It thus constitutes the theoretical basis of the magnificent Christian artistic achievement, which from the late third century onwards, with the aid of experiments carried out by secular Roman art, replaced the still classical symbolism of the funerary art of the hypogea with an art novel in idiom, conception and function.

The thought of Plotinus, in fact, encouraged his immediate successors, the Fathers, to undertake a doctrinal exposition that reached its highest practical importance in the aesthetics of Augustine, but did not therein exhaust the continuous process of scriptural application, and presented Christian teaching with a powerful organ capable of absorbing, transfiguring and thus preserving the classical tradition in art. It was the rank accorded in Plotinian eschatology to instruction in the nature of Beauty that permitted an aesthetic application of the final divine act of creation – 'Let us make man in our own image and likeness' – by introducing into Christian preaching an ontological reference which of itself accounted for the earthly form, and the very act of shaping it, as an imitation of the beauty of the Creator. It was the Plotinian image of the Beautiful as light shared by the soul 'not measured in terms of size nor enclosed by outline, but actually immeasurable, greater than any measure and superior to any quantity' (I, 6, 9), that enabled Ambrose, following Basil, to define the beauty of light as 'not in number nor measure nor weight but *in aspectu*'.[27] This aesthetic of resemblance to the divine and of light beyond qualification, which withdraws every support from the old naturalistic canons of beauty, is also an aesthetic of the transfiguration of the soul and of the world, again extraordinarily consonant with Plotinus ('. . . to be transmuted finally, resplendent with thoughts, from "seer" to "sight", the vision, I mean, of another who contemplates, such as is he who manifests himself to us from above') (V, 8, 11). That was the ideologico-cosmological basis of the decoration of the religious building, summed up in the splendour of the gold and light of its domes according to the doctrine of Pseudo-Denys (*Celestial Hierarchy* and *Ecclesiastical Hierarchy*), such as it appears, for example, in the account of Santa Sofia given by Paul the Silentiary in his *Ekphrasis tōn naou tēs hagias sophias*.[28]

Through this eschatological plan of the aesthetic of

27 Ambrose, *Hexaemeron*, I, 34: Lucis natura huiusmodi est, ut non in numero, non in mensura, non in pondere ut alia, sed omnis eius in aspectu sit gratia.' The passage from Basil about 'simple' beauty, not arising from the symmetry of its parts, that is, from their relations, of gold, the sun and so on, is in *Hexaemeron*, II, 8.
28 Pseudo-Denys, *The Celestial Hierarchy and The Ecclesiastical Hierarchy*; Paulus Silentiarius, *Description of the Church of St. Sophia. See also* Grabar (1947).

29 'Corporis est quaedam apta figura membrorum cum coloris quadam suavitate, eaque dicitur pulchritudo' (Cicero, *Tusculan Disputations*, IV, 31). 'Quid est corporis pulchritudo? Congruentia partium cum quadam coloris suavitate' (Augustine, *Letters*, III, To Nebridius,

30 De Bruyne (1947, p. 18; 1946).

31 But see the different view expressed in *Enneads*, VI, 7, 22: 'It should be recognised that beauty consists not so much in symmetry as in that which shines forth from symmetry'. So also in I, 6, 1.

32 '*Hinc est profecta in oculorum opes, et terram coelumque collustrans, sensit nihil aliud quam pulchritudinem sibi placere, et in pulchritudine figuras, in dimensiones, in dimensionibus numeros.*' (Augustine, *De Ordine*, II, 15, 42.) Riegl (1953, p. 372, n. r), after quoting part of this passage, adds: 'The word *figuras* denotes separate forms, while *dimensiones* means those, i.e. of height and breadth, operative on the plane. For the identification of *numeros* and rhythm *see De Ordine* etc.' A certain distortion by Riegl of Augustine's ideas on art has been deplored by Karel Svoboda (1933, p. 8).

33 Augustine, *De Doctrina Christiana*, iv, 13, 41, and elsewhere.

34 *Ibid.*, ii, 18, 28.

35 *Ibid.*, ii, 25, 39.

36 *Ibid.*, i, 4, 4.

37 Marrou (1958), pp. 296–7). Cf. Augustine, *De Ordine*, ii, 14, 41: '*In hoc igitur quarto grado* (musica), *sive in rhythmis, sive in ipsa modulatione intelligebat regnare numeros, totumque perficere.*'

Plotinus and the Fathers, the evident dependence of Augustine on the classical teaching as presented by Cicero loses the significance of an inconsistent adoption of the laws of rhetoric and approaches that of a merely formal acceptance, subsequently much modified in practice. In fact, the formula which Augustine himself employs, having derived it from Cicero,[29] is nothing, as De Bruyne has pointed out,[30] but a commonplace repeated in various ways throughout Antiquity, even by Plotinus (I, 6, 1);[31] its meaning would be sought with new interpretations of the words from the third century onwards. Thus, it cannot be said that a contradictory attachment to outmoded principles is inherent in the Augustinian acceptation of dimensions and numbers.[32] As is generally apparent from all the theoretical writings of the late age, the rigidity (with scarcely appreciable variants) of the canons of classical rhetoric, of literary genera, of styles, and of the distributive arrangement of the arts, was an almost inevitable result of the continuous reference to the great masters of thought, misunderstood though they now were in the connexion and validity of individual statements.

Indeed, any cultivation of artistic form for its own sake was strongly condemned by Augustine after his conversion. His censure is directed in the first place to the excesses of the 'second sophistic'.[33] But even musical performances are *nugae*[34] and the figurative arts are *superflua*.[35] They should be resorted to only in so far as they may be accepted as means to the pleasurable contemplation of divinity. As Plotinus had already taught (I, 6, 8), man is a traveller who must not stop to enjoy sensible beauty, since God, to whom he is voyaging, is the one Beauty worthy of his attention.[36] The liberal arts may indeed serve to lead the soul beyond the realms of sense to the nature of intelligibles. But that means nothing more than a reduction of aesthetic pleasure to philosophic judgment, based on the one hand upon the Neoplatonic consideration of a metaphysical reference in earthly beauties, and on the other upon the Neopythagorean presupposition, well brought out by Marrou, that musical rhythm can be reduced to a mathematical entity and that all sensible beauty (by extension even if not musical) can be described as having 'a certain *numerositas* or participation in the beauty of number'.[37]

But this transfer of the aesthetic attribute to a character in some way rational and scientific (though certainly not in the modern experimental sense), an attribute significantly capable of transferring music from the domain of the 'mechanical' to that of the 'liberal' arts, is by no means a return to Vitruvius. Actually, it is such as in itself to render mathematical entities symbolical, as had been done in the *Theologumena Arithmetica* of Nicomachus of Gerasa and other similar treatises known to have been written in the imperial period. Augustine recognised that numbers 'in the mind given over to the things of this world have a certain beauty of their own'.[38] But they are no more than images of the spiritual and eternal numbers. As Assunto has recently shown, this Augustinian theory of musical quantities was still held valid for the other arts in the late Middle Ages.[39] When Augustine with the help of Pythagoras shows in *De Musica*[40] that there is a certain perfection in the number 3 because it is a 'whole' which 'has a beginning, a middle and an end' (perhaps the simplest case of the aesthetic qualification of number, which went to incredible lengths of artifice, especially in Biblical exegesis), or proves in *De Civitate Dei*[41] the perfection of the number 6 ('the first to be composed of each of its parts, the sixth, the third and the half of itself, the numbers 1, 2 and 3, which when added make 6'), he reveals a very clear tendency to a symbolist concept of the beautiful, with which numerous analogies can be found in the frequent employment of *exempla* in contemporary literature and in the solving of problems almost as though they were cryptograms, which characterises grammatical studies of the great classical authors (Vergil particularly) in the late imperial age. It is a tendency to figural exegesis, to often fantastic etymological analysis and to allegorical interpretation, which in both literature and the illustrative arts, in both words and numbers, leads to the mystical and moral figuralism of the Middle Ages, going so far as to combine with the geometrical study of surfaces or volumes, in which the greatest beauty is held to be that of figures composed 'of equal lines',[42] and finally, through the circle,[43] with the discipline of astronomy, etc.[44] The Neoplatonic symbolism of the inexpressible and the sublime, founded by Plotinus and taken to a deeper level by Proclus, thus acquired in the thought of Augustine a grammar of signs and a repertory of meanings which assured its secular diffusion for a thousand years throughout 'Romania' and the Eastern Mediterranean.

These elements of aesthetic symbolism so patiently worked out by the culture of antiquity, and not in Pythagorean circles alone, seem to have constituted the systematic reconstruction of what had been studied for centuries in the mysterious books of the new religions and of such ideas as had been advanced by Augustine in the course of his Biblical exegesis. The process suggests that the search for the hidden meaning, the figural significance, of the Biblical story was considered an exercise at least as useful as the discovery of truth itself.[45] The stimulus thus applied to the keenest possible participation of the faithful in obscure truth, and of the spectator in hidden beauty, was enough in itself to restore in the aesthetic field the combined utilitarian and spiritual trend of the culture of late antiquity, whether Christian or

38 Augustine, *De Musica*, vi, II, 33.
39 Assunto (1961), pp. 31, 32 and 40, note 7.
40 Augustine, *De Musica*, i, 12, 20.
41 Augustine, *De Civitate Dei*, xi, 30.
42 A. '. . . *Quaenam tibi figura melior videatur et pulchrior? Eam quae paribus, an quae imparibus lineis constat? E. Quis dubitet eam esse meliorem in qua aequalitas praevalet?*' (Augustine, *De Quantitate Animae*, 8, 13).
43 Augustine, *De Quantitate* . . ., 10, 16.
44 Augustine, *De Ordine*, ii, 15, 43: '*In his igitur omnibus disciplinis* (geometry and astronomy) *occurrebant ei omnia numerosa, quae tamen in illis dimensionibus menifestius eminebant*'.
45 Augustine, *De Doctrina* . . ., iv, 6, 9.

pagan. The goal of learning as sought by the profane – from the field of rhetoric to that of the sciences – and the eschatological aim of religious thought, encountered one another in a restoration, to some extent independently achieved, of the dimension of the beautiful, which came to be understood in that weighty, mysterious, enigmatic and sacramental sense common to all the artistic production utilised in the society of the late Empire.

Nor can the art which triumphed with this taste, shortly before the secular collapse, be described as incapable of movement, insignificant and unable to take risks. It might perhaps have assumed such a character in consequence of Neoplatonic influences, for it is significant that records of official and secular painting during the fourth century show some traces of it, especially in the more classically determined phases. But it must be emphasised that with Augustine we have a strongly dramatic moral impulse, and a qualification of the *iter* of life which was optimistic though tragic and subject to the vicissitudes of time. Both those factors, projected against the providential though not undisturbed background of the Christian redemption of the cosmos, imposed on a steadily growing market the acquisition of a new *habitus* capable of response in the ecclesiastical as well as in the individual sphere to the deep significance and harsh realism of the New Testament message. The artistic taste present in the literary manner used to describe the story of the abominable crucifixion of the Galilean was continued in Augustine's psychological and moral realism, and was transmitted, as Riegl[46] was the first to emphasise, through that aesthetic illustration of the providential nature of evil and sin which provides a typical illustration of the African's artistic taste. Ethics and aesthetics meet in the concept that likens the beauty of the cosmos, despite the presence there of sinners in themselves deformed, to that of a picture which rightly includes the colour black.[47] Nor does this assertion appear unique in the thought of Augustine;[48] it recurs persistently throughout his writings, and shows that ugliness and deformity, evil and sin, have necessarily to be reintegrated in an aesthetic and moral order that now excludes classical beauty, though the ancient definition of it remains in use. Even with specific reference to rhetoric this view, often supported by theory,[49] proves that Augustine, despite his general hostility to the arts or at any rate to some of them (e.g. the theatre), which he based on ethical and religious grounds, shared profoundly in the aesthetic opinions of his day.

He both shared them and expressed them, whether or not we agree with Svoboda[5] that his 'aesthetic system', though much indebted to the philosophy that preceded it, was 'the most complete bequeathed by antiquity to modern times'. It may at any rate be acknowledged that

46 Riegl (1953), pp. 374–5; (1959), p. 271.
47 Augustine, *De Civitate Dei*, xi, 23. *See also De vera religione*, 76, and *Sermones*, cxxv, 5.
48 Augustine, *De Civitate Dei*, xi, 15, 18 and 22; *Enarratio in Psalmus* CXLVIII, 9, 10; *De Ordine*, i, 7, 18. Concerning the latter *see* Assunto (1961), pp. 33, 34, 40, note 9 and 41, note 17. As Svoboda has observed (1933, pp. 22–4): 'As well as the public executioner who, according to Plotinus, is necessary in a city, he (Augustine) mentions the prostitute, taking the Roman point of view, and replaces the Plotinian example of the painter with that of the mosaicist, whose art was then flourishing, and with those of the antitheses, barbarisms and solecisms' usually adduced by grammarians and rhetoricians), and also Marrou (1958, p. 240 and note 8), this argument follows one by Plotinus. (*Enneads*, iii, 2, 2; iii, 2, 3).
49 Augustine, *De Ordine*, i, 18; ii, 12. *See* especially in this connection Balmus (1930), p. 152 ss.
50 Svoboda (1933), p. 199.

his system is 'in more than one respect still of interest to posterity, for example in its formalist substructure, its notion of organic unity, its opposition between the perception and the significance of a work of art, its appreciation of rhythm and the need for classification of this feature, and finally in its analysis of emotion and aesthetic judgment'. Accordingly, it is not by chance that the art of his time, misunderstood for so many centuries, speaks to us in terms that sound familiar.

Centres of Imperial
painting cited in text
(1st to 5th centuries)

KEY

- – – – Boundaries of the Empire under Diocletian
- • • • • • Boundaries of Prefectures
- – – – – Boundaries of Dioceses
- ◉ Capital of Prefecture
- ○ Capital of Diocese
- C Rome – Illuminated Manuscripts
- M Antioch – Mosaics
- A Stabia – Frescoes
- S Antinoe – Textiles
- T Ostia – Marble Inlay
- R Fayyum – Portraits on wood or textile
- □ Paris – Works of uncertain provenance preserved in museums
- ○ Boscoreale – References in text to pictorial works of a different epoch
- X Pergamum – References in text to sculptures
- Δ Sabratha – References in text to architectural works
- ·········· Greco–Latin linguistic boundary

□ Leningrad

□ Moscow

□ Berlin

Inset circle (Rome region):

C A M
T

O X △ ● ROME

A M T

C A M Tivoli
M Palestrina

A Grottaferrata
M Genazzano

M Tuscolo
A Marino L.

Ostia

M Baccano

Capua A

Napoli M □

Boscoreale

A Ercolano

A Pompei

X Benevento

A Caivano

M Campagna

A Stabia

ORUM

Munich □

M Salzburg

Vienna □

Malles ○

Sirmione ●

Oderzo □

ia

□ M   M □ Aquileia

A M   Concarona

Verona □ Venezia

o

O X △
Ravenna
Ancona □

Chiusi M

Second inset circle:

C A M
□ T
O X △ ● ROME A
A M T   M
M
A X
M □ A
A   A
A   A

Casanarello ○

Palermo
M

M Piazza Armerina

X A Syracuse

Henchir
Toungar

Oudna
uburbo M.
Susa

El Djem

Henchir
Thina

ratha △ O M
Tripoli □
Gargaresh A
AMT   Leptis Magna
AMT
Zliten

SIRMIUM
Belgrade □

Gamzigrad

M Ulpia
Oescus
M

A Silistra

A Kerc

SARDICA ●

● PHILIPPOPOLIS

Constantinople ●

THESSALONICA
M ● X △

A C M X □ △ ○ NICOMEDIA

CAESAREA ●

Edessa
M

X Pergamum

EPHESUS ●

Aspendos

X
Afrodisias

M Sparta

M
Cos

Rhodes

M. Staurin
Seleucia M ● ANTIOCH
MM Daphne

Palmyra A
Dura Europos

Apamea A X

Damascus ○

Bishapur M

Città del
○ Nebo

Scheik Zueda
M

Petra △

ALEXANDRIA ●

S M X □

R
Saqqāra
Fayyūm
R

St. Catherine
○ Sinai

M
Qasr el-Lebia

Antinoë
R S

Akhimim
R S

A Luxor

A El Baghawat
R
Assuan

Achelis, Hans (1926), 'Die gnostike Katakombe an Viale Manzoni in Rom', *Kunst und Kirche*, pp. 65–71

Achelis, Hans (1932), *Römische Katakombenbilder in Catania*, Berlin.

Achelis, Hans, (1935), *Die Katakomben von Neapel*, Leipzig.

Adriani, Achille (1958), 'Alessandrina arte', *Enciclopedia dell'arte antica classica e orientale*, i, Rome, pp. 218–35.

Agnello, Giuseppe (1952), *La Pittura paleocristiana in Sicilia*, Vatican City.

Aletti, Ezio (1948), *Lo stile di Ludio e l'impressionismo ellenistico romano*, Rome.

Aletti, Ezio (1951), *La tecnica della pittura greca e romana e l'encausto*, Rome.

Alföldi, Andreas (1939), 'The Crisis of the Empire', *Cambridge Ancient History*, vol. xii ch. 6, Cambridge.

Alföldi, Andreas (1955), 'Zur Erklärung der Konstaninischen Deckengemälde in Trier', *Historia*, IV, pp. 131–50.

Allais, Yvonne (1957), 'Mosaiques du Musée de Djemila (Cuicul): La Toilette de Venus', *Actes du LXXIX Congrès National des Sociétés Savantes* (Algiers), Paris.

Altheim, Franz (1960), *Il dio invitto*, Milan.

Altheim, Franz (1961), *Dall'Antichità al Medioevo*, Florence.

Ambrose, St. *Hexaemeron.*

Apollony-Ghetti, Bruno M., *et al.* (1951), *Esplorazioni sotto la confessione di S. Pietro in Vaticano eseguite negli anni 1940–1949*, Vatican City.

L'Art copte (1964; catalogue of the exhibition at the Musée du Petit-Palais), Paris.

Arte e civiltà romana nell'Italia Settentrionale dalla Republica alla Tetrarchia (1964; catalogue of the exhibition at the Palazzo dell'Archiginnasio), Bologna.

Assunto, Rosario (1961), *La critica d'arte nel pensiero medioevale*, Milan.

Aubert, Marcel (1934), 'Les fouilles de Doura Europos. Notes sur l'origine de l'iconographie chrétienne', *Bulletin Monumentale*, IV, pp. 397–407.

Auerbach, Erich (1956), *Mimesis. Il realismo nella letteratura occidentale*, Turin.

Auerbach, Erich (1960), *Lingua letteraria e publica nella tarda antichità latina e nel Medioevo*, Milan.

Augustine, St. *De Civitate Dei; De Doctrina Christiana; De Musica; De Ordine; De Quantitate Animae; De Vera Religione; Enarratio in Psalmum CXLVIII; Epistulae;* and *Sermons.*

Aurigemma, Salvatore (1926), *I Mosaici di Zliten*, Rome-Milan.

Aurigemma, Salvatore (1954), *Le terme di Diocleziano e il Museo Nazionale Romano*, Rome.

Aurigemma, Salvatore (1957–9), 'Il restauro di consolidamento del Mosaico Barberini, condotto nel 1952', *Rendiconti della Pontificia Accademia Romana di Archaeologia*, XXX–XXXI, pp. 41–98.

Aurigemma, Salvatore (1960), *L'Italia in Africa–Tripolitania: I. I monumenti d'Arte decorativa. Part I. I mosaici*, Rome.

Aurigemma, Salvatore (1962), *Ibid.*, Part II. *Le Pitture d'età romana*, Rome.

Avi-Yonah, Michael (1960a), 'Giudaica arte', *Enciclopedia dell'arte antica classica e orientale*, iii, Rome, pp. 917–21.

Avi-Yonah, Michael (1960b), *Israele. Mosaici parimenti antichi*, Milan.

Aymard, J. (1937), 'Quelques scènes de chasse sur une mosaique de l'Antiquarium', *Mélanges d'Archéologie et d'Histoire* (École Française de Rome), LIV, 65–6.

Bagatti, Bellarmino (1936), *Il cimitero di Commodilla e dei martiri Felice e Adautto, presso la via Ostiense*, Vatican City.

Bagatti, Bellarmino (1952), 'Il mosaico dell'Orfeo a Gerusalemme', *Rivista di Archeologia Cristiana*, XXVIII, pp. 145–60.

Bagatti, Bellarmino (1962), *L'archeologia cristiana in Palestina*, Florence.

Balil, A. (1958), 'Consideraciones sobre el mosaico hispano-romano', *Revista di Guimaraes*, LXVIII, p. 337 ff.

Balmus, Constantin J. (1930), *Étude sur le style de Saint Augustin, dans les Confessions et la Cité de Dieu*, Paris.

Bartoli, P. S. and Caylus, C. Ph. (1783), *Recueil des peintures antiques trouvées a Rome*, i.

Basil, St., *Hexaemeron.*

Battisti, Eugenio (1961), 'Per la datazione di alcuni mosaici di Ravenna e di Milano', *Scritti di storia dell'arte in onore de Mario Salmi*, Rome, pp. 201–13.

Baur, Paul V. C. (1933), 'Les Peintures de la chapelle chrétienne de Doura', *Gazette des Beaux-Arts*, X, pp. 65–78.

Becatti, Giovanni (1951a) *Case ostiensi del tardo Impero*, Rome.

Becatti, Giovanni (1951b), *Arte e gusto negli scrittori latini*, Florence.

Becatti, Giovanni (1960), *La colonna coclide istoriata*, Rome.

Becatti, Giovanni (1961), *Scavi di Ostia. IV, Mosaici e parimenti marmorei*, Rome.

Becatti, Giovanni (1962), *L'arte romana*, Milan.

Beckwith, John (1958), 'Tissus coptes', *Les Cahiers Ciba*, 83.

Beckwith, John (1961), *The Art of Constantinople. An Introduction to Byzantine Art, 330–1453*, London.

Bendinelli, Goffredo (1922), 'Il monumento sepulcrale degli Aureli al viale Manzoni in Roma', *Monumenti antichi publicati per cura della R. Accademia Nazionale de Lincei*, XXVIII, pp. 289–519

Bérard, Jean (1935), 'Mosaiques inédites de Cherchel', *Mélanges d'Archéologie et d'Histoire* (École Française de Rome), LII, p. 113 ff.

Berenson, Bernard (1952), *L'Arco di Costantino e la decadenza della forma*. Florence.

Beschi, Luigi (1960), *Verona romana. I monumenti, in Verona e il suo territorio*, i, Verona.

Bettini, Sergio (1942), *Mosaici cristiani*, Novara.

Bettini, Sergio (1943), *Quaderni di Archeologia e Storia dell'Arte Paleocristiana e Bizantina*, i, Padua.

Bettini, Sergio (1946), *L'architettura di San Marco*, i, Padua.

Bettini, Sergio (1948), *L'arte alla fine del mondo antico*, Padua

Bettini, Sergio (1952), *Pittura delle origini cristiane*, Novara

Bettini, Sergio (1953), *Introduzione a Alois Riegl, Industria artistica tardo romana*, Florence.

Beyen, Hendrik G. (1938), *Die pompejanische Wanddekoration vom zweiten bis zum vierten Stil*, volume i, The Hague.

Beyen, Hendrik G. (1960), *Die pompejanische Wanddekoration vom zweiten bis zum vierten Stil*, vol. ii, The Hague.

Biagetti B. (1937), 'Osservazione sui mosaici della navata centrale nella basilica di S. Maria Maggiore in Roma', *Rendiconti della Pontificia Accademia Romana di Archeologia*, XIII, pp. 101–16.

Biagetti, B. (1939), 'Intorno ai mosaici della navata centrale nella basilica liberiana di S. Maria Maggiore', *Rendiconti della Pontificia Accademia Romana di Archeologia XV*, pp. 47–56.

Biagetti, B. (1946–7), L'antica struttura della navata centrale della basilica di S. Maria Maggiore ed i suoi mosaici e stucchi', *Rendiconti della Pontificia Accademia Romana di Archeologia*, XXII, pp. 241–51.

Bianchi Bandinelli, Ranuccio (1950), *Storicità dell' arte Classica*, Florence.

Bianchi Bandinelli, Ranuccio (1951), 'Schemi iconografici nelle miniature dell'Iliade Ambrosiana', *Rendiconti dell'Accademia Nazionale dei Lincei*, CIII, 6, pp. 421–53.

Bianchi Bandinelli, Ranuccio (1952), 'La crisi artistica della fine del mondo antico', *Società*, VIII, pp. 427–48.

Bianchi Bandinelli, Ranuccio (1953a), 'Recensione e ricostruzione del codice originario dell'Iliade Ambrosiana', *Rendiconti dell'Accademia Nazionale dei Lincei*, VIII, 8, pp. 466–84.

Bianchi Bandinelli, Ranuccio (1953b), 'Continuità ellenistica nella pittura di età medio e tardoromana', *Rivista dell'Istituto Nazionale di Archeologia e Storia dell'Arte II*, pp. 77–6;. Now in *Archeologia*, pp. 360–444.

Bianchi Bandinelli, Ranuccio (1954), 'Virgilio Vaticanus 3225 e Iliade Ambrosiana', *Nederlands Kunsthistorisch Jaarboek*, V, pp. 225–40. Now in *Archeologia*, p. 340.

Bianchi Bandinelli, Ranuccio (1955), *Hellinistic-Byzantine Miniatures of the Iliad (Ilias Ambrosiana)*, Olten.

Bianchi Bandinelli, Ranuccio (1956), *Organicità e astrazione*, Milan.

Bianchi Bandinelli, Ranuccio (1957a), 'Sulla formazione del ritratto romano' *Società*, XIII, pp. 18–35.

Bianchi Bandinelli, Ranuccio (1957b), 'Problemi della pittura tardoromana e protobizantina', *Corsi di cultura sull'arte ravennate e bizantina*, Ravenna, I, pp. 5–8.

Bianchi Bandinelli, Ranuccio (1961), *Archeologia e cultura*, Naples.

Blaise, Albert (1955), *Manuel du Latin chrétien*, Strasbourg.

Blake, Marion Elizabeth (1930), 'The Pavements of the Roman Buildings of the Republic and Early Empire', *Memoirs of the American Academy in Rome*, VIII.

Blake, Marion Elizabeth (1936), 'Roman Mosaics of the Second Century in Italy', *Memoirs of the American Academy in Rome*, XIII.

Blake, Marion Elizabeth (1940), 'Mosaics of the late Empire in Rome and Vicinity', *Memoirs of the American Academy in Rome*, XVII.

Blanco Freijero, A. (1950), 'Mosaicos romanos con escenas de circo y anfiteatro en el Museo Arqueologico Nacional', *Arquivo Español de Arqueologia*, XXIII, p. 127 ff.

Bloch, Herbert (1963), 'The Pagan Revival in the West at the End of the Fourth Century', *The Conflict between Paganism and Christianity*, Oxford, pp. 193–218.

Böckler, Albert (1930), *Abendlandische Miniaturen bis zum Ausgang der romanischen Zeit*, Berlin–Leipzig.

Bolten, J. (1937), *Die Imago clipeata*, Paderborn.

Bonicatti, Maurizio (1959), 'In margine ai problemi

310 della cultura figurativa di Alessandria nella tarda antichità', *Commentari*, X, 2–3, pp. 75–8.

Bonicatti, Maurizio (1963), *Studi di Storia dell'Arte sulla tarda antichità e sull' alto medioevo*, Rome.

Borda, Maurizio (1958), *La pittura romana*, Milan.

Bovini, Giuseppe (1941), 'Gallieno: la sua iconografia e i riflessi in essa delle vicende storiche e culturali del tempo', *Atti della R. Accademia d'Italia. Memorie*, VII, pp. 115–159.

Bovini, Giuseppe (1949), *I sarofagi paleocristiani. Determinazione della lora cronologia mediante l'analisi dei ritratti*, Vatican City.

Bovini, Giuseppe (1957a), 'Momenti tipici del linguaggio figurativo della pittura cimiteriale d'età paleocristiana', *Corsi di cultura sull'arte ravennate e bizantina*, Ravenna, I, pp. 9–30.

Bovini, Giuseppe (1957b), 'Il mosaico paleocristiano dalle origini alla meta del V secolo', *Corsi di cultura sull'arte ravennate e bizantina*, Ravenna, I, pp. 31–50.

Bovini, Giuseppe (1959), 'I mosaici del battistero de S. Giovanni in Fonte a Napoli', *Corsi di cultura sull'arte ravennate e bizantina*, Ravenna, I pp. 5–26.

Bovini, Giuseppe (1963a), 'I mosaici romani dell'-epoca di Sisto III (432–440), I., I mosaici di S. Sabina dell'atrio del Battistero Lateranense e di S. Pietro in Vincoli', *Corsi di cultura sull'arte ravennate e bizantina*, Bologna, pp. 67–80.

Bovini, Giuseppe (1963b), 'I mosaici romani dell'epoca di Sisto III (432–440). II., I mosaici della navata mediana e dell'arco trionfale di S. Maria Maggiore', *Corsi di cultura sull'arte ravennate e bizantina*, Bologna, pp. 81–109.

Brandi, Cesare (1956), *Arcadio o della Scultura; Eliante o dell' Architettura*, Turin.

Bréhier, Louis (1928), *L'art chrétien*, Paris.

Brett, Gerard L. (1947), *The Great Palace of the Byzantine Emperors, First Report*, Oxford.

Brezzi, Paolo (1961), 'Impero romano e regni barbarici nella valutazione degli scrittori cristiani alla fine del mondo antico', *Studi romani* IX, pp. 260–70.

Brezzi, Paolo (1963), 'L' idea d'impero nel IV secolo', *Studi romani*, XI, pp. 265–79.

Brodsky, N.A. (1961), L'iconographie oubliée de l'arc éphésien de Sainte Marie Majeure à Rome', *Byzantion XXXI*, pp. 413–503.

Brown, P. R. L. (1961), 'Aspects of the Christianisation of the Roman Aristocracy', *Journal of Roman Studies*, LI, pp. 1–11.

Bruns, G. (1935), 'Der Obelisk und seine Basis auf dem Hippodrom zu Konstantinopel', *Istanbuler Forschungen*, VII.

Brusin, Giovanni (1923), in *Notizie degli scavi*, XXI.

Brusin, Giovanni (1948), *La Basilica del Fondo Tullio alla Beligna de Aquileia*, Aquileia.

Brusin, Giovanni (1950), 'Il mosaico antico nel Veneto. Quadro compendiario', *Arte Veneta*, IV, p. 95 ff.

Brusin, Giovanni (1961), *Due nuovi sacelli cristiani di Aquileia*, Aquileia.

Brusin, Giovanni, and Zovatto, Paolo L. (1957), *Monumenti paleocristiani di Aquileia e di Grado*, Udine.

Buberl, P. (1922), *Die griechisch–ägyptischen Mumienbildnisse der Sammlung Th. Graf*, Vienna.

Budde, L. (1960), 'Die frühchristlichen Mosaiken von Misis–Mopsuhestia in Kilikien', *Pantheon*, XVIII, p. 116 ff.

Bulas, K. (1929), *Les illustrations antiques de L'Iliade*, Lwow.

Bultmann, Rudolf (1964), *Il cristianesimo primitivo nel quadro delle religioni antiche*, Milan.

Burckhardt, Jacob (1880), *Die Zeit Constantins des Grossen*, Leipzig.

Byvanck, Alexander W. (1931), 'Het Mozajek in de Doopkerk bij de Kathedral te Naples', *Medeelingen van het Nederlandisch Historisch Instituut te Rome*, I, pp. 45–64.

Byvanck, Alexander W. (1938), 'Antike Buchmalerei. Die Datierung der Berliner Itala', *Mnemosyne*, VI, pp. 241–51.

Byvanck, Alexander W. (1958), 'Il problema dei mosaici di S. Maria Maggiore di Roma', *Corsi di cultura sull'arte ravennate e bizantina*, Ravenna, I, pp. 41–7.

Byvanck, Alexander W. (1961a), 'Das Problem der Mosaiken von Santa Maria Maggiore', *Festschrift H.R Hahnloser zum 60 Geburtstag*, Basel-Stuttgart, pp. 15–26.

Byvanck, Alexander W. (1961b), 'Rome en Constantinopel in de vierde eeuw', *Mededeelingen van het Nederlandisch Historisch Instituut te Rome*, XXXI, pp. 71–122.

Cabrol, Fernand, and Leclercq, Henri (1924), *Dictionnaire d'Archéologie chrétienne et de Liturgie*, Paris.

Cagiano de Azevedo, Michelangelo (1947–9), 'Osservazioni sulle pitture romane di un edificio di via de Cerchi', *Rendiconti della Pontificia Accademia Romana di Archeologia*, XXII–XXIV, pp. 253–8.

Cagiano de Azevedo, Michelangelo (1954), 'La Dea Barberini', *Rivista dell'Istituto Nazionale di Archeologia e Storia dell' Arte*, III, pp. 108–46.

Cagiano de Azevedo, Michelangelo (1958), 'Ritratti o personificazioni, li figure del soffitto dispento di treviri?', *Archeologia classica*, X, pp. 60–63.

Cagiano de Azevedo, Michelangelo (1960), 'Nota in margine ai restauri del Mosaico Barberini', *Archeologia classica*, XII, pp. 224–5.

Cagiano de Azevedo, Michelangelo (1961), 'I proprietari della Villa di Piazza Armerina', *Scritti di Storia dell'arte in onore di Mario Salmi*, Rome pp. 15–27.

Cagiano de Azevedo, Michelangelo (1962a), 'I cosiddetti Tetrarchi di Venezia', *Commentari*, XIII, pp. 160–81.

Cagiano de Azevedo, Michelangelo (1962b), 'L' eredità dell'antico nell'Alto Medioevo', *Il passaggio dall' Antichità all'Medioevo in Occidente*, Spoleto, pp. 449–76.

Cagnat, R. and Chapot, V. (1916 and 1920), *Manuel d'Archéologie Romaine*, vols. i and ii, Paris.

Calderini, Aristide (1950), *I Severi, la crisi dell'Impero nel III secolo*, Bologna.

Calderini, Aristide, et al. (1951), *La Basilica di San Lorenzo maggiore in Milano*, Milan.

Calderini, G., et al. (1896), *Die Marcus Säule auf Piazza Colonna in Rom*, Munich.

Calza, Guido (1940), *La necropoli del porta di Roma nell'Isola Sacra*, Rome.

Calza, Raissa, and Nash, Ernest (1959), *Ostia*, Florence.

Calza, Raissa, and Squarciapino, Maria Floriani (1962), *Museo Ostiense* Rome.

Camprubi Alemany, F. (1942), 'I mosaici paleocristiani de Centcelles', *Rivista di Archeologia Cristiana*, XIX, pp. 87–110.

Camprubi Alemany, F. (1952), *El monumento paleocristiano de Centcelles*, Barcelona.

Caprino, Caterina, et al. (1955), *La colonna di. M. Aurelio illustrata a cura del Comune di Roma*, Rome.

Caputo, Giacomo (1959), *Il teatro di Sabratha e l'architettura teatrale in Africa*, Rome.

Carandini, Andrea (1962a), 'Ricerche sui problemi dell'ultima pittura tardoantica nel bacino del Mediterraneo meridionale', *Archeologia classica*, XIV, 201–35.

Carandini, Andrea (1962b), 'Metodo e critica nel problema dei mosaici di Sousse (Hadrumetum)', *Archeologia classica*, XIV, pp. 244–50.

Carcopino, Jérome (1956), *De Pythagore aux Apôtres*, Paris.

Casalone, C. (1962), 'Note sulle pitture dell'ipogeo di Trebio Giusto in Roma', *Cahiers Archéologiques*, XII, pp. 53–64.

Cecchelli, Carlo (1922), 'Origini del mosaico parietale cristiano', *Architettura e Arti decorative*, II, p. 3 ff.

Cecchelli, Carlo (1927), *L'Ipogeo eretico degli Aureli*, Rome.

Cecchelli, Carlo (1933), 'Gli edifici e i mosaici paleocristiani nella zona della Basilica', *La Basilica di Aquileia*, Bologna.

Cecchelli, Carlo (1944), *Monumenti cristiano-eretici di Roma*, Rome.

Cecchelli, Carlo (1956), *I mosaici della basilica di Santa Maria Maggiore*, Turin.

Cecchelli, Carlo (1958a), 'Mosaici romani del V e VI secolo', *Corsi di cultura sull'arte ravennate e bizantina*, Ravenna, II, pp. 37–44.

Cecchelli, Carlo (1958b), 'La pittura dei cimiteri cristiani dal V al VII secolo', *Corsi di cultura sull'arte ravennate e bizantina*, Ravenna, II, pp. 45–56.

Ceriani, A. M. and Ratti, A. (1905), *Homeri Iliadis pictae fragmenta Ambrosiana*, Milan.

Chatzidakis, Manolis, and Grabar, André (1965), *La pittura bizantina e dell'Alto Medioevo*, Milan.

Cicero, *Tusculanae*.

Cilento, Vincenzo (1961), *Trasposizioni dell'antico. Saggi sulle forme della grecità al suo tramonto*, Milan.

Clédat, J. (1915), 'Fouilles à Cheikh Zouede', *Annales du Service des Antiquités de l'Egypte*, XV, pp. 15–48.

Clement of Alexandria: *Paidagogos; Stromateis;* and *Hupotuposeis*.

Coche de la Ferté, Etienne (1952), *Les portaits romano-egyptiens du Louvre*, Paris.

Cohen, Henri (1880–92), *Description historique des monnaies frappées sous l'Empire Romain*, Paris.

Cohn, E. (1904), 'Le miniature dell'Agada', *Rivista Israelita*, I.

Colini, Antonio Maria (1944), 'Storia e topografia del Celio nell'Antichità', *Memorie della Pontificia Accademia Romana di Archeologia*, VII.

Courcelle, Pierre (1939), 'La tradition antique dans les miniatures médiévales d'un Virgile de Naples', *Mélanges d'Archéologie et d'Histoire (École Française de Rome)*, LVI, pp. 249–79.

Courcelle, Pierre (1944), 'Quelques symboles funéraires du neoplatonisme latin–Le vol de Dédal, Ulysse et les Sirenes', *Revue des Etudes Anciennes*, XLVI, pp. 65–93.

Courcelle, Pierre (1963), 'Anti-Christian Arguments and Christian Platonism–from Arnobius to St. Ambrose', *The Conflict between Paganism and Christianity in the Fourth Century*, Oxford, pp. 151–92.

Croce, Benedetto (1950), *Estetica come scienza dell'espressione e linguistica generale*, Bari.

Cumont, Franz (1926), *Fouilles de Doura-Europos (1922–1923)*, Paris.

Cumont, Franz, and Rostovtzev, Mikhail (1939), *The Excavations at Dura-Europos. Seventh and Eighth Season 1933–34 and 1934–35*, New Haven.

Curtius, Ernst Robert (1956), *La littérature européenne et le Moyen Age latin*, Paris.

Curtius, Ludwig (1929a), *Die Wandmalerei Pompejis*, Leipzig.

Curtius, Ludwig (1929b), 'Geist des romischen Kunst', *Die Antike*, V, p. 187 ff.

Cyprian, St, *Ad Demetrianum*.

312   Daremberg, Ch., and Saglio, E. (1887–1916),
Dictionnaire des Antiquités grecques et romaines, Paris.

De Bruyne, Edgar (1946), *Études d'esthétique médiévale*,
Bruges.

De Bruyne, Edgar (1947), *L'Esthétique du Moyen Age*,
Louvain.

De Dios De La Rada, Juan (1880), 'Mosaicos romanos
representando carreras de carros en el circo',
Museo español de Antiquedades, XI.

De Franciscis, Alfonso (1963), *Antichi mosaici al
Museo di Napoli*, Cava dei Tirreni.

De Francovich, Geza (1951), 'L'arte siriaca e il suo
influsso sulla pittura medioevale nell'Oriente e
nell'Occidente', *Commentari*, II, pp. 3–16, 75–92,
143–52.

De Francovich, Geza (1963), 'L'Egitto, la Siria e
Constantinopoli; problemi di metodo', *Rivista
dell'Istituto Nazionale di Archeologia e Storia dell'Arte*,
XI–XII, p. 83 ff.

Degering, Hermann, and Böckler, Albert (1932), *Die
Quedlinburger Itala-Fragmente*, Berlin.

Degrassi, Nevio (1960), 'Desenzano', *Enciclopedia
dell'arte antica classica e orientale*, III, Rome, pp.
79–80.

De Grüneisen, W. (1911), *Le Portrait. Traditions
hellénistiques et influences orientales*, Rome.

Deichmann, Friedrich W. (1948), *Frühchristliche
Kirchen in Rom*, Basel.

Delbrück, Richard (1929), *Die Consulardiptychen und
verwandte Denkmäler. Studien sur spätantiken
Kunstgeschichte*, Berlin.

Delbrück, Richard (1932), *Antike Porphyrwerke*,
Berlin–Leipzig.

Delbrück, Richard (1933), *Spätantike Kaiserporträts
vom Konstantinus Magnus bis zum Ende des
Westreiches*, Berlin–Leipzig.

Delbrück, Richard (1940), *Münzbildnisse vom
Maximinus bis Carinus (235–285)*, Berlin.

Delbrück, Richard (1952), *Probleme der
Lipsanothek in Brescia*, Bonn.

Deonna, Waldemar (1942), *L'art romain en Suisse*,
Geneva.

De Pachtère, F. G. (1911), *Inventaire des Mosaïques de
la Gaule et de l'Afrique. III., Afrique Proconsulaire,
Numidie, Mauretanie (Algérie)*, Paris.

Devoto, Giacomo (1944), *Storia della lingua di Roma*,
Bologna.

Devoto, Giacomo (1953), *Profilo di storia linguistica
italiana*, Florence.

De Wit, Joseph (1935–6), 'Die Datierung der
spätantiken illustrierten Vergilhandschrift',
Mnemosyne, III, pp. 75–82.

De Wit, Joseph (1938), *Spätrömische Bildnismalerei*,
Berlin.

De Wit, Joseph (1959), *Die Miniaturen des Vergilius
Vaticanus*, Amsterdam.

Diehl, Charles (1953), *La peinture byzantine*, Paris.

Diesner, H. J. (1963), *Kirche und Staat im spätromischen
Reich. Aufsatze sur Spätantike und zur Geschichten
der Alten Kirche*, Berlin.

Dimitrov, D. P. (1960), 'La pitture murali del
sepolcro romano di Silistra', *Arte antica e moderna*,
pp. 351–65.

Dimitrov, D. P. (1962), 'Le Système décoratif et la
date des peintures murales du tombeau antique de
Silistra', *Cahiers Archéologiques*, XII, pp. 35–52.

Doresse, Jean (1958), *Les livres secrets des gnostiques
d'Egypte*, Paris.

D'Orsi, Libero (1959), 'Les nouvelles fouilles de
l'antique Stabiae', *Revue archeologique*, I, pp. 78–87.

Drack, W. (1950), *Die römische Wandmalerei der
Schweiz*, Basel.

Drerup, Heinrich (1933), 'Die Datierung der
Mumienporträts', *Studien zur Geschichte und Kultur
des Altertums*, XIX, i, Paderborn.

Du Bourguet, Pierre (1959), 'Datation des tissus
coptes en fonction des mosaïques
méditerranéennes. Précisions nouvelles', *Ars
Orientalis*, III, pp. 189–92.

Du Bourguet, Pierre (1965), *La Pittura cristiana
primitiva*, Milan.

Ducati, Pericle (1938), *L'arte in Roma dalle origini al
secolo VIII*, Bologna.

Ducati, Pericle (1952), *L'arte classica*, Turin.

Du Mesnil du Buisson, Comte R. (1939), *Les
peintures de la Synagogue de Doura–Europos*, Rome.

Dvořak, Max (1924), *Kunstgeschichte als
Geistesgeschichte*, Munich.

Dyggve, Ejnar (1957a), 'Excursus sulla
"Basilica Herculis" ricordata da Cassiodoro',
Corsi di cultura sull'arte ravennate e bizantina,
Ravenna, II pp. 75–8.

Dyggve, Ejnar (1957b), 'Fouilles et recherches faits
en 1939 et en 1952–53 à Thessaloniki. Recherches
sur le palais impérial de Thessalonique–architecture
et mosaïques', *Corsi di cultura sull' arte ravennate et
bizantina*, Ravenna II, pp. 79–88.

Egger, H. (1906), *Codex Escorialensis*, Vienna.

Egger, Rudolf (1953), 'Ein Collegium Castorum in
Trier. Betrachtungen zum Figurenmosaik',
*Trierer Zeitschrift für Geschichte und Kunst des Trierer
Landes und seiner Nachbargebiete*, XXII, pp. 56–63.

Ehrle, Franz (1902), *Picturae ornamenta complura
scripturae specimina codicis Vaticani 3867, qui codex
Vergilii Romanus audit, phototypice expressa, consiliis
et opera curatorum Bibliothecae Vaticanae*, Rome.

Ehrle, Franz (1945), *Fragmenta et picturae Vergiliana
codicis Vaticani Latini 3225 phototypice expressa
consilis et opera curatorum Bibliothecae Vaticanae*, 3rd
edition, Vatican City.

Eiden, Hans (1950), Spätrömisches Figurenmosaik am

Kornmarkt in Trier', *Trierer Zeitschrift für Geschichte und Kunst des Trierer Landes und seiner Nachtbargebiete*, XIX, pp. 52–69.

Elia, Olga (1931), 'L'ipogeo di Caivano', *Monumenti antichi pubblicati per cura della R. Accademia Nazionale dei Lincei*, XXXIV, cc. 421–92.

Elia, Olga (1951), 'Scoperta di dipinti a Stabiae', *Bollettino d'Arte* XXXVI, p. 40 ff.

Elia, Olga (1957), *Pitture di Stabia*, Naples.

Elia, Olga (1962), 'La villa stabiana di S. Marco', *Napoli nobilissima*, II, 2, pp. 43–51.

Epictetus, *Encheiridion*.

Felletti Maj, Bianca Maria (1941), 'Contributo alla iconografia del IV secolo d. C. Il ritratto femminile', *La Critica d'Arte*, VI, pp. 74–90.

Felletti Maj, Bianca Maria (1960), 'Ostia. La casa delle volte dipinte', *Bollettino d'Arte*, XLV, pp. 45–65.

Ferri, Silvio (1931), *Arte romana sul Reno*, Rome.

Ferri, Silvio (1933a), *Arte romana sul Danubio*, Rome.

Ferri, Silvio (1933b), *Studi nodi e sviluppi della critica intorno alla questione dell'arte romana*, Rome.

Ferri, Silvio (1936), 'Plotino e l'arte del III secolo', *La Critica d'Arte*, I p. 166 ff.

Ferrua Antonio (1956a), 'Una nuova catacomba cristiana scoperta sulla via Latina', *La Civiltà Cattolica*, II, pp. 118–31.

Ferrua, Antonio (1956b), 'Un nuova cimitero cristiano scoperto sulla via Latina', *L'Osservatore Romano*, 6th April, p. 4.

Ferrua, Antonio (1958), 'Scoperta di una nuova regione della catacomba di Commodilla, II', *Rivista di archeologia cristiana*, XXXIV.

Ferrua, Antonio (1960a), ' "Qui Filius diceris et Pater inveniris". Mosaico novellamente scoperto nella catacomba di S. Domitilla', *Rendiconti della Pontificia Accademia Romana d'Archeologia*, XXXIII, pp. 209–24.

Ferrua, Antonio (1960b), *Le Pitture della nuova catacomba di via Latina*, Vatican City.

Focillon, Henri (1931), *L'art des sculpteurs romains. Recherches sur L'histoire des formes*, Paris.

Focillon, Henri (1933), *Vie des formes*, Paris.

Forlati Tamaro, Bruno (1962), 'L'ipogeo di S. Maria in Stelle, Verona', *Stucchi e mosaici altomedioevali. I., Lo stucco, il mosaico, studi vari*, Milan, pp. 245–59.

Foucher, L. (1960), *Inventaire des mosaïques*, Sousse. Tunis.

Frank, T. (1959), *An Economic Survey of Ancient Rome*, Paterson.

Fremersdorf, Franz (1949), *Dionysos–Mosaik in dem römischen Haus vor dem Südportal des Kölner Domes*, Cologne.

Fremersdorf, Franz (1956), *Das römische Haus mit dem Dionysos-Mosaik vor dem Südportal des Kölner Domes*, Berlin.

Fremersdorf, Franz (1957), *Dionysos–Mosaik in dem römischen Haus vor dem Südportal des Kölner Domes*, Cologne.

Friedlander, Paul (1912), *Johannes von Gaza und Paulus Silentiarius. Kunstbeschreibungen Justinianischer Zeit*, Leipzig.

Frova, Antonio (1943), *Pittura romana in Bulgaria*, Rome.

Frova, Antonio (1943), 'Peinture romaine en Bulgarie', *Cahiers d'Art*, XXIX pp. 25 ff.

Frova, Antonio (1961), *Arte di Roma e del mondo romano*, Turin.

Gabriel, Mabel M. (1952), *Masters of Campanian Painting*, New York.

Gabriel, Mabel M. (1955), *Livia's Garden Room at Prima Porta*, New York.

Galassi, Giuseppe (1930), *Roma o Bisanio. Vol. i, I mosaici di Ravenna e le origini dell'arte italiana*, Rome.

Galassi, Giuseppe (1953), *Roma o Bisanzio. Vol. ii, Il congedo classico e l'arte dell'alto Medioevo*, Rome.

Garcia y Bellido, Antonio (1957), *Arte Romana*, Madrid.

Gasdia, Vincenzo Eduardo (1937), *La Casa pagano-cristiana del Celio*, Rome.

Gauckler, Paul (1896), *Monuments et Mémoires publiés par l'Académie des Incriptions et Belles Lettres (Fondation Piot)*, III.

Gauckler, Paul (1910), *Inventaire des mosaïques de la Gaule et de l'Afrique. II. Afrique Proconsulaire (Tunisie)*, Paris.

Gentili, Gino V. (1950), 'Piazza Armerina', *Notizie degli scavi*, p. 291 ff.

Gentili, Gino V. (1952), 'I mosaici della villa romana di Piazza Armerina', *Bollettino d'Arte*, XXXVII, p. 33 ff.

Gentili, Gino V. (1952b), *La villa imperiale di Piazza Armerina* (Itinerari dei musei e monumenti d'Italia), Rome.

Gentili, Gino V. (1957), 'Le gare nel circo nel mosaico di Piazza Armerina', *Bollettino d'Arte*, XLII, pp. 7–27.

Gentili, Gino V. (1959), *La Villa Erculia di Piazza Armerina. I mosaici figurati*, Rome.

Gerke, Friedrich (1935), 'Das Verhältnis von Malerei und Plastik in der Theodosianisch–Honorianischen Zeit', *Rivista di Archeologia cristiana*, XIII, pp. 199–63.

Gerke, Friedrich (1936), *Der Sarkophag des Junius Bassus*, Berlin.

Gerke, Friedrich (1940), *Die christlichen Sarkophage der vorkonstantinischen Zeit*, Berlin.

Gerke, Friedrich (1947), 'Altchristliche Philosophie', *Beiträge zur christlichen Philosophie*, 2.

314 Gerke, Friedrich (1964), 'Il mosaico absidale di Hosios David di Salonicco', *Corsi di Cultura sull'arte ravennate e bizantina*, Bologna, pp. 179–99.

Ghirshman, Roman (1956), *Bichapour. II, Les mosaïques sassanides*, Paris.

Ghirshman, Roman (1962), *Arte persiana. Parti e sassanidi*, Milan.

Ghislanzoni, Ettore (1965), *La Villa romana di Desenzano*, Milan.

Giannelli, G., and Mazzarino, S. (1956), *Trattato di Storia Romana*, ii, Rome.

Gilson, Etienne (1952), *La Philosophie au Moyen Age*, Paris.

Gioseffi, Decio (1955), 'La terminologia dei sistemi di parimentazione marmorea e una pagina della "Naturalis Historia",' *Rendiconti dell'Accademia Nazionale dei Lincei*, VIII, 10, p. 272 ff.

Giuliano, Antonio (1955), *L'Arco di Costantino*, Milan.

Gonzenbach, Victorine von (1961), *Die römischen Mosaiken der Schweiz*, Basel.

Goodchild, Richard (1957), 'The Finest Christian mosaics in Libya, in perfect condition and with a unique picture of the Pharos of Alexandria', *Illustrated London News*, p. 1034.

Grabar, André (1945), 'Plotin et les origines de l'esthétique médiévale', *Cahiers Archéologiques*, I, pp. 15–34.

Grabar, André (1947), 'Le Temoignage d'une Hymne syriaque sur l'architecture de la Cathédrale d'Edesse au VI siècle', *Cahiers Archéologiques*, II.

Grabar, André (1953), *La peinture byzantine*, Geneva.

Grabar, André (1962a), 'Le portrait en iconographie paléochrétienne', *Revue des sciences Religieuses*, CXXXIII–CXXXIV, pp. 87–109.

Grabar, André (1962b), 'Recherches sur les sources juives de l'art paléochrétienne. II, Les mosaïques de pavement', *Cahiers Archéologiques*, XII, pp. 115–52.

Gregoire, Jacques (1953), 'La nativité des Dioscures dans la mosaïque de la Johann-Philipp-Strasse à Trèves', *La Nouvelle Clio*, pp. 451–64.

Grossi-Gondi, Felice (1913), *L'Arco di Costantino*, Rome.

Gsell, Stephane (1902), *Musée de Tébessa*, Paris.

Gsell, Stephane (1926), *Promenades archéologiques aux environs d'Alger*, Paris.

Guidi, Giacomo (1933), 'La Villa del Nilo', *Africa Italiana*, V, pp. 1–56.

Guidi, Giacomo (1935), 'Orfeo, Liber Pater e Oceano nei mosaici della Tripolitania', *Africa Italiana*, VI, pp. 110–55.

Guimet, E. (1912), *Les Portraits d'Antinoé au Musée Guimet*, Paris.

Guitton, Jean (1933), *Le temps et l'éternité chez Plotin et Saint Augustin*, Paris.

Gullini, Giorgio (1956), *I mosaici di Palestrina*, Rome.

Gullini, Giorgio, and Fasolo, Furio (1953), *Il Santuario della Fortuna Primigenia a Palestrina*, Rome.

Hanfmann, G.M.A., and Detweiler, H. (1963), 'Sardis. A Season of Varied Discoveries. Some Splendid Mosaics and a third century AD Synagogue', *Illustrated London News*, pp. 340–4.

Haseloff, Günther (1962), 'I principi mediterranei dell'arte barbarica', *Il passaggio dall'Antichità al Medioevo in Occidente*, Spoleto, pp. 477–96.

Hauschild, T., and Schlunk, H. (1961), 'Vorbericht über die Arbeiten in Centcelles', *Madrider Mitteilungen*, II, p. 119 ff.

Heland, Madeleine von (1964), *Mosaïques Romaines de Tunisie*, Brussels.

Helbig, Wolfgang (1868), *Wandgemalde der von Vesuv verschütteten Städte Campaniens*, Leipzig.

Helbig, Wolfgang, and Amelung, W. (1912–3), *Führer durch die öffentlichen Sammlungen Klassischer Altertümer in Rom*, Leipzig.

Hermann, A. (1962), 'Agyptologische Marginalien zur spatantiken Ikonographie', *Jahrbuch für Antike und Christentum*, V, pp. 60–92.

Hermann, P. and Bruckmann, F. (1904–31), *Denkmaler der Malerei des Altertums*, Munich.

Hinks, Roger P. (1933), *Catalogue of the Greek, Etruscan and Roman Paintings and Mosaics in the British Museum*, London.

Hoppe, H. (1903), *Syntax und Stil des Tertullians*, Leipzig.

Hübinger, P.E. (1952), 'Spätantike und frühes Mittelalter', *Deutche Vierteljahrschrift für Literaturwissenschaft und Geistesgeschichte*, XXVI, pp. 1–48.

Ihm, Chr. (1960), *Die Programme der christlichen Apsimalerie vom IV Jahrhundert bis zum Mitte des VIII Jahrhunderts*, Wiesbaden.

Ivanov, T. (1954), *Une mosaïque romaine de Ulpia Oescus*, Sofia.

Jacopi, Giulio (1943), 'Scavi in prossimità del porto fluviale di S. Paolo, località Pietra Papa', *Monumenti antichi pubblicati per cura della R. Accademia d'Italia*, XXXIX, 1, cc. 1–166.

Jacopi, Giulio (1959), *Il Santuario della Fortuna Primigenia e il Museo archeologico di Palestrina*, Rome.

Jerome, St, *Epistulae*.

Jones, H.A.M. (1963), 'The Social Background of the Struggle between Paganism and Christianity', *The Conflict between Paganism and Christianity in the Fourth Century*, Oxford.

Jones, H. Stuart (1926), *The Sculptures of the Palazzo dei Conservatori*, Oxford.

Josi, Enrico (1928), 'Le pitture rinvenute nel cimitero dei Giordani', *Rivista di Archeologia cristiana*, V, pp. 167–227.

Junyent, Edoardo (1932), *Il titolo di San Clemente in Roma*, Rome.

Justin Martyr: *Apology* and *Second Apology*.

Kähler, Heinz (1962), *Die Stiftermosaiken in der Konstantinischen Südkirche von Aquileia*, Cologne.

Kaschnitz, von Weinberg, Guido (1926), 'Spätrömische Porträts', *Die Antike*, II, pp. 36–60.

Keil, Heinrich (1856–79), *Grammatici Latini*, 6 vols., Leipzig.

Kempf, Theodor (1950a), 'Konstantinische Deckenmalerein aus dem Trierer Dom', *Trierer Zeitschrift für Geschichte und Kunst des Trierer Landes und seiner Nachbargebiete*, XIX, pp. 45–51.

Kempf, Theodor (1950b), 'Die Ezforschung einer altchristlichen Bischofkirche auf deutsche Boden', *Forschungen und Fortschritte*, no. 19–20, pp. 244–7.

Kempf, Theodor (1951a), 'Die vorläufigen Ergebnisse der Ausgrabungen auf dem Gelände des Trierer Domes', *Germania*, XXIX, pp. 47–58.

Kempf, Theodor (1951b), *Aus der Schatskammer des antiken Trier*, Trier.

Kempf, Theodor (1959), *Überlieferung, Forschung–Untersuchungen über der Trier, Ill. Rock*, Trier.

Kennedy, A. (1925), *Petra, its history and monuments*, London.

Kenner, H. (1950), 'Antike römische Wandmalereien in Kärnten', *Carinthia*, I, p. 149 ff.

Kesser, Armin (1960), 'Koptische Textilien aus ägyptischen Gräbern', *Graphis*, XVI, n. 90, pp. 336–60.

Kinch, K. F. (1890), *L'arc de triomphe de Salonique*, Paris.

Kirsch, Johann P. (1927), 'Sull'origine dei motive iconografici nella pittura cimiteriale di Roma', *Rivista di Archeologia cristiana*, IV, pp. 259–87.

Klauser, Theodor (1941 ff.) *Reallexicon für Antike und Christentum*, Leipzig-Stuttgart.

Kollwitz, Johannes (1933), *Die Lipsanothek von Brescia*, Berlin-Leipzig.

Kollwitz, Johannes (1941), *Oströmische Plastik der theodosianischen Zeit*, Berlin.

Kollwitz, Johannes (1956), *Die Sarkophage Ravennas*, Freiburg i. Br.

Kömstedt, Rudolf (1929), *Vormittelalterliche Malerei. Die künstlerischen Probleme der Monumental- und Buch-Malerei in der frühchristlichen und frühbyzantinischen Epoche*, Augsburg.

Kötting, B. (1961), *Christentum und heidnische Opposition in Rom am Ende des 4. Jahrhunderts*, Munster i W.

Kraeling, Carl H. (1956), *The excavations at Dura Europos, Final Report*, VIII, 1, *The Synagogue*, New Haven.

Kraeling, Carl H. (1961–2), 'Colour Photographs of the Paintings in the Tomb of the three Brothers at Palmyra', *Les Annales Archéologiques de Syrie*, XI–XII, pages 13–18.

Krautheimer, Richard (1938), *Corpus Basilicarum Christianarum Romae*, i, Vatican City.

Krautheimer, Richard (1961), 'The Architecture of Sixtus III: A Fifth-Century Renaissance?' *Essays in Honor of Erwin Panofsky*, New York, pp. 291–302.

Krüger, Emil (1933), 'Römische Mosaiken in Deutschland', *Archäologischer Anzeiger*, XLVII, cc. 656 ff.

Künzle, Paul (1960–1), in *Rendiconti della Pontificia Accademia Romana di Archeologia*, XXXIII, pp. 9–10.

Künzle, Paul (1961), 'Zur Basilica Liberiana: Basilica Sicinini Basilica Liberii', *Römische Quartalschrift*, LVI, pp. 129–66.

Künzle, Paul (1961–2), 'Per una visione organica dei mosaici antichi d. S. Maria Maggiore', *Rendiconti della Pontificia Accademia Romana de Archeologia*, XXXIV, pp. 153–90.

La Baume, Peter (1958), *Colonia Agrippinensis. Kuzzer Rundgang durch das römische Köln*, Cologne.

Lafaye, Georges, and Blanche, Adrien (1909), *Inventaire des Mosaïques de la Gaule et de l'Afrique. I. 1, Narbonnaise et Aquitaine; I. 2, Lugdunaise, Belgique et Germanie*, Paris.

Lazarev, Victor (1959), 'Bizantino (Pittura)', *Enciclopedia Universale dell'Arte*, II, Rome, cc. 666–91.

Leclercq, Henri (1907), *Manuel d'archéologie chrétienne*, Paris.

Lehmann Hartleben, Karl (1926), *Die Traianssäule: ein römisches Kunstwerk zu Beginn der Spätantike*, Berlin.

Leroy, J. (1957), 'Mosaïques funéraires d'Edesse', *Syria*, XXXIV, pp. 306–42.

Levi, Doro (1935), *Il Museo Civico di Chiusi*, Rome.

Levi, Doro (1946–8), 'L'arte romana. Schizzo della sua evoluzione e sua posizione nella storia dell'arte antica', *Annuario della Scuola Archeologica italiana di Atene*, XXIV–XXVI, p. 229 ff.

Levi, Doro (1947), *Antioch Mosaic Pavements*, 2 vols., Princeton.

Levi, Doro (1949), *L'Ipogeo di S. Salvatore de Cabras in Sardegna*, Rome.

Lippold, Georg (1922), 'Herakles–Mosaik von Liria', *Jahrbuch des Deutschen Archäologischen Instituts*, XXXVII, p. 1 ff.

L'Orange, Hans Peter (1933), *Studien zur Geschichte des spätantiken Porträts*, Oslo.

L'Orange, Hans Peter (1952), 'E un palazzo di Massimiano Erculeo quello portato alla luce dagli scavi di Piazza Armerina?', *Symbolae Osloenses*, XXIX, p. 114 ff.

L'Orange, Hans Peter (1953), 'Aquileia e Piazza Armerina', *Studi Aquilejesi in onore di Giovanni Brusin*, Aquileia, pl 185 ff.

L'Orange, Hans Peter (1955), 'The Adventus ceremony and the slaying of Pentheus as represented in two Mosaics of about AD 300',

316   *Late Classical and Mediaeval Studies in honor of Albert Mathias Friend, Jr.*, Princeton, pp. 7–14.

L'Orange, Hans Peter (1956), 'Il Palazzo di Massimiano Erculeo di Piazza Armerina', *Studi in onore di Aristide Calderini e Roberto Paribeni*, III, Milan, p. 693 ff.

L'Orange, Hans Peter (1958), *Frå Principat til Dominat*, Oslo.

L'Orange, Hans Peter (1961), 'Der subtile Stil. Eine Kunstströmung aus der Zeit um 400 nach Christus', *Antike Kunst*, IV, pp. 68–75.

L'Orange, Hans Peter, and von Gerkan, Armin (1939), *Die spätantike Bildshmuck des Konstantinsbogens*, Berlin.

L'Orange, Hans Peter, and Nordhagen, Per Jonas (1958), *Mosaikk frå antikk til Middelalder*, Oslo.

Louis, René (1953), 'Notes iconographiques sur la mosaïque de la Naissance des Dioscures au Musée de Trèves', *Mémorial d'un voyage d'études de la Société Nationale des antiquaires de France en Rhenanie–Juillet 1951*, Paris, p. 217 ff.

Lowe, Elias A. (1934), *Codices Latini Antiquiores. A paleographical guide to Latin Manuscripts prior to the 9th century*, vol. i, Oxford.

Lowe, Elias A. (1935), *Codices Latini antiquiores. A paleographical guide to Latin Manuscripts prior to the 9th century*, vol. ii, Oxford.

Lubke, Wilhelm, *et al.* (1958), *Die Kunst der Römer*, Vienna.

Lugli, Giuseppe (1924), *La zona archeologica di Roma*, Rome.

Lugli, Giuseppe (1953), 'Edifici rotundi del tardo Impero in Roma e suburbio', *Studies to D. Robinson*, II, Washington.

Lugli, Giuseppe (1963), 'Contributo alla storia edilizia della villa romana di Piazza Armerina', *Rivista dell'Istituto Nazionale di Archeologia e Storia dell'Arte*, XI–XII, pp. 28–82.

Maiuri, Amedeo (1951), 'La scoperta di Stabiae', *Atene e Roma*, I.

Maiuri, Amedeo (1953), *La peinture romaine*, Geneva.

Maiuri, Amedeo (1954), *Saggi di varia antichità*, Venice.

Maiuri, Bianca (1957), *Museo Nazionale di Napoli*, Novara.

Mancini, Gioacchino (1910), 'Genezzano, scoperta di un parimento a mosaico policromo presso il convento di S. Pio', *Notizie degli scavi*, VII, pp. 517–8.

Managanaro, Giacomo (1960), 'Grifo', *Enciclopedia dell'arte antica classica e orientale*, III, Rome, pp. 1056–63.

Mango, Cyril (1951), 'Autour du Grand Palais de Constantinople', *Cahiers Archéologiques*, V, pp. 179–86.

Mano-Zisi, Djordje (1956), 'Le castrum de Gamzigrad et ses mosaïques', *Archaeologia iugoslavica*, II, p. 67 ff.

Mansuelli, Guido Achille (1958), *Le ville del mondo romano*, Milan.

Marconi, Piero (1929), *La Pittura dei Romani*, Rome.

Marco, Aurelius, *Meditations*.

Marrou, Henri-Irénée (1950), *Storia dell'educazione nell'antichità*, Rome.

Marrou, Henri-Irénée (1958), *Saint Augustin et la fin de la culture antique*, Paris.

Marucchi, Orazio (1911), 'L'ipogeo sepolcrale di Trebio Giusto recentemente scoperto sulla via latina e proposta di spiegazione gnostica delle sue pitture', *Nuovo Bollettino di Archeologia Cristiana*, XVII, pp. 209–35.

Marucchi, Orazio (1921), 'L'Ipogeo del Viale Manzoni', *Nuovo Bollettino di Archeologia Cristiana*, XXVII, pp. 44–7.

Marucchi, Orazio (1922), 'Un singolare gruppo di antiche pitture nell'ipogeo del Viale Manzoni', *Nuovo Bollettino di Archeologia Cristiana*, XXVIII, pp. 1–11.

Marucchi, Orazio (1933), *Le catacombe romane*, Rome.

Matthiae, Guglielmo (1937–9), 'Il mosaico romano di S. Pudenziana', *Bollettino d'Arte*, XXXI, pp. 418–25.

Matthiae, Guglielmo (1962a), *Le chiese di Roma dal IV al X secolo*, Bologna.

Matthiae, Guglielmo (1962b), 'La cultura figurativa di Salonicco nei secoli V e VI', *Rivista di Archeologia cristiana*, XXXVIII, pp. 162–213.

Mattingly, H. (1928), *Roman Coins from the Earliest Times to the Fall of the Western Empire*, London.

Mau, August (1882), *Geschichte des dekorativen Wandmalerei in Pompeji*, Berlin.

Maurice, J. (1908–12), *Numismatique constantinienne*, 3 vols, Paris.

Mazzarino, Santo (1951), *Aspetti sociali del quarto secolo. Ricerche di storia tardoromana*, Rome.

Mazzarino, Santo (1953), 'Sull'otium di Massimiano Erculio dopo L'abdicazione', *Rendiconti dell' Accademia Nazionale dei Lincei*, VIII 8, pp. 417–21.

Mazzarino, Santo (1954), *Storia romana e storiografia moderna*, Naples.

Mazzarino, Santo (1959), *La fine del mondo antico*, Milan.

Mazzarino, Santo (1962), 'Si può parlare di rivoluzione sociale alla fine del mondo antico?', *Il passaggio dall'Antichità al Medioevo in Occidente*, Spoleto, pp. 410–25.

Meates, G. W. (1955), *Lullingstone Roman Villa*, London.

Merlin, Alfred (1921), 'La Mosaïque du Seigneur Julius a Carthage', *Bulletin Archéologique*, XXXVIII, pp. 95–114.

Merlin, Alfred, and Poinssot, L. (1950), *Guide du Musée Alaoui (Musée du Bardo), I., Musée Antique*, Tunis.

Michelis, P. A. (1959), *Esthétique de l'art byzantin*, Paris.

Mingazzini, Paolo (1942–3), 'Sull'carattere eretico del sepolcro degli Aureli', *Rendiconti della Pontificia Accademia Romana di Archeologia*, XIX, pp. 355–69.

Mirri, L. and Carletti, G. (1776), *Le antiche camere esquiline*, Rome.

Mohrmann, Christine (1947), 'Le Latin commun et le Latin des chrétiens', *Vigiliae Christianae*, I, pp. 1–12.

Mohrmann, Christine (1948), 'Les éléments vulgaires du Latin des chrétiens', *Vigiliae Christianae*, II, pp. 89–101 and 163–84.

Mohrmann, Christine (1956), *Latin vulgaire, Latin des chrétiens, Latin médiéval*, Paris.

Mohrmann, Christine (1958), *Études sur le Latin des chrétiens*, Rome.

Mohrmann, Christine (1962), 'La problème de la continuité de la langue littéraire', *Il Passaggio dall'Antichità al Medioevo in Occidente*, Spoleto, pp. 329–49.

Momigliano. Arnaldo (1963), 'Pagan and Christian Historiography in the Fourth Century', *The Conflict between Paganism and Christianity in the Fourth Century*, Oxford, pp. 79–99.

Monneret de Villard, Ugo (1953), 'The Temple of the Imperial Cult at Luxor', *Archaeologia*, XCV, pp. 86–105.

Moreau, Jacques (1960), *Das Trierer Kornmarktimosaik*, Cologne.

Morey, Charles R. (1932), 'A Note on the date of the Mosaic of Hosios David, Salonica', *Byzantion*, VII, pp. 339–46.

Morey, Charles R. (1938), *The Mosaics of Antioch*, New York.

Morey, Charles R. (1953), *Early Christian Art*, Princeton.

Morgan, T. (1886), *Romano-British Mosaic Pavements*, London.

Müller, D.H., and von Schlosser, Julius (1898), *Die Haggada von Serajevo*, Vienna.

Neuss, Wilhelm (1926), *Die Kunst der alten Christen*, Augsburg.

Nogara, Bartolomeo (1907), *Le nozze Aldobrandini, i paesaggi con scene dell'Odissea e altre pitture murali antiche conservate nella Biblioteca Vaticana e nei Musei Pontifici*, Milan.

Nogara, Bartolomeo (1910), *I mosaici antichi conservati nei palazzi pontifici del Vaticano e del Laterano*, Milan.

Nordenfalk, Carl (1936), *Der Kalender von Jahre 354 und di lateinische Buchmalerei des IV Jahrhunderts*, Goteborg.

Nordenfalk, Carl (1957), 'L'Enluminure', in A. Grabar and C. Nordenfalk, *Le Haut Moyen Age du quatrième au onzième siècle*, Geneva.

Nordenfalk, Carl (ed.) (1961), *5000 Ar Egyptisk Konst*, Stockholm.

Nordhagen, Per Jonas (1963), 'The Mosaics of the Great Palace of the Byzantine Emperors', *Byzantinische Zeitschrift*, LCI, pp. 53–68.

Origen, *Contra Celsum*.

Orti Manara, Giovanni (1848), *Di un antico monumento dei tempi romani che trovasi nella terra delle Stelle presso Verona*, Verona.

Pace, Biagio (1939), *Arte e civiltà della Sicilia antica*, ii, Milan.

Pace, Biagio (1951), 'Note sulla villa romana di Piazza Armerina', *Rendiconti dell'Accademia Nazionale dei Lincei*, VIII, 6.

Pace, Biagio (1955), *I Mosaici di Piazza Armerina*, Rome.

Pallottino, Massimo (1938–9), 'L'orientamento stilistico della scultura Aureliana', *Le Arti*, I, pp. 32–6.

Panofsky, Erwin (1961), *La prospettiva come "forma simbolica" e altri scritti*, Milan.

Paribeni, Roberto (1921), 'Antichissime pitture cristiane a Roma', *Bollettino d'Arte*, XV.

Paribeni, Roberto (1923), in *Notizie degli scavi*, XXI, p. 380 ff.

Paribeni, Roberto (1932), *Le Terme di Diocleziano e il Museo Nazionale Romano*, Rome.

Paribeni, Roberto (1934), *Il ritratto nell'arte antica*, Milan.

Paribeni, Roberto (1941), *Da Diocleziano alla caduta dell'impero d'Occidente*, Bologna.

Parlaska, Klaus (1950), *Die Mosaiken des römischen Germanien*, Göttingen.

Parlaska, Klaus (1951), 'Das Trierer Mysterienmosaik und das ägyptische Ur Ei', *Trierer Zeitschrift für Geschichte und Kunst des Trierer Landes und seines Nachbargebiete*, XX, pp. 109–25.

Parlaska, Klaus (1959a), 'Bemerkungen zum römischen Peristylhaus beim Kölner Dom und Mosaik', *Germania*, XXXVII, pp. 155–70.

Parlaska, Klaus (1959b), *Die römischen Mosaiken in Deutschland*, Berlin.

Parlaska, Klaus (1965), *Studien zu den Mumienporträts und verwandten Denkmälern*, Wiesbaden.

Paul, St, I Corinthians.

Paul the Silentiary, Description of the Church of S. Sophia.

Pauly, A.F., and Wissowa, G. (1894 ff), *Realencyclopädie der Klassischen Altertumswissenschaft*, Stuttgart.

Pavlov, Vsevolod, V. (1965), *Fajumskij Portret* (with catalogue by R. Schurinova, Moscow.

318 Peirce, Haiford, and Tyler, Royall (1932), *L'art byzantin*, vol. i, Paris.

Peirce, Haiford, and Tyler, Royall (1934), *L'art byzantin*, vol. ii, Paris.

Pellizzari, A. (1915), *Le opere di Francisco de Hollanda*, Naples.

Perler, Othmar (1933), *Die Mosaiken der Juliergruft im Vatikan*, Freiburg i. d. Schw.

Pesce, Gennaro (1949), 'La decorazione del frigidario delle Piccole Terme di Leptis', *Bolettino d'Arte*, XXXIV, p. 36 ff.

Pfuhl, Ernst (1923), *Malerei und Zeichnung der Griechen*, 2 vols., Munich.

Picard, Charles (1945), 'La grande peinture de l'hypogée funéraire du Viale Manzoni', *Comptes rendus de l'Académie des Inscriptions et Belles Lettres*, pp. 26–51.

Picard, Gilbert Charles (1959), 'Africo–romani centri', *Enciclopedia Universale dell'Arte*, i, Venice–Rome, c. 147 ff.

Picard, Gilbert Charles (1960), 'Mosaïques africaines du IIIe siècle après J.C.', *Revue Archéologique*, II, p. 17 ff.

Picard, Gilbert Charles (1963), 'Mosaico', *Enciclopedia Universale dell'Arte*, IX, Venice–Rome, cc. 673–83.

Piganiol, André (1947), *Histoire romaine. L'empire chrétien (325–395)*, Paris.

Pliny, the Elder, *Historia naturalis*.

Plotinus, *Enneads*, edited with commentary (in Italian) by Vincenzo Cilento, 4 vols. Bari, 1947–9.

Poinssot, Louis, and Quoniam, Pierre (1953), 'Mosaïques des bains des protomés a Thuburbo Majus', *Karthago*, IV, pp. 153–67.

Pörtner, Rudolf (1961), *Civiltà romana in Europa dal Reno al Danubio*, Milan.

Prandi, Adriano (1936), *La Memoria Apostolorum in Catacumbas*, Vatican City.

Prandi, Adriano (1942–3), 'Osservazioni su Santa Costanza', *Rendiconti della Pontificia Accademia Romana di Archeologia*, XIX, pp. 281–304.

Prandi, Adriano (1953), *La basilica celimontana dei SS. Giovanni e Paolo*, Rome.

Premerstein, Anton, *et al.* (1906), *Dioscurides, codex Aniciae Julianae phototypice editus*, Leipzig.

Pseudo-Denys, *Celestial Hierarchy* and *Ecclesiastical Hierarchy*.

Puech, H. Ch. (1938), 'Position spirituelle et signification de Plotin', *Bulletin de l'Association Guillaume Budé*, 61, pp. 13–46.

Quintilian, *Institutiones oratoriae*.

Quoniam, Pierre (1951), 'Une mosaïque à scènes de chasse récemment découverte à Henchir-Toungar (Tunisie)', *Karthago*, II.

Radford, C. A. R., and Dewar, H. S. (1954), *The Roman Mosaics from Low Ham and East Coker* (Somerset County Museum Publications, II).

Ragghianti, Carlo Ludovico (1954), 'Personalità di pittori a Pompei', *Critica d'arte nuova*, pp. 202–38.

Ragona, A. (1961), *Un sicuro punto di partenza per la datazione dei mosaici della Villa romana di Piazza Armerina*, Caltagirone.

Ragona, A. (1962), *Il proprietario della Villa romana di Piazza Armerina*, Caltagirone.

Reinach, Adolf (1914), 'Les Portraits gréco-égyptiens', *Revue Archéologique*, pp. 32–54.

Reinach, Adolf (1915), 'Les Portraits gréco-égyptiens', *Revue Archéologique*, pp. 1–36.

Reinach, S. (1904–10), *Répertoire de la statuaire grecque et romaine*, 6 vols. Paris.

Reinach, S. (1909–12), *Répertoire des reliefs grecs et romains*, 3 vols. Paris.

Reinach, S. (1922), *Répertoire des peintures grecques et romaines*, Paris.

Richardson, L. Jnr. (1955), 'Pompeii: The casa dei Dioscuri and its Painters', *Memoirs of the American Academy at Rome*, XXIII.

Riegl, Alois (1893), *Stilfragen*, Berlin.

Riegl, Alois (1901), *Die spätrömische Kunstindustrie nach den Funden in Osterreich–Ungaru*, Vienna; (1953) Italian translation by Bruna Forlati Tamaro and Maria Teresa Ronga Leoni, *Industria artistica tardoromana*, with introduction by Sergio Bettini, Florence; (1959) Italian translation, by Licia Ragghianti, *Arte tardoromana*, Turin.

Rizzo, Giulio E. (1929), *La pittura ellenistico-romana*, Milan.

Rizzo, Giulio E. (1936), *Le pitture della casa dei Grifi (Palatino)*, Rome.

Rizzo, Giulo E. (1937), *Le pitture della casa di Livia (Palatino)*, Rome.

Rocchetti, Luigi (1961), 'Il mosaico con scene di arena al Museo Borghese', *Rivista dell'Istituto Nazionale di Architettura e Storia dell'Arte*, X, pp. 79–115.

Rodenwaldt, Gerhart (1909), *Die Komposition der Pompejianischen Wandgemälde*, Berlin.

Rodenwaldt, Gerhart (1923–4), 'Römisches in den antiken Kunst', *Archäologischer Anzeiger*, XXXVIII–XXXIX, c. 364 ff.

Rodenwaldt, Gerhart (1927), *Die Kunst der Antike*, Berlin.

Rodenwaldt, Gerhart (1935), 'Ueber den Stilwandel in der Antoninischen Kunst', *Abhandlungen der Preussischen Akademie der Wissenschaften*, III, pp. 1–27.

Rodenwaldt, Gerhart (1936), 'Zur Kunstgeschichte der Jahre 220 bis 270', *Jahrbuch des Deutschen Archäologischen Instituts*, LI, pp. 82–113.

Romanelli, Pietro (1922), 'Tomba romana con

affreschi del IV secolo d.C. nella regione di Gargaresc (Tripoli)', *Notiziario Archeologico del Ministero delle Colonie*, III, p. 21 ff.

Romanelli, Pietro (1942), *La colonna Antonina*, Rome.

Roscher, W.H. (1884–1937), *Ausführliches Lexicon der Griechischen und Römischen Mythologie*, Leipzig.

Rostovtzev, Mikhail (1922), *Iranians and Greeks in South Russia*, Oxford.

Rostovtzev, Mikhail (1926), *The Social and Economic History of the Roman Empire*, Oxford.

Rostovtzev, Mikhail (1934), *Preliminary Report of Fifth Season of Work, October 1931–March 1932*, New Haven.

Rostovtzev, Mikhail (1935), 'Dura and the problem of Parthian Art', *Yale Classical Studies*, V, p. 157 ff.

Rostovtzev, Mikhail (1938), *Dura Europos and its Art*, Oxford.

Rostovtzev, Mikhail, and Baur, Paul V.C. (1931), *The Excavations at Dura Europos. Second Season, October 1928–April 1929*, New Haven.

Roth, Cecil (1963), *L'Haggadah de Serajevo*, Belgrade.

Rumpf, Andreas (1953), 'Malerei und Zeichnung', *Handbuch der Archäologie* IV, 1, Munich.

Rumpf, Andreas (1957), *Stilphasen der spätantiken Kunst. Ein Versuch*, Cologne.

Ruysschaert, José (1962–3), 'Essai d'interprétation synthétique de l'Arc de Constantin', *Rendiconti della Pontificia Accademia Romana di Archeologia*, XXXV, pp. 79–100.

Ruysschaert, José (1963), 'Unità e significato dell'arco di Costantino', *Studi Romani*, XI, pp. 1–12.

Saletta, Vincenzo, *Ludi circensi*, Rome.

Salomonson, Jean W. (1965), *Konst från Kartago – Tunisisk Konst fr ån Romersk Tid.* Stockholm.

Schefold K. (1952), *Pompejanische Malerei. Sinn und Ideengeschichte*, Basel.

Schlosser, Magnino Julius von (1901), *Zur Genesis der Mittelalterlichen Kunstanschauung*, Vienna (later in *Präludien. Vorträge und Aufsätze*, Berlin (1927), pp. 180–212.

Schlosser, Magnino Julius von (1956), *La letteratura artistica*, Florence.

Schlunk, Helmut (s.d.), *Die frühchristlich-byzantinische Sammlung*, Berlin.

Schlunk, Helmut (1939), *Kunst der Spätantike in Mittelmeerraum*, Berlin.

Schlunk, Helmut (1954), 'Archäologische Funde in Spanien', *Archäologischer Anzeiger*, LXIX, C. 455 ff.

Schlunk, Helmut (1959), *Untersuchungen in frühchristlichen Mausoleum von Centcelles*, Berlin.

Schmidt, Eva (1929), *Studien sum Barberinischen Mosaik in Palestrina*, Strassburg.

Schoppa, Helmut (1957), *Die Kunst der Römerzeit in Gallien, Germanien und Britannien*, Munich.

Schrijnen, Joseph (1932), *Charakteristik des altchristlichen lateins*, Nijmegen.

Schumacher, W.N. (1959), 'Eine römische Apsiskomposition', *Römische Quartalschrift*, LIV, pp. 137–202.

Schumacher, W.N. (1963), 'Cubile Sanctae Helenae', *Römische Quartalschrift*, LVIII, pp. 196–222.

Schurinova, R. (1960a), *Koptskie Tkani*, Moscow.

Schurinova, R. (1960b), *Fajumskie Portreti*, Moscow.

Schweitzer, Bernhard (1963), 'Die spätantiken Grundlagen der mittelalterlichen Kunst', *Zur Kunst der Antike*, Tubingen, pp. 280–303.

Sedlmayr, Hans (1962), 'Ars humilis', *Hefte Kunsthistorisches Seminar Universität Munchen*, IX, pp. 7–21.

Seeck, Otto (1910–21), *Geschichte des Untergangs der antiken Welt*, 6 vols., Stuttgart.

Segal, J.B. (1959), 'New Mosaics from Edessa', *Archaeology*, XII, pp. 150–7.

Seneca, *Ad Lucilium Epistulae morales*.

Sestan, Ernesto (1962), 'Tardo antico e alto Medievale: difficolta di una periodizzazione', *Il passaggio dell'Antichità al Medioevo in Occidente*, Spoleto, pp. 13–37.

Shepperd, D.C. (1954), 'A late Hellenistic Tapestry from Egypt', *Bulletin of the Cleveland Museum of Art*, XLI, pp. 4–6.

Simon, Marcel (1945), *Hercule et le Christianisme*, Strasbourg.

Setiriou, Georges A. (1950), Ἐγκαυστίκη εἰκὸν τοῦ Ἀποστόλου Πέτρου τῆς Μονῆς Σινό, *Melanges Gregoire*, Brussels, II, pp. 607–10.

Spitzer, Les (1954), *Critica stilistica e storia del linguaggio*, Bari.

Stefanini, Luigi (1956), 'La Prospettiva tolemaica', *Rivista di Estetica*, I, pp. 97–106.

Stein, E. (1928), *Geschichte des spätrömischen Reiches*, Vienna.

Stenico, Arturo (1963), *La pittura etrusca e romana*, Milan.

Stern, Henri (1953), *Le Calendrier de 354. Étude sur son texte et ses illustrations*, Paris.

Stern, Henri (1955), 'La Mosaïque d'Orphée de Blainzy-les-Fismes', *Gallia XIII*, pp. 41–47.

Stern, Henri (1957), *Recueil général des mosaïques de la Gaul. I. Province de Belgique, 1 Partie ouest*, Paris.

Stern, Henri (1958), 'Les mosaïques de l'Église de Sainte Constance à Rome', *Dumbarton Oaks Papers*, XII, pp. 157–218.

Stern, Henri (1960), 'Les peintures du Mausolée de l'Exode à El-Bagouat', *Cahiers Archeologiques*, XI, pp. 93–119.

Stillwell, R. (1961), 'Houses of Antioch', *Dumbarton Oaks Papers*, XV, pp. 45–57.

Stockmeir, P. (1963), 'Konstantinische Wends und Kirchengeschichtliche Kontinuität', *Historisches Jahrbuch*, LXXXII, pp. 1–21.

320 Strelkow, A.S. (1936), *Fajumskij Portret*, Moscow.

Strong, Eugenia (1916), 'Forgotten fragments of Ancient Wall Paintings in Rome. I. The House in the via dei Cerchi', *Papers of the British School at Rome*, VIII, p. 91 ff.

Strong, Eugenia (1923), *La scultura romana da Augusto a Costantino*, vol. i, Florence.

Strong, Eugenia (1926), *La scultura romana da Augusto a Costantino*, vol. ii, Florence.

Strzygowski, Joseph (1888), *Die Kalenderbilder des Chronographen von Jahre 354*, Berlin.

Strzygowski, Joseph (1936), *L'ancien art chrétien de Syrie*, Paris.

Styger, Paul (1927), *Die Altchristliche Grabeskunst*, Munich.

Styger, Paul (1933), *Die römischen Katakomben*, Berlin.

Styger, Paul (1935), *Die römischen Märtyrergrufte*, Berlin.

Svoboda, Karel (1933), *L'esthétique de Saint Augustin et ses sources*, Brunn.

Swift, E.H. (1951), *Roman Sources of Christian Art*, New York.

Swodboda, K.M. (1961), 'The problem of the Iconography of Late Antique and Early Mediaeval Palaces', *Journal of the Society of Architectural Historians*, XX, pp. 78–89.

Talbot Rice, David (1953), *Byzantine Art*, London.

Talbot Rice, David (1955), 'Les Mosaïques du Grand Palais des Empereurs byzantins à Constantinople', *La Revue des Arts*, V, pp. 159–66.

Talbot Rice, David (1957a), 'The Great Palace of the Byzantine Emperors', *Archaeology*, X, pp. 174–80.

Talbot Rice, David (1957b), *The Beginnings of Christian Art*, London.

Talbot Rice, David (1958), '*The Great Palace of the Byzantine Emperors*'. Second Report, Edinburgh.

Talbot Rice, David (1959), *Kunst aus Byzanz*, Munich.

Thieme, U., and Becker, F. (1907–50), *Allgemeines Lexicon der bildenden Kunstler von der Antike bis zur Gegenwart*, Leipzig.

Thompson, E.A. (1963), 'Christianity and the Northern Barbarians', *The Conflict between Paganism and Christianity in the Fourth Century*, Oxford, pp. 56–78.

Toesca, Pietro (1927), *Storia dell'Arte italiana. I. Il Medioevo*, Turin.

Torp, Hjalmar (1955), 'Quelques remarques sur les mosaïques de l'église de S.Georges à Thessalonique, Πεπραγμενα διεθν. Βυζ. συνεδ. Θεσσαλονικη, Athens, pp. 489–98.

Torp, Hjalmar (1953), *Mosaikkene I st. Georg– Rotunden I Thessaloniki*, Oslo.

Toynbee, Arnold (1939), *A Study of History*, London.

Toynbee, Jocelyn M.C. (1958), *Guide to the Antiquities of Roman Britain in the British Museum*, London.

Toynbee, Jocelyn M.C. (1962), *Art in Roman Britain*, London.

Toynbee, Jocelyn M.C., and Ward-Perkins, John B. (1956), *The Shrine of St.Peter and the Vatican Excavations*, London.

Traversari, Gustavo (1960), *Gli spettacoli in acqua nel teatro tardo-antico*, Rome.

Van Berchem, Marguerite, and Cluzot, Étienne (1924), *Mosaïques chrétiennes du IV au X siècle*, Geneva.

Van der Meer, F. (1960), *Atlas de l'Antiquité chrétienne*, Paris-Brussels.

Venturi, Adolfo (1901), *Storia dell'Arte italiana*, i, Milan.

Verdiani, Carlo (1946), *L'Ipogeo di Durostorum e pitture nelle Provincie Orientali dell'Impero Romano*, Padua (unpublished).

Verzone, Paolo (1958), 'I due gruppi in porfido di S.Marco in Venezia ed il Philadelphion di Costantinopoli', *Palladio* VIII, pp. 8–14.

Vilaro, J. (1937), 'I sepolcri della necropoli di Tarragona, *Rivista di Archeologia cristiana*, XIV, pp. 253–80.

Vitruvius, *De Architectura libri X*.

Voelkl, L. (1963), 'Zusammenhänge zwischen der antiken und der frühchristlichen Symbolwelt', *Das Münster*, XVI, pp. 1–50.

Volbach, Wolfgang F. (1932), *Spätantike und frühmittelalterliche Stoffe*, Mainz.

Volbach, Wolfgang F. (1952), *Elfenbeinarbeiten der Spätantike und des frühen Mittelalters*, Mainz.

Volbach, Wolfgang F., and Hirmer, Max (1958), *Frülichristliche Kunst. Die Kunst der Spätantike in West- und Ost-Rom*, Munich.

Wagner, Friedrich (1908), *Die römische Villa und der Mosaikboden zu Nennig*.

Ward-Perkins, John B. (1948), 'Severan Art and Architecture at Leptis Magna', *Journal of Roman Studies*, XXXVIII, pp. 59–80.

Ward-Perkins, John B. (1958), 'A new group of sixth-century mosaics from Cyrenaica', *Rivista di Archeologia cristiana*, XXXIV, pp. 183–92.

Ward-Perkins, John B., and Toynbee, Jocelyn M.C. (1951), 'The Hunting Baths at Leptis Magna', *Archaeologia*, XCIII, p. 165 ff.

Weber, Wilhelm (1929), *Römische Kaisergeschichte und Kirchengeschichte*, Stuttgart.

Wegner, Max (1931), 'Die Kunstgeschichtliche Stellung der Marcussäule', *Jahrbuch des Deutschen Archaeologischen Instituts*, XLVI, pp. 61–174.

Weidlé, Vladimir (1954), *Mosaici paleocristiani e bizantini*, Milan-Florence.

Weis, Adolf (1960), 'Die Geburtsgeschichte Christi am Triumphbogen von S. Maria Maggiore in Rom', *Das Münster*, XIII, pp. 73–88.

Weitzmann, Kurt (1947), *Illustrations in Roll and Codex. A Study of the Origin and Method of Text Illustration*, Princeton.

Weitzmann, Kurt (1954), 'Observations on the Milan Iliad', *Nederlands Kunsthistorisch Jaarboek*, V, pp. 241–61.

Weitzmann, Kurt (1955), 'Observations on the Cotton Genesis', *Late Classical and Mediaeval Studies in honor of Albert Mathias Friend, jr.*, Princeton, p. 112 ff.

Weitzmann, Kurt (1959), *Ancient Book Illumination*, Cambridge.

Weitzmann, Kurt (1960), 'The Survival of Mythological Representations in Early Christian and Byzantine Art and their Impact on Christian Iconography', *Dumbarton Oaks Papers*, XIV, pp. 43–68.

Werbel, A. G. (1952), *Two Thousand Years of Textiles*, New York.

Wessel, Klaus, (1957), *Rom-Byzanz-Russland. Ein Führer durch die Frühchristlich-byzantinische Sammlung*, Berlin.

Wessel, Klaus (1963), *Koptische Kunst. Die Spätantike in Ägypten*, Recklinghausen.

Wheeler, Mortimer (1963), *La civiltà romana oltre i confini dell'impero*, Turin.

Wheeler, Robert E. M., and Wheeler, T. V. (1936), *Verulamium: and two Roman Cities* (Reports of the Society of Antiquaries of London, no. XI).

Wickhoff, Franz (1895), *Die Wiener Genesis*, Vienna.

Wilpert, Joseph (1903), *Le pitture delle Catacombe romane*, Rome.

Wilpert, Joseph (1913), 'Die Malereien der Grabkammer des Trebius Justus', in Dolger, *Konstantin der Grosse und seine Zeit*, Freiburg i Br., pp, 276–96.

Wilpert, Joseph (1917), *Die Römischen Mosaiken und Malereien der Kirchlichen Bauten vom IV bis XIII Jahrhundert*, Freiburg i. Br.

Wilpert, Joseph (1923–4), 'Un battistero "ad Nymphas Beati Petri" ', *Rendiconti della Pontificia Accademia Romana di Archeologia*, II, pp. 53–83.

Wilpert, Joseph (1924), 'Le pitture dell'Ipogeo di Aurelio Felicissimo presso il Viale Manzoni in Roma', *Memorie della Pontificia Accademia Romana di Archeologia*, X, pp. 1–42.

Wirth, Franz (1934), *Römische Wandmalerei vom Untergang Pompejis bis aus Ende des III Jahrhunderts*, Berlin.

Wolska, Wanda (1962), *La topographie chrétienne de Cosmos Indicopleustes. Theologie et Science au VIe Siecle*, Paris.

Wulff, Oskar (1914), *Altchristliche und byzantinische Kunst*, 2 vols., Berlin.

Wulff, Oskar, and Volbach, Wolfgang F. (1923), *Die Altchristlichen und mittelalterlichen Bildwerke*, Berlin-Leipzig.

Wulff, Oskar, and Volbach, Wolfgang F. (1926), *Spätantike und koptische Stoffe aus ägyptischen Grabfunden in den Staatlichen Museen*, Berlin.

Xyngopoulos, A. (1931), Το Καθολικόν τῆς Μόνης τοῦ Λατόμου ἐν Θεσσαλονίκη καί το ἐν αὐτῆ Φηφιδωτον, 1931.

Zaloscer, Hilde (1961), *Porträts aus dem Wüstensand. Die antiken Mumienbildnisse aus der Oase Fayuum*, Vienna-Munich.

Zaloscer, Hilde (1963), *Tissus Coptes*, Lausanne.

Zovatto, Paolo L. (1956), Scene di caccia e di ucellagione nei mosaici opitergini, *Noncello*, pp. 3–22.

Zovatto, Paolo L. (1963), *Mosaici paleocristiani delle Venezie*, Udine.

Page numbers in italics refer to the notes

Names of (i) ancient and modern authors; (ii) other historical persons (e.g. *Constantine*); (iii) mythical or legendary persons and personifications in classical and Christian literature; (iv) artists (printed in capitals), whether historically known or styled by the author; (v) peoples.

Not included are the names of (i) historical persons incorporated in the denomination of monuments (e.g. Arch of *Titus*); (ii) mythical or legendary persons contained in the denomination of artists (e.g. *Dionysus* Master); (iii) persons known only through the evidence of monuments (e.g. Hypogeum of *Trebius Justus*).

Places where are kept or where were excavated the works of art and other monuments referred to, even if only by the name of the locality. *Not* included are places mentioned in bibliographical titles and the denomination of artists.

Works of art are printed in inverted commas. Their category is indicated as follows: c., painted codices; f., frescoes; i., inlays; m., mosaics; t., textiles. *Not* included are the frequent textual references without specific mention of titles. Place names within brackets indicate that the work in question is preserved there but was discovered or executed eleswhere. The numbers of illustrations are given in square brackets, bold figures referring to coloured plates.

Photographic references

The numbers in ordinary type refer to the illustrations in this volume and those in bold type to the coloured plates. Numbers and letters in italics within brackets are those of the original negatives.

Alinari, Rome, 3 (*12138*), 4 (*43180*), 10 (*41216*), 16 (*39135*), 23 (*12000a*), 43 (*27189*), 52 (*46979*), 100 (*P.1, 12365*), 101 (*55465*), 127 (*55467*), 166 (*285517*)

Anderson, Rome, 1 (*40855*), 5, 12 (*23433*), 14, 15, 24 (*23462*), 34 (*41156*), 46 (*24397*), 84 (*6219*), 107 (*17889*), 111 (*24167*), 114 (*31267*), 115 (*31277*), 116 (*31278*)

Arborio Mella, Milan, 33, 51, 53, 96, 142, 143, 144, 218, 222, **18, 19, 20, 32**

Archivio Fotografico Gallerie Musei Vaticani, Vatican City, 210 (*XXVIII.13.20*)

Bildarchiv Foto Marburg, Marburg, 147 (*180630*), 148 (*180628*)

British Museum, London, 45, 198

Central Office of Information, London, 205 (*GOV. 12822*), 206 (*GOV.12824*)

Detroit Institute of Arts, Detroit, 155

Direzione Scavi Ostia Antica, Ostia, 197

Dorigo, Venice, 84, 99, 123, 134, 135, 136, 161, 199

Gabinetto Fotografico Nazionale, Rome, 46 (*E 40863*), 47 (*E 40888*), 93 (*F 10266*), 102 (*F 10290*), 109 (*F 10272*), 110 (*F 10292*), 128, 129 (*F 10249*), 130 (*F 10309*), 131 (*F 10279*)

Hirmer Fotoarchiv, Munich, 215 (*FK 126*), 216, 217 (*FK 123*), 219 (*B 39*)

Istituto Archeologico Germanico, Rome, 2 (*56.937*), 25 (*61.1866*), 26 (*61.1848*), 27 (*61.1839*), 28 (*61.1880*), 29 (*41.1347*), 37 (*62.1437*), 38 (*64.705*), 39 (*64.706*), 48 (*37.1261*), 49 (*55.853*), 54 (*64.700*), 55 (*64.699*), 59 (*35.1672*), 60 (*34.1485*), 67 (*34.136*), 80 (*54.709*), 97 (*61.237*), 137 (*56.1001*), 139 (*56.1003*), 145 (*36.1089*), 146 (*61.532*), 160 (*64.707*), 165 (*56.1662*), 167 (*30.647*), 180 (*58.1535*), 200 (*41.607*), 208 (*64.2324*), 209 (*64.2323*)

Kunsthistorisches Museum, Vienna, 202, 203

Landesmuseum, Trier, 40 (*RB 54.48*), 41 (*RD 56.60*), 42 (*RB 54.58*), 185, 186 (*RB 57.33*), 187 (*RD 57.69*), 188 (*RD 57.72*), 189 (*RB 50.41*), 190 (*RC 50.113*), 191 (*RC 50.104*), 192 (*RC 50.101*), 493 (*RC 50.102*), 194 (*RC 56.95*), 195 (*RE 56.26*), 196 (*RE 56.27*)

Meledandri, Castellamare di Stabi, 20, 22

Metropolitan Museum of Art, New York, 207 (*Gift of Edward S. Harkness, 1931*–*85329*)

Pontificia Commissione di Archeologia Sacra, Rome, 9, 75 (*9133*), 81 (*3139*) 85 (*7130*), 86 (*5021*), 87 (*7131*), 88 (*7138*), 162 (*19108*), 164 (*10013*), 168 (*26552*), 169 (*26588*), 170 (*26579*), 171 (*26681*), 172 (*26680*), 173 (*26682*), 174 (*26604*), 175 (*26614*), 176 (*26584*), 177 (*26672*), 178 (*16041*), 179 (*5140*)

Powell, Rome, 220 (*T 2–25*), 221 (*T 2–16*), **39, 40, 41**

Scala, Florence, 11, 13, 17, 36, 95, 113, 132, 133, 138, 140, 141, 150, 151, 163, 211, 212, 213, 214, **1, 2, 3, 4, 5, 6, 13, 15, 16, 17, 21, 22, 23, 24, 25, 26, 27, 29, 30, 31, 33, 34, 35, 36, 37, 38**

Soprintendenza Alle Antichità Della Campania, Naples, 12 (*Stabia, B4*), 19 (*Stabia, B 14*), 21 (*Stabia, B 7*)

Staatliche Museen, Berlin, 35

Yale University Art Gallery, New Haven, 62 (*1936. 127.14*), 64 (*1936.127.15*), 65 (*1936.127.2*), 66 (*1936.127.16b*)

The remaining illustrations are taken from: Agnello, Apollony-Ghetti, *L'Art Copte*, Baur, Bendinelli, Borda, Brusin, Coche de la Ferté, Cumont, De Wit, Ferrua, Frova, Galassi, Gentili, Ghirshonan, Ghislanzoni, Kempf, Levi, Pace, Parlov, Rizzo, Salomonson, Van der Meez, Wilpert (*see* Bibliography) and Feltrinelli's archives.

and in particular by the textiles of the Byzantine age. Many specimens of Coptic, Syrian and Constantinopolitan textiles surviving from antiquity in fact show their fidelity to the originals. It is easier in these copies to appreciate the adequacy with which the actual function of repetition to infinity of the figurative motives employed was carried out.

14 Brett (1947), pl. 37.

the varied torsions of their bodies and the diversity of superimposed planes in no way recall the paratactical, monotonous character of tetrarchic figures.

Similarly, in the extreme north-east corner, we have the group of 'Griffin and Prey',[15] in which the body of the monster is yellow and maroon, the head modelled in dark strokes, the beak grey and green; also the damaged 'Mounted Hunter',[16] where the brilliant colours of the clothing are skilfully associated. The Alexandrianism of these figures, which are clearly quite late, should not deceive the critic. He should be put on his guard, in particular, by certain idiomatic details in the capacity of the artists to achieve complex unitary and harmonious effects through the more extended, distributed and daring use of the chromatic *vermiculatum* line. It becomes, by union with the lines preceding and following it, something other than itself, as if the *tessellarius* had succeeded in distilling from an ancient compost of colour its simple, basic essentials and had materialised them in his stone cubes, trusting to their subsequent masterly arrangement for his customary result.

Look, for example, at the tree-trunk in the background.[17] It receives light and volume from an arrangement of strips of yellow, emerald green and light brown tesserae alternating along a considerable part of the trunk in the following order: first a row of monochrome tesserae, then one of two colours alternating, then another in monochrome and another in two colours as before, then two more in monochrome, the second being brown and constituting the shaded front of the trunk. At its base a different, still bolder structure is substituted, in the shape of a true chessboard pattern of yellow and brown tesserae. It is obvious that linked idiomatic formations of this kind were the outcome of the chromatic disunion and two-dimensional flattening typical of the crisis at the end of the third century. The resultant Hellenistic form cannot therefore deceive an observer who examines the pictorial line idiomatically.

A similar explanation will serve in the case of the 'Incomplete Fisherman', holding a fish he has just caught and with one foot in the transparent water of a stream. The figure appears in the upper part of the north-east corridor,[18] on the same level as the winged and horned griffin with a lizard in its talons. The organic laying on of colour, though in separate and alternate lines, along the dry part of the man's leg is found to result from the combined use of two bright chromatic tones to express the colour of flesh. But at the point where the foot enters the veiling element of water a system of alternating lines comes into play. This time they are horizontal, in white and blue, crossing the others in such a way as to produce a chequered pattern in four colours and achieving a surprisingly accurate im-

15 *Ibid.*, pl. 38.
16 *Ibid.*, pl. 39a.
17 *Ibid.*, pl. 37.
18 *Ibid.*, pl. 33.

12 Talbot Rice (1958), p. 158.

13 The zoophytic arabesque on a white abstract background in fan-shaped layers of tesserae was very widespread at Antioch from the fifth century onwards, the composition being derived from the decorative disorder of North African pavements which has been called *asaroton*-like (El Djem: Gauckler (1910), no. 71; Carthage, Gauckler (1910), no. 640). *See* in this connection for example the pavements of the 'Lion with Ribbons', probably of the age of Theodosius II (Levi (1947), ii, pl. LXX b) in the House of the Phoenix, which dates from the early sixth century (Levi (1947), ii, pl. LXXXIII a, c) and of the 'Beribboned Parrots' (Levi (1947), ii, pl. LXXXV) and others. An interesting variant, influenced by the redundant decorative partitions much in vogue at the beginning of the fourth century, displays animals, mainly birds, and fruit framed geometrically in squares or rhombs, collectively identical in their formal significance. Relevant examples include the Antioch mosaics of the 'Striding Lion' from the second half of the fourth century; (Levi (1947), ii, pl. LXXIV) and Room 2 of the House of *Ktisis* from the beginning of the following century; (Levi (1947), ii, pls. LXXXV b and CXXXVII c). This last specimen is of particular interest as being an exact replica of the mosaics of the vaults of certain large niches at St. George's, Salonika, reproducing their 'Alternate Birds and Fruit' organisation in quadrangular settings. They give a clear impression of being vulgarised and poor copies, thus enabling possible active influence to be conjectured of the comparatively restricted region of Constantinople, including Salonika, on the wider late Hellenistic area, with its long tradition of artistic independence, to which Antioch belonged. All these productions should be compared with the 'Phoenix Mosaic' (Levi (1947), i. pp. 351–5) from the house of the same name at Antioch and now at the Louvre. This wonderful pavement repeats to infinity the motive of a stylised flower and is surrounded by a border of goats' heads, with at the centre, almost like an *emblema*, the haloed bird in question. In these types of formal organisation the ancient *emblema* is almost always present in centralised isolation, as if to indicate the association of the late Roman *emblema* structure, open and multiplied in the background area and its extension to the cornices, with the Hellenistic convention of the closed, separate *emblema* which conveyed the narrative elements of the work. These arrangements were taken over directly by applied art

their presence on the ivory mantle of the background, whereon the tesserae, arranged like fish-scales, composed an infinite procession of repetitive arabesques in the void.

These presences bear a certain resemblance to phantoms, thanks to the revolutionary perspectives of late Roman art, which comes between them and their authentic Hellentistic models, freeing them from the close ties that bound them to the environmental scenery, in which the great art of Alexandria had flourished for centuries. The language which those rules had imposed continued relevant, though objectively it was no longer a classical idiom but a structure which had undergone profound alteration in the climate of late Roman times that had presided at its conception. By its recovery, due to cultural reorientation, of some of the stylistic features of Hellenistic civilisation, it had attained in effect a new synthesis of modes of expression, in taste related to Hellenism, but in morphological structure entirely changed. The resultant forms cannot be regarded as less than astonishing in their restraint and elegance, which have been correctly, at least in some respects, described as neo-Attic.[12]

As this effect leaves out the homogeneous background of the ancient models by the severely abstract method of delineating individual forms against empty space, it constitutes the result of the new spatial conception and may appear at first sight the outcome of a deliberately polemical technique. But this is not in fact the case.

The matter may be clarified by a careful analysis of line, colour and perspective in the separate figures, showing how remote Alexandrian civilisation had now become and how organic, finally, the connection between the structure of the images and their situation in space. This was the only way, it might as well be mentioned at this point, in which at a later date the repetitive arabesques of plant-like forms could be set against a background, a method splendidly exemplified in pavements at Antioch, even before it came to be adopted in Coptic and Byzantine textiles.[13]

Let us start from the north-east angle of the four-sided portico, with the wonderful picture of 'Two Hunters Confronting a Tigress':[14] the over-all effect is one of plastic solemnity, though it depicts a tense movement of attack. The body of the animal is represented in very warm tones, harmonised and fused in a gradual lowering of accentuation; the muzzle in particular expresses, by its solidity of form, a highly realistic ferocity. In a comparison with the heads of beasts of Piazza Armerina, to take one striking parallel, one cannot fail to notice how far the two-dimensional flatness and atonality of the latter had undergone a process of linear reorganisation, thus indubitably restoring the natural physical volume. The same considerations apply, indeed, to the two hunters:

40